BUSINESS AND GOVERNMENT IN CANADA

Stephen Brooks
Department of Political Science
University of Windsor

Andrew Stritch
Department of Political Studies
Bishop's University

Prentice-Hall Canada Inc., Scarborough, Ontario

Canadian Cataloguing in Publication Data

Brooks, Stephen, 1956-
  Business and government in Canada.
Includes bibliographical references.
ISBN 0-13-098427-2

1. Industry and state—Canada.
I. Stritch, Andrew J. II. Title.
HD3616.C22B76 1991   338.971   C90-095041-2

Prentice Hall, Inc., Englewood Cliffs, New Jersey
Prentice-Hall International, Inc., London
Prentice-Hall of Australia, Pty., Ltd., Sydney
Prentice-Hall of India Pvt., Ltd., New Delhi
Prentice-Hall of Japan, Inc., Tokyo
Prentice-Hall of Southeast Asia (Pte.) Ltd., Singapore
Editora Prentice-Hall do Brasil Ltda., Rio de Janeiro
Prentice-Hall Hispanoamericana, S.A., Mexico

ISBN 0-13-098427-2

Production Editor: Doris Wolf
Proofreader: Patti Giovannini
Production Coordinator: Florence Rousseau
Cover Design: Monica Kompter
Book Design: Marjorie Pearson

1 2 3 4 5 JD 95 94 93 92 91

Printed and bound in Canada by John Deyell Company

To
Paul and Thomas Brooks
and
Joan and Terry Stritch

TABLE OF CONTENTS

LIST OF TABLES

LIST OF FIGURES

PREFACE

This textbook is intended to provide a general introduction to business-government relations in Canada. It is written from a political science perspective and is designed primarily for use in undergraduate courses in politics, public administration and public policy. As such, it seeks to fill a significant gap in the literature of a growing area of interest in political science. The lack of an appropriate text has been a frustrating handicap in teaching business-government relations to politics students, and our own teaching experience in this area has made us acutely aware of the deficiency. Instructors have so far been forced to accept alternative options that, for one reason or another, have not been very satisfactory. These include: (1) books written specifically for business students which are essentially "how-to-do-it" manuals for influencing government; (2) books written for economics students, often in fairly technical jargon, with more graphs and formulas than most politics students (or instructors) can stomach; (3) an expensive combination of more narrowly focussed works, each dealing with some specific aspect of business-government relations; (4) collections of readings, which are too often a bit like old jewellery boxes—the gems are mixed in with the glass, and nothing really goes together; (5) the "do-it-yourself" approach, involving a painstaking compilation of journal articles, book chapters and other bits and pieces, which are photocopied with dubious legality and more certain tedium.

This book aims to overcome some of the foregoing problems by providing a reasonably comprehensive text which addresses issues of power, conflict and policy formation that are of central concern to students of politics. However, such concerns are certainly not irrelevant to the study of economics or business administration.

The book is divided into six parts. Part 1 (Introduction) introduces the main actors in Canadian business-government relations. Part 2 (History and Theory) provides an outline of the major developments in the interaction of business and government from the first staple industries to the present day. It also provides some theoretical grounding by introducing students to leading theories concerning the power of business in capitalist society. Part 3 (Structure) investigates the structure of Canadian industry. It focusses particularly on sectoral and regional divisions, foreign ownership, public ownership and privatization, and the concentration of corporate power. It also examines the federal structure of Canadian government and its impact on both the power of business and on the character of industrial policy. Part 4 (Business Influence) deals with the political organization of business, and with business efforts to influence public policy through means such as lobbying, the media, and electoral finance. Part 5 (Public Policy) looks at a selection of important policy areas with central relevance for business-government relations. These include competition policy, business regulation, international trade, and industrial relations. A separate chapter is devoted to the Canada-United States Free Trade Agreement. In each of these, an attempt is made to strike a balance among the analyses of historical developments, political processes and contemporary issues. In Part 6 (Conclusion), we reflect on the possible future course of business-government relations. This is done by looking at a couple of key developments—public opinion and structural economic change—affecting business power in Canada.

During the writing of this book we asked various colleagues to review some of the chapters. We would like to express our gratitude for the thoughtful suggestions of Kenneth Kernaghan (Brock), Hugh Thorburn (Queen's) and Glen Toner (Carleton). Kathy Cusack provided some much appreciated research assistance for this project. The complete manuscript was read by several reviewers, including Professor Mark Baetz of Wilfrid Laurier University and Professor S. Drabek of the University of Calgary. Their comments and advice helped us to improve the final product. None of these colleagues, known and unknown, is responsible for those shortcomings that remain.

We would also like to thank Barbara Faria of the University of Windsor for typing much of the manuscript, and Lucia Brown, Diane Dupuis, and Patricia Jolie, also of Windsor, for putting the material on disk.

This book would not have been written had it not been for the confidence of Prentice-Hall's college editor, Pat Ferrier. The careful assistance of Maurice Esses and Doris Wolf, both of Prentice-Hall, helped guide this project from draft chapters to the final book.

Finally, we would like to thank our respective spouses, Christine Brooks and Rose Morelli. Their support made it possible for us to write this book.

PART 1

Introduction

Chapter 1

Business - Government Relations

Business and government, it sometimes seems, are natural antagonists. Complaints about excessive government regulation, heavy taxation and the inefficient bureaucracy of politicians who "have never had to meet a payroll" are voiced frequently by business people. A recent survey of business executives and senior federal public officials found evidence of a huge gulf separating the attitudes and beliefs of these two groups. Seventy per cent of the public sector respondents felt that business-government relations ranged from "good" to "excellent," compared with 71 per cent of private sector respondents who felt that these relations were only "poor" to "fair."[1] Business people overwhelmingly believed that the government's social and economic policies were too left-wing while the majority of public officials thought they were appropriate. A majority of business executives (53 per cent) expressed the view that business-government relations had become worse over the previous ten years, while an even larger majority of public officials (69 per cent) felt that they had improved or remained the same.[2]

From this survey, it seems clear that those in business and those in government are not interpreting the world in the same way. However, popular and academic writing often conveys an opposite notion—one of close cooperation between business and government. Here, there is an impression of powerful corporations and business associations generally getting their way in dealing with government. One of Canada's leading business journalists, Diane Francis, writes:

> [The concentration of corporate power] has become so significant that the country is hurtling towards a new form of economic and political feudalism, a twentieth century version of Upper Canada's Family Compact back in the 1800s, when agrarian Ontario was politically and financially controlled by the few.[3]

In a more academic vein, Canadian political scientist Leo Panitch argues that "[it] is not that political and bureaucratic officials *decide* to favour capitalist interests in case after case; it is rather that it rarely even *occurs* to them that they might do other than favour such interests."[4]

What sense is one to make of these contradictory messages? Are business people right when they maintain that government is unresponsive to their needs, too likely to interfere in economic and social matters, and interested mainly in what needs to be done to ensure their election (politicians) or preserve their administrative turf (bureaucrats)? Or is government the normally compliant tool of business as others have argued? The reality of business-government relations is complex and provides a basis for both of these views. To understand these relations, we first need to examine the basic features of both political democracy and the capitalist economy.

DEMOCRACY AND CAPITALISM

The relationship between business and government is a complex one that involves both conflict and cooperation. The media is inclined to portray government and business as natural antagonists whose goals regularly conflict. Academics are more likely to see them as having a wide range of shared interests and to attribute to business a degree of political influence that no other group possesses. The conflict is real, but so too are the shared interests and the cooperation. This tension between confrontation and cooperation has its roots in the basic social organization of capitalist democracies in which two very different distributive mechanisms operate.

Democracy is a political system based on universal suffrage and its fundamental principle is equality. A second distinguishing feature of the Western-style democracies of North America, Western Europe and Japan is competition between political parties. These two factors — universal suffrage and competitive political parties — provide a basis for the political influence of groups whose only real resource is their voting power. The demands that workers, consumers, women, regional populations and other non-business groups make upon governments are often opposed by business interests. Therefore, governments which are receptive to these demands may give the impression of being unsympathetic or even hostile to business. This impression is usually a false one for reasons we will discuss later. The point to be made here is that the distributive mechanism that characterizes Western-style democracy enables non-business interests to influence the behaviour of government in ways that do not always accord with the preferences of business. The allocation of valued resources which fall within the scope of the state's influence is determined by the political power of those interests that are competing to have their goals expressed in public policy. Business interests occupy a privileged position in this competition, leading us to the second distributive mechanism that operates in capitalist democracies—the market economy.

A market economy is an economy in which most productive assets are privately-owned and in which most decisions regarding employment, technology, investment, the location of production facilities, and other matters of clear social importance are in the hands of private individuals. In the division of labour that characterizes capitalist societies, this vast range of distributive choices is left to a relatively small segment of the population—those who control the instruments of production—in the belief that their responsiveness to market signals is the most efficient system of allocating economic resources. The distributive mechanism that characterizes capitalism may be competitive, but it is not democratic in the egalitarian sense. When it comes to decisions regarding a business, the preferences of the individual who owns the business will necessarily count for more than those of his or her employees. Investors are unlikely to consult popular opinion before deciding whether to build a new facility in Toronto or in Moncton. In brief, the relatively small segment of society that controls most of society's productive assets determines the distribution of economic activity *within the bounds of the government's intervention in the economy*.

This distributive mechanism operates according to a principle that is fundamentally opposed to the one which characterizes the political system. The capitalist economy is based on inequality because not everyone is able to own or control productive assets. Even in populations where the ownership of private property and the investment in corporation shares are widespread, great inequalities in effective power will exist because of unequal distributions made in the past and differences in individual endowments and motivations. Inequalities also exist in the political system. Not all individuals or interests possess equal resources with which to influence government, nor are they all equally motivated to press their demands on the state. But the opportunities for non-business interests to influence decisions and outcomes is clearly greater in the democratic political system than in the capitalist economic system.

In capitalist democracies, the tension between one distributive mechanism which is based on formal equality in political status and another distributive mechanism which is based on inequality in property ownership is reconciled by a couple of widely held assumptions about society. One of these is individualism. *Capitalist* democracies are *liberal* democracies, where the principle of freedom of choice is a cornerstone of society. Historically speaking, the development of the market economy—an economy based on "the impersonal market allocation of work and rewards in response to individual choices"[5]—preceded the spread of liberal political institutions. The market economy dissolved the glue of tradition and status which had characterized social arrangements in pre-liberal times. Individual choice in the economy inevitably led to the break-up of barriers to individual choice in other spheres of society. It also led to a fundamental restructuring of power relations. Control over the new forms of wealth such as factories, transportation companies and investment capital contributed to the increased social prestige and political power of people in business.

The consequences of economic change were far-reaching. Freedom in the marketplace led to the break-up of traditional class divisions and to growing pressures for the extension of political rights throughout the (male) population. The form of democracy that emerged was one that accommodated itself to liberal capitalism. It was not a democracy that demanded the levelling of all social and economic differences. It was, however, opposed to the idea that the differences between individuals should be determined by the ascriptive characteristics related to one's birth. By the end of the 19th century, mainstream democratic thought was also solidly opposed to the existence of differences in the formal political status of citizens.[6]

An important shift had taken place in the concept of social class. The rigid lines of distinction based on one's hereditary social and economic status were no longer considered to be legitimate. Obviously, traditional class divisions did not dissolve overnight or even completely. But the basic premise of the market economy—free choice as embodied in the contractual relationship — was fundamentally at odds with non-voluntary social arrangements determined by birth and family status and it followed that the social and political inequalities that had characterized pre-liberal times were increasingly seen to be unacceptable. Inequalities in the economic sphere, however, were acceptable because they did not offend the liberal principle of individual freedom. Class distinctions in liberal society came to be associated with the differences in income and property, generated by the capitalist economy. So long as it was believed that competition in the economic marketplace was relatively open or, in other words, that upward socio-economic mobility and the acquisition of property were *available* to anyone, the inequalities generated by the economy were not seen to be a problem. The democratic principle of social and political equality was able to co-exist with an economic reality where inequalities were produced by the market economy.

Historically speaking, the market economy created pressures for a liberal state before it generated pressures for a democratic one. By "liberal state" we mean a system of government based on competition between political parties, enfranchisement of those who effectively ran the market economy (i.e., the owners of property) and supremacy of the elected legislature. This was a political system suited to the social power of the *bourgeoisie*, the business people who controlled the levers of the capitalist economy. It was not a democratic state as is demonstrated by the fact that universal voting rights were not achieved until the late 19th and early 20th centuries in most capitalist societies. The liberal state and the market economy ultimately generated pressures for the extension of full political rights to the general population. Industrialization created an urban working class which, as it grew in size, gained more and more political strength. The demands of this class for the vote eventually became irresistible. This was due both to the sheer size of the class, and therefore its potential for social disruption, and to the logic of the liberal state. Liberalism was based on free individual choice and equality of opportunity. The denial of these rights to a large segment of the population simply because they were not property-owners became less and less justifiable as the propertyless grew in number.

The extension of democratic rights to the working class transformed the liberal state into a liberal-democratic one and this had important consequences for the relationship between business and government. The political demands of the working class were often in conflict with the interests of business. Demands for state regulation of workplace conditions, minimum wage laws, social benefits and legal recognition of labour unions were generally resisted by the business community. Just how receptive governments were to these demands depended on the particular economic and social structures of their societies. Regardless of how ready political elites were to concede these demands for economic and social reform, the balance of political forces was changed significantly by the entry of the working class onto the political stage.

Business people had once been society's reformist element. They had been at the forefront of the movement to end hereditary privilege and non-representative government. The liberalism that they championed involved a challenge to the social and political status quo. In the societies of Western Europe, this challenge was resisted in varying degrees by the landed aristocracy, the crown and the church. In new world societies like Canada and the United States, liberalism had a somewhat different character. Its essential beliefs were the same as those of European liberalism, but it did not have the anti-establishment quality of its old world counterpart. The reason for this difference was simple enough: New world societies were established after the liberal state had consolidated itself in Europe. Business people in Canada and the United States did not have to overcome the entrenched power of a traditional aristocracy. As H.G. Wells has aptly written, these were societies without a past, with no memory of pre-liberal social arrangements.[7] To be opposed to the established powers in North America was to be opposed to business.

The coexistence of capitalist economic structures and democratic political structures has been viewed both pessimistically and optimistically by some of the major thinkers of modern times. During the 19th century the prevailing view was one of pessimism. Alexis de Tocqueville expressed this attitude in his monumental study *Democracy in America*. His arguments about the dangers that democracy can pose for individual freedom are certainly better known than his views on the social consequences of industrial capitalism. Nevertheless, his brief observations on the relationship between capitalism and democracy are important because of the way they anticipate later critics of capitalism like Karl Marx and Thorstein Veblen and also because of their contemporary relevance.[8]

De Tocqueville argued that political democracy and the working of the market economy produced a society in which the social conditions of individuals became more and more equal. He did not mean by this that all differences in possessions and income would be eliminated. What he meant was that the differences in manners, rights and duties associated with traditional class lines were dissolved by the democratic principle of equality. In place of the landed and hereditary aristocracy of pre-modern times, a new "aristocracy" of business emerged in capitalist democracies. The social power of those who owned the new manufacturing establishments of an industrializing economy was, according to de Tocqueville, no less than that of a traditional aristocracy. But there were some important differences between them. The manufacturers of this industrial economy constituted a distinct class because of their control over instruments of generating wealth that were not restricted to any group by birth or traditional right. This meant that their ranks were fluid and that the ties of class solidarity among the aristocracy of business were weak. They formed a class only in the sense of having certain material interests in common. Their relationship to other groups in society was one of increasing dominance which was based on control over the technology of industrialization. De Tocqueville argued that the tendency towards the increasing division of labour and the replacement of workers by machines—what 20th century industrial sociologists would call "de-skilling"—would lead to increasing inequality between capitalists and workers. The greatest danger to democracy, according to de Tocqueville, came from the inequality generated by industrial capitalism.

The inequality and conflict generated by capitalism was also a central issue in the work of Karl Marx. Like de Tocqueville, Marx recognized that the capitalist economy was the solvent of the ties that bound individuals to particular social ranks and occupations in pre-modern times. In place of these ties the market economy substituted "the cold cash nexus" between the buyers and sellers of labour. The feudal system of social relations was replaced by one in which an individual's class was determined by his or her relationship to the means of production in the capitalist economy. As capitalism developed, society would increasingly be polarized between two classes: the capitalists who controlled the factories, the mines, the banks and all the other means for the production and distribution of wealth, and the propertyless working class.

The existence of economically-determined classes was, according to Marx, inconsistent with a truly democratic society. He viewed the state as an expression of class domination; a view that was totally at odds with the widely held belief (as articulated by de Tocqueville) that liberal-democratic governments were responsive to popular demands. Marx argued that the inequality generated by the capitalist economy ultimately would lead to the demise of the capitalist system. In one of the more memorable lines from *The Communist Manifesto* he wrote, "What (capitalism). . . produces, above all, is its own gravediggers."[9]

This pessimistic view of the ability of capitalism and democracy to coexist needs to be understood in the context of an era in which capitalism was widely associated with "dark satanic mills," "robber barons" and rapacious industrialists. Illustrations of this are found in the obsessive materialism of Mr. Gradgrind in Charles Dickens' *Hard Times*, the biting satire of the *nouveau riche* portrayed in Stephen Leacock's *Arcadian Adventures of the Idle Rich*, the journalism and fiction of the American "muckrakers" Upton Sinclair and Lincoln Steffans and the critical sociology of Thorstein Veblen in his *The Theory of the Leisure Class*. The common theme of these diverse writings was their depiction of the dark side of capitalism: the inequalities it produced, the debased values that characterized it and the human suffering that accompanied it. The politics of "one man, one vote" were not enough to overcome the fundamentally undemocratic nature of capitalism.

Not everyone shared this bleak view. The philosophy of social Darwinism—the belief in competition and the "survival of the fittest" as natural conditions of society—achieved widespread popularity in the Anglo-American societies of the late 19th and early 20th centuries. This philosophy provided a perfect justification for capitalism on two grounds: (1) The competitive market economy accorded with the laws of nature; and (2) The inequalities produced by capitalism were socially beneficial because they were necessary for the achievement of the greatest social good. The economic crisis of the Great Depression and the positive reports that many English-speaking intellectuals brought back from the Soviet Union were factors that shook the faith in the viability of capitalist democracy. Social Darwinism lost its appeal when unemployment was widespread, real incomes were falling and the ability of the capitalist economy to deliver the material goods that had been its chief claim to popular support looked dubious.

Capitalism recovered from the global crisis of the 1930s and experienced a long period of expansion after World War II. Concern over the reconciliation of democracy and capitalism faded during the postwar years due to close to full employment and rising standards of living. Mass consumer goods industries such as automobiles, televisions and domestic appliances both fuelled this economic expansion and were the beneficiaries of increasing real personal incomes. The social reforms instituted by governments in Western societies and the increased economic management responsibilities assumed by the Keynesian state appeared to demonstrate that capitalism could be modified to be less harsh and more democratic. But as government interference in society and the economy increased, the relationship between capitalism and democracy became the subject of a very different critical perspective developed by those who worried about the consequences of *excessive* democracy.

In order to understand this perspective one must remember that democracy in capitalist societies developed as *liberal* democracy. The idea of rule by the people—the *demos*—emerged after the basic principle of the market economy—the individual's freedom to choose—had been established as part of the liberal state. Individual freedom was limited through the operation of the fundamental democratic principle of majority rule. But it was not until the scope of state activities became very large that encroachments on individual freedom of choice came in for intense criticism.[10] We may label this the *anti-collectivist critique*. It was not opposed to political democracy, but instead to the limits imposed by state regulation and taxation on the individual's freedom to choose. Economists like Frederick von Hayek[11] and Milton Friedman[12] have been the main exponents of the anti-collectivist critique.

The market economy provides the basis for the anti-collectivist argument. It becomes the model for the best protection of individual freedoms through voluntary agreements between individuals. It is also, according to this view, the cornerstone of a liberal-democratic political system. Capitalism and the private ownership of property are argued to be the necessary *economic foundation* for the maintenance of a free society. The reasoning behind this claim is that individual freedom is inconsistent with centralized decision-making power. A large and intrusive state which taxes a large share of individuals' incomes and places numerous restrictions on their economic and social activities is enforcing conformity (supported by the state's coercive power to punish those who violate its rules) at the expense of diversity. In Friedman's words: "The preservation of freedom requires the elimination of [concentrated power] to the fullest possible extent and the dispersal and distribution of whatever power cannot be eliminated—a system of checks and balances."[13]

This idea of checks and balances, or competition, as the surest guarantee of individual freedom goes back at least to the 18th century French political theorist Montesquieu. Friedman and the anti-collectivists give the idea a 20th century twist by arguing that (1) the practical operation of checks and balances is seen in the competitive capitalist economy, and (2) anything that limits freedom in the economic marketplace necessarily undermines political freedom. The anti-collectivist argument is not opposed to an extensive welfare state and state management of the economy on the grounds that these activities are undemocratic. Indeed, a majority of the population may well support what effectively are limitations on the individual's freedom to choose. The anti-collectivists' opposition to "big government" (and for that matter to private concentrations of economic power) is based on their belief that the competitive marketplace is the best guarantee of individual freedom. Their ideal state would still perform important regulatory (i.e., freedom-limiting) functions. But it would not attempt to substitute its judgements for those of private economic decision-makers, nor would it carry out most of the redistributive functions associated with the modern welfare state.

The anti-collectivists maintain that competitive capitalism is a necessary condition for a democracy in which individual freedoms are protected rather than trampled on by government. This is a contemporary restatement of the philosophy of economic liberalism which rose to ideological dominance in the 19th century. It is a philosophy that glorifies the market and the private economic decision-maker and it is suspicious of anything that interferes with them. The equality that it prizes is equality of opportunity. Competition is valued both because it enshrines the liberal value of individual freedom, and because it is supposed to maximize the collective well-being of society.

This brand of economic liberalism has enjoyed a renaissance since the 1970s. It has been given a variety of names—neo-conservatism, Reaganomics, Thatcherism, "Orange County anarchism"[14]—but in every case the central idea has been that interference with the market has reached excessive proportions. Capitalist business and its values of private ownership, individual initiative and profits appear to have acquired a renewed respectability. On the other side of the coin is the reputation of the welfare state. The renaissance of economic liberalism is directly related to the tarnished image of the welfare state. To put this more precisely, the apparent failure of the welfare-interventionist state in sustaining the economic prosperity of postwar expansion has contributed to a greater openness to market-oriented policies and to the widespread view that government has grown too large for the collective good. The fairness of this assessment should not concern us at this point. In the present context, what is important is that the issue of how to reconcile capitalism and democracy (and whether they are even reconcilable at all) has once again come to the fore—this time in the guise of a debate over the appropriate size and functions of government.

THE SPECTRUM OF BUSINESS-GOVERNMENT RELATIONS

Media reporting on business-government relations is replete with terms like "business reaction," "business pressure" and "business's position." Academic writing on these relations is likewise inclined to use terms that imply a consensus of opinion or objective interests that, in actual fact, usually do not exist among business people. This tendency to overgeneralize what business has in common is understandable. But at the same time it may lead to some very wrong conclusions about the nature of business-government relations.

The political interests of business can be arranged along a spectrum from the most general, those shared by virtually all businesses, to the most specific. The positions on this spectrum coincide with different levels of political orgazation among businesses and with different sorts of policy interests. At the most general level are the interests of *capital*. These include protection for those fundamental principles of the capitalist economic system that we discussed earlier in this chapter: the private ownership of property, the social respectability and economic importance of private profits, and the market as the chief mechanism for allocating the economy's resources. In addition, capital has an objective interest in the maintenance of social order. Dramatic change and an unpredictable future obviously pose the greatest risks for those who have the most to lose from such changes. For this reason a stable social-political climate is valued highly by investors and established businesses.

Table 1.1

Spectrum of Business Interests and Organization			
	Level of Business Fragmentation	Principal Level of Policy Interests	Level of Political Organization
General	Capital "as a whole"	Highly generalized and diffuse. eg. private property rights; continuity of capital accumulation; social acquiescence to capitalism.	No Formal organization
	Sectoral; regional	National issues. eg. taxation; monetary policy; social programs; industrial relations; national trade policy.	Broad-based business associations
	Single industries	Specific industry measures. eg. industry regulations and standards; specific tax breaks; particular tariffs and NTBs; patent protection; R & D assistance	Trade associations
	Individual corporations	Narrow corporate interests. eg. government contracts; grants; loans; subsidies; licences.	Lobbying firms; government relations/public affairs departments.; personal contact by executives.
Narrow			

Business is rarely organized at this very general level. In Canada, broad-based associations, such as the Business Council on National Issues, The Canadian Chamber of Commerce, The Canadian Manufacturers' Association and Quebec's Conseil du Patronat, come closest to representing the general interests of business. They fall far short, however, of operating as organizational voices for all parts of the business community. Nor do they "represent" business in such activities as collective bargaining with labour or national economic planning. These functions are attributed to the nationally-integrative associations for business and labour that exist in so-called "corporatist" societies like Austria, Sweden and West Germany (see Chapter Five). Broad-based associations in Canada also tend to have problems in maintaining internal cohesion because they try to cover a wide range of business interests that sometimes conflict.

Trade associations which are organized around particular industries, as in the cases of the Canadian Petroleum Association and The Canadian Bankers' Association, tend to be more cohesive organs for making political demands on governments. But, by the same token, they are more limited in scope. This intermediate level of business interests is one of intense political activity, with a large number of trade associations that vary enormously in terms of their membership size, financial resources and internal structures. Using a fairly conservative definition, we located over four hundred trade associations that were active at the national level in Canada in 1988.[15] Divisions within the business community are obvious at this level of objective interests.

At the most specific level of business-government relations, one finds the individual corporation. Here, the political interests of business appear in their most fragmented form. Corporations do not rely exclusively nor in most cases even primarily on the business associations they belong to for political representation. They often act individually, hiring lobbyists and public relations professionals. In the case of large corporations, particularly in regulated industries, it is common to employ a full-time public affairs staff to handle the firm's relations with the state and its dealings with the media and the public.

Like the intermediate level of business-government relations, the fragmentation of interests among individual corporations is reflected in their contacts with the state. Business associations and corporations do not have dealings with government as a whole, but with *particular* departments (and specifically with specialized divisions within these departments), agencies, cabinet ministers and bureaucratic officials. Through a process of mutual reinforcement, the divisions among business interests contribute to fragmentation within the state, whose specialized structures reinforce the lines of division among economic interests. These divisions among business interests create a sort of tower of Babel—a discordant chorus of voices, each demanding that its own special interests be protected or promoted by the state. Adding to the dissonance are the demands made by non-business groups. The overall impression is one of an unceasing competition among a multitude of different groups whose interests coincide and collide depending upon the issue and its political and economic context.

Business-government relations at the intermediate and individual corporation levels are characterized by both cooperation and confrontation. The confrontational side of these relations may seem to dominate (agreement and cooperation usually are not considered to be newsworthy). But conflict between business and government is kept within limits by the factors responsible for the privileged position of business in capitalist society. However, given this privileged position and the overall interdependence of business and government, how do we explain the various instances of conflict that occur?

THE SOURCES OF BUSINESS-GOVERNMENT CONFLICT

Conflict between business and government in capitalist democracies can be explained along four principal dimensions. These are (1) Business fractions, (2) Democratic pressures, (3) State autonomy and (4) State fragmentation.

Business Fractions

In the preceding section we looked at the divisions within the business world and the cacophony of disparate interests subsumed under the general heading of "business." Different fractions of the business community have different policy needs, and the particular demands of one section of business quite often conflict with the demands of another section. Given the existence of these conflicts, it is impossible for government to satisfy all business groups equally. From time to time, governments must make difficult choices in which some particular industry, association or corporation is a loser. One possible solution is to try to reconcile these interests and engineer some sort of policy compromise. But if this is not possible, then state policy-makers have to adjudicate in favour of some business interests and against others. In this process, the most dominant or highly-aggregated sets of business interests are likely to be favoured over weaker and subordinate ones.

In reconciling and adjudicating between business fractions, government must give top priority to the overall health of the capitalist economy. The general needs of capital take precedence over the narrower goals of individual business groups, and government officials must consider the bigger economic picture, not just particular corporate demands. Failure to do this may ultimately jeopardize the long-term vitality of the capitalism. Consequently, governments cannot always do what individual corporations or business associations want, and thus we have one basis for conflict between business and government.

Democratic Pressures

Public policy formation is not simply a response to the conflicting needs of different sections of business. In democratic political systems, governments also have to take public opinion or pressure from significant, well-organized sections of the population seriously. Here, too, calculations are far from simple. Public opinion is frequently divided and non-business pressure groups are often at loggerheads with one another. Trying to form an aggregate picture of public opinion is no easier for government than trying to form an aggregate picture of business interests. For instance, the demands of voters in Quebec may clash with the demands of voters in Western Canada, or, in another example, "Pro-Choice" groups may clash with "Pro-Life" groups on the issue of abortion. Reconciling these interests and constructing compromises is not always easy, and again, government may have to make difficult choices. As with the consideration of business needs, government is likely to give priority to the more aggregated and dominant interests over the subordinate ones; for example, when government favours Central Canada, where voter concentration is greatest, over Western and Atlantic provinces.

So far, we have noted two sets of calculations for governments in considering public policy. There is the "economic calculation" which addresses the balance of business needs, and there is the "political calculation" which addresses the balance of public pressure and opinion. On some policy issues these calculations lead to compatible conclusions, but on others there is conflict between the two sorts of factors. In such circumstances, elected officials may well decide that the political calculation takes precedence over the economic one (especially if an election is approaching). Thus we have another reason why policy-makers may reject business demands, and another basis for business-government conflict.

State Autonomy

In addition to conflict between business fractions and the exigencies of democratic pressure, there is a further reason why business demands are sometimes denied by public officials. Conflict can arise when the demands of particular businesses run counter to the "autonomous preferences"[16] of state policy-makers. Bureaucrats and politicians have motivations for policy decisions which are independent from societal pressures (including business and the public). These fall under two basic headings.

The first is self-interest, where policy-makers adopt a course of action in order to promote their own career advancement, power and prestige. Politicians try to extend the scope of their personal authority and political clout and bureaucrats have a vested interest in expanding the size of their bureaus, budgets and programmes. This is part of the well-known process called "bureaucratic empire-building." As Fred Block has suggested, such pursuit of self-interest raises the possibility that state managers might act against capital if it improves their own position to do so.[17]

The second type of motivation comes under the heading of national interest. Policy-makers can pursue goals that they consider to be in the national or regional interest (such as economic nationalism, national unity, minority rights, sovereignty-association, etc.), regardless of whether these things serve business needs, public demands or personal gains. We have become accustomed to being cynical about politics (often with some justification). Yet we miss something if our view of politics emphasizes *only* the self-serving, moral flexibility of politicians who bow to the strongest pressure. Although politicians often *do* see national interests as coincidental with business needs, personal goals or the latest opinion polls, this is not inevitable or universal. Policy-makers can have objectives which are more high-minded or ideologically committed, and examples of "conviction" politicians can occasionally be found in all political parties.

The essential point here is that independent motives of self-interest or national interest (whether stemming from rational calculation or from ideology) can form the basis for state action that goes against the demands of business. Thus we have another potential source of business-government conflict.

State Fragmentation

Finally, conflict is also evident if we shift the focus of attention from explaining government action to explaining business action. Government industrial policy is typically concerned with getting private business to behave in a certain manner, such as investing in particular regions or conforming to certain regulatory standards. In a country like Canada where jurisdiction over many aspects of industrial policy is split among different levels of government, businesses can be pushed in different directions by different sets of policy-makers. When corporations are subject to conflicting pressures from federal and provincial governments, it is not always possible to accommodate them both. In these cases, business-government conflicts occur when business fails to do what a particular government wants, rather than the other way around. This problem occurs in any complex and functionally differentiated system of government. However, it is especially noticeable in federations such as Canada, where authority over major aspects of public policy is shared among different levels of government.

It is clear that the governments of democratic societies are not the mere instruments of business. It is equally clear that "business" does not speak with a single voice—a fact reflected in the hundreds of different associations that represent business interests. But one should not conclude from these facts that business interests are *comme les autres* in the politics of capitalist societies. Nor should one conclude that the hundreds of separate business associations do not have politically important interests in common. Although their common interest in the fundamental values and institutions of capitalism is not expressed through unified organization and concerted political action, the general interest of capital operates as a sort of ideological-structural stage that limits the movement of state actors. By distinguishing between the various levels of business-government relations, one can reconcile the reality of conflict over particular issues with that of a general consensus on the fundamentals of capitalism. This consensus is one of several factors that underpins business power in modern industrial democracies.

HOW POWERFUL IS BUSINESS?

To hear some business people tell it, governments are not especially receptive to the needs and demands of the business community. On the contrary, they argue, politicians' obsessive concern with votes means that business's voice— or its many voices—must compete with all of those other interests that press their demands upon the state. While there is no doubt that business does not have matters all its own way in the political system (the diversity of material interests within the business community alone ensures that there will be both winners *and* losers among business interests), there also is no doubt that business occupies a privileged position in the politics of capitalist societies. This privileged position is based on a combination of the *cultural dominance* of business values, the *structural dependence* of governments on the behaviour of business, *elite linkages* and the *lobbying power* that business interests wield through pressure politics.

The cultural dominance of business values—what we will refer to here as business ideology—has three dimensions. These are (1) the widespread belief in the non-political character of private economic decision-making; (2) the values associated with the basic unit of capitalist enterprise, the corporation; and (3) the materialist culture that pervades Western societies. We will examine each of these in turn.

Cultural Dominance

The fact that governments interfere with the activities of private business demonstrates their awareness of the public consequences of these activities. Pollution controls, minimum wage laws, grants and tax deductions to encourage investment, price regulations for certain goods: these are only a few examples of the ways in which the state intervenes in the economic marketplace in pursuit of public policy goals. The extent of such interventions in the modern capitalist economy does not undermine the fundamental belief that business decision-making should be primarily a private affair. Charles Lindblom makes this point in arguing that business people make decisions that, by any reasonable standard, have broad public consequences. A decision to shut down a factory, to invest in a particular community, to produce a certain product or to use a particular technology may in each case affect the lives of hundreds and even thousands of people. Whether a decision is made by private sector decision-makers or by public officials is not determined by the consequences of that decision for society. Instead, most economic decisions on investment, employment, production and pricing are generally believed to be matters for private determination. These are matters that lie outside of the public realm. The state may (and does) influence the choices that business people make. But as Lindblom observes, the essential point is that "in any private enterprise system, a large category of major decisions is turned over to businessmen, both small and larger."[18] A vast area of decision-making is delegated to private decision-makers who, within the bounds of the law, are accountable only to their shareholders for the consequences of their choices. Business people are, according to Lindblom, public officials in terms of the social importance of their actions. But they are public officials whose behaviour is neither controllable by nor accountable to the public through the political system.

In liberal societies we tend to associate politics with government and to distinguish the political (governmental) system from the economic system. This conception of politics has the unfortunate consequence of obscuring the fact that "private" decisions may be every bit as political as "public" ones in every important respect except in who actually makes and executes them. For example, when public authorities decide to change the zoning classification of a particular area, build an airport or alter the budget allocated for social services, these decisions have very real distributional, and therefore political, consequences. They may affect such matters as property values (zoning, airport), pattern of employment (zoning, airport), quality of life for a segment of the population (zoning, airport, social services) and ideological conflicts (most obvious in the social services' example). When private decision-makers (business people) choose to close down a mining operation, open a new factory, advertize a product using sexual imagery or implement a particular employment policy, the decision will also carry distributional and political consequences.

The difference between the choices of public and private decision-makers is not even one of the magnitude of their effects. When the Iron Ore Company of Canada decided to close down its operations at Schefferville, Quebec, the consequences for the local community could hardly have been greater. In the other direction, investment decisions by Honda (Alliston, Ontario) and Toyota

(Cambridge, Ontario) provided real income benefits for the communities where the new plants were built and for both the Ontario and national economies. When the Thompson-owned *Ottawa Journal* closed on the same day as the Southam-owned *Winnipeg Tribune*, leaving the Southam-owned *Ottawa Citizen* as the sole daily in Ottawa and the Thompson-owned *Free Press* with a monopoly in Winnipeg, the possible social consequences of these private decisions were considered to be serious enough to warrant the appointment of a royal commission to investigate the newspaper industry. More generally, the level of business confidence in the future health of the economy is a factor that has an enormous influence on employment and income levels, public revenues and the choices available to public decision-makers.

Obviously, the difference between the choices of public and private decision-makers is not that those of public authorities have political (distributional) consequences and those of business people do not. Instead, the difference is essentially one of process: public authorities are elected or appointed to their positions of power according to different rules than those that apply to private sector organizations. This distinction only exists because of the cultural beliefs associated with a market economy. Where the market economy does not exist or is a very minor part of the total economy (as in communist societies), there is no basis for the distinction between business (private) decisions and political (public) decisions.

The fact that immense public power is exercised by private decision-makers has its roots in certain premises about the market economy. In non-market societies, it is understood that decisions about what to produce, how much to produce, with what technology and at what price are policy decisions that are undertaken by state officials. In market societies, on the other hand, the general expectation is that these decisions should be made by private individuals and that state interference with the economic marketplace needs to be justified on grounds that the public interest is not being served by the market. The dominant ideology of capitalist society—the belief system that most people share— includes a faith in the socially beneficial consequences of private markets. From this faith there follows a number of related beliefs about the individual's right to private property, the social desirability of private profits and the removal of most decisions about the allocation of the economy's resources from governmental control.

In short, the belief system that characterizes capitalist society builds a wall between economics and politics, and between the private realm of executives, investors, workers and consumers and the public realm of government. The separation between these realms has never been watertight and, in fact, has grown increasingly leaky throughout the 20th century. But the idea of the market operating as a sort of protective barrier that insulates a vast area of socially important decision-making from direct political control remains. This has crucial implications for the distribution of resources in society. The political marketplace provides greater opportunities than does the economic marketplace for those groups whose influence rests on collective action rather than on the control of capital.

A second dimension of business ideology that reinforces the cultural dominance of business values is the concept of the corporation. In a capitalist society we take it for granted that most economic activity will be carried out by privately-owned businesses. A vast body of commercial law has been developed to specify the rights and responsibilities of those who own businesses. This body of law provides legal support for the market economy. As Peter Russell puts it: "The legal systems of western liberal democracies continue...to attach great value to protecting individuals in the enjoyment of their personal property, a value essential to maintaining capitalist economic relations; in the same way, the legal systems of communist states emphasize the importance of promoting behaviour which conforms with an ideological conception of communist society."[19] The corporation is woven into the legal fabric of capitalist society.

The fact that the corporation is the basic unit of economic life is significant in two ways. First, it means that economic decision-making is a *fragmented* process centring on individual firms. This fragmentation reinforces the social power of private business by associating property rights with the individuals who own corporations rather than with the community and its political arm, the state. Second, it has contributed to the belief that modern capitalism is free of the sort of class divisions that beset market societies at an earlier stage of their development. For decades now the conventional wisdom has been that the people who actually control the large corporation are its managers, not its owners. As John Kenneth Galbraith has argued, power in the modern corporation has passed from the classical individual entrepreneur heralded in economics textbooks, to the reality of an organizational "technostructure" that is dependent on planning.[20] Sociologists like Talcott Parsons, Daniel Bell and Ralf Dahrendorf have argued that the separation of ownership from control of the large corporation has led to the decline of a dominant class in advanced capitalist societies.[21] This claim will be examined in Chapter Five.

A third dimension of the cultural dominance of business involves the pervasive materialism that characterizes capitalist societies. This materialism is reinforced by the mass media through commercial advertizing and entertainment programming. The values purveyed through these powerful instruments of social learning include consumerism (the identification of material achievement with one's social status, personal worth and sexual desirability) and the middle-classness of society. Some sociologists have argued that the historical roots of capitalism's acquisitive materialist culture lie in certain protestant ethical values which view worldly success as a sign of grace.[22] Whatever its origins may be, there can be no doubt that the modern consumer culture which sustains capitalism does not depend on religion for its inspiration. It is a secular culture that mirrors the basic values of the market economy: individualism, private profits, equality of opportunity and apparently boundless growth. Dissent from mainstream materialism is marginal in all capitalist societies.[23]

The Structural Basis of Business Power

Culture is an important part of the explanation for the privileged position of business, but it is not a complete account. We also need to consider the structural basis of business power. By "structural" we mean the material factors which establish the state's dependency on capital.

One of the crucial factors in this relationship is the *mobility of capital*. Investors enjoy a wide although not absolute freedom to shift their capital between sectors of the economy and from one national economy to another. The epitome of this mobility is found in the multinational corporation—an enterprise whose activities span a number of national economies and whose international character often is used as a lever in dealing with the government of a particular country. In addition to being territorially mobile, investment capital also has the capacity to expand and contract in response to investors' perceptions of the political-economic climate for business. Short of imposing punitive tax rates on savings, governments cannot force business and private investors to invest. Governments in all capitalist societies are concerned with levels of business confidence and are reluctant to take actions that carry a high risk of causing a cutback in investment. The consequences of such a cutback are felt politically by governments. Weak economic activity tends to translate into popular dissatisfaction and a loss of political support.[24]

This relationship between government action and business confidence is labelled by Lindblom the "automatic, punishing recoil of the market."[25] He argues that the existence of the market imprisons the behaviour of public policy-makers by placing objective limits on their responsiveness to non-business interests. Politicians need to care about business confidence because of the very real possibility that they will not be re-elected if business's unwillingness to invest causes unemployment and falling incomes. But another factor that gives pause even to governments which can count on strong popular backing is the state's financial dependence on business. A decline in the levels of investment or profit will soon be felt as a drop in government revenues from the taxation of corporate and employment income and from the taxation of consumption. The problem of falling revenues is almost certain to be compounded by an increase in state expenditures on social programmes whose costs are sensitive to changes in the level of economic activity. Borrowing on the public credit is only a temporary solution to this dilemma—and one that experience has shown to be both costly and subject to the limits of international investor confidence.

In summary, the privileged position of business rests upon cultural and structural factors that are, in fact, related to one another. A government's popular support and the state's ability to finance its activities are heavily dependent on the level of business confidence and the level of private investment in the economy. Two constraints on state action flow from this relationship. One is ideological: the belief that the market is the most desirable system for allocating economic resources. Although interference with the market is sometimes desirable, its elimination is unthinkable. The second constraint is based on the fact that capital and capitalism are international. A government intent on reforms opposed by the business community might be able to weather a drop in domestic business confidence if the economy of such a country had no important links to the rest of the capitalist world. Businesses could be nationalized and currency controls could be imposed to stem the outbound flow of capital. The strength of liberal values makes such a scenario unlikely in most capitalist societies. But even assuming there was the political will to take such measures, the economic ties that exist between capitalist economies mean that anti-market reforms of this scale would be met by a negative reaction on the part of foreign investors, currency traders, and creditors. International business confidence is, therefore, another brake on the actions of governments.

Elite Linkages

Reinforcing the cultural and structural bases of business power is a network of linkages at the elite level between business leaders and political leaders. In its most simple form, elitism is manifest in the under-representation of important sections of society in the higher reaches of power. Those at the top are predominantly white, Anglo-Saxon males, few of whom have been drawn from working-class backgrounds. With some exceptions, elite members tend to have similar socio-economic origins and experiences, as well as similar outlooks and ideologies. This is sometimes reinforced by friendship, kinship and frequency of personal contact that produces an easy familiarity between economic and political elites.

These ties are further strengthened by institutional linkages. Amongst the Canadian economic elite, the elaborate network of interlocking directorships and corporate cross-ownerships has a unifying tendency which is exacerbated by high levels of corporate concentration (see Chapter Five). Institutional links with the political world are established both through the frequent participation of business representatives on public boards and commissions, and through the recruitment of business executives into senior political positions. As shown in

Chapter Nine, since the end of World War II nearly half of the federal cabinet ministers with economic portfolios came from, or returned to, the ranks of the economic elite. Prominent political figures such as Brian Mulroney, John Turner and Paul Martin Jr. provide individual examples of top politicians who were presidents or directors of large corporations.

This system of intimate elite connections constitutes a further reason why business's demands frequently receive a sympathetic political hearing. However, in itself, elitism is only a partial explanation of business power. Ultimately, elite linkages are underpinned by the structural interdependency of the state and capital. In addition, elite theory has problems in dealing with the manifest divisions and conflicts that characterize both the corporate and political worlds (see Chapter Three). At a more disaggregate level, lobbying and political pressure from particular fractions of the business community play an important role in determining "who gets what."

The Lobbying Power of Business

In the real world of pressure politics there are large inequalities between the tools of influence that different groups have at their disposal. Studies of pressure-group behaviour show that political influence tends to be associated with permanent organization, a professional staff, extensive financial resources and direct access to political and bureaucratic decision-makers. Organizations representing business interests are more likely to possess these characteristics than other groups. The clientele of Canada's most important lobbying firms and political survey/market research companies read like a Who's Who of the Canadian (and international) corporate world. Canada's election spending legislation and democratic norms prevent business interests from "buying" political candidates and political parties through campaign contributions. Nonetheless, there is still a good deal of room for influence through money and the Liberal and Progressive Conservative Parties continue to be heavily dependent on corporate support to finance their election campaigns. The relationship between money and influence tends to be even starker in municipal politics. It is here that property developers focus much of their efforts in order to influence public policy.

Not all business interests are well-heeled and highly organized. The difference between oil and gas producers and convenience store owners, for example, is enormous. Petroleum companies, especially the large ones, are capable of both independent influence and collective influence through their umbrella organization, the Canadian Petroleum Association. Convenience store operators, despite their numbers, are largely unorganized. Some belong to the Canadian Federation of Independent Business and others do not. They tend to organize sporadically around issues like Sunday closing laws. Therefore, when we say that business interests have superior financial and organizational resources for lobbying, for politically-oriented advertizing, and for contributing to political parties, this should be understood as a generalization. It does not imply that all business interests possess the same political muscle, nor does it follow that non-business groups can not also deploy impressive resources.

But equality is not the prevailing condition in the world of pressure politics. It is inconceivable that any single local labour union, parish or community social organization could marshal the political resources of an individual corporation like Bell Canada. Non-business groups typically rely upon collective organization which allows them to pool their resources for influencing government. Business also organizes collectively. But in the case of large corporations, independent action is often an effective way to influence public policy. Bell Canada annually spends far more money on preparing and arguing its case for rate changes before the Canadian Radio and Telecommunications Commission, and on advertizing intended to generate positive public feelings about the company, than the Canadian Consumers' Association, the principal representative for consumer interests at CRTC hearings, does on its entire budget. Only a small fraction of the CCA's budget goes toward telephone rate hearings.

The lobbying power of business interests does not derive wholly from the power of money. There are also extensive personal links between government and business. These links are less important today than they were in Canada's early history, when cabinet ministers regularly were drawn from the business elite and saw no reason to sever their business connections simply because they held public office. The concept of "conflict of interest" was much less developed in an era when government was frankly looked upon as an instrument for economic development and when politics was seldom a full-time occupation. The circumstances that led to charges of conflict of interest against Conservative Cabinet minister Sinclair Stevens in 1985 would not have caused a ripple in the politics of 19th century Canada.

The personal links between business and government may be less intimate today than in the past, but they are still important. After the legal profession, business is the major recruiting ground for public office. Of course many lawyers are also part of the business world, working on a daily basis with a corporate clientele. In the 1988 Conservative government, 51 per cent of the cabinet ministers had a previous background in either business or law.[26] These figures are not unusual. Legislative studies have shown that lawyers and business people have tended to be even more heavily represented in Cabinet than in the government as a whole. The tradition of having "representatives" of the Montreal and Toronto business communities in the federal cabinet is a long one, and the Finance portfolio in particular has been dominated (with rare exceptions) by individuals whom the corporate world could call their own. The importance of these personal links between business and government is discussed in greater detail in Chapter Five. For now, we simply want to make the point that other interests like teachers, organized labour, farmers and native peoples, to name only a few, do not enjoy the same level of personal representation in government.

This examination of the sources of business power should not be interpreted as meaning that business gets everything it wants, whenever it wants, from government. This is obviously far from the truth. "Business" is in fact a highly fragmented community whose members often make irreconcilable demands on the state. Nor is business the only voice that governments listen to in democratic societies. The point of the preceding analysis was to understand the basis for the privileged position that business occupies in the politics of capitalist societies. We have identified four bases of business power, namely cultural dominance, structural dependence, elite linkages and lobbying power; and we have argued that the first two factors are the most fundamental. To put it simply, if there were no personal links between the state and business, and if business's financial resources were no greater than those of other groups attempting to influence the behaviour of governments, business interests would still occupy a privileged position in politics for the cultural and structural reasons we have discussed. This is the fundamental political significance of the capitalist economy. It establishes limits to government's ability to respond to non-business interests and to alienate economically powerful groups of corporate decision-makers.

ENDNOTES

1. D. Wayne Taylor and Victor V. Murray, "An Interpretive Understanding of the Non-fulfilment of Business-Government Relations," in *Canadian Public Administration* 30:3 (Fall 1987), 424.
2. *Ibid.*, 425-26.
3. Diane Francis, *Controlling Interest: Who Owns Canada?* (Toronto: Macmillan, 1986), 3.
4. Leo Panitch, ed., *The Canadian State: Political Economy and Political Power* (Toronto: University of Toronto Press, 1977), 14, emphasis in the original.
5. C.B. Macpherson, *The Real World of Democracy* (Toronto: CBC Enterprises, 1966), 7.

6. The category of "citizen" was sometimes far from inclusive, women in particular being left out. The prominent liberal thinker J.S. Mill was opposed to the idea of formal equality of status for all citizens, advocating instead a system in which property-owners would have greater electoral weight than citizens without property.

7. H.G. Wells, *The Future in America* (New York: Harper, 1906).

8. Alexis de Tocqueville, *Democracy in America,* Book II (New York: New American Library, 1956), 34.

9. Karl Marx and Frederick Engels, *Manifesto of the Communist Party* (Moscow: Foreign Languages Publishing House, 1959), 61.

10. There were some earlier exceptions like Henry David Thoreau's "Civil Disobedience" in Henry Canby, ed., *The Works of Thoreau* (Boston: Houghton Mifflin, 1937), 789-808.

11. Frederick von Hayek, *The Road to Serfdom* (Chicago: University of Chicago Press, 1944).

12. Milton Friedman, *Capitalism and Freedom* (Chicago: University of Chicago Press, 1962).

13. *Ibid.,* 15.

14. The flamboyant term "Orange County anarchism" was coined by political philosopher Tom Darby in describing the politics of the middle class tax revolt in the U.S.

15. Based on authors' survey, 1988 (see Chapter Seven).

16. Everyone's preferences are, of course, shaped by some process of socialization, but autonomy refers to the ability of policy-makers to resist the specific pressures emanating from civil society and to act with a high degree of independence from these forces in making particular policy choices.

17. Fred Block, "Beyond Relative Autonomy: State Managers as Historical Subjects" in Ralph Miliband and John Saville, eds., *The Socialist Register 1980* (London: The Merlin Press, 1980), 230.

18. Charles E. Lindblom, *Politics and Markets* (New York: Basic Books, 1977), 172.

19. Peter Russell, *The Judiciary in Canada* (Toronto: McGraw-Hill Ryerson, 1987), 21.

20. John Kenneth Galbraith, *The New Industrial State*, 4th edition (New York: Mentor, 1985), 53-90.

21. Daniel Bell, "The Breakup of Family Capitalism," in *The End of Ideology* (New York: Collier, 1961); Ralf Dahrendorf, *Class and Class Conflict in Industrial Society* (Stanford: Stanford University Press, 1959); Talcott Parsans and Neil Smelser, *Economy and Society* (London: Routledge & Kegan-Paul, 1957).

22. The classic statements of this argument are Max Weber's, *The Protestant Ethic and the Spirit of Capitalism* (London: Unwin, 1965); and R.H. Tawney's, *Religion and the Rise of Capitalism* (Gloucester, Mass.: Peter Smith, 1962).

23. Anti-materialist political movements have made inroads in some societies. West

Germany's Green Party and the "Ecos" in countries like France, Belgium and New Zealand have even achieved some small electoral success (5-10 per cent of the popular vote). But perhaps more significant than these minor electoral breakthroughs is the fact that the generation which appeared to reject the materialist society during the 1960s has become the current vanguard of consumerism.

24. Bruno S. Frey, *Modern Political Economy* (New York: John Wiley & Sons, 1978), chapter 11.
25. Charles E. Lindblom, "The Market as Prison" in Thomas Ferguson and Joel Rogers, eds., *The Political Economy* (Armonk, New York: M.E. Sharpe, 1984), 3-11.
26. Canada, Parliament, *Parliamentary Guide* (Kanata: Normandin, 1988).

PART 2

HISTORY AND THEORY

Chapter 2

Business and Government in Historical Perspective

HISTORICAL DEVELOPMENT

When he wrote, "The role of the state in the economic life of Canada is really the modern history of Canada,"[1] Alexander Brady could have omitted the reference to "modern." From the first European settlement to present day society, the interwoven character of politics and business has been at the centre of Canada's development. Government has from the beginning acted on the assumption that one of its major roles—indeed its principal role—is to provide the conditions for economic growth. While the precise form that this growth should take and the policy goals which allow for interference with market forces have varied over time, the overriding significance of economic issues and the political importance of business interests have been constant factors in Canada's history. It is no accident that many of Canada's most prominent historians (English Canada's at least) are best known for their work on economic history.[2]

The idea that business operates in a laissez faire environment which asks nothing of government and which subjects business to no significant limitations except for those imposed by the criminal law and the law of civil damages (tort) is a fiction that has never had any basis in the Canadian reality. The myth of laissez faire is based upon very limited historical evidence; mainly the emergence of industrial capitalism in Britain and the rapid growth of the American economy in the late 19th and early 20th centuries. Its wide acceptance as a characterization of historical fact, and not simply as an idealized model of a capitalist economy of the sort described in Adam Smith's *The Wealth of Nations*,[3] has been due largely to the *ideological role* that this myth has played. Laissez faire is a doctrine that includes a belief in the private ownership of property, in the rights of individuals to dispose of their property as they so choose, and in the superiority of the free market as a means for promoting the well-being of individuals and society as a whole. It coincides with the objective interests of those who benefit most from the operation of capitalism and who have the most to

28

lose from interference with their right to buy, sell, produce or invest as they wish. In other words, a belief in laissez faire either as an historical fact or as a doctrine that, like a religious one, can be only imperfectly attained in the real world supports the social position of those who control private property. State interference with the rights that go with property ownership needs to be justified on grounds that a greater social good is expected from such intervention in the free market. In a capitalist society where the principal tenets of the laissez faire creed are still strong at the level of the popular culture, the rights of an employer to lay off workers, to shut down a factory and to earn profits (subject to some limits) are not questioned. It is the state's right to question these things that needs to be defended. In exercising this conditional right, governments generally do not challenge the fundamental premises of capitalism.

In this chapter we survey the historical development of business-government relations in Canada. The purpose of this survey is to provide the reader with an idea of the nature and extent of these relations during earlier periods of Canada's history. This tour d'horizon is highly selective. The history of business-government relations is the subject for a book (indeed several books!) by itself.[4] We restrict ourselves to a discussion of some of the main features of these relations. Many of the issues raised in the following pages are discussed in greater detail in later chapters.

History may be written in two ways: chronologically or thematically. A straightforward chronological approach that begins at a particular point and moves forward toward the present is the one most commonly adopted by historians. Other social scientists are inclined to favour the thematic approach, where historical material is organized into "bunches" that, in the writer's view, reflect the analytically significant features of historical development. The two approaches are not mutually exclusive. Historians almost inevitably end up identifying "eras" and "turning points" and pointing their fingers at what they believe to be the main reasons for change.

The approach adopted in this chapter is thematic, but the themes represent what in our view are the major successive stages in the evolution of business-government relations in Canada. The break between these stages is seldom abrupt. Transition is usually a gradual process, and for this reason there is some moving backwards and forwards between the various sections in this chapter. For those who prefer their history in a chronological fashion, the Addendum at the end of this chapter should provide some comfort.

EARLY STAPLE INDUSTRIES

The links between government and business may be more extensive and more visible today than they were in the past, but they have always been important. In its very origins Canada was an outpost for the economic empires of

France and then Britain. As such, its importance (which admittedly was not very great) was as a source of fish, furs and timber. The colonial economy was a staples economy, an economy based upon the extraction or harvesting of certain natural resources and the export of these resources to an industrially more diversified trading partner. It was also a *dependent* economy in the sense that business activity in the colonies was tied to demand in the export market. The capital investment for economic production came at first entirely and then largely from abroad and, therefore, the pattern of commercial development was determined by the needs of a much larger trading partner. The politics of New France and, after 1760, of British North America were determined by their trading relationship to a European imperial power.

The main demand that business made on government was for protection from competition. Monopoly—or at least the attempt to establish monopoly—had roots in Canada's first capitalist ventures: fishing and fur trading. In each case, vested business interests were quick to request various sorts of exclusive privileges like charters that assigned them the sole right to trade in an area claimed by the imperial government, although the practical effect of "official" monopoly was seldom to eliminate competition entirely. The granting of commercial monopolies was generally tied to the territorial and political ambitions of home governments during an era in which control of overseas possessions and sources of natural resources was viewed as being crucial to a nation's wealth and political glory. The ambitions of business interests (or at least of *some* business interests) coincided with those of government to create the basis for early efforts to restrict economic competition.

Fish

Exploitation of the Atlantic coast fisheries was the first business enterprise engaged in by Europeans in Canada. From the late 1500s until the fur trade took off in the early 1700s, exports of fish caught on the Grand Banks of Newfoundland and in the Gulf of St. Lawrence constituted the only commercial venture of any significance. During wartime, the French and British navies were occasionally called on to protect their respective fishing fleets from pirating. Eventually, some fishermen decided to pass the winter on the shores of Newfoundland and in the process established a claim on the best port locations and facilities built for curing the fish catch. Conflict quickly emerged between them and the migratory fishermen accustomed to setting up their shore operations each spring. The history of the early fisheries, as of the fur trade, reads as a struggle between those who attempted to protect their market position by securing privileges from government and those whose interests lay in unrestricted trade; for example, Britain's Navigation Act of 1651 attempted to regulate the industry by establishing charters (effectively monopoly rights), a policy that had always been opposed by the independent fishermen. In fact, policy regarding the Atlantic fisheries was an element in Britain's first major debate on free trade during the early 1600s.

Fur

The early trade in fish had very limited consequences for the pattern of settlement and economic development in the territories that would eventually become Canada. The opposite was true of the fur trade. In *The Fur Trade in Canada*,[5] Harold Innis identifies the following consequences that this trade had on the economic and political development of Canada:

(1) The export of furs to Europe was the basis for the first significant import trade in manufactured goods. Canada's trading relationship with the outside world really dates from the commerce generated by furs.

(2) The pattern of communication and settlement in Canada was largely determined by the needs of the fur trade. The extension of the fur trade was supported at convenient intervals by agricultural development extending from the lower St. Lawrence basin in the east to the agricultural communities of the Columbia River in the west. (In the end, the fur trade and agriculture proved to be incompatible. The spread of agriculture and permanent settlement detroyed the habitat of fur-bearing animals and pushed the trade ever further into the interior.)

(3) Related to the preceding point, the fur trading empires of the Hudson's Bay Company and the North West Company laid the basis for the political territory of Canada. The boundaries between Canada and the United States were largely determined by the fur-trading areas of these businesses, and the "northern half of North America remained British because of the importance of fur as a staple product."(This claim is disputed by Michael Bliss who contends that the political boundaries between Canada and the U.S. do not coincide very closely at all with those of the fur traders' territories.)[6]

Like the fisheries, the fur trade was characterized by the struggle between monopoly and competition. This struggle was between the chartered companies which held an official monopoly over all trade within a designated territory and the independent traders. But there was another conflict. This was between the fur trade generally and the expansion of agriculture and settlement into what previously had been the domain of the industry. The political influence of the fur industry receded as the economic importance of the agricultural and manu-facturing industries advanced.

Timber

Timber is usually considered to be the third staple whose production and export left a significant mark on the economic development and politics of Canada. A.R.M. Lower shows that wood products accounted for about three-quarters of all Canadian exports in 1825 to about one-fifth by 1900.[7] In fact, the timber industry of Canada owed its export trade to the extremely high duties Britain imposed on timber imported from non-colonial sources (the Baltic being Europe's main source of supply) while imports from the colonies were allowed in duty-free. British protectionism was the result of that government's desire for a secure supply of the wood, mainly pine, on which its navy depended. The American Revolution and the Napoleonic wars had cut off Britain's supply of this vital commodity. The Canadian trade in timber began as a "hot-house war industry," as Britain attempted to protect itself from the loss of much needed pine masts for ship building. The duties that sheltered the industry continued during peacetime due to the vested business interests that developed behind them. These included the British shipowners who benefited from the cheap sup-ply of wood and the British timber companies whose Canadian export operations were centred in Quebec City and St. John, New Brunswick. When these duties were swept away in 1846 by the strength of the free trade sentiment in Britain, the Canadian industry was well-established and internationally competitive.

The industry did, nonetheless, suffer an immediate shock from the removal of protectionist duties. The interrelatedness of business and government and the sheer importance of the timber industry were shown in the fact that the Canadian government[8] also suffered a financial blow. Government's interest was in the steady removal of timber from crown lands both for the revenue this provided[9] and in order to clear the way for settlement. Therefore, it was not sur-prising when the end of a protected export market was compensated for by new forms of support for the industry at home. In addition to the state's financial dependence on taxation of the industry, the politicians making the laws and the lumbermen were often the same people. H.V. Nelles notes that Canada's first statutory framework for regulating the forest industry, The Crown Timber Act of 1849, was drawn up by a legislative committee that included several spokes-men for the Ottawa-based lumber community.[10]

Wheat

Fish, furs and trees were not staple industries that generated much in the way of population growth. Wheat, on the other hand, was closely tied to the settlement of Western Canada and the building of an East-West economic and political union. While economic historians differ over how important the expanding wheat economy of the late 19th and early 20th centuries was to Canada's overall economic development, there can be no doubt that wheat became the country's chief staple during this period.

The economy of the Prairie provinces was a wheat economy. The years between 1900 and 1914 were particularly buoyant ones: the Prairie population more than tripled; railroad mileage increased almost three-fold; and a vast amount of investment capital flowed into the region to finance the expanding wheat economy.[11] By 1931 about 40 per cent of all Prairie farmland was planted with wheat. By 1920 wheat had become the country's most valuable export.[12] Like the fur trade and the lumber trade before it, wheat exports were vulnerable to the great instabilities of the world markets. The wheat economy was a classic "boom and bust" industry in which the severity of the downturns was augmented by the debts that farmers took on during periods of high prices and optimistic expansion. Instability in prices (and therefore in farmers' incomes), heavy indebtedness to Eastern-based banks, dependence on the Canadian Pacific Railway and the wheat-purchasing grain elevator companies and the political muscle of farmers in the West provided the basis for a number of important state interventions in the market.

These interventions focussed on transporting, marketing and financing wheat production. The CPR's monopoly position on the Prairies was a perennial grievance for Western farmers during the late 19th century. Their complaints became less strident after the freight rate reductions were enacted under the Crow's Nest Pass Agreement (1897-1981): this was a federal regulation that fixed the permissible rates that could be charged by the railroads on freight moving east. In return the railroads received a subsidy to compensate them for the losses they incurred in transporting grain. Another monopoly which affected the incomes of wheat producers was the one held by the privately-owned grain elevators which purchased the grain for shipment to market. In 1900, 5 companies owned about 70 per cent of the 447 grain elevators on the Prairies. Beginning in 1903, the activities of the private elevators were coordinated through the North West Grain Dealers' Association—an industry cartel whose main goal, in the words of a 1906 Royal Commission, was "the regulating of the buying of grain in the country."[13] This was a euphemistic way of saying that the grain elevators engaged in price-fixing. The inability of the farmers to break this monopoly by charging it with illegality under the federal anti-combines law demonstrated the ineffectiveness of Ottawa's competition policy. This failure led to the expansion of cooperative elevator companies owned by farmers. It also led to some direct state intervention in the industry, as in the case of the

Manitoba government's purchase of 164 privately-owned elevators which were eventually sold to farmers' cooperatives.

Even after the expansion of producer cooperatives broke the monopoly hold of the privately-owned elevator companies, the marketing of wheat remained an essentially free market affair. Farmers' demands for a government monopoly in wheat marketing to replace the private transactions on the Winnipeg Grain Exchange were resisted by Ottawa. As in the case of grain elevators, some wheat growers turned to the cooperative solution and established wheat pools in the mid-1920s. The wheat pools purchased grain from members under contract and sold directly to domestic and foreign buyers through a jointly controlled Central Selling Agency. The pool system was a precursor to the Canadian Wheat Board (1935). The initial function of this federal crown corporation was to provide a minimum price floor for wheat producers, rather than be a marketing monopoly. But in 1943 the Canadian Wheat Board was assigned a monopoly over the buying and selling of Prairie wheat, a monopoly that it continues to hold.

In addition to state interventions affecting the transportation and the marketing of Canada's wheat staple, governments also became involved in the financing of wheat production. The Eastern-based banks were perhaps the most reviled institutions in the West. They symbolized to farmers an economic and political system in which they were exploited for the benefit of others. During World War I the governments of Manitoba, Saskatchewan and Alberta all passed legislation that prohibited bank foreclosures on farmers who failed to make their scheduled payments. These were temporary measures only. A more lasting form of intervention involved direct state loans to farmers. All three provincial governments established credit agencies after the war, and Ottawa entered the field in 1929 when the Canada Farm Loans Board was created. Government's importance in financing the wheat economy and agriculture in general increased substantially in the Depression of the 1930s when the private banks virtually withdrew from this sector. The state responded to political pressure and filled the void.

It is impossible to find a contemporary analogue to the staple industries that were at the centre of Canada's economic and political development until the early 20th century. As we will see in Chapter Four, business activity—including Canada's pattern of exports—is much more diversified today. It has been argued by some that the staple economy has bequeathed to Canada a legacy of industrial underdevelopment as a result of the earlier concentration of private and public capital on the production and export of particular natural resources. For example, Tom Naylor argues that the development of Canada's manufacturing base was stunted by a financial sector "geared to the international movement of staples, rather than abetting secondary processes for domestic markets."[14] The contemporary significance of the staple economy is perhaps best seen in the cases of some provinces whose economies are heavily dependent on the income generated from the export of natural resources. British Columbia (forest products), Alberta (petroleum), Saskatchewan (grain), and Quebec (hydro-electric power) all fall into this category. As in the eras of fish, fur, lumber and wheat, today's economic dependence on the production and exportation of natural resources shapes the relationship between business and government.

BUILDING THE ARTERIES OF COMMERCE

Confederation changed the political environment of business. In the most basic sense it did this by creating a new level of government to which the Constitution (the Constitution Act, 1867) assigned a broad range of economic powers. The enumerated list of these powers included the regulation of trade and commerce, the collection of revenue by any mode or system of taxation, the exclusive control over a number of functions essential to business activity including currency, postal service, banking, weights and measures, copyright and the incorporation of businesses with national objects. At the time of Confederation it certainly appeared that Ottawa had been given all of the major economic responsibilities in the new Dominion. (A combination of aggressive provincial governments, regionally-oriented business interests and controversial judicial interpretations led to a very different outcome.) Confederation presented the business community with a new field of opportunity: a market that could eventually stretch across the continent. At the same time it complicated the business-government relationship by entrenching in the Constitution two levels of government, each capable of influencing economic affairs. The fact that the scope of state interference with the marketplace was much narrower then than now meant that the complications of a federal political system intruded less significantly into the daily decision-making of business people. Nonetheless, the division of legislative powers did have important consequences for some businesses during this earlier period—and business rivalries had an important influence on the federal-provincial relationship.

This influence was most apparent in the case of railroads. By the time of Confederation, railroads occupied such an important place in Canadian politics that a promise of a line linking Halifax to Montreal was needed to entice Nova Scotia's politicians to join the new dominion. Confederation itself was strongly supported by railroad promoters who saw the greater borrowing power of Canada as a necessary condition for fulfilling their own business plans. The head of the Grand Trunk Railway, Edward Watkin, was certainly immodest when he referred to himself as *the* Father of Confederation. But there can be little doubt that the business of building railroads was an important influence in the Confederation decision: an influence that continued during the subsequent decades of nation-building. Indeed, the politicians and railroad promoters were often the same people.

It is important to realize that the prevailing views on what constituted acceptable personal relationships between business and government were very different in 19th century Canada from those held today. Frequently, politicians were on the boards of directors of corporations, and business people saw no need to divest themselves of their investments and business affairs when they entered politics. John A. Macdonald was the first president of Manufacturers Life—an insurance company—while he was prime minister of Canada. Several of Canada's founders and most prominent politicians, including Alexander Galt, Francis Hincks and Joseph Howe, were also railroad promoters. The limits on how far one's business interests could carry over into politics were fairly generous. But they did exist. When it came to light that Prime Minister John A. Macdonald had accepted an enormous campaign contribution from Canadian Pacific's Hugh Allan in return for the promise that Allan would be made president of the company chartered to build a transcontinental railroad, the limit had been reached. The Pacific Scandal brought down Macdonald's government in 1873. Though conflict of interest was not considered a very serious problem in the politics of 19th century Canada, bribery was.

Government financial support for transportation lines predates Confederation. In fact, Canada's first crown corporation was created when the Welland Canal Company was bailed out. This was a venture in which the colonial government had sunk vast sums of money and imperilled the colony's credit abroad. The westward spread of population and the expansion of trade created the *expectation* of future business activity. The canals and railroads that were constructed in the 19th century to link up the trading system of the Great Lakes region and eventually the region west to the Pacific were with rare exceptions not built in response to existing market demand. They were, however, widely considered necessary in order to facilitate the expansion of commerce and population. In both pre-Confederation Canada and in the United States, governments invested heavily in the arteries of trade and in most cases it took years before the canal or railroad carried enough traffic to earn a profit. In some cases profitability was never achieved.

THE NATIONAL POLICY AND INDUSTRIAL DEVELOPMENT

The domination of Canadian economic history by the staples theory and the importance of railroads in the politics of post-Confederation Canada combine to obscure the industrialization that was proceeding rapidly during this early period. At the time of Confederation, primary industries—particularly agriculture and to a lesser degree forestry—constituted the main area of economic activity. Manufacturing accounted for about one-fifth of the national income in 1871; a figure that conceals the small, decentralized character of most of this activity. The Royal Commission on Dominion-Provincial Relations estimated that the average capital invested in a manufacturing business in 1870 was $1,900.[15] O.J. Firestone put the figure even lower, at about $930.[16] Small as it was, the manufacturing base of 19th century Canada was sufficient for most of the economy's needs. In 1871 domestic production accounted for over 80 per cent (and usually well over 90 per cent) of domestic consumption in all manufacturing sectors except sugar (60 per cent Canadian production), cotton and denim (24 per cent) and earthenware (39 per cent).[17]

Most writers point to the Conservative Party's 1878 election platform, which was based on the National Policy, and the Wheat Boom of 1896-1914 as marking the beginning of significant industrialization in Canada.[18] The problem with this interpretation is that it underrates the importance of more general changes that were taking place in capitalism. Moreover, it overrates the extent to which the National Policy marked a departure from the economic policies of previous governments and exaggerates the contribution of railroad construction and Western wheat to Canada's industrialization.

The Canadian economy was already undergoing important transformations before either the National Policy or the expansion of the Western wheat economy. These changes were brought about by the growth of urban centres, the implementation of the factory system of production, and increasing specialization of production.[19] As the size of the Canadian market grew and as the transportation links between urban centres improved, the threat posed by foreign competition increased. The 1870s saw mounting political pressure from manufacturers for increased protection from foreign competition.

These demands were nothing new. Protectionist tariffs were first imposed in British North America in 1847, and were increased to a general level of 20 per cent in 1857-58. Part of the motivation for these early tariffs was government's search for revenue in an era before direct taxation. But particularly in the case of the 1857-58 tariff increases, the lobbying of Montreal-based manufacturers was an important factor influencing government policy.[20] What was new about the protectionist demands of the 1870s was the greater political muscle of the manufacturers and the fact that Ontario business people had become as vociferous as their Montreal counterparts in demanding a protected domestic market.

The 1878 national election was fought largely on the issue of laissez faire versus protectionism. Most of Canada's major capitalists lined up on the side of interference with the marketplace, or protectionism, against the Liberal Party's refusal to increase tariffs. Their demands received a sympathetic hearing in the Conservative Party, as demonstrated by the following passage from one of John A. Macdonald's campaign speeches:

If we had a protective system in this country, if we had a developed capital, we could, by giving our manufacturers a reasonable hold on our home trade, attain a higher position among the nations. If our factories were fenced round to a certain extent with protection and[we] impose a tariff such as the necessities of Canada may demand, our national prosperity would be enhanced.[21]

Macdonald and the manufacturers were making what was at the time already an old argument: infant industries needed state protection so that some day they could stand on their own feet against foreign competitors. The very same argument had been made in the United States over half a century earlier.[22] The increasing number of manufacturers in Canada, the growing size of their businesses, and the expanding workforce employed by them combined to increase the political weight of this argument in Canada in the 1870s. The failure of the American government to ratify a 1874 reciprocity (i.e., limited free trade) agreement that was favoured by the Canadian government may also have contributed to the surge of protectionist pressure. Canadian trade policy has always been heavily influenced by political developments in our major trading partners (see Chapter Twelve).

The 1879 tariff increases have been described by one historian as "a frank creation of vested manufacturing interests living on the bounty of government."[23] This view is shared by most observers. Politics aside, the economic question is "Did they work?" Did tariffs that averaged at about 30 per cent result in a burst of industrialization and the development of competitive manufacturing industries? The consensus among economists is that historically high tariff levels have resulted in (1) a loss for consumers who have had to pay higher prices; (2) employment benefits in Ontario and Quebec at the expense of incomes in other parts of Canada (particularly the West); and (3) lower real incomes in Canada than in the United States because of the sheltered inefficiency of Canadian industry.[24] Another consequence of the National Policy tariffs—one that was experienced immediately and which has had lasting political repercussions—was the flow of foreign (mainly American) investment into Canada. Businesses that would otherwise have exported their products found it economic to set up branch plants in Canada to supply the Canadian market. The overall consequence has been a level of foreign ownership in Canada that is without parallel among advanced capitalist economies. The debate over the economic consequences of foreign ownership has been a heated one since the 1960s.

There were limits to how far the Canadian government would go to protect domestic industry. These limits were very clearly seen in the case of steel. The construction of the CPR—one of the other planks of the National Policy—required thousands of miles of steel rail. The rails that eventually spanned

Canada were purchased almost entirely from the huge steel mills of Pittsburgh. The fledgling steel industry of Hamilton would have required enormous tariff barriers to be able to compete for the railroad's business. Ottawa's solicitude for the interests of the central Canadian manufacturers stopped short of intruding upon the interests of the politically powerful railroad companies.

The transcontinental railroad was a necessary condition for achieving the third goal of the National Policy: settlement of the vast western territories that Canada had purchased from the Hudson's Bay Company in 1871. In retrospect it is tempting to attribute remarkable vision to Canada's early nation-builders. The West was populated by settlers coming mainly from Europe, the United States and Ontario. Wheat production soared so that by 1920 wheat surpassed lumber as Canada's main export.[25] But this expansion did not take off until the late 1890s (and particularly after 1901) when the international demand for wheat pushed prices upward and made farming on the Prairies an economically attractive venture. An expanding wheat economy meant the construction of more railroad lines, the purchase of agricultural machinery, and the emergence of a new consumer market in the West.

The industrial activity generated by the production and export of Western wheat—what economists call "backward linkages" between sectors of the economy—provides one of the key pieces of evidence for the staples theory of Canada's economic development. A considerable debate has been waged over the extent of wheat's contribution to national economic growth.[26] It certainly is wrong to suggest, as some early economic historians did, that the wheat boom was a necessary condition for the diversification and growth of Canada's manufacturing economy.[27] As mentioned earlier, many of the industrial benefits from railroad construction spilled over into the American steel industry. On the other hand, the tariff-sheltered agricultural machinery industry of Ontario benefited enormously from farmer demand on the Prairies. Furthermore, population expansion created a Western consumer market whose needs provided considerable economic benefits to other tariff-sheltered manufacturers in central Canada.

To summarize the above discussion, John A. Macdonald's National Policy had three parts:

(1) Tariff protection for the manufacturers of central Canada.

(2) The building of a continental railway.

(3) The settlement of the vast territory between Ontario and British Columbia.

It was a comprehensive and daring attempt at nation-building and an important example of state intervention shaping the nation's economic destiny.

The National Policy has left an enduring mark on both the politics and the economic development of Canada. The infant industries nurtured by high tariffs in most cases never reached maturity—at least if one defines maturity as the ability both to compete with foreign producers at home and to sell abroad. Lured by the protected domestic market, the foreign-owned branch plants took root and became a characteristic feature of Canadian industry. High tariffs were not favoured by everyone. They would become one of the sources of Western discontent, as that region would be burdened with much of the cost but experience few of the economic benefits of protection. Tariffs were favoured neither by import-dependent commercial interests nor by farmers. The fact that they were implemented and that there was a bi-partisan consensus on protectionism up until the Liberal government's decision to fight the 1911 national election campaign on its proposal for reciprocity with the United States attested to the growing political influence of the manufacturing community.

The building of the CPR and, more to the point, its monopoly position in the West proved to be another source of political and economic division. We have already mentioned farmers' grievances over the CPR's ability to set freight rates without fear of losing customers to competitors (that is, until the Crow's Nest Pass rates were imposed as a sort of compromise between the railroad's interests and those of the Western wheat producers). The CPR's monopoly was also the cause of a protracted conflict between Ottawa and the government of Manitoba. That provincial government responded to the interests of Manitoba's business people and consumers by repeatedly chartering lines that would link the province to the American railroads running through Minnesota. This would pose direct competition to the CPR and therefore break its monopoly stranglehold on prices. Ottawa repeatedly used its constitutional authority to disallow provincial legislation in order to protect the CPR's monopoly. In 1888 the company agreed to the elimination of its formal monopoly status in exchange for a federal loan guarantee. A Manitoba line, the Northern Pacific, was built but freight rates did not fall. Not surprisingly, the two railroad companies both found it in their interest to fix rates rather than compete.[28]

The Western Wheat Boom and the end of the CPR's monopoly led to overexpansion in the railroad industry. By 1915 there were three transcontinental lines and only one, the CPR, was profitable. In each case the railroad received large government subsidies during their construction phase. Although the CPR's competitors were not economically viable, the federal government was not willing to see them go under because of the interests of investors and the country's credit rating abroad (much of the capital had been raised from foreign sales of bonds). The CPR's Western competitors and three other bankrupt railroads were nationalized and consolidated into Canadian National Railways between 1917 and 1923.[29]

THE MANUFACTURING ECONOMY

Industrialization produced important changes in business-government relations. The expansion in the relative importance of manufacturing and the decline in that of agricultural production led to a shift in the political power of these different producer groups. The increasing strength of manufacturing interests had already been evident at the time of the National Policy. But railroad construction and western expansion obscured the extent to which Canada's centre of economic gravity was changing. In a real sense, the roots of Canada's modern economy and of contemporary business-government relations can be traced to the industrialization that took place during the early 20th century.

Canada was undergoing a transformation that had been experienced about 50 years earlier in the United States. A predominantly agricultural economy was giving way to industrialization. In 1881 almost half of the Canadian workforce was in the agricultural sector. By 1911 the percentage was down to about one-third. In terms of absolute numbers, the size of the farm workforce had grown by 40 per cent over this period. But the non-agricultural workforce had grown by 150 per cent.[30] The absolute size of the agricultural workforce would not decrease until World War II, after which it shrank rapidly. As the major producer group in the post-Confederation economy, farmers were politically powerful: a large part of the electorate for most politicians was comprised of farmers. An important feature of Canadian politics in the early part of the present century was farmers' attempts to resist the decline in their social influence by organizing politically.[31]

They were, however, fighting a rearguard and largely unsuccessful battle as Canada's economy became steadily more industrialized. In terms of its contribution to national income, manufacturing was as important as agriculture by 1910.[32] By the late 1920s the contribution of manufacturing to gross domestic product exceeded that of agriculture and all other primary industries combined.[33] The manufacturing workforce grew less dramatically, from about 14 per cent of the total workforce in 1881 to about 20 per cent in 1911.[34] The growth of the manufacturing sector provided the basis for even more rapid employment growth in the service industries (retailing, banking, insurance, public administration and so on) which were concentrated in the expanding urban centres. Expansion was particularly rapid in such industries as rubber and plastics, chemical, electrical, paper, and non-ferrous metals. These were the growth sectors of what some economic historians have labelled a "second industrial revolution," one brought on by the application of new industrial technologies.[35] In Canada they developed as branch-plant sectors, dominated by foreign-owned firms which produced essentially for the small Canadian market.

The manufacturing sector was changing in other ways as well. In 1880 the size of the "average" manufacturing establishment was 5.3 employees, producing a gross value of $6,470. By 1905 the average size had increased to 25.2 workers with the gross value of production at $45,960. On the eve of the Depression the average manufacturing business employed 30 people and produced a gross value of $173,130.[36] Not only was the average size of a manufacturing establishment becoming larger, very big firms were beginning to dominate the industrial landscape. In 1910 only one-tenth of one per cent of all manufacturing businesses had a gross value of production exceeding one million dollars. But these firms accounted for 30 per cent of the gross value of production in the manufacturing sector. By 1925 the number of very big firms was up to half of one per cent of all manufacturing establishments. They together accounted for 55 per cent of the gross value of all manufacturing production.[37]

One of the first political consequences of the increasing economic importance of manufacturing was the mounting demands for protection from foreign competition. We have seen that the 1879 tariffs represented Ottawa's response to those business people who draped their self-interest in the claim that protection was necessary if Canada was to develop along the lines of the more advanced industrial economies of the United States and Britain. From some quarters there were also demands for protection from internal competition; that is, state regulation to assure businesses of a fair return on their investment. Michael Bliss has documented how business people attempted to shelter themselves from the risks posed by a competitive marketplace. He writes that "in the real world of business most participants in the market would have amended the formula for material success to read Industry, Integrity, Frugality, and Fixed Prices."[38] Government could provide protection from some of the rigours of competition through a measure such as laws restricting the hours of retail business. But for the most part, businesses relied upon their own associations to achieve and enforce price-fixing agreements reached between themselves. These anti-competitive business practices became a matter of public concern in the late 19th century. (Canada's first investigation into uncompetitive business practices was the 1888 Select Committee of the House of Commons inquiry into price-fixing arrangements of the Wholesale Grocers' Guild.) Despite anti-combines legislation that dates from 1889, it is clear that the lack of unity within the business community was far more effective in maintaining competition than was government policy.

The self-interest of business people—as of other groups in society—has often led them to demand government intervention. The tariff provides a classic illustration of this. Another instance that demonstrated the growing political muscle of the manufacturers involved the movement for cheap electrical power in Ontario. The province's manufacturers, who were important consumers of electricity, were quite prepared to accept public ownership of electrical utilities if this meant cheap power and lower costs for them.[39] Business was also pleased to accept the public assistance provided by municipal governments, including such inducements to industry as free land, tax exemptions, loans or free utilities.[40]

World War I and the subsequent reconstruction period were marked by unprecedented state intervention in the economy. The requirements of war had led to state control over production and prices in many industries. After the war these state powers were not immediately dismantled, but were in fact extended by Ottawa through the creation of the Board of Commerce in 1919. There was a general feeling that the end of wartime production would result in economic instability. The Canadian Reconstruction Association—an association created in 1918 which spoke for the interests of big business—was initially supportive of state regulation that would have protected the domestic market from foreign competitors and reduced competition at home.[41]. The CRA's demand for regulation of domestic competition was soon shelved, leaving support for continued high tariffs and protection against labour unrest and social disorder as big business's main political demands. What spokespersons for the large manufacturers wanted was a stable market and social environment that would enable them to maintain the profitability that had characterized the war years. They were, however, unable to achieve the sort of political dominance that characterized American big business during the same period.[42] The reasons for this failure had to do with the greater political strength of agricultural producers in Canada, as well as the decentralist features of Canada's constitution that effectively limited Ottawa's capacity to act on behalf of nationally-organized business interests.

The end of the war meant the return of thousands of soldiers to civilian life. With the widespread expectation of economic recession and the general strains that were developing in relations between management and labour, there was an urgency to business's demand for a stable social climate for industrial activity. These elements of demobilization, recession and more general stresses in industrial relations came together to produce the Winnipeg General Strike of 1919 (see Chapter Fourteen). This was a highly visible demonstration of the social disruption that manufacturers feared. It was, however, only symptomatic of more general changes that industrialization had produced.

Industrial capitalism had altered the social landscape. The technology of factory production spawned the growth of cities and, in turn, of the service industries that lived off of these urban centres. The urban working class gained in numerical importance as Canada became an industrialized and predominantly urban society. By 1921, the percentage of the population living in cities about equalled the rural population.[43] Traditional employer-employee relationships increasingly gave way due to the advance of the factory system, the increasing division of labour, and the growth in the size of business establishments. Large numbers of workers concentrated in single businesses set the stage for the growth of the labour movement and for profound changes in industrial relations. Unions representing workers in highly skilled trades had long existed and had been legal in Canada from 1872. They had grown out of the guild system of pre-industrial Europe and were imported to North America by emigrating artisans and tradesmen. The new ideas of organizing unskilled workers and of grouping different sorts of workers into the same union were products of industrial capitalism. Industrial unionism and collective bargaining were highly contentious issues in early 20th century Canada. Business for the most part resisted the development of unions, arguing that they violated the "natural laws" of supply and demand and were essentially combinations against the interests of the community.[44] Despite business's hostility, the unionization of workers increased from 7 per cent of the non-agricultural workforce in 1911 to 16 per cent in 1921.[45]

The development of an industrial workforce was accompanied by an increasing incidence of employer-employee conflict. The federal Department of Labour recorded more than 1,300 strikes against more than 7,100 employers between 1901 and 1911.[46] Paul Craven argues that the years of rapid economic growth at the beginning of this century resulted in "unprecedented tensions in industrial relations."[47] The state's response to Canada's changing industrial scene was to establish the Department of Labour in 1900 and to pass the Industrial Disputes Investigation Act in 1907. The major thrust of Ottawa's labour policy during this early period was toward the prevention of work stoppages through state arbitration—an orientation that reflected the personal philosophy of Canada's first Deputy Minister of Labour, Mackenzie King. King's influence aside, Ottawa's intervention into the field of industrial relations reflected the state's response to the new class tensions generated by industrialization (see Chapter Fourteen).

CAPITALISM IN CRISIS: THE GREAT DEPRESSION

Economic depressions were not new. The world capitalist economy had sunk into a deep depression in the early 1870s and had only begun to move into recovery about twenty years later. What was unique about the Depression of the 1930s was not its depth or duration. Instead, the fact that it had greater social and political repercussions than previous downturns in the capitalist economy was what made it unique. The reason for this was that capitalist societies of the 1930s were heavily urbanized ones in which unemployment and falling incomes posed a much greater threat of social disruption and outright class warfare than was true of capitalist societies at an earlier stage of their development.[48] The social bonds of traditional societies had been dissolved by industrialization and had not been replaced by anything. There was also the dramatic stock market crash of October 1929 and the failure of the market to recover. The crash seemed to indicate that the economy of the capitalist world's emerging power, the United States, rested on unsound foundations. The then fresh experiment with a collectivized system of economic production in the Soviet Union was another factor that led many—intellectuals in particular—to question not only the economic viability but also the social desirability of capitalism.

Business was on the defensive. Economic collapse provided fertile ground for reform movements of both the political right and left.[49] As the Depression deepened, with no end in sight, increasingly, concern was voiced that the economic chaos would ultimately undermine liberal democratic government. In 1931 Mackenzie King wrote that "the old capitalist system is certain to give way to something more along communist lines.[50] With the rise of fascism in Germany and Italy and the increasing class polarization in Britain, the link between economic and political instability seemed evident.

The circumstances of the Depression provided the basis for important changes in the relationship of business to the state. The "New Deal" introduced by American president Franklin Delano Roosevelt in 1933 was generally taken to symbolize the more interventionist role that government was prepared to play in the economic marketplace. Canada's own version of the New Deal was introduced by Prime Minister R.B. Bennett in a desperate attempt to fend off what appeared to be certain defeat in the 1935 federal election. Like the American original, it included reforms to the banking and credit system, protection for agricultural producers, labour reforms and public works. And like its American counterpart, many of the Canadian New Deal reforms were ruled unconstitutional by the courts.

But despite some setbacks, a major change was taking place in the state's role. Economic crisis at home and in the world capitalist economy (the international monetary system collapsed and international trade contracted dramatically during the early 1930s) created the political space for important reforms which can be summarized in the term the *positive state*. This was a more interventionist state than had existed previously—a state that regulated more aspects of the economic marketplace. It was not, however, an anti-business state. Not all business people were converts to the New Deal-type reforms. But it soon became apparent to all but hide-bound dogmatists that the Bank of Canada, the Canadian Wheat Board, financial assistance for debt-ridden farmers, unemployment insurance [51] and some changes to Ottawa's competition policy did not constitute a radical political agenda. Judged from the viewpoint of concrete policy changes, very little of the positive state was actually implemented during the Depression. While most of the reforms would come later, the economic chaos of the 1930s had created a receptive climate for change.[52]

KEYNESIAN ECONOMICS AND THE POSITIVE STATE

The positive state was consolidated by the onset of World War II and the postwar adoption of Keynesian economic policies by Western governments. The war saw unprecedented state management of the economy, including price controls administered by the Wartime Prices and Trade Board, the creation of about 30 new federal crown corporations and numerous other forms of regulation established under the authority of the War Measures Act. This management involved the active cooperation of most of the country's leading business figures—the so-called "dollar-a-year men" who were recruited from the private sector to head up the boards and crown corporations established during the war. Moreover, one of business's own, American-born engineer C.D. Howe, was the central figure in the wartime Liberal government. The relationship between business and government was close and generally congenial during this period. The real test would come with the transition to peace and the expected end to the economic prosperity that war production had fuelled.

When the war ended the size of the federal government contracted sharply. All but one of the crown corporations created during the war were wound up or sold (virtually given away in some cases) to the private sector. Federal spending shrank by 50 per cent between 1945 and 1946, with virtually all of the decrease being the result of reduced defense expenditures. But while the frontiers of state intervention were rolled back, the wartime experience had reinforced the changes set in motion during the Depression. What emerged from this extended period of economic crisis, followed by wartime mobilization, was a new belief in the capacity of government to promote the well-being of capitalist economies.

The positive state of the postwar era found its intellectual justification in the writings of the British economist John Maynard Keynes.[53] Prior to Keynes, the dominant view among economists had been that a market in equilibrium—where demand matched supply—equalled full employment. This view provided no basis for state intervention in the economy, other than policies intended to prevent monopolistic practices. Keynes argued that equilibrium might in fact be reached at a point below full employment and that government could influence the level of economic activity through its spending and taxation policies. Keynesian economics was interventionist economics. The circumstances of the Depression had undermined economists' faith in the old orthodoxy and opened the way for a theory of the economic world that was not obviously at odds with reality.

Ideas seldom, however, triumph by their sheer intellectual force. The fact that policy-makers in Western capitalist societies soon became converts to Keynesian economics was due to the evident crisis that capitalism had undergone during the Depression, followed by the experience of state economic management during the war and the widespread expectation of economic collapse with the return to peace. In the case of Canada, rising popular support for the socialist Cooperative Commonwealth Federation (the predecessor to the New Democratic Party) was another factor that nudged the governing Liberals and Prime Minister Mackenzie King towards a commitment to more interventionist policies. The Liberal Party's 1945 election platform and the government's 1945 White Paper on Employment and Income expressed two pillars of the postwar deal: management of the economy and the social welfare state.

What did this mean for government's relations with business? First of all, it should be kept in mind that none of the fundamental elements of capitalism were challenged by Keynesian economics and the positive state. What had taken place was a reform—not a revolution—in methods of managing the economy. Despite the ideological protests of some business people and economic liberals,[54] the positive state of the postwar era operated in support of capitalism, rather than as an attack on the market. It did so in three ways:

(1) The state assumed responsibility for maintaining full employment and stable economic growth. One of the consequences of the Keynesian belief in government's ability to influence the level of economic activity is to absolve the capitalist economy of blame for undesirable conditions. If unemployment is too high, economic growth too weak, or inflation too rapid, the fault must lie with government's choice of counter-cyclical policies.

(2) The successful use of economic stabilization policies serves the general interests of private business by maintaining the conditions for profitability. Some economists have argued that one of the most important of these conditions in the postwar era was the political climate for investment. Governments' commitment to maintaining economic growth and reconstructing the shattered economies of Western Europe contributed, they argue, to investor confidence and to the long period of economic expansion that followed World War II.

(3) Social welfare policies geared to supplementing the incomes of particular groups (like families through family allowances) or individuals (like the jobless through unemployment insurance) were tied to economic stabi-

lization policy. The origins of family allowances in Canada show very clearly that this social policy was shaped by macro-economic policy considerations.[55] The fact that this and other planks of the social welfare system have been politically popular has served to weaken dissatisfaction with the inequalities that inevitably are generated by a capitalist economy. In this sense, the welfare state has the practical effect of being an investment in social stability (and therefore in the conditions for business profitability). The cost of the welfare state has been paid for mainly through the increased taxation of individuals, not of business income and profits.[56]

The war years were significant in more ways than consolidating the positive state. Canada's economic ties with the United States were reinforced through a 1941 agreement to share defense production. This wartime agreement was extended in the 1959 Defense Production Sharing Agreement, a treaty that established limited free trade between the defense industries of the two countries. A further step toward formal economic integration was taken in 1965 with the signing of the Auto Pact. This agreement established continental free trade in automobiles and automotive parts, with production guarantees for Canada linked to the volume of domestic sales.

The formal steps taken toward integration of the Canadian and U.S. economies were less important than the informal integration that resulted from the postwar growth of American investment in Canada. The share of Canadian industry controlled by non-residents increased from 21 per cent in 1939, to 27 per cent in 1951, to over a third by the mid-1960s.[57] The vast majority of this foreign investment was American. The inflow of American capital was greatest in the manufacturing, petroleum and gas, and mining and smelting sectors. All of these were predominantly foreign-controlled by the 1950s.[58] Along with this growth in foreign control of the Canadian economy, there emerged increasing concerns over what some maintained were adverse political and industrial consequences of foreign ownership. We discuss these concerns in Chapter Four.

Industrial relations assumed a different face after the war, as an increasingly large share of the Canadian workforce belonged to unions. In 1939 about 17 per cent of non-agricultural workers were union members, a figure that increased to 28 per cent by 1946 and to about a third by the mid-1950s.[59] Full production and increased demand for labour during the war were factors that contributed to this increase. Postwar prosperity provided the basis for generally amicable employer-employee relations; a pattern of industrial peace that lasted until the mid-1960s. The average annual working time lost due to strikes and lockouts was 0.16 per cent between 1946 and 1965, but this figure more than doubled to 0.36 per cent for the period 1966-1975.[60]

THE CHANGING INTERNATIONAL CONTEXT OF BUSINESS-GOVERNMENT RELATIONS

The world capitalist economy of the postwar period has been characterized by two main developments. One is the enormous growth in the volume of international trade and, related to this growth, the increasing interdependence of national economies. The other involves the changing balance of economic power in the global economy. Both of these developments have influenced the context of business-government relations in Canada, including the demands business makes on government and the role of the state.

It has become a cliche to observe that economies are more interdependent today than in the past. The links of international trade involve more than commodities and services. They also involve capital. Borrowing by corporations and by governments has become international. The internationalization of finance has been promoted by four main developments: (1) the creation of international organizations like the International Monetary Fund and the World Bank; (2) the growth of private banks' international lending activities; (3) the spread of the multinational corporation; and (4) the accumulation of enormous foreign exchange reserves by particular national economies which become exporters of capital to the rest of the world. (In the first couple of decades after World War II, the United States was by far the world's major exporter of investment, a distinction that has more recently been assumed by Japan.)

Growing trade interdependence has given rise to increasing calls for protection from those industries whose ability to compete in their home market is undermined by imports. While tariff barriers on manufactured goods have fallen sharply from an average level of 40 per cent in 1947 to around 5 per cent today,[61] governments have increasingly resorted to other trade barriers to protect domestic producers. In 1986 about 16 per cent of the total imports of all industrial countries were subject to non-tariff barriers,[62] such as import quotas, discriminatory regulations and voluntary export restraints. This does not even include the protectionism involved in various direct and indirect state subsidies to business. The evidence shows that the new protectionism represented by NTBs and subsidies has grown since the 1970s.

The balance of economic power in the world economy has also changed. In the period of economic reconstruction and expansion after the war, American dominance in the world capitalist economy prevailed. This dominant position has been eroded by the increasing strength of other capitalist economies, particularly those of the newly industrialized countries (NICs), Japan and the European Economic Community. The combined share of the Organization for Economic Cooperation and Development (OECD) imports of manufactured products held by Japan and the NICs (principally South Korea, Taiwan and Hong Kong) increased from about 8 per cent of the total in 1965 to about 23 per cent in 1985.[63] The emerging world economic order is one in which the policies of American governments still have a major impact on the economies and policies of other countries—an impact that in the Canadian case is magnified by the fact that about three-quarters of our external trade is with the United States. But the American economy itself has become increasingly vulnerable to economic conditions and government policies in other countries.

The world in which Canadian business operates and in which governments make economic policy is one where "there is less and less place to hide."[64] The reaction of business when faced with competition has always been to try to limit the threat. When cooperation between them is not possible or is ineffective they often have turned to the state for some form of protection. The increasingly competitive world economy has contributed to the growing interpenetration of business and state as vested economic interests seek to protect themselves and governments attempt to protect their revenue base (which depends on continued business investment) and their popular support (which is likely to decline if investment dries up and jobs are lost). The federal Task Force on Program Review characterized as "giving with both hands"[65] the complex and expensive network of industrial incentives that Ottawa and the provinces provide to business. But Canada is by no means unique in this respect. State subsidization of private business in all capitalist economies has made the issue of international trade a heavily politicized one.

In the case of Canada, the increasingly competitive world marketplace has not only heightened business's exposure to international challenges, it has also increased the political importance of Canada's economic dependence on the United States.

While the level of American ownership of economic assets in Canada declined in the 1970s, all other aspects of our country's trade with the United States have been intensified. One needs to keep in mind that the Canada-United States economic relationship is not a balanced one. Although we are the Americans' most important trading partner, imports from Canada accounted for only 17.9 per cent of total U.S. imports in 1987, and exports to Canada accounted for only 23.6 per cent of total U.S. exports.[66] The brushfires that break out periodically over particular features of Canada-U.S. trade are invariably more prominent items on Canada's political agenda than on that of the United States. In the competitive world economy of the late 20th century some Canadians hold the view that Canada's trade dependence can be transformed into an opportunity through a free trade agreement (FTA) with our dominant trading partner (see Chapter Thirteen).

The free trade debate of the 1980s is, in a sense, simply the most recent production of an old favourite of the Canadian political stage. And as was true of previous productions, the timing has been triggered by developments in the larger world economy—developments that have posed the question of whether

Canada's best hope lies in even greater economic integration with the United States. The current free trade debate has been significantly different from previous ones in that nobody views conventional protectionism as a viable economic strategy. The major political alternative to a FTA involves some sort of state-centred economic planning which its advocates argue would enable Canadian business to compete internationally.[67]

HAVE BUSINESS-GOVERNMENT RELATIONS DETERIORATED?

There is a tendency among some writers to divide the postwar history of business-government relations into the periods before and after Pierre Trudeau came to power in 1968.[68] The period before is viewed as something of a golden era during which the business community could count on sympathetic ears in Ottawa and the avenues for influencing public policy were well understood. C.D. Howe was the symbol of this close cooperation, but he certainly was not the only personal link between the business and state elites. Sociologists like John Porter argued that there existed a "confraternity of power" in Canada: an informal network of business and political leaders who had often graduated from the same schools, belonged to the same elite clubs, frequently had kinship ties, and in many cases moved between business and political careers.[69] A system of "elite accommodation"—a seamless web often existing between private and governmental elites at the bureaucratic level[70]—was argued by some to grease the gears of business-government relations. Interest group studies tended to confirm the picture of regular and generally cooperative relations between business representatives and bureaucrats.[71]

According to this interpretation, the Trudeau era was one of "mutual misunderstanding"[72] between business and government. The change was caused largely by the policy-making reforms instituted under Trudeau: reforms intended to strengthen cabinet's control over the determination of policy and reduce the influence of the departmental bureaucracy. Familiar avenues for dealing with government were no longer as effective. Moreover, the increasingly powerful central agencies (particularly the Privy Council Office and the Prime Minister's Office) which operated as extensions of cabinet decision-making were perceived as being out of touch with the world outside of Ottawa, including the business world.[73] Added to this was Prime Minister Trudeau's personal coolness toward business and the gradual departure of Liberal cabinet ministers like John Turner, Mitchell Sharp and Donald Macdonald who had been a bridge between the government and the business community.

Not all of the blame for the alleged deterioration in business-government relations has been placed on Trudeau and the institutional reforms he set in motion. Some argue that business and government increasingly were becoming two solitudes, separated by a wall of incomprehension and different beliefs.[74] The shared values and ties of social background and professional experience that provided the basis for the "confraternity of power" during the 1950s and 1960s were becoming weaker. Another strand of the declining business influence argument points to the growing vociferousness and political organization of non-business interests. As the interest group playing field has become more crowded, the ability of business to dominate the action has declined. Moreover, the rules of the game have changed. Both the media and public opinion must be taken into account to a greater extent than when business had fewer rivals for government's ear.[75]

Although there is some truth in each of these particular arguments, this thesis of deterioration of business-government relations is defective in three major ways. First, the claim that business-government relations passed from a state of cooperation to confrontation during the Trudeau years overemphasizes the conflict side of these relations. The claims and perceptions of any group should not be taken at face value. In a study of the social thought of business, Michael Bliss shows that business people at the turn of the century were convinced that the democratic form of government led politicians to pander to farmers and workers at the expense of business interests.[76] The reality was quite different. Likewise, the fact that the business people in the Trudeau era sincerely believed that they constituted a badly treated minority interest is not proof that this was the case.

Second, business-government relations in capitalist democracies are always characterized by the coexistence of conflict and cooperation (see Chapter One). To focus on conflict over the last couple of decades is to understate the large element of cooperation that characterizes the daily relationship between corporations and business associations and those departments and agencies of the state with which they have regular contact. It also attaches insufficient weight to the structural and cultural limitations to state actions that challenge the general interests of business. We have seen in Chapter One that these general interests exist at a fairly abstract level, but that they are practically important in limiting government's responsiveness to the demands of non-business groups. Conflict is generally more visible than cooperation, and certainly more widely reported by the media. For this reason an increase in conflict is likely to generate an exaggerated impression of deterioration in business-government relations.

Third, the various explanations put forward to account for the alleged deterioration of business-government relations all point to domestic determinants of those relations. External determinants are also important. Among the most important of these are changes in the world economy that have influenced business-government relations. Increased competition abroad and from foreign imports at home, and the increased vulnerability of the American economy to the outside world have changed the context of business-government relations in

Canada. The stakes appear to have become higher, as the political debate over free trade has demonstrated. However, this has not meant a deterioration of business-state relations. Instead, it has raised the visibility of these relations by focussing attention on the political choices facing the governments that preside over Canada's capitalist economy. At the same time, the structural constraints on government persist. These include the need to maintain business confidence for fiscal and electoral reasons, and to be (or appear to be) responsive to popular pressures for the regulation of many aspects of business activity.

Addendum to Chapter Two

A Chronology of Selected Important Developments in Canadian Business-Government Relations

Date	Event	Significance
1600s	Laws regulating Grand Banks fisheries	Attempt to limit competition
1660s	First import quotas in New France	Protection for wine and spirits producers
1670	Hudson's Bay Company (HBC) trade	English fur trade initiated from Hudson's Bay in competition with the French St. Lawrence system
1663-72	Jean Talon, first intendant of New France	Attempt at state-directed economic growth; Canada's first failed state enterprise
1760	Fall of New France	Replacement of much of the francophone business class by anglophones
1776	American War of Independence	Beginnings of the U.S. as a separate economic market
1784	North West Co. set up in Montreal	Dominates St. Lawrence fur trade in competition with HBC
1809	Heavy British tariff on non-colonial timber	Major stimulus to Canadian timber trade
1812	Law restricting land ownership by Americans	First attempt to regulate foreign ownership
1821	North West Co. and HBC merge	Horizonal integration creates fur trade monopoly

Date	Event	Significance
1825	Erie Canal built, linking Lake Erie with New York	New trade route competes with St. Lawrence/Montreal system
1830-40	Family compact in Upper Canada	Fusion of political and business power; criticism of a closed elite
1839-40	First canal subsidy	State underwrites a commercially weak venture
1841-45	Government of Upper Canada buys into the Welland Canal	First bail-out of a private sector business; first mixed ownership corporation in Canada
1846	Repeal of British Corn Laws; Colonial timber preferences	End of Imperial preferential tariffs that gave a sheltered market to Canadian grain products and timber
1849	Annexationist demands in Montreal	First demands from business people for political and economic union with the U.S.
1850s	Construction of the first Canadian railroads	Beginning of massive state support for railroads
1854	Canada-U.S. Reciprocity Treaty	U.S. tariffs abolished on many Canadian resources
1857	Canadian tariffs raised on imported manufactured goods	Raised revenue for government subsidies to railway interests
1866	U.S. abrogates Reciprocity Treaty	Canadian access to U.S. market restricted
1867	Confederation	Changed the politics of business; close personal connections between politicians and railroad interests
1870	Transfer of HBC territories to Canada	Responsibility for economic development of Western Canada was now in the state's hands
1873	Pacific Railway Scandal	Questions raised about the propriety of party donations by business in apparent return for favours

Date	Event	Significance
1874	Ontario Manufacturers' Association formed	Forerunner of Canadian Manufacturers' Association
1879	National Policy	Increased and extended tariff protection for manufacturers; commitment to build the CPR; Western expansion-oriented immigration policy. Stimulates rise of U.S. branch plants
1881	Canadian Pacific Railway formed to build line to the Pacific	Massive state subsidies to private railway interests
1889	Passage of first anti-combines law	Response to the increasing concern with anti-competitive business practices
1889	Ontario passes amendment to the Crown Timber Act	An industrial strategy to generate processing of timber in the province
1892-96	Court rulings on the division of powers	First in a string of judicial decisions that tended to place a narrow interpretation on Ottawa's power to regulate business
1900	Department of Labour created	Recognition of the ever-increasing industrial character of Canada's labour force
1906	Creation of Ontario Hydro	Supported by municipalities and manufacturers who saw in public ownership the promise of lower cost of electricity
1910	Combines Investigation Act passed	First of many half-hearted attempts to control mergers and monopolies
1911	Free trade election	Liberals defeated on a free trade policy platform
1917	Nationalization of Canadian Northern Railway	State assumes debts of nearly bankrupt railway and establishes CNR as a crown corporation

Date	Event	Significance
1914-18	World War I	Unprecedented state intervention in economy and centralization of powers in Ottawa (would not outlast the war)
1917	Introduction of the income tax	Introduced as a "temporary" measure, income tax would become the most important source of government revenue
1918	Publication of *Industry and Humanity*	Mackenzie King's ponderous tome addressed the problem of reconciling democracy and capitalism by proposing corporatist forms of business-labour-government cooperation
1919	Winnipeg General Strike	Unprecedentedly large conflict between labour and capital; troops called in to support business; labour leaders jailed
1929	Stock market crash; beginning of the Great Depression	Fundamental questioning of capitalism's stability
1935	R.B. Bennett's "New Deal"	Proposed a much broader scope of state intervention in business including marketing boards, a central bank and vastly extended labour legislation
1936-37	Courts rule that most of the New Deal laws are unconstitutional	Appears to limit the federal government's ability to intervene in the economy
1936	Bank of Canada created	Originally having private shareholders, it would soon play an important role in economic policy
1939-45	World War II	Centralization of economic management in Ottawa
1941	Constitutional amendment assigning responsibility for UI to Ottawa	Recognition of the inadequacy of private and municipal relief

Date	Event	Significance
1941	Defense Production Sharing Agreement between Canada and the U.S.	Limited free trade agreement (continued after the war)
1945	White Paper on Employment	Official adoption of Keynesian economic policy, with Ottawa assuming responsibility for steady employment
1948	Discovery of oil at Leduc, Alberta	Oil would provide the basis for Alberta's new economic muscle in the 1970s and for major conflicts between producer provinces and Ottawa
1956	Royal Commission on the Economy	Suggested that not all the effects of foreign investment might be beneficial
1963	Liberal government's nationalist budget	Proposed a 30 per cent takeover tax on foreign purchases of Canadian companies; proposal withdrawn in the face of intense business and U.S. opposition
1965	Autopact between Canada and the U.S.	Free trade in the automotive industry; carried production guarantees linked to Canadian sales
1968, 1972	Watkins and Gray reports on foreign investing	Foreign ownership linked to industrial inefficiencies and intrusions on political sovereignty
1969	Creation of the Department of Regional Economic Expansion	Provides subsidies to businesses located in designated areas (mainly the Maritimes and eastern Quebec)
1974, 1977	Bill 22 and Bill 101 in Quebec	One of their goals was the increased use of French in Quebec's business life
1974	Creation of the Foreign Investment Review Agency	Assigned the power to screen foreign takeovers

Date	Event	Significance
1975	Creation of Petro-Canada	Within a decade would become Canada's largest petroleum company
1975-78	Anti-Inflation Board	Placed controls on incomes and prices
1976	Business Council on National Issues estab-lished	Represents big business and is probably Canada's most powerful pressure group
1978	Twenty-three industry sector task forces set up to advise government	Formal mechanism for busi-ness-government consulta-tion. Ends in failure
1980	National Energy Policy	Attempt to increase domes-tic control of the Canadian oil and gas industry; viru-lently opposed by producer provinces, most of the busi-ness community and the U.S. government
1985	FIRA transformed into Investment Canada	Screening of foreign invest-ment relaxed and emphasis shifted to active encourage-ment of foreign capital
1985-	Privatization and deregu-lation by Ottawa and some provinces	The "market" achieves renewed respect and state intervention falls into disre-pute
1986	New Competition Act passed	New approach to mergers and monopoly practices
1987	Free trade pact signed between Canada and the U.S.	Proposes the gradual elimi-nation of all barriers to trade between these economies

ENDNOTES

1. Alexander Brady, "The State and Economic Life in Canada," in G.W. Brown, ed., *Canada* (Los Angeles: University of California Press, 1950), chapter 15.

2. The list includes the likes of Harold Innis, W.A. Mackintosh, James Careless, Donald Creighton, Adam Shortt, A.R.M. Lower, W.L. Morton, Michael Bliss and R.H. Naylor.

3. Adam Smith, *An Inquiry into the Nature and Causes of the Wealth of Nations* (London: George Routledge, 1890).

4. The only integrated survey of the history of Canadian business is Michael Bliss's *Northern Enterprise: Five Centuries of Canadian Business* (Toronto: McClelland and Stewart, 1987). Bliss does not focus explicitly on business-government relations but, inevitably, much of his book deals with this subject. Among the more specialized volumes that have been written on the history of business and business-government relations in Canada, some of the most useful include Tom Traves, ed., Essays in Canadian Business History (Toronto: McClelland and Stewart, 1967)

5. H.A. Innis, *The Fur Trade in Canada: An Introduction to Canadian Economic History* (Toronto: University of Toronto Press, 1956), especially see summary on pages 386-92.

6. Bliss, *Northern Enterprise*, 105.

7. A.R.M. Lower, "The Trade in Square Timber," in Easterbrook and Watkins, *Approaches to Canadian Economic History*, Diagram No. 1, 29.

8. The Canadian government referred to here is that of Canada East and Canada West.

9. H.V. Nelles, *The Politics of Development* (Toronto: Macmillan, 1975), 18. Nelles estimates that between 1867 and 1899 revenue from the lumber industry accounted for 28 per cent of Ontario's total public revenue.

10. Ibid., 13.

11. Richard Pomfret, *The Economic Development of Canada* (Toronto: Methuen, 1981), 147.

12. Vernon C. Fowke, "The National Policy—Old and New," in Easterbrook and Watkins, *Approaches to Canadian Economic History*, 246.

13. Quoted in Pomfret, *The Economic Development of Canada*, 151.

14. Quoted in Paul Grayson, ed., *Class, State, Ideology and Change* (Toronto: Holt, Rinehart and Winston, 1980), 378.

15. Royal Commission on Dominion-Provincial Relations, Report (Ottawa: King's Printer, 1940), 27.

16. O.J. Firestone, *Canada's Economic Development*, 1867-1953 (London: Bowes, 1958), Table 74, 202.

17. O.J. McDiarmid, *Commercial Policy in the Canadian Economy* (Cambridge, Mass.: Harvard University Press, 1946), 148.

18. This is certainly true of O.D. Skelton's influential *General Economic History of the Dominion* (Toronto: Publishers' Association of Canada, 1913). A more restrained interpretation of the impact that the National Policy and the Wheat Boom had on Canada's industrialization is offered by O.J. Firestone, Canada's Economic Development, 202-203.

19. O.J. Firestone, *Canada's Economic Development*, 230. See also G.W. Bertram, "Economic Growth in Canadian Industry, 1870-1915: The Staple Model," in Easterbrook and Watkins, Approaches to Canadian Economic History, 96-97.

20. Bliss, *Northern Enterprise*, 247.

21. Quoted in Bliss, ibid., 251.

22. The classic statement of this argument is by Alexander Hamilton, "Report on Manufactures," in Samuel McKee Jr., ed., *Alexander Hamilton: Papers on Public Credit, Commerce, and Finance* (New York, Bobbs-Merrill), 175-276.

23. A.R.M. Lower, Colony to Nation, 4th edition. (Don Mills: Longmans, 1964), 373-74.

24. John Dales, *The Protective Tariff in Canada's Development* (Toronto: University of Toronto Press, 1966) and Eastman and Stykolt, *The Tariff and Competition in Canada* (Toronto: Macmillan, 1967).

25. Fowke, "The National Policy—Old and New," in Easterbrook and Watkins, *Approaches to Canadian Economic History*, 246.

26. This debate is reviewed in Pomfret, *The Economic Development of Canada*, 157-64.

27. The "necessary condition" view is argued by, among others, O.D. Skelton, *General Economic History of the Dominion* and Kenneth Buckley, *Capital Formation in Canada, 1896-1930* (Toronto: University of Toronto Press, 1955).

28. Pomfret, *The Economic Development of Canada*, 107-108.

29. Marsha Gordon, *Government in Business* (Montreal: C.D. Howe Institute, 1981), 54.

30. Canada, *Historical Statistics of Canada*, 2nd ed., (Ottawa: Supply and Services, 1983), D1-7.

31. Louis A. Wood, *Farmers' Movements in Canada* (Toronto: University of Toronto Press, 1924).

32. Firestone, *Canada's Economic Development*, Table 67, 188.

33. Canada, *Historical Statistics of Canada*, F56-65.

34. Firestone, *Canada's Economic Development*, Table 66, 185.

35. Eric J. Hobsbawn, *Industry and Empire* (London: Penguin, 1969), 174.

36. Canada, *Historical Statistics*, R1-22.

37. *Ibid.*, R783-794.

38. Bliss, *A Living Profit* (Toronto: McClelland and Stewart, 1976), 54.

39. Nelles, *The Politics of Development*, 304.

40. Bliss, *Northern Enterprise*, 303.

41. Tom Traves, *The State and Enterprise* (Toronto: University of Toronto Press, 1979), 17-22.

42. Gabriel Kolko, *The Triumph of Conservatism* (New York: The Free Press, 1963).

43. Canada, *Historical Statistics*, A94-109.

44. Bliss, *A Living Profit*, chapter 4.

45. Canada, *Historical Statistics*, E175-177.

46. Paul Craven, *"An Impartial Umpire": Industrial Relations and the Canadian State* (Toronto: University of Toronto Press, 1980), 113.

47. *Ibid.*, 113.

48. A good sense of these class tensions, as they were experienced in Canada, is provided in Michiel Horn, *The Dirty Thirties: Canadians in the Great Depression* (Toronto: Copp Clark, 1972).

49. See the essays in Ramsay Cook, ed., *The Politics of Discontent* (Toronto: University of Toronto Press, 1967).

50. Quoted in Doug Owram, *The Government Generation* (Toronto: University of Toronto Press, 1986), 163.

51. Unemployment Insurance did not come into effect until the constitutional amendment of 1941.

52. The lag between changing ideas and actual reforms is discussed in great detail by Owram, *The Government Generation*, chapters 7 and 8.

53. Keynes most famous work is *The General Theory of Employment, Interest and Money* (New York: Harcourt, Brace and Company, 1936).

54. The best example is Frederick von Hayek's attack on the interventionist state in *The Road to Serfdom* (Chicago: University of Chicago Press, 1944).

55. Owram, *The Government Generation*, 310-15.

56. National Council of Welfare, *The Changing Tax Pie: Trends in Federal Tax Revenues* (Ottawa: Health and Welfare, June 1987), 2.

57. Canada, *Historical Statistics*, G291-302. "Industry" is defined to include manufacturing, petroleum and natural gas, mining and smelting, railways, utilities, merchandising and construction.

58. *Ibid.*, G291-302.

59. *Ibid.*, E175-177.

60. *Ibid.*, E190-197.

61. "Survey of the World Economy," in *The Economist*, (26 September 1987), 36.

62. *Ibid.*, Chart 11, 41.

63. *Ibid.*, 45.

64. Canada, Royal Commission on the Economic Union and Canada's Development Prospects, *Final Report* (Ottawa: Supply and Services, 1985).

65. Canada, Task Force on Program Review, *Services and Subsidies to Business* (Ottawa: Supply and Services, 1985), 11.

66. Jeffrey J. Schott and Murray G. Smith, eds., *The Canada-United States Free Trade Agreement: The Global Impact* (Halifax: Institute for Research on Public Policy, 1988), 9.

67. This position has become associated with the Science Council of Canada. See any of the SCC's recent annual reports and the essays in Laurier Lapierre, ed., *If You Love This Country* (Toronto: McClelland and Stewart, 1987).

68. This periodization is critically examined in Michael Atkinson and William Coleman, "Is There a Crisis in Business-Government Relations?," in *Canadian Journal of Administrative Studies* 4:4 (December 1987), 321-40. The following section is heavily influenced by their analysis.

69. John Porter, *The Vertical Mosaic* (Toronto: University of Toronto Press, 1965), especially chapter XVII.

70. Robert Presthus, *Elite Accommodation in Canadian Politics* (Toronto: Macmillan, 1973), 215.

71. *Ibid.*, chapters 7, 8 and 9.

72. James Gillies, "Where Business Fails Revisited," in V. Murray, ed., *Theories of Business-Government Relations* (Toronto: York University, 1985).

73. Colin Campbell, SJ, "The Growth of Central Agencies and the State of Bureaucratic Consultation with Business," in V. Murray *ibid.*.

74. Litvak, "The Ottawa Syndrome: Improving Business-Government Relations," in *Business Quarterly* 44:2 (1979), 22-29.

75. Litvak, "The Lobbying Strategies of Business Interest Groups," in James D. Fleck, ed., *Business Can Succeed* (Toronto: Gage, 1984) and William T. Stanbury, *Business-Government Relations in Canada* (Toronto: Methuen, 1986), chapter 11.

76. Bliss, *A Living Profit*, chapter 6.

Chapter 3

Political Theory and Business Power

The power and position of business and the nature of business relations with government in developed capitalist democracies are addressed by a wide variety of competing theories. In these societies the significance of private business in economic and political life is so substantial that no theory of social power and public policy-making could realistically ignore it. The major theories all have a direct relevance for the study of business power and this chapter aims to introduce these different theoretical perspectives. While the list is not exhaustive, the discussion does focus on what we consider to be the principal approaches in an attempt to evaluate their strengths and weaknesses, starting with elite theory.

ELITE THEORY

The basis of modern elite theory lies in the contention that the political systems of Western industrial societies are far from democratic. Despite democratic forms such as elections, competitive political parties and interest groups, in reality power is concentrated in the hands of a tightly knit cabal of individuals which is largely unaccountable to the general public. Leaders of the corporate world are an integral part of this elite group as are the formal political leaders. These "men at the top" form a cohesive, consensual and conspiratorial clique constituting a "power elite" or a "confraternity of power."[1]

American sociologist C. Wright Mills has developed one of the best known formulations of the elite approach in his work, *The Power Elite*. Here, Mills argues that the key decisions in American politics are controlled by a "troika" or three-pronged elite consisting of those who occupy the highest positions in three dominant institutional hierarchies, namely the military, business and government. "The warlords, the corporate chieftains, [and] the political directorate" are linked together to form a single unified power elite at the pinnacle of the U.S. political system.[2] The elite's power is derived from the institutional positions that its members occupy, but these people are linked by common membership in the top social stratum, and also by similar origin, education and life style. They are not representative of the mass public, nor in practice are they responsible to it.

In Canada, elite theorists tend to be less concerned about the role of the military because it does not have the same significance as in the United States. Yet there is no shortage of concern about the power of a Canadian corporate elite and its links with the higher echelons of politics. A classic study here is John Porter's *The Vertical Mosaic*, which identifies a number of institutional hierarchies in Canada—in the political system, in the economic system and in the ideological system (including mass media, churches and education). Each hierarchy is dominated by an elite which is not proportionately recruited from Canadian society with regard to factors such as class background or ethnicity. The elites are readily accessible to one another and are coordinated into a "confraternity of power" by a variety of links. These include both informal links, like kinship, friendship and common social characteristics, and formal links, such as participation on the same boards and commissions and personnel interchanges between the elite groups. The "confraternity" is not as tightly knit as Mills' power elite and there is a greater potential for internal disagreements, but its power is sufficient for Porter to conclude that Canada is a long way from being a "thoroughgoing democracy."[3]

Subsequently, other studies have examined elite groups in Canada, focussing both on the specific character and social origins of the corporate and state elites, as well as on the direct personal linkages between the two.[4] These studies reveal a picture of intimate personal ties between the state and corporate worlds and a pattern of economic and political recruitment to the top positions in Canada which heavily under-represents major sections of society, including women, non-Anglo-Saxons and members of the working class in particular. It is stretching the bounds of credibility to suggest that such a pattern could occur by chance; instead it provides strong evidence that there is a systematic structural bias operating throughout Canadian society. This is a finding that cannot be dismissed lightly in a nominally democratic society which professes equality of opportunity. Elite studies have thus made a major contribution to our social knowledge in this regard. However, when it comes to understanding public policy or the relations between business and government, elite theory has a number of problems that diminish its utility.

By conceiving of a single elite, or in focussing on the common social bonds between corporate and political leaders, elite theory has difficulty explaining instances of discord between business and government. If personal connections and shared attributes have a crucial impact in determining public policy outputs, then how do we account for business-government conflict? And how is it that non-elite sections of society are sometimes successful in achieving their policy goals in opposition to corporate preferences? There are several possible responses by elite theorists to these questions.

The first response would be to deny that much business-government conflict takes place, or to suggest that any conflicts are essentially trivial. There are of course many areas where business and political elites are in substantial agreement, yet there are also enough examples of conflict to raise questions about elite unity. Government and big business have clashed from time to time on a diverse range of issues, including the role of crown corporations, environmental and some other regulations, certain social programmes, taxation, foreign investment and national energy policy. While these issues may not be "fundamental" in the sense of posing a serious threat to capitalist production, they are nevertheless more than just trivial and have provided a basis for notable conflicts.

In trying to explain business-government conflict it can also be argued that the business world is fragmented into different, and sometimes competing, sections and that in satisfying some business demands government must necessarily deny others. Yet this suggests a picture of an economic elite that is internally divided and non-consensual, and a political elite that has some autonomy to pick and choose between competing sections. On both counts elite cohesion is weakened. Alternatively, even if business is united it may be short-sighted or mistaken about where its real interests lie. In such circumstances, conflict could occur when government leaders refuse to satisfy immediate corporate demands in order to fulfill the broader, longer-term interests of the economic elite, that is, government acts in accordance with what business really needs rather than what business people say they want. But here again government would be seen to have an autonomy that overrides the personal bonds between members of the political and economic elites, and thus in regard to public policy objectives the two groups would be "de-coupled."

Elite theorists are normally quick to dismiss the electoral process as something that provides only an illusion of popular control rather than genuinely democratic government. They point to such things as the capacity of elites to shape public opinion, the role of business in funding election campaigns and the often limited choices presented by the major parties to the electorate. Yet the periodic accountability of elected officials to a mass public (albeit imperfect) is not purely fictitious, and at least once in a while government has to be sensitive to mass preferences. We cannot simply assume that electoral outcomes will slavishly reflect business needs or that the electorate is a sheep-like herd waiting to be manipulated. Popular demands do sometimes conflict with the goals of business, and politicians have been willing to oppose business interests when the electoral pressures are sufficient. Despite the deficiencies of elections, political leaders must maintain some legitimacy in the eyes of the electorate. They cannot simply service corporate needs; they must also march to another drummer, namely voters, and the beats are not always in harmony with the business drum.

A further problem with elite theory is that it assumes a degree of unity and centralization in government that is unrealistic in any complex and functionally diverse political system like Canada's. In particular, elite theorists must come to terms with intergovernmental conflict in Canadian federalism, and its structural division of authority which weakens the cohesion and unity of any prospective political elite.

Finally, elite theory overrates the significance of personal ties in explaining government policy towards business. Within the context of a developed capitalist society, no government can ignore the need to maintain the vibrancy and profitability of private enterprise, regardless of the social origins of corporate chieftains or political leaders. Even if, hypothetically, the largest corporations and the principal institutions of government were run by people from very diverse social backgrounds proportional to Canadian society as a whole, it would probably not make very much difference to the structural constraints which government faces in trying to manage a mature industrial capitalist economy. Government would still need to foster profitability, encourage investment, provide incentives, subsidize production, regulate the market, underwrite a transportation infrastructure, protect private property, intervene in industrial disputes, secure access to foreign markets and so on. This hypothetical shift in the socio-economic characteristics of the top personnel would mean that significant changes had taken place in the pattern of recruitment and the structure of opportunities of individuals, but it would not signal a fundamental transformation in the underlying character of government relations with business in a capitalist economy.

PLURALISM

Pluralism constitutes one of the most dominant sets of beliefs about the distribution of power in Western industrial societies and, as a general theory of social power, it necessarily has implications for the way business power is interpreted. Although it enjoys widespread popularity, pluralism is not always explicitly defined by those who write from within this perspective. In fact, quite often the approach is left unstated as a set of implicit assumptions about the policy process. Implicit or not, pluralism has shown a remarkable resilience as an interpretation of politics, in spite of being extensively criticized.

In large measure, modern pluralism is a reaction to elite theory and constitutes an attack against those who believe that the political process, at either the national or local community levels, is controlled by a "power elite" or a clique of notables dominated by business interests.[5] This attack was led, in the 1950s and 1960s, by a number of American political scientists (such as Robert Dahl and Nelson Polsby) and it relied heavily on empirical studies of local community power structures.[6] To the extent that local communities were seen as analogous to national political systems, conclusions drawn from these studies provided a basis for pluralist theories of national politics, and subsequently pluralism was incorporated into "mainstream" political science textbooks in Canada as well as the United States.

In essence, pluralism can be expressed as a series of broad contentions about power and policy-making in Western societies. Firstly, power in these societies is seen as widely dispersed rather than concentrated in the hands of any single elite. There is no single centre of power to be captured by an elite because sovereignty is split up amongst multiple and competing centres, none of which has absolute authority. We have little to fear from the powerful because power is divided and checked and balanced. As Robert Dahl has stated, "Because one centre of power is set against another, power itself will be tamed, civilized, controlled, and limited to decent human purposes."[7] Power in this view is *situational* in the sense of being tied to individual issue-areas, and those policy actors who prevail in one issue-area rarely prevail in others.[8] Thus, contrary to elite theorists, pluralists see power as *non-cumulative* across issue-areas, and the answer to the question of who dominates the policy process is that *nobody* dominates.[9]

Secondly, society is organized into a myriad of independent interest groups which are composed of individuals who freely and voluntarily associate together in order to promote their policy goals. For pluralists, interest groups and "the public" are the "social collectives most relevant to the analysis of political processes."[10] Government is open and responsive to this plurality of groups and "all the active and legitimate groups in the population can make themselves heard at some crucial stage in the process of decision."[11] Not all groups are equal in the skills and resources they possess, but virtually every legitimate group in society has "the capacity and opportunity to influence some officials somewhere in the political system in order to obtain at least some of their goals."[12] The system is thus inclusive rather than exclusive.

Thirdly, although pluralism involves competition between groups, the system as a whole is harmonious, consensual and stable. In order to achieve their goals groups need to build coalitions with other groups in society, and this involves a bargaining process characterized by compromise and conciliation as well as conflict.[13] As salient issues change over time, what emerges is a shifting pattern of group coalitions that are formulated, broken-up and reformulated on a continuing basis. Different coalitions of interests prevail at different times and there is no persistence in the social distribution of power.[14] Consequently, there is no persistent bias of government policy towards some groups rather than others, and thus there is no persistent problem with the structure of power in our societies.

The power of some groups, such as those representing business interests, is supposedly checked by the countervailing power of other groups, such as those representing labour, consumers, environmentalists, etc. The need for coalition-building amongst a plurality of groups and the need for negotiations between multiple centres of power mean that "citizens and leaders will perfect the precious art of dealing peacefully with their conflicts, and not merely to the benefit of one partisan but to the mutual benefit of all the parties to a conflict."[15]   The intensity of conflict is also reduced because people are members of more than one group and are simultaneously pulled in different directions by different allegiances. The cross-pressuring that results from these overlapping group memberships serves to limit the intensity of any single line of political cleavage and helps to bring about a reconciliation of different interests.[16]

Finally, this pluralist vision of the political system is one that places great emphasis on the societal forces (e.g. interest groups) and very little emphasis on the role of the state. For pluralists the institutions of government are fragmented, are set against one another and are little more than "centres of interest-based power."[17]   The state is seen either as just another interest group in the same category as churches or trade unions, or as a sort of neutral referee in the group battle that maintains the rules of the game, preserves a measure of order and allocates the policy spoils to the winners in each particular contest.[18] Government decisions simply reflect the balance of societal forces, and "what may be called public policy is actually the equilibrium reached in the group struggle at any given moment."[19]

In sum, pluralists draw a picture of a political system that is open, accessible and democratic; where virtually everyone has an opportunity to influence policy in some way; where power is widely distributed; where all legitimate groups can achieve some of their policy goals and nobody consistently loses; where group coalitions balance each other out; where there is no single elite or dominant class but a competition between policy elites in different issue-areas; where there is a premium on bargaining, compromise and peaceful accommodation; and where the state plays a rather passive and secondary role as a neutral arbiter between group interests. This largely rosy picture is presented by pluralists as a reasonably accurate description of how industrial democracies actually operate. In this respect pluralism has some notable shortcomings as numerous critics have pointed out.

One problem with seeing group pluralism as an open, inclusive and democratic system is that interest group activity (and political participation generally) tends to be biased toward the wealthier, better-educated and higher-status sections of the population. As E.E. Schattschneider has pointed out in an often quoted passage,

"The flaw in the pluralist heaven is that the heavenly chorus sings with a strong upper class accent."[20]   Whether it is a matter of having more knowledge, more resources, a greater sense of political efficacy, more trust in the political process, or other structural biases, it is simply easier to organize associations of bankers, industrialists, lawyers or doctors, than it is to form effective associations amongst the poor, the sick, the homeless or the unemployed. The pluralist assumption that interest group activity is virtually ubiquitous ignores the fact that there are serious barriers to the mobilization of some interests, and that some sections of society are not organized into the pluralist competition at all. Furthermore, because the internal structure of interest groups, like most organizations, tends to be hierarchical, concentrating effective control at the top with a minimal level of active rank-and-file participation, further doubt is cast on the universalist suppositions about interest group activity and on the democratic claims of pluralism.

Pluralists sometimes object, with justification, to the criticism that they see all groups as being equal in their capacities, resources, influence, etc.[21]   While it is true that pluralists do not go this far in claiming equality, they do nevertheless substantially ignore or downplay the gross inequalities that exist between groups in the associational universe. In particular, they overlook the persistent privileged position of business interests in the system of policy formation. This is not just a matter of corporate interests having vast resources and organizational capacities that can be mobilized for lobbying, electoral funding, political advertizing or other mechanisms of persuasion, though this is certainly part of the story; but it is the strategic power inherent in the private control of the nation's industrial and commercial base that is of crucial importance.

This is recognized by writers from a variety of perspectives. For example, one of the foremost modern marxists, Ralph Miliband, writes that "the existence of this major area of independent economic power is a fact which no government, whatever its inclinations, can ignore in the determination of its policies," and that business power is effective, "without the need of organization, campaigns and lobbying."[22]   In a similar vein, Charles Lindblom, who was once a collaborator with Robert Dahl, argues that

> Because public functions in the market system rest in the hands of those in business, it follows that jobs, prices, production, growth, the standard of living, and the economic security of everyone all rest in their hands. Consequently, government officials cannot be indifferent to how well business performs its functions.[23]

Business people are not just the representatives of another special interest; they fulfill indispensable functions for government officials. Officials must therefore grant business a privileged position, and they do "not have to be bribed, duped, or pressured to do so."[24]

This strategic power lies in the extensive private control over production, distribution and employment in the national economy, and the dependency of state policy-makers on those who hold this power. Ultimately the sanction rests on the mobility of capital, that is, the possibility that business will "dis-invest" and move production to another country. While the state may be able to survive individual business "defections," any mass exodus would have devastating economic and political consequences. State officials are necessarily sensitive to this power. Policy-makers automatically avoid (or do not even begin to consider) actions that might threaten to provoke such mass business hostility; thus public policy is ultimately constrained by bonds that are never tested.

Giant corporations can move vast quantities of capital across international borders at the touch of a computer key, normally with very few restrictions. Labour, particularly unskilled labour, has no such comparable strategic power as it is more tied down by territorial loyalties, personal attachments, immigration restrictions, etc. Nor is labour as easily coordinated as capital, because the ownership of capital is relatively concentrated while the ownership of labour power is as dispersed as the multitude of individuals who are its "proprietors." This strategic dissimilarity between business and labour undermines the pluralist belief in countervailing powers. As Miliband has put it:

> In the light of the strategic position which capitalist enterprise enjoys in its dealings with governments, simply by virtue of its control of economic resources, the notion, which is basic to pluralist theory, that here is but one of the many 'veto groups' in capitalist society, on a par with other 'veto groups', must appear as a resolute escape from reality.[25]

Pluralism has also been heavily criticized on methodological grounds. For instance, some of this criticism focussed on the empirical studies of local communities, such as those conducted by Dahl and Polsby. These studies examined a few different issue-areas (typically three) where there were observable instances of decision-making in progress. The analyses revealed that different policy actors were involved in different issue-areas, from which it was concluded that power was dispersed and noncumulative. Critics of this method, for instance Bachrach and Baratz or Stephen Lukes,[26] argue that pluralists have an unduly restricted conception of power, and that power is not simply contained in the overt decision-making battles on any "given" issue; power is also involved in the way the political agenda is shaped so that overt political conflict is confined to relatively "safe" issues (safe in the sense of not threatening the dominant interests in society whichever way the decision goes). The principal use of power is not to determine the outcome of observable political conflict, but in Stephen Lukes's words, "The most effective and insidious use of power is to prevent such conflict from arising in the first place."[27] This is done through the systems of socialization that shape people's perceptions and preferences.

Pluralists are thus remiss in just focussing on decision-making, they also need to consider "non-decision-making," or the structured biases in Western political systems that prevent certain questions from getting on the political agenda or certain conflicts from ever arising.

These shortcomings of the pluralist approach to power have inspired a modified version of pluralism which retains some of the descriptive aspects of the original, but which interprets the system in a much more negative way as an undesirable and undemocratic distortion in which power has been parcelled out to special interests, frequently those representing business. This version has become known as "neopluralism" and involves a network of "clientele relations" established between sections of government and particular special interests. It is to these concepts that discussion now turns.

NEOPLURALISM AND CLIENTELE RELATIONS

Neopluralism takes as its starting point the pluralist notion that the policy system is decentralized and fragmented among different issue-areas. Like pluralists, neopluralists emphasize a lack of centralized coordination and control in the structure of government, but unlike pluralists, they do not see this fragmentation as providing an inclusive, benign, democratic system in which power has been dispersed, tamed and civilized. Instead it is suggested that, within each issue-area, special relationships develop between the government department, bureau or agency, and the principal organized interests from the private sector that are concerned with that area of policy. In this view, organized business interests typically constitute the main private participants.

These networks or "sub-governments" enjoy a high degree of autonomy from any central political control, and they are seen as islands of delegated authority free to shape the direction of public policy in their own area as they see fit. Policy-making power has been parcelled out to coalitions of organized private concerns and quasi-independent subsections of government, which determine policy outputs in their own interests rather than in the public interest.

The basis for the development of these sub-governmental coalitions lies in a mutual exchange of benefits and favours between the government agency and the interest group. The two sets of actors are locked together in a system of "clientele relations" with the government agency being the "patron" and the private sector organization being the "client." Such relationships are often thought to be particularly prevalent in the United States where the highly fragmented structure of government provides a fertile ground for their development. However, they have also been identified as an important political phenomenon in other countries, including Canada, and the model of patron-client relations enjoys a widespread popularity as an interpretation of business-government interaction.[28]

Joseph LaPalombara was one of the pioneers in applying the concept of clientelism to group-government relations, and he has provided a general definition of the phenomenon. For LaPalombara:

> The clientele relationship exists when an interest group, for whatever reasons, succeeds in becoming, in the eyes of a given administrative agency, the natural expression and representative of a given social sector which, in turn, constitutes the natural target or reference point for the activity of the administrative agency.[29]

It is a situation characterized by trust and cooperation, in which a well-established, legitimate, institutionalized group has been informally incorporated into the structure of state policy-making itself.

The symbiotic nature of clientele relations, ie. the specific basis for jointly rewarding exchange, has been described by B. Guy Peters as a system of mutual dependency. Government agencies depend on client groups for information, advice, technical support, cooperation in policy implementation and political support in battles with other government agencies, while in return, the groups get privileged access to policy-makers and favourable policy outputs. Peters writes:

> The administrative agency depends upon the pressure group for information, advice, prior clearance of policy decisions, and, most importantly, for political support in its competition with other agencies for the scarce resources within government. The pressure groups, on the other hand, depend upon the agency for access to decision-making and ultimately, then, for favourable decisions on certain policy choices.[30]

In Peters' view clientelism is common in many industrial societies where the institutions of central policy coordination are weak.

In Canada, several writers have suggested that significant aspects of the policy process can be understood in terms of clientelism. For example, Robert Presthus claims that "a network of clientele relations exists between government and interest groups," and that relations generally are cooperative and consensual, and are characterized by symbiotic exchange.[31] Paul Pross also makes extensive use of the concept of "subgovernments" in interpreting group politics in Canada, while M. Bucovetsky notes that "the symbiotic relationship between government agencies and their clientele is a well-known administrative phenomenon."[32] More recently, William Coleman has looked at clientelism in a broader work on Canadian business associations, and has concluded that clientele relations are most highly developed in connections between government and the finance industry.[33]

Frequently, neopluralist structures of clientele relations are viewed in negative terms, and one of the most comprehensive critiques of these subsystems has been provided by Theodore Lowi in his work, *The End of Liberalism*. Lowi argues that the parcelling-out of power to those who have the most at stake allows a network of privilege to be maintained. Programmes become self-governing and nonaccountable. The public is shut out, and the institutions of representative government are undermined. The pluralist vision of freely competitive groups exercising countervailing power is largely mythical, because programme specialization reduces the number of potentially competitive groups involved, and the policy process becomes oligopolistic. The delegation of authority to self-governing coalitions makes any large-scale, policy-planning difficult, and for the most part allows only incremental change. The system is thus inherently conservative. Furthermore, in Lowi's view, it is fundamentally unjust, because the uniform application of general principles has been sacrificed to a system of informal group bargaining and special pleading.[34] Such criticisms are not confined to the U.S. system, but also strike a chord amongst leading Canadian analysts of group-government relations such as Hugh Thorburn.[35]

In Canada, however, the opportunities for business to develop clientele relations may be shrinking due to the growing centralization of policy authority within the federal government. Changes that have taken place in the structure of the federal government over the last 20 years or so have placed limitations on the role of interest groups. In particular, the increased role of central coordinating agencies, such as the Privy Council Office, the Prime Minister's Office and Treasury Board Secretariat, and the enhanced power of Cabinet committees have injected a degree of central control over federal government policy that makes decentralized clientele relations harder to establish and less productive for the groups concerned. Peter Aucoin, for example, suggests that the growth of central bureaucratic agencies has important implications for the position of interest groups because these "super bureaucrats" are less accessible to special interest organizations and have a greater degree of independence from them. Groups can no longer rely solely on departmental contacts because the line departments no longer have the independent authority they once enjoyed. The diminished influence of the regular departments means that any special relationships between departments and pressure groups are of less benefit, and the groups have been "dropped one step in the hierarchy of policy influence."[36]

Although policy-making within the federal government has been subject to centralizing tendencies, it is worth inserting a note of qualification here. The central agencies themselves are not all-powerful organizations and they generally do not have the staff or resources to become involved in the details of policy, which must still be left up to the regular departments. Writers such as Richard Schultz have suggested a variety of ways in which departments can thwart attempts by central agencies to "coordinate" them, ranging from the selective provision of information to playing off one agency against another.[37] In addition,

Richard French has described, in detail, the problems of coordinating the coordinators in making industrial policy in the 1970s, while Paul Pross has argued that attempts to centralize policy-making simply created additional policy actors and served to make the process even more diffuse.[38]

Rather than seeing clientelism either as an ubiquitous phenomenon, or alternatively as totally constrained by central agencies, it is more realistic to see clientelism as a limited occurrence that is more likely to emerge in some contexts than in others. The question then becomes one of identifying factors that are conducive to the development of clientele relationships. In this regard we would include the following points:

(1) Where policy authority is institutionally fragmented, we would expect self-governing subsystems to be more common and intra-governmental battles to be more frequent. Consequently, there would be more incentive for bureaucrats to mobilize the support of client groups.

(2) Clientelism is more likely to occur when a single government agency has a clearly defined jurisdiction over a particular policy issue. In such cases there is no confusion about the location of the government "patron," and no encroachment on the discrete symbiotic links by other government divisions.

(3) Clientelism is also more likely when the agency's clientele group is clearly defined and internally united. If an agency has to deal with a wide variety of business groups then the prospects for developing exclusive, privileged relationships with any one group are reduced. Similarly, if the agency receives conflicting messages from its clientele then its focus is less clear.

(4) Technically complex issues also promote clientelism because here government bureaucrats may well be dependent on the specialized expertise that only client groups can provide. On issues where there is little public controversy then there will be little outside pressure to break up these self-contained coalitions.

(5) The prospects for clientelism also improve when the particular objectives of client groups can easily be reconciled with the broader economic, social and political goals of

government. Where particular and general objectives cannot be reconciled then clientelism is likely to break down.

(6) Where the successful administration of policy depends to a large extent on the cooperation or "voluntary compliance" of business organizations then we can expect consensual clientele relations to be more characteristic of business-government interaction.

Clientelism can thus be seen as a particular form of consensual business-government relations, found in some circumstances and not in others. In general, clientelism is a "micro" level relationship; in other words, it concerns the interaction of fragmented subsections of both government and the business universe. At a more "macro" or centralized level, there is also an extensive body of literature that suggests a consensual incorporation of business interests into state policy-making structures, though here there is an additional contention that organized labour is a joint partner. This body of theory is known as "corporatism."

CORPORATISM

Corporatism, like pluralism, provides a model of policy-making in advanced industrial countries that gives a crucial role to organized societal interests. And like pluralism, corporatism has direct implications for the way business power and state power are interpreted. In addition, both contain a combination of descriptive and prescriptive elements. Theorists of each persuasion attempt to paint a picture of how existing policy systems operate, while at the same time suggesting that these systems are desirable in some way and that they should be preserved, extended or adopted in other contexts.

However, beyond these rather superficial similarities, pluralism and corporatism are quite different: While pluralism has its roots in an analysis of the fragmented structures of American government, corporatism is rooted in the more centralized policy systems of some of the smaller European countries like Sweden, Austria and Holland. Although the epicentres are in different parts of the globe, these conceptions, like earthquakes, have little respect for national boundaries and countries such as Canada have no immunity from their intellectual tremors.

Although there are several competing definitions of corporatism, in essence it is a tripartite political structure in which the business elite and the trade-union elite have been jointly incorporated with the state elite into a centralized system of authority dominating the policy making process in capitalist societies. In a more elaborate conceptualization, Philippe Schmitter has provided what is now one of the best known and most popular definitions of corporatism:

Corporatism can be defined as a system of interest representation in which the constituent units are organized into a limited number of singular, compulsory, non-competitive, hierarchically ordered and functionally differentiated categories, recognized or licensed (if not created) by the state and granted a deliberate representational monopoly within their respective categories in exchange for observing certain controls on their selection of leaders and articulation of demands and supports.[39]

This definition is by no means self-explanatory and some clarification is necessary here. The constituent interests being represented in corporatism are few in number, principally the categories of business and labour, although sometimes agricultural producers are also included. These interests are organized politically into a single association for each category. The associations in the different categories do not overlap one another and their relationship is characterized by cooperation rather than competition. Internally, the structure of each association consists of a disciplined hierarchy in which members are effectively controlled by the leadership, which in turn is subject to some controls imposed by the state. This monopolistic and authoritarian system of interest representation has been given the blessing of the state, and the state may even play a role in setting it up.

Within this view of corporatism, the position of the state can vary from one of almost total domination over business and labour organizations, to one in which business, labour and the state are roughly equal partners. The first case, known as *state corporatism*, is akin to Italian fascism under Mussolini, where business organizations and unions were rigidly controlled by the state, and where political parties were suppressed. In the second case, known as *liberal corporatism* or *societal corporatism*, business and labour associations have greater independence from the state and may even play leading roles in pushing the state towards the adoption of corporatist arrangements. In this form, corporatist structures can co-exist with other forms of representative politics, such as parties, elections and legislatures.

Another distinction often made by writers on corporatism concerns the level at which corporatist structures exist. At a macro level it involves a form of interest representation in which the whole range of businesses, associations and labour unions throughout society are integrated with few exceptions. This sort of aggregated and centralized system characterizes corporatism in countries like Austria where businesses, workers and farmers each are represented by all-encompassing organizations with compulsory memberships.[40]

In Canada, the organizational fragmentation of business and labour, as well as the fragmentation of the state, makes macro-level corporatism difficult to engineer, although some writers nevertheless see Canada as corporatist.[41] Others, such as William Coleman, recognize the structural barriers to be a more corporatist form of politics in Canada yet suggest this as a desirable direction for Canadian industrial policy. In a massive study, Coleman documents the disunity of Canadian business associations, and argues that socio-economic producer groups are too fragmented to develop a "viable strategic framework" for industrial policy in consultation with government. In lamenting this fragmentation he contends that Canada would benefit from adopting a more centralized pattern of interest representation, modelled on the smaller European democracies, such as Austria, where corporatism along with Keynesian macroeconomic policies are credited with fostering political stability and an "impressive" economic record.[42]

However, it is also possible to conceive of corporatism at a different level—one characterized by relations between the state and individual sectors of industry and labour. Here, corporatist relations do not require such a macro level of interest aggregation, but can exist at the less centralized, sectoral or *meso* level (middle level).[43] At the sectoral level, the problems of associational fragmentation are less daunting, but here there is a problem of conflict between sectors. It can be difficult, and sometimes impossible, for the state to reconcile the policy needs of one economic sector with those of others.

In its weakest form, sectoral corporatism is diluted into a tripartite system of policy consultation. Exercises of this nature took place in 1978 when the federal government set up 23 sectoral task forces involving representatives of business and labour, along with provincial and federal government officials. The task forces constituted "Tier I" of the consultation process, and dealt with a broad array of issues including taxation, trade policy, government regulation, competition policy and so on.[44] At a more centralized level, a "Tier II" committee then tried to integrate the recommendations of the various task forces into some general policy proposals for an industrial strategy. Unfortunately, this job was extremely difficult because each task force drew up a shopping list of special concessions for its own sector, including a basketful of tax breaks that would have drained government revenues.[45] Sectoral special pleading undermined attempts to find a consensus on industrial policy, and government was provided with no basis for choosing between the competing claims of different sectors.[46] The failure of this consultative process to provide a coherent guide to industrial strategy is not an encouraging precedent for those who advocate some form of sectoral corporatism as an instrument of Canadian industrial policy.

One of the reasons why corporatism holds an attraction for some people is due to the fact that it offers the possibility of fostering political stability by anaesthetizing class conflict and promoting more harmonious industrial relations. Corporatist structures can weaken labour militancy by incorporating union elites into an alliance with business and the state, and in return for formal participation, labour leaders are required to ensure that their members maintain industrial peace. It is a vision of policy-making in which the labour movement is docile and all sections of society work together to make the capitalist economy run more smoothly. Naturally enough, unionists are often wary of any such attempts to incorporate them. The acceptance of such a structure by labour is necessarily debilitating to any serious challenge to the capitalist system itself, which is why corporatism is criticized heavily by marxists such as Leo Panitch.

Panitch argues that corporatist forms are associated with a particular stage in the development of capitalism in which: (a) business is becoming increasingly monopolistic; (b) the working class is economically and politically strong; and (c) the state is pursuing policies of "full employment, economic planning and wage restraint."[47] Where the working class is strongly organized, the bourgeoisie and those who control the state have a great problem in trying to get workers to accept wage restraint. In these circumstances, especially if the working class has been scoring some political and economic victories, the bourgeoisie and the state are prepared to join together to offer labour greater participation in return for more moderation. Corporatism is thus a mechanism for reducing labour militancy, and integrating working class organizations into the capitalist state where they can be controlled.[48] Thus from a perspective of class analysis, corporatism can be seen as:

> a political structure within advanced capitalism which integrates organized socioeconomic producer groups through a system of representation and cooperative mutual interaction at the leadership level and mobilization and social control at the mass level. (Emphasis in original) [49]

Panitch also maintains that we need to distinguish between corporatism as an ideology and corporatism as existing political structure. While corporatist ideas have emerged from time to time in Canada, corporatists structures have not. In Canada, corporatist ideas have been put forward on a number of occasions, but have been stymied by the weakness and fragmentation of the labour movement, the lack of centralized business associations, and the balkanized character of the Canadian state.[50] If corporatism were to develop in Canada, labour would still face the problem of being co-opted into a system designed principally to control workers rather than to represent them.

More generally, corporatism can also be criticized for undermining established democratic institutions. If the real decisions in society are made by a tripartite coalition of business, labour and the state, then parliament and electoral politics are pushed further out of the picture. Furthermore, if policy is determined solely by producer groups then many sections of the public would be excluded. Consumers, environmentalists, homemakers, pensioners, the unemployed and many others would all be shut out of the representational system. These problems exist regardless of whether corporatism is analyzed at a macro or meso level. Calls for the introduction of corporatist relations therefore face not only the practical difficulties posed by institutional fragmentation, but also the more trenchant problems of trying to reconcile and harmonize conflicting interests within capitalism in a democratic fashion.

MARXISM AND NEOMARXISM

Marxism is much more than the analysis of the relations between the state and capital. Among other things it is (a) a general theory of social, economic and political development aimed at explaining the transformation of societies and the sweep of human history; (b) an analysis of the essential features of capitalism—its motive forces and contradictions, the nature of the human condition under this mode of production and a critique of bourgeois political economy; (c) a methodology or approach to the study of history, society and politics which focusses on class conflict as the fundamental explanatory and predictive category; (d) an intellectual challenge to the dominant philosophical ideas of Marx's day, chiefly those of Hegel and his followers; and (e) a practical endeavour as a mobilizing ideology for revolutionary action. Marx's writings on the state in general and on the capitalist state in particular comprise only a small part of his writing, and references to the state are dotted throughout his work rather than incorporated systematically into a single volume. While Marx had intended to write a systematic book on the state, death intervened before the project could be undertaken, and it has been left to Marx's many followers to develop his ideas in an effort to achieve a fully-fledged marxist theory of the state—an endeavour that is still in progress

For Marx, the state can only be understood in the context of relations between economic classes in society. It is the relationship between those who own the means of production (the bourgeoisie in capitalist societies) and the producers who actually do the work (the proletariat) that provides the base upon which the rest of social, political and intellectual life is built.[51] The state, along with laws, ideologies, culture, etc., forms the *superstructure* of society which rises from the economic *base*. Yet this does not mean that the superstructure is simply an inert dead-weight supported by the economic base and mechanistically determined by it; state action shapes the contours of the base and plays an important role in managing class antagonisms.

From a marxist perspective, the capitalist state is thus inextricably bound up with class conflict, and as a set of related institutions (including the executive, the bureaucracy, the legislature, the judiciary, sub-national governments, etc.) it arises and is shaped in the midst of a battle between warring classes. It is not a detached and disinterested entity, overseeing class conflict in an even-handed fashion. Instead, the state is actively involved on the side of the capitalist class and is a means by which class domination is maintained.[52] The state's role in this battle is to defend the interests of the dominant class and to regulate class antagonisms so that working-class challenges to the capitalist system are defeated or are prevented from occurring in the first place.

For marxists, capitalism is a self-destructive system. Ultimately, the state must fail in its task of regulating the internal contradictions and conflicts that push capitalism towards collapse and a revolutionary transformation into socialism. As capital becomes progressively centralized in fewer and fewer hands, as the working class becomes larger and better organized, as the mass of exploitation and misery grows, so the working class grows into a revolutionary force that will burst capitalism asunder.[53] Whatever the functions of the state in trying to prop up capitalism, eventually the system will explode from within, despite the state's efforts.

However, in an attempt to postpone capitalism's apocalypse, the capitalist state performs three basic functions. First, it must try to ensure that capital accumulation continues to take place and that capitalist enterprises generally remain profitable. The purpose behind this is that the state is dependent on the profitability of the private economy to supply the money that pays for everything the state does. Part of the surplus generated by capitalist production is taken by the state in the form of taxes on sales, profits and dividends, and also taxes on the incomes of people that the economic system is able to employ, as well as other forms of payments from employers and employees. This money is then used to fund government programmes, to pay the salaries of those who are employed by the state and to provide the overall financial basis of state power. State officials, whether elected or non-elected, cannot be insensitive to the needs of capital because, in the words of marxist economist James O'Connor:

> A state that ignores the necessity of assisting the process of capital accumulation risks drying up the source of its own power, the economy's surplus production capacity and the taxes drawn from this surplus (and other forms of capital).[54]

O'Connor also elaborates on a second function of the state, namely *legitimization*. Here the state must try to preserve social harmony in the face of class divisions and the continual possibility of open class conflict. In an attempt to preserve the stability of the capitalist system, the state must make this system seem legitimate and acceptable to those who are likely to pose the most serious challenge to it, that is, the working class. The state must also make its own role seem legitimate in order to maintain mass loyalty, and this requires a variety of social expenses that provide benefits to the "have-nots," such as those aspects of the welfare state that are "designed chiefly to keep social peace among unemployed workers."[55] These expenditures are thus seen as attempts to "buy-off" working-class dissent and to defuse social conflict within capitalist societies. Even if business people vociferously oppose many social expenditures, they are nevertheless the ultimate beneficiaries because the capitalist system is rendered more stable.

For O'Connor, the state has a fundamental problem in trying to perform these first two functions simultaneously because they are seen as contradictory. If the state openly intervenes to help one class (the capitalist class) over the others in order to ensure continued capital accumulation, then it simultaneously loses legitimacy in the eyes of subordinate classes.[56] The state is more clearly revealed as serving class interests rather than national interests. This apparent contradiction is part of the reason that O'Connor thinks there is a crisis of the capitalist state, yet O'Connor himself provides a qualification that may overcome the contradiction between accumulation and legitimization. He suggests that the state is capable of disguising, of "mystifying", what it is doing, so that interventions to support capital accumulation are seen as conducive to the general or national interest. Such policies become defined as "job development" or as measures aimed at "stability and growth"; they are certainly not defined in class terms. But if the state can successfully "mystify" its policies in this way, then the contradiction between accumulation and legitimization disappears. If the working-class people accept that actions on behalf of capital are in the national interest, then such interventions will be a means by which legitimacy is enhanced, not undermined. If for cultural and ideological reasons most people have been persuaded that capitalism is legitimate and worth preserving (as is clearly the case in developed capitalist democracies), then efforts by the state to support capital may well receive public applause, not public hostility.[57]

Besides accumulation and legitimization, the state also performs another important function in capitalist societies, and this is the *coercive function*.[58] Where the working class cannot be controlled and pacified by policies falling under the heading of legitimization, the coercive arm of the state, which includes the judicial system, the police and the armed forces, can be used to crush working-class dissent through physical means. Included here are such things as declaring strikes illegal, breaking up picket lines, jailing union leaders, using the security services to infiltrate and intimidate left-wing organizations, and arresting protestors. Such state repression has been the exception rather than the rule in Canada, in part because the docility and disorganization of the Canadian working class has made it unnecessary. In addition, Canadian capitalism has allowed a tolerable degree of prosperity for most people which has reduced the stimulus to widespread, radical activism. In general, the capitalist state's use of physical coercion only becomes evident as other less overtly repressive mechanisms for controlling the working class start to break down and fail.

In examining marxist interpretations of the state's basic functions in a capitalist society, a crucial question arises, namely, why does the state perform these functions on behalf of capital? This question addresses the central issue of the relationship between the state and the capitalist class, and has given rise to an extensive debate amongst neomarxists about how this relationship should be understood.

Broadly speaking there are two competing neomarxist views of state-capital relations that have become characterized as *instrumentalism* and *structuralism*. In the instrumentalist view, the ruling class, ie. those who own and control the means of production, is able "to use the state as its instrument for the domination of society," and the state is an "instrument in the hands of the possessing class."[59]   Here, the capitalist class is reasonably cohesive and unified, and is capable of having a clear and common set of interests that can be represented by the state. State action and the determination of public policy can be best understood as a function of interpersonal relations between the economically dominant class and the state elite. Attention centres on such things as their common social origin, their similar upbringing and life experiences, their similar ideologies, etc. These sociological linkages and mutual sympathies are augmented by an extensive interchange of personnel between the state elite and the capitalist class, with individuals frequently moving from business to politics and back again. In this explanation the state has very little autonomy from the capitalist class. Instrumentalism is often associated with the earlier views of Ralph Miliband as expressed in *The State in Capitalist Society*, and these have a lot in common with elite theory, particularly in concentrating its attack on the pluralist "assumption that power, in Western societies, is competitive, fragmented and diffused."[60]

Structuralist critics, such as Nicos Poulantzas, have argued that Miliband has largely missed the point in looking at the state in this way, as it is not just an instrument in the hands of the bourgeoisie. Poulantzas and other structuralists try to move away from an emphasis on individuals and personal interactions as a means for understanding state-capital relations. Instead, both the state and the class system are seen as objective structures and relations between them are impersonal and systemic. Any personal ties between state officials and members of the ruling class do not matter very much; they are an *effect* of the objective relations, not a *cause*, and may just be coincidental.[61] Miliband defends himself by arguing that he does not totally ignore structural forces as constraints on state action, and that Poulantzas "goes much too far in dismissing the nature of the state elite as of altogether no account."[62]

One intrinsic element of the attack against instrumentalism has been to emphasize that the capitalist state (while still embedded in the class structure) has a significant degree of independence, or *relative autonomy*, from the capitalist class—a view that Miliband himself quickly came to accept. This perspective of the state recognizes that the capitalist class is not a monolithic entity, but is divided into different fractions, each with somewhat different interests. These divisions can be based on a wide variety of possible cleavages, for instance, between the manufacturing sector and the resource sector, between industries in different regions of the country, between foreign-owned firms and domestically-owned ones, and between big business and small business. Because of this disunity it is impossible for the state simply to carry out the wishes of the dominant class—the dominant class is too politically disorganized to provide any coherent set of instructions for the state to follow. Instead, the state must try to interpret what is in the best interests of capitalism as a whole, and must try to reconcile or choose between the sometimes conflicting interests of different segments of the business world.

The state thus performs a crucial function as a sort of political glue, unifying and organizing the chaotic and contradictory interests of the many disparate fractions of capital. In order to do this the state has to have some autonomy from the particular demands placed upon it by the various sections of business. This is not just because specific business demands may contradict one another, but also because business people tend to be preoccupied with their own immediate profits rather than with the longer-term health of the capitalist system. The state must be concerned with the bigger picture, and sometimes this means responding to working-class demands in order to enhance legitimacy, or enacting policies such as social welfare programmes or environmental regulations that business has generally opposed. In this way neomarxists are able to explain why the capitalist state does not always do what business wants. The state has some life of its own and acts on *behalf* of capital, not at its *behest*.[63] Miliband maintains that this is implicit in Marx and Engels' own work, even in their most famous dictum on the state from the *Communist Manifesto* where they say that "the modern state is but a committee for managing the common affairs of the whole bourgeoisie."[64] Miliband argues that

> the notion of common affairs assumes the existence of particular ones; and the notion of the whole bourgeoisie implies the existence of separate elements which make up that whole. This being the case, there is an obvious need for an institution of the kind they refer to, namely the state; and the state *cannot* meet this need without enjoying a certain degree of autonomy.[65]

However, the capitalist state does not enjoy complete autonomy because it is still rooted in the class structure of society and is restrained by the overall need to serve the interests of capital.

One of the main strengths of modern marxism is in analyzing the constraints on state action imposed by the fact that investment, production and distribution—the key elements of a nation's economic livelihood—are largely in private hands. This fact prompts the state to perform functions that serve the interests of capital over other classes and that are directed towards the long-term stability of the capitalist system. At the same time, neomarxists recognize that public policy is not just a response to the demands of capitalists, and that the state has some degree of autonomy from dominant classes or class fractions. However, the thrust of this analysis is not without its problems.

The first problem is that this approach frequently comes close to sinking into a "functionalist swamp" in which all state policies are necessarily construed as functional to the interests of capital and the stability of capitalism. Even policies that seem to benefit the working class, such as unemployment insurance or minimum wage laws, are interpreted in a negative way as things that make the capitalist system seem more acceptable, thus helping to prolong the life of a system that is still fundamentally based on exploitation. Consequently, any real gains made by workers are disparaged, and hard-fought, working-class struggles are written off as counterproductive.

The functionalist perspective also implies that policy-makers have a substantial prescience in designing policies to serve the long-term needs of capital. But the ample history of policy failures, in numerous fields, would suggest that the state is quite capable of acting against capital by mistake. This goes against the notion that there is some functional imperative in capitalist societies which requires that the state must act on behalf of capital. Furthermore, it is difficult for marxists to maintain a view of the state as being functional to stability in capitalist society, while at the same time portraying capitalism as a dysfunctional system doomed to self-destruction.

Secondly, the overall dependency of the state on capitalist production needs to be qualified. Given the existing fact of capitalism, the state obviously does depend on this system of production to provide revenues (directly or indirectly) for most of the state's activities. Yet state structures can also exist under other systems of production, and the state does not need capitalism per se. What it needs is *some* form of production that provides an effective mechanism for generating a sufficient economic surplus. Part of this surplus can then be used to support the state. Under current circumstances, capitalism seems the most effective way of doing this. However, if capitalism should dramatically fail in this task, at some future date, then it is quite possible that some alternative revenue-generating mechanism would seem more attractive to state officials. In short, the state's dependency on capital is contingent, not absolute.

Finally, the concept of relative autonomy disassociates state action, at least to some extent, from the interests of capital. But how much autonomy can the state be granted before it is no longer appropriate to label it definitively as a capitalist state? The state still exists within the context of a capitalist society, but if it has considerable autonomy in responding to capital, or in accommodating the interests of subordinate classes, then its links with dominant class power start to become more tenuous. It is by no means clear how far one can go in granting autonomy to the state before the essential class-based character of a marxist analysis of state power is lost. If neomarxists interpret the state just as a "strategic battlefield" or an arena where class struggle takes place, then a significant step has been taken towards a more pluralistic form of analysis.

Despite the concept of relative autonomy, neomarxists still see the state as ultimately serving the needs of a capitalist class. It is this ultimate lack of detachment from capital that distinguishes marxist conceptions of the relative autonomy of the state from modern "statists" who go further in granting the state an even greater degree of independence from societal forces in general and from business in particular.

STATISM

Most of the preceding interpretations of business-state relations have given primacy to societal forces (whether they are elites, classes or interest groups) as the key actors in determining the course of public policy.[66] In contrast to these theories, statism, as its name implies, takes the state rather than society to be the central focus of attention. The state is seen as distinct and largely independent from societal pressures, and as having a dominant position over society in the determination of public policy. This state-centred orientation is a relatively recent development in public policy theory, although loose historical connections can be made with the works of Weber and Hegel. In large measure, statism is a reaction to the popularity of many of the theories previously discussed because these are generally seen as either ignoring or undervaluing the role of the state. The result has thus been a resurgence of interest in the state, and a growing concern with "bringing the state back in" to the centre of political analysis.[67]

Within this general resurgence, there are nevertheless a number of specific differences in emphasis and approach among different writers, and these can be broadly differentiated into two main groups. The first group consists of those writers whose views have emerged as both a critique and extension of neomarxism. The second group consists of more "mainstream" political scientists who have become disenchanted with the assumptions and limitations of pluralism or neopluralism, and who have challenged the dependent and secondary role accorded to state actors in these models of policy-making. By and large the first group looks at state autonomy in relation to "class" while the second looks at state autonomy in relation to "interest groups." Where these terrains overlap is in regard to business interests.

The first group, represented by writers such as Theda Skocpol and Fred Block, argues that the state does not inevitably act in the interests of a dominant class, and that state power is not reducible to class power.[68] For Block, those who manage the state are reliant on capitalists to provide the economic surplus necessary to fund state activity, but at the same time these state managers also have their own self-interests that can be separated from those of capitalists. They are "interested in maximizing their power, prestige and wealth" which they can do by expanding the realm of state activity, and this can bring them into conflict with the interests of capital.[69]

For Skocpol, the departure from neomarxism is more clear cut. She attacks neomarxism for not giving sufficient weight to state and party structures as "*independent* determinants of political conflicts and outcomes," and for not taking these organizations seriously enough.[70] Autonomy is more than just "relative" and neomarxists are criticized for failing "to grant true autonomy to states." She also argues that they have generalized about the state in too abstract a fashion, and that more attention needs to be paid to cross-national variations in state structures.[71]

This emphasis on a more substantial autonomy for the state has had an impact even on neomarxists; for example, Miliband has gone so far as to reinterpret state-capital relations in terms of a "*partnership between two different, separate forces*, linked to each other by many threads, yet each having its own separate sphere of concerns," where the state cannot "be taken necessarily to be the junior partner."[72] For a marxist such an interpretation is a significant step towards the analytical Rubicon where "relative autonomy" becomes "true autonomy," and where the state is seen not as a state of the dominant class but as a separate force in itself and *for* itself. If the state is autonomous to this extent then there is the possibility that, at some future date, key state officials may see the continuation of capitalism as inimical with their own interests—especially if capitalism were to fail as a revenue-generating mechanism for the state. Under such circumstances we have a potential for radical social transformation orchestrated by the state rather than resisted by it.

At a more mundane level, the second group of statists, best exemplified by Eric Nordlinger and Stephen Krasner, look at state autonomy in relation to organized groups in society, including business. Here autonomy is seen as the capacity of the state to act upon its preferences even "when its preferences diverge from the demands of the most powerful groups in civil society."[73] As Nordlinger asserts, "Public officials have at least as much independent impact or explanatory importance as any and all private actors in accounting for the public policies of the democratic state."[74]

In a more empirically-oriented work, Krasner sees the state pursuing goals "that are separate and distinct from the interests of any particular societal group," and he labels these the "national interest." He then uses a case study of U.S. raw materials policy to demonstrate that "central decision-makers did not always follow the preferences of private corporations," and concludes that "the state has it own needs and goals, which cannot be reduced to specific societal interests."[75]

In Canada, various versions of statism are becoming increasingly popular as interpretations of business-government relations. For example, Elizabeth Riddell-Dixon analyzes a specific case study of deep-seabed mining and argues that policy outputs reflected state preferences "in spite of opposition from the Canadian business community."[76] In the area of Canadian foreign policy more generally, Kim Nossal maintains that government officials are able to define "national interests" in policy-making with a fair degree of immunity from societal pressure. Yet civil society does impose very broad limits on what officials can do, and Nossal recognizes that conceptions of the national interest do not emerge in a political and economic vacuum. Such concepts "are inevitably affected by Canada's capitalist economic structure and by the state's basic commitment to the maintenance of that structure."[77] Here we can see that there is often a fine line between statism and structural marxism, which is something that Stephen Krasner is also prepared to admit.[78]

Canadian political scientist Les Pal perhaps goes furthest in trying to distance statism from structural marxism, and in a study of the origins of unemployment insurance he maintains that policy development is best understood not in terms of class conflict, but as a product of the internal dynamics and structure of the state. These could not simply "be reduced to controlling labour or accumulating capital."[79]

Statism as an approach to business-government relations attempts to redress some of the shortcomings of other theories that allocate only a secondary and contingent role to state structures, and this seems all the more appropriate in light of the considerable expansion of the state in Western capitalist societies throughout most of this century. However, the statist approach also has some problematic areas, leaving a number of questions unanswered. Writers, such as Nordlinger, who emphasize the autonomous preferences of state actors ignore the question of where these preferences come from. Clearly they are not just accidental and there is some process of socialization at work which accounts for the attitudes and preferences of state policy-makers. In this process the ideological dominance of capital cannot be ignored, and it is no coincidence that policy-makers are overwhelmingly predisposed towards a capitalist system of production. Preferences are also shaped by the structural constraints of a capitalist economy in which business is mobile across national borders. The need to attract and retain investment from the private sector puts limits on what policy-makers can "prefer" to do if they are not to scare off private capital and jeopardize economic performance.

Statism also needs to avoid the mistake of seeing the state as a unitary actor, especially in a federal political system such as Canada's. Clearly, the state is not a monolith, but a complex interrelation of many separate institutions.[80] It seems reasonable to suggest that where the state is highly centralized, its prospects of dominating civil society will be enhanced. But this does not mean that more fragmented states are necessarily lacking in autonomy. Just as the state is a set of institutions existing at different levels, so autonomy from business or other societal interests can also exist at different levels. Various substructures of the state, such as departments, agencies, commissions and provincial governments, are capable of acting independently from sections of the business world, and they can do this either separately or as part of a broader institutional network. Even a highly fragmented system such as the United States has provided a fertile ground for the application of state-centred analysis. In fact, it has sometimes been argued that the U.S. is a "crucial case" for testing the statist model—if state autonomy exists there it can exist virtually anywhere.[81]

Perhaps the most useful way of looking at state autonomy is not as an all-or-nothing category, with the state being either autonomous or dependent, but as a matter of degree, with states having variable levels of autonomy depending on the context. However, no state is totally autonomous because state institutions themselves typically emerge in response to societal forces, and indeed it would be difficult to account for the origins of the state without reference to the society within which it is embedded. Thus, while the potential for autonomous state action exists with regard to the immediate policy process, this scope is ultimately limited by a broad set of societal constraints in which business and the economic system in general play an important part.

ENDNOTES

1. C. Wright Mills, *The Power Elite* (New York: Oxford University Press, 1956) and John Porter, *The Vertical Mosaic* (Toronto: University of Toronto Press, 1965).
2. Mills, *The Power Elite*, 9.
3. Porter, *The Vertical Mosaic*, 557.
4. See for example: Wallace Clement, *The Canadian Corporate Elite: An Analysis of Economic Power* (Toronto: McClelland and Stewart Ltd., 1975); Jorge Niosi, *The Economy of Canada: Who Controls It?* (Montreal: Black Rose Books, 1978); Dennis Olsen, "The State Elites" in Leo Panitch, ed., *The Canadian State: Political Economy and Political Power* (Toronto: University of Toronto Press, 1977), 199-224; and Wallace Clement, "The Corporate Elite, the Capitalist Class and the Canadian State," in Panitch, ed., *The Canadian State*, 225-48.
5. Some of the main targets include Mills, *The Power Elite*; Floyd Hunter, *Community Power Structure* (Chapel Hill, N.C.: University of North Carolina

Press, 1953); and Robert S. Lynd and Helen M. Lynd, *Middletown* (New York: Harcourt, Brace, 1929).

6. Two principal works in this area are Robert A. Dahl, *Who Governs?* (New Haven: Yale University Press, 1961) and Nelson W. Polsby, *Community Power and Political Theory* (New Haven: Yale University Press, 1963). Other prominent contributions to pluralism include, David B. Truman, *The Governmental Process* (New York: Alfred A. Knopf, 1951); Robert A. Dahl, "A Critique of the Ruling Elite Model," in *American Political Science Review*, 52 (June 1958), 463-69; Robert A. Dahl, *Pluralist Democracy in the United States* (Chicago: Rand McNally and Co., 1967); Earl Latham, "The Group Basis of Politics: Notes for a Theory," in Heinz Eulau, Samuel Eldersveld and Morris Janowitz, eds., *Political Behavior: A Reader in Theory and Research* (Glencoe, Illinois: The Free Press, 1956), 232-45.

7. Dahl, *Pluralist Democracy in the United States*, 24.

8. Polsby, *Community Power and Political Theory*, 90.

9. *Ibid*, 113, emphasis in original.

10. *Ibid*, 117.

11. Robert A Dahl, *A Preface to Democratic Theory* (Chicago: University of Chicago Press, 1956), 137.

12. Dahl, *Pluralist Democracy in the United States*, 386.

13. *Ibid.*, 455.

14. Polsby, *Community Power and Political Theory*, 115.

15. Dahl, *Pluralist Democracy in the United States*, 24.

16. Truman, *The Governmental Process*, 510 and Dahl, *Pluralist Democracy in the United States*, 369.

17. Truman, *The Governmental Process*, 506.

18. Truman, *Ibid.*, 45 and Latham, "The Group Basis of Politics," 233, 235.

19. Latham, "The Group Basis of Politics," 239.

20. E.E. Schattschneider, *The Semisovereign People* (Hinsdale, Illinois: The Dryden Press, 1960), 34-35.

21. Robert A Dahl, *Dilemmas of Pluralist Democracy* (New Haven: Yale University Press, 1982), 207-209.

22. Ralph Miliband, *The State in Capitalist Society* (London: Quartet Books, 1973), 132.

23. Charles Lindblom, *Politics and Markets* (New York: Basic Books Inc., 1977), 172.

24. *Ibid.*, 175.

25. Miliband, *The State in Capitalist Society*, 139.

26. P. Bachrach and M.S. Baratz, "The Two Faces of Power," in *American Political Science Review*" Vol. 56, No. 4 (December 1962), 947-52 and Stephen Lukes, *Power: A Radical View* (London: Macmillan, 1974).

27. Lukes, *Power: A Radical View*, 23.

28. The literature in this area is extensive and includes Joseph LaPalombara, *Interest Groups in Italian Politics* (Princeton: Princeton University Press, 1964); J.J. Richardson and A.G. Jordan, *Governing Under Pressure* (New York: Basil Blackwell, 1985); B. Guy Peters, "Insiders and Outsiders: The Politics of Pressure Group Influence on the Bureaucracy," in *Administration and Society*, Vol. 9, No. 2 (1977), 191-218; Grant McConnell, *Private Power and American Democracy* (New York: Alfred A. Knopf, 1966); Randall Ripley, *Congress, Process and Policy* (New York: W.W. Norton, 1979); and Theodore Lowi, *The End of Liberalism*, 2nd edition (New York: W.W. Norton, 1979).   In Canada, writers who deal with this concept include Robert Presthus, *Elite Accommodation in Canadian Politics* (Toronto: MacMillian, 1973); K.Z. Paltiel, "The Changing Environment and Role of Special Interest Groups," in *Canadian Public Administration*, Vol. 25, No. 2 (Summer 1982), 198-210; M. Bucovetsky, "The Mining Industry and the Great Tax Reform Debate," in A. Paul Pross, ed., *Pressure Group Behaviour in Canadian Politics* (Scarborough, Ont.:   McGraw-Hill Ryerson, 1975), 89-114; A. Paul Pross, *Group Politics and Public Policy* (Toronto: Oxford University Press, 1986); and William D. Coleman, *Business and Politics* (Kingston and Montreal: McGill-Queen's University Press, 1988).

29. LaPalombara, *Interest Groups in Italian Politics*, 262.

30. Peters, "Insiders and Outsiders," 202.

31. Presthus, *Elite Accommodation in Canadian Politics*, 211, 224-26.

32. Pross, *Group Politics and Public Politics*, 240 and Bucovetsky, "The Mining Industry," 107.

33. Coleman, *Business and Politics*, 74, 172-92.

34. Theodore Lowi, *The End of Liberalism*, 2nd edition (New York: W.W. Norton, 1979).

35. Hugh Thorburn, *Interest Groups in the Canadian Federal System* (Toronto: Royal Commission on the Economic Union and Development Prospects for Canada, Research Studies, Vol. 69, 1985), 125.

36. Peter Aucoin, "Pressure Groups and Recent Changes in the Policy-Making Process," in Paul Pross, ed., *Pressure Group Behaviour in Canadian Politics* (Scarborough, Ont.:   McGraw-Hill Ryerson, 1975), 180.

37. Richard Schultz, "Prime Ministerial Government, Central Agencies and Operating Departments: Towards a More Realistic Analysis," in T.A. Hockin, ed., *Apex of Power*, 2nd edition (Scarborough, Ont: Prentice-Hall, 1977), 229-36.

38. Richard French, *How Ottawa Decides* (Toronto: James Lorimer and Co., 1980) and A. Paul Pross, "Governing Under Pressure: The Special Interest Groups— Summary of Discussion," in *Canadian Public Administration* Vol. 25, No. 2 (Summer 1982), 170-82.

39. Philippe Schmitter, "Still the Century of Corporatism?" in Philippe C. Schmitter and Gerhard Lehmbruch, eds., *Trends Toward Corporatist Intermediation* (Beverly Hills: Sage, 1979), 13.

40. Coleman, *Business and Politics*, 224.

41. Presthus, *Elite Accommodation in Canadian Politics*, 24-28 and K.J. Rea and J.T. McLeod, eds., *Business and Government in Canada*, 2nd edition (Toronto: Methuen, 1976), 338-39.

42. Coleman, *Business and Politics*, 7, 223-29, 265-68.

43. See for example A. Wassenberg, "New Corporatism and the Quest for Control: The Cuckoo Game," in G. Lehmbruch and Schimitter, eds., *Trends Toward Corporatist Intermediation* (Beverley Hills: Sage, 1979), 33-108 and Gibson Burrell, "Corporatism in Comparative Context," in V.V. Murray, ed., *Theories of Business-Government Relations* (Toronto: Trans-Canada Press, 1985), 221-41.

44. Douglas Brown and Julia Eastman with Ian Robinson, *The Limits of Consultation: A Debate Among Ottawa, the Provinces and the Private Sector on an Industrial Strategy* (Ottawa: Science Council of Canada, 1981), 150.

45. *Ibid.*, 152.

46. *Ibid.*, 176.

47. Leo Pantich, "Corporatism in Canada?," in *Studies in Political Economy*, I (1979), 45.

48. *Ibid.*, 83-84.

49. *Ibid.*, 44.

50. *Ibid.*, 78-82.

51. Karl Marx, *Preface to Contribution to the Critique of Political Economy* (Moscow: Progress Publishers, 1970), 20-21.

52. Ralph Miliband, *Marxism and Politics* (Oxford: Oxford University Press, 1977), 67.

53. Karl Marx, *Capital*, Vol. 1 (New York: International Publishers Co. Inc., 1967), 763.

54. James O'Connor, *The Fiscal Crisis of the State* (New York: St. Martin's Press, 1973), 6.

55. *Ibid.*, 7.

56. *Ibid.*, 6.

57. This whole question of cultural and ideological hegemony is largely ignored in *The Fiscal Crisis*.

58. Leo Panitch, "The Role and Nature of the Canadian State," in Leo Panitch, ed., *The Canadian State: Political Economy and Political Power* (Toronto; University of Toronto Press, 1977), 8.

59. Ralph Miliband, *The State in Capitalist Society* (London: Quartet Books, 1973), 23. [First published by Weidenfeld and Nicholson Ltd., 1969] and Ernest Mandel, *The Marxist Theory of the State* (Merit Publishers, 1969), 11.

60. Miliband, *The State in Capitalist Society*, 4.

61. Nicos Poulantzas, "The Problem of the Capitalist State," in *New Left Review*, No. 58 (November-December 1969), 67-78. Poulantzas had developed the structuralist position at great length (and complexity) in an earlier work, *Political Power and*

Social Classes (London: NLB and Sheed & Ward, 1973). [First published as *Pouvoir politique et classes sociales* (Paris: Francois Maspero, 1968)].

62. Ralph Miliband, "The Capitalist State, Reply to Nicos Poulantzas," in *New Left Review*, No. 59 (January-February 1970), 53-60.

63. Ralph Miliband, "Poulantzas and the Capitalist State," in *New Left Review*, No. 82 (November-December 1973), 83-92.

64. Karl Marx and Frederick Engels, *Manifesto of the Communist Party* (Peking: Foreign Languages Press, 1972), 33.

65. Miliband, "Poulantzas and the Capitalist State," 85.

66. With the possible exception of corporatism in its strongest version.

67. See for example: Peter B. Evans, Dietrich Rueschemeyer and Theda Skocpol, eds., *Bringing the State Back In* (Cambridge: Cambridge University Press, 1985); Eric Nordlinger, *On the Autonomy of the Democratic State* (Cambridge, Mass.: Harvard University Press, 1981); Stephen D. Krasner, *Defending the National Interest: Raw Materials Investments and U.S. Foreign Policy* (Princeton: Princeton University Press, 1978); and Fred Block, "Beyond Relative Autonomy: State Managers as Historical Subjects," in Ralph Miliband and John Saville, eds., *The Socialist Register 1980* (London: Merlin Press, 1980).

68. Theda Skocpol, *States and Social Revolutions* (Cambridge: Cambridge University Press, 1979), 30 and Block, "Beyond Relative Autonomy," 229.

69. Block, *ibid.*

70. Skocpol, *States and Social Revolutions*, 199-200.

71. Theda Skocpol, "Bringing the State Back In: Strategies of Analysis in Current Research," in Evans et al., *Bringing the State Back In*, 5-6.

72. Ralph Miliband, *Class Power and State Power: Political Essays* (London: Verso Editions and NLB, 1983), 72.

73. Nordlinger, *On the Autonomy of the Democractic State*, 1.

74. *Ibid.*, 8.

75. Krasner, *Defending the National Interest*, 10, 32, 333.

76. Elizabeth Riddell-Dixon, "State Autonomy and Canadian Foreign Policy: The Case Deep Seabed Mining," in *Canadian Journal of Political Science*, 21:2 (June 1988), 297-317.

77. Kim Richard Nossal, *The Politics of Canadian Foreign Policy* (Scarborough, Ont.: Prentice-Hall Canada Inc., 1985), 62.

78. Krasner, *Defending the National Interest*, 6.

79. Leslie A. Pal, "Relative Autonomy Revisited: The Origins of Canadian Unemployment Insurance," in *Canadian Journal of Political Science*, 19:1 (March 1986), 77.

80. Riddell-Dixon, "State Autonomy and Canadian Foreign Policy," 314.

81. Krasner, *Defending the National Interest*, 7.

PART 3

STRUCTURE

Chapter 4

Canadian Industrial Structure

The relationship between business and government in Canada, or in any other capitalist country, takes place within the context of a particular national industrial structure. This structure plays an important role in shaping the character of business-government relations, and at the same time is itself shaped by the continuing interaction of these two forces. On a very general level, the industrial structure consists of the basic pattern of production and distribution of goods and services within a given geographic area, and encompasses the principal characteristics and cleavages in the overall network of economic activity. The balance between different sectors of industry, regional economic divisions, the level of foreign ownership and the degree of corporate concentration, all play a part in making up the particular configuration of attributes that is a country's industrial structure. While such configurations are not static, they are not normally prone to sudden and dramatic changes; therefore, structural patterns tend to exhibit a measure of stability, at least in the short-term.

The nature of a country's industrial structure is important because it provides a direct stimulus to industrial policies. Structural change can cause severe economic dislocation for those regions and sections of the population that are adversely affected, and this often inspires government efforts to compensate particular groups or to shape the course of restructuring. In particular, the regional division of business activity and the associated economic inequalities between different parts of the country have been a continual source of friction in Canada, giving rise to a range of industrial policies from both federal and provincial governments. In provinces where the industrial structure is more biased towards resource extraction, governments have frequently tried to promote greater diversification and have sought to alter the structure of provincial economic activity by encouraging the growth of manufacturing. Governments at all levels have been sensitive to problems of industrial structure and have made efforts to influence business behaviour, especially concerning location, level and type of investment.

Besides being a stimulus to government action, economic structures also impose a set of constraints on policy-makers by limiting the options that can realistically be pursued in the area of industrial policy. The nature of the industrial structure makes some policies seem more feasible and attractive than others. For instance, the extent of foreign ownership of the Canadian economy and Canada's trade dependency on the United States imposes severe constraints on Canadian foreign policy, while the small number of large firms that dominate many industries makes it more difficult for governments to ensure real competition amongst producers. This does not mean that these problems cannot be addressed, but it does show that it is easier for governments to pursue some options rather than others.

Structural divisions within the economy also have an impact on the way business is organized politically. Regional, sectoral, linguistic and other cleavages provide a basis for political disunity within the business world, and the conflicting interests of different segments of capital create problems for government in responding to business needs. Against this, capital in Canada is highly concentrated, and corporations are frequently locked together by a variety of personal and financial linkages. These have a unifying tendency in opposition to the divisive aspects of the industrial structure. In the following sections of this chapter, we will examine briefly the sectoral and regional characteristics of the Canadian industrial structure, as well as the issue of foreign ownership. The next chapter will look specifically at the question of corporate concentration.

THE SECTORAL BALANCE

Industrial activity in developed societies is commonly divided into three broad sectors, each consisting of a group of loosely related industries. These sectors are known as primary, secondary and tertiary industries.[1]

The primary sector covers all industries whose principal activity is the extraction of natural resources from land or water. Included under this heading would be agriculture, fishing, forestry, mining, drilling, quarrying, etc. The secondary sector encompasses a wide range of industries concerned with the secondary processing of natural resources and with the manufacture or construction of material goods. Examples include the traditional heavy industries such as steelmaking, shipbuilding and construction, as well as a variety of manufacturing industries involved with the production of textiles, chemicals, automobiles, plastics, furniture, household appliances and numerous other goods. Finally, in the tertiary sector, industries are not involved with the extraction or manufacture of tangible products, but with the distribution of goods or the provision of services and public utilities. This category is a broad one covering such things as finance, insurance, real estate, the transportation and communications industries, wholesaling, retailing, personal and commercial services, and public administration.[2]

The balance between these sectors has been the subject of some concern in Canada, and a number of political economists have argued that we are too dependent on the extraction and exportation of natural resources. The traditional stereotype of Canadians as "hewers of wood and drawers of water" still persists in the minds of many people, and from this perspective, it is commonly argued that Canada is qualitatively different from other industrialized countries. We are sometimes seen as a resource hinterland with a weak and underdeveloped manufacturing sector that relies too heavily on exports of raw materials and not heavily enough on finished products. In this view the sectoral balance of the economy is distorted to such an extent that we scarcely qualify to be called an industrial country. It is also claimed that this imbalance is getting worse and that Canada is actually undergoing a process of "de-industrialization."[3]

In assessing this contention, a careful look at the changing balance of employment between different sectors of the economy is useful. By examining the long-term picture, shown in Figure 4.1, we can see that throughout this century there

FIGURE 4.1

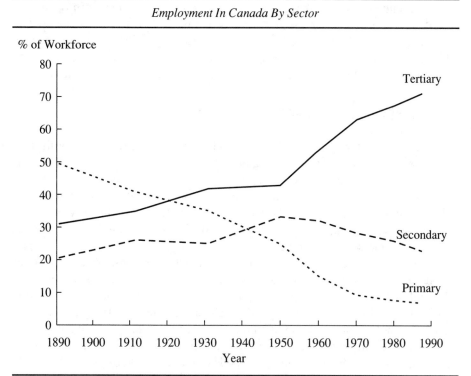

Employment In Canada By Sector

% of Workforce

Sources: M.C. Urquhart and K.A.H. Buckley, eds., *Historical Statistic's of Canada* (Toronto: MacMillan, 1965); F.H. Leacy, ed., *Historical Statistics of Canada, 2nd edition* (Ottawa: Statistics Canada, 1983); and Statistics Canada, *Historical Labour Force Statistics* (71-201).

has been a dramatic decline in the primary sector as Canadian society continued to shift from an essentially rural/agricultural base to an urban/industrial one. The proportion of the workforce in primary occupations has fallen consistently while the tertiary sector has experienced a substantial growth, so that by the early 1920s more people were employed in tertiary industries than primary ones. By 1989 the proportion of the labour force earning its living from tertiary occupations was 71.1 per cent, while the primary sector—including the traditional staple industries of forestry, fishing, agriculture, as well as mining, and drilling—accounted for only 5.7 per cent of the workforce.[4]

Against this, it might be argued that the employment figures tend to underestimate the economic significance of the resource sector because this sector is not very labour intensive, that is, it does not employ many people relative to the value of its output. If, instead, we examine the proportion of gross domestic product that each sector contributes, then the significance of primary industries in the Canadian economy increases. In 1989 the primary sector accounted for 8.8 per cent of Canada's GDP, but was still far outweighed by the tertiary sector which made up 64.3 per cent of the total.[5]

This historical pattern in both employment and GDP is not distinctively Canadian but has characterised the economic developement of virtually all advanced capitalist nations. If we compare Canada today with other mature economies, then broad structural similarities are evident in the balance between economic sectors. As can be seen from the pie charts in Figure 4.2, there is a basic pattern, which runs across these countries, in the division of employment between sectors and Canada does not stand out as being radically different from the rest. Canada does have a smaller proportion of employment in the secondary sector than other top capitalist economies (G-7), but it also has a larger proportion in the tertiary sector. The proportion employed directly in the primary sector was roughly the same as the G-7 average. What needs to be explained, then, is not Canada's deviance or distortion (although all countries have some unique aspects in their economic development), but the common historical pattern across different countries, involving a decline of the primary sector and the growth of tertiary industry.

In the primary sector, the principal component in the decline has been a shift away from agriculture that can be explained as a function of rising per capita incomes and changing technology. Demand for food is *income inelastic*, i.e., it does not increase very much even when personal incomes rise substantially. If someone's income doubles, he or she is not likely to eat twice as much, but is more likely to spend the extra money by increasing his or her consumption of manufactured goods or services, for which demand is more *income elastic*. This stimulates the expansion of these latter sectors at the expense of agriculture. At the same time, the growing mechanization of farming has meant that more output can be produced by fewer people, and this productivity

FIGURE 4.2

Employment by Sector — Various Countries, 1987

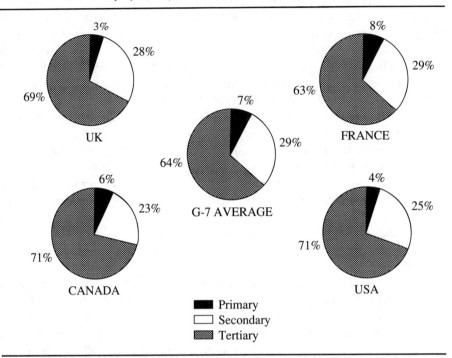

Source: UN International Labour Organization, *Yearbook of Labour Statistics, 1988.*

increase, along with inelastic demand, has resulted in a proportional reduction in the agricultural labour force.

In the tertiary sector, growth has been stimulated by a variety of social, economic and political developments that have taken place in the 20th century, as suggested by Simon Kuznets.[6] Higher per capita incomes have provided more leisure time and a greater demand for services associated with recreational pursuits; concentration of production in particular locations, combined with the dispersion of markets, has led to the development of distribution and retailing networks; growing urbanization has increased demands for services such as police, sanitation and public health; wider availability of consumer durables, such as automobiles, has stimulated the growth of labour-intensive occupations involved with servicing and repair; and government regulatory functions have expanded as society has become more complex.[7]

If these trends toward services are a sign of de-industrialization, then we would have to conclude that Canada is not alone in making a transition to "post-industrial society." This questions the notion that "de-industrialization" in

Canada is a product of our specific economic relationship with the United States. Instead, it suggests that changes in the sectoral structure of the Canadian economy are in line with common developments taking place in most industrial countries, including the United States itself.

If we look specifically at manufacturing industry, the proportion of people employed here has indeed declined over the last 25 years or so. In 1961 manufacturing employed 24 per cent of the labour force, but by 1989 this figure had fallen to 17 per cent. [8] However, before we can conclude that the economy is de-industrializing we also need to look at the level of output in manufacturing, not just the level of employment. What proportion of gross domestic product (GDP) does manufacturing occupy, and how has this changed? From 1961 to 1989 the percentage of GDP taken up by manufacturing industry has remained virtually unchanged: it was 19.6 per cent in 1961 and 19.2 per cent in 1989.[9] Contrary to the data on employment, this suggests that manufacturing has held its ground and is not in decline. How do we explain this apparent contradiction?

The answer is that labour productivity has increased more quickly in manufacturing than in the economy as a whole.[10] Manufacturing industries are squeezing more output from proportionately fewer workers, through increased automation of the workplace and the adoption of new production technologies. For instance, between 1980 and 1988 General Motors in Oshawa tripled its capacity from 250,000 vehicles to 750,000 with no increase in the labour force, because 95 per cent of the welding on car and truck bodies is now done by robots.[11] As the manufacturing industry has become increasingly automated, so have more workers been forced to seek jobs in other sectors of the economy, principally in services.

These changes reflect a continual process of restructuring, both between economic sectors and within them, as some industries rise while others decline. We can get some idea of what has been happening in Canada by looking at the varying rates of employment growth in different industries, as set out in Table 4.1. Between 1960 and 1989, the fastest rates of manufacturing growth have been experienced in motor vehicles, motor vehicle parts, telecommunications equipment and machinery, with the automotive parts industry showing an impressive growth in employment of 295 per cent, compared with an increase of 70 per cent for manufacturing as a whole. On the other side of the coin, the slowest (or negative) growth has been in textiles and clothing, leather goods, shipbuilding, railway stock and agricultural implements. In the tertiary sector, employment growth has been by far the strongest. Air transport and airports, trucking, broadcasting and trade, all grew by over 250 per cent; while finance, insurance and real estate grew by over 300 per cent. These were topped by commercial, business and personal services which expanded by 1111 per cent. This included an 867 per cent increase in hotels and restaurants, and a massive 1281 per cent increase in business services (such as employment agencies, computing, security and investigation, engineering and scientific services, accounting,

Table 4.1

Growth in Employment in Canada by Selected Industries
1960-89 (thousands)

	Dec. 1960	Dec. 1989	% change
Forestry	64.3	52.7	–18
Mining and Drilling	99.6	143.7	+44
Manufacturing	1119.8	1856.3	+66
Leather Industries	28.1	16.1	–43
Textiles	57.1	60.9	+ 7
Clothing	92.3	101.7	+10
Wood Products[b]	61.5	110.5	+80
Pulp and Paper Products	91.4	125.7	+38
Primary Iron and Steel[c]	32.8	53.5	+63
Machinery[d]	31.8	93.4	+194
Agricultural Implements	10.5	9.4	–11
Electrical Apparatus and Appliances	77.4	126.6	+64
Telecommunications Equipment	17.4	56.0	+222
Transportation Equipment	115.9	213.2	+84
Aircraft and Parts	29.4	45.7	+55
Motor Vehicles[e]	29.6	73.3	+148
Motor Vehicle Parts	17.8	70.3	+295
Railroad Stock	19.7	7.7	–61
Shipbuilding and Repairs	17.0	10.7	–37
Chemical Products	53.3	103.6	+94
Construction	226.6	467.9	+107
Transportation & Communications	335.3	729.7	+118
Air Transport and Airports	16.8	64.8	+286
Railways	137.1	68.3	–50
Trucking	28.9	106.2	+268
Broadcasting	13.6	48.1	+254
Public Utilities	58.7	131.8	+125
Trade	496.3	1892.7	+281
Wholesale Trade	161.9	553.0	+242
Retail Trade	334.4	1339.7	+301
Finance, Insurance and Real Estate	156.9	646.1	+312
Commercial, Business & Personal Services[f]	141.5	1713.9	+1111
Hotels and Restaurants	67.4	651.7	+867
Business Services	40.3	556.6	+1281
Industrial Aggregate	2699.0	7637.7	+183

(a)Includes knitting mills   (b)Excludes pulp and paper products and furniture
(c)Includes foundries and pipe and tube mills   (d)Excludes electrical and farm machinery
(e)Includes trucks   (f)Excludes public administration, health services and education

Sources: Dominion Bureau of Statistics, Employment and Payrolls (Dec. 1960), 72-002 and Statistics Canada, Employment, Earnings and Hours (Dec. 1989), 72-002.

advertizing, management consultancy and legal services). From 1960 to 1989 employment in hotels and restaurants jumped from 67,400 to 651,700, while business services went from 40,300 to 556,600.[12]

Although some of the occupations in the growing tertiary sector are relatively well-paid (lawyers and accountants, for example), many others, particularly in hotels, restaurants and retailing, are very poorly paid. In retailing, for instance, average earnings at the end of 1989 were $302 per week, compared with $582 in manufacturing. In the service industry, salaries as a whole were nearly $120 per week lower than manufacturing salaries.[13] Service industries also contain a higher proportion of part-time jobs, which may be attractive for some people, but which generally mean a less secure livelihood. As the structure of employment continues to shift away from manufacturing towards services there is a general shift towards lower-income occupations. This is a worrying trend, firstly because it implies a relative decline in living standards, and secondly because high levels of industrial production are dependent on high levels of consumption. If high mass consumption is becoming harder to maintain, due to the changing occupation structure and a trend towards lower-paying jobs, then high levels of industrial production may be harder to sustain. For every consumer product manufactured by robots there has to be a human employee with a big enough wage packet to afford it. If not, a crisis of overproduction may result.

Besides these problems associated with the growth of the service economy, we must also recognise that many service occupations are not self-sustaining but are directly dependent on goods-producing industries. For example, employment in wholesaling or retailing could not function without goods to be sold; the transportation and trucking industries would not exist without goods to be moved; and many business services such as advertizing, engineering and accountancy rely extensively on manufacturing businesses for their customers. This is not to belittle the contribution that service industries make to the economy, but at the same time we cannot assume that a modern capitalist economy can exist without a viable goods-producing sector. The two sectors are interdependent.

With regard to exports, Canada does have a massive international trade deficit in end-products, amounting to $32.5 billion in 1989.[14] Yet if we examine the historical trends in relation to other sectors, end-products have taken up an increasing share of Canada's exports while the proportion of primary products has declined. Figure 4.3 shows that end-products constituted only 8 per cent of Canada's total exports in 1960, but increased to 44 per cent of the total by 1989. If anything, this would indicate that Canada is becoming more industrialized, not less so. Much of this growth is due to the exportation of automobiles and auto parts which increased dramatically as a result of the Canada-U.S. Auto Pact of 1965. In 1989, auto exports constituted 60 per cent of total end-products, and 96.4 per cent of auto exports went to the United States.[15] Canada thus has an extremely high reliance on one industry and one foreign market for its exports of manufactured end-products.

FIGURE 4.3

Canada's Domestic Exports by Category ^a

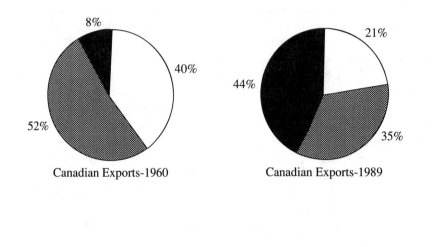

Canadian Exports-1960   Canadian Exports-1989

☐ Primary
▦ Fabricated
■ End Products

^a Excluding special transactions.

Sources: Dominion Bureau of Statistics, *Exports*, 1961-62 (65-202) and Statistics Canada, *Summary of Canadian International Trade*, Dec. 1989 (65-001).

The changes that have taken place in the sectoral balance of the Canadian economy indicate some possible problems for the future. However, these changes and problems are common to most Western industrial nations, and the argument that Canada is undergoing a process of de-industrialization in relation to other countries is weak. In sum, there is too much evidence that Canada fits in with the general pattern of other capitalist countries, and not enough evidence that Canada is a retarded economic hinterland.[16] However, generalizations that are true for Canada as a whole are not necessarily true for every single region of the country. Regional economic differences constitute one of the most distinctive characteristics of Canada's industrial structure and it is to this issue that our analysis now turns.

REGIONAL INDUSTRIAL STRUCTURES

Canada is the second largest country in the world by area (after the USSR), and like any large country it is characterized by significant regional differences within the overall national economy. Territorial divisions in the pattern of economic activity are of concern because they can give rise to marked inequalities between one region of the country and another. This can lead to political discord, regional rivalries and threats to national unity. It is not just that some regions are more prosperous than others, but also that different parts of the country have different types of industries and different types of economic interests. Because these interests are not always compatible, national policy-makers can face severe problems in trying to reconcile the competing needs of different regions when industrial policy is being formulated.

Problems of regional diversity have been a prominent feature of Canadian political economy since Confederation, and the federal structure of Canadian government is itself a response to such diversity. Federalism has an impact in diminishing regional conflicts by allowing the provinces some measure of freedom to decide their own policies, and yet it still preserves an overall economic and political union. At the same time, federalism has a contradictory impact in heightening regional conflicts. Provincial governments are a permanent institutional expression of regional demands and they act as mechanisms by which regional dissent is channelled and organized, thereby making it more potent. Aside from questions of national unity and conflict, federalism also has an important role in shaping business-government relations in Canada (see Chapter Six). However, first it is necessary to outline briefly the main regional divisions in the structure of economic activity across Canada.

The Atlantic Provinces

For much of the first half of the 19th century, the Maritime provinces of Nova Scotia and New Brunswick enjoyed a period of considerable prosperity based on the success of shipbuilding and the timber trade with Britain. Today the Atlantic provinces constitute an economic backwater, almost totally eclipsed by the industrial development of central Canada. By 1989 Ontario and Quebec accounted for over 62 per cent of Canada's GDP and nearly 80 per cent of Canada's manufacturing industry. In comparison, the four Atlantic provinces together accounted for only 6 per cent of the national GDP and less than 4 per cent of manufacturing.[17] This region had, in 1989, a per capita income that was $5,000 lower than the national average and $7,450 lower than in Ontario. The disparity between Newfoundland (the poorest province) and Ontario (the richest) was $8,894 [18] The Atlantic provinces have also experienced unemployment rates consistently above the national average, with Newfoundland topping the list. For the period from 1980 to 1989, Canada had an average unemployment rate of 9.3 per cent, whereas in Newfoundland the rate was 17.3 per cent.[19]

This region of Canada is characterized by the significance of resource-based staple industries, especially forestry, mining and fishing, and closely associated industries such as fish processing and pulp and paper. Newfoundland depends largely on fishing, pulp and paper and iron ore mining in Labrador, although the prospect of offshore oil and gas production could radically transform the economy in the 1990s. New Brunswick is heavily reliant on forest products and mining, while the economy of Prince Edward Island revolves around agriculture, food processing and tourism. Nova Scotia is the most diversified of the four, and although fishing, mining and forest products are still very important, the province also contains a wider range of manufacturing industries including transportation equipment, textiles, auto parts, tires, machinery, metal fabricating and an integrated (and perennially unprofitable) steel mill on Cape Breton. In spite of all of this, Nova Scotia has nowhere near the range of manufacturing or the level of industrial activity found in Ontario or Quebec.

Besides a relatively low per capita income, the Atlantic region's weak industrial structure creates a number of other problems. As natural resources become depleted and more expensive to extract, so the economic base gradually erodes. Furthermore, if provincial economies are based on a narrow range of industries, then they are especially vulnerable to changing world conditions in those industries. For instance, iron ore mining in Labrador is vulnerable to changes in demand from the steel industry, and both fishing and forestry face threats of protectionism in key export markets. If a relatively diversified economy like Ontario is hit by protectionism against one of its industries, it is a matter for concern; if a relatively undiversified economy like New Brunswick is hit by protectionism against one of its industries, it could be disastrous.

Awareness of the vulnerability of the Atlantic provinces has provoked efforts by both federal and provincial governments to encourage industrial diversification through a variety of incentives and initiatives designed to stimulate economic growth, prop up declining industries and attract new capital to the region. These have included grants, loans and tax credits, as well as a number of large-scale, high profile projects, many of which turned out to be expensive failures. In the 1970s the New Brunswick government entered into a partnership with American entrepreneur Malcolm Bricklin to produce sports cars, but costs escalated and after the provincial government had spent $19 million, the project collapsed.[20] In Newfoundland, the province had invested nearly $22 million in a joint venture with Calgary entrepreneur, Philip Sprung, to produce cucumbers in hydroponic greenhouses, but the project turned into a fiasco and collapsed into receivership. In 1989 the Newfoundland government was forced to sell it to a private company for the token price of one dollar. In Nova Scotia, the privately-owned steel mill on Cape Breton Island was on the point of bankruptcy when, in 1967, the provincial government bought it and created the Sydney Steel Corporation (Sysco) as a provincial crown corporation. While it is an antiquated and uneconomic mill, it is important for the Cape Breton economy and the province has been absorbing its debts and losses ever since.

Other instances of state support include grants paid by federal, provincial and local governments to Michelin Tire as an inducement to set up tire production in Nova Scotia in 1969. This French tire manufacturer was also encouraged by the provincial government's willingness to pass legislation making it more difficult to unionize the tire plants. Unfortunately, export production from the plants was subjected to countervailing duties by the United States, which ruled that the grants paid to Michelin were unfair trade subsidies. More recently in New Brunswick, federal government procurement policy has played a role in regional development with a contract for 12 new patrol frigates. The contract, with a value of $6.3 billion, was awarded to Saint John Shipbuilding (owned by the Irving family), and production started in 1989. In addition there has been a refocussing of the federal government's industrial assistance programmes to the region through the creation of the Atlantic Canada Opportunities Agency in 1988. However, despite the various efforts of different governments, Atlantic Canada remains a region of relative industrial underdevelopment.

Quebec

Compared with the Atlantic provinces, Quebec is a large, thriving economy with a diversified industrial base, an extensive manufacturing industry and a high standard of living. However, when compared to Ontario the economic picture is not so favourable, and Quebec continually has had to live in the shadow of Ontario's more vigorous industrial and commercial development. In 1989 Quebec's GDP per capita was less than 83 per cent of the level in Ontario and Quebeckers' personal incomes were lower on average by $3,500 per year.[21] Unemployment rates have been consistently higher in Quebec, averaging 11.2 per cent from 1980 to 1989, as opposed to 7.4 per cent in Ontario for the same time period. By the first quarter of 1990 Quebec's unemployment rate was at 10.0 per cent compared to Ontario's rate of 5.4 per cent.[22]

Part of the reason for this relatively poor performance lies in the structure of Quebec's manufacturing, which contains a high proportion of so-called "sunset" industries that are generally labour intensive and are characterized by low technology and slow growth. These include textiles, knitted goods, clothing and leather, which together accounted for over 20 per cent of Quebec's manufacturing employment in 1986.[23] These industries in particular are now facing intense international competition, especially from newly industrializing countries (NICs) where labour costs are lower, and Quebec has relied heavily on the federal government to provide tariff barriers and other forms of import protection. Quebec also derives a considerable proportion of its livelihood from resource industries, such as forest products and mining, which face some of the same problems that Atlantic Canada faces with respect to volatile world demand and resource depletion.

However, there is another, more positive side to Quebec's industrial structure. This revolves around new, high technology industries such as telecommunications equipment, electronics, transportation equipment, aircrafts and avionics. These "sunrise" industries now constitute an important part of Quebec's commodity exports, offering the prospect of continued industrial restructuring away from traditional and less competitive sectors. Another bright spot is Quebec's abundance of cheap hydro-electric power, which serves Quebec industries in general, and is of particular benefit to the aluminum industry which uses vast quantities of electricity. Consequently, Quebec has a prosperous aluminum smelting industry even though the province has no bauxite (the raw material for aluminum).

While Quebec industry now appears to be undergoing a significant restructuring process, the business world has also been transformed by the enormous changes that have taken place in Quebec society since 1960. The Quiet Revolution of the 1960s, under Jean Lesage's Liberals, helped to bring about a gradual reorientation of francophone Quebec, altering it from an essentially anti-business culture in which the Catholic Church was the dominant institution, towards a more modern, secular and entrepreneurial disposition. Through a revised educational system that emphasized business, science, engineering and technical skills, and increased government activity in promoting industrial development, the path was laid for the rise of a strong francophone business class in the subsequent decades. Intrinsic to this development was a challenge to the anglophone domination of Quebec business, which began under Lesage, but carried to fruition under René Lévesque and the Parti Québecois in the 1970s and early 1980s. In retrospect, the flight of anglophone capital following the election of the PQ in 1976 was probably a positive development, because it opened the door to the new and dynamic class of francophone entrepreneurs. It is partly as a result of these changes that, by the late 1980s, Quebec had achieved one of the strongest rates of economic growth of any province in Canada.

Ontario

Ontario is the industrial heartland of Canada, with over 40 per cent of national GDP in 1989, and 54 per cent of all manufacturing industry.[24] It has the most diversified range of industries of any province, and close to half of all Canada's exports originate in Ontario.[25] For 1989, per capita income was higher in Ontario than in any other province and the unemployment rate was the lowest in the country.[26] Between 1982 and 1989 real economic growth in Ontario averaged 5.6 per cent per year—compared with the rate for all of Canada which was 4.2 per cent in the same period.[27] In comparison with other parts of Canada,

Ontario's position is thus a strong one, and yet there are still certain features of the province's industrial structure that give cause for concern.

Although the provincial economy is reasonably diversified, the automobile industry nevertheless occupies a key position. Over 100,000 people in Ontario are directly employed in the assembly or production of motor vehicles, parts and accessories, and this industry accounts for over 11 per cent of manufacturing employment and 18 per cent of manufacturing output.[28] Automobile production also provides a major market for some of the province's other industries, such as steel, and thus makes an additional, indirect contribution to employment. To a large extent, Ontario's economic fate is closely tied to the performance of the auto industry, and the Canadian auto industry is closely tied into a continental North American system of production and sales. This makes the province vulnerable to downswings in demand or longer-term declines in the industry's competitiveness on a continental basis. With the current state of intense international competition amongst car makers and with the growth of new car plants throughout the world, the auto industry may well be heading for a crisis of surplus capacity and overproduction. Almost certainly this would hit the Ontario economy hard, and although several new car plants have been opened in Ontario, especially by Japanese car makers, the resulting overcapacity may add to the problem and undermine the profitability of the entire industry.

A second potential problem is that Ontario, like much of the rest of Canada, is dependent on the U.S market for its exports. Eighty-six per cent of the province's exports go to the United States[29] and this puts a lot of eggs in one nation's basket. As a result many of Ontario's industries are very sensitive to any political moves in the U.S. that are designed to raise protectionist barriers. If access to the American market becomes more restricted, then large segments of the provincial economy will suffer.

Not only does Ontario export a lot to the United States, it also imports a lot too, making the U.S. a major source of competition for Ontario's manufacturers. The problem here is that, with some notable exceptions, the productivity of Ontario's industries tends to lag behind that of the United States by as much as 25 to 30 per cent. [30] This is normally attributed to the smaller size of Canadian plants and the consequent failure to achieve greater economies of scale and lower unit costs. In addition, spending on research and development is lower than in the United States on a per capita basis, and Ontario is too dependent on imported "trickle-down" technology transmitted by U.S. multinationals to their Canadian branch plants.

Finally, there is the problem of uneven development within Ontario, as the bulk of the province's manufacturing industry is concentrated in the south, particularly in the "Golden Horseshoe" area from Oshawa down through the Niagara Peninsula. This contrasts markedly with northern Ontario where the economy is largely resource-based and relies principally on mining, metals and the forest products industries. Here employment and incomes are less secure as single industry communities are buffeted by fluctuating world demand for their commodities. In this respect the northern region of Ontario more closely resembles the industrial structure of other resource-based provinces rather than the more developed south. Regional imbalances across Canada are also reflected within Ontario.

The Prairie Provinces

Historically, the Prairie provinces of Manitoba, Saskatchewan and Alberta owed their economic development to the production of wheat and to the railway that facilitated both the export of wheat and the influx of new settlers. Today, agriculture continues to play an important role in the prairie economy and accounts for over 9.5 per cent of all employment in the three provinces and over 17.3 per cent of employment in Saskatchewan.[31] In international trade, over 26 per cent of the region's exports are agricultural products which includes livestock as well as grains, and Saskatchewan is again the most dependent, with over 50 per cent of exports being produced on the farm.[32] Besides this traditional emphasis on agriculture, other natural resources also make up an important part of the regional economy, particularly in Alberta and Saskatchewan. These include oil and gas, uranium, potash, metals, minerals and forest products. In 1989 the primary sector comprised 25.2 per cent of the region's GDP, with Alberta deriving nearly a third of its gross provincial product directly from this sector.[33]

Natural resources are the source of the region's strength but they also account for a large measure of the region's economic instability. Reliance on agriculture means suffering through periodic crop failures due to drought or pestilence, and having incomes that are dramatically affected by the weather, not just on the Prairies but throughout the world. It also means battling for export markets against heavily subsidized farmers in the United States and Europe and being dependent on credit from banks in central Canada, not all of which have a great empathy with farming life on the Prairies.

Resource products generally are subject to more violent swings in world prices than are manufactured goods, and dependence on resources tends to produce a "boom and bust" pattern of economic activity as exemplified by the history of the oil industry in the 1970s and 1980s. The massive increases in world oil prices in the 1970s provoked a tremendous growth in exploration and production in Western Canada, especially in Alberta where the value of oil reserves increased several times over. New capital flowed into the province, to be encouraged further by incentives from the Alberta government, and many new people arrived, attracted by conspicuous prosperity and the prospect of well-paying jobs. Along with this bonanza came a runaway boom in land prices and construction, including very rapid real estate development in Calgary and Edmonton. Jobs were plentiful, incomes rose and banks were eager to lend the money to finance new development projects and new personal spending.

However, during this period other changes also took place in the world economy. Partly as a result of higher energy costs, economic growth in developed countries slowed down, thus reducing the demand for oil. In addition, a number of countries began to implement conservation measures and look for alternative energy sources, both of which reduced demand even more. On the other side of the equation, an enormous effort was directed towards discovering new sources of oil supply, not just in Alberta but across the globe. By 1982 the combined forces of supply and demand caused world oil prices to collapse, and suddenly Alberta's oil reserves significantly decreased in value. Revenues declined, development projects were shelved, workers were laid off, bankruptcies were widespread and the construction industry went into a tailspin. In just one year Alberta's unemployment rate doubled, and the boom turned to bust.

This pattern of boom and bust has been a common feature of Canada's economic history, but it has the hardest impact on provinces such as Alberta where the structure of the provincial economy is heavily skewed towards resources. Manitoba has a greater degree of immunity to these swings in fortune because its economy is a little more diversified and it has a larger proportion of manufacturing than the other two provinces. However, even in Manitoba a single renewable resource, namely wheat, is still by far the province's major commodity.

As in Eastern Canada, Prairie governments are acutely aware of the problems posed by structural imbalances in the pattern of economic activity, and efforts have been made to encourage broader industrial development. Manitoba has developed hydro-electricity and transportation equipment and some capacity in electronics, clothing and other manufacturing industries. Saskatchewan is involved, to a modest extent, with steel production, electronics and metal fabricating, while Alberta has focussed on the secondary processing of natural resources, for example in petrochemicals and food processing. The Alberta government has also played a role in providing incentives for the development of large scale Albertan corporations such as Nova Corp. (formerly Alberta Gas Trunk Lines), which is a privately-owned company established with the sponsorship of the provincial government. However, despite the efforts of both provincial and federal governments to bring about economic diversification in the region, any progress towards substantial industrial restructuring has been slow and intermittent.

British Columbia

In the course of this regional survey it has become evident that industrial production in Canada's "peripheral" provinces focusses around natural resources. Outside the central provinces of Ontario and Quebec, manufacturing, with few exceptions, is either weak or closely tied to the extraction of a particular staple product, as with the manufacture of pulp and paper or petrochemicals. Canada's most peripheral Western province is a prime example of this phenomenon, and the provincial economy is dominated by forestry and mining, with agriculture, fishing and tourism being of secondary significance. Productive forests cover 46 per cent of British Columbia's land mass and the forest industry alone accounts for 57 per cent of the province's exports.[34] Manufacturing industry accounts for only 16 per cent of the province's GDP, and 65 per cent of this manufacturing is directly tied to the province's resource base, involving wood and paper products, food processing and primary metals.[35] Indirectly, the prosperity of the resource industries underpins much of the province's tertiary sector activity as well, and thus has a fundamental impact throughout the economy. In 1988, forestry, mining and fishing accounted for roughly three-quarters of British Columbia's exports and in international trade, British Columbia is different from the rest of Canada because over 50 per cent of its exports do not go to the United States.[36] The province has a substantial trade with the Pacific Rim countries, especially Japan, and its export growth is bound up with the prosperity of the Japanese economy, not just the American one.

As with most of Canada's other provinces, rich endowments of natural resources have proved to be a mixed blessing for British Columbia. The prosperity of forestry and mining has brought big export revenues and high wages, yet these industries are capital intensive and they do not generate very high levels of employment. Nor are employment levels very stable due to the cyclical boom-bust character of production. In the short term there are further problems posed by the expensive costs of modernization and the threat of foreign protectionism, while in the long term there are problems of resource depletion and difficult access to supplies.

Capital intensity also means that these industries are dominated by a small number of large corporations like MacMillan Bloedel and Fletcher Challenge (owner of B.C. Forest Products) that can afford the huge investment outlays required. A high degree of corporate concentration both reduces the level of competition and, more importantly, places extensive regional economic power in a few private hands, which necessarily has political implications. The significance of forestry and mining to the provincial economy means that government officials must continually be concerned about the profitability of these industries and must be sensitive to the needs of the major companies. Inevitably this gives the companies a strategic influence over provincial government policy, even before they start lobbying or trying to influence policy-makers in other ways. This situation is not unique to British Columbia but applies to any jurisdiction where government has been forced to rely for its revenue on a few industries dominated by a few giant corporations.

In British Columbia, as in other parts of Canada, concern with business performance and industrial structure has led provincial governments to take an interventionist role in promoting regional economic development. This takes a wide variety of forms, from the provision of a publicly funded transport infra-structure—crucially important in British Columbia's rugged terrain—to an array of financial assistance programmes, including grants, tax credits, low interest (or no interest) loans, cost sharing schemes and equity investments. In 1989 the B.C. government maintained 18 separate programmes designed specifically to provide financial incentives to business in an attempt to promote provincial economic development.[37]

Government strategy has taken two main directions. The first has been to encourage diversification by trying to increase the level of secondary processing of resources and by promoting the development of new manufacturing industries. The second has been to provide assistance to the existing resource industries. The problem here is that the profitability of resource extraction tends to make investment in manufacturing seem less attractive and this diverts capital away. Attempts at industrial diversification are thus counteracted by the very strength of the resource sector, and the structural imbalances in the economy become self-reinforcing.

The Yukon and the Northwest Territories

Canada's two northern territories have a combined population of only 82,000 and a GDP of less than 0.5 per cent of the Canadian total.[38] Most of the population is concentrated in a few urban centres, such as Whitehorse and Yellowknife, while the rest is scattered in tiny and very remote communities.

Primary sector industry is concerned mostly with mining and exploration—focussing on oil and gas, gold, silver, lead and zinc—and large quantities of oil are known to exist under the Beaufort Sea and Mackenzie Valley regions. Manufacturing industry is extremely underdeveloped and is mainly limited to a small amount of resource processing, plus some "cottage" industries which produce hand-made artifacts. In general, the industrial structure of the territories is weak, poorly integrated and undiversified.[39] There is a great vulnerability to fluctuations in world commodity prices, and the closing of a single mine can have a dramatic impact. However, alongside this vulnerability is a centuries-old subsistence economy that is relatively immune from global economic trends.

Predominantly, the Yukon and the Northwest Territories are dependent on the service sector, especially government. In the Yukon, for example, over 82 per cent of the workforce is employed in services.[40] In this sector, tourism provides an important supplementary source of revenue, but it is government that constitutes the mainstay of these economies. Government expenditures on goods and services account for 49 per cent of GDP in the Northwest Territories and 60 per cent of GDP in the Yukon.[41] In this respect the territories differ from the northern parts of most provinces because "federal-territorial relations and sizeable bureaucracies" reduce the overall dependency on resources.[42]

FOREIGN OWNERSHIP

One of the most striking features of the Canadian economy is that large sections of it are controlled by non-Canadians. In 1987, foreign interests controlled $385.8 billion in corporate assets in Canada. For non-financial corporations, 24.6 per cent of all assets were foreign-controlled, while for manufacturing industries, the figure was as high as 45.6 per cent.[43] The United States took the lion's share of this, accounting for 67.5 per cent of foreign-controlled assets in non-financial industries.[44] At the end of 1989, 34 of Canada's 100 largest corporations were foreign-owned and the majority of these were subsidiaries of United States multinational companies. The 20 largest foreign-owned corporations in Canada are shown in Table 4.2, and American firms account for nearly two-thirds of these.

The History of Foreign Investment in Canada

Historically, Canada has always relied heavily on foreign capital for economic development. In the 19th century shortages of indigenous capital meant that finances for industrial growth had to come from abroad. Governments at all levels actively courted foreign investment, and much of the money used to build roads, railways, canals and other elements of Canada's early commercial infrastructure was obtained from British investors. Most of this British capital was in the form of portfolio investment, such as bonds that earn interest without conferring ownership of assets, rather than direct investment which involves stock ownership. Consequently, at the time of Confederation, Canada was heavily in debt but without high levels of foreign ownership.

Table 4.2

Twenty Largest Foreign-Owned Companies in Canada

Company	Revenues (C$billion)	Foreign Ownership (%)	Parent	Country
1. General Motors of Canada	19.7	100	General Motors Corporation	U.S.
2. Ford Motor Company of Canada	15.3	97	Ford Motor Company	U.S.
3. Alcan Aluminum	10.5	56	Widely held	
4. Imperial Oil	10.0	70	Exxon Corporation	U.S.
5. Chrysler Canada	8.2	100	Chrysler Corporation	U.S.
6. Shell Canada	4.9	78	Shell Petroleum	Holland
7. Inco	4.7	54	Widely held	
8. Sears Canada	4.6	61[a]	Sears Roebuck & Company	U.S.
9. Canada Safeway	4.2	100	Safeway Inc.	U.S.
10. IBM Canada	4.2	100	IBM Corporation	U.S.
11. Amoco Canada	3.4	100	Amoco Corporation	U.S.
12. Ensite	2.9	94[b]	Ford Motor Company	U.S.
13. Mitsui (Canada)	2.8	100	Mitsui & Company	Japan
14. United Westburne	2.7	79	Dumez	France
15. Total Petroleum	2.6	51	Total	France
16. Great Atlantic & Pacific of Canada	2.3	100	Great Atlantic & Pacific Tea Company	U.S.
17. F.W. Woolworth	2.3	100	Woolworth World Trade Corporation	U.S.
18. Honda Canada	2.2	100	Honda Motor Company	Japan
19. Dow Chemical of Canada	2.0	100	Dow Chemical Company	U.S.
20. Rio Algom	1.7	59	R.T.Z. Corporation	U.K.
Total Revenues	110.4			

[a] percentage held by Sears Roebuck [b] percentage held by Ford

---

Source: Financial Post 500, Summer 1990.

The dependence on British portfolio investment meant that Canadian politicians continually had to be sensitive to the wishes of British financial institutions and had to tailor their policies accordingly. These linkages have been investigated at some length by economic historian R.T. Naylor, who has traced the crucial role of British banking houses, such as the Barings and the Glyns, in Canada's economic development. Naylor goes so far as to conclude that Confederation itself was, to a substantial degree, an exercise in public finance designed to instill confidence in nervous British financiers.[45]

Later, in the 20th century, this pattern of foreign investment changed radically. As Britain's economic and imperial power declined, British investment was increasingly overshadowed by investment from the United States. However, not only did the geographic source change, but the type of investment changed as well. American capital contained a much higher proportion of direct investment, which meant that U.S. individual and corporate investors had an ownership stake in Canada through stock purchases or the establishment of branch plants. As early as 1930 the United States accounted for 61.2 per cent of all foreign investment in Canada, while Britain's share dropped to 36.3 per cent. Direct investment made up only 14 per cent of Britain's total, whereas the figure for the United States was 43 per cent.

While the shifting balance of economic and political power between Britain and the United States helped to shape this development, one specific Canadian policy initiative had a major impact in promoting the growth of direct foreign investment. This was the system of National Policy tariffs set up in 1879 and extended at various times in the following decades. By imposing import duties of over 30 per cent on a variety of imported goods, John A. MacDonald's government sought to protect Canadian manufacturing industries from foreign competition. The tariffs were part of a broad nationalist strategy aimed at fostering domestic economic development, political integration and independence. Yet one of the major consequences of this policy was the growth of direct foreign investment, particularly from the United States. American companies who wanted to sell in Canada found themselves penalized by the high tariffs, but many soon realized that there was an simple solution. Instead of shipping goods to Canada from the United States, and thus paying the tariff, American companies could jump the tariff walls by establishing branch plants north of the border that would supply the Canadian market. By the early 1900s many prominent American corporations had been persuaded to set up plants in Canada, including Singer Sewing Machine, Edison Electric, American Tobacco, Gillette, Swift's, Parke Davis and Coca-Cola.[46] Business historian, Michael Bliss, reports that by 1913 as many as 450 American branch plants had been established in Canada, involving an investment of $135 million.[47]

The tariff was not the only government measure that encouraged this movement of capital. The Patent Act of 1872 stipulated that foreign inventors would only receive patent protection in Canada for two years unless they set up production in Canada and stopped importing. Upon failure to do so, their inventions legally could be produced by anyone once the two years were up. Naturally, this spurred many foreign patent holders to open branch plants in Canada. At the municipal level, politicians tried to attract both foreign and domestic investment to their communities by offering businesses a variety of incentives and "bonuses," and a system of intense competition often existed amongst municipalities.

The invasion of U.S. branch plants, which was stimulated by these policies, was not seen as a threat to national sovereignty, but as a positive contribution to national economic development. As Michael Bliss recounts:

> No one thought foreign ownership of factories in Canada was in any way harmful. On the contrary, the 'Canadianization' of American business in this migration was exactly the result economic nationalists wanted. The National Policy helped move jobs, technology, capital and capitalists into Canada.[48]

Ironically, it was this continued migration and the persistence of foreign ownership that would become the prime target for economic nationalists in the 1960s and 1970s.

Direct investment from the United States increased substantially in the 1920s and expanded further in the 1950s and 1960s. In the period after the Second World War, a large portion of U.S. direct investment involved the exploitation of Canada's natural resources, particularly oil, natural gas and mining. As U.S. resources became more and more depleted, American corporations had to look further afield, and Canada was a conveniently located source of supply. Foreign investment in manufacturing also expanded rapidly in this period as giant U.S. multinationals established themselves throughout the world. By 1971, 37 per cent of corporate non-financial assets in Canada were foreign-owned, and for manufacturing industries the figure was just under 60 per cent.[49]

Public opposition to foreign investment increased in the 1960s and Gallup polls showed that the proportion of Canadians who thought there was enough U.S. investment had risen from 46 per cent in 1964 to 67 per cent in 1972.[50] In addition, three major reports on foreign investment were written during this period and all of them were critical of U.S. ownership. The most comprehensive and influential of these studies was the Gray Report of 1972, published under the authority of the Canadian federal government.[51] In over 500 pages, the Gray Report identified a litany of problems associated with direct foreign investment and recommended that a government review agency be established to screen investment proposals from abroad.

Faced with a new climate of economic nationalism, and prodded by the NDP, the minority Liberal government accepted the main recommendation of the Gray Report and in 1973 set up the Foreign Investment Review Agency (FIRA). FIRA's initial mandate was to review foreign acquisitions of Canadian businesses, and this was soon extended to cover the establishment of new businesses in Canada. The agency was required to determine whether such foreign investments were likely to be of "significant benefit" to Canada in areas such as job creation, local procurement, exports, technological development, etc. If there were few significant benefits, then FIRA could recommend to Cabinet that the proposed investment be disallowed.

FIRA represented the first attempt at across-the-board regulation of direct foreign investment, although previous restrictions had been applied in specific strategic areas such as financial institutions, broadcasting, telecommunications and uranium mining. However, in the course of its operation, FIRA became the target of simultaneous criticisms from different political directions, and was charged both with being too restrictive and with not being restrictive enough. Between 1973 and its demise in 1985 only about seven per cent of the proposals reviewed by FIRA were rejected. Because of its low "hit-rate" nationalist critics accused FIRA of being a predominantly symbolic instrument, paying lip-service to economic nationalism while actually doing very little to block U.S. take-overs or to justify the vehement hostility of the Reagan administration.[52] Continentalist critics, including the MacDonald Commission, argued that FIRA's restrictive impact went beyond a mere seven per cent, because an unknown number of foreign corporations were discouraged from making an application by the simple fact of FIRA's existence.[53] Yet it could also be argued that FIRA had an unknown positive effect. We do not know how many foreign corporations improved the "significant benefits" in their investment proposals prior to submitting them for FIRA's scrutiny.

Whatever the real impact of FIRA, the proportion of foreign ownership in the Canadian economy did drop in the 1970s and early 1980s. Foreign-owned assets in Canada comprised 37 per cent of the total in 1971, but fell to 23.4 per cent by 1985. Other policies besides FIRA had an impact on this development. One of the goals of the National Energy Program, which was introduced in 1980, was to increase the Canadian ownership of the oil and gas industry to 50 per cent by the end of the 1980s. This would be achieved through a combination of government incentives, regulations and public ownership. Although the NEP proved to be short-lived, it nevertheless encouraged a substantial "buy-back" of foreign-owned assets in the energy sector. By July 1981 this repatriation was taking place at such a rate that the Federal government became concerned about the amount of money being paid out to foreign interests. Ten Canadian companies had paid $6.6 billion buying subsidiaries of foreign oil firms and this was causing problems for the country's current account and the Canadian dollar.[54] In response, the Department of Finance placed pressure on the Canadian banks to slow down their lending to Canadian companies for acquisitions in order to restrict the outward flow of capital.[55]

Both FIRA and the NEP caused considerable displeasure in Washington, and by the mid-1980s both had disappeared. The NEP collapsed along with the drop in world oil prices, and FIRA was scrapped in 1985 in accordance with the new Conservative government's more open attitude towards foreign investment. In its place a new agency, Investment Canada, was created. The new agency still retained a role in screening direct foreign investment, but the main difference was that foreign investors now only had to show "net benefit" to Canada rather than "significant benefit," and investments below a certain value would not be screened at all. Canadian firms with assets under $5 million could be directly acquired without review, and for indirect acquisitions (when a foreign firm with a Canadian subsidiary is taken over by another foreign firm) the threshold was set at $50 million. Investment Canada's principal mandate has been to encourage investment in Canada, not to restrict it. If we look at the record, it is clear that Investment Canada could hardly be less restrictive in screening foreign takeovers. From Table 4.3, it can be seen that between 1985 and 1989 Investment Canada reviewed 651 foreign acquisitions of Canadian companies, valued at $55 billion. Approval was granted in every single case.

A more substantial revision of the rules on foreign investment is included in the Canada-United States Free Trade Agreement (FTA), which also deals with investment and other matters besides trade. Under the terms of the agreement the threshold for review of direct acquisitions by U.S. companies has been raised to $150 million and the threshold for indirect acquisitions has been abolished altogether. The result may well be a resurgence of U.S. ownership in Canada. In addition it will probably bias the distribution of direct foreign investment

Table 4.3

	Investment Canada - Reviews of Foreign Acquisitions of Canadian Companies 1985-1989.			
	Acquisitions Reviewed	Value ($ billion)	Approved	Not Approved
1985-1986	105	8.6	105	0
1986-1987	160	11.1	160	0
1987-1988	178	18.6	178	0
1988-1989	208	16.7	208	0
Total	651	55.0	651	0

Source: Investment Canada , Annual Reports.

further in favour of the United States because other countries will still be subject to pre-existing thresholds.[56]

The new investment proposals under the FTA are the latest development in a continuing controversy over the role of foreign ownership in Canada. They are part of a wider battle between the "nationalists" who oppose U.S. domination of the Canadian economy and the "continentalists" who welcome closer ties with the United States. We will now examine this debate.

The Foreign Ownership Debate

The debate on foreign ownership in Canada has centred both on the costs and benefits and on the extent of government regulation of direct foreign investment. Positions for and against regulation depend on whether or not high levels of direct foreign investment are seen as beneficial in themselves and on the beliefs about the appropriate role of the state in capitalist economies.

Criticism of foreign ownership has enjoyed considerable popularity in Canada over the last couple of decades and has become incorporated into a mainstream interpretation of Canadian political economy known as "left-nationalism."[57] Left-nationalists argue that domination by U.S. multinationals has turned Canada into a dependent economic satellite of the United States and has had a debilitating effect on the Canadian economy. In the resource sector U.S. branch plants have been set up to exploit Canadian raw materials for the benefit of the American manufacturing industry. Our natural resources are exported in an unprocessed or semi-processed form, largely to the United States, meaning that it is in the United States, not Canada, that the better jobs are created turning these raw materials into the higher-value end products we then buy back.

In the manufacturing sector branch plants have been established specifically to supply the relatively small Canadian market and are not intended to compete on the world stage as independent actors. The head office generally keeps a tight control over any major decisions, and subsidiaries are prevented from exporting goods because exports would compete with production by the parent company or by the parent's subsidiaries in other countries. Not only is the export capacity of Canadian plants restricted, their efficiency also suffers because they are less able to take advantage of economies of scale. The branch plants are "miniature replicas" of their parents, producing a full range of similar products but on a smaller scale and with higher unit costs.

Canada also loses out because these firms are "truncated," i.e., they do not perform the full range of functions of an autonomous corporation. For instance, they rarely carry out much research and development because multinationals generally centralize this function at the head office. Consequently, the Canadian subsidiaries have to rely on imported technology and this removes a potential stimulus to the development of the Canadian scientific and technical community.

Branch plants also have a tendency to import machinery and components from the parent country rather than buy them locally, and they often depend on the head office to perform the bulk of supporting services, which further reduces the economic benefit to Canada.

Other claims are also made against foreign multinationals. They are accused of draining capital out of Canada by repatriating the profits of their subsidiaries and of artificially manipulating the prices of goods shipped between branches in different countries. The latter problem, concerning transfer-pricing, can occur when companies want to reduce the profits made in a particular country in order to reduce the amount of tax they have to pay there. In addition, the dominance of foreign multinationals can discourage independent Canadian entrepreneurship, "as local firms are bought out and potential local entrepreneurs become the salaried employees of the multinational corporation."[58] The indigenous class of Canadian industrialists is thought to be too weak to challenge this predatory domination by the multinationals.

Finally there is the problem that foreign-owned subsidiaries may be more responsive to foreign laws than to Canadian ones. Foreign laws may force a subsidiary in Canada to act in a certain way even though it is outside the territorial jurisdiction of the other country. For example, U.S. parent corporations can force their Canadian branch plants to comply with laws formulated in Washington, even if it is against the wishes of the Canadian government. This is known by the rather cumbersome title of *extra-territoriality*, and constitutes an infringement of Canadian national sovereignty. The most notorious example concerns a piece of U.S. legislation called the Trading with the Enemy Act which allows the U.S. president to prohibit American firms from trading with certain countries. This law covers the foreign subsidiaries of American corporations and has normally been used to restrict exports to selected communist nations, even though Canada and other countries have no such restriction.

In total, left-nationalists present a picture of Canada as a dependency of the United States with a distorted and semi-developed economy resulting from foreign ownership, and with little national autonomy in the face of U.S. imperialism.

Some of the claims made by left-nationalists are not very easy to assess because they rely on hypothetical assumptions about what the Canadian economy would have been like if foreign branch plants had not played such an extensive role. For instance, if U.S. branch plants had largely been absent, would Canadian entrepreneurs have filled the gap, or would we just have been left with a lower level of economic development? The MacDonald Commission has argued that foreign direct investment has allowed "the Canadian economy to achieve levels of industrial development not otherwise possible."[59] However, surveys of U.S. multinationals suggest that one of the main reasons why these American firms set up plants in other countries is to pre-empt local competition.[60] Such a finding indicates that foreign multinationals may have had a negative impact on Canadian entrepreneurship and economic development. On the other hand, a study by Richard Caves and Grant Reuber indicates that direct foreign investment in Canada has stimulated additional investments by domestic firms. They examined the period 1951-1962 and found evidence that every dollar of direct foreign investment stimulated additional domestic investment of as much as three dollars.[61] The central problem in the balance of these arguments is that we do not know how much additional investment might have been created had Canadian companies developed on their own.

One of the left-nationalists' principal contentions, namely that Canada is an underdeveloped and structurally distorted resource hinterland, contradicts evidence presented earlier in this chapter that the sectoral structure of the Canadian economy is not radically different from other industrial capitalist nations. Furthermore, in comparison with other developed countries Canada's economic performance has been strong. Canada is not a de-industrial colony but a "principal economy" in its own right.[62] The notion that Canadian economic development has been "distorted" raises the question of what undistorted development would look like, and as William Carroll points out, "The tacit comparison is always with an idealized condition of autonomous development."[63] Canada's deviations from the idealized norm are no greater than those of other countries such as France or Italy, both of which have large primary sectors.[64]

Looking more specifically at some of the other arguments against foreign ownership, even avid continentalists recognize that foreign multinationals do most of their research and development in their home country,[65] and that foreign-owned firms "spend less on indigenous R & D than their Canadian-owned counterparts in the same industry."[66] This admission is normally qualified by arguments that Canada benefits from the transmission of foreign technology by multinationals and that further government intervention to promote Canadian R & D is unnecessary. In the words of the MacDonald Commission:

> Foreign investment is a major source of valuable technology, managerial 'know-how' and entrepreneurship. Since innovative products, practices and concepts will be the key to Canada's economic success, our policies towards foreign-controlled enterprises must avoid restrictions that impede the importation of these elements.[67]

Again it is hard to know how much more (or less) Canada would have benefited from developing its own technology in the absence of branch plants, assuming that such a development would have taken place. Other countries such as Sweden and Japan, which placed severe restrictions on foreign ownership at an early stage in their industrialization, do not appear to have suffered unduly from this lack of technology transfer.

As for the "miniature replica" syndrome in which branch plants are accused of being unspecialized and inefficient, economists John Baldwin and Paul Gorecki conducted an extensive empirical study and found that "Canadian-owned plants, across the manufacturing sector as a whole, were unequivocally more specialist than their similar sized U.S.-owned counterparts in Canada."[68] They attributed this to trade barriers rather than foreign ownership *per se*, although branch plants and trade barriers are of course historically related. In their analysis, the nationalist argument for restricting foreign ownership has been spun into an argument for free trade and continentalism.

Finally, on the question of extra-territoriality, Canada's national sovereignty obviously has been compromised by the application of U.S. laws such as the Trading with the Enemy Act, but short-term remedies have their drawbacks. Canada could pass its own laws to counteract this intrusion, but statutes compelling branch plants to trade with certain countries would be very difficult to enforce. Some form of subsidy or tax incentive could be offered to encourage branch plants to trade with particular countries, but such non-compulsive measures would probably be ignored in the face of legal prohibitions by the U.S. government. In the past, Canada has frequently been able to negotiate special exemptions from the extra-territorial application of U.S. laws, but this puts us in a position, in Kari Levitt's words, "of begging favours from the metropolitan power to lift restrictions which violate Canadian sovereignty in the first place."[69]

In the case of the Trading with the Enemy Act, the insult to national sovereignty is probably of more significance than any economic injury because of the small volume of trade that is actually affected. The Gray Report speculates that there may even be some gains, because if U.S. companies withdraw completely from a foreign market then this opens up the field for indigenous Canadian firms.[70] The Trading with the Enemy Act is not the only example of extra-territoriality, and it is not inconceivable that future U.S. laws may force branch plants to do something that has a more serious economic impact on Canada. But so far, it has been the political affront rather than the economic effect that has been of most concern.

PUBLIC OWNERSHIP

Another prominent feature of Canada's industrial structure is the extent to which the state actually owns companies in various sectors of the economy. At the end of 1989, 6 of Canada's 40 largest industrial companies were *crown corporations*—corporations owned wholly by either the federal or a provincial government.[71] Among this country's financial institutions, 8 of the top 60 were crown corporations.[72] The single largest equity investor in Canada today, la Caisse de dépôt et placement du Québec, is an agency of the Quebec government. Overall, state-owned and state-controlled businesses together account for about 5 per cent of total employment in Canada, but just over 20 per cent of all productive assets (see Figure 4.4). The distribution of public ownership between

sectors of the economy is very uneven. As Figure 4.4 demonstrates, public ownership is most prominent in the electrical power, transportation, communications and mining sectors of the economy.

FIGURE 4.4

*The Share of Assets and Employment Accounted
for by Federal and Provincial State
Enterprises in Canada, by
Sector for 1983*

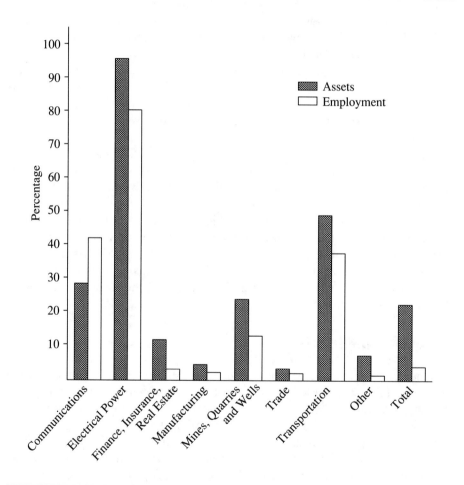

Source: Economic Council of Canada, *Minding the Public's Business* (Ottawa: Supply and Services, 1986), adapted from Charts 2-1 and 2-2, pages 8-9.

Many of the most important publicly-owned corporations have existed for decades, some going back to the beginning of this century. Ontario Hydro (1906), Manitoba Telephone (1908), Canadian National Railways (1917-1923), the Canadian Broadcasting Corporation (1932) and Air Canada (1937) fall into this group (although the sale of Air Canada to private investors began in 1988.) Early public enterprises were concentrated in the public utilities and communications sectors, along with provincial liquor monopolies. While public ownership continues to be important in these sectors, the period since about 1960 has seen a proliferation in both the functions and sheer number of public enterprises. The Economic Council of Canada estimates that about two-thirds of existing public enterprises were created after 1960.[73] Many of these newer enterprises operate in financial and industrial sectors of the economy, often in competition with privately-owned corporations. The rapid expansion of public ownership in the 1960s and 1970s—about 60 per cent of all provincial public enterprises and about 55 per cent of federal ones were created during these decades[74]—cooled off in the 1980s. Indeed, both Ottawa and some provincial governments have been busy rolling back the frontiers of the state by selling publicly-owned companies to private investors.

The broad justification for public ownership in a capitalist economy is that it promotes policy goals that privately-owned corporations would not pursue. These goals may be related to industrial development, to protection and promotion of cultural values or to social objectives like redistributing economic activity and providing jobs in economically disadvantaged regions. The defenders of public enterprise argue that the social benefits of public ownership are worth whatever costs are imposed on the taxpayer and the economy. For example, no one would seriously argue that most of the Via Rail regional services axed during the 1980s were economically viable without government subsidies. But some would argue that Via's annual infusion of $400-500 million was justified by the social and economic benefits that regional rail services bestowed on communities outside of the more densely populated corridors.

Critics of public ownership maintain that public enterprise is often an economically inefficient way for achieving whatever policy goals are associated with the enterprise. They argue that publicly-owned businesses are generally less efficient than their privately-owned counterparts. Moreover, the critics claim that the putative benefits of public ownership seldom match the economic waste that results from government-imposed corporate goals and from a weakened dependence on private capital markets. The policy role of a public enterprise may be a valid one, they concede, but it could be accomplished more efficiently in some other way. Finally, the critics argue that the policy goals that originally gave rise to a public enterprise have either become less relevant over time, or disappeared altogether.[75]

Privatization

If public ownership leads to inefficient economic performance, and if the policy goals associated with a public enterprise either are *passé* or can be achieved more cheaply using some other policy instrument, what is the point of public enterprise? This question has been asked more and more frequently since the 1979 election of Margaret Thatcher's Conservative government in Great Britain. The "solution" pioneered by the Thatcher government—a solution that has gained a foothold in economies as different as Canada, Japan and Turkey— has been to sell publicly-owned companies to private investors. This is referred to as *privatization*. It may involve either the complete or partial transfer of ownership to the private sector. The advocates of privatization argue that once the corporation is in the hands of private shareholders it will perform efficiently.

Have privatized corporations experienced efficiency improvements? This question is by no means an easy one to answer. Most of the state enterprises that have been privatized in countries like France, Britain and Canada were profitable (in some cases very profitable) *before* their privatization. In some instances, publicly-owned corporations targeted for privatization have had part or all of their debt assumed by the government, leaving them in more saleable condition and making their post-privatization record look much better because of this pre-privatization subsidy. This was true of British Aerospace, which received £100 million to repay its debt before its privatization, and this was also true of Canadair, whose debt of $1.1 billion was transferred to the government before being sold to Montreal-based Bombardier. In several cases of privatized monopolies, like British Telecom and Teleglobe Canada, sale to private investors has been accompanied by government assurances that the corporation's monopoly status will be retained for at least a period of several years. While such assurances are necessary in order to maximize the sale price of a publicly-owned monopoly, they clearly represent a public subsidy for the corporation's post-privatization owners. However, they also muddy the waters for a proper comparison of pre- and post-privatization performance.

Using profitability as a crude measure of efficiency it is clear that in most cases privatization has been followed by either no significant change in commercial performance or by an improvement. One might be inclined to accept this as sufficient proof that the transfer to private ownership tends to result in greater efficiency. It is arguable, however, that the more remarkable phenomenon is that this transfer often makes little difference in terms of profitability. Table 4.4 shows the pre- and post-privatization profitability for three privatized companies in the United Kingdom. The Table includes both the pre-taxation profits for each corporation and the pre-taxation profits expressed as a

Table 4.4

Profit Performance of Selected Privatized Corporations
in the U.K., 1978-1986

	1978	1979	1980	1981	1982	1983	1984	1985	1986
British Aerospace (1981)									
a) £m	66.3	49.1	49.8	70.6	84.7	82.3	120.2	150.5	182.2
b) Profits/ Turnover	.07%	.04%	.03%	–	.04%	.03%	.04%	.05%	.05%
Cable & Wireless (1981)									
a) £m	55.4	59.4	61	62	89.2	156.7	190.1	245.2	295
b) Profits/ Turnover	31%	28%	23%	21%	24%	37%	28%	28%	32%
Britoil (1982)									
a) £m	(22)	70	303	437	542	612	715	759	134
b) Profit/ Turnover	(40%)	26%	59%	52%	49%	48%	46%	42%	13%

Note: Figures to the right of the line are for the post-privatization period and include
the year of transfer to the private sector.
Figures in parentheses indicate losses.

Sources: Annual Reports for Britoil plc, British Aerospace plc, and Cable and Wireless plc; various
years.

percentage of turnover. Both of these are, admittedly, very crude as measures of
efficiency. The reason for providing both sets of figures is that they suggest
very different conclusions about the efficiency consequences of privatization.

In its recent study, *Minding the Public's Business*, the ECC reports only the
annual pre-taxation profits for privatized companies in the UK. The British
Treasury does the same in its public briefing material on privatization.[76] The
three corporations included in Table 4.4 are among those whose post-privatization records lead the ECC to conclude that privatization has resulted in "generally favourable profit performance."[77] But if change in the volume of the
corporation's business is accounted for, as in the second measure of profits as a
percentage of turnover, one finds no reason to conclude that privatization tends
to be associated with improved efficiency.

Table 4.5 presents similar data for four of Ottawa's accomplished privatizations. As in the case of the British privatizations displayed in Table 4.4, there is
no evident pattern to be discerned from pre- and post-privatization profitability.

A more thorough examination of pre- and post-privatization performance—

one that uses better measures of efficiency than either of the profitability yardsticks used in Tables 4.4 and 4.5—would be needed before firm conclusions could be drawn about whether transfer to the public sector has tended to make a difference for commercial efficiency. Such an examination would have to estimate the extent to which efficiency gains have resulted from eliminating whatever political-social goals were associated with public ownership. It would also have to account for the effects of market circumstances and other economic developments on corporate performance, irrespective of ownership.

Finally, it would seem only reasonable to look at how the commercial performance of firms that have *not* been privatized has changed. In other words, a fair assessment of the relationship between privatization and performance should include a control group of commercially oriented state enterprises that have not been sold to the private sector. Britain's electrical utilities, water utilities and post office, all of which remain publicly-owned as this is written, have

Table 4.5

Corporation[a]	Profitability	1983	1984	1985	1986	1987	1988
Profit Performance of Selected Privatized Corporations in Canada 1983-1988							
Canada Development Corp./Polysar (1985, 1987)	a) $ Millions	(48.7)	56.2	159.2	(296.8)	227.5	319.0
	b) %	(1.9)	2.0	5.4	(11.4)	7.9	12.6
Canadair (1986)	a) $ Millions	(184.5)	6.0	27.6	4.9	15.3 c	40.6
	b) %	(47.7)	1.6 a	6.3		6.5	(184.5)
Teleglobe (1987)	a) $ Millions	50.0	46.1	53.2	63.0	64.6	33.5
	b) %	26.2	21.1	22.1	23.0	18.7	9.1
Air Canada (privatization began in 1988)	a) $ Millions	3.1	28.1	(14.8)	40.4	45.7	98.9
	b) %	0.1	1.1	(0.5)	1.4	1.5	2.9

Note: Figures to the right of the line are for the post-privatization period and include the year of transfer to the private sector. Figures in parentheses indicate losses.

a   Year in parentheses is the date of privatization.

b   Canadair underwent financial restructuring on March 30, 1984 with its accumulated debt being assumed by the government.

c   The sale of Canadair to Bombardier was concluded December 23, 1986. These figures are for 17 months.

Sources: Annual Reports for Air Canada, Canadair (Bombardier), Canada Development Corporation (Polysar), Teleglobe Canada (Memotec Data); various years.

experienced large increases in profitability over the last couple of years. Indeed, the British Treasury reports that the country's nationalized industries experienced average productivity growth of 4.7 per cent between 1979-80 and 1986-87, compared to 2 per cent for the economy as a whole, and 3.7 per cent for the manufacturing sector.[78] All of this at least raises some doubts about the alleged economic superiority of private over public ownership.[79]

In this chapter, we have characterized Canada's industrial structure in terms of sectoral and regional divisions, as well as levels of foreign investment and public ownership. However, one further aspect cannot be ignored. We must confront the fact that economic power in Canada is highly concentrated and that a small number of giant enterprises, often controlled by single families, dominate a substantial part of the industrial landscape. This issue is the subject of the next chapter.

ENDNOTES

1. A.G.B. Fisher is normally credited with pioneering this terminology. See A.G.B. Fisher, *The Clash of Progress and Security* (New York: Augustus M. Kelley, 1966; original publication 1935), 25-43.

2. There are some differences of opinion as to which industries should be allocated to which sectors, but this classification follows Statistics Canada, *The Labour Force* (71-001).

3. See for example Mel Watkins, "Resources and Underdevelopment," in Robert M. Laxer, ed. *(Canada) Ltd.: The Political Economy of Dependency* (Toronto: McClelland and Stewart, 1973), 107-26; C.W. Gonick, "Foreign Ownership and Political Decay," in Ian Lumsden, ed. *Close the 49th Parallel etc.: The Americanization of Canada* (Toronto: University of Toronto Press, 1970), 41-73; and James Laxer, *Canada's Economic Strategy* (Toronto: McClelland and Stewart, 1981).

4. Statistics Canada, *The Labour Force* (71-001).

5. Statistics Canada, *Gross Domestic Product Industry*, March 1990 (15-001).

6. Simon Kuznets, *Modern Economic Growth: Rate, Structure and Spread* (New Haven: Yale University Press, 1966).

7. Kuznets, *Modern Economic Growth*, 150.

8. F.H. Leacy, *Historical Statistics of Canada*, 2nd edition (Ottawa: Statistics Canada, 1983) and Statistics Canada, *The Labour Force* (71-001).

9. Statistics Canada, *Gross Domestic Product by Industry*, March 1990 (15-001).

10. For a discussion of this point see Michael F. Charette, Robert Henry and Barry

Kaufmann, "The Evolution of the Canadian Industrial Structure: An International Perspective," in D.G. McFetridge *Canadian Industry in Transition*, Vol. 2 of the research studies prepared for the Royal Commission on the Economic Union and Development Prospects for Canada (Toronto: University of Toronto Press, 1986), 108.

11. *Globe and Mail*, (23 May, 1988), B1.

12. Dominion Bureau of Statistics, *Employment and Payrolls*, December 1960 (72-002) and Statistics Canada, *Employment Earnings and Hours*, December 1989 (72-002).

13. Statistics Canada (72-002).

14. Statistics Canada, *Summary of Canadian International Trade*, December 1989 (65-001).

15. Statistics Canada, *Summary of Canadian International Trade*, Dec. 1989 (65-001) and Statistics Canada, *Exports*, 1989 (65-202).

16. See, amongst others, Paul Kellogg, "Canada as a Principal Economy: A Comparative Critique of the 'Counter-Discourse' of Political Economy," paper presented to the annual meeting of the Canadian Political Science Association, (June 1987); Steve Moore and Debi Wells, *Imperialism and the National Question in Canada* (Toronto: Better Read Typesetting, 1975); Roy A. Matthews, *Structural Change and Industrial Policy* (Ottawa: Economic Council of Canada, 1985); D.G. McFetridge, "The Economics of Industrial Structure: An Overview," in D.G. McFetridge, ed. *Canadian Industry in Transition*, Vol. 2 of the research studies prepared for the Royal Commission on the Economic Union and Development Prospects for Canada (Toronto: University of Toronto Press, 1986), 1-59; Charette, Henry and Kaufmann in *Canadian Industry in Transition*, 61-133; and William K. Carroll, "Dependency, Imperialism and the Capitalist Class in Canada," in Robert J. Brym, ed. *The Structure of the Canadian Capitalist Class* (Toronto: Garamond Press, 1985), 21-52.

17. The Conference Board of Canada, *Provincial Outlook*, Vol.5, No. 2 (Spring 1988).

18. Conference Board of Canada, *Provincial Outlook*, Vol.5, No. 2 (Spring 1990) and Statistics Canada (91-210).

19. Financial Post, *Report on the Nation* (Winter 1989).

20. Allan Tupper, *Public Money in the Private Sector* (Kingston, Ont.: The Institute for Intergovernmental Relations, Queen's University, 1982), 50.

21. Conference Board of Canada *Provincial Outlook*, Vol. 5, No 2 and Statistics Canada (91-210).

22. Conference Board of Canada, *Provincial Outlook*, Vol. 5, No.2 (Spring 1990) and Financial Post, *Report on the Nation* (Winter 1989).

23. Quebec, Ministere de l'Industrie et du Commerce, *The Manufacturing and Trade sectors in Quebec: Review of 1986 and Outlook for 1987*.

24. Conference Board of Canada, *Provincial Outlook*, Vol. 5, No. 2 (Spring 1990).

25. Statistics Canada, *Summary of Canadian International Trade*, December 1989 (65-001).

26. Conference Board of Canada, *Provincial Outlook*, Vol. 5, No. 2 (Spring 1990) and Statistics Canada (91-210).

27. Ontario, Ministry of Treasury and Economics, *Ontario Economic Accounts* (May 1990) and the Financial Post, *Report on the Nation* (Winter 1989).

28. Ontario, Ministry of Industry, Trade and Technology, *The Sectoral and Regional Sensitivity of Ontario Manufacturing Industries to Tariff Reductions* (November 1987).

29. Statistics Canada, *Exports*, 1989 (65-202).

30. Ontario, *The Sectoral and Regional Sensitivity of Ontario Manufacturing of Industries to Tariff Reductions*, 14.

31. Statistics Canada, *The Labour Force*, December 1989 (71-001).

32. Statistics Canada, *Summary of Canadian International Trade*, December 1989 (65-001).

33. Conference Board of Canada, *Provincial Outlook*, Vol.5, No. 2 (Spring 1990).

34. British Columbia, Ministry of Finance and Corporate Relations, *British Columbia Economic and Statistical Review* (1989), 62.

35. *Ibid.*,76.

36. *Ibid.*, 53-54.

37. *Ibid.*, 130-31.

38. Yukon, Economic Development: Mines and Small Business, *Yukon Economics Forecast* (January 1989); Northwest Territories, Economic Development and Tourism, *NWT Trade and Investments* (1989); Northwest Territories, Bureau of Statistics, *Newstats*, (April 28, 1989).

39. Northwest Territories, Economic Development and Tourism, *NWT Economic Review and Outlook* (1988), 5.

40. *Yukon Economic Forecast*, 10.

41. NWT, *Newstats*; Yukon, *Yukon Economic Development Perspective Update* (1987-88), 5.

42. Duncan Knowler, "Basic Industry Activity in Remote Canadian Regions," paper submitted to *The Northern Review* (January 1989), 17.

43. Statistics Canada, *Corporations and Labour Unions Returns Act 1987*, March 1990 (61-210).

44. *Ibid.*

45. R.T. Naylor, *The History of Canadian Business 1867- 1914*, Vol. 1, 254.

46. Michael Bliss, *Northern Enterprise: Five Centuries of Canadian Business* (Toronto: McClelland and Stewart, 1987), 304

47. Michael Bliss, "Canadianizing American Business: The Roots of the Branch Plant," in Ian Lumsden, ed., *Close the 49th Parallel*, 31.

48. Michael Bliss, *Northern Enterprise*, 304.

49. Statistics Canada, *Corporations and Labour Unions Returns Act* (61-210).

50. Alan M. Rugman, *Multinationals in Canada: Theory, Performance and Economic Impact* (Boston: Martinus Nijhoff Publishing, 1980), 127.

51. Government of Canada (The Gray Report), *Foreign Direct Investment in Canada* (Ottawa: Information Canada, 1972).

52. See for example Stephen Clarkson, *Canada and the Reagan Challenge* (Toronto: James Lorimer and Co., 1982), 83-113.

53. MacDonald Commission, *Report*, Vol. 2, 239.

54. Clarkson, *Canada and the Reagan Challenge*, 77-78.

55. *Ibid.*

56. Mel Watkins, "Investment," in Duncan Cameron, ed., *The Free Trade Deal* (Toronto: James Lorimer and Co., 1988), 84.

57. Proponents include Kari Levitt, *Silent Surrender: The Multinational Corporation in Canada* (Toronto: MacMillan of Canada, 1970); Mel Watkins, "Resources and Underdevelopment," in Robert M. Laxer, ed., *(Canada) Ltd.: the Political Economy of Dependency* (Toronto: McClelland and Stewart, 1973), 107-26; C.W. Gonick, "Foreign Ownership and Political Decay," in *Close the 49th Parallel*, 41-73; James Laxer, *Canada's Economic Strategy* (Toronto: McClelland and Stewart, 1981); and Glen Williams, *Not For Export: Toward a Political Economy of Canada's Arrested Industrialization* (Toronto: McClelland and Stewart, 1983).

58. Levitt, *Silent Surrender*, 104.

59. MacDonald Commission, *Report*, Vol. 2, 232.

60. Findings from a wide range of U.S. studies are summarized in I.A. Litvak and C.J. Maule, *The Canadian Multinationals* (Toronto: Butterworths, 1981).

61. Richard E. Caves and Grant L. Reuber, *Capital Transfers and Economic Policy: Canada 1951-1962* (Cambridge, Mass.: Harvard University Press, 1971), 170.

62. See for example Paul Kellogg, "Canada as a Principal Economy: A Comparative Critique of the "Counter-Discourse of Political Economy."

63. Carroll, "Dependency, Imperialism and the Capitalist Class in Canada," 27.

64. *Ibid.*, 28.

65. William Watson, *A Primer on the Economics of Industrial Policy* (Ontario Economic Council, 1983), 48.

66. D.G. McFetridge, "The Economics of Industrial Structure," 22.

67. MacDonald Commission, *Report*, Vol. 2, 235.

68. John R. Baldwin and Paul K. Gorecki, "The Relationship Between Trade and Tariff Patterns and the Efficiency of the Canadian Manufacturing Sector in the 1970s: A Summary," in John Whalley, ed., *Canada-United States Free Trade* Vol. II of the studies for the Royal Commission on the Economic Union and Development Prospects for Canada (Toronto: University of Toronto Press, 1985), 185.

69. Levitt, *Silent Surrender*, 117.

70. *Gray Report*, 259.

71. *Financial Post 500* (Summer 1990). These six were Ontario Hydro (11th), Hydro-Québec (14th), Petro-Canada (23rd), Canadian Wheat Board (25th), Canadian National Railway (26th) and the Canada Post Corporation (31st).

72. *Financial Post 500* (Summer 1990). The eight were la Caisse de dépôt et place-ment du Québec (8th), the Canada Mortgage & Housing Corporation (28th), the Province of Alberta Treasury Branches (31st), the Export Development Corporation (32nd), the Farm Credit Corporation (47th), the Alberta Mortgage & Housing Corporation (53rd), the Insurance Corporation of British Columbia (58th) and the Federal Business Development Bank (60th).

73. Economic Council of Canada, *Minding the Public's Business* (Ottawa: Minister of Supply and Services, 1986), Chart 2-3, 11.

74. *Ibid.*.

75. All of these criticisms are found in the Economic Council of Canada's *Minding the Public's Business*.

76. United Kingdom, Her Majesty's Treasury, *Privatisation in the United Kingdom: Background Briefing* (May 1988).

77. Economic Council of Canada, *Minding the Public's Business*, 142.

78. United Kingdom, Her Majesty's Treasury, *The Government's Expenditure Plans 1988-89 to 1990-91* (January 1988), 85.

79. The arguments for privatization are investigated more fully in Stephen Brooks, "Evaluation des arguments émis en faveur de la privatisation," Revue Politique et Management Public, 7:1 (1989), 35-55.

Chapter 5

Corporate Concentration and the Canadian Business Elite

In liberal societies concentrated power is viewed with distrust. The basis for this distrust is the belief that those who hold this power are likely to use it to enrich themselves at the public's expense. Economists associate concentrated power with monopoly, where the competitive forces of the market are distorted by the dominance of a particular firm. A monopolistic firm produces less and charges more than would businesses in a competitive industry. Monopoly is economically inefficient and, therefore, contrary to society's best interests. Political scientists and sociologists also tend to be critical of concentrated power. Their concern is with its political dimension; the degree to which the uneven distribution of power violates the democratic value of equality and the liberal value of individual freedom. In place of "monopoly," political scientists and sociologists substitute terms such as "elites" and "dominant class." But like economists, they generally view concentrated corporate power as being contrary to society's best interests.

The concept of "corporate power" requires some explanation. In general, power is the ability to influence what happens. When applied to business, power has three distinct though interrelated dimensions. These are economic (influence in the marketplace), political (influence over government), and social (influence on society). The Royal Commission on Corporate Concentration (1978) offered the following definitions of each of these dimensions of corporate power:

> The corporation is thought to have *economic power* if it can control the prices at which its products are offered, control the quantity of its products produced and, through its ability, due to its size, to withstand losses, influence the price at which it purchases labor, capital and raw materials. Large corporations are thought to have *political power* due to the resources at

their disposal and their ability to inform and persuade the politicians and civil servants who make decisions in government. They are thought to have *social power* because of the influence they have directly over their employees and indirectly over consumers who are affected by their decisions and, in some instances, by their ownership, or influence over the mass media.[1]

The concentration of corporate power in Canada has been the subject of numerous studies by academics, journalists and publicly appointed commissions. Concern with the possible economic, political and social consequences of industrial concentration has ebbed and flowed in response to particular events like price-fixing arrangements and major corporate takeovers, and to more general trends in merger activity. The first wave of public concern was prompted by the price-fixing activities of the Dominion Wholesale Grocers' Guild in the late 1880s. These collusive practices led to Canada's first investigation of anti-competitive business practices and to the passage of the country's first anti-combines legislation in 1889. A hundred years later another wave of concern has been mounting, this time due to a series of major corporate takeovers that have raised fears that the competitive forces in Canada's economy may become significantly weaker.

The issue of corporate concentration is linked to the broader question of the social power of business. Since the publication in 1965 of John Porter's book, *The Vertical Mosaic*,[2] the proposition that big business is perched atop the power structure of Canadian society has been widely accepted within sociology and political science. This view has been popularized through books like Peter C. Newman's *The Canadian Establishment*,[3] Walter Stewart's *Towers of Gold, Feet of Clay*[4] and Diane Francis's *Controlling Interest: Who Owns Canada?*[5] But while the political and social dominance of business has the status of received truth among many intellectuals and political writers, there exists considerable disagreement over the character of business dominance and the sources of corporate power. Moreover, the Canadian public is unconvinced that corporate power poses a serious problem. Table 5.1 shows that "big labour" and "big government" are more likely to be seen as threats to the country than is "big business."

In this chapter we examine the two main issues that are raised by concentrated corporate power: (1) the economic consequences of concentrated ownership; and (2) the effects on Canadian society and politics. Governments have acted in ways intended to redress, or at least reduce, what are perceived to be the negative economic and social consequences of corporate power. Private groups, especially small producers and consumers, have also organized to counter the power of "big business." In looking at the nature and effects of corporate power we will examine these government and private responses. The public-policy dimension of this issue is addressed in Chapter Ten's discussion of competition policy.

Table 5.1

		Canadians' Attitudes Toward Concentrated Power		
Question: Speaking of our future, which do you think will be the biggest threat for the country in the future—big business, big labour or big government?				
	Big Business	Big Labour	Big Government	Unknown
1977	19%	38%	32%	11%
1983	14%	34%	45%	7%
1987	15%	30%	42%	14%
1988	17%	24%	47%	11%

Source: Gallup Canada, *Gallup Report*, various press releases.

THE CONCENTRATION OF ECONOMIC POWER IN CANADA

The concentration of enormous economic power in the hands of a relatively few individuals and wealthy families was an important theme of social criticism in turn-of-the-century America. "Robber barons" was the term used to describe what some argued was the new aristocracy of money, whose power rested on their ownership of factories, railroads and banks. Figures like William Randolph Hearst, Henry Ford, Andrew Carnegie and J. P. Morgan were viewed as the personal embodiment of business power. The economy whose heights they occupied was characterized by what John Kenneth Galbraith refers to as "entrepreneurial capitalism": an economy in which the biggest corporations were extensions of their owners' personal power and ambitions.

In his book *The New Industrial State*,[6] Galbraith argues that the era of entrepreneurial capitalism has passed. He popularizes the idea that the economies of advanced capitalist societies have two distinct components. One comprises huge businesses that employ thousands of people, are controlled by their managers rather than their shareholders, and are generally found in sectors of the economy in which a small number of firms dominate the market. The other comprises smaller businesses that are more likely to be controlled by their owners, and that generally are found in sectors of the economy where the level of competition is high. Galbraith argues that it is the big business component of the economy—what marxists refer to as "monopoly capital"—that is the characteristic feature of modern capitalism. It is also, he claims, the part of the economy that has the greatest impact on the structure and actions of government.

Canada's economy certainly fits this dual model. Since 1987, about two-thirds of corporate assets, 60 per cent of business profits and over one-half of total sales are accounted for by the 500 largest companies in this country. These 500 represent less than one per cent of all non-financial companies in the country.

The leading 25 enterprises alone account for about 40 per cent of all corporate assets, a quarter of profits and over a quarter of sales. (See Figure 5.1)

These big businesses are not distributed evenly across sectors of the economy. Instead, corporate concentration is greatest in the financial and utilities sectors. It is also high in some manufacturing industries like tobacco products, automobiles, rubber and primary metals and in many mining and extractive industries like gold, nickel and petroleum.[7]

Studies comparing the level of corporate concentration in Canada and the United States have been undertaken since 1954.[8] They all reach the same conclusion: concentration is significantly greater in the Canadian economy.

FIGURE 5.1

*Cumulative Share of Total Assets, Revenues, and Profits
Accounted for by Canada's Largest 500 Companies,
1985*

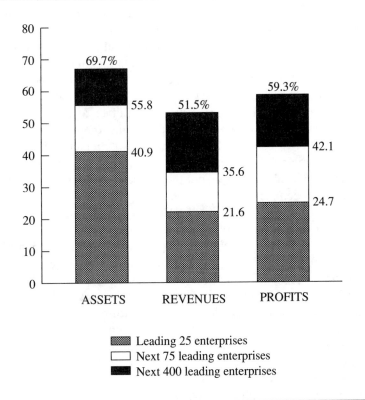

Leading 25 enterprises
Next 75 leading enterprises
Next 400 leading enterprises

Source: Based on Statistics Canada, *Corporations and Labour Unions Returns Act,* Report for 1987, Part 1 - Corporations, cat. 61-210 Annual (Ottawa: Supply and Services, March 1990), 71, Table 4.1.

The 1980 average industry CR_4 in Canada's manufacturing sector was 49.8 per cent, while the United States' 1977 average was 38.8 per cent.[9] R. S. Khemani observes that about three-fifths of Canadian GDP is produced in industries that are either oligopolistic or state regulated, while the comparable share is about two-fifths in the United States.[10] Not only are concentration levels higher in Canada than in the United States, they also appear to be higher than in most other advanced capitalist economies. The Royal Commission on Corporate Concentration found that when Canada was compared to the United States, West Germany, France, Japan and Sweden, only Japan came close to having the level of corporate concentration found in Canada.[11]

One needs to approach such comparisons with caution. They do not take into account the fact that competition in an industry may be provided by imports. Nor should one conclude that a high level of concentration in an industry is necessarily bad from either an economic or a political point of view.

From the economic point of view, the defenders of corporate concentration argue that size is an important advantage if a firm is to compete internationally. A corporation may dominate in the relatively small domestic market, and yet be dwarfed by its foreign competitors. In fact, only three of the capitalist world's 100 largest industrial companies are Canadian (General Motors of Canada, Ford Motor of Canada and Canadian Pacific).[12] Following the logic of this argument, the size of Canadian firms should not be measured against the domestic market, but against the international marketplace. If this is the standard, the "problem" of corporate concentration disappears. It becomes, in fact, a virtue.

The relationship between the size of firms and their efficiency, which includes their ability to compete internationally, is extremely complex. Based on a review of a large number of studies,[13] the Royal Commission on Corporate Concentration concluded that it was not the typically smaller size of Canadian production units as compared to, say, American plants that caused lower efficiency in Canadian industry. Instead, the Commission identified product specialization (manufacturing a smaller range of products with longer production runs) and research and development spending as more influential upon efficiency at the level of the individual plant. At the level of the firm (which might comprise numerous plants), size appeared to provide competitive advantages in terms of raising capital, marketing products and taking risks. The Commission was sympathetic toward the growth of Canadian firms so that they could take advantage of these economies of scale. This would imply even higher levels of economic concentration in Canadian industry. In the Commission's view, this was a problem that could be dealt with through a competition law that would "preserve the advantages of market competition in an oligopolistic economy."[14]

On the political side, the advocates of state economic planning have sometimes supported corporate concentration. This was particularly true during the 1960s' heyday of French economic planning, when the case for a few dominant firms was explicitly formulated as the "80:20 rule": 80 per cent of an industry's output should be accounted for by 20 per cent or fewer of the firms in that industry. The reasoning was that government would be better able to influence economic activity if it had to deal with only a few large businesses. This argument had at least a certain plausibility given that performance contracts between the state and corporations were an important tool of French industrial policy-making. In a political economy like Canada's, where the structures and tradition of comprehensive state economic planning are almost wholly absent, this argument for corporate concentration lacks any basis in reality.

The Canadian economy certainly does have the dual character that Galbraith claims is a feature of modern capitalism. This is not, however, a recent development. In 1921, 55 per cent of all sales by Canadian manufacturing establishments were accounted for by only half of one per cent of the companies in that sector.[15] Corporate concentration declined somewhat between the end of World War II and the mid-1960s. Since then the share of total business activity accounted for by the very largest companies has increased, but the current level of concentration appears to be no greater than existed forty years ago (see Figure 5.2).

A different picture emerges, however, if one looks at the share of total busi-

FIGURE 5.2

Assets of the 70 Largest Industrial Companies as a Percentage of All Canadian Industrial Assets, 1946-1987

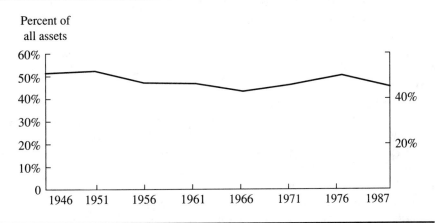

Source: Adapted from William K. Carroll, *Corporate Power and Canadian Capitalism* (Vancouver: University of British Columbia Press, 1986), 65, Figure 4.2; data for 1987 calculated from Statistics Canada, *Corporations and Labour Unions Returns Act,* Report for 1987, Part 1 - Corporations (Ottawa: Supply and Services, 1990), 71, Table 4.1.

ness activity controlled by a *constant fraction* of all firms. The justification for measuring corporate concentration in this way is that the total number of companies in Canada has grown enormously over time, so that a given number of firms in 1946 constituted a greater fraction of all firms than it does today. Measuring corporate concentration in this way, the Royal Commission on Corporate Concentration found that corporate power became much more concentrated over the period 1946-1976. This trend towards increasing concentration of economic power has continued (see Figure 5.3). We should keep in mind, however, that explosive growth in the sheer number of businesses has meant that this top 0.08 per cent of industrial enterprises is comprised of many more firms in 1985 than in either 1946 or 1976.

The postwar trend toward the increasing concentration of corporate power has been marked by the growth of sprawling business empires, many of which are under the control of individual capitalists and wealthy families. In this respect, Canada's corporate map does not conform to Galbraith's characterization of modern capitalism. The list of Canada's twenty-five largest non-financial companies includes eleven in which a particular Canadian capitalist holds a controlling interest.[16] Several of the remaining companies are part of other corporate empires. For example, Bell Canada Enterprises (ranked second by sales in 1987) and Canadian Pacific Ltd. (ranked fourth) each control several large subsidiaries. Business writer Diane Francis notes that in 1985 only 5 per cent of the 400 largest publicly traded corporations in Canada were widely held (with "widely held" defined to mean that no single investor held 15 per cent or more of the stock). Of the remaining 380 firms, she estimates that in 374 of them a family or conglomerate investor held at least a 25 per cent ownership stake.[17] Not only is corporate power concentrated in Canada, it is concentrated in the hands of a relatively small network of wealthy families and conglomerates.

The extent to which corporate power in Canada is concentrated may be seen from the fact that in the mid-1980s a mere nine families controlled 46 per cent of the value of the 300 largest companies on the Toronto Stock Exchange.[18] The largest of these family empires, Edper Investments (Peter and Edward Bronfman), has a voice in companies whose combined assets have been estimated to be worth as much as those of a major Canadian bank.[19]

The prominence of Canada's leading capitalist families raises serious doubts about one of the most widely accepted claims of modern capitalism. This is the belief that corporate ownership and corporate control have become separated due to the emergence of the large publicly-traded corporation. This argument goes back to Berle and Means's *The Modern Corporation* (1932).[20] They showed that ownership of large businesses was typically fragmented between a large number of shareholders, no one of whom was able to exercise a controlling influence over the corporation. Those who really determined the corporation's direction

FIGURE 5.3

Share of Total Industrial Assets Held by the Leading 0.08 Percent of Industrial Firms, Selected Years.

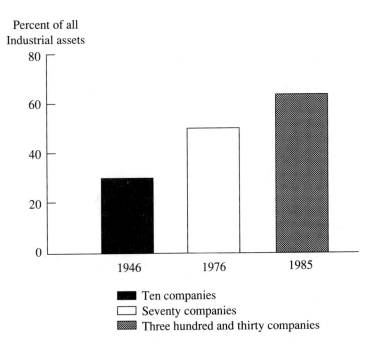

Percent of all
Industrial assets

■ Ten companies
□ Seventy companies
▦ Three hundred and thirty companies

Source: Data provided by William K. Carroll, *Corporate Power and Canadian Capitalism* (Vancouver: University of British Columbia Press, 1986), 66 and Statistics Canada, *Corporations and Labour Unions Returns Act,* Report for 1985, Part 1 - Corporations (Ottawa: Supply and Services, 1987), 72, Table 2.

were its managers, whose interests were not necessarily identical to those of the shareholders. This stage of capitalist development is referred to by Galbraith as "managerial capitalism." It is an economy in which corporate power has passed from the capitalist owners to the career managers. If this proposition is true, and to the degree that opportunities to advance into the managerial elite are greater than the likelihood of either inheriting or acquiring great wealth, this would appear to involve a democratization of economic decision-making.

It is difficult to determine the precise degree to which Canada's leading capitalist families actually involve themselves in the management of the companies they own. But there can be no doubt that the potential for real control exists. The list of Canada's 50 largest industrial companies in 1987 contains 8 crown corporations and another company, Domtar, that was controlled by an agent of the Quebec government. Of the remaining 41 corporations, 18 clearly had dominant shareholders.[21] Even if one assumes that some of these investments were "passive"—that the dominant shareholder had no desire to influence the corporation's management—it still is the case that a very great potential existed for personal influence by a relatively small number of wealthy individuals and families. In a later section of this chapter we look at the personal characteristics of Canada's business elite.

The main features of corporate concentration can be briefly summarized:

> (1) Canada has a dual economy. One part consists of very large companies that dominate the economic landscape. The other part is comprised of hundreds of thousands of small businesses that operate in much more competitive market circumstances.

> (2) A small number of corporations account for most of the assets, sales and profits in the Canadian economy. The 25 largest non-financial enterprises (representing about 0.00005 per cent of all non-financial enterprises) alone accounted for one-third of all assets, almost one-third of profits and almost one-quarter of sales in Canadian industry. Concentration is also heavy in the financial sector of the economy, where the five largest banks account for about two-thirds of total assets.[22]

> (3) The concentration of corporate power in Canada appears to be greater than in most advanced capitalist economies.

> (4) Depending on how one measures concentration, the period since World War II has seen either no increase or a sharp increase in the degree to which corporate power is concentrated in relatively few hands (see Figures 5.2 and 5.3).

> (5) At the top of Canada's business world are a number of corporate empires, many of which are controlled by a small coterie of wealthy families.

MERGERS: THE FUSION OF CORPORATE POWER

The takeover of one corporation by another is often the occasion for expressions of concern over the power of business. For example, the attempted takeover of Argus Corporation by Power Corporation in the mid-1970s led to the appointment of the Royal Commission on Corporate Concentration. More recently, the 1987 purchase of Dome Petroleum by Chicago-based Amoco, the 1986 takeover of Windsor-based Hiram Walker's by Allied Lyons of Britain, the 1989 purchase of Carling O'Keefe by Molson's and the takeover of Texaco Canada by Imperial Oil were corporate mergers that received much attention in the business press. These high-profile mergers represent only the tip of an iceberg of takeover activity that grows and shrinks over time, and which has been growing significantly since the mid-1980s. Figure 5.4 shows the trend in merger activity in Canada since 1960.

A merger involves the joining together of what previously were separate firms. There are three types of merger, each of which raises a particular set of concerns.

Horizontal Merger   This is a merger of two firms operating in the same industry and producing the same products, as in the case of Amoco's takeover of Dome and Molson's purchase of Carling O'Keefe. The chief concern here is that merger may lead to a significant reduction in market competition, with adverse economic consequences for consumers and for efficiency within the industry.

Vertical Merger   This involves a takeover where there is a buyer-supplier relationship between the two firms. It may make sense for a corporation to internalize some market transactions by buying the firm (or firms) with which it deals. A look at the corporate family trees of many large businesses shows that this is precisely what they have done. Thomson-owned Woodridge controls both newspapers and publishing companies *and* newsprint producers. Canadian Pacific, Bell Canada Enterprises and Air Canada are other Canadian examples of extensive vertical integration. The economic consequences of such mergers vary between cases, but they appear to have the greatest negative potential when an oligopolist purchases a supplier company in what is a competitive industry. The possibility that the oligopolist might favour the merged firm in its purchasing decisions means that such a merger could lead to a reduction in competition in the supplier industry.

Conglomerate Mergers   This happens when one powerful network of corporate holdings acquires control of another such network. The concern here is that if two big kids join forces, their capacity to bully others on the block increases. In other words, conglomerate mergers are sometimes argued to have the potential of leading to an undesirable concentration of economic and political power.

We return to the issue of mergers in Chapter Ten on competition policy. For now we will leave the subject with the observation that the recent past has seen an increase in the pace of merger activity, and has also witnessed several major

FIGURE 5.4

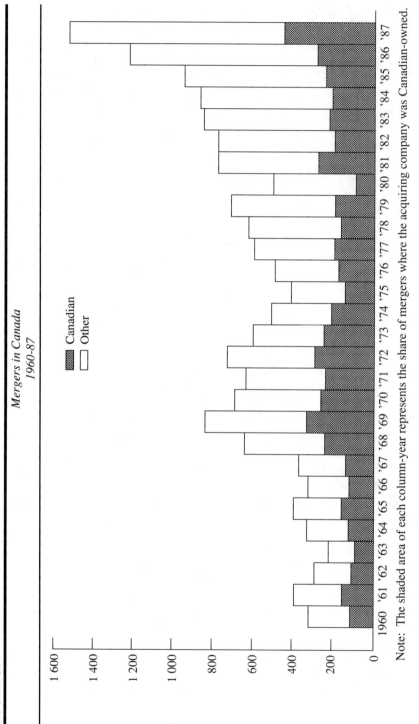

Mergers in Canada
1960-87

Canadian
Other

1600 1400 1200 1000 800 600 400 200 0

1960 '61 '62 '63 '64 '65 '66 '67 '68 '69 '70 '71 '72 '73 '74 '75 '76 '77 '78 '79 '80 '81 '82 '83 '84 '85 '86 '87

Note: The shaded area of each column-year represents the share of mergers where the acquiring company was Canadian-owned.

Source: Data from Consumer and Corporate Affairs Canada, *Annual Report*, Director of Investigations and Research: Competition Act, various years.

takeovers of Canadian businesses by foreign corporations. Other consequences aside, this has not led to an increase in the level of foreign ownership in the economy due to the rapid expansion of domestic capital.

NETWORKS OF INFLUENCE

From the economist's point of view, concentrated economic power is a problem only to the extent that it results in inefficient business practices—inefficient not for the company that exercises monopoly power, but for consumers and the overall economy. From the standpoint of the political scientist or the sociologist, concentrated corporate power raises concerns that domination of the economic system by a small segment of the population will produce undesirable inequalities in society at large. For Canadian nationalists (a category that includes a large number of this country's sociologists and political scientists) the issue of corporate power is also tied to that of American influence. They argue that the economic elite, or dominant class, is to a great degree an extension of American business power. This fact, they argue, has harmful consequences for the Canadian economy, for Canadian politics and for Canadian culture.

When one uses terms like "corporate elite" or "dominant economic class" this implies some sort of cohesion among the members of these groups. According to elite analyses, this cohesion is the result of the social background characteristics that elite members share and the fact that they occupy positions of power within society. Marxian class analysis is more likely to find the sources of business cohesion in the relationship that this group has to private property. Control over the means of production, they argue, gives the capitalist class a common interest in maintaining a system of economic relations that depends on the expropriation of some part of the value provided by those who sell their labour to make a living.

Family ties, private schooling at Upper Canada College (or some other upper class establishment) and the possession of extraordinary wealth certainly reinforce class solidarity. But from the standpoint of Marxian class analysis, the fundamental point is that one's relationship to property determines one's class. The glue that binds capitalists together is, therefore, in the very nature of the capitalist economic system (see Chapter Three).

The ties that bind Canada's corporate elite take several forms. These may be grouped into three categories of linkages: structural, social and cultural. Structural linkages involve formal connections between different parts of the business world. For example, when a corporation relies on a particular bank for a significant part of its financial needs this establishes a formal/legal relationship between these organizations. Ownership linkages may also exist; linkages that frequently are reflected in corporate interlocks between boards of directors. By this we mean that some of the same individuals are directors of several corporations. As we will see, Canada's corporate elite does in fact cluster around a number of interlocking networks that are based on ties of ownership and financial dependence. The largest banks play a prominent role in cementing these intercorporate networks.

Social linkages within the corporate elite are, to a degree, an extension of the material relations established by money. Terms like the "Canadian establishment" (popularized by Peter C. Newman's book of the same name), the "corporate elite" and "Bay Street" are often used in a sort of anthropological sense to signify a social community. The community is an exclusive one, marked off from the rest of society by private education at elite schools, club memberships, cultural philanthropy, residence in expensive neighbourhoods and even kinship ties.[23] Its boundaries are not impenetrable, but entry into the social networks of the corporate elite requires far more wealth than most Canadians can even hope to possess. Not surprisingly, the community is not representative of Canadian society. Women comprise only a small fraction of this male-dominated network. Visible minorities are conspicuous by their visible absence.

The third set of linkages that serve to distinguish the corporate elite from the rest of society are cultural. By this we mean the values and beliefs held by those who occupy positions of power in the business community, or what may be called *business ideology*. The difference between business ideology and the ideologies of other social groups and the general population is one of degree. Moreover, as we argued in Chapter One, the general culture of Canadian society, or of any capitalist society, is strongly influenced by business ideology.

STRUCTURAL LINKAGES[24]

Canada's largest businesses are integrated through a network of complex financial relations. These relations take concrete form in three ways: ownership ties, lending ties, and interlocking corporate directorships. The *interpenetration of capital* is not a distinctively Canadian phenomenon.[25] Nor is it a condition that only recently developed. The reason why anyone frets over this interpenetration is because it appears to provide the basis for self-interested cooperation among a small number of business people who together control most of the economy's productive assets. This is a situation that runs afoul of the economists' concern with market competition and the democrat's concern that the power to make decisions with important social ramifications not be concentrated in the hands of a small, unelected group.

Analysis of capital interpenetration in Canada reveals the existence of several major *cliques*—distinct intercorporate networks—each of which focusses on a major financial institution. Table 5.2, below, shows William Carroll's identification of the major intercorporate cliques in 1946 and in 1976. Carroll finds evidence of both stability and change in the interpenetration of capital. Seven of the eight cliques existing in 1946 continued to exist in 1976.[26] They were joined by three others, centred around the Toronto Dominion Bank, and Brascan and Canadian Pacific Investments.

The identification of a clique's geographic centre is important. As Carroll demonstrates, there is a regionalized pattern in the distribution of capitalist power. Corporate interlocks between the network of the Toronto-based Canadian Imperial Bank of Commerce and the Brascan and Argus (also Toronto-based) groups are frequent. Likewise, the networks centred on the Montreal-based Royal Bank and Bank of Montreal tend to interlock with the Canadian Pacific and Power Corporation (also Montreal-based) cliques.

The existence of concentrated economic power in the hands of relatively few people is more easily demonstrated than are its consequences. Conglomerates, those networks of corporations linked by ownership ties, have long been a standard feature of the industrial landscape in Canada and other capitalist economies. To the extent that they permit cost reductions through such potential advantages as greater managerial talent or transfers between firms, conglomerates may be argued to have economic virtues. From the firm's point of view, it may make sense to acquire businesses with whom it has regular dealings (vertical integration). Or it may be considered desirable to acquire shares in corporations that operate in totally separate sectors of the economy, in order to reduce the acquiring firm's risk or simply to take advantage of profit opportunities. But to the extent that they reduce competitive pressures, as when one firm acquires control over a rival, the negative economic potential of conglomerates becomes apparent.

The economic problem of conglomerates has received a good deal of attention. Much less attention has been devoted to the social problem of conglomerates. Regardless of whether ownership links between businesses reduce market competition and increase costs for the consumer, the resulting concentration of corporate power means that control over economic decisions rests with a small number of people. Concentrated power in the economy inevitably translates into concentrated power in society. The social consequences of the interpenetration of capital have been the subject of numerous studies since the publication of John Porter's *The Vertical Mosaic*. The Royal Commission on Corporate Concentration devoted some minor attention to the issue in a couple of its research studies.[27] On the whole, however, the social problem of concentrated corporate power has taken a backseat to concerns over the market distortions that concentration may produce. We return to the social issue in the next section of this chapter.

Table 5.2

Major Intercorporate Cliques in Canada, 1946, 1976		
Focal Firm	Size of Clique[a]	Density of Clique[b]
1946		
Bank of Montreal	15	53%
Royal Bank of Canada	14	37%
Canadian Bank of Commerce	8	39%
Bank of Nova Scotia	5	50%
Banque Canadienne Nationale	4	83%
Imperial Bank of Canada	4	50%
Power Corporation	4	100%
Argus Corporation[c]	6	53%
1976		
Bank of Montreal	22	19%
Royal Bank of Canada	21	18%
Canadian Imperial Bank of Commerce[d]	26	18%
Bank of Nova Scotia	11	29%
Toronto-Dominion Bank	16	18%
Power Corporation	9	47%
Argus Corporation[c]	7	67%
Canadian Pacific Investments[e]	11	58%
Brascan[f]	6	73%

a A clique is comprised of firms that shared one or more directors with the focal bank.

b The greater the number of directors in common among members of the clique, the greater the clique's density. A density of 100% indicates all of the members of the clique have directors in common. A density of 50% indicates that half the firms share multiple directors, and so on.

c Most of Argus Corporation's assets were sold off by Conrad Black in the early 1980s. Argus no longer exists as a holding company.

d The CIBC was formed from a merger of the Canadian Bank of Commerce and the Imperial Bank of Canada.

e The holding company is today called Canadian Pacific Ltd.

f Brascan is now 48 per cent controlled by Brascan Holdings, which in turn is controlled by Edward and Peter Bronfman through Edper Investments and Hees International.

Source: William K. Carroll, *Corporate Power and Canadian Capitalism* (Vancouver: University of British Columbia Press, 1986), 151, Table 6.6

Linkages between industrial capital and finance capital (banks, trust companies, insurance companies) are another feature of the interpenetration of capital that emerges from Carroll's study. It would be surprising if such linkages did not exist. Banks and other financial institutions are in the business of loaning money in order to earn a profit. Industrial corporations frequently require more money than their own cashflow and retained earnings provide, in order to expand, develop or market a new product, or even simply to survive when their profitability is down. It is natural enough that a financial institution with a significant investment in a business should want to have a representative on the board of directors of that corporation. From the other side, an industrial enterprise may well find that the presence of its financiers on the board is a useful means for reinforcing its access to commercial credit.

As noted earlier, financial institutions tend to be at the centre of the networks of interlocked business interests that one finds in Canada. This is likewise the case in other capitalist economies.[28] Historically, it appears that finance capital played a central role in the transformation of capitalism from an earlier stage of development to the modern era of giant corporations—what some call

FIGURE 5.5

Share of Total Chartered Bank Assets in Canada Held by the Five Largest Banks, 1880-1985 (selected years)

Source: Adapted from E.P.Neufeld, *The Financial System of Canada* (New York: St. Martin's Press, 1972), 99, Table 4.6; figure for 1985 calculated from *The Financial Post 500* (Summer 1986), 132.

the age of monopoly capital. In the case of Canada, banks and investment companies were involved in the growth of this country's first major industrial groupings. This was most obviously true of the links that developed between Canadian Pacific and the Bank of Montreal, but was also seen in the links between the Toronto-based Bank of Commerce, Canada Life Assurance and Dominion Securities and several Ontario-based industrial corporations.[29]

Domestic finance capital developed rapidly in the late 19th and early 20th centuries, increasing from 31 per cent of Canada's 1870 GNP to 80 per cent in 1910.[30] As Canada's financial sector expanded, it also became more concentrated through mergers and the failure of smaller chartered banks. Figure 5.5 shows that the banking system has increasingly become dominated by a handful of very large banks. The 1982 revisions to the Bank Act, which opened the door to foreign banks operating in Canada, has not led to a reduction in this dominance.[31] At the same time as the banking sector has become more oligopolistic, the banks' share of total domestic financial assets has fallen sharply over the course of this century. Figure 5.6 shows that other financial intermediaries, particularly life insurance companies, private pension funds and public sector financial institutions, have captured an increasing share of Canada's financial system.

As we observed in Chapters Two and Three, Canadian businesses have not relied exclusively on domestic sources for their capital requirements. Especially during the period of railroad construction and western expansion, British investors provided much of the money needed for economic growth. With the influx of branch plant investment, particularly after World War I, a large share of the economy's capital requirements were met from foreign sources. This evidence of early dependence on British and then American investment has led some commentators to argue that the influence of finance capital on the development of Canadian business is also the influence of foreign investors on that development.

Without underestimating the importance of foreign capital, there is hardly any solid evidence to suggest that Canada's financial-industrial elite has been dominated by non-Canadians. Looking at the boards of directors of Canada's largest corporations between 1900 and 1930, Gilles Piedalue found that the percentage of Canadian directors increased from 73 per cent to 81 per cent.[32] Thus, even at this earlier stage of economic development the corporate elite was overwhelmingly comprised of Canadian capitalists.

The nationality of directors provides only a crude and perhaps misleading impression of the influence of foreign capital. Some have argued that the Canadian managers and directors of branch plants in this country represent a *comprador* faction of the Canadian capitalist class. This is a group—some of whose members are in fact Canadian-born—that represents the interests of foreign

FIGURE 5.6

*Relative Size of Canadian Assets of Canadian Financial
Intermediaries, 1870-1985 (selected years)*

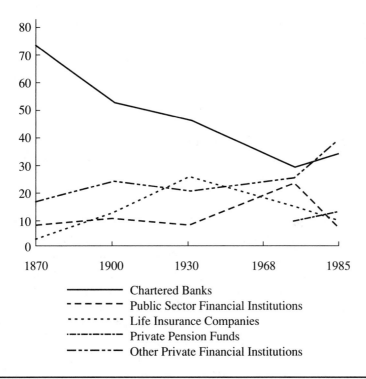

——————— Chartered Banks
- - - - - - Public Sector Financial Institutions
· · · · · · · · · Life Insurance Companies
·—·—·—·— Private Pension Funds
—·—··—·— Other Private Financial Institutions

Source: Adapted from Neufeld, *The Financial System of Canada,* 52, Table 2.2; figures for 1985 taken
Statistics Canada, *National Balance Sheet Accounts 1961-85* (Ottawa: Supply and Services Canada, 1986),
Cat. 13-214, xvii, Table VI.

capital in Canada. They are, according to the left-nationalist critics discussed in
Chapter Four, that part of the corporate elite most oriented towards continentalist economic policies. Their influence is greatest in those sectors of the economy—like manufacturing and mineral resources—where the level of foreign
ownership is highest. Political scientist Stephen Clarkson has interpreted the
policy preferences of Prime Minister Brian Mulroney as being the products of
Mulroney's early membership in this comprador group. As the president of the
American-owned Iron Ore Company of Canada, Clarkson has argued, Mulroney
grew accustomed to thinking of the Canadian economy in terms of a continentalist vision of development.[33] The American-born architect of Canada's postwar

economic policies, Liberal Cabinet minister C.D. Howe, is said to have had a similar continentalist mindset.

Canadian capitalists, it is sometimes argued, have been most influential in commercial sectors of the economy like finance and transportation. The stereotype of a Canadian bourgeoisie of commercial capitalists who have little interest in, and sometimes an outright hostility to, investment in secondary industry has little basis in reality.[34] In fact it appears that from an early stage in Canada's industrial development there have been extensive linkages between the financial and industrial elites. A study of the 44 heads of the main banks, railways, steamship lines, manufacturing plants, insurance companies, stock brokerages and mining companies in this country in 1910 found that 36 of them held directorships in *both* financial companies and manufacturing or mining firms. A single member of this capitalist elite held directorships in the financial and merchandising sectors only.[35] Another study of Toronto's corporate elite during the 1920s confirmed the fact of extensive interlocks between finance and industry. A majority of the 164 members of this elite held directorships in both the financial and industrial sectors of the economy.[36]

If there is little factual basis for the claim that Canadian capitalists historically were not very interested in industrial sectors of the economy, preferring to leave this field to the representatives of foreign capital, the more recent past provides even weaker grounds for such a claim. Earlier in this chapter we examined the corporate empires of Canada's leading capitalist families. They comprise the nucleus of the country's domestic business elite and evidence suggests that the scope of their influence is enormous and has increased since the 1970s. This increase has resulted from both the creation and growth of indigenous private sector enterprises like Nova Corporation, Norcen Energy Resources and Magna Corporation, and the takeover of what previously were foreign-controlled firms, including Bell Canada, Inco, Alcan Aluminum, the Hudson's Bay Company and Gulf Canada. In addition, the expansion of state capital through industrial companies like Petro Canada, la Société Nationale de l'Amiante (Québec), Potash Corporation of Saskatchewan, Alberta Energy Corporation and the Canada Development Corporation has contributed to the repatriation of foreign-controlled assets. As the share of Canadian industry under the control of foreign capitalists has decreased since the mid-1970s, falling most dramatically in the manufacturing and mining sectors, the position of the domestic corporate elite has been consolidated.

Networks of domestic capital span the finance and industrial sectors of the economy. Perhaps the best way to illustrate this is to look at the "family trees" of a couple of this country's leading corporate empires. Figures 5.7 and 5.8 show the extensive networks that branch out from two of Canada's largest capitalist families, Edper Enterprises (Edward and Peter Bronfman) and Olympia & York Developments (the Reichmann family).

FIGURE 5.7

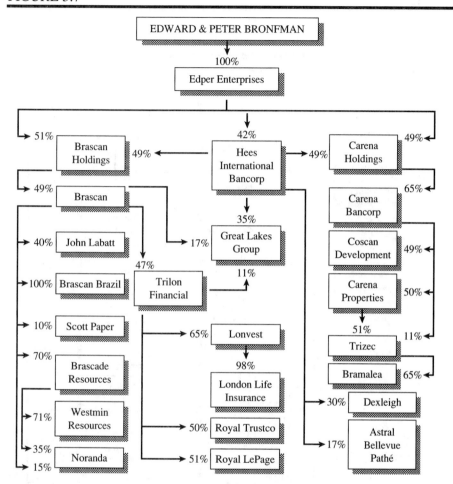

Noranda has significant interest in, among others, Noranda Forest, Norcen Energy, MacMillan Bloedel, Hemlo Gold Mines, Brunswick Mining, Brenda Mines and Lumonics.

Source: *The Financial Post 500* (Summer 1988), 166.

Arguments that the Canadian economy is dominated by foreign capital, whose power is exercised through direct ownership and a comprador elite of branch plant managers and directors, run up against the reality of a mature and indigenous Canadian corporate elite. This is an elite whose activities span all sectors of the economy, and whose mature development has involved increasing investment outside of Canada. While it is tempting to emphasize the fact that the level of foreign ownership in Canada continues to be higher than in any other advanced capitalist economy, this difference should not be allowed to

FIGURE 5.8

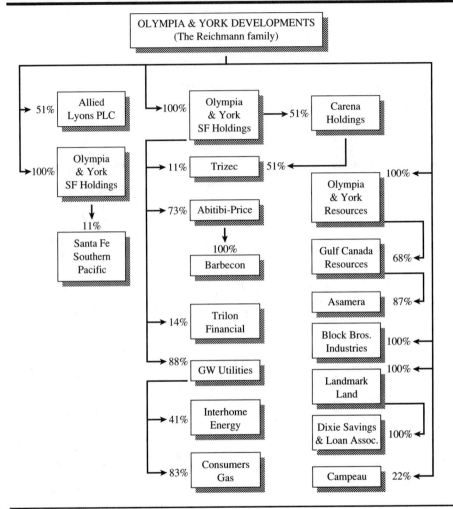

Source: *The Financial Post 500* (Summer 1988), 172.

overshadow an important similarity between Canada and these other economies. This involves the extent to which capital has become international. As we will see later in this chapter, Canadian capitalists have been important participants in this global trend toward the *internationalization of capital*. The fact that several of this country's leading corporations are the subsidiaries of foreign parents has become less and less remarkable. For example, nine of the 35 largest industrial corporations in Canada in 1987 were foreign-owned;[37] but in the U.K. the presence of foreign capital among the largest industrial companies was about as strong, at seven of 30 firms.[38] Indeed, the U.K. and U.S. economies have been the major recipients of the increasing worldwide volume of foreign investment. Looked at from this perspective, Canadian exceptionalism and economic "dependence" disappear. What the left-nationalist critics of foreign investment interpret as evidence of Canadian underdevelopment turns out to be broadly similar to developments that have been overtaking other capitalist countries (see Chapter Four). We would conclude with William Carroll that "relative to other capitalist classes experiencing internationalization, the comprador elements within the bourgeoisie in Canada are not particularly exceptional.... While there is no doubt that a continental elite of leading Canadian and American capitalists exists, it can perhaps be most fruitfully viewed as a segment of a larger, international network of finance capital that has developed with capitalist cross-penetration in the post-Second World War era."[39]

Let us summarize the discussion to this point. We have seen that economic power in this country is concentrated in relatively few hands. Within this corporate elite we find several distinct networks of capital that are held together through shared corporate directors, ownership ties and borrowing relationships. Banks and other financial institutions constitute the focal points of these networks that bridge the financial and industrial sectors of the economy. Foreign capital has historically occupied an important place in the Canadian economy, especially in the manufacturing and mining sectors. Some have argued that the representatives of foreign capital—the comprador element of the corporate elite—have been the dominant faction of Canada's capitalist class. The evidence suggests, however, that domestic capitalists have had a significant stake in the industrial sectors of the economy since the beginning of this century, and that foreign capital has not been closely tied to the centres of finance capital in this country. Moreover, the period since about the mid-1970s has seen considerable repatriation of what previously were foreign-owned companies, resulting in both a decline in the overall level of foreign investment and an increase in the prominence of domestic conglomerates, such as Edper Enterprises, Bell Canada Enterprises, Canadian Pacific and Olympia & York Developments, to name only a few. Canadian capitalists have also expanded their activities abroad, participating in the internationalization of capital. This should not be interpreted to mean that the Canadian corporate elite does not include an important foreign element. It certainly does, but then this is also true (to varying degrees) of such economies as those of West Germany, the U.K., France, the Netherlands, Belgium and even the United States. Canada has become less and less exceptional in this respect.

The politically important question is, "What follows from all of this?" Does it matter particularly that as of a few years ago nine families controlled 46 per cent of the value of the 300 largest companies on the TSE?[40] Would it be better if business power were more widely dispersed? What are the possible adverse *social* consequences that worry the critics of concentrated corporate power?

First of all, it bears repeating that economic consequences—the effects that corporate concentration may have on the allocation of resources between sectors of the economy and on the distribution of wealth in society—are politically relevant. Uncompetitive practices and inefficient commercial performances are contrary to consumers' interests. They may cause real incomes to be below their potential level. They may also contribute to an inefficient allocation of capital between sectors of the economy (i.e., capital is encouraged to remain in inefficient sectors due to the fact that lack of competition makes these investments profitable). Much of government policy is intended to deal with problems of industrial performance and inadequate incomes. To the extent that corporate concentration aggravates these problems, it has social consequences in addition to economic ones.

Second, it may be taken as a sort of physical law of politics that as the number of agents pressing their claims on government decreases, the political weight of any one of these agents increases. This can be expressed more concretely. When there is only a handful of powerful businesses operating in an industry, government finds it more difficult to be responsive to demands that are contrary to those of these dominant business interests. Division within the business community and competition between its members allow government a wider margin to respond to non-business interests and to impose its independently established preferences on business (factors that, in the language of political scientists, increase state autonomy). Concentrated corporate power means that these divisions are likely to be fewer and inter-business competition weaker, thus increasing the political influence of the dominant business interests. This is seen in its most extreme form in the case of the one-industry town, or in any economy in which a small number of corporations dominate the economic landscape.

Third, if foreign capital controls a large share of the economy, this raises the question of how the behaviour of foreign capitalists differs from that of their domestic counterparts. In Chapter Four we examined the criticisms that left-nationalists have made of foreign investment. In the present chapter we have argued that, regardless of whether behavioural differences exist, foreign capital does not dominate within this country's corporate elite. Canada possesses a mature, indigenous capitalist class whose activities span the commercial and industrial sectors of the economy, and have increasingly extended abroad. The signficance of this refutation of the left-nationalists' claims about the dominance of a comprador corporate elite is that related arguments about Canadian economic dependency and industrial underdevelopment are weakened. The concepts of "dependency" and "underdevelopment" imply an aberration from what should be the normal course of economic development. But the post-World War II trend toward the growing internationalization of capital has meant that Canada's situation has come to look more and more like the norm for capitalist economies.

Finally, and perhaps most basic, is the concern with the enormous social power of individual capitalists. Thousands of jobs, often the livelihood of an entire community, may be affected by the decisions of a single person or capitalist family. They are not accountable to those affected by their actions, but to their shareholders and to the market. While it is in the very nature of capitalism that business people are not accountable for their actions in the way that public officials are, it usually is argued that competition limits the impact of each decision. But where competition is weak, the magnitude of the effects of each corporate decision is greater. This creates the potential for enormous power to be concentrated in the hands of a few, with neither the restraints that we associate with public accountability nor the checks that competition provides. This seems to be the principal worry of those like business writer Diane Francis, when she argues that Canada is in the grip of an "economic oligarchy."[41]

SOCIAL-CULTURAL LINKAGES WITHIN THE CORPORATE ELITE

Business has its social dimension. The corporate expense account is the modern day symbol for the dining, entertaining and socializing that is part of doing business. At the top of the business world, these social activities have an exclusiveness conferred on them by the money required to move in these circles.

Peter C. Newman is probably most responsible for popularizing the belief that the "Canadian Establishment," the capitalists who occupy the commanding heights of the Canadian economy, breathes an atmosphere compounded of power, expensive tastes and superficial judgements about politics and politicians. The image of Conrad Montegu Black moving toy battalions and armaments around the floor of the "battle room" in his Toronto mansion, or of big deals consummated by the denizens of Bay Street when they "do lunch" at Winston's, capture the distinct and exclusive quality of social life as it is pursued in Establishment circles.

There are really two questions here. One has to do with the distinctive social and cultural characteristics of the corporate elite. The other asks what difference (if any) this distinctiveness makes for Canadian society.

Social Characteristics

Academic and journalistic writing on Canada's corporate elite agree that this group is highly unrepresentative of the general population, and that access to it appears to be much greater for those from certain backgrounds than from others. The most systematic studies of the social characteristics of the corporate elite have been carried out by sociologists John Porter and Wallace Clement.[42] Porter's study was based on data for 1951 and Clement's on data for 1972. They both found that of the members of this elite (which they defined as the directors of Canada's dominant corporations)[43] most were overwhelmingly male, about a third had attended private schools like Upper Canada College or Ridley, most had upper class backgrounds (50 per cent 1951 and 59.4 per cent in 1972), those with non-Anglo-Saxon ethnic origins were under-represented (comprising 13.8 per cent of Clement's 1972 group, compared to 55.3 per cent of the Canadian population), and about half (51.1 per cent in 1972) belonged to one or more of the six most prominent private clubs in Canada.[44] The picture they sketch is one of a self-perpetuating group whose social backgrounds and adult activities set them sharply apart from the general population.

This is especially true of what we might call the inner circle of the corporate elite. Those who held multiple directorships constituted 28.9 per cent of Clement's 1972 elite, accounting for 53.8 per cent of all dominant directorships. Almost three-quarters (72.8 per cent in 1972) had upper class backgrounds. This provides further confirmation of the clear head start that social status confers in moving up the corporate ladder. This conclusion requires a small qualification. Clement found that the comprador element of the corporate elite—those whose principal corporation affiliation was with a Canadian subsidiary of a foreign corporation—was more likely to include people from middle class backgrounds than the indigenous part of the elite (50.4 vs. 29.9 per cent). One might be tempted to conclude from this fact that foreign capital has produced a certain democratization of Canadian business, at least compared to domestic capital. But Clement notes that while foreign investment in Canada was growing and greater middle-class representation was being introduced through the comprador elite, the corporate elite as a whole was becoming more upper class (from about 50 per cent in 1951 to about 60 per cent in 1972).

The corporate elite operates as a social network that reproduces itself largely through self-recruitment. Education at elite schools adds to what John Porter calls the "social capital" of its members; reinforcing elite ties that are maintained in the adult world of business. Club membership provides a complement to the boardroom; a social setting that is very much part of the personal relations essential in business life. It is for this reason that the question of private club membership has become a matter of political controversy in recent times. Women's groups especially have charged that the exclusively male character of these clubs reinforces men's dominance of the business world by excluding women from its social network. In addition to challenging the exclusionary policies that traditionally have existed at some private clubs, women in business have established their own clubs like the Toronto-based McGill Club. These are intended to provide women in business with the sort of social support system that has always existed for men.

Values

Do the upper-class origins, private schooling and exclusive club membership that characterize much of this elite contribute to the formation of attitudes and beliefs (we will simply call these "values") that are significantly different from those held by other groups? There is an abundance of anecdotal, biographical and impressionistic writing which suggests that the answer is "yes." Peter C. Newman paints a picture of an Establishment in which what he refers to as the "theology of free enterprise" runs strong, continually placing the leaders of the business world at odds with politicians and bureaucrats.

As we observed in Chapter One, however, rhetoric and action may sometimes be out of sync. There can be little doubt that business people have accustomed themselves to the general idea of state intervention, though they may often bridle at its scope or object to particular instances. But certainly Canadian business people, like their counterparts elsewhere, have never been shy about asking for and accepting state subsidies. To speak, then, of the values of Canada's corporate leaders runs up against two problems. One is to determine the nature of those values. (Should the exaggerated rhetoric of Chamber of Commerce speeches, or the platitudes of an after-dinner talk be taken for evidence of the speaker's values? Should anyone's public declarations necessarily be taken at face value?) The other is to decide how closely these values correspond to actual behaviour. We cannot even attempt to unravel the complicated issues posed by these problems. Perhaps the least controversial way to approach the subject is to assume that an individual's value system will tend to coincide broadly with his or her material self-interest. If this is true then we would expect to find that the attitudes and beliefs of the corporate elite set them apart from other groups in Canadian society.

One of the few systematic investigations of these value differences was carried out by sociologist Michael Ornstein.[45] He surveyed a sample of executives from large corporations (drawn from the *Financial Post 500* for 1980), along with a sample of small business people, labour union leaders, corporate lawyers and public officials. Ornstein asked all respondents a number of questions dealing with aspects of what he refers to as "bourgeois ideology." These included questions about the relations between capital and labour, about social programmes, about policies on civil liberties and about state economic policy. His study reveals significant differences between the values of business people and those of the other groups surveyed. Within the business world, Ornstein found that the executives of large corporations tended to take positions that were ideologically more right wing than those of small business people and lawyers. This was true for most of the issues on which respondents were surveyed, with the notable exception of attitudes toward organized labour. Here, small business people were clearly more hostile to unions than were the other two business groups.

Ornstein also examined the uniformity of attitudes within both the business community and the state. This study suggests that the divisions among business people are no greater than those that exist among public officials. The degree of ideological unity is greatest among the representatives of big business, and is greater than for Ornstein's sample of public officials on two-thirds of the political attitude scales used in his study.[46] What this suggests is that there exists a relatively high level of class cohesion among Canadian capitalists, particularly within big business. Given what we know about the concentration of corporate power in this country, this evidence of considerable like-mindedness among members of the corporate elite is perhaps grounds for concern. Not only do they occupy positions of enormous power in the capitalist economy, but their ideological unity appears to provide them with the capacity for acting as a class in defence of their collective interests. If one believes, however, that these interests in fact coincide broadly with those of society as a whole then there is no reason for concern.

CANADIAN MULTINATIONALS

In the past we have been accustomed to thinking about multinational corporations as organizations based elsewhere that have established branch plants in the Canadian market. The term "multinational," at least as used by political scientists and sociologists, often carries connotations of domination and exploitation. Multinational corporations have often been viewed as international extensions of the economic power of countries like the United States, West Germany, France and Japan. Their rise to prominence in the post-World War II period has been accompanied by claims ranging from the charge that they are agents of cultural imperialism (the "coca-cola-ization" of societies) to the argument that they have facilitated the global transfer of technology. Whether multinationals are viewed positively or negatively, the capacity to generate these international businesses is usually taken as an indication of an economy's maturity. Any discussion of corporate power in Canada must therefore consider the external activities of this country's businesses.

There is a growing awareness that Canadian business has become more internationally oriented. This awareness has been driven home by the much publicized foreign investments of capitalists like Robert Campeau (who purchased the

U.S.-based Allied Stores and Federated Department Stores for US$6.6 billion in 1988), the Reichmanns (who in 1977 purchased a large share of Manhattan's office district, and who have major office property holdings in London, England), Robert Bata (whose shoe production facilities are spread throughout the less-developed world) and Conrad Black (who purchased London's *Daily Telegraph* in 1985). As can be seen from Table 5.3, Canadian direct investment abroad has jumped from $6.2 billion in 1970 to nearly $60 billion in 1987, and has more than doubled since 1980. Outgoing investments have also increased relative to direct foreign investments (d.f.i.) in Canada. In 1970, Canadian direct investment abroad was less than a quarter of the value of d.f.i. in Canada. By 1985 the figure was nearly 60 per cent. This ratio has declined only slightly in the last few years despite the Conservative government's friendlier policy towards foreign investment than its Liberal predecessor.

By far the largest portion (roughly two-thirds in 1987) of Canada's direct investments abroad are located in the United States. Several of Canada's multinational corporations are really bi-national enterprises whose operations are primarily in the U.S. and Canada. Table 5.4 lists the top 20 Canadian MNCs, which in 1989 had combined revenues of $98 billion. On average, these companies have 46 per cent of their assets outside Canada. These figures may well underestimate the true extent of Canadian capital abroad because they exclude some giant private multinationals such as Olympia and York and Bata Shoes, for which information is incomplete. Bata, for example, is known to employ 83,000 people in 90 countries, with only about 5 per cent of its production in Canada. Olympia and York has extensive investments in the United States and, among other things, is the biggest real estate owner in New York City.

Of the corporations in Table 5.4, many have recently expanded their U.S. or offshore operations, often through takeovers. For example, in the fiscal year 1987,

Table 5.3

Canadian Direct Investment Abroad 1970-87		
	Canadian Direct Investment Abroad	Relative to Direct Foreign Investment in Canada
Year	($ billion)	(%)
1970	6.2	23.5
1975	10.5	28.1
1980	27.0	43.8
1985	49.9	59.7
1987	59.9	58.1

Source: Statistics Canada (67-202).

Table 5.4

Canada's Leading Multinationals, 1987		
Company[a]	Sales/Revenue (Cdn, $billion)	Non-Canadian Assets [b] (%)
1. Canadian Pacific Ltd.	11.0	19.5
2. George Weston Ltd.	10.5	24.9
3. Noranda Inc.	9.3	25.7
4. Northern Telecom Ltd.	7.2	65.2
5. Thomson Corp.	6.1	93.2
6. Seagram Co. Ltd.	5.3	95.3
7. John Labatt Ltd.	4.9	48.1
8. Imasco Ltd.	4.4	35.9[c]
9. Abitibi-Price Inc.	3.3	16.8
10. Moore Corp.	3.2	85.6
11.TransCanada Pipelines.	3.1	39.6
12. Domtar Inc.	2.5	15.5
13. Molson Co. Ltd.	2.1	27.7
14. Bombardier Inc.	2.1	42.7
15. Ivaco Inc.	2.1	37.4
16. Magna International Inc.	1.9	18.5
17. Onex Corp.	1.8	18.2
18. Dylex Ltd.	1.7	26.5
19. Southam Inc.	1.7	23.7
20. Cominco Ltd.	1.6	30.3

a Does not include privately traded corporations for which segmented information is not generally available. Subsidies are only listed if parent companies themselves do not qualify.
b Excludes companies with less than 15% non-Canadian assets.
c Estimate based on revenues.

Sources: *Financial Post 500* (Summer 1990) and corporate annual reports.

Labatts acquired six food and drink processing companies for $388 million. One of these companies was in Quebec and the remaining five were in the United States. In 1981 Seagrams spent over $3 billion to obtain a 20 per cent stake in Du Pont, and recently it spent $1.2 billion acquiring Tropicana Products in the U.S. and a further $1.19 billion buying Martell in France. For a number of years, Ivaco has been acquiring primary and secondary steel producers in the United States; Canadian Pacific's subsidiary, Amca International, has been buying up U.S. metal fabricating, engineering and manufacturing firms; and Northern Telecom has been creating new subsidiaries in the U.K., Europe and the Pacific rim. Such developments get less media attention than Campeau's well-publicized acquisitions of Allied Stores and Federated Department Stores, but they are all part of a general trend.

The examples cited above provide an indication of how Canadian business has participated in the internationalization of capital. The last decade particularly has been characterized by increasing volatility in the pattern of cross-national investment. The U.S. market has been a major focus of much of this activity, as is suggested by the fact that the level of direct foreign investment in the United States increased from US$34.6 billion in 1977 to US$261.9 billion in 1987. U.S. direct investment abroad also increased during this period—from US$145.9 billion to US$308.8 billion—but the ratio has consistently changed in favour of foreign investment coming into the United States. In 1977, d.f.i. in the U.S. was 24 per cent of American direct investment abroad. By 1987 the figure was 85 per cent. Canadian direct investment made a significant contribution to the foreign penetration of the American economy, growing from US$5.9 billion in 1977 to US$ 21.7 billion in 1987. Ten of the 11 largest Canadian acquisitions abroad since 1977 have been takeovers of American-based companies (see Table 5.5, below).

What are the political consequences of this expansion in the international activities of Canadian business? First and most obviously, it seems likely that as Canadian capital becomes more mobile and its foreign operations more important, the ability of government to control the domestic economy is weakened. This is not a uniquely Canadian dilemma, but is true for capitalist democracies generally. Multinationals desire the maximum freedom to locate production in areas of the world where the greatest return can be achieved, regardless of national boundaries or national loyalties. The state, in contrast, is rooted in a particular territory, and is dependent on production within its geographic boundaries for employment and for tax revenue.

The threat that businesses may transfer production elsewhere is an important form of structural power that businesses hold over governments, and one which state policy-makers recognize as a real constraint on their actions. The highly competitive international trading system makes global restructuring a necessary consideration for some corporations. The choice of which countries will lose and which will gain is likely to involve a range of factors, including government policies (especially taxation, regulation and industrial subsidies) and the environment of industrial relations.

The argument on the negative consequences of growth in Canadian multinationals can be summarized as follows. These corporations are part of the trend toward the internationalization of capital; a trend that has blurred the "national identity" of corporations whose activities are spread across international borders. From the standpoint of governments whose political fortunes are influenced by the jobs and tax revenues generated from domestic investment, an

Table 5.5

			Eleven Largest Canadian Acquisitions Abroad, 1977-87		
Rank	Purchase Price $million	Acquiring Company	Acquired or Merged Company	Date of Acquisition	% of Stock Acquired
1	8,000	Campeau Corp.	Federated Department Stores, Cincinnati	1986	100
2	5,004	Campeau Corp.	Allied Stores, Corp., New York	1986	100
3	3,120	Seagram Co.	Du Pont, Wilmington, Del	1981	20
4	1,099	Northern Telecom Ltd.	STC PLC, Britain	1987	28
5	914	Olympia & York Developments	Santa Fe Southern Pacific Corp., Chicago	1987	10
6	737	Hiram Walker Resources Ltd.	Davis Oil Co., Denver	1982	100
7	834	People's Jewellers Ltd.	Zale Corp., Irving, Tex.	1986	100
8	718	Bank of Montreal	Harris Bankcorp Inc., Chicago	1984	100
9	740	First City Financial Corp.	Scoville Inc., Stamford, Conn.	1985	100
10	447	Genstar Corp.	Flinkote Co., Stamford, Conn.	1979	100
11	655	Alcan Aluminum Ltd.	Aluminum assets, Arco, Los Angeles	1985	100

Source: *Financial Post 500* (Summer 1988), 27.

increase in the international mobility of capital subjects them to additional pressure to accommodate policy to the demands of businesses whose capacity to "pull up stakes" appears credible. On the other hand, one might also argue that the internationalization of capital presents governments with the opportunity to try to capture an increasing share of international investment. The automotive industry provides a good illustration of how the internationalization of production and sales has led governments, like those in Canada and the United States, to adopt policies designed to induce foreign automakers to establish production facilities in their countries. Whether one views the internationalization of capital—in which Canadian MNCs have participated—as a problem or an opportunity, it certainly appears that it has strengthened the hand of these mobile businesses in relation to governments.

If, however, we use the logic of left-nationalists who have been critical of MNCs in Canada, we might well conclude that the expansion of Canadian MNCs is a positive development. After all, one of the criticisms laid at the feet of MNCs operating in Canada has been that they contribute to a balance of payments problem by taking money out of the country in the form of dividends, repatriated profits and intra-firm transfers that benefit the parent corporation at the subsidiary's expense. Presumably, then, Canadian multinationals contribute positively to Canada's balance of payments. The picture is complicated, however, if one accepts the view that businesses that invest abroad may be exporting jobs and the income that goes with production. Supporters of Canadian MNCs counter that this is not necessarily the case, because intra-firm trade between a parent and its foreign subsidiaries generates income (and jobs) within the domestic economy.

ENDNOTES

1. Canada, Royal Commission on Corporate Concentration, *Report* (Ottawa: Supply and Services, 1978), 6., emphasis added.
2. John Porter, *The Vertical Mosaic* (Toronto: University of Toronto Press, 1965).
3. Peter C. Newman, *The Canadian Establishment*, Vol. 1 (Toronto: McClelland and Stewart, 1975).
4. Walter Stewart, *Towers of Gold, Feet of Clay* (Don Mills, Ontario: Collins, 1982).
5. Diane Francis, *Controlling Interest: Who Owns Canada?* (Toronto: Macmillan, 1986).
6. John Kenneth Galbraith, *The New Industrial State*, 2nd edition (New York: New American Library, 1972).
7. See R.S. Khemani, "The Extent and Evaluation of Competition in the Canadian Economy," in Donald G. McFetridge, research coordinator, *Canadian Industry in Transition* (Toronto: University of Toronto Press, 1986), particularly 146-50.
8. Gideon Rosenbluth," "Industrial Concentration in Canada and the United States," in *Canadian Journal of Economics and Political Science* (August 1954), 332-46.

9. R.S. Khemani, "Extent and Evaluation of Competition in the Canadian Economy," in D.G. McFetridge, research coordinator, *Canadian Industry in Transition* (Toronto: University of Toronto Press, 1986), 152.

10. *Ibid.*, 147.

11. Royal Commission on Corporate Concentration, Report, 40-42.

12. *Fortune*, (1 August 1988), D3-D9.

13. Royal Commission on Corporate Concentration, *Report*, chapter 3.

14. *Ibid.*, 406.

15. F.H. Leacy, ed., *Historical Statistics of Canada*, 2nd edition (Ottawa, Statistics Canada, 1983), R783-794.

16. Galen Weston controls George Weston Ltd.; Edgar and Peter Bronfman control Noranda Inc., Brascan Ltd., John Labatt Ltd., Seagram Co. and MacMillan Bloedel Ltd.; the Sobey family controls Provigo Inc.; the Thomson family controls Hudson's Bay Co. and International Thomson Organization Ltd.; the Steinberg family controls Steinberg Inc.; and Robert Campeau controls Campeau Corporation. Based on *Financial Post 500* (Summer 1988).

17. Francis, *Controlling Interest*, 4.

18. Figures cited in William K. Carroll, *Corporate Power and Canadian Capitalism* (Vancouver: University of British Columbia Press, 1986), 182.

19. The *Financial Post* (12 November 1983), 1 put the value of the Edper corporate empire at $70 billion.

20. A.A. Berle and C.G. Means, *The Modern Corporation and Private Property* (New York: Macmillan, 1932).

21. Calculated from information in the *Financial Post 500* (Summer 1988), 65.

22. Calculated from the *Financial Post 500* (Summer 1987), 136.

23. See Porter, *The Vertical Mosaic*, 303-8; Newman, *The Canadian Establishment*, chs. 11, 12; and Wallace Clement, *The Canadian Corporate Elite* (Toronto: McClelland and Stewart, 1975), chapter 6.

24. This section draws heavily on William Carroll's analysis in *Corporate Power and Canadian Capitalism*.

25. See Ernest Mandel, *Marxist Economic Theory* (1968), 411; and William G. Domhoff, *Who Rules America Now?* (Englewood Cliffs, N.J.: Prentice-Hall, 1983).

26. The Canadian Bank of Commerce and the Imperial Bank of Canada merged during this period. They are counted separately for 1976 to allow for comparison to 1946.

27. See "Corporate Social Performance," research study No. 21; "The Newspaper Firm and Freedom of Information," research study No. 23; and "The Social Characteristics of One-Industry Towns in Canada", research study No. 30 (Ottawa: Ministry of Supply and Services, 1977).

28. See, for example, James C. Knowles, "The Rockefeller Financial Group," in R.L. Andreano, ed., *Superconcentration/Supercorporation* (Andover, Mass.: Warner

Modular Publications, 1973); Joel Levine, "The Sphere of Influence", *American Sociological Review,* 37 (1972), 14-27; and Oliver Pastre, *Multinationals: Bank and Corporation Relationships* (Greenwich, CN: JAI Press, 1981).

29. Ian Drummond, "Canadian Life Insurance Companies and the Capital Market, 1890-1914," in *Canadian Journal of Economics and Political Science,* 27, 204-24.

30. E.P. Neufeld, *The Financial System of Canada* (New York: St. Martin's Press, 1972) Table 1.2, 23.

31. These revisions to the Bank Act placed limitations on the activities of foreign banks, as well as on their total share of the Canadian market.

32. Gilles Piedalue, "Les groupes financiers au Canada 1900-1930," in *Revue d'Histoire de l'Amerique Fran*çaise, 30:1, 24-5.

33. Interview with CBC Radio, 1985.

34. The main source of this "commercial bourgeoisie" thesis is R.J. Naylor, *The History of Canadian Business 1867-1914,* 2 Vols. (Toronto: James Lorimer, 1975).

35. Richard P. DeGrass "Development of Monopolies in Canada from 1907-1913," Master's thesis (University of Waterloo, 1977); cited in Carroll, *Corporate Power and Private Property,* 52.

36. R.J. Richardson, "Merchants Against Industry: An Empirical Study," in *Canadian Journal of Sociology,* 7 (1982), 287.

37. *Financial Post 500* (Summer 1988), 64-65.

38. *Times 1000,* (London, 1987-1988), 26-27.

39. Carroll, *Corporate Power and Private Property,* 197.

40. *Ibid.,* 182.

41. Francis, *Controlling Interest,* 3.

42. Porter, *The Vertical Mosaic*; and Clement, "Inequality of Access: Characteristics of the Canadian Corporate Elite," in Clement, *Class, Power and Property* (Toronto: Methuen, 1983).

43. Porter looked at the 170 largest corporations, the banks, insurance corporations and some other businesses, finding adequate information on 985 individuals, or 78 per cent of those in this group. Clement collected biographical data for the directors of the 113 dominant corporations, for a total of 946 individuals, or 82 per cent of all those in this elite.

44. These are listed by Clement as the National, the York, the Toronto, the Mount Royal, the St. James, and the Rideau.

45. Michael Ornstein, "Canadian Capital and the Canadian State," in Robert Brym, ed., *The Structure of the Canadian Capitalist Class* (Toronto: Garamond Press, 1985).

46. *Ibid.,* Table 8,154.

Chapter 6

The Impact of Federalism

Federalism pervades Canadian politics. Divided policy responsibilities, administrative coordination and political rivalry between Ottawa and the provincial governments provide a frequent backdrop to many political issues in this country. Political issues involving business are no exception. Canada's federal constitution has had important consequences for the way in which business interests have organized their political activities, and for the relative degree of success that different segments of the business community have had in influencing public policy. At the same time, the actions of business have influenced the development of Canadian federalism, with some business forces pulling in the direction of greater centralization of power in Ottawa and others pulling toward greater power in the provincial capitals.

Business operates in a legal-political environment in which both Ottawa and the provinces have the constitutional right to tax producers and consumers, to regulate economic activity, and to assist or hamper the fortunes of particular corporations and industries. As business people thread their way through the intricate maze of intergovernmental relations, a knowledge of how legal jurisdiction and effective power are divided between governments is as indispensable as a compass is to a mountaineer. Governments, for their part, preside over economies in which the different, often contradictory, demands of regionally-concentrated business interests add to the confusion created by sectoral and other divisions in the business community. They must be sensitive to the regional dimension of business activity, if only because their own financial basis and political support are affected by it.

Where are citizens in all this? Does it matter to Canadians as consumers, workers and taxpayers how the jurisdictional rivalries between Ottawa and the provinces are worked out? Is there any reason for them to care about which level of government regulates what business activity? Are they personally affected by business actions that strengthen or weaken one level of government vis-à-vis another? We think so. Federal-provincial relations are part of the warp and woof of Canadian politics, influencing the way issues are conceived (and even what the issues are), how they are resolved and what policies are finally arrived at. As we will see, federalism constantly spills over to affect economic life in this country.

Our starting point in this chapter is the complex web of relations between the federal constitution, the national/provincial governments and business interests. We discuss how court decisions on the federal division of powers have also had important consequences for business-government relations. After this, we examine how federalism has affected the political activities of business. The final sections of this chapter are devoted to what the federal and provincial governments do to encourage regional business activity.

THE CONSTITUTIONAL DIVISION OF ECONOMIC POWERS

Whatever the intentions of the founders may have been when the Constitution Act, 1867 was drafted, it is clear that both levels of government exercise significant legislative and taxation powers with which they influence economic activity within their borders. The provisions of the Constitution that enable them to do so include the following:

Federal Government

• Sections 55 and 90 permit the federal government to withhold approval for a law passed by a provincial legislature for a period of up to a year, or to disallow it. These powers were widely used during the first few decades after Confederation, and were used periodically during the first half of this century. In most instances, Ottawa was reacting to provincial economic policies that challenged its own priorities and jurisdiction. Despite the fact that two major rounds of constitutional reform during the 1980s left these powers formally intact, the consensus is that they are effectively dead letters of the Constitution.

• Section 91 contains most of the specific jurisdictional headings under which Ottawa can intervene in the economy. The section starts with a preamble that includes what appears to be a general grant of legislative power: the "peace, order and good government" (POGG) clause. Judicial decisions have limited the scope of Ottawa's general legislative power to the point that laws cannot be based on the POGG clause alone, except during exceptional circumstances (see the subsequent section on judicial interpretation). The enumerated legislative powers set forth in section 91 are of greater practical importance. These include: the regulation of trade and commerce (ss.2); unemployment insurance (ss.2A); "raising of money by any mode or system of taxation" (ss. 3: the limits on Ottawa's capacity to tax stem from economic and political circumstances—including the level of taxes imposed by the provinces—not from the Constitution); exclusive powers relating to a national monetary system (ss.14, 15, 16, 18, 19, 20); exclusive powers over commercial standards (ss.17, 22, 23); the post office (ss.5); and the incorporation of companies having national objectives, implied under (ss.2). Section 91, ss.10 and 12 provide the basis for Ottawa's jurisdiction over international waters like the commercially vital Great Lakes-St. Lawrence Seaway System, and over offshore waters and the resources that lie underneath them.

• Section 92 sets out the legislative powers of the provincial governments. It includes, however, a section (Section 92, ss.10c) that gives Ottawa the authority to intervene in a provincial economy by declaring that the construction of a public work (this could be anything from the development of an oil field to a new highway) is in the national interest. This power has been used 470 times, but has not been used since 1961.

• Section 121 prohibits provincial governments from levying duties on imports coming from other provinces. This is reinforced by section 6 of the Constitution Act, 1982, that guarantees the free mobility of individuals within the Canadian economy (subject only to provincial restrictions that need to be justified on the grounds that the unemployment rate in the province is higher than the national average). By depriving provincial governments of the constitutional right to discriminate against other provincial economies, these provisions reinforce the idea of a national economic union under Ottawa's stewardship.

Provincial Governments

• Section 92 contains four main headings that have provided a basis for provincial intervention in the economy. These include the rights to raise money through direct taxation (ss.2), to carry out public works within the province (ss.10), to incorporate companies with provincial objectives (ss.11) and to maintain control over "property and civil rights" (ss.13).

• Section 92A, added in 1982, expands provincial powers of taxation over natural resources to include indirect taxation. It also reaffirms provincial authority over natural resources within their borders.

• Section 109 establishes provincial ownership of natural resources that lie within their borders and gives provincial governments the right to levy royalties and other direct taxes on these resources.

During the couple of decades immediately following Confederation, the federal government made aggressive use of its economic powers under the Constitution—including its reservation and disallowance powers—in order to carry out its programme of western expansion and railroad construction. Ottawa's attempted monopoly over all important levers of economic policy was very quickly and persistently opposed by several provincial governments. The "provincial rights" movement of the 1880s reflected provincial politicians' unwillingness to accept the glorified municipality status that the government of John A. Macdonald appeared to have in mind for them. In asserting the constitutional rights of the provinces to make economic policy, these politicians were responding both to the demands of regionally-concentrated business interests and to the revenue needs of their provincial governments.

The constitutional division of economic powers very quickly became contested terrain. Ottawa's links to monopoly railway capital and the Macdonald government's nationalist-expansionist aspirations were factors that supported a centralist interpretation of federalism. This coalition of national politicians and nationally-oriented business interests might have been better able to withstand provincial challenges had it not been for the fact that the long economic depression of 1873-1896 largely discredited Ottawa's economic policies. As the Report of the Royal Commission on Dominion-Provincial Relations (Rowell-Sirois) put it, "The achievement of Confederation and the spectacular activity of the Federal government in the early years had merely overshadowed or, at most, temporarily subordinated the separate interests of the distinct regions and communities."[1] These separate interests surfaced in intergovernmental conflicts over railways (particularly Ottawa vs. Manitoba), over the 1879 tariff increases (Ottawa vs. British Columbia, and Ottawa vs. the Maritime provinces), over the control of natural resources (Ottawa vs. Ontario) and over public finances (particularly Ottawa vs. the Maritime provinces), but all provincial governments felt the need to develop new sources of tax revenue, including corporation taxes.[2]

Relations between Ottawa and the Ontario government at the turn of the century provide a classic illustration of politics as the clash of business interests.[3] Lumber companies in the west of Ontario increasingly came to favour protectionist measures intended to encourage the domestic processing of timber before its export to the United States. They turned first to Ottawa for help, but when they got no action from that quarter they turned to the Ontario government. Under the combined pressure from the industry (a major source of provincial revenue), public opinion and a looming election, the province amended the Crown Timber Act to include what was called the "manufacturing condition." This required that pine cut on provincial crown lands be sawn into lumber in Canada. (This was a countervailing action against American tariffs on Canadian lumber, imposed in 1898). Ottawa was pressured by American-owned lumber companies operating in Ontario, and by the United States government, to disallow the Ontario legislation. One of the American arguments was that the law was *ultra vires* (outside the jurisdiction) of the province because it interfered with the federal government's responsibility for trade and commerce. This constitutional question came before the Ontario Court of Appeal, which ruled that the law was a valid exercise of the province's authority over property and civil rights. Despite the pressures on Ottawa to disallow the Ontario law, the Laurier government let it stand.

The manufacturing condition soon was extended to spruce pulpwood, thus providing a boost for the province's fledgling pulp and paper industry. It was when the Ontario government attempted to extend the manufacturing condition to mining that the clash of business interests generated a more serious federal-provincial conflict.

The mineral in question was nickel, mined in the Sudbury region by the American-owned Canadian Copper Company and exported as ore to its refineries in the United States. A group of Ontario businessmen approached the Laurier government to impose an export tax on nickel which they argued would provide an economic basis for a refining industry in the province. Rebuffed by Ottawa, they turned to the Ontario government which was flushed with the apparent success of the manufacturing condition in the lumber and pulpwood industries. The province amended the Mines Act in 1900 to gear the license fee on nickel so as to punish exports of unprocessed ore. If the ore was refined in Canada the entire amount of the substantial license fee would be refunded. The Canadian Copper Company pressured Ottawa to disallow the legislation, on the grounds that it interfered with the federal trade and commerce power. Weighing heavily in the balance was the federal government's belief, urged on by some influential businessmen, that the Ontario government's actions were likely to make foreign investment more difficult to attract. A series of exchanges between Ottawa and the Ontario government followed that ultimately resulted in an agreement to refer the law to the courts in order to test its constitutionality. As time passed the Ontario government became increasingly convinced that its position rested on very shaky constitutional grounds; therefore, the law was never officially proclaimed and was repealed altogether in 1907. Commenting on the failure of this particular attempt by Ontario to extend the manufacturing condition, H.V. Nelles writes: "[T]hose parties injured most by its actions were financially and politically powerful enough to play off the federal and provincial governments."[4]

If these were merely isolated cases they would be of limited interest to us. But in fact, they are part of a pattern that extends from the post-Confederation years down to the present. It is a pattern in which the alliances between business interests and governments are determined by the self-interest of these parties, not by deeply felt beliefs about what the constitutional division of powers ought to be in some abstract sense (much less by what the founders expected this division to be). Business interests have interpreted the Canadian Constitution and have used the fact of two levels of government to suit their own convenience. This is not surprising, and of course the same thing can be said of other interests in Canadian society.

Business interests have played an important role in shaping the division of powers between federal and provincial governments. Powers to regulate economic activity, including the capacity to raise public revenue, are the key to determining one level of government's strength and independence vis-à-vis the other level, as the literature on Canadian federalism attests.[5] These economic powers have been the ones that have most concerned business, providing the basis for political alliances between business interests and governments, for legal challenges to jurisdictional claims and for various retaliatory actions by capital. As we will see, many of the key judicial decisions on the federal division of powers have resulted from business interests directly challenging the legislative authority of a particular level of government, or from a government acting on businesses' behalf to challenge the constitutionality of another government's actions. In some other cases business has not been a primary party to constitutional squabbles, but has intervened in one way or another in proceedings between governments.

BUSINESS, THE CONSTITUTION AND THE COURTS

The courts have had an important influence on the shape of business-government relations in this country. This influence has resulted from the courts' role as the interpreter of the Constitution when its meaning is in dispute. Judicial interpretation is not the only mechanism available for settling such disputes. In fact governments have often preferred negotiations and the political resolution of their jurisdictional struggles to the sort of "winner-take-all" solution that tends to be associated with a judicial ruling. Nonetheless, since Confederation the courts have regularly been called upon to decide whether Ottawa or a provincial government has acted within the legitimate scope of its constitutional authority. A very large number of these cases, and most of the landmark ones in defining the federal balance of power, have resulted from actions brought by companies and business associations against forms of regulation that they have perceived as harmful to their economic interests.

One of the few efforts to relate these judicial decisions on federalism to broader social forces is James Mallory's study, *Social Credit and the Federal Power in Canada.*[6] Mallory argues that the industrialization and urbanization that Canada was undergoing during the half century after Confederation compelled governments—both federal and provincial—to assume new functions. This expansion in the scope of state activity was, he argues, opposed by "a steady litigious pressure which sought to exploit the federal division of legislative power in the constitution as a means of minimizing the change which was taking place in the statute law."[7] An identical phenomenon was occurring in the United States, with the difference being that American business opposed the extension of the state's regulatory reach using the due process clause of the United States' Bill of Rights. Lacking a similar protection for individual property rights in the Canadian Constitution, businesses resorted to the claim that an impugned law was *ultra vires* (outside the jurisdiction) of the government that passed it.

Based on his review of the leading constitutional decisions between 1867 and 1939, Mallory concludes that one-half of these cases involved attempts by either Ottawa or a provincial government to interfere with individual property rights. In half of these cases the charge of *ultra vires* was upheld by the courts, and the legislation struck down as unconstitutional. Mallory writes, "It is impossible to avoid the conclusion that the resulting spheres of authority of the Dominion and the provinces are the incidental outcome of a clash between individualism and collectivism."[8] The "individualism" he refers to took the concrete form of business people defending what they perceived to be a private right to dispose of their property without limitation. The "collectivism" assumed the form of governments that increasingly felt compelled to interfere with these rights. "Only on the surface," says Mallory, "has this struggle been a conflict between two conceptions of federalism."[9]

The fact that the courts so often struck down legislation as being *ultra vires* is attributed by Mallory to the judges' general predisposition against collectivism (as used above). He argues that the self-interested opposition of business interests to laws that restricted their freedom received a sympathetic hearing from judges whose habits of mind and legal training inclined them to look unfavourably on state interference with private property. The Constitution made no explicit mention of the rights of individuals, let alone of property. It did, on the other hand, deal extensively with the legislative rights of governments. Judges could not oppose the interventionist state *per se*, but they could use the division of powers in the BNA Act and the rules of judicial interpretation to slow down its expansion. There is a widespread view that the courts, and particularly Britain's Judicial Committee of the Privy Council, acted mainly to limit Ottawa's legislative powers. But in fact, provincial laws were at least as likely to be ruled *ultra vires* as were federal ones.[10]

Judges, according to this view, were important participants in shaping the relationship between government and business. Conflicts over state interference with vested economic interests regularly were fought in the courts disguised as disputes over the federal division of powers. With the passage of time, judges, like other groups in society, came increasingly to accept the expanded state functions that were the inevitable accompaniment of changes in the capitalist economy and in the structure of society. The courts continue to be an important arena where conflicts between the state's regulatory authority and the freedom of economic interests are played out, as well as conflicts that have governments as the chief protagonists. But these conflicts now occur against a broad acceptance of the principle of the positive state, if not of its precise features and limits.

The extension of the state's frontiers—both federally and provincially—has not resulted in fewer legal challenges to the constitutional authority of governments to interfere with private property rights. Far from subsiding, the "steady, litigious pressure" that Mallory argues was a characteristic feature of business's reaction to the emergence of the positive state has continued during more recent times. Some of this country's leading constitutional experts have seen in more recent Supreme Court decisions a trend toward a narrow interpretation of the federal government's economic powers, with the chief beneficiary of this trend being the business interests that have successfully challenged federal regulation. This argument is developed at length by James MacPherson.[11] Based on his analysis of several Supreme Court decisions handed down between 1978 and 1980, he concludes that Ottawa's capacity for economic regulation was being left to rest on shaky constitutional foundations. Macpherson's conclusion is almost identical to that reached by Mallory thirty years earlier:

> ... the consistent winners (in these cases) have been the corporate interests who use the vehicle of constitutional challenge as another weapon in their fight against government regulation.... At a time when, realistically, corporate litigants have easier access than ordinary citizens to the highest court and at a time when corporate interests are well represented in the legislative and executive branches of government, it would be discouraging if the Supreme Court of Canada picked up the collected works of Milton Friedman and began to strike down major federal laws regulating the corporate and consumer markets.[12]

In fairness to the Court, it has upheld major federal economic laws on several occasions in recent years. This was true in *Caloil Inc. v. A.-G. Can* (1971) and the Reference re Anti-Inflation Act, 1976.[13] The Supreme Court also implicity supported Ottawa's regulatory powers in striking down provincial laws in the *Canadian Industrial Gas & Oil Ltd. v. Government of Saskatchewan* (1978) and *Central Canadian Potash Co. Ltd. v. Government of Saskatchewan* (1979) cases.[14] What legal scholars like Macpherson[15] are saying is that the *overall effect* of recent judicial decisions on economic regulation has been to narrow the bases of federal power and to create uncertainty over the constitutional foundation of Ottawa's authority. Not everyone agrees. Years later, Queen's constitutionalist John D. Whyte, for example, reaches opposite conclusions.[16] Whether the judicial pendulum is swinging towards or away from Ottawa's authority to regulate the economy in pursuit of national objectives, we can at least conclude that the courts continue to play a significant intermediary role in the triangular relationship between business interests, Ottawa and the provinces.

Leaving aside the consequences of recent judicial rulings for the federal-provincial balance of power, there remains the question of why, in an age where the positive state and the mixed economy are established facts of life, business interests are often successful in exploiting the federal Constitution by challenging state regulation before the courts. Patrick Monahan argues that a large part of the answer lies in the fundamental conservatism of the judicial method.[17] Judges' reasoning, he maintains, has tended to be based on an implicit assumption that state intervention in society (which of course includes interference with individual property rights) can be compared to what he calls a pre-political condition of society. This condition is the free market. It is not necessary that judges be passionate devotees of Milton Friedman; all that is required is that the liberal concept of the market (see Chapter One) be the implicit reference point for judicial evaluation of state economic regulation. If judicial interpretation was based on some other premise, say, a particular conception of the general welfare of society, the likelihood of individual property rights being upheld over state regulation would probably be less. But the use of a yardstick that involves a communitarian conception like the "collective good" or the "general welfare" or "social benefits" is obviously repugnant to the idea that the courts should not pass judgement on the political desirability of legislation (this being the job of elected legislators). On those occasions when the courts have invoked some communitarian conception as the basis for a constitutional decision, the value they have been defending has always been public order.[18]

To argue that the judicial method, as described above, is conservative means that its application tends to produce results that are favourable to the protection of individual property rights. As Monahan puts it, "[State] interference is not necessarily illegitimate. But derogations from 'natural liberty' should be accepted only with misgivings and doubt."[19] It needs to be stressed here that business interests are not always successful in their legal challenges to restrictions on their freedom of action. But if the jurisprudential rules used by judges are predisposed toward the protection of the individual freedoms associated with the pre-political ideal of the market, as Monahan claims, then corporations' frequent recourse to the courts is understandable.

There is a danger in all of this of overestimating the importance of the courts as a factor determining both government's ability to regulate business and the division of regulatory powers between Ottawa and the provinces. Supreme Court rulings usually are simply a part of a continuing process of conflict and negotiation, rather than the final chapter to these disputes. As Leslie Pal and Ted Morton observe, "Judicial decisions have no intrinsic finality. A Supreme Court decision may appear on its own merits to favour one or another side of a dispute, but the final political resolution of that dispute depends on the determination, organization, resources, and wit of the combatants."[20] The truth of this assessment can be seen in the case of one of the most prominent fields of modern business-government and federal-provincial conflict—that of natural resource regulation.

Federalism and the Regulation of Natural Resource Industries

Increasing world prices for oil and gas during the 1970s was the basis for escalating conflict between Ottawa and the petroleum-producing provinces over regulation of that industry. While energy disputes received most of the attention, the decade was marked by a more general intensification of federal-provincial conflict over the regulation of natural resources. This began as early as 1971 when Ottawa attempted to eliminate longstanding tax deductions enjoyed by the mining industry. Mining interests were able to enlist the support of provincial governments to successfully oppose these tax reforms.[21] In the case of energy, the wrangle was primarily between governments; each level was keen on capturing a larger share of the growing revenue generated by higher prices for a heavily taxed natural resource. But private sector interests were by no means indifferent to how this intergovernmental struggle was resolved. Its outcome would shape the location of new petro-chemical refineries, the price that industrial consumers (located mainly in central Canada) would have to pay for Canadian petroleum, the possibility of exports (Ottawa, through the National Energy Board, must approve all energy exports) and the competitiveness of investment in Canada's petroleum industry in comparison to that of other countries.

The disputes over regulation of natural resources moved onto judicial terrain in two important cases. One of these involved Saskatchewan's taxation of oil produced on provincial crown lands. The other was a legal challenge to a production management scheme organized by the Saskatchewan government for that province's potash industry. The details of these cases have been analyzed at length by others.[22] What is important about them for our purposes is that each conformed to the time-honoured tradition of business interests challenging a government's regulatory authority by arguing that the government in question was acting outside of its constitutional sphere.

In the oil tax case, *CIGOL v. Government of Saskatchewan*, the challenge came from what was a relatively united industry that decided that one of its members (Canadian Industrial Gas and Oil Ltd.) should initiate a legal action. In the potash case, *Central Canada Potash v. Government of Saskatchewan*, the courts became involved because of a dispute within the province's potash industry. Two dissatisfied members of the industry refused to keep to the production quotas that the provincial government imposed on them, and challenged the constitutionality of the supply management scheme before the courts. Ottawa intervened in support of the private plaintiffs in both of these cases. In each case, provincial laws were ruled unconstitutional: in the *CIGOL* case on the grounds that the impugned law involved a form of indirect taxation, and in the *Potash* case on the grounds that the supply management scheme intruded upon Ottawa's exclusive responsibility for interprovincial and international commerce.

Matters did not end here. In the potash case, the Saskatchewan government had decided on a policy of nationalizing the private producers even before the first court ruling on its production management scheme was handed down. Public ownership of the industry was in a sense forced on the government by the judicial ruling that the province's regulatory scheme was unconstitutional.[23] This was not the only time that the question of constitutional jurisdiction became associated with provincial public ownership. In both British Columbia and Quebec, the decision to nationalize the private producers of electricity appears to have been partly inspired by the desire to avoid federal taxation of the industry, given that crown corporations of one level of government are not required to pay taxes to the other level.

The Alberta government's 1974 purchase of Pacific Western Airlines precipitated a conflict with Ottawa over whether provincial ownership posed a threat to federal regulatory authority in air transportation. Finally, the investment activities of Quebec's Caisse de dépôt et placement during the early 1980s led Ottawa to introduce legislation that would have placed limits on the ability of provincial governments and their agents to purchase ownership shares in private sector transportation companies. In all of these cases direct provincial ownership of business had an important federalism dimension. In the *CIGOL* case the court's ruling that the impugned royalty surcharge constituted a form of indirect taxation met with a quick response by the Saskatchewan government: it replaced the royalty surcharge with an income tax on producers.

The constitutional setbacks that *CIGOL* and *Potash* dealt to the provinces' capacity to control their natural resource industries were largely, but not entirely, swept away after the constitutional reforms of 1982.[24] As part of the package of changes that accompanied the patriation of the Constitution, Ottawa and the signing provinces agreed to amend the constitutional powers to manage natural resources. It appears that the intention was to give to the provinces politically what had been denied them judicially as a result of the *CIGOL* and *Potash* cases. Although no judicial interpretation of Section 92A of the Constitution Act exists to this point, it would seem to permit the form of resource taxation that was ruled *ultra vires* in the *CIGOL* case. Whether the production management scheme at issue in *Potash* would survive is open to greater doubt, because the resource amendment does not enable the provinces to intrude upon Ottawa's exclusive authority to make laws respecting international commerce.[25]

From the standpoint of business-government relations, the significance of the 1982 resource amendment is two-fold. First, it shows that a successful court challenge by business to the regulatory power of a government may be reversed through political negotiations between the two levels of government. In fact, intergovernmental bargaining is commonly the rule even where constitutional jurisdiction is clearly established. For example, the Supreme Court has twice ruled that Ottawa has exclusive jurisdiction over offshore resources.[26] Despite this, provinces like Newfoundland, Nova Scotia and Quebec are able to make policy in this area because of the federal government's willingness to effectively share authority over offshore resources. A second effect of the 1982 resource amendment is that it appears to reduce the likelihood that future court challenges to provincial resource regulation would succeed. As Cairns, Chandler and Moull put it, private interests are less likely to "reach for the judicial lever"[27] due to the expanded resource taxation and interprovincial trade powers that are conferred on the provinces by the resource amendment. This does not necessarily mean that the provinces' hand over resource industries has been strengthened. What it does mean is that the political resolution of disputes between industry interests and provincial governments is less likely to focus on jurisdictional matters.

If court rulings are seldom the last word in business-government conflicts—as they certainly were not in the area of resource regulation, discussed above—is it reasonable to argue that the courts have been an important factor limiting the state's ability to regulate private business? After all, if a government runs up against a constitutional roadblock the chances are good that it can find some other route to reach the same destination. What is required in these circumstances is the political will to circumvent the constitutional obstacles to business regulation. This may or may not exist.

FEDERALISM AND THE POLITICAL ACTIVITIES OF BUSINESS

So far in this chapter we have presented the case that federalism strengthens the political influence of business by increasing the number of access points, including the courts, where private interests can attempt to influence the political system. Federalism provides business with an opportunity to exploit a constitutional division not present in a unitary political system. This has been labelled the "multiple crack hypothesis."[28] The existence of two levels of government, each of which is equipped with a range of taxing, spending and regulatory powers, provides business with an opportunity to seek from one government what it cannot get from the other. We have examined a number of cases where business interests attempted—sometimes successfully and at times not—to exploit the federal division of powers for their own ends. The tendency of some business interests to enter strategic "alliances" with one or another level of government will be discussed at greater length in a subsequent section on what has been called *province-building*.

There is, however, another interpretation of federalism's impact on business-government relations. This is the view that a federal constitution tends to weaken the political influence of business by reducing the internal cohesion of organized business interests. Where both the national and regional governments have the power to make policy in areas of concern to an industry, the representative associations in the industry will be likely to adopt a federal form of organization. This is a natural enough response to the realities of divided legislative authority. But it may reduce the ability of business associations to speak with a single voice and to persuade governments that they have the capacity for collective action to back up their demands. Their influence may be weakened even further when the two levels of government are in serious conflict; a situation that may spill over to create division within the industry and its representative associations.[29]

A further twist on this second view involves what we might call the *statist* interpretation of federalism's impact. According to this view it is governments and their sprawling bureaucracies that more and more dominate the policy-making scene, particularly when jurisdictional issues are involved. Societal groups, including business interests, may be largely frozen out of the process of intergovernmental relations. Alan Cairns implies as much in arguing that modern Canadian federalism is mainly about conflicts between governments and their political and organizational goals in "governmentalized societies."[30] Societal interests react to the intergovernmental rivalry by adopting federated structures themselves. As Cairns puts it, "The increasing politicization and governmentalization of society elicits a proliferation of pressure groups struggling to fit the federal system's requirements for influencing policy."[31] Unlike the "federalism as opportunity" view, this interpretation sees federalism—at least the modern federalism of large, bureaucratic state structures at both the national and regional levels—as a constraint on the influence of business and other societal interests.

The "federalism as opportunity" and "federalism as constraint" views are best thought of as representing the two ends of a continuum along which actual cases fall. Examples can be found to support either of these interpretations. Between them are other instances (probably the majority) where the federal division of powers and the intergovernmental rivalry that it sets up provide opportunities for business interests (the "multiple cracks" referred to earlier) but also place limits on their influence. Opportunity or constraint, federalism does influence the way in which business interests (and other interests) organize for political action, the strategies they adopt when trying to influence policy, and the likelihood of their success.

The long-accepted claim that Canada's federal constitution has led most associations to adopt a federal form of organization is not supported by the facts—at least not in the case of business associations. A recent survey by William Coleman finds that about three-quarters of business associations have unitary structures.[32] In order to provide a more precise test of the relationship between the constitution and the political organization of business, Coleman breaks down business associations according to whether they fall into industries that are primarily under federal, provincial or shared jurisdiction (see Table 6.1).[33] Those associations in industries falling primarily under Ottawa's jurisdiction are the most likely to have unitary structures (87 per cent) while those in industries falling primarily under provincial jurisdiction are the most likely to have decentralized structures (50 per cent have either federal, confederal or affiliated structures). The data does not, however, support the claim that provincial or divided jurisdiction leads groups to adopt a decentralized form of political organization. Associations with centralized structures (unitary or unitary with regional sub-units) comprise about half of all associations in both the "shared jurisdiction" and "primarily provincial jurisdiction" categories.

Coleman's conclusion is that Canada's industrial structure has a far greater impact on how business associations organize themselves than does the

Table 6.1

Structural Type	Primarily Federal Jurisdiction	Shared Jurisdiction	Primarily Provincial Jurisdiction	Total
Business Association Structures and Federalism				
Unitary	41(87%)	11(44%)	6(37%)	58(66%)
Unitary with regional sub-units	4(9%)	1(4%)	2(13%)	7(8%)
Federal	1(2%)	5(20%)	5(31%)	11(13%)
Confederal	0	3(12%)	2(13%)	5(6%)
Affiliate	1(2%)	2(8%)	1(6%)	4(4%)
Informal affiliate	0	2(8%)	0	2(2%)
Independent regional associations only	0	1(4%)	0	1(1%)
Total	47	25	16	88

Source: William D. Coleman, *Business and Politics: A Study of Collective Action* (Montreal: McGill-Queen's University Press, 1988), 242.

Constitution. He finds that the fragmentation of business interests in Canada is not significantly greater than in the more centralized political systems he examined, for instance, the United Kingdom and West Germany. The two versions of the "federalism as constraint" position that we described earlier would seem, therefore, to have little empirical basis.

We should not draw the conclusion, however, that Canada's federal Constitution makes little difference for the political organization of business. The federal division of powers reinforces regional divisions in the business community when the issue at stake is one that clearly pits territorially-based business interests against one another. Tariff protection and energy prices are two issues that historically have divided both governments and business interests along regional lines. As Coleman observes, Canada's federal system "does not encourage the bridging of the structural divisions already present in the Canadian business community."[34] The solution, he feels, lies in the adoption of *corporatist* policy-making structures that would better integrate the fragmented interests of business along with those of other "functional" groups like labour and consumers (see Chapter Three).

EXPLAINING INTERPROVINCIAL DIFFERENCES IN POLICY TOWARDS BUSINESS

If the economies of Canada's provinces were broadly similar, the impact of federalism on business-government relations would be much less. But as we saw in Chapter Four, the Canadian economy is regionalized; particular industries are concentrated within the boundaries of one province or a small number of provinces. The fact that the economy is regionalized is not in itself surprising. The United States, Germany and Australia are federal political systems that also have sharp inter-regional differences in the distribution of economic activity. But Canada's Constitution, more than the constitutions of these other federal states, divides the levers of economic policy between the national and regional governments in such a way as to provide both levels with the *constitutional* capacity to have a major impact on the policy environment within which private business operates. And because their political and administrative fortunes are tied to the health of the economies over which they preside, politicians and bureaucrats take a keen interest in what policies are pursued and which level of government receives credit (or blame) for them. In short, the regional divisions in the Canadian economy are invested with a heightened political significance by this country's federal Constitution. This nurtures a situation where business-government conflicts often assume the form of intergovernmental disputes.

We have said that both Ottawa and the provinces have the constitutional capacity to shape the environment within which private business people make decisions. But while it is true in theory that all provincial governments may have recourse to the same policy levers (taxation, direct regulation, public ownership, subsidies and so on), in practice there are wide variations in the provinces' objective capacity and political willingness to use these policy instruments. Consider, for example, the difference between provinces like Ontario and Alberta, on the one hand, and New Brunswick and Newfoundland, on the other, in their ability to raise revenue from taxation. The weaker economies of the latter two provinces place greater limits on their governments, as compared to those of more economically robust provinces, in raising revenue from the taxation of individuals and corporations. In addition, economically weaker provinces incur greater costs when they borrow money, paying higher interest rates to lenders than do provinces considered more creditworthy by the private financial companies that determine these matters.

Higher rates of taxation do not represent a solution to the financial dilemma of these provinces. Indeed, they have the perverse economic effects of driving out business and contributing to the outmigration of workers and consumers. The Canadian "solution" has involved transfers from Ottawa to the so-called have-not provinces. In 1980-81, these transfers ranged from a low of 12 per cent of provincial revenue in Alberta's case, to over half of provincial revenue in each of the Maritime provinces.[35] This does not even include the income transferred to business and workers as a result of federal programmes like Unemployment Insurance (which effectively subsidizes seasonal industries and weak economies at the expense of industries and regions where the level of claims on UI is relatively low), and regional economic development policies.

Dependency on money from Ottawa reduces the capacity of these provincial governments to deploy the range of policy levers *realistically* available to more affluent provinces. Economic policy decisions are very likely to be shaped by intergovernmental considerations. An idea of how important these constraints are in the have-not provinces is conveyed in the proportion of their total investment that is accounted for by the public sector, and in the revenue dependence of governments in these provinces on transfers from Ottawa (See Figures 6.1 and 6.2).

There is no automatic correspondence between what we have called a province's objective capacity to independently finance and, therefore, determine its policies—including those policies that make the province attractive to private business—and its *political willingness* to use the levers it has available. Governments vary in their propensity to intervene in the market, and also in terms of the policy instruments they favour.

The choice of publicly-owned telephone systems in Saskatchewan, Manitoba and Alberta, instead of state-regulated privately-owned ones, can only be understood in the context of the special social and economic structures that prevailed in each of these provinces when the public ownership decision was made. Quebec's extensive intrusions into the economic marketplace since the Quiet Revolution can only be understood against the backdrop of the unique historical circumstances and socio-economic developments of that province. Forays into public ownership, direct regulation, heavy taxation and public subsidization of the petroleum industry under Alberta's putative Conservative government during the 1970s need to be interpreted in light of the complex relationships that existed between the industry and both levels of government, as well as between Ottawa and the Alberta government. The examples could be multiplied infinitely, but the point has already been made: a provincial government's willingness to use the policy levers available to it under the Constitution, in order to interfere with the economic marketplace, depends upon the constellation of social and economic forces that exists in the province.

Province-Building

When the political needs of governments are reinforced by the demands of provincially-oriented economic interests this may give rise to what has been called *province-building*. As the very term suggests, this is the provincial counterpart to the nation-building orientation of Sir John A. Macdonald's post-Confederation government. Province-building has been defined as the "recent evolution of more powerful and competent provincial administrations which aim to manage socio-economic change in their territories and which are in essential conflict with the central government."[36] The fact that the concept generally is associated with the provincial governments of Alberta and Quebec[37] demonstrates that visible and intense conflict with Ottawa is an important dimension of province-building. After all, the provincial state in Ontario is as "powerful and competent" as these other provincial states, and no one would accuse Ontario governments of being indifferent toward the direction of "socio-economic change" within their borders. But Ontario's pivotal status in Canadian politics, a status based on its large population and economic importance, has meant that it generally has been able to count on a sympathetic hearing in Ottawa. Overt "fed-bashing" has not been a popular blood sport among that province's politicians, simply because it has not been necessary for the achievement of their goals. In other respects, however, Ontario governments have not lagged behind their more aggressive counterparts, and in fact have often been at the forefront in expanding the political-administrative reach of the provincial state.

A comparison of Quebec and Alberta demonstrates the very different impulses and developments that have been associated with the growth of more interventionist provincial states. In the case of Quebec, most commentators point to the period of the Quiet Revolution during the early to mid-1960s as the decisive break with that province's tradition of limited state intervention.

FIGURE 6.1

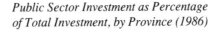

Public Sector Investment as Percentage
of Total Investment, by Province (1986)

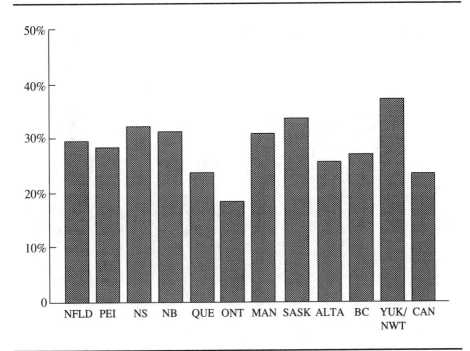

Source: Data provided in Statistics Canada, *Private and Public Investment in Canada,* cat. 61-205 annual, 24-25.

Province-building in Alberta invariably is dated from the early-1970s, when the Conservative Party under Peter Lougheed replaced the longstanding Social Credit government. In each case the impetus behind an aggressive and expansionist provincial state has been linked to the demands of a "new middle class," which is argued to have benefited more than other segments of the provincial society from this expansion. However, this similarity is a superficial one. The so-called "new middle class" assumed very different forms in these two provinces, and the business community's reaction to state expansion in Quebec has been much more ambivalent than that of its Alberta counterpart. We do not propose to examine these two provincial cases in great detail. Our focus is limited to what province-building in Quebec and Alberta reveals about the relationship of business to the provincial state.

Turning first to Quebec, the reforms ushered in by the Quiet Revolution were accomplished in spite of the opposition of much of that province's business

FIGURE 6.2

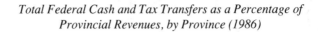

Total Federal Cash and Tax Transfers as a Percentage of
Provincial Revenues, by Province (1986)

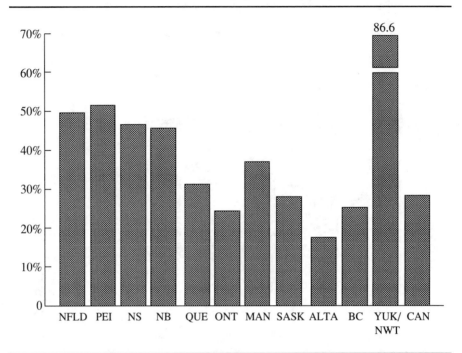

Source: Data provided in Statistics Canada, *Provincial Economic Accounts, Historical Issue 1961-1986,*
cat. 13-2BS (June 1988); and Federal Provincial Relations Office, *Federal-Provincial Programs and*
Activities 1986-1987 (May 1987), iii.

community—including francophone business people. The most persuasive
interpretation of the proliferation of state enterprises, the public sector growth
and the expansion of provincial state functions that characterized these years
sees them as evidence of *rattrapage* (catching-up) in a province where the
forces of modernization had been repressed under an increasingly tenuous
alliance of conservative political, social and corporate elites. A new middle
class of educated francophones had been developing in Quebec. With the rise to
power of the provincial Liberal Party under Jean Lesage in 1960, this segment
of the provincial population achieved the opportunity to institute its agenda of
social and economic reform. The instrument for this reform was the Quebec
state, and the new middle class was a beneficiary—many have argued that it
was the *main* beneficiary—of the state expansion that was the hallmark of the
Quiet Revolution.

Some of the most prominent economic reforms of the period were directed at providing benefits to the province's francophone business community. The Société générale de financement, a source of capital for francophone business, and the Conseil d'orientation économique, an advisory planning agency on which francophone business was well represented, were probably the major instances of such reforms under the Lesage government. It would be a mistake to conclude, however, that francophone business was strongly supportive of the new interventionist state that was being built in Quebec. The measures mentioned above were ones that had been advocated by the francophone business class, as was the creation of a provincial steel industry (set in motion in 1964 with the creation of provincially-owned Sidérurgie Québécoise). But other economic reforms, notably the nationalization of several privately-owned hydro-electric companies and the creation of the Caisse de dépôt et placement du Québec, were opposed by the representatives of francophone business in tones no less critical than those of anglophone business. Kenneth McRoberts argues that "francophone businessmen readily welcomed reforms that promised to give business greater influence over economic policy or to make available additional sources of capital, but they had little apparent enthusiasm for direct state intervention."[38]

Francophone business was ambivalent in its reaction to the province-building undertaken during the Quiet Revolution. It was not part of the alliance of social groups that enthusiastically embraced the provincial state as the agent for restructuring Quebec's social-political order. This alliance was comprised mainly of the province's new middle class, for whom an expanded provincial state meant a greater field of career opportunities, and organized labour. The presence of labour in this political alliance was a factor guaranteed to give capitalists—whether anglophone or francophone—reason to be uneasy about the direction of Quiet Revolution reforms.

As the francophone business community has expanded to establish a solid presence in the worlds of big business and finance, it has retained its ambivalence toward the provincial state. On the one hand, public institutions like Hydro-Québec and the Caisse de dépôt et placement are now widely accepted—and sometimes staunchly defended by spokespersons for francophone capital. On the other hand, the province's self-confident and politically-powerful business community has been at the forefront of calls that the Quebec state be trimmed through the privatization of many of the state enterprises created between the Quiet Revolution and the Parti Québécois's term in office.[39] It is always dicey to speak of business as though it had a single voice, but one can reasonably argue that the francophone business community is supportive of a provincial state that facilitates its desire to expand nationally and internationally. The support that most of Quebec's francophone business community gave to

Ottawa's free trade initiative (support echoed by the Bourassa government) demonstrated these aspirations. But when it comes to provincial state intervention that it perceives as a drag on the private sector's ability to make profits, the francophone business community has been outspokenly critical. In present day Quebec it is possible to talk the language of conservative politics—to talk of rolling back the provincial state—without being anti-nationalist.

Province-building in Alberta has followed a very different course. As in the case of Quebec, the impetus towards a more interventionist and intergovernmentally assertive provincial government has been credited to an ascendant new middle class. But at this point the similarity ends. Alberta's new middle class is argued to have solid roots in the private sector of the provincial economy. It is, in the words of Larry Pratt and John Richards, an "arriviste bourgeoisie" comprised of Alberta-based entrepreneurs, managers and professionals (lawyers, engineers, financial experts) who "[link] private and public sectors in a quasi-corporatist alliance of interests."[40] The dramatic escalation of world petroleum prices in the early to mid-1970s generated the wave of investment and unbounded enthusiasm that formed the basis for the social ascendance of this urban-based bourgeoisie. The proliferation of high-rise office towers, booming land prices and projections that Calgary's population would reach two million by the year 2000 (it has fluctuated between 600,000 and 670,000 for several years now) all testified to the rising economic importance of the new West.

But the increased wealth of the province also led to escalating conflict between Alberta and Ottawa over the price of petroleum, over the intergovernmental division of tax revenue from the industry and over the location of new petrochemical facilities. The provincial government of Peter Lougheed was defending its own state interests in a growing revenue base and in provincial economic growth and industrial diversification. It was at the same time defending the private interests of Alberta's new middle class whose incomes and numbers were linked to an expanding provincial economy. Calgary had long been the centre for the multinational petroleum companies operating in Canada, whose managers comprised a "comprador bourgeoisie" (see Chapter Five) within the provincial economy. This segment of the business community usually occupied common ground with local capitalists over such issues as Ottawa's energy pricing policies, taxation of the industry, early opposition to Petro-Canada and vociferous opposition to the National Energy Program (1980-84). It did not, however, have the same material interest in expansion of the provincial state as had been argued to characterize the province's indigenous new middle class.

The period of the 1970s saw rapid expansion of the Alberta state's activities in facilitating capital accumulation and in financing the social conditions necessary to maintain popular support for the high-powered capitalism that the province's political and corporate elites preached. The Lougheed government was no less committed to capitalist values and no less sympathetic to business interests than its Social Credit predecessor. Where it parted company with Socred philosophy and practice was in its willingness to use the state as an engine for provincial economic development, including reducing the economy's dependence (and, by extension, the state's dependence) on the production and exportation of petroleum. So long as this did not interfere with its own commercial objectives, the petroleum industry was not opposed to province-building. After all, Alberta's brand of state expansionism did not have redistributive goals (except to redistribute wealth from the industrial heartland of Canada to Alberta).

Unlike the state expansion undertaken in Quebec during the Quiet Revolution, few of Alberta's new economic interventions during the 1970s were met with cries of "socialism" from the business community. While involving itself heavily in the petroleum industry, the provincial government tended to avoid outright public ownership. Instead, it opted for relatively unconventional policy instruments like the mixed ownership corporation (Alberta Energy Company), and generally provided capital for the private sector in forms that did not carry influence. The provincial government's investment in the Syncrude consortium is a good example of this. Another involves the activities of the province's investment fund, the Alberta Heritage Savings Trust Fund (AHSTF). From its creation the AHSTF has operated under severe restrictions—much more limiting than those imposed on Quebec's Caisse de dépôt et placement—on its capacity to own shares in private sector businesses. There is no doubt that this limitation has carried a cost in terms of the Fund's profitability.[41] But in Alberta's conservative political climate, where public ownership is usually equated with socialism,[42] the financial cost of this restriction needs to be weighed against the political cost of appearing to interfere too much with the capitalist economy.

These political costs were evident in another instance of the 1970s province-building—the Lougheed government's 1974 decision to purchase Pacific Western Airlines. The decision was supported by Alberta's two major daily papers (the *Edmonton Journal* and the *Calgary Herald*). But it was criticized by many of the smaller dailies which reflected the views of the province's staunchly conservative ranchers and small independent business people. There was dissent in the business community over whether this particular state intervention was warranted; dissent that the government reacted to with repeated assurances that PWA would operate according to private sector standards and that the future return of part or all of PWA to private ownership was very possible (this was accomplished with PWA's privatization in the 1980s). The PWA case demonstrated the ideological limits within which province-building in Alberta has been contained.[43]

State expansion in Alberta has followed a very different path from that in Quebec, one that can be linked very clearly to the distinctive features of Alberta's economy and the interests of that province's business community. As in Quebec, province-building in Alberta was tied up with intergovernmental struggles. But these struggles were mainly about competing visions for economic development and the rivalry between Ottawa and Edmonton for tax revenues.

The Bill S-31 Episode

The intermingling of conflicts between regional segments of the business community with battles between Ottawa and the provinces was classically illustrated in 1982. At the centre of events was The Corporate Shareholding Limitation Act (Bill S-31) introduced in the Senate by a Liberal government.[44] This federal bill proposed a limit of 10 per cent on the ownership share that any provincial government or its agent (for example, a provincial crown corporation) could hold in a private sector company involved in interprovincial or international transportation of any sort. The purpose of this limitation on provincial investment was very clearly to protect certain large national corporations from the possibility that a province might acquire a significant ownership share that could be used to influence corporate decision-making. In fact, the impetus for Bill S-31 was precisely such a scenario. Quebec's Caisse de dépôt et placement had been increasing its investment in Canadian Pacific, to the point where the chairman of the Caisse indicated to CP's president that the Caisse wanted to be "represented" on the board of directors. Canadian Pacific's president turned to Ottawa for help. The corporation received a sympathetic hearing from a Liberal government that already was uneasy about what it perceived to be the excessive economic powers of the provinces.

The reaction to Bill S-31 was intense. While Quebec's Parti Québécois government led the counterattack, it was not alone. Several important representatives of francophone capital spoke out against the legislation, most notably Pierre Lortie, then president of the Montreal Stock Exchange (afterwards president of Provigo, the Quebec-based food retailing giant), but others as well, including Serge Saucier, chairman of the Montreal Chamber of Commerce. The provincial governments of British Columbia, Alberta, Saskatchewan, Ontario and Newfoundland lined up against Bill S-31, turning the tables on Ottawa by accusing it of centralizing tendencies.[45] The federal government was unable to count on the solid support of big business. A common reaction among business spokespersons was that the investment limitation was a good idea, and should be extended to Ottawa as well. The federal government argued that as a *national* government it would be less likely than provincial governments to abuse its investment power. This argument impressed no one. In the face of the opposition that Bill S-31 generated, the Liberal government allowed the legislation to die on the order paper after committee hearings.

The debate over Bill S-31 really had two themes. One was the question of the legitimate role of the state in the economy. The other was that of the appropriate balance between the economic powers of Ottawa and the provinces. The fact that these issues were raised simultaneously was due to the level that provincial economic intervention had reached. The activities of Quebec's Caisse, the single largest equity investor in the Canadian economy and the largest investor on the Montreal Stock Exchange, provided the sharpest demonstration of this intervention. But Quebec was not unique, as was shown by the opposition of several other provincial governments to S-31. Province-building had by this point led to extensive economic activity—including direct investment in the private sector—on the part of most provinces.

It is impossible to identify a coherent business position on provincial investment activities. As the Bill S-31 controversy showed, nationally-oriented business interests tended to favour investment restrictions on *all* governments, while regionally-concentrated business interests were more likely to recognize and support the provincial state's role as a source of capital. Thus, the jurisdictional rivalry between Ottawa and the provinces was reinforced by divisions within the business community.

CONSTITUTIONAL DISCORD AND BUSINESS

Investors dislike instability. Whether it is caused by economic problems, social unrest, religious strife or political conflict, instability increases the risk of doing business and therefore threatens the profitability of invested capital. Switzerland—the word is synonomous with unflinching reliability in the business world—has no problem selling its government bonds or persuading investors that their factories or offices will not be blown up, nationalized or rendered unprofitable by a sharp change in government policy. Countries like Lebanon and Iran face a tougher selling job.

In Canada, one of the chief sources of instability has been the federal division of powers. Constitutional conflict has on occasion reached proportions where the impact on the economy was palpable. For example, in 1966 a Union Nationale government was elected in Quebec under the campaign slogan "Québec d'abord!" (Quebec first!) It was headed by a premier Daniel Johnson who had authored a book entitled *Egalité ou indépéndance* (Equality or Independence). The business community, particularly the English Canadian and American investors who dominated Quebec's economy at that time, was ill-disposed towards the Johnson government's demands that Quebec receive special status within Canadian federalism. They expressed their disapproval by not buying Quebec government bonds immediately after the 1966 election. This sort of investor pressure would generally bring a government to heel. As it happened, the province's public investment fund, the Caisse de dépôt, filled the breach, making massive purchases of Quebec government bonds. The Caisse again played this role around the time of the 1970 FLQ crisis and after the 1976 election of the PQ. On both occasions institutional investors were cool towards the province's bonds because of their anxiety over Quebec's political stability and the future of that province's relationship to the rest of Canada.

Federal-provincial squabbles have affected business in other provinces as well. Throughout most of the 1970s Ottawa was at loggerheads with some of the provinces, particularly Alberta, over the regulation and development of the petroleum industry. The 1980 National Energy Program (NEP) provoked howls of outrage from the Alberta government and the multinational oil companies operating in that province. They charged that the NEP's Canadianization provisions were unfair and confiscatory. Exploration activity in Alberta's oil and gas fields dropped off sharply; the multinational petroleum companies' response to this federal-provincial wrangle.

The impact of intergovernmental conflict on business activity became a major issue during the 1990 stalemate over the Meech Lake Accord. The Accord was a set of proposed amendments to the Canadian Constitution. These amendments represented the Quebec government's conditions for signing the earlier federal-provincial agreement that had produced the Constitution Act, 1982 giving Canada the Charter of Rights and Freedoms and a formal procedure for amending the Constitution. Ottawa and most of the provincial governments agreed to the changes proposed by the Accord.

As the June 23 1990 ratification deadline approached, the likelihood of unanimous agreement—necessary under the 1982 rules for constitutional amendment—appeared to be increasingly remote. It was widely believed that Canada was facing a major constitutional crisis which, if not resolved, could end in the separation of Quebec. Stories about the damaging effects of the Meech Lake controversy on investor confidence and on the value of the Canadian dollar became daily fare in the media during the months of May and June. Many of these stories were inspired by the comments of political leaders, including Prime Minister Brian Mulroney and Finance Minister Michael Wilson, and others by the remarks of business spokespersons. The chairman of Montreal-based Power Corporation, Paul Desmarais, stated publicly that his company had lost two deals with foreign investors, "worth hundreds of millions of dollars," because of the political uncertainty generated by the Meech Lake conflict. "There are so many places to invest money these days," said Desmarais, "that people can withdraw their investment—and do it very quickly."[46]

The impact of the Meech Lake constitutional imbroglio, and the Accord's death after the June 23rd deadline, may not be limited to short-term investor skittishness. Quebec business leaders were outspokenly critical of the Accord's detractors, and many went so far as to talk about the economic viability of an independent Quebec. This was a dramatic turnaround from a decade earlier, when none of the province's francophone business leaders supported the PQ's proposal for Quebec sovereignty. The political break-up of Canada would certainly have an impact on the relationship between business and government. These consequences could include the following:

- The authority of the national government in a Canada without Quebec would probably be seriously weakened. The prospect of a strong federal government confronting powerful economic interests would diminish.
- The competition between Canada and Quebec for investment capital would intensify. Government finances could be squeezed even harder between the cost of expensive social programmes, on the one hand, and the price of attracting business investment, on the other.
- International economic relations, including the future of the Canada-United States Free Trade Agreement and the economic relationship between a sovereign Quebec and Canada, would become open questions.

REGIONAL INDUSTRIAL POLICY

Regional industrial policy can exist without federalism. Indeed, in unitary political systems like those of Italy, France and Great Britain, the impact of state policies on the location of business investment—and therefore on the distribution of wealth and jobs—has long been the subject of political controversy. But under a federal Constitution (and particularly under one like Canada's, where the provinces have at their disposal important levers of economic policy-making), there is the possibility that each government will pursue its own regional industrial policy, geared to its particular political and administrative needs and to those of the regional business interests that are grouped around it. To paraphrase Allan Tupper, *federalism institutionalizes regionalism.*[47] In the case of industrial policy, it does so by ensuring that virtually any important investment choice between regions involves an element of intergovernmental conflict.

Just as governments across the capitalist world have become increasingly involved in an intense subsidies competition to attract internationally mobile business investment, governments in Canada have also been competing with each other. The costs of this competition are extremely difficult to calculate. In addition to the public money spent on attracting private capital (which, after all, can be argued to generate offsetting benefits in the form of direct and indirect job creation, tax revenue and reduced outlays on income security programmes), one must also take into account the possible costs for the overall efficiency of the national economy. Capital that is attracted to or remains in a particular region because of public sector subsidies might be more efficiently invested elsewhere. This standard economic criticism of state assistance to private business no doubt has merit. But the reality is that governments' perception of the political costs of not providing assistance, of not participating in the intergovernmental and international competition for business investment, ensures that they remain in this highly competitive bidding game.

In this section we examine the impact that federalism has had on industrial policy in Canada. We turn first to provincial industrial policies, considering their general significance and some of the particular features of industrial policy in three provinces. Ottawa's regional industrial policies (or regional development policies, as they are more often called) are then examined. Finally, we discuss the general consequences that Canadian federalism has had for industrial policy-making.

Provincial Industrial Policies

The principal theme of this chapter has been that Canada's federal Constitution, as it has been used by governments and interpreted by the courts, heightens the political significance of regional divisions in the business community. It does so in two main ways. First, business interests often make common cause with one level of government or another, depending on their perception of which level is most sympathetic to their demands and capable of advancing their interests. Second, provincial governments naturally find that their self-interest lies in paying greater attention to the demands of business interests within their borders (except where they are trying to entice capital located elsewhere to invest in their province). Industrial policy provides a clear illustration of how these decentralizing tendencies operate in practice.

Provinces in Canada, like nations in the world economy, practise protectionism in varying degrees. The main instruments they use to favour provincially-based business interests over those outside their borders are well known and include the following:

State Purchasing   It is common for provincial governments (and their agents, like crown corporations) to favour businesses within their borders when buying goods and services. While there is little evidence that any provincial government has used its considerable spending power as part of an integrated industrial strategy, there is abundant evidence that the provinces have regularly used this power to support particular industries and individual firms. Provincially-owned electrical utilities are perennially among this country's leading capital spenders. At least in the case of Hydro-Québec, it is well known that this corporation has had an explicit policy of favouring Quebec-based suppliers since the first phase of the huge James Bay project.

Investment Incentives   These may take numerous forms, including the provision of physical infrastructures like the construction and maintenance of roads, electrical power supply systems and industrial parks, as well as pro-business labour laws and outright grants to businesses locating in a province. Virtually all provinces actively seek to attract new capital investment through advertising what they offer to business. The last few years have seen provinces vying with one another to attract, among other things, Japanese automobile plants, high-technology industry and immigrating Hong Kong business people (and their capital).

Regulation   The power to determine who may practise in a profession or trade that is subject to provincial regulation has sometimes been used to exclude out-of-province individuals or businesses from competing with those already working in a province. For example, the development of interprovincial law firms has been impeded by the barriers erected by provincial law societies.[48] Ontario and Quebec, a decade ago, were engaged in border skirmishes on a couple of occasions over Quebec's imposition of restrictions on the right of non-residents to work on construction sites in that province. One of the most significant instances of protectionist regulation has been through those sections of Quebec's language law, commonly known as Bill 101, that require businesses in that province to acquire "francisation" certificates as a condition for doing business in Quebec.

Provincial Investment   The prominence given to the privatization of state assets in recent years has somewhat obscured the extent to which Canadian governments continue to be important investors in the economy. Most of the provinces have created corporations which provide capital assistance, sometimes in the form of equity, for provincial businesses. Some, like Alberta, operate specialized venture capital funds. The amounts invested through these development corporations and venture capital funds are slight alongside the state capital invested through the numerous provincial crown corporations, mixed ownership corporations and provincial investment funds like the Caisse de dépôt et placement du Québec and the Alberta Heritage Savings Trust Fund. Financially disastrous provincial attempts to "force" the pace of economic activity are well-known---New Brunswick's investment in Bricklin, Newfoundland's construction of the Come-by-Chance petroleum refinery, Quebec's attempt to develop a provincial steel industry through Sidbec—as are provincial rescue operations and life-support systems for firms that are important employers in the provincial economy, like Nova Scotia's Sydney Steel Corporation.[49] While there have certainly been some spectacular and sometimes apparently ludicrous failures (remember the Sprung cucumbers in Newfoundland?), there are also many cases where provincial investment has been successful in promoting regional economic development. The Potash Corporation of Saskatchewan (currently a mixed-ownership corporation) and the Quebec investments of the Caisse de dépôt et placement are prominent examples of this.

There are wide variations in the particular mix of policy instruments employed by provincial governments, and in the relative importance of the public sector in the provincial economy. We examine some of these differences by looking at Ontario (a "have" province), Québec (a special case) and Nova Scotia (a "have-not" province).

Ontario

Ontario has sometimes been characterized as a relatively non-interventionist province when it comes to industrial policy.[50] Nonetheless, the province does support Ontario business through a variety of policy instruments. These include such diverse measures as traditional tax incentives (like the Manufacturing Investment Incentive, introduced in 1988, that allows Ontario firms to deduct 15 per cent of the cost of new manufacturing machinery and equipment from their taxable income), the subsidization of employers' wage costs through the province's Skills Training and Youth Opportunities programmes, business loans made by Ontario's four development corporations, support for high-technology industries channelled through the IDEA Corporation, and the preference for provincial suppliers imposed by the government on the Urban Transportation Development Corporation.

Unlike Quebec, Ontario has shown a reluctance to use direct public ownership as an instrument of industrial policy. At the end of 1987, the provincial government owned 24 business enterprises, counting subsidiaries, compared to 99 in the case of Quebec.[51] Ontario governments have, however, made extensive use of outright grants to attract new capital investment, particularly grants to auto companies. Moreover, high-technology industry has been identified as an industrial policy priority since the rash of plant closures in the late 1970s and early 1980s. Despite the high political visibility of some of these interventions, Ontario governments have pursued what Richard Bird characterizes as a "cautious" approach that has steered clear of anything resembling an industrial strategy.[52]

Compared to the other provincial economies, Ontario's is the least dependent on public sector investment. In 1987, private investment exceeded public investment by a ratio of about 5 to 1 ($44.5 billion v. $9.4 billion). For Canada as a whole the ratio was closer to 3 to 1 ($106.9 billion v. $30.6 billion). New Brunswick, Nova Scotia and Manitoba had the greatest dependence on public investment, with ratios of about 2 to 1.[53]

Presiding over the economic loadstar of Confederation, the centre of manufacturing and finance in this country, Ontario governments have been immune from the industrial adventurism that produces Bricklins. Nor has the province felt the need to bail out failing private businesses. When a company the size of Massey-Ferguson (now called Varity) closes its doors, as it did on its Brantford production facility in 1986, it is a serious matter. But its economic and political ramifications are not great enough that the province feels compelled to step in. This is a luxury that a province like Nova Scotia would be hardpressed to afford if Michelin Tire, for example, was going under.

Quebec

In the latest edition of the standard textbook on Quebec politics, Kenneth McRoberts observes that "the whole notion of the interventionist state has fallen into disrepute."[54] Evidence of this seems to be everywhere. Since the provincial Liberal Party was elected to power in 1985, Quebec has gone further than any other government in Canada—Ottawa included—in privatizing state enterprises. Public ownership had been a favourite instrument of Quebec industrial policy since the Quiet Revolution. One of the main reasons for this predilection was the fact that the state enterprise was a ready vehicle for the promotion of French in the economy, in a province where francophones had traditionally been excluded from the centres of economic power. With the emergence of a mature, self-confident, francophone business class in contemporary Quebec, the negative aspects of the province's large stable of state enterprises—particularly the money that many of them lose—have received increasing attention. Nonetheless, Quebec still has a more extensive state enterprise sector than any other province, with 99 crown corporations and subsidiaries at the end of 1987.

Industrial policy in the new Quebec represents a mix of the interventionist legacy that has been built up since the early 1960s, with the market-oriented reforms that have been introduced under the Bourassa government. Important pillars of the Quiet Revolution like the Caisse de dépôt et placement and Hydro-Québec continue to enjoy widespread support in the province as a whole and in the francophone business community. But many other aspects of state regulation and ownership have been subject to attack, particularly from the representatives of francophone capital. Their views were given forceful expression in three task force reports issued during the first year after the provincial Liberals gained power. These reports dealt with the functions and structures of the Quebec state, provincial state enterprises and regulation, respectively. All three were dominated by prominent members of Quebec's francophone business community, and all three produced reports calling for a major withdrawal of the provincial state from Quebec's economic life.[55]

While it is clear that the province's francophone business class is highly critical of the interventionist industrial policy that has been built up over the years, the Bourassa government's sympathy for business's views has been tempered in practice by its unwillingness to incur the full force of the political opposition that would follow if the more radical reforms favoured by business were implemented. Consequently, the province's industrial policy remains more interventionist than that of Ontario, even though the political momentum has been towards a less intrusive Quebec state.

Public sector investment continues to account for a larger share of total investment in Quebec than in Ontario. In 1987 the ratio of private to public capital was about 3.5 to 1, compared to 5 to 1 in Ontario. This gap between the two most industrialized provinces has been consistent over the last several years. Thus, despite the emergence of an assertive, outward-looking francophone business class that is impatient with the structures of economic nationalism, the provincial economy remains considerably more dependent on the state than is true of the province to which Quebec's business and political leaders regularly compare it. As we will see later in this chapter, the federal government is an important investor in the Quebec economy, spending a greater share of its regional development dollars in that province than in any other.

In the new Quebec that includes firms like Bombardier, Lavalin, Culinar, Power Corporation and Provigo, it is difficult to argue that an intrusive provincial government is needed to promote francophone capital. But the provincial economy still has weaknesses that Ontario's economy does not. The problem of economic underdevelopment is even more serious in eastern Quebec than it is in northern Ontario. The eastern end of Montreal continues to experience deindustrialization. A mega-project/export mentality—embodied in the James Bay II decision—continues to run strong in the province, and Quebec remains more dependent on the export of natural resources than does Ontario. In short, the province's economy does not have the vitality of Ontario's. It was this gap in economic well-being that was largely responsible for the growth of the interventionist Quebec state. And it would be unrealistic to expect that any Quebec government, even one as sympathetic to business as the Bourassa government, can survive politically with the relatively non-interventionist industrial policy that Ontario governments can afford.

Nova Scotia

It has often been said that Nova Scotia's most valuable export is its people. Indeed, during 17 of the 24 years between 1961-62 and 1984-85 more people left Nova Scotia to go to other provinces than came to Nova Scotia from other parts of Canada—a record of outmigration surpassed only by Quebec and Newfoundland.[56] This captures the dilemma of a province whose economy is unable to generate enough jobs to retain its young people. One of the consequences of this is a relatively high level of dependence on both federal and provincial transfers to businesses and consumers. About 16 per cent of gross provincial product is accounted for by public administration and defense, compared to about 7 per cent for Canada as a whole.[57] Nova Scotia's private sector economy, like those of the other Atlantic provinces, is relatively weak. The ratio of private to public investment is about 2 to 1 (1987), compared to about 3.5 to 1 for the national economy. Three of Nova Scotia's most prominent private sector manufacturing establishments, Michelin Tire, Volvo and Litton Industries, were attracted to the province partly on the strength of the public subsidies they received from the provincial government.

The weakness of the private sector economy has provided the basis for provincial intervention through the tax system (for example, the sales tax exemption for purchases of machinery and equipment used in R&D), through grants to companies locating in the province, through indirect subsidies like provincial labour legislation and through direct investment. Support for industrial R&D activity through the Nova Scotia Research Foundation Corporation, equity for higher-risk businesses through the Venture Capital Program, manpower training programmes that effectively subsidize the labour costs of provincial businesses and preference for provincial suppliers in government procurement are additional instruments of industrial policy in Nova Scotia.

There is nothing remarkable about this catalogue of policy instruments. Indeed, the complete list of government assistance for business is less extensive than in either Ontario or Quebec; a fact that partly reflects the much more diversified state of those two larger economies.[58] A couple aspects of Nova Scotia's industrial policy are, however, worth highlighting for what they reveal about the business-government relationship in an economically weak province.

One of these is public investment. The province has relatively few crown corporations—many fewer than in Manitoba and Saskatchewan, provinces of roughly comparable size, but where state ownership has been a favoured policy instrument of CCF-NDP governments. But a couple of Nova Scotia's crown corporations are noteworthy. One of these is the Sydney Steel Company (Sysco), taken over by the province in 1967 when its private owner proposed to shut down its foundries. This would have left 4,000 workers without jobs, and would have devastated a local economy that was already in serious decline because of its uncompetitive coal industry. Since its takeover, Sysco has been a regular drain on the public purse, receiving $865 million in combined federal and provincial support between 1967 and 1986, at the same time as employment dropped to about 1,200 jobs.[59] A perennial money-loser, it almost certainly would have lost more over the years had it not been for state purchases like those of Canadian National, and the subsidy provided by DEVCO, a federal crown corporation, which has sold coal to Sysco at below cost. Sysco represents a classic case of a state bail-out, followed by a steady flow of public money for political reasons rather than for any reasonable expectation of eventual profitability. Its history is one of political reaction to economic events.

A rather different role was intended for another of the province's crown corporations, Industrial Estates Limited (IEL). When IEL was established in 1957 it was Canada's first industrial development corporation, whose role was "the promotion, diversification and development of industrial activity in Nova Scotia."[60] It was a model that would be followed by several other provincial governments. Much of IEL's financial assistance has been directed to smaller firms, but it is the larger subsidies—often to foreign-owned corporations—that have captured the most attention. Some of these have ended in financial collapse, notably IEL's support of Clairtone (a manufacturer of colour televisions) and of Deuterium (a heavy water plant). Others, notably the investment subsidies used to attract Michelin Tire to the province, have been more successful if judged from the standpoint of generating long-term employment.

Provincial assistance to private investors has often been accompanied by financial support from Ottawa. For example, the federal government subsidized the training of Clairtone's Nova Scotia workforce in the 1960s. More recently, Ottawa has provided $42 million to Michelin Tire for investment in a new production facility, with the province contributing an additional $14 million. This money is paid under a General Development Subsidiary Agreement between DRIE and the government of Nova Scotia. Subsidiary agreements were also entered into during the 1980s for industrial development in the Strait of Canso region of the province, and to encourage ocean industries. Ottawa has also subsidized the province's money-losing steel industry, most recently through agreeing to cover 70 per cent of a $150 million modernization for Sysco's production facility.

Combined federal and provincial support for the same firm is not something one finds only in Nova Scotia and other have-not provinces. But what is noteworthy about this dual assistance in these economically weaker provinces is that it is rare for any major new investment to be made *without subsidies from both levels of government*. The latitude that a government like that of Nova Scotia has in making industrial policy is seriously constrained by the weakness of provincial public revenues. Not only is the province more dependent on federal personal income transfers to subsidize purchasing power than are the wealthier provinces, it is also more dependent on Ottawa for a large part of its ability to attract and keep private sector investment in Nova Scotia.

Federal Regional Industrial Policy

In a broad sense, Ottawa has always had something that could be called regional industrial policy. Tariffs and railway lines were hotly contested political issues in the post-Confederation period precisely because they were expected to have different economic consequences for different regions. A perennial complaint of the Western and Eastern provinces has been that Ottawa's economic policies (and the activities of the Department of Industry, Trade and Commerce) have favoured industrial development in Ontario and Quebec, at the expense of consumers and industries in the "hinterland" regions. The political weight of business interests in central Canada, and the votes at stake in Ontario and Quebec, have translated into federal economic policies that have favoured the "industrial heartland." On perhaps the only occasion when a federal government (Liberal) chose to align itself with regional economic interests outside of central Canada, squarely against the preferences of the industrial heartland, the result was a resounding defeat in the 1911 election. The issue was free trade with the United States, a policy overwhelmingly opposed by the Ontario and Quebec industrialists whose markets were protected by high tariff walls.

While Ottawa's economic policies have always had consequences for the pattern of regional industrial development in this country, the beginnings of *regional industrial policy* as a specialized field of economic policy with its own bureaucratic apparatus date from the late 1960s. The creation in 1968 of the Department of Regional Economic Expansion (DREE) raised the profile of regional industrial policy by giving it an institutional focus. DREE provided both a symbolic affirmation of Ottawa's commitment to assisting the economies of the have-not provinces and a channel through which this assistance would flow. Since then Ottawa's regional economic policy has undergone several major reforms, affecting the manner in which economic assistance decisions are made and implemented. Primary responsibility for this policy field currently rests with the Department of Regional Industrial Expansion (DRIE). The evolution of federal policy in this field has been extensively documented by others.[61]

Federal assistance from DREE to DRIE, and through business investment incentives available under the tax system, have been geared toward encouraging the sort of industrial activity that characterizes central Canada's industrial economy. This emphasis, economist Harvey Lithwick argues, may well run counter to an optimal strategy for *national* economic development.

Lithwick suggests that if the well-being of the national economy is best promoted by specialization—which means in effect that different regions of the country will have different sectoral mixes, depending on their particular advantages—then a policy that encourages economic diversity within all regions is economically wrongheaded.[62] The federal Task Force on Program Review acknowledged this contradiction in its assessment of regional development programs. In the words of its *Report*:

> Unfortunately national economic efficiency does not easily fit with interregional equity....for example, while the expansion of a plant may provide benefits for the region in which it is located, it could be adding capacity to an industry which on the whole is already suffering from an over-capacity situation.[63]

Of course such a policy may carry political advantages; for instance, recall the controversy over the Conservative government's 1988 decision to award a multi-million dollar service contract for the CF-18 fighter planes to Montreal-based Bombardier instead of to Winnipeg-based Bristol Aerospace, despite a bureaucratic recommendation that the Winnipeg company be chosen. The CF-18 decision confirms how important political considerations are in Ottawa's decisions on where to locate job-creating investments. This and other procurement decisions constitute an important part of Ottawa's regional economic assistance. Indeed, the shipbuilding industry of Eastern Canada has been sustained for decades by federal purchases. New Brunswick's share of the Canadian Patrol Frigate contract awarded in 1984 caused the level of federal procurement dollars spent in that province to jump five-fold to about $1,000 per capita (compared to $321 per capita for Canada as a whole in 1983-84).[64]

We should not conclude, however, that the economies of the have-not provinces have been the only (or even the main) beneficiaries of Ottawa's procurement policy. The Task Force on Program Review reported that the per capita level of spending by the federal government between 1979-1984 was higher in Ontario than in any other province.[65] Despite Ottawa's efforts to decentralize purchasing, the locational and industrial advantages of Ontario continue to give its economy a formidable edge in the competition for federal government contracts.

There is a consensus that the billions of dollars of economic assistance that successive federal governments have channelled into the economically-weaker provinces has not promoted the ostensible goal of economic development. The economies of these provinces show no signs of having become less dependent on the state life-support system. Public sector investment accounts for close to half of all investment in Atlantic Canada. The investment incentives provided under DRIE and through the tax system have been accused of multiple sins: of encouraging an inefficient pattern of investment; of having a bias towards investment in new capital rather than job creation; and of transferring income to businesses that would have invested anyway, without producing new jobs in a self-sufficient private sector. But as Donald Savoie and John Chenier observe:

> The fact remains that no researcher has ever been able to state clearly the full impact of regional incentives either on slow-growth regions or on the location intentions of firms, even those that did receive a grant. *About all that can be said is that things could have been worse for slow-growth regions if no regional incentives had been available.*[66]

ENDNOTES

1. Canada, *Report of the Royal Commission on Dominion-Provincial Relations* (Ottawa: King's Printer, 1940), Vol. 54.
2. *Ibid.*, 54-65.
3. The following discussion is based on H.V. Nelles, *The Politics of Development* (Toronto: Macmillan, 1974), chapter two.
4. *Ibid.*, 102.
5. All of the major writers on Canadian federalism agree on this point. See, for example, Garth Stevenson, *Unfulfilled Union*, revised edition (Toronto: Gage, 1988); Alan C. Cairns, *Constitution, Government and Society in Canada*, edited by Douglas E. Williams (Toronto: McClelland and Stewart, 1988), especially Part III; Donald V. Smiley, *Canada in Question: Federalism in the Eighties*, 3rd edition (Toronto: McGraw-Hill Ryerson, 1980); Peter Leslie, *Federal State, National Economy* (Toronto: University of Toronto Press, 1987); and Richard Simeon, "Federal-Provincial Relations," in *The Canadian Encyclopedia*, 2nd edition, Vol. 2 (Edmonton: Hurtig Publishers, 1988), 754-55.
6. James Mallory, *Social Credit and Federal Power in Canada* (Toronto: University of Toronto Press, 1954).
7. *Ibid.*, 37.
8. *Ibid.*, 55.
9. *Ibid.*, 55.
10. *Ibid.*, 54.
11. James Macpherson, "Economic Regulation and the British North America Act," in *Business Law Journal*, 5 (1980-81), 172-220.
12. *Ibid.*, 219-20.
13. *Caloil v. Attorney-General of Canada* (1971) S.C.R., 543 and *Reference re Anti-Inflation Act* (1976) 2 S.C.R., 373.
14. *Canadian Industrial Gas & Oil Ltd. v. Government of Saskatchewan* (1978) 2

S.C.R., 545; *Central Canadian Potash Co. Ltd. v. Government of Saskatchewan* (1979) 1 S.C.R., 42.

15. Canadian constitutional expert Peter Hogg agreed with Macpherson's argument. See Hogg's "Comments," in *Business Law Journal*, 5 (1980-81), 220.

16. John D. Whyte, "Federal Powers Over the Economy: Finding New Jurisdictional Room," in *Canadian Business Law Journal*, 13:3 (December 1987), 257-302.

17. Patrick Monahan, "The Supreme Court and the Economy," in I. Bernier and A. Lajoie, research coordinators, *The Supreme Court of Canada as an Instrument of Political Change*, Vol. 47 of the research studies for the Royal Commission on Economic Union and Development Prospects for Canada (Toronto: University of Toronto Press, 1986), 105-78.

18. The interpretation of the P.O.G.G. clause in s.91 of the Constitution Act as an emergency power has been probably the major instance where the courts have used a communitarian conception as the basis for their reasoning. In cases involving such things as censorship and charges under so-called "hate laws," the courts generally have been unwilling to substitute their conception of the social good for that of elected legislatures—although since the passage of the Chart of Rights and Freedoms they have certainly weighed the law-makers' conception of the social good against both the individual guarantees set forth in the Charter and the "reasonable limits" provision of that document.

19. Monahan, "The Supreme Court and the Economy," 165.

20. Ted Morton and Leslie Pal, "Bliss v. Attorney General Canada: From Legal Defeat to Political Victory," in *Osgoode Hall Law Journal*, 24:1 (Spring 1986), 158-60.

21. M.W. Bucovetsky, "The Mining Industry and the Great Tax Reform Debate," in A. Paul Pross, edition, *Pressure Group Behaviour in Canadian Politics* (Toronto: McGraw-Hill Ryerson, 1975), 89-114.

22. See the discussion in John Richards and Larry Pratt, *Prairie Capitalism: Power and Influence in the New West* (Toronto: McClelland and Stewart, 1979), chapter eleven.

23. Jeanne Kirk Laux and Maureen Appel Molot, "The Potash Corporation of Saskatchewan," in Allan Tupper and G. Bruce Doern, eds., *Public Corporations and Public Policy in Canada.* (Montreal: Institute for Research on Public Policy, 1981), 194. See also Aidan Vining, "Provincial Hydro Utilities," in Tupper and Doern, *Public Corporations*, 161, 165.

24. This paragraph draws on the interpretation in Cairns, Chandler and Moull, "Constitutional Change and the Private Sector: The Case of the Resource Amendment," in *Osgoode Hall Journal*, 24:2 (Summer 1986), 299-313.

25. *Ibid.*, 302-304.

26. *Reference re Offshore Mineral Rights of British Columbia* (1967) S.C.R., 792; *Reference re Mineral and Other Natural Resources of the Continental Shelf* (1983) 145 D.L.R. (3d) 9.

27. Cairns, Chandler and Moull, "Constitutional Change and the Private Sector," 310.
28. Richard J. Schultz, *Federalism, Bureaucracy and Public Policy: The Politics of Highway Transport Regulation* (Montreal: McGill-Queen's, 1980), 148.
29. See *Ibid.*, especially chapter eight.
30. Cairns, "The Governments, and Societies of Canadian Federalism," in Cairns, *Constitution, Government and Society in Canada*, 167.
31. *Ibid.*, 158.
32. William D. Coleman, *Business and Politics: A Study of Collective Action* (Montreal: McGill-Queen's University Press, 1988), Table 3, 37.
33. This text is based on a sample of 88 business associations that constitute the most influential organizations in each three-digit category of the Canadian Standard Industrial Classification.
34. Coleman, *Business and Politics*, 260.
35. Statistics Canada, *Provincial Economic Accounts*, Cat. 13-213.
36. R.A. Young, Philippe Faucher and André Blais, "The Concept of Province-Building: A Critique," in *CJPS* XVII:4 (December 1984), 785.
37. Two of the major works using this concept are Richards and Pratt, *Prairie Capitalism* and Kenneth McRoberts, *Quebec: Social Change and Political Crisis*, 3rd edition (Toronto: McClelland and Stewart, 1988).
38. McRoberts, *Ibid.*, 164.
39. Francophone business leaders were prominent members of the task forces on regulations, privatization and government functions and structures, established by the Bourassa government in 1986. The reports of these three task forces all called for significant trimming of the provincial state.
40. Richards and Pratt, *Prairie Capitalism*, 167.
41. Rolf Mirus, "Opportunities for Portfolio Diversification" and comments by Stephen Jarislowsky in the special issue of *Canadian Public Policy*, VI (1980), 236-44, 251-53.
42. There are exceptions to this general rule. Alberta Government Telephone Limited is the province's publicly-owned telephone utility. It behaves and performs in ways indistinguishable from privately-owned, regulated telephone monopolies in other provinces. Like Saskatchewan and Manitoba, which also have publicly-owned telephone companies, the political power of farmers and rural constitutions earlier in this century helps to explain the choice of public ownership.
43. See All Tupper, "Pacific Western Airlines," in Tupper and Doern, *Public Corporations*, 317.
44. A first-rate analysis of these events is provided in Allan Tupper, *Bill S-31 and the Federalism of State Capitalism* (Kingston: Institute of Intergovernmental Relations, Queen's University, 1983), discussion paper #18.
45. *Ibid.*, 24.
46. Barrie McKenna, "Power Says Meech Row Lost Firm Two Big Deals," in *The Globe and Mail* (10 May, 1990), B1.

47. Allan Tupper, *Public Money in the Private Sector* (Kingston: Institute of Intergovernmental Relations, Queen's University, 1982), 83.

48. Colin Languedoc, "Lawyers' fortunes tied to local economy," in *Financial Post 500* (Summer 1988), 194.

49. The "doom and gloom" view of provincial investment has been popularized by books like Philip Mathias, *Forced Growth* (Toronto: Lorimer, 1971) and Walter Stewart, *Uneasy Lies the Head: The Truth about Canada's Crown Corporations* (Toronto: Collins, 1987).

50. See Michael Jenkin, *The Challenge of Diversity* (Ottawa: Science Council of Canada, 1983), background study No. 50 and Richard Bird, *Industrial Policy in Ontario* (Toronto: Ontario Economic Council, 1985). Bird agrees that Ontario has a tradition of non-intervention, but notes increasing state activity in recent years (see pages 54-65).

51. Statistics Canada, *Provincial Government Enterprise Finance 1988*, Cat. 61-204, 98-101.

52. Bird, *Industrial Policy in Ontario*, 65.

53. All of these investment figures are calculated from the data in Statistics Canada, *Private and Public Investment in Canada 1988*, Cat 61-206 annual, 14-15.

54. McRoberts, *Quebec*, 434.

55. A summary of these reports and their political context, is provided in *ibid.*, 404-10.

56. Statistics Canada, *Postcensual Annual Estimates of Population by Marital Status, Age, Sex and Components of Growth for Canada, Provinces and Territories*, Cat. 91-210 annual.

57. Nova Scotia, Department of Development, *Building Competitiveness: A White Paper on Economic Development* (1984), 9.

58. See the inventories of provincial programme in J. Peter Johnson, *Government Financial Assistance Programs in Canada*, 4th edition (Toronto: Butterworths, 1986).

59. "Sydney's Costly Symbol," in *Maclean's* (8 December 1986), 26-27.

60. Quoted in Roy E. George, *The Life and Times of Industrial Estates Limited*, No. 93 (Halifax: Institute of Public Affairs, Dalhousie University), 7.

61. See Donald Savoie, *Federal-Provincial Collaboration* (Montreal: McGill-Queen's, 1981); Savoie, *Regional Economic Development: Canada's Search for Solutions* (Toronto: University of Toronto Press, 1986); W. Coffey and M. Polese, eds., *Still Living Together: Recent Trends and Future Directions in Canadian Regional Development* (Montreal: Institute for Research on Public Policy, 1987); and W. Lithwick, "Federal Government Regional Economic Development Policies: An Evaluative Survey," in Norrie, research coordinator, *Disparities and Interregional Adjustment*, Vol. 64 for the Royal Commission on the Economic Union and Development Prospects for Canada (1986).

62. Lithwick *Ibid.*, 110-111.

63. Canada, Task Force on Program Review, *Economic Growth: Services and Subsidies to Business* (Ottawa: Supply and Services, 1985), 108.

64. Canada, Task Force on Program Review, *Management of Government: Procurement*, 201,205.

65. This is based on contracts awarded through the Department of Supply and Services, and does not include purchases by federal crown corporations.

66. Donald Savoie and John Chenier, "The State and Development: The Politics of Regional Development Policy" in Coffey and Polese, eds., *Still Living Together*, 416, emphasis added.

PART 4

BUSINESS INFLUENCE

Chapter 7

Business Organization and Lobbying

In this chapter, attention focusses on the political organization of business in Canada, and on the methods and channels used by business organizations to influence government policy. Here we look at different sorts of business organizations, and at business lobbying and pressure politics. In the next chapters we examine the relationship between business, the media and political parties.

The enormous resources that organized business can muster for the purposes of influencing public policy provide a significant advantage over most other groups in the battle for the ear of government. Yet this advantage in the realm of resources and pressure politics is just one of a number of complementary bases of business power, and it is worth recalling the three other aspects of business power mentioned in Chapter One.

BUSINESS POWER REVISITED

First and foremost, business power has a *structural* base resting on the state's dependency on private business to provide the economic surplus that ultimately funds everything the state does. If profits start to dry up and bankruptcies begin to occur on a large scale, or if many companies pack up and move to other parts of the world, then the loss of employment and tax revenue would have an extremely serious impact on the ability to fund state programmes and pay the salaries of state personnel. Needless to say, such a situation would also have a detrimental impact on the re-election chances of incumbent politicians.

The structural basis of business power means that the state simply cannot ignore the question of business profitability because the state itself suffers if business fails. Consequently, state policy must be directed towards providing the necessary support, subsidies and incentives for profitable business enterprise, and must maintain a favourable climate for private investment. As James O'Connor has argued (see Chapter Three), the state must intervene to assist capital because the state's own power rests on the revenue it gets from the capitalist economy (through taxation, etc.).[1]

Limitations on this structural power are imposed by the nature of the democratic process in which policy-makers have to respond (albeit infrequently and imperfectly) to the voice of the people. This voice is not always in tune with the overall requirements of business, and sometimes politicians are forced to bow to popular pressure even when this conflicts with business needs.

More commonly, however, the public is sympathetic towards business profitability and supportive of government measures to maintain the health of the private economy. Thus the imperatives of capital accumulation and the imperatives of the democratic process are often in substantial harmony. State intervention to assist private business is frequently supported even by sections of society that are normally hostile towards business, such as the labour movement. In the long-run, labour may have an "objective" interest in destroying capitalism, but in the short-run, the immediate employment prospects, job security, income levels and standards of living of most working people are objectively tied to the prosperity of capitalism. If business fails, the first victims are often the workers.

The structural basis of business power is in itself an extremely potent force impelling state policies in a pro-business direction, but business also has cultural and ideological forces in its favour. Business power has a *cultural-ideological* dimension based on a widespread faith in the legitimacy of the private market system and the private corporation, underpinned by a predominantly materialist and individualist culture. The dominant sets of ideas and values to which policy-makers (and the rest of the population) are exposed throughout their lives are ones sympathetic to private enterprise and hostile to the consideration of radical alternatives. This is particularly true in North America, and is buttressed by the fact that most of the communications media are owned by private sector corporations (see Chapter Eight). The cultural and ideological dominance of business has a diffuse impact in shaping attitudes, and is so pervasive that most people take it for granted and accept the business system as normal, natural or inevitable, without question.

In addition to the structural and the cultural-ideological bases of business power, there is another set of factors that works in business's favour, namely *elite linkages* that exist between the upper reaches of the corporate and political worlds. Control over economic activity is itself highly concentrated in Canada (as illustrated in Chapter Five), and at the highest levels the business world is interconnected by ownership linkages, interlocking directorships, social ties and common values. Socio-economic linkages also help to provide a basis for mutual understanding and empathy between corporate and political elites, and this is reinforced by an exchange of personnel between the two spheres. For instance, in the period 1945-89, nearly half of the federal cabinet ministers with economic policy responsibilities had backgrounds in big business (see Chapter Nine). In an earlier epoch the two realms were even more closely connected, with many individuals simultaneously being involved in business and politics. For the period around Confederation, such links were particularly evident in regard to financial and railway interests. As Leo Panitch points out, "A list of the board of directors of the Grand Trunk Railway reads like a list of the Fathers of Confederation."[2]

Today the rules concerning conflict of interest are a little stricter and ministers are required to give up their corporate directorships on taking office and to put stock holdings into a blind trust. But as Ralph Miliband notes, "It is easier for ministers to ditch their stocks and shares when appointed to public office than it is to ditch their basic sympathies and predispositions towards the business world."[3]

Elite linkages are compounded with structural and cultural-ideological factors in shaping state action towards business, and it is not always easy to identify which set of factors is most significant in explaining state policy. In general, these aspects of business power are more useful in accounting for broad patterns of policy rather than particular government decisions, and in the latter regard we also need to consider the fourth side of business power, namely *pressure politics*. It is here that political organizations representing various subsections of the business world are active in trying to influence policy-makers, sometimes in competition with one another. The rest of this chapter focusses on this aspect of business-government relations and examines business organizations, lobbying and political influence.

THE POLITICAL ORGANIZATION OF BUSINESS

Compared with many other Western capitalist countries, business organization in Canada is characterized by fragmentation rather than centralization. Unlike some European countries, Canada has no single comprehensive business association representing the collective interests of industry as a whole. Instead, several different organizations represent different sectors or fragments of Canadian business, and the presentation of business demands to government is disaggregated rather than collective. This group mosaic includes broad-based business associations, such as the Canadian Manufacturers' Association and the Business Council on National Issues, and it also includes a disparate array of trade associations that represent the interests of single industries. In addition to these, many larger corporations maintain their own "in-house" government relations divisions, while others use the services of lobbying firms to get their messages across to government decision-makers. These various organizational forms by which business interests are articulated will now be examined, starting at the most general level with broad-based business associations.

Broad-based Business Associations

These associations represent firms operating in many different industries, and serve as mechanisms for aggregating business interests across industrial boundaries. Yet none of these organizations is truly comprehensive, and each represents some subsection of the business world. The Business Council on National Issues represents big business; the Canadian Federation of Independent Business and the Canadian Organization of Small Business both represent small business; the Canadian Manufacturers' Association represents both big and small business, but exclusively in the manufacturing sector; the Conseil du Patronat du Québec and the Business Council of British Columbia are prominent regional organizations; and the Canadian Chamber of Commerce is a loose confederation of provincial and local chambers of commerce and boards of trade, mixed up with individual companies and other business associations.

The Business Council on National Issues

The Business Council on National Issues (BCNI) is a very exclusive club. Its members consist of the chief executive officers from 150 of the largest corporations in Canada which together generate annual revenues of over $275 billion, employ around 1.5 million people, and control assets of more than $750 billion (roughly 7 times the bookvalue of the federal government assets).[4]

Membership cuts across all sectors of Canadian business, although large crown corporations such as CN, Petro-Canada, Ontario Hydro and Hydro-Québec are excluded. All of Canada's big banks are represented, along with most of the largest insurance companies and investment dealers. Next to these are major names from manufacturing and resource industries such as Inco, Alcan, Stelco, Dofasco, Noranda, Dominion Textiles and Seagrams, as well as Canadian-owned conglomerates like BCE, Canadian Pacific, Brascan, Imasco and Power Corporation. There is no requirement that corporations be Canadian-owned, and the BCNI represents a large number of branch plants of foreign multinationals including Ford of Canada, General Motors of Canada, General Electric Canada, Imperial Oil, Shell Canada, IBM Canada, Mitsui (Canada), Mitsubishi Canada and many others. This reflects the high proportion of foreign ownership in the Canadian economy. The members of the BCNI constitute the "big boys" of the corporate elite in Canada (not one of the 150 CEOs is a woman), and although some of the corporate barons such as the Reichmans, the Westons and the Bronfmans are not members themselves, they nevertheless have a voice through the CEOs of the companies that they control.

The BCNI was established in 1976 in order to defend corporations against an increasing barrage of criticism from the public and from a growing level of government regulation and intervention. The early 1970s was a period when changes in the world economy, such as the OPEC oil price increases in 1973-74 and the growth of new international competition, started to undermine the position of many Western industries. At the same time business in Canada was under attack from nationalists, environmentalists, consumer groups and other sections of society who were critical of corporate self-interest. Government was also becoming more active in regulatory policy, notably in the areas of foreign ownership and price controls and it had intervened directly in the oil industry with the establishment of Petro-Canada as a crown corporation in 1975. Corporations saw themselves being threatened from all directions, and business's image had become tarnished in the eyes of the public. The BCNI was a response to these challenges and an attempt to brush-up the image of big business in order to present the corporate world as being more socially responsible.

The model for the BCNI was the Business Roundtable in the United States which is a similar organization of CEOs set up in 1972 to facilitate lobbying by big business. However, the BCNI has a more visible public profile than the Business Roundtable, and is concerned not just with high level contacts with senior policy-makers, but also with the presentation of briefs and submissions to parliamentary committees, royal commissions and other official bodies.[5] Its president, Thomas D'Aquino, is also very active in touring the country, lecturing and speaking to the media, and presenting the Council's views on just about any subject in any forum. In this manner, the Council battles for the hearts and minds of the public as well as for those of top government policy-makers.

Rather than engaging in special pleading for the narrow interests of particular member corporations, the BCNI focusses on national public policy issues, and over the last ten years it has been involved with such issues as competition law reform, pension reform, defence policy, the federal deficit and free trade, to name but a few. In dealing with these issues the Council is organized into various task forces, each of which covers a broad policy area such as "international economy and trade" or "national finance." These are supported by a professional secretariat that conducts research and handles communications and administration. The Council also draws on the resources and specialist knowledge of its member corporations, and from time to time employs the services of outside experts as well. The BCNI prides itself on its ability to build a consensus on national issues within the big business community, despite the disparate interests of the different corporations it represents. It also tries to avoid an openly adversarial approach towards the labour movement and other groups in society, seeing itself as "building bridges" rather than undertaking frontal attacks. Its relations with government are characterized by quiet diplomacy and regular contact rather than confrontation, and it claims to be non-partisan (provided, of course, that your party has no objection to massive concentrations of corporate wealth).

The strength of the BCNI as an advocate of big business interests lies principally in its ability to speak for such a strategically important portion of

Canadian capital. Whatever the professionalism of its research, the eloquence of its arguments or the quality of its diplomacy, when an organization that controls $750 billion says something, then government has to listen seriously. In many respects policy-makers are quite happy with this situation, because it is a lot easier for government to consult with an association that has "collectivized" the inputs of 150 corporations, rather than trying to consult with each corporation separately. The BCNI thus plays an integrative role across business divisions and this is strengthened further by contacts with other business organizations such as the Canadian Manufacturers' Association (CMA), the Canadian Chamber of Commerce (CCC) and the Conseil du Patronat du Québec (CPQ) that are also members of the BCNI.

The Canadian Manufacturers' Association

The CMA is one of the oldest business associations currently in existence in Canada, and unlike the BCNI it represents firms solely in the manufacturing sector. Its roots can be traced to the early 1870s, with the efforts of Ontario-based manufacturers to organize themselves to lobby for higher levels of tariff protection. Spurred by persistent economic crises, the Ontario Manufacturers' Association was formed in 1874. Over the next few years it "carried on a vigorous campaign in favour of tariff protection."[6] During this period protectionist sentiment was growing, and by 1878 the Association's position was supported by commercial interests in Montreal that had previously been staunch free traders. The input of the Manufacturers' Association was apparent in the redirection of Canadian trade policy and the organization has been credited with playing a key role in drafting the National Policy tariffs of 1879.[7]

The organization's name was changed to the Canadian Manufacturers' Association in 1887, and today the CMA provides both political representation and information services to more than 3,000 member firms accounting for over 80 per cent of Canadian manufacturing output. All sizes of firms are represented, though to be eligible for membership a firm must have five or more employees and must be engaged in manufacturing in Canada. Seventy-five per cent of the members have less than 100 employees.[8] Membership fees are proportionate to the size of the company, and official positions within the CMA are generally dominated by the largest corporations that pay the most. With one exception all of the chairmen of the CMA's ten standing committees are representatives of large Canadian corporations or foreign multinationals.[9]

The CMA provides a variety of information services for its members and has a staff of specialists on numerous topics such as government grants and incentives, labour relations, taxation, exports and technology. It also conducts surveys, organizes seminars, publishes a newsmagazine and a trade index, provides low-cost insurance and offers a telephone "hotline" on product liability. Besides serving its corporate members, it also manages the affairs of 37 national and provincial trade associations, from the Adhesives and Sealants Manufacturers' Association of Canada to the Western Food Processors Association. These associations retain their independence but benefit from the expertise and resources that the CMA provides in such areas as presenting views to government, organizing conferences and mounting public relations campaigns.[10]

In the political arena the CMA monitors the activities of federal and provincial governments and engages in extensive lobbying across a wide spectrum of issues. In recent years it has claimed a major success in pressing for deregulation of the trucking industry, with the expectation that this would reduce manufacturers' freight rates. It, along with other business groups, was also very active in pushing for the adoption of the Canada-U.S. Free Trade Agreement and claimed that Ottawa's decision to initiate negotiations was "a major victory for the CMA's lobbying efforts."[11] In regard to taxation, the CMA has campaigned to have the manufacturers sales tax replaced by the broader Goods and Services Tax that would include service industries, and thus reduce the proportionate burden on manufacturing. It has also lobbied for a reduction in corporate income tax rates and, following the lead of the United States, for lower personal tax rates. Despite advocating tax cuts, the CMA also wants governments to reduce their budget deficits, and in this vein, the CMA has advocated large cuts in social programmes. In particular, it has targeted unemployment insurance and workers' compensation as areas where cuts should be made. At the same time, the CMA has lobbied for the retention (or extension) of wide-ranging tax breaks for corporations.[12] These issues are ones on which at least a minimal degree of consensus can be obtained across the organization's membership, and understandably the CMA tends to steer away from taking strong stands on issues where its membership is divided.

As is to be expected, the CMA has claimed a number of successes in its lobbying efforts, including free trade, deregulation, sales tax reform, the freeze on UI premiums for a number of years and opposition to a worldwide ban on the use of asbestos. But along with these it has also had policy defeats—for example, in the leaked budget of 1989 when the Conservative government increased Unemployment Insurance premiums, transferred the costs of UI entirely to employers and employees and imposed a new tax on the capital of large corporations.

In looking at these policy measures it is never easy to determine the impact that business groups like the CMA have had in influencing government actions. In this respect it is often easier to say when a particular organization has failed to influence public policy rather than when it has been successful. If a group wants something, lobbies government and fails to get it, then we have a reasonable indication of a lack of influence. However, if a group gets what it wants there is still the possibility that group pressure was not a decisive factor and government would have done it anyway for other reasons. Yet it is clear that as a well-funded, well-respected, institutionalized pressure group representing a major sector of Canadian economic activity, the CMA enjoys ready access to key policy-makers at the highest levels, and its demands always receive a hearing even if they are not always granted.

The Canadian Chamber of Commerce

While the CMA is the oldest broad-based business association in Canada, the Canadian Chamber of Commerce (CCC) is the largest. Founded in 1925, the CCC currently claims a membership of over 170,000, divided into five categories.[13]

> (1) *Organization Members.* In this category there are more than 500 community and provincial chambers of commerce or boards of trade (the terms are synonymous).
>
> (2) *Corporation Members.* The CCC gets the vast bulk of its financial support from several thousand corporations that are directly represented at the national level. These span across all regions and sectors of the economy and include both large and small business.
>
> (3) *Associate Members.* These consist of over 95 trade and professional associations representing particular industries or occupations. The CCC coordinates its activities with these groups in order to achieve a broader base of business pressure when dealing with government.
>
> (4) *Individual Members.* The CCC also has members who are individuals closely connected with Canadian business life, even if they do not represent specific corporations or associations.
>
> (5) *International Organization Members.* A number of international business organizations are also affiliated with the CCC, such as the Canada Taiwan Business Association, the Canada-Arab Business Council and the Canadian East European Trade Council. These are mostly concerned with trade development and they provide channels of communication between business people and government officials in different countries.

At the local level, chambers of commerce exist in most reasonably sized communities representing the business interests of firms and individuals in over 500 locations across Canada. These organizations are then affiliated both with a provincial chamber and the CCC. The CCC claims that it has these affiliated organizations in every federal riding throughout the country,[14] and these can be used to exert grassroots pressure on individual MPs.

Although community chambers pay fees to the provincial and national organizations, they are not subordinate entities, and the CCC has the character of a loose federation rather than a disciplined hierarchy. Concern with provincial government affairs is largely left up to the provincial associations while the community chambers focus on such things as industrial development, tourism and taxation at the local level.

At the national level the CCC makes representations to government on a long list of policy issues, including finance, external affairs, regional development, labour relations and other areas. Over recent years the Chamber's main policy objectives have included (a) reducing the federal deficit and the national debt while lowering personal and corporate tax rates; (b) cutting social programmes, especially unemployment insurance; (c) ending universality by "taxing-back" old age pensions and family allowances; (d) supporting the Free Trade Agreement; (e) reducing government regulation of business in many areas; and (f) privatizing crown corporations. Many of the CCC's positions are quite similar to the BCNI and the CMA. Together these business groups are sometimes referred to as the "Gang of Three," and their policy demands constitute the central core of the business agenda in Canada.

Like its affiliated chambers (and many other business associations) the CCC's functions fall into two main categories, namely political representation and membership services. Membership services include the provision of management training courses and business-government relations seminars for executives; a legislative intelligence programme called "Ottawa Watch" which provides custom-tailored information about legislative developments for subscribing members; a general counselling service incorporating a toll-free information "hotline"; and a variety of publications such as the *Ottawa Directory* and the *Parliamentary Directory* which give information about cabinet ministers, MPs, senators and their staffs, plus a bimonthly newsletter *Ottawa Update* and a quarterly magazine *Impact.*

As for political representation, the CCC sends out numerous briefs and position papers to federal government departments, agencies and parliamentary committees, as well as engaging in more personal lobbying at all levels of decision-making. Its annual reports are packed with photographs of meetings with senior cabinet ministers and the prime minister, and the CCC enjoys reasonably good access to top policy-makers and generally smooth relations with state officials. Interaction is regular and cordial and takes place both formally and informally, for instance at working dinners where CEOs meet with Department of Finance officials for off-the-record discussions. Good access is of course no guarantee of political influence, but nonetheless it is an important first step—one that many other groups would like to have.

One of the main strengths of the Canadian Chamber of Commerce is that it is a federal network and can exert pressure on government at different levels simultaneously. This is particularly useful given that many issues in Canadian public policy cut across the jurisdictional boundaries between federal and provincial governments. The network of regional and local organizations also provides a geographically diverse base for putting pressure on policy-makers.

The main weakness of the CCC is that it attempts to aggregate the views of a complete cross section of business in Canada, and this makes its more difficult to develop a consensus position on many issues. Consequently, the CCC's policy stands tend to be more diluted and less focussed than other business groups that speak for particular sections of capital such as the BCNI (big business), the CMA (manufacturing) and the CFIB (small business).

Canadian Federation of Independent Business

The CFIB is the principal organization in Canada specifically representing small-and medium-sized businesses. It was founded in 1971 by John Bulloch, whose father was a politically vocal, small businessman in Toronto, and by 1989 it had a membership of over 82,000. Its origins lie in a mini tax-revolt in 1969 against a federal government proposal to raise corporate tax rates for small businesses. Bulloch was outraged by this proposal and published an attack against it in a newspaper. The attack struck a chord with many others in small businesses and several hundred contacted Bulloch offering their support, and from this response he set up the Canadian Council on Fair Taxation which organized rallies across Canada and began fundraising.[15] In 1971 Bulloch disbanded this ad hoc body and set up the CFIB as a permanent association in its place.

The Federation (which is actually a unitary organization) was modelled on the National Federation of Independent Business in the United States, and the bulk of its members have under 10 employees, with the majority being involved in retailing and other service industries.[16] It is arguably one of the more democratic business associations in Canada and its policy positions are based on regular surveys of members' views which are then conveyed to politicians, bureaucrats and the media. The professional staff of the CFIB maintains regular contact with federal and provincial policy-makers, and continually monitors public policy developments. It conducts detailed research into issues that concern its membership and draws up briefs that are submitted to government. The Federation is also involved in a publicity programme using the media, schools and numerous speaking engagements to get its message across to the public and keep itself and its goals in the spotlight.

In addition, the CFIB provides information services to its members on such things as government programmes and regulations and advice on taxation. Although the CFIB deals with over 4,000 individual requests from members per year, it is still primarily an organization that is concerned with political action and lobbying rather than member services. In some respects the CFIB's political goals are similar to other broad-based business associations, and it favours deficit reduction without tax increases, free trade, privatization, less regulation, more tax breaks, etc. However, it also has some more particular bugbears. These include Statistics Canada which it accuses of harassing its members with interminable surveys, and Canada Post where the CFIB campaigned vigorously to have the right to strike removed. On some issues it has been in direct conflict with other business groups, for example, with the BCNI concerning the latter's attempts to end special concessionary tax rates for small businesses. It also has a more credible interest in an effective competition policy than organizations representing big business.

In contrast with most of the other broad-based business associations the CFIB has adopted a more confrontational style, and its literature speaks of countering big business, standing up to big labour and challenging government.[17] It is particularly militant in its opposition to organized labour, and while the BCNI talks about "building bridges" to other groups in society, the CFIB is more inclined to reach for the dynamite. This is reflected in its demands for easier union decertification, tighter controls on picketing, denial of the right to strike in the public sector and opposition to pay equity.

Its lobbying activities are also more aggressive, more publicity-oriented and less reliant on quiet diplomacy. In 1974, for example, the CFIB protested against an increase in employers' UI contributions by encouraging members to make the payments to Ottawa on cheques 3 feet long and 15 inches wide, and in 1981 John Bulloch was hardly moderate in describing the federal budget as a "cancerous abortion" and a "bag of snakes."[18] In more recent years, however, this stridency and showmanship seem to have dissipated somewhat.

Ideologically the CFIB is an anti-statist champion of individual enterprise, and this disposition is also reflected in a rival small business association, namely the Canadian Organization of Small Business. This group is much smaller than the CFIB, with around 6,000 members, and it was formed in 1979 as a splinter group that broke away from the CFIB in fairly acrimonious circumstances. Both organizations aim to represent the same clientele and the main difference between them is that the COSB tends to put greater emphasis on member services rather than lobbying.

Unlike large corporations, small businesses have very few resources for dealing with government on their own, and consequently associations play an important part in their political representation. Yet in Canada small businesses have several organizations from which to choose. In addition to the CFIB and COSB, they are wooed by the Chamber of Commerce and individual trade associations, and (if they are in manufacturing) by the CMA as well. Besides these, there are also regional associations such as the Conseil du patronat du Quebec and the Business Council of British Columbia.

The Conseil du Patronat du Québec

The Conseil du Patronat du Québec (CPQ) was founded in 1969 as an organization representing the interests of employers in Quebec. Its members are either individual corporations or Quebec employers' associations such as the Association des proprietaires d'autobus du Québec and the Fédération de la construction du Québec. In 1989 the CPQ had 430 corporate members and 116 affiliated associations providing a budget of approximately $1 million per year. The corporate membership is dominated by giant enterprises, many of which are foreign-owned multinationals such as BP, Honeywell, Marconi, GE, Gillette, RCA, Unilever and the big three automakers. Among the Canadian companies are Bell Canada, Eatons, Bombardier, Noranda, CP, Dominion Textile, Stelco and all the big banks, as well as some lesser lights such as Noel and Eddy Verchere and Les Croustilles Yum Yum Inc.[19]

Unlike most of the other business associations discussed previously, the CPQ admits crown corporations as members; therefore, CN, Hydro-Québec, Atomic Energy of Canada Ltd., Petro-Canada, Sidbec-Dosco and other public sector institutions are represented. The CPQ also represents members from all sectors of the economy and thus is in a good position to act as a spokesperson for a wide range of business interests in Quebec. But there is the usual trade-off between diversity of membership and coherence of policy positions, and the CPQ, like other broad-based business associations, has difficulty manufacturing a consensus on some issues.

The CPQ's main focus of activity is lobbying the Quebec government (although it does occasionally involve itself with federal issues), and to this end it makes presentations, provides briefs and information, issues press releases, etc. It also provides information services to its members on particular problems or general legislative issues.

One of the CPQ's principal preoccupations is with labour legislation, on which it takes fairly militant anti-union positions. It has lobbied for stricter controls over unions; removing the right to strike for public utility workers and those in the health services; making it easier to hire replacement ("scab") labour; and opposing employee participation on boards of directors. Other policy objectives include privatization, a reduction in the public debt, lower taxation, free trade, unrestricted foreign investment and less state intervention generally.[20] These goals are, in the main, congruent with the objectives of other broad-based business associations, which is perhaps not surprising as there is a considerable overlapping membership across these organizations.

The Business Council of British Columbia

The Business Council of British Columbia was formed in 1966 and represents 185 large and medium-sized corporations in different sectors of the regional economy. Its member companies employ over 250,000 people in British Columbia.[21]

In common with the CPQ, one of the BCBC's main preoccupations is with industrial relations, and its formation was a response to the perceived power of trade unions in British Columbia. However, it has now become concerned with a more diverse range of policy interests.[22] It focusses its attention at both provincial and federal levels of government, and has recently been involved with issues of privatization, workers' compensation and free trade.[23] It has a permanent staff of policy experts, an ability to conduct research into a variety of issue-areas, and a legitimacy provided by the financial significance of its member companies for the B.C. economy. These factors make it reasonably easy for the BCBC to get its message across to the provincial government, especially when the Social Credit Party holds the reins of power.

In conclusion, the picture of broad-based business associations in Canada is one of a disparate collection of different organizations, frequently with overlapping memberships, each competing for the ear of government, and each representing a slightly different portion of the business community. In short, it is a picture of fragmentation rather than centralization.

Trade Associations

Trade associations, representing the interests of firms operating in the same industry or segment of an industry, are a widespread phenomenon in business-government relations in Canada. They are more narrowly focussed than broad-based associations, and their membership is generally smaller and more exclusive. Politically they cannot claim to speak for such extensive segments of business, but by the same token they have less difficulty in reconciling internal policy conflicts amongst their members. Because they are narrower they tend to be more cohesive and are better able to take clear-cut stands on policy issues that affect them. In terms of policy objectives they are normally less concerned about national issues such as the deficit, privatization or macro-economic policy, although they do sometimes add their voice to the broad-based associations on these issues. Instead they are normally more concerned with narrower measures that affect their industry in particular, such as specific tax breaks, trade barriers and regulations.

Estimates vary as to the number of national trade associations in Canada, with Isaiah Litvak calculating that there were over 700 in 1981, while William Coleman, using a different definition, puts the figure at 482 for 1980.[24] Using a more restrictive definition of trade associations than either Litvak or Coleman, we managed to locate 403 national trade associations in Canada in 1988.[25] Of these, 40 (10 per cent) were in the resource sector, 171 (42 per cent) in the manufacturing and construction sector and 192 (48 per cent) in the service sector.

Membership size varies according to the structure and scope of the industry. For example, in automobile manufacturing where domestic production is highly concentrated, the Motor Vehicle Manufacturers' Association has only eight members, whereas in the travel industry, the Alliance of Canadian Travel Associations has approximately 3,000 members dispersed across the country.

Frequently, a single industry will contain more than one trade association, with different subsections of an industry each having its own organization. In the food processing industry Coleman and Jacek analyzed 14 "nationally relevant" associations,[26] while in the insurance business we found 18 different trade associations covering a hodge-podge of industry segments including underwriters, adjusters and brokers in separate fields such as marine, fire, automobile and life insurance. There were even separate organizations for boiler and machine underwriters, and for those concerned specifically with nuclear power insurance. These sorts of organizational divisions are indicative of the high degree of political fragmentation of business in Canada.

Other industries are also divided, with a pattern of trade associations corresponding to the internal divisions and political conflicts that take place within the industry. For instance, in drug manufacturing a major battle has taken place between the Pharmaceutical Manufacturers' Association of Canada (PMAC), which represents almost exclusively the interests of multinational drug companies, and the Canadian Drug Manufacturers' Association (CDMA), which represents the generic drug makers. PMAC wanted a longer period of patent protection for brand-name drugs to prevent generic manufacturers from selling cheap substitutes. Despite increased costs to consumers, PMAC's lobbying campaign was largely successful, and a bill granting extended patent protection was passed and given royal assent in November 1987. On this issue competing products and opposing policy goals provided a basis for organizational conflict within the industry.

The Functions of Trade Associations

While trade associations are not solely concerned with lobbying and political action, it is nevertheless one of their principal functions, and a survey by Isaiah Litvak showed that 90 per cent of these associations ranked government relations amongst their top four activities.[27] In general, trade associations fulfill five political functions for their members:

> (1) *Monitoring.* Trade associations act as the political eyes and
> ears of an industry, monitoring legislation and legislative
> proposals, government regulations, political appointments,

judicial rulings, ministers' speeches, articles in the press and emerging public issues. In this regard the association is able to provide information to its members on issues of common interest more cheaply than if each company tried to do it on its own.

(2) *Direct Lobbying.* This involves maintaining contacts with key policy-makers at all levels and attempting to persuade government officials of the industry's position. Included here are personal contacts on both a formal and informal basis and the presentation of briefs to government departments, regulatory agencies, parliamentary committees, task forces, commissions, tribunals, etc.

(3) *Indirect Lobbying.* Trade associations attempt to influence government policy indirectly by working on public opinion. Through public relations, advocacy advertising and use of the media, associations try to boost the industry's image and provide a more favourable climate for achieving the industry's goals.

(4) *Alliance-Building.* Associations try to broaden their political impact by forming political alliances with like-minded groups on particular issues in order to give greater weight to their lobbying efforts. This requires trade associations to engage in liaison with other groups on a regular basis, and also requires the political flexibility to realize that opponents on one issue may be friends on another.

(5) *Research.* In order to carry out all the previous functions, trade associations need to maintain a continuous research effort, both in regard to the substance of policy issues, and also in regard to the changing structures, processes and personnel of the political decision-making system.

In addition to these explicitly political functions, trade associations also maintain other 'non-political' services for their members; for instance, disseminating marketing and product information, setting technical standards and providing a forum for cooperation between the various companies in an industry.

Trade associations also perform functions that are useful to government policy-makers. Firstly, they constitute a means for aggregating and rationalizing the political input of numerous firms in any one line of business. It is much easier for bureaucrats and politicians to deal with a single organization representing an industry than it is to speak with a gaggle of individual companies each making its own special demands, sometimes in contradiction with one another. It is less confusing for policy-makers if the necessary discussions and compromises within the industry have been worked out prior to submitting demands to government. Government officials sometimes encourage the establishment of trade associations for this very reason—the Canadian Ocean Industries Association and the Canadian Railway and Transit Manufacturers' Association were both set up with encouragement from the federal Department of Regional Industrial Expansion. Occasionally financial assistance is also provided. For example, the Canadian Outdoor Power Equipment Association and the Canadian Die Casters' Association both have received federal government funding for some aspects of their operations.

Secondly, government policy-makers rely on trade associations for technical information and specialized knowledge about the nature of their industries. This is essential if costly mistakes are to be avoided in formulating industrial policies, and trade associations can be a great help in providing a level of specialized expertise that most government officials do not possess. It is unlikely that bureaucrats would propose changes to industry regulations or tariff rates for an industry's products without first consulting the relevant trade associations. In this way they can check that possible adverse side-effects have not been overlooked.

Thirdly, trade associations can be effective mechanisms for policy implementation, and can be instrumental in ensuring industry compliance with government regulations. In food processing, for example, industry associations were continuously involved in implementing regulations on product grading and standards, health protection, labelling and packaging, inspection and quality control.[28] Authority for policy implementation is in many cases delegated to the industry itself, reflecting the fact that government regulators simply do not have the manpower and resources to check up on every business to ensure that regulations are being enforced. Consequently, government is often forced to rely on the "voluntary compliance" of industry for the administration of policy, and trade associations play a role in encouraging such compliance and self-regulation. Because government bodies often depend on cooperation from trade associations to implement regulations, these industry organizations are normally closely consulted in formulating regulatory policy (see Chapter Eleven). If an industry objects vehemently to a particular regulation then "voluntary compliance" will be unlikely, and this acts as a constraint on government in setting regulatory policy for the industry.

The basis for mutual cooperation between government departments and trade associations can result in a close and consensual interaction between the two, with industry associations becoming incorporated into clientele relationships with sections of government (see Chapter Three). In this manner trade associations can be co-opted into the policy process and be granted a privileged position in both the formation and implementation of policy outputs.

These cordial and mutually supportive relationships are often further enhanced by personnel linkages, and trade associations are renowned for giving high paying jobs to former bureaucrats and politicians. Practising bureaucrats and politicians are, needless to say, aware of this phenomenon and they are also aware that associations do not normally give jobs to people who have been antagonistic towards the industry or overly strenuous in imposing regulations. This practice has the effect of helping to integrate government more closely with business, and it offers the association the advantage of obtaining high quality personnel who are familiar with the relevant components of the policy process and who also have personal contacts in government. Examples of former public officials who were subsequently hired by trade associations are numerous: William Neville who was chief of staff in the Prime Minister's Office under Joe Clark, and who was responsible for setting up the PMO under Brian Mulroney, went on to become president and chief lobbyist of the Canadian Tobacco Manufacturers' Council; former minister of Consumer and Corporate Affairs, Judy Erola, became president of the Pharmaceutical Manufacturers' Association of Canada; Jean Bélanger was director of the Chemicals Branch of the Department of Industry, Trade and Commerce before becoming president of the Canadian Chemical Producers' Association; Dan Romanko was hired as managing director of the Canadian Steel Producers' Association after being group manager of the Primary Industries division of Revenue Canada. The list goes on.

Personal contacts and specialized experience can help grease the wheels of political influence, but trade associations still face a number of problems in trying to shape government policy. Firstly, the structure of power *within* the federal government has become more centralized. Central agencies such as the Privy Council Office, the Prime Minister's Office, and the Treasury Board have assumed greater responsibility for the direction of policy, and these agencies are not very accessible to trade associations. It is no longer sufficient for industry representatives to influence departmental officials because the line departments have less autonomy in policy-making than they used to.[29]

Secondly, the fragmentation of associations in Canada means that rival groups are competing for the attention of government. Trade associations can face opposition not only from non-business groups, but from other business associations as well.

Finally, the narrow demand of trade associations must be evaluated by government in the context of broad policy objectives. If the goals of a particular trade association are in conflict with a major segment of Canadian capital, or if they conflict with the government's overall political agenda, then it is unlikely that the trade association will be successful, no matter who is at the helm.

Trade associations also have another limitation as far as some corporations are concerned, in that they articulate general industry goals but are not able to represent all the idiosyncratic needs of each individual company. For this reason some corporations also maintain their own custom-tailored lobbying capacity, either through their own in-house government relations/public affairs division, or through an outside firm of hired lobbyists or consultants.

Individual Corporate Action

Individual corporate action in the political arena has a number of advantages over the use of trade associations or other business organizations, but it also has a number of shortcomings. One of the main advantages is that corporations have greater control over the direction and content of lobbying when they do it themselves. Using business associations means making compromises with other firms over policy goals and political tactics, and this may not effectively serve the special objectives of particular companies.

Also, trade associations are not well placed to represent the needs of conglomerate enterprises. Trade associations deal with the interest of a distinct industry or industry segment, but conglomerates have operations in several different industries. Consequently, the political needs of such corporations cannot be completely fulfilled by a single trade association. Even if the corporation belongs to several trade associations, none of these in isolation can cover the unique mixture of subsidiary interests contained within a diversified conglomerate.

Finally, trade associations are inadequate when rival companies within an industry are competing for the ear (and pocketbook) of government, for instance, in the competition for government contracts. In these circumstances companies have to deal with government on their own.

The disadvantages of individual action include, for one, the expense. It is more costly for companies to fund their own customized lobbying activities than to share the costs of joining an association with other firms. Whether it is in the form of in-house government relations or hired lobbying firms, this option is not a cheap one, and risks duplicating the research and lobbying efforts of other companies or associations. Because of the expense, a formal structure for individual corporate action is more feasible for larger firms than it is for smaller ones.

Another disadvantage is that individual action foregoes the benefits of collective pressure. Hard pressed politicians and bureaucrats normally prefer to deal with broad aggregations of businesses rather than an array of individual companies or associations because it is quicker and less complicated that way. Thus, individual corporations may have difficulty getting access to policy-makers. In addition, they lose any claim to be representing broad segments of business opinion, and by focussing on individual self-interest they are denied the political asset of strength in numbers.

As mentioned previously, lobbying activity by individual corporations is organized in two principal ways: either within the corporate structure as a separate division handling government relations/public affairs, or alternatively, outside the corporate structure by hiring outside lobbyists and consultants. Both of these will now be examined briefly.

In-house Government Relations/Public Affairs

Government relations/public affairs is an important and expanding area of Canadian corporate activity, and in many corporations this function has become formalized in a separate division within the company. One of Canada's leading analysts of corporate public affairs, Andrew Gollner, conducted a survey of corporations drawn from the *Financial Post* list in 1982, and found that 68 per cent of responding firms had a distinct public affairs department and over half of these departments had been set up in the last decade.[30] Gollner identified three principal reasons why corporations had established a public affairs department:

(1) The increasing socio-political complexity of the business environment.

(2) The growth of government intervention.

(3) The impact of external issues on profits.

Each factor was rated as significant or highly significant by well over 60 per cent of the responding firms.[31]

Public affairs departments normally do not just deal with government policy-makers, but are also concerned with the media, the general public, interest groups, the academic world and various internal and external stakeholders such as unions, customers, creditors and shareholders.[32] However, with specific regard to government relations, Gollner found that Canadian corporations ranked four functions as the most important, as shown in Table 7.1.

Public affairs staff play an advisory role for senior executives in a corporation by anticipating trends in government policy and providing advance warning of any relevant developments. In this way corporations aim for a more proactive involvement in policy formation, rather than just reacting to the latest crisis.

Table 7.1

The Most Significant Government Relations Activities of Canadian Corporations

| Activity | % of corporations consider this to be: | | | | |
| | Highly significant | | | Insignificant | |
	1	2	3	4	5
Alerting governments to possible impacts of various legislative scenarios upon the company	34.1	34.8	23.5	6.1	1.5
Systematically anticipating legislative and regulatory needs	34.8	23.5	27.3	12.9	1.5
Projecting favourable corporate image to rule-makers	26.3	34.6	29.3	8.3	1.5
Keeping governments advised on a regular and systematic basis about company's special needs	24.8	33.1	25.6	11.3	5.3

Source: Gollner, *Social Change and Corporate Strategy*, 116.

This is especially important for companies that are heavily involved with government procurement, or that are highly regulated.

The greater the role of government in determining corporate livelihood, the greater the stakes in business-government relations and the greater the need for effective public affairs management. This function is a substitute for the personal involvement of senior executives, but is integrated with other mechanisms of corporate political action. Public affairs staff act as intermediaries in setting up meetings between executives and government officials, and an enthusiastic and hard-working staff may mean that the amount of time senior executives spend in Ottawa is increased rather than reduced.[33] It has been estimated that chief executive officers used to spend 5 to 10 per cent of their time dealing with public issues prior to the 1970s, but by the mid-1980s this figure had risen to around 70 per cent.[34] In between dealing with government and engaging in that other great contemporary corporate pastime, namely fighting takeover battles, it is amazing that some CEOs still actually find time to run a business.

Public affairs divisions also play an important role in educating the rest of the corporation about government and public policy, and encouraging executives to use this knowledge in the planning process.[35] But this task is not always successful, and public affairs is sometimes viewed internally as a peripheral activity. In an interview, one public affairs specialist complained that this activity was seen as a "soft" part of the corporate organization and was one of the first things cut back in periods of economic downturn. Paradoxically, it is often during such periods that the corporation needs government support the most, and would benefit most from a systematic public affairs effort.

However, Gollner suggests that corporate public affairs, in general, is undergoing a transformation in Canada, as in the United States. The function is changing from one that is an irregular, informal, reactive "add-on" with limited legitimacy, to one that is increasingly formalized, sophisticated, systematic and institutionalized with the full support of senior management. Public affairs is thus moving from an age of adolescence to one of maturity.[36] So in the long run, this function can be seen as "hardening-up" in terms of corporate priorities.

One problem for corporate lobbying is to coordinate the activities of in-house public affairs staff with inputs from other sources such as external consultants and lobbyists. Tema Frank cities a case where an organization was faced with a conflict between its Ottawa representative and its external consultant, with each accusing the other of "stealing" information.[37] This sort of problem is likely to become increasingly apparent as both in-house public affairs and external lobbying/consulting firms continue to expand.

Professional Lobbyists and Consultants

One of the principal developments in Canadian business-government relations over the last decade or so has been the growth of firms specializing in lobbying and political consultancy. These firms hire themselves out to corporations, business associations and anyone else who can afford their fees, and they provide their clients with political advice and assistance in dealing with government. Their advice can be sought on just about any subject, but often they are asked to help corporations win government procurement contracts or get grants, subsidies and loans from the public purse.

Some firms, such as Public Affairs International (PAI) or Government Consultants International (GCI), are substantial organizations employing dozens of senior analysts and consultants, and offering a wide range of services to their clients. Others are small independent consultants, sometimes consisting of just one person who can offer highly specialized assistance in one specific policy area. Several law firms are also part of the professional lobbying fraternity, undertaking government relations work as well as their more traditional legal services. In some cases, the government relations work has grown so much that law firms have created their own separate consultancy organizations, for example, Lang Michener Lash & Johnston who set up Strategicon Inc. in 1988.

The growth of these firms is related to the increased size and complexity of government in Canada, and to the upsurge of business regulation that took place in the 1970s. The expansion of government, the shifting structures of federal and provincial bureaucracies, the complexity of policy issues and the criss-crossing lines of departmental and agency responsibility make it difficult for many businesses to figure out who does what in government, or to identify where the decisions that affect them are really made. In trying to achieve their policy objectives it is no longer possible for business people simply to rely on a few discrete words to their cabinet friends over cocktails at the Rideau Club. Such cozy informal string-pulling, based on the "old boy network," has largely passed into history.

In addition, by the early 1980s, business had been stung by government policies, such as the National Energy Program and the tax hikes in the 1981 budget, and government appeared to many corporations as both a dangerous and perplexing entity. Dealing with government was beginning to seem like walking through a mine field without a map, and some of the first government consultancy firms, such as Executive Consultants Ltd., acted largely as guides for confused corporations.

In the early 1980s some of the pioneering lobby firms rather coyly avoided the term "lobbying." Instead they preferred to call themselves "consultants" in order to avoid adverse connotations of influence-peddling, arm-twisting and political-fixing. However, since Brian Mulroney's victory in 1984, lobbying firms have come out of the closet, and have adopted a more aggressive and self-publicizing stance. Firms now proudly parade their political connections and openly admit they are selling political influence, not just policy expertise.

Lobby firms are very much concerned with inside contacts and personal relations with policy-makers at the highest levels, and they normally place heavy emphasis on hiring former politicians, aides to cabinet ministers and senior bureaucrats. Many former public officials are thus recruited as "for hire" lobbyists on behalf of business, which is one of the few sections of society that can afford their services. Naturally, while still in office, top public servants are aware that they may well land a lucrative job serving business when they leave. This, of course, assumes that they do not alienate business too much during their term of public office.

By April 1990 there were 295 "for hire" lobby firms registered with Ottawa—matching exactly the number of MPs—and many of these enterprises employed a large number of individual lobbyists.[38] Some of the most prominent firms are outlined below.

Public Affairs International PAI was set up in 1973 by Torrance Wylie who had worked for Prime Minister Lester Pearson and had been an adviser in the Prime Minister's Office of Pierre Trudeau. By 1990 it had become the largest lobbying firm in Canada with 51 clients, including AT&T, Canadian Pacific, Ciba-Geigy, CNCP, Ferranti, H.J. Heinz, Imperial Oil, IBM and Proctor and Gamble. Its lobbyists are no strangers to the inner circle of power in Canadian government. For example, its president, Pierre Fortier, was national director of the Progressive Conservative Party. Other lobbyists include the

Honourable Doug Frith (former Liberal cabinet minister); Paul Curley (former national director of the PC Party); and David Crapper (former assistant to Deputy P.M. Don Mazankowski). PAI's parent company, the Public Affairs Resource Group, also controls Decima Research, the Conservative Party's polling firm, and in 1989, the whole operation was taken over by the British conglomerate, the WPP Group.

Government Consultants International   One of the more flamboyant firms is Government Consultants International, which was set up in 1984 by former Newfoundland premier, Frank Moores, following Brian Mulroney's electoral victory. Unlike some other firms, GCI flaunts its partisan ties to the federal Conservatives, and Moores, along with co-founders Gerry Doucet (now with Fred Doucet Consulting International) and Gary Ouellett, is a high place Tory and a friend of the prime minister. Moores himself was a principal organizer of Mulroney's successful bid for the PC leadership in 1983. GCI also hired Patrick MacAdam who was one of Mulroney's senior officials in the PMO, and hedged its partisan bets by hiring former Liberal Minister of Communications, Francis Fox. It also dipped into the bureaucracy, hiring Ramsey Withers, who was a deputy minister in the Department of Transport and a former chief of the Canadian defence staff. He is considered to be of great value in advizing business clients about obtaining government contracts in these two major spending areas. In 1990, GCI counted many prominent corporations, such as Anheuser-Busch, Bell Canada, British Aerospace, GEC, Hiram-Walker, Irving Pulp and Paper and the Upjohn Company among its 50 clients.

Fred Doucet Consulting International   Fred Doucet was Brian Mulroney's chief of staff in 1983 and up until 1987 was his top policy adviser in the PMO. In 1989, he and his brother Gerry (also a prime ministerial confidant) set up their own lobbying firm, including another top Mulroney staffer, Pierre Nolin. Nolin was formerly the Conservatives' chief organizer in Quebec. Within a year, the firm had 38 clients, including Brascan, Labatts, Nestlé, Merrill Lynch, Noranda and Royal Trustco, all seeking to influence government policy.

Other prominent lobby firms include Osler, Hoskin and Harcourt with 38 clients; S.A. Murray with 30; and Government Policy Consultants with 20. All employ well-connected former government officials or politicians, and all work primarily for a changing collection of big name corporations. GPC, for example, employs Jon Johnson and James Crossland, formerly senior advisers to Brian Mulroney, as well as William Kennett, formerly Canada's Inspector General of Banks. Kennett undoubtedly enhances GPC's reputation in financial policy, and its client list includes American Express, Citibank, Confederation Life Insurance, Metropolitan Life Holdings and Power Financial Corporation.

One of the earliest and most prominent firms, Executive Consultants Ltd., was started in 1968 by Bill Lee and Bill Neville, both of whom had been aides to cabinet ministers. Lee subsequently became election campaign director for Prime Minister John Turner in 1984, while Neville became chief of staff for Prime Minister Joe Clark in 1979 and set up the Prime Minister's Office for Brian Mulroney in 1984. Neville later joined PAI, before becoming a tobacco industry lobbyist.

In the area of trade policy, Simon Reisman, Canada's chief negotiator of the Free Trade Agreement, set up the Trade and Investment Advisory Group Inc., while the deputy negotiator, Gordon Ritchie, joined Strategicon. In December 1988 Strategicon announced that it was also employing three other political heavyweights as policy associates. These were Jean Chrétien, the former senior Liberal cabinet minister and party leadership contender; Mitchel Sharp, the former Minister of Finance; and William Teschke who had been deputy minister in a variety of portfolios.

The fees charged by lobbyists vary, and firms are not required to disclose the amounts. But PAI and Government Consultants International have charged up to $6,000 per month for their assessments of political trends,[39] and the Pharmaceutical Manufacturers' Association of Canada paid GCI $100,000 for help in its successful bid to get great patent protection from the federal government.[40] This was undoubtedly a smart move, given GCI's close personal links with Prime Minister Brian Mulroney. As John Sawatsky points out, while "Gerry Doucet handled the PMAC file in GCI's office, his brother Fred handled the issue in the Prime Minister's Office."[41]

This whole litany of personal links and recruitment by lobbying firms sends a clear message. If you look carefully at many of today's elected politicians and senior civil servants, you will see tomorrow's business lobbyists waiting to emerge. Any sections of Canadian society who find themselves in conflict with business interests may thus be forgiven if they occasionally have doubts about the impartiality of government officials.

LOBBYING: TARGETS AND TACTICS

Lobbying can be defined as any form of direct or indirect communication with government that is designed to influence public policy. Direct communication occurs when an individual, group or organization contacts policy-makers themselves, for instance by visiting or writing to an MP or a government agency. Indirect communications, on the other hand, are aimed at influencing public opinion or sections of the public in the hope that government policy-makers will then respond to the public mood.

Anyone can engage in the process of lobbying, and the activity is not confined just to interest groups or manifestly political associations. Individuals, corporations, trade unions and churches, all attempt to influence government policy from time to time, with varying degrees of success. One section of government can even lobby another, as when provincial governments try to convince Ottawa to do something, or when one cabinet minister tries to persuade others.

Despite popular images of corruption, manipulation and sleazy politics, lobbying is, in principle, a basic democratic right involving the freedom to petition government for redress of grievances, and the freedom to associate with other people for that purpose. It is a widespread activity in Canada, but those groups that lobby government on a regular basis continually have to fight against the "sleazy" image. In an attempt to foster "innocence by association," the president of the BCNI, Thomas D'Aquino, has even gone so far as to claim that "the Pope is a lobbyist"[42]—but perhaps this is stretching things a little.

Not only are there numerous groups and individuals in Canadian society who get involved in lobbying, there are also numerous points in the political system where lobbying efforts are directed. Government is not a single-celled organism, and decision-making authority is vested in a diverse array of state institutions, each of which has some power. To be successful in lobbying, it is necessary for business organizations (or anybody else) to identify the points in the political system where pressure is likely to be most effective. In short, it is necessary to identify appropriate lobbying targets.

Lobbying Targets

The plurality of different government institutions can present a confusing picture to anyone intent on lobbying, and choosing a target or targets is by no means a simple decision. The main targets will vary according to the nature of the issue, and the politicians and bureaucrats who are crucial on one issue may not be involved in others. Nor is a written constitution always a reliable guide to the location of power in the system of government. Written constitutions tell us how the system *ought* to work and where power *ought* to reside, not necessarily where it actually does in practice. Experienced lobbyists are well aware of this distinction between theory and practice, and the actual pattern of lobbying and the targets chosen can provide an indication of the real location of power in the system.

The way in which the governmental system is structured, and the power relations between different institutions, such as Parliament, Cabinet and the bureaucracy have a crucial impact on lobbying targets. Understandably, these structures vary from one country to the next, and lessons drawn from one country's experiences are not necessarily valid in other contexts. For instance, in the United States the structure of government institutions is very different from that in Canada, and generalizations about lobbying in the U.S. cannot simply be transferred across the border.

In Canada the specific framework of government institutions provides a complex target structure for lobbying, and lobbyists frequently try to hit several different targets at the same time (provided, of course, that they have sufficient resources to do so). In analyzing the most important targets it is first necessary to recognize that lobbying takes place at different levels of government, i.e., at federal, provincial and municipal levels. In a federal system such as Canada's it is vital for lobbyists to identify which level of government has jurisdiction over which issues. It is largely a waste of time trying to convince policy-makers in Ottawa if decision-making power over an issue rests with the provinces.

One problem here is that the Canadian political system has evolved in such a way that jurisdiction over most policy issues is divided between Ottawa and the provinces. Garth Stevenson notes that the federal government has exclusive jurisdiction only in the areas of "military defense, veterans' affairs, the post office and monetary policy."[43] Even where jurisdiction is not formally divided, a myriad of intergovernmental consultation mechanisms gives each level of government some input into the other's policy domains.

This blurring of jurisdictions provides both burdens and opportunities for lobbyists. The burdens are, firstly, that lobbyists must expend effort discovering which level of government does what. Secondly, they frequently need to lobby more than one level of government simultaneously, and victories at one level may be nullified by defeats at another. And finally, on controversial political issues, lobbyists are liable to get shunted around between federal and provincial governments, as each tries to pass the buck. On the opportunities side, business interests are sometimes able to mobilize support from a provincial government in order to put pressure on the federal government, or vice versa. In addition, if a business is unable to get what it wants from one level of government, such as an industrial assistance subsidy, then it may be able to milk the other level. It is not uncommon for business to be subsidized by both levels of government simultaneously.[44]

In terms of the basic pattern of government institutions, the provinces are in many respects microcosms of the federal level, and the target structure for lobbyists is roughly comparable. Focussing explicitly on the federal government, the principal lobbying targets fall into several categories:

Cabinet Ministers   Cabinet ministers individually and the Cabinet as a whole constitute the pinnacle of the decision-making system in Canada. A minister has authority over a substantial area of public policy, and if business groups can get the relevant cabinet minister interested in a proposal then their lobbying effort is off to a flying start. However, ministers should not be overrated as lobbying targets for a number of reasons. Firstly, they are extremely busy and it can be difficult getting access to them. Secondly, they are not normally experts in their areas of policy jurisdiction, and they rely heavily for advice on their departmental bureaucrats and on their own political staff. If a minister is being advised against something by his or her staff, then it is unlikely that a lobby group will change the minister's mind. Thus it is important for lobbyists to convince ministers' executive assistants and senior bureaucrats if they want their message to receive a sympathetic hearing. Finally, individual ministers do not have complete discretion concerning policies in their area. This is particularly true when it comes to spending decisions, and ministers are subject to constraints imposed by the Department of Finance, the Treasury Board, the expenditure management system, as well as by their cabinet colleagues and the prime minister.

Departmental Bureaucrats   These are one of the prime targets of lobbyists. Many public policies start out as proposals formulated within the bowels of the civil service, which subsequently make their way up through the hierarchy (being modified as they go), until they are submitted to Cabinet under the authority of the minister. By the time legislative proposals are discussed in Cabinet, or in a cabinet committee, most of the work has already been done. It is in the middle-levels of the bureaucracy, particularly around the level of director-general, where a lot of this work takes place, and where the details of subsequent legislation first start to crystallize. This level of the bureaucracy is also relatively accessible and receptive to groups that can provide needed technical information.

Central Agencies   Central bureaucratic agencies such as the Prime Minister's Office, the Privy Council Office and the Treasury Board[45] are general coordinating bodies at the top of the governmental machine, and have a substantial veto power over departmental proposals. The scope of their activity spans across the whole range of public policy at the federal level, but compared to regular departments they are a relatively small elite corps. They do not have the staff to deal with the technical details of most issues arising from other departments, and they have limited time for negotiating with outside interests. These two things make them difficult targets for business lobbyists or interest groups generally.

The House of Commons   By the time legislative proposals are introduced into Parliament, they are very difficult to change in any substantive way. The government has become publicly committed to a particular line of action by submitting a bill for parliamentary approval, and in the House of Commons the ability to amend or reject executive proposals is highly constrained—at least in times of majority government. On any important issue, the ruling party will almost invariably use its majority to force the measure through, and this is made possible by the strong party discipline that is characteristic of all parliamentary parties in Canada (see Appendix).

In the House of Commons much of the work takes place in committees which examine the details of legislative proposals, review public expenditures and conduct investigations on various topics. Like the House itself, committees are dominated by MPs from the majority party and the constraints of party discipline still pertain. Business groups often submit briefs and make presentations before parliamentary committees, but the changes that committees make to government legislation are usually minimal because the majority of MPs will follow the government line. Despite reforms of the committee system designed to give MPs more autonomy and resources, the utility of these committees for lobbyists remains slight. Of somewhat more use are special committees that occasionally investigate particular topics before legislation is actually drafted. At this earlier stage there is greater flexibility, and business input here can have some affect on the formation of the government's legislative proposals.

The Senate   As the non-elected chamber of Parliament, the Senate has little real legitimacy in interfering with legislation from the House of Commons. However, this does not stop it from trying. Despite formal powers which are in many respects equivalent to those of the House, the Senate has in the past had a reputation for doing very little to alter the course of legislation. Under Liberal governments with a Liberal-dominated Senate, this reputation was largely justified. However, under Brian Mulroney's Conservative government, the Senate, up until 1990, was dominated by Liberals, and was more conflictual and obstructionist. In particular it delayed passage of the controversial drug patent bill of 1987 (much to the chagrin of the PMAC), and it held up the free trade legislation in 1988 until after a general election had decided the issue. In response to the Senate's obstruction of the Goods and Services Tax, Brian Mulroney appointed eight new Conservative senators in 1990, removing the Liberal majority. This was a step towards re-establishing the Senate's subservience to the House of Commons.

Despite its normally subservient position, the Senate should not be written off as a target of business lobbying. It is stacked with well-connected, professional politicians, many of whom have close business ties. As John McMenemy has shown, many senators are far from "has-beens," in that they are still actively involved in politics behind the scenes.[46] As such, they can be useful allies and intermediaries in dealing with cabinet ministers and the bureaucracy.

Backbench MPs   Backbench MPs are often regarded as being of little significance in the policy process because they are bound by party discipline, and because they have few resources at their disposal. Furthermore, vigorous support from backbench MPs who belong to opposition parties can mean the "kiss of death" for a group's goals. Opposition MPs are in the business of publicly attacking the government, and this is not always the most productive method of gaining favour.

However, MPs do have some advantages as far as lobbyists are concerned. They can be helpful in getting information out of the bureaucracy; they can provide publicity for an issue by asking questions in the House of Commons; they have a voice in party decision-making through weekly caucus meetings; and of course there is always a chance that one day a backbench MP may become a cabinet minister. For these reasons many business groups are loathe to ignore MPs altogether, and some give them quite a high priority in their lobbying efforts. For instance, in 1988 the Grocery Products Manufacturers of Canada (GPMC) developed a computerized "Political Support Data Base" which allows the organization to generate information about plants, warehouses, investments, numbers of employees, etc., on a riding-by-riding basis. This information is then used in lobbying MPs from any ridings the GPMC chooses.

The Public And The Media   Business organizations can have an indirect impact on public policy by influencing the climate of public opinion, and to do this it is necessary for business to get its message across via the mass media. This can take various forms ranging from simple statements to newspaper or television journalists, for instance when business groups are asked for their reaction to the budget, to more systematic campaigns to influence the public through advocacy advertising. These forms of activity, and the overall pattern of business relations with the media, are analyzed more extensively in the next chapter. But first it is useful to look at some of the tactics used by business lobbyists to influence government policy.

Lobbying Tactics

The sorts of tactics used by business in trying to influence government policy depends, firstly, on the targets that have been chosen. If a business group decides to focus on departmental bureaucrats, then this will require a very different strategy from one that focusses on mobilizing public opinion.

Secondly, tactics are conditioned by the level of resources available for political action. Expensive publicity campaigns involving advocacy advertising will be beyond the reach of most small or medium-sized companies, and the use of in-house government relations or professional, hired lobbyists may not be a realistic option for smaller firms. Such firms may have to rely on representations by the CEO, or on the services of trade associations and broad-based business groups.

Finally, tactics are conditioned by the nature of the issue. On complex technical issues, detailed discussions and exchanges of information between bureaucrats and corporate specialists will be at a premium. It is unlikely that cabinet ministers will have the time or competence to deal with technicalities (however important they are to the corporation), and trying to get the public interested in such things as procedural changes in the administration of countervailing duty regulations is virtually impossible.

Whatever targets are chosen, lobbyists must necessarily be sensitive to timing. In the later stages of the policy process (for instance, after a bill has been introduced into Parliament), it is difficult to change matters because, by this time, the governing politicians have committed themselves publicly to a course of action. It is much easier for lobbyists to influence policy formation if they get involved at the earlier stages of the process when things are first starting to take shape. In order to do this, any organization must have an effective intelligence gathering and early warning system to provide information about policy developments when they are still in embryonic form.

Although there is an advantage in early involvement, the battle is not necessarily over in the later stages, even after legislation has been passed. In order for legislation to be implemented, detailed sets of regulations have to be drawn up by the bureaucracy, specifying the rules and procedures by which the law will be administered. These regulations are typically put together after the statute has been passed by Parliament, and they can sometimes have a substantial bearing on the impact of the legislation. The drafting of regulations is an area where authority has largely been delegated to bureaucrats, and it thus becomes worthwhile for lobbyists to concern themselves with this area of activity.

One example of this occurred with the Tobacco Products Control Act which was passed in June 1988. The final regulations for the Act were only published in January 1989, and in the interim the Canadian Tobacco Manufacturers' Council, through its president and lobbyist, Bill Neville, managed to bring about a number of significant changes. Documents obtained by the Non-Smokers Rights Association showed that officials in the Department of Health and Welfare originally wanted warnings on tobacco packages that covered 30 per cent of the surface, and that stated that tobacco is addictive, and a cause of lung cancer, heart disease and birth defects. Attention would be drawn to the warning by means of a prominent circle and arrow displayed on the package. According to *The Globe and Mail*, Neville wrote a long memo protesting these proposed regulations in August 1988, claiming that it was wrong to say that tobacco is addictive. A meeting was sought on August 23, and the next day a departmental memo was written weakening the regulations, and removing any reference to addiction. By November the regulations were further weakened when the size of the warning was reduced. It is not clear how much impact Neville's personal connections had on this process, though during the fall election campaign he acted as a senior adviser to the government and worked on speeches for the Prime Minister. Neville clearly had access to the draft regulations at an early stage, and even requested that the CTMC's participation be kept secret until after the regulations were finally published. Health groups that had opposed the CTMC were not so privileged, and were kept in the dark about the regulations until they were published.[47]

In lobbying the bureaucracy one of the key components of success is the ability to supply information. If a business organization can provide accurate, thorough and relevant information that can help civil servants do their jobs, then access will not be much of a problem. If a group has not done its homework and has a reputation for half-baked or unreliable research, then it will be of less use to officials, and access will be more restricted. Successful interaction with the bureaucracy is based on exchange, and business must have something to offer, whether it is information, assistance in policy implementation or political support for the relevant sections of the bureaucracy in battles with other government departments and agencies.

Any private interest seeking to influence government policy has to overcome the problem of appearing preoccupied with its own narrow concerns. Obviously groups *are* concerned with their own interests, but government officials have a broader set of considerations to weigh. Business lobbying has a much greater chance of success if it shows some sensitivity to broader societal needs and to the government's overall political agenda. Groups therefore try to present their narrow interests in a way that is congruent with the government's conception of the "national" interest, and naturally this is easier to do with some issues than with others. It also helps if some other groups or sections of society can be recruited in coalition, so that the base of support can be broadened.

In terms of specific goals for individual corporations, such as winning government grants or procurement contracts, the utility of lobbying can be exaggerated. Despite occasional revelations of attempted influence-peddling, reliance on personal connections and partisan attachments is probably the exception rather than the rule. In many cases the secret to winning government contracts is not wrapped in political mystique; it rests instead on more prosaic bases, such as completing the paperwork correctly, fulfilling the specification for the job and having the lowest bid.[48]

One tactic that is normally unsuccessful, or even counterproductive, is to make threats or to engage in public attacks on government. For instance, the PMAC was unsuccessful in getting Pierre Trudeau's Liberal government to extend patent protection for multinational drug companies when they used what John Sawatsky has described as "one of the most odious lobby campaigns in the history of Canada."[49] Their aim was to prevent generic companies from making lower-priced copies of brand-name drugs and according to Sawatsky, PMAC tried bullying cabinet ministers and bureaucrats, accusing the government of "licensing legalized theft," threatening to move their plants out of Canada, spreading scare stories about unsafe generic drugs, yelling at the Minister of

Consumer and Corporate Affairs, Ron Basford, and launching lawsuits against generic companies.[50] It was not until there was a change of government, with a more favourable attitude towards foreign investment (especially from the United States), and the employment of Government Consultants International with its close Conservative connections, that PMAC eventually had some success.

Even though business has a powerful sanction against government, namely the ability to move production out of the country or out of a region, this weapon is a last resort, and the threat cannot be used repeatedly without some devaluation. Moving production also involves major costs for business, and to threaten such a move for every adverse policy proposal would just result in a speedy loss of credibility. In addition it is not a threat that can be made directly by trade associations or broad-based business groups because, as Leo Panitch has pointed out, these associations do not actually control capital; it is the corporations themselves, not their associations, that have this power.[51] Threats and public criticism can do more harm than good for business interests, and while corporate executives may sometimes have a strong desire to vent their frustrations in this way, they risk alienating the very people they are trying to influence.

This is not to say that business groups shy away from publicity-oriented campaigns designed to influence public opinion. Publicity campaigns and attempts to mobilize grassroots opinion are often used to complement other forms of lobbying. These tactics do not just involve advocacy advertizing and corporate image-building, but also employ other techniques such as direct mail campaigns. For example, in an attempt to block a proposed ban on tobacco advertizing, the Canadian Tobacco Manufacturer's Council contacted 200,000 tobacco retailers and provided computer-generated letters for the owners to sign and mail to their MPs.[52] This was in addition to high-level lobbying, running a national advertising campaign and making extensive submissions to legislative committees. A lobby firm called Policorp uses direct-mail extensively, and can send out tens of thousands of personalized letters by hooking up 200 typewriters to a mainframe computer.[53]

On major policy issues, such as the free trade debate, where public opinion plays an important role, business interests have an advantage because they control extensive financial resources that can be made available for advertising and media campaigns. Prior to the election of 1988, prominent business associations spearheaded a coalition of 35 pro-free trade groups called the Canadian Alliance for Trade and Job Opportunities, which spent over $2 million even before the campaign got going.[54] On this issue it was superfluous trying to persuade government policy-makers because government was already firmly committed to the Free Trade Agreement. The public became the real target because the public had the ability to kill the deal by choosing an alternative government in the November election.

In general the pattern of business lobbying is not restricted to any single set of targets or tactics. Business groups are frequently able to devise a lobbying "package" that incorporates a plurality of different approaches, both public and behind the scenes. The control over a substantial level of resources makes this possible and gives business a political edge over the other sections of society, in addition to the other bases of business power mentioned at the beginning of the chapter. Concern about corporate pressure and the growth of business lobbying has provoked recent attempts to control this activity, or at least to make it more visible through a system of registration. Not surprisingly, these attempts were opposed by the lobbying industry itself.

Registration of Lobbyists

Unlike the United States which has had legislation since 1946 that requires lobbyists to register, in Canada there has been no such legislation at either the federal or provincial levels.[55] This situation changed in 1989 when the federal Lobbyists Registration Act came into effect. The new Act was part of a response by the Conservative government to the problems over conflict of interest which dogged its first term in office.

The Act divides lobbyists into two groups. The first group, or Tier I lobbyists, are those who hire themselves out to various clients and who provide a service for a fee. Tier II lobbyists are those who work for a single company or group, and who lobby just on behalf of their employer. For Tier I lobbyists the new requirements are quite minimal; lobbyists must register the names of their clients, and indicate the issue on which they are lobbying by checking off one of several possible subject areas on a form. If their clients are corporations they must also provide some extra information about ownership and subsidiaries. Data on Tier 1 firms from the Register of Lobbyists showed that the 10 largest enterprises in 1990 employed a total of 93 individual lobbyists working on behalf of 317 clients, almost exclusively from the corporate world.

For Tier II lobbyists, the rules are even less burdensome. Once a year they must provide the registry with their name, title and employer, which takes about as much effort as sending in a business card.[56] Although there are penalties for violating the requirements, no special mechanisms are established for carrying out investigations or enforcing the rules. Unlike in the United States, Canadian lobbyists are not required to disclose their fees. Despite their objections, lobbyists have really very little to complain about in terms of the new "burden" imposed on them, and public disclosure of their activities is still decidedly limited.

ENDNOTES

1. James O'Connor, *The Fiscal Crisis of the State* (New York: St. Martin's Press, 1973), 6.

2. Leo Panitch, *The Canadian State: Political Economy and Political Power* (Toronto: University of Toronto Press, 1977), 11-12.

3. Ralph Miliband, *The State in Capitalist Society* (London: Quartet Books, 1973), 55.

4. Statistics Canada, *National Balance Sheet Accounts 1986*, 13-214.

5. Ben Forster, *A Conjunction of Interests: Business, Politics, and Tariffs 1825-1879* (Toronto: University of Toronto Press, 1986), 115.

6. S.D. Clark, *The Canadian Manufacturers' Association* (Toronto: University of Toronto Press, 1939), 6.

7. *Ibid.*, 7.

8. The Canadian Manufacturers' Association, "Looking Outward: The CMA and Trade," (official pamphlet) and CMA, "The Canadian Manufacturers' Association: Helping Manufacturers Grow."

9. CMA, "Bulletin," No. 4951 (October 1987), 2.

10. CMA, *President's Report 1986-87*, 19.

11. CMA, *President's Report 1985-86*, 4.

12. The above policy positions are expressed in various CMA publications including *President's Reports* (1985-86, 1986-87); "Competing on Industrial Research and Development" (March 1987); "The Importance of Trade Negotiations" (May 1987); "Tax Reform" (September 1987); "Issues" (October 1987); and "The Canadian Manufacturer" (various issues).

13. Information in this section is taken from CCC publications including *Annual Reports* (various years), *By-Laws*, *Impact* (Winter 1988), *Ottawa Update* (March 1988) and *Positions on Selected National Issues 1987-1988*.

14. CCC, "Positions on Selected National Issues 1989-1988."

15. Mark Baetz, "The Canadian Federation of Independent Business and the MacEachen Budget," in Mark C. Baetz and Donald Thain, eds. *Canadian Cases in Business-Government Relations* (Toronto: Methuen, 1985), 326.

16. *Ibid.*, 328-29.

17. CFIB, "Action Report."

18. Baetz, "CFIB," in Budget, *Canadian Cases*, 337 and 344.

19. CPQ, "Conseil du patronat du Québec, 1988-89," and CPQ, "Some Facts About the C.P.Q." (February 1989).

20. *Ibid.*

21. Business Council of British Columbia, *Annual Report* (1988), 1.

22. William D. Coleman, *Business and Politics: A Study of Collective Action* (Kingston and Montreal: McGill-Queen's University Press, 1988), 95.

23. BCBC, *Annual Report*, 1988.

24. Isaiah A. Litvak, "National Trade Associations: Business-Government Intermediaries," in *Business Quarterly*, Vol. 47, No. 3 (Autumn 1982), 34-42 and Coleman, *Business and Politics*, 31.

25. Our research excluded farmer's groups, professional associations or institutes, broad-based associations and regional or provincial groups, many of which were included in the other studies.

26. William D. Coleman and Henry J. Jacek, "The Roles and Activities of Business Interest Associations in Canada," in *Canadian Journal of Political Science*, Vol. 16, No. 2 (June 1983), 257-80.

27. Litvak, "National Trade Associations," 36.

28. Coleman and Jacek, "Roles and Activities of Business Interest Associations," 269.

29. For discussion of this tendency see Peter Aucoin, "Pressure Groups and Recent Changes in the Policy-Making Process, in A. Paul Pross, ed., "*Pressure Group Behaviour in Canadian Politics* (Scarborough, Ont.: McGraw-Hall Ryerson, 1975); Colin Campbell and George Szablowski, *The Superbureaucrats* (Toronto: Gage, 1979); and James Gillies, *Where Business Fails* (Montreal: The Institute for Research on Public Policy, 1981).

30. Andrew B. Gollner, *Social Change and Corporate Strategy: The Expanding Role of Public Affairs* (Stanford, Conn.: Issue Action Publications Inc., 1983), 105.

31. *Ibid.*, 25.

32. *Ibid.*, 111-19.

33. Tema A. Frank, "The Lobbyists," in *Canadian Business Review* (Summer 1988), 36-38.

34. Andrew B. Gollner, "Managing Public Affairs," in *Canadian Business Review* (Autumn 1984), 29-33.

35. Frank, "The Lobbyists," 38.

36. Gollner, *Social Change and Corporate Strategy*, 154-56.

37. Frank, "The Lobbyists," 38.

38. Based on information obtained from the Lobbyists Registration Branch of Consumer and Corporate Affairs Canada, April 23, 1990.

39. *Financial Post* (20 March, 1989), 17.

40. *Globe and Mail* (5 June 1989), 827.

41. John Sawatsky, *The Insiders: Government Business and the Lobbyists* (Toronto: McClelland and Stewart, 1987), 316.

42. *Globe and Mail* (14 December 1987), 13.

43. Garth Stevenson, "Federalism and Intergovernmental Relations," in Michael S. Whittington and Glen Williams, eds., *Canadian Politics in the 1980s*, 2nd edition (Toronto: Methuen, 1984), 378.

44. For a broader discussion of the impact of federalism see Chapter Six.

45. The Department of Finance is sometimes included in this list.

46. John McMenemy, "Business Influence and Party Organizers in the Senate," in Paul W. Fox, ed., *Politics in Canada*, 5th edition (Toronto: McGraw-Hill Ryerson Ltd. 1982), 541-49.

47. The documents were obtained by the Non-Smokers Rights Association using the provisions of the Access to Information Act, and were reported in the *Globe and Mail*, (26 June, 1989), A1 and A13.

48. A possible exception is in government advertizing, where the partisan connections of advertizing agencies are more important.

49. Sawatsky, *The Insiders*, 315-16.

50. *Ibid.*

51. Leo Panitch, "Trade Unions and the Capitalist State," in *New Left Review*, 125 (January-February 1981), 26.

52. *Globe and Mail* (16 December, 1987), B4.

53. *Globe and Mail* (18 April, 1988), B23.

54. *Financial Post* (5 December, 1988), 15

55. Bruce Carson, "Registration of Lobbyists," in *Current Issue Review*, 86-18E, Library of Parliament, Research Branch (September 1987), 1-12.

56. "*Canada Gazette*, Part 1, Vol. 123, No. 23, (10 June, 1989), 2798-799.

Chapter 8

Business and the Media

In a capitalist economy we take for granted that a primary goal of business is to make profits. In a democratic society we assume that the role of the media is to provide information in its various forms: news and entertainment. But most media organizations are also businesses, for whom making a profit is crucial for their survival. To what extent is their role as purveyor of information—of "all the news that's fit to print" as the *New York Times'* slogan goes—influenced by the fact that media organizations are usually privately-owned, profit-oriented businesses? Is the media's relationship to business affected by the fact that newspapers, television broadcasters and radio broadcasters usually are privately-owned businesses themselves?

These questions are not new. They have been asked since the turn of the century when print was the only medium of popular communication. Two opposing images of the media-business relationship have contended since then. One of these sees them as adversaries who regularly clash when the media's interest in the "news"—which may involve exposing the negative public consequences of corporate actions—runs up against business's aversion to public controversy over its activities. This image of the media-business relationship goes back to the muckraking journalism that achieved prominence in the United States during the first decades of this century.[1] A very different image of the relationship sees business and the media as having a fundamental sympathy of interests. This comes about largely because of the privately-owned media's dependence on the advertizing revenue of business, and because of the ownership of media companies by non-media interests. These are argued by some to be forms of economic censorship, imposing limits on the media's capacity to criticize the activities of business.

Which of these images is correct? Are business people right when they accuse journalists of having an anti-business bias? Or does the media in fact serve to reinforce the social power of the corporate elite, as some critics charge? To answer these questions, let us start by comparing two different models of the media's role in society.

MODEL I: THE MEDIA AS GATEKEEPER

Newspapers, magazines, broadcasters and film-makers produce a version of reality that is selective. Confronted with more information than could possibly be conveyed to their readerships/audiences, they must choose what images, ideas and "facts" to convey. In making these choices, they offer a definition of reality to those who consume what they produce. Journalists, editors and producers exercise discretion in deciding what messages to send out to the public. They are the gatekeepers of ideas and information in modern societies. As the American journalist Walter Lippman put it, "The facts of modern life do not spontaneously take a shape in which they can be known. They must be given a shape by somebody."[2]

The responsibility for deciding the "shape" given to the "facts of modern life" rests largely with the mass media. Everyone agrees that the responsibility is a heavy one in democratic societies, societies in which the average person devotes more of his or her time to consuming what the media offer than to any other activity except sleeping and working.[3] Where disagreements arise is over the neutrality of the gatekeeper. What are the factors that influence how "reality" is constructed and how news is reported by the media?

Those who subscribe to the gatekeeper model do not argue that there are no important sources of media bias. Indeed, there are several that are routinely mentioned as either potential or actual sources of bias. They are listed below.

Advertizing

The vast majority of a newspaper's or broadcaster's revenue comes from the sale of advertizing space or time to organizations that want to persuade the public (or at least that part of the public represented by the media company's market) to behave in a particular way. The reliance of the mass media on advertizing income has two consequences. One of these is the possibility that information and interpretations of events that put an important advertizer (or group of advertizers) in a bad light will be suppressed for fear that the advertizer will withdraw its business. The likelihood of this happening depends on a number of factors including, on the media side, the importance of the advertizer's account and, on the advertizer's side, its ability to do without the exposure its products receive through that media outlet.

This sort of "advertizer blackmail" is much less important than a second consequence of dependence on advertizing, the need for mass markets. Newspapers and broadcasters that do not attract large readerships/audiences, or that do not reach markets of sufficient affluence to buy what advertizers want to sell, are at a serious disadvantage in the competition for advertizing dollars. The result is, most media experts agree, pressure on media companies to avoid the sort of information and analysis that is not likely to have mass appeal. It is not that controversy does not sell. It does, as demonstrated by the longstanding success of the CBS exposé programme *60 Minutes* and of programmes like *Donahue* (NBC), *Geraldo* (CBS), *20/20* (CTV) and *the fifth estate* (CBC), as well as by the extensive media coverage of such matters as industrial pollution, large corporate takeovers, insider trading and business closures and layoffs. But although controversy sells, fundamental criticism of the social and economic systems in which these controversies occur does not. We return to this point subsequently.

Ownership

Monopoly and oligopoly are the rule in the newspaper industry. This raises the question of whether the "marketplace" of ideas and information is open and competitive, or whether the range of what is produced and disseminated by the print media is seriously narrowed by the lack of competition. Ownership is much less concentrated in broadcasting and, in the case of television, competition has actually increased in recent years due to the widespread distribution of cable reception. This has not, however, resulted in significant gains in terms of programme diversity: but this raises another issue that we will examine later in this chapter.

A second aspect of media ownership that has received enormous attention involves the possibility that the interests of the owner may influence the ideas and information conveyed by the mass media. Newspapers and broadcasters (and, for that matter, publishers and film companies) are often part of corporate networks that include non-media businesses. Is their capacity to report critically on businesses with whom they have ownership ties diminished? Is there evidence that the political views of their owners percolate down to influence editorial, reporting and programming decisions? In the case of newspapers, the Southam and Thomson chains together account for about 60 per cent of total circulation in English Canada, while Quebécor, Power Corporation and Unimédia control over 90 per cent of Canada's French-language market. Does chain ownership have any effect on how the news is reported? Finally, it is frequently the case in Canada, the United States and elsewhere that one company controls different media—say a newspaper and a television station—in the same regional market. This is referred to as media cross-ownership, and it has been argued by some to carry the danger of narrowing, even further, the range of information and ideas conveyed through the mass media.

Technology

Few things date more quickly than news. The technology of broadcasting is instantaneous, and that of newspapers involves a matter of hours. The mass media are thus capable of providing their audiences with the latest developments, and indeed our general expectations are that they will communicate what is happening now. What is happening now can, of course, be reported in the context of the larger background against which events unfold. The practical problem is that "stories" must be edited down to a length suitable for inclusion in a 30-minute news programme or the pages of a newspaper.

Television is the medium relied upon by most people for their knowledge of national and international events.[4] The visual character of this medium lends itself to the personalization of reality—an emphasis on individuals and personalities at the expense of broad social forces that are not captured by the eye of a camera. Consequently, the media, and in particular the technology of television, are disposed towards the personal, the immediate and the concrete. Reality becomes a constantly shifting pastiche of images; a portrayal of the world that is attenuated, but not overcome, by the more sustained reporting and documentary programming provided by programmes like *The Journal*, *Le point*, *Sunday Report* (television); CBC's *Ideas*, *Sunday Morning* and *Morningside* (radio); and some of the feature sections of newspapers.

Journalists

A constant lament of business people is that the media are either uninformed or wrongly informed about the world of business. The result, they argue, is news coverage that tends to be unfairly critical of corporate decision-makers, profits and the capitalist economy.

Are business and the media two solitudes? Those who report the news are often accused by business people of having a "liberal," anti-business bias. Surprisingly, there have been no systematic attempts in Canada to determine, one, whether this is true and, two, what the nature and causes of these differences in belief systems might be. An American study, however, confirms the existence of significant differences in social background, personality, ideology and world view between that country's media and business elites.[5] Researchers found that members of their media and business samples tended to "interpret the same information quite differently, in ways that correspond to their very divergent views of the world."[6] Media respondents typically gave more liberal responses to such statements as, "Government should substantially reduce the income gap between rich and poor."[7] Rothman and Lichter conclude that "leading journalists seem to inhabit a symbolic universe which is quite different from that of businessmen, with implications for the manner in which they report the news to the general public."[8]

A different angle on why journalists themselves may bias the media in its gatekeeping role is provided by public choice theory.[9] Journalists, it is argued, operate within a structure of incentives that provides material and status rewards for work that supports their newspaper's circulation, or audience in the case of television. There are few rewards for sustained reporting and in-depth analysis of a story. Indeed, there are likely to be serious disincentives to carry out this sort of journalism.[10] The problem is greater in business/economic journalism than in general political reporting because, historically, the business field has had a comparatively low prestige. The "stars" of journalism have, with a few exceptions such as Don McGillvray, Peter Newman and Diane Francis, covered the political field. As a result, the organizational incentives for journalists to develop an expert understanding of business, and to place corporate actions in a larger economic context, are weak.

The image of the media as gatekeeper needs to be qualified, then, by a recognition that there are sources of bias that influence the selection and communication of information and ideas. Whether the biases of the media are anti-business is, within the terms of the gatekeeper model, an open question. Advertizing and ownership generally are viewed as factors likely to tilt the media in favour of business, or at least to rein in outspoken criticism. Not everyone, however, is in agreement on this. Some argue that media profitability in fact permits higher quality journalism. In the words of an American business professor, "Adequate profits enable the news media to probe deeply into the events of the day, to attract and retain high quality personnel, to withstand any pressures from government, industry, and other special interest groups."[11] Disagreement also exists over the relationship between ownership and media behaviour. A number of Canadian studies have found no empirical evidence of a relationship.[12] It should be added, however, that these studies have looked at ownership's effect on the political coverage and partisan orientation of newspapers. The question of how ownership influences media treatment of the owner's other economic interests has not, surprisingly, received the same sort of rigorous examination.

The bias of technology has been argued to cut both ways. The need to condense reality into a 30-minute newscast or a couple of column inches in a newspaper results, some argue, in a superficial treatment of economic and business affairs. Corporate spokespersons have claimed that these matters receive too little coverage for the public to acquire a reasonable (and sympathetic) understanding of the complexities of corporate decision-making.[13] The implication is that if business received more and "better quality" media coverage the public would become more sympathetic to business's perspective on the world. Those who maintain that the media has a pro-business bias argue that both the relatively small proportion of all news that is devoted to business affairs and the tenor of that coverage work to business's advantage. Their reasoning is that superficiality helps to perpetuate public ignorance of the darker side of the capitalist economy and, secondly, they argue that most business coverage is favourable to corporate interests.

Agreement that journalists are usually poorly trained in business and economics is not matched by agreement on the consequences of their weak knowledge of these subjects. Corporate spokespersons often lament that this weakness means that business's side of a story is not communicated properly to the public, and that business's image suffers because of inexpert reporting. There is, however, another factor that needs to be taken into account. This involves the enormous quantity of information provided free of charge to the media by corporations and business associations, as well as by the economic bureaucracy of the state. Given the time and resource constraints under which these inexpert journalists operate, this information represents an important source of material for what ultimately reaches the printed page or the airwaves.

Specialized business journalism has acquired greater prominence over the last several years. Business weeklies like *The Financial Post* and *The Financial Times* have had a market for decades. They were joined in the 1980s by an expanded daily "Report on Business" section in *The Globe and Mail*; by the growth of French-language business weeklies like *Finance*, geared to the Quebec market; and by television and radio programmes like *Venture* (CBC television), *Business Week* (TVO) and CBC radio's weekly half-hour during *Morningside*, devoted to current business topics. The market for business news has expanded enormously as the "yuppie" segment of the baby-boom generation moves through the professional-managerial ranks.

With the arguable exception of the weekly business coverage of *Morningside*, the growth in specialized business journalism has tended to be favourable towards the corporate image in society. One needs to keep in mind, however, that the business press is largely preaching to the converted. Its "congregation" is an influential one, being comprised of more highly educated and affluent Canadians who, political participation studies show, are more likely to be active in politics than their less-educated and less-affluent fellow citizens. We would argue, therefore, that the expansion of the specialized business press in Canada has been both a consequence of changes in society—most notably the growth of the affluent professional-managerial class and the increased popularity

of neo-conservative political values[14]—and a factor that has reinforced the privileged position of business.

To conclude this section, the gatekeeper model is not tied to any particular
conclusions about either the biases that influence the information and images
conveyed by the media or the effects of these biases on the media-business relationship. The main point of agreement is that the mass media in some fashion
shape popular perceptions of the world through their decisions on what to communicate. The media are not simply messengers; they are to some degree
authors of the message. We will see that the *propaganda model* of the media-
business relationship reaches very definite conclusions about the biases that
affect media coverage of business.

MODEL II: THE MEDIA AS PROPAGANDIST

In a democratic society in which the idea of state control of the media is
repugnant to most people, how can the media be viewed as an instrument of
propaganda? The term "propaganda" is usually associated with the official state
press of communist societies—media organs like *Pravda* in the Soviet Union—
or with the sort of emergency controls on information that Canada and other
capitalist democracies have resorted to in wartime. Propaganda is not generally
considered to be a function of the mass media in capitalist democracies.
Admittedly, the state regulates the media, and in most Western societies even
participates directly as a television and radio broadcaster. But it is generally
expected that governments will not use their powers to impose a particular ideological perspective on the media, or in any way undermine the "freedom of the
press and other media of expression."[15]

Our usual understanding of propaganda is linked to state control and political manipulation of the media. But if it could be shown that the images and
information conveyed by the media are systematically biased in favour of the
most powerful interests in society, and therefore operate to maintain their dominance, would this not also count as propaganda? In other words, for the media
to perform a propaganda function, it is not necessary that newspapers and
broadcasters be controlled by the state. This is the argument advanced by those
who view the media as an agent of propaganda on behalf of dominant business
interests.

The potential for the media to play a propaganda role in democratic societies has long been recognized. Several decades ago, before electronic broadcasting, Walter Lippman used the term "the manufacture of consent"[16] to
describe the process whereby governments attempt to shape public opinion
through their selective use of information. When Lippman spoke of the "manufacture of consent" he had in mind the use of "psychological research" and "the

modern means of communication"[17] by *political elites* to influence popular opinion. But the propaganda model of the media that has developed in more recent times focusses on how the organs of mass communication support the general interests of *economic* elites and the capitalist system.

This model is laid out in Edward Herman and Noam Chomsky's *Manufacturing Consent*.[18] They argue that the information and images purveyed by the media are influenced by a number of "filters." These include the following: the structure of the mass communications industry; advertizing; media reliance on information provided by the state, businesses and socially recognized "experts"; the media's aversion to criticism; and anti-communist ideology. "The raw material of news," Herman and Chomsky maintain, "must pass through [these] successive filters, leaving only the cleansed residue fit to print."[19]

This is a sweeping claim. It goes beyond the gatekeeper model's acknowledgement of media bias to argue that these biases—"filters" as the propaganda model calls them—operate to maintain the social dominance of those who benefit most from the capitalist system. We need to look more closely at the components of this propaganda model before we can judge whether its conclusions about the media-business relationship are fair. The last two components of the propaganda model, media aversion to criticism and anti-communist ideology, are far more relevant to understanding media-business relations in the United States than in Canada. Our focus will therefore be restricted to the argued effects of industry structure, advertizing and the sources of media news.

Industry Structure

"Look, we are running a business organization. They happen to be newspapers."

—Kenneth Thomson to the Royal Commission on Newspapers[20]

As the costs associated with producing a newspaper have increased, competition has suffered. The daily newspaper industry in Canada (as in the United States) is characterized by local monopoly. In only six Canadian cities (Toronto, Edmonton, Calgary, St. John's, Montreal and Quebec) is there competition between same language, mass-circulation dailies that have different owners. Chain ownership is a feature of both the English- and French-language markets. About 60 per cent of daily circulation in the English market is controlled by the Southam and Thomson chains, and about 90 per cent of the French market by the Québecor, Power Corporation and Unimédia groups.

Broadcasting markets are more competitive. The 1986 federal Task Force on Broadcasting found that the largest television audience market share held by any single ownership group in Toronto (Autumn 1985) was 19 per cent; 28 per cent in Montreal; 29 per cent in Vancouver; and 44 per cent in Halifax.[21] About half (49.4%) of all privately-owned television stations were owned by the nine largest ownership groups—broadcasting's equivalent of newspaper chains—with the largest of these groups owning only 8.6 per cent of all stations.[22] Ownership in cable television is more concentrated, with the five largest companies accounting for 53 per cent of the total Canadian market in 1985.[23] One company, Vidéotron, has about 60 per cent of the Quebec cable market.

Ownership in the radio broadcasting industry is also much more dispersed than is characteristic of daily newspaper markets. In 1985, the 13 largest corporations in the industry accounted for 31.4 per cent of all radio stations in Canada, ranging from a high of 40 per cent in Ontario to 13 per cent in British Columbia.[24] Seven private groups of radio stations broadcasting in Toronto captured 66 per cent of that market; in Montreal four groups controlled 57 per cent; in Vancouver four radio groups held 57 per cent; and in Halifax two groups accounted for 57 per cent of radio listeners.[25] This may not look like rip-roaring competition, but compared to the monopoly and occasional oligopoly that is typical of daily newspaper markets, the radio broadcasting market is much more open.

But ownership is a misleading measure of concentration in the *content* of broadcasting. The vast majority of Canadian television stations (85 per cent in 1980)[26] belong to one of the three major television networks: CBC, CTV and CTV's French-language counterpart, TVA. Over half of all viewing time in English Canada is accounted for by the CBC and CTV networks; their French-language counterparts (Radio Canada and TVA) account for over half of total viewing time in that market.[27] Much of their programming, including national news and public affairs programmes, is received through the network affiliation. The considerable presence of American broadcasters in the English Canadian market—33 per cent of all viewing time, 38 per cent of public affairs viewing time and 19 per cent of news audiences[28]—does not add much to programme diversity. The three big American networks, ABC, CBS and NBC, still dominate the United States market. Consequently, the uniformity in programming that characterizes that market is imported into the Canadian scene. The explosion of new broadcasting technologies—notably cable and direct satellite broadcasting—has not resulted in increased programme diversity in the case of either radio or television. Duplication of existing programme formats is usually more profitable for new entrants into a broadcasting market.[29]

We mentioned earlier that media firms are sometimes part of a larger corporate conglomerate that may include non-media businesses. Thomson Newspapers, for example, owns Thomson Newsprint and controls Augusta Newsprint, while itself is a holding within the Woodbridge conglomerate whose other assets span retailing, information services, North Sea oil and publishing.

Power Corporation, which owns Montreal's most popular daily newspaper, *La Presse*, has important holdings in the pulp and paper and financial services industries. In 1986 Power Corporation attempted to acquire control of Télé-Métropole, the largest privately-owned French television station in Canada. Its application to the CRTC was turned down, although not explicitly on the grounds of cross-media ownership in the same market.

Perhaps the most remarkable Canadian instance of a conglomerate that combines media and non-media interests is the corporate empire of New Brunswick's Irving family. In addition to owning all five of that province's English-language daily newspapers, as well as television and radio stations in Saint John, the Irving family has wide-ranging interests in shipyards, all phases of the petroleum industry, forest products, transportation, construction and retailing. The Royal Commission on Newspapers expressed the view that the Irving's hammerlock on English newspapers in New Brunswick, combined with their extensive industrial holdings, was contrary to the public interest: "Irving papers are noteworthy for their obeisance to every industrial interest. They are not known for probing investigations into pollution, occupational health dangers, industrial wastes or any of the other darker consequences of industrial power."[30]

Canada's mass-media industry also includes some large corporate networks whose holdings are mainly or exclusively in communications industries. The largest of these media conglomerates is Southam Incorporated (1987 revenue of $1.45 billion), which includes the Southam Newspaper Group (accounted for 27 per cent of total Canadian newspaper circulation in 1987),[31] printing companies, Canada's largest book retailer (Cole's) and specialized information services like business and professional periodicals. Southam also has a 30 per cent interest in Torstar Corporation (publisher of *The Toronto Star*, among other communications interests); a large stake (20 per cent voting shares; 42 per cent non-voting shares) in Selkirk Communications, which operates television and radio stations in numerous Canadian cities; a 35 per cent interest in Telemedia Publishing (publisher of several consumer magazines); and a 48 per cent ownership share in JEMCOM Inc., which publishes the *Kitchener-Waterloo Record*. Almost as big in terms of corporate revenue is Maclean Hunter Limited ($1.125 billion, 1987). Its activities include periodicals (including *The Financial Post*, *Maclean's* and some of the country's most popular consumer magazines); daily newspapers (*The Financial Post* and *The Sun* newspapers); printing services; cable television in Ontario, Michigan and New Jersey; radio and television stations across Canada; and specialized communications services.

The propaganda model makes a number of claims about how industry structure influences media content. First, concentrated ownership is argued to impose some degree of censorship on journalists and programmers who must tread carefully where their owners' interests are involved. Second, media companies are often part of larger corporate networks that extend into non-media industries. They are interlocked by ownership, directorship ties and financing relationships to the world of corporate power. This is argued to limit their independence. Third, the profit imperative of the market is a factor that has both weakened competition and imposed limits on what is printed and broadcast.

What is the evidence for these claims? We have already mentioned that studies of the relationship between ownership and media behaviour have failed to substantiate the existence of such a link. But these studies have focussed mainly on the partisan political orientation of the media, and have largely ignored the crucial question of whether ownership affects the media's treatment of business. There exists, nonetheless, some less systematic evidence from both Canada and elsewhere that points to the occasional influence of owners on how (and whether) business news is covered.[32] Herman and Chomsky suggest that it is a mistake to look for direct correlations between ownership and the way particular issues or stories are handled by the media. Instead, they argue, owners exercise their influence more diffusely through "establishing the general aims of the company and choosing its top management."[33] The fact that ownership is considered to make a difference by corporate interests was demonstrated in very stark terms during the mid-1980s. American Senator Jesse Helms and media giant Ted Turner attempted (unsuccessfully) to acquire a controlling interest in CBS. The takeover bid featured the slogan "Become Dan Rather's boss," and was largely motivated by the conservative perception that CBS and Rather were biased against business and against conservative political values.

Where there is competition between newspapers or between broadcasters operating in the same market, the likelihood that stories unfavourable to owners' interests will be suppressed is expected to be less. This is the reasoning that lies behind calls for greater competition in these industries. It is also the basis for calls that cross-media ownership—control of more than one media in a single local market—be regulated.

Profit orientation, more than ownership, exerts a general influence on media treatment of business. It would stretch credibility to claim that the privately owned media, because of their dependence on advertizing revenue from business, engage in a tacit conspiracy of silence where business "misdeeds" are concerned. This obviously is not true. The environmental consequences of industrial activity, corporate takeovers, bank service charges and corporate investments in South Africa are among the recent subjects that have tended to cast business in a negative light. And of course individual corporations are placed daily under the light of media scrutiny; sometimes favourably and other times not.

Profitability in the newspaper and television industries depends on large markets. This is due to a combination of enormous production costs and the fact that even a slight shift in market share vis-à-vis that of competitors is likely to result in serious losses of advertizing revenue. Chain ownership in the newspaper industry and the domination of television production by a handful of networks can both be traced to the economics of the market. Mass audiences and circulations are sold by broadcasters and newspapers to advertizers. Anything that reduces the reach of a media company necessarily reduces its appeal to advertizers, and therefore weakens profitability. The question then becomes, "What sort of media product succeeds in reaching the markets that advertizers want to attract?"

There is no simple or single answer to this question. Sellers of BMW automobiles or of Rolex watches will seek a different sort of media vehicle than those who want to sell aspirin or domestic beer. But in the case of both newspapers—where people expect to pay a low price that in fact covers only a fraction of production costs—and broadcasting—where the media product is provided "free," or at a relatively small charge in the case of cable television—profitability depends on the ability to deliver to advertizers a large circulation/audience. The fate of those newspapers that have tried to rely upon subscriber revenues to cover their costs demonstrates the dilemma that confronts media organs whose orientation limits either the size or affluence of their market. James Curran and Jean Seaton show that the eclipse of the left-wing press that emerged in Britain during the mid-19th century was due largely to the economics of the industry.[34] Rising production costs and the fact that other newspapers were able to provide advertizers with mass circulations, combined to squeeze these newspapers out of the industry. This also happened in the United States, where a couple of ad-less newspapers, which were launched early in this century, quickly disappeared from the scene.[35]

Private broadcasters, for whom advertizing revenue is their only source of income, could never even contemplate the possibility of ignoring the needs of corporate advertizers. The advent of cable technology, direct broadcast satellites and pay-TV have radically changed the economics of broadcasting and have loosened the grip of the major networks in the area of entertainment programming. Despite these changes, the major networks retain their dominance in news programming. The emergence of what has been called "infotainment" or "soft news," news that is packaged using an entertainment, celebrity-journalist format, has become prevalent in the United States. The Canadian industry has not gone as far in breaking down the traditional barriers between entertainment and news programming.[36] But the economics of broadcasting in Canada also work against the viability of programming that does not attract a mass audience.

Important as industry structure is, it is easy to exaggerate the influence that this factor has on how the media treat business. The values and beliefs of those who write, edit and communicate the news have something to do with the final product that reaches the reader/viewer/listener. This needs to be kept in mind so as to avoid the impression that media-business relations are simply a matter of economic structures.

Advertizing

In the propaganda model, the role of advertizing is compared to a "license to do business."[37] Without advertizing dollars, privately-owned and even (to a lesser degree) publicly-owned media companies are not economically viable. These media companies are in competition for the advertizing patronage of business. It follows, then, that they will be sensitive to their patrons' needs and adverse to reporting or programming that reduces their attractiveness in the eyes of advertizers. In the words of an American network executive, "[Television] is an advertizing-supported medium, and to the extent that support falls out, programming will change."[38] The advertizing base of a newspaper or radio broadcaster is typically more local than that of a television network, but the maxim still holds: advertizers' preferences cannot be ignored by an ad-dependent media.

Does this have any particular consequences for the way in which business is portrayed? The answer is "yes," but not in the simplistic sense of advertizers holding a power of economic blackmail over the heads of media organs. There are cases—many cases—where particular programmes have been boycotted by corporate sponsors or where their broadcast was followed by advertizer reprisals. In some instances, the anticipated reaction of corporate advertizers is enough to either kill a story or moderate its tone.[39] But the influence of advertizing is much more subtle and pervasive than is implied by a term like sponsor blackmail. Moreover, there have been cases where the victim of an advertizer boycott has gone ahead with the offending programme. One of the most spectacular of such cases occurred in the 1970s, when CBS broadcast a special documentary that portrayed hunting in an unfavourable light. The powerful National Rifle Association attempted to suppress the programme, and corporate sponsors were unwilling to advertize during that hour. CBS went ahead and broadcast the programme during prime time, scoring a public relations coup by standing firm behind freedom of the press, while losing the revenue from that time slot. A similar situation occurred in 1989 when "pro-life" groups (those opposed to abortion) threatened to boycott sponsors of the American television documentary, *Roe V. Wade*.

But when a 30-second commercial spot during prime time on a major American network can cost up to US$320,000 (1990), the economic costs of broadcasting material that offends powerful corporate advertizers obviously are great. Most television broadcasting and most viewing time are devoted to enter-

tainment programming. Because audiences are largest for entertainment programmes, the most lucrative advertizing slots are also associated with this sort
of programming. There is, therefore, an economic pressure on ad-dependent
broadcasters to maximize the amount of high audience-appeal programming
during prime-time hours. Most public-affairs programming does not have the
draw of a popular sitcom or drama, and consequently is subject to pressures that
it be marginalized (relegated to off-peak viewing times, or left up to state-
owned or viewer-supported broadcasters) or that it adopt an entertainment format. We have already discussed the emergence of "infotainment," a development that is clearly linked to the high price fetched by advertizing spots during
popular viewing hours. The popular news times, sandwiched around prime time
and in the morning before work, account for a relatively small share of advertiz-
er-attractive broadcasting time. Business stories must compete for space during
these news programmes with politics, disasters, crime, human interest stories,
sports and weather.

In short, an advertizing-based media system operates to minimize the
amount of broadcast time devoted to public affairs programming generally, let
alone news and documentaries on business. Mass circulation newspapers are
subject to similar pressures. They are read primarily as sources of local news
and information and sports, and for nationally popular columnists. Business
news is usually in short supply and is dominated by pages of stock market and
other financial data. For more extensive treatments of business, it is necessary
to turn to the specialized business press (*The Financial Post, The Financial
Times* and *The Globe & Mail*'s "Report on Business"). These are papers whose
principal market is already sympathetic to corporate values, so that advertizing
probably does not have much of an impact on the way they portray business.

State-owned media organs like the CBC, TV Ontario and Radio-Québec in
Canada, and the viewer-supported Public Broadcasting Stations (PBS) network
in the United States, are not immune from the influence of advertising. Both the
CBC and Radio-Québec rely on advertizing for part of their revenue. In the case
of the CBC, advertizing income accounts for about a fifth of its annual budget.
Viewer-supported broadcasters like the American PBS system rely upon state
subsidies (directly and through the tax system) and corporate sponsorship of
programmes for part of their revenue needs. Some critics have argued that corporate sponsorship, like advertising, tends to filter out socially divisive and
controversial programming, including criticism of business and the capitalist
system.[40]

Dependence on state subsidies does not necessarily remove all constraints
on public affairs and business reporting. Public broadcasters must constantly be
sensitive to charges of bias and ideological favouritism. Over the years CBC
television programmes like *This Hour Has Seven Days, the fifth estate* and

Marketplace and CBC Radio's *Sunday Morning* have been accused of having a leftist political bias and of being anti-business. The in-house monitoring of CBC broadcasting for "fairness" has reached unprecedented levels of sophistication. Much of this, as during election campaigns, is intended to ensure that the Corporation is even-handed in its treatment of the major political parties and their leaders.[41] But monitoring also focusses on the treatment of social and economic groups, including business. In the world of public broadcasting, culture-crats' and politicians' aversion to controversy may substitute for the check that dependence on advertizing imposes on private broadcasters.

There is another dimension to advertizing's influence which is not captured by the economics of programming decisions. This involves the cultural reinforcement that capitalism receives from an advertizing-based media system. In addition to the intended message conveyed by a product ad—the attempt to influence consumer behaviour—commercial advertizements carry an incidental message. In seeking to inform and persuade, advertizing also lets us know that we live in a society in which goods and services are produced mainly by private corporations, and that it is the market—the collective power of individual consumers—that is the key mechanism for determining what is produced. Advertizing reinforces, at a cultural level, the objective reality of the capitalist economy. And it does so in ways that are overwhelmingly favourable to business. Corporations do not, after all, pay millions of dollars to publicize any negative or controversial aspects of their products or activities. Instead, they naturally attempt to create a positive image of their products and themselves. Commercial advertizing is not always successful in promoting a favourable public image for a corporation or an industry. Public relations advertizing (advertizing that is geared specifically to the corporate or industry image, rather than attempting to sell a particular product) has become increasingly important for those businesses that receive an unfavourable press. But the vast majority of commercial advertizing is still centred around selling products and services. The unintended cultural support that an ad-based media system provides for the capitalist economy is not an easy thing to measure, but should not be underestimated on that account.

The Sources of Business News

Journalists are seldom trained specialists in economics or business matters. In one sense this may be just as well. Those who have received a formal education in these subjects are not necessarily the best-equipped to cast an independent, critical eye on corporate activities. On the other hand, lack of familiarity with the terrain may have as a downside an inability to break free of the processed information that is provided to the media by corporations, business associations and the state's economic bureaucracy. *Toronto Star* business writer

Diane Francis argues that this dependence has a strong influence on how the media covers business: "Most of the reporters (for Canada's financial press) run around and do rewrites of Dow Jones wire copy and put their bylines on it. They print press releases verbatim, intact: they don't do any big pictures or trend pieces."[42]

Reliance on corporations and state agencies for much of the business news purveyed by the mass media is inevitable. Alternative ways of sourcing the news involve more time and expense, and require greater journalistic skills, than does buying wire service news (Canadian Press, the American wire services and Dow Jones) and using the vast amount of information provided free by business and the state. Even a casual examination of international business and economic news demonstrates the heavy dependence of Canada's mass media on foreign wire services. Domestic coverage is far more likely to be produced by a newspaper or broadcaster's own reporters, but there still remains the question of how they source their stories. Given the pressure of deadlines, it would be surprising if journalists did not rely heavily on the material provided to them by the public relations bureaucracies of the state and business, as Diane Francis claims they do.

The public relations arms of corporations, business associations and public sector bureaucracies provide the mass media with a constant flow of information. This information ranges from press releases and briefing materials, to organized press conferences and other media-tailored events, all the way to the "canned editorials" produced by some business associations and distributed to newspapers.[43] Unlike advocacy advertizing (discussed later in this chapter), this is information that businesses do not pay the media to carry. It finds its way into the news in the form of data, positions and arguments that have been provided as information, not as advertizing. Inevitably, much of the raw material of the news that journalists report on business activities will be based on the information provided by corporations and their representative bodies. While there obviously is no automatic correspondence between business's "side of the story" and the way the media reports it, there are two reasons for thinking that the general impact of business's investment in media relations helps to legitimize business activities.

First, we need to consider the process by which media stories are generated. When a large business shuts down, or a product is linked to damaging health effects, or a major corporate takeover occurs, or an investor decides to open a new facility that will create new jobs, these events immediately have the status of news. They become part of the media agenda by virtue of their intrinsic public importance and the wide interest they are bound to generate. But much business news is not automatically determined. It emerges, instead, largely from the information provided by the public relations arms of business organizations, by the news wire services and by the specialized business press (domestic and international). In other words, the agenda of business reporting—what is covered, if not necessarily how it is covered—is to a large extent shaped by the steady stream of information coming from business and from the specialized business press. It requires no great acuity to realize that the Dow Jones wire service (New York), *The Wall Street Journal* (New York), *Business Week* (New York), *The Financial Times* (London), *The Economist* (London) and *The Financial Post* (Toronto), to mention only some of the more prominent members of the specialized business press, are not in the business of producing anti-business news. Together they constitute a sort of nerve centre for the media's coverage of business, sending out impulses that are received by journalists, editors and producers working for daily newspapers, television and radio.

Second, spokespersons for important business organizations have a credibility with the media that is cultivated by the routine day-to-day relationships between them. This does not mean that their version of events is always believed, but simply that they can be fairly certain that it will receive a hearing in the papers or over the airwaves. They may be supported by other socially prominent sources of expert information, like spokespersons for business/economics-oriented research agencies, private think tanks and some academics. We are not arguing that business is always successful in influencing popular opinion when it considers its interests to be threatened. Rather, we are simply making the point that the day-to-day, highly professional media relations that are practised by many large corporations and business associations establish a presumption of expertise ("The spokesperson for this organization has a point of view worth hearing") and a guarantee of access to the media—and thus to public opinion.

News management is a term used to connote the deliberate manipulation of what the media covers and, so far as possible, how it is reported. It is a practice that has been associated mainly with the state and with private interests that are well enough endowed to pay for information campaigns that may start with expensive public opinion surveys and culminate in advocacy advertising. Its prosaic but probably most important side involves the continuous flow of information that is provided to the mass media in formats that are readily useable and that are timed to "meet the journalist's scheduled needs."[44]

ADVOCACY ADVERTIZING

The 1988 federal election will no doubt go down in history as the "free trade election." A few weeks into the autumn campaign, the Liberal Party made the Free Trade Agreement (FTA) with the United States *the* issue, and it dominated the last several weeks leading up to the pro-free trade Conservative Party's victory. Only a couple of weeks before voting day, the election outcome, and thus the fate of the FTA, seemed uncertain. A minority Liberal or

Conservative government seemed probable. At this point, business interests entered the fray, spending tens of millions of dollars on advertizing intended to assuage public fears that free trade might not be such a good thing after all.

This is *advocacy advertizing*. It involves the purchase of newspaper space or broadcast time in order to convey a political message. Corporations and business associations are not the only interests to buy advertizing time/space in an effort to influence public opinion on some issue. During the 1988 federal election campaign, for example, labour unions, nationalist coalitions like the Council of Canadians, and some agricultural groups were among those who used paid advertizing to get their message across to voters. But it is business that uses advocacy advertizing most extensively, and there is no doubt that business groups far outspent other groups during the 1988 election campaign.

Advocacy advertizing has achieved its most developed form in the United States. One estimate placed the total value of advocacy advertizing by American business in 1984 at US$1.6 billion.[45] Institutional features of the American political system—especially the use of referendums in state and local politics, and weak party discipline that has provided the basis for the proliferation of political action committees (PACs) which are tremendously active in American elections at all levels of government[46]—have encouraged the growth of advocacy advertizing. But some of the characteristics of American business, notably the enormous size of leading American companies, the extent of their overseas interests and the prominence of the defense industry, probably explain much of business expenditure on issue- and image-related advertizing.

An ad that advocates a particular position on some issue is clearly advocacy advertizing. But what about advertizing that relates to a corporation's or an industry's public image, or that promotes something as general as profits or the "national interest?" This is not product advertizing, but neither is it directly tied to a specific issue. Matters are complicated further by product advertisements that also contain a message about a corporation's relationship to broad social and economic values like national security, economic growth, individual freedom or preservation of the environment and natural resources. Petro-Canada advertizements in the early 1980s contained the message "Pumping your dollars back into Canada," thus making a direct link between the product and nationalist political values.

Distinctions are usually made between product advertizing, image or institutional advertizing and advocacy or issue advertizing. The first aims to persuade consumers. The second may also be geared towards influencing consumer behaviour, but is usually targeted at specialized publics whose views about the advertizer are felt to have an influence on its ability to achieve its goals. Billboard and other advertizing by Canadian breweries and distilleries, reminding people that drinking and driving do not mix and generally promoting moderation in alcohol consumption, clearly represent an investment in protecting these industries' right to advertize their products—a right that has been severely curtailed in the case of the tobacco industry. The third category of advertizing is the most explicitly political in its content and its aims. Advocacy advertizing is not geared toward *consumer* behaviour, but instead seeks to influence *citizen* behaviour. It may be closely tied to specific issues like abortion, free trade or the National Energy Policy (NEP), or it may have a more general focus. "Advertorial" campaigns, whereby large corporations or business associations regularly purchase space in newspapers or magazines in order to express their point of view on a variety of public issues, are more prominent in the United States than in Canada. Perhaps the best known and most longstanding Canadian case was the regular advertorials run in *The Globe and Mail* by Toronto's Bulloch the tailor (father of John Bulloch, head of the CFIB). Over the years, these paid ads provided a forum for the expression of ideologically conservative business viewpoints on a wide range of policy issues.

Distinctions aside, the crucial question raised by any form of advertizing that carries a political message is whether the ability to pay for media time/space should determine what views get expressed. The critics of advocacy advertizing were quick to denounce the blitz of pro-free trade advertizing by business during the 1988 election campaign. They argued that the deep pockets of the corporate interests ranged behind free trade made a sham of the democratic political process and totally undermined the intention of the statutory limits on election spending by political parties (see the discussion in Chapter Nine). Similar fears have for years been expressed in the United States, where well-heeled PACs make extensive use of media advertising (probably about half of these are the political arms of business interests, and in dollar terms corporate PACs outspend all others by a large margin.)[47]

Is advocacy advertizing undemocratic? The defenders of advocacy advertizing by corporate interests argue that it is a way for businesses to overcome the anti-business bias of the media and to bridge the "credibility gap" that has developed between business and the public. Mobil Oil, one of the pioneers of this advertising technique, has called it a "new form of public disclosure,"[48] thereby associating it with freedom of information. Business and economic issues are complex, and advocacy advertizing—most of which is done through the print media—provides an opportunity for business to explain its actions and to counter public misconceptions. And in any case, argue corporate spokespersons, the biggest spender on advocacy advertizing is government, whose justification for this spending is essentially the same as business's.[49]

Criticisms of advocacy advertizing by business are based on the assumption that it works—that the public is influenced by the arguments business pays to have circulated through the mass media. But the evidence on effectiveness is not conclusive. Seymour Martin Lipset and William Schneider claim that corporate efforts to "educate" the public and dispel misperceptions do almost nothing to counter the causes of negative public attitudes toward business. They argue that "business leaders, like the leaders of other institutions, need to recognize that they have been caught in a downdraft that has swept across the entire social landscape...Only if major social changes generate a renewal of public confidence can business and other institutions expect to rise significantly in [public] esteem."[50]

Issue advertising faces a credibility problem, as numerous studies have demonstrated.[51] It appears that advocacy advertising is more likely to make a difference when it is targeted at the elite level, when it is geared toward correcting errors of fact or interpretation and when authoritative spokespersons whose public credibility is high are used to express the advocacy message.[52] Nonetheless, the evaluation of advocacy advertising's impact is largely a matter of guesswork, as is true of product advertising as well. Lipset and Schneider argue that the billions of dollars spent by American corporations on image and advocacy advertising has not reversed the downward slide in public confidence in business.[53]

But there are notable cases where advertising is generally believed to have made a difference in the attitudes of targeted publics.[54] Many of those campaigns considered to have been successful are ones where advocacy advertising generated a good deal of secondary media coverage, thus expanding the reach of paid advertizements. This does not always work to the advertizer's advantage. The Canadian government's 1981 television campaign to promote constitutional reform (the campaign consisted mainly of 30-second "feel good" ads showing Canada geese winging across the landscape) received a good deal of criticism, both directly from the media and indirectly through media coverage of opposition politicians who accused the Liberal government of engaging in taxpayer-subsidized propaganda. The advertizing blitz paid for by Canadian businesses during the 1988 "free trade" election generated considerable controversy about the appropriateness of this spending, although much of the public debate on whether business had helped "buy" a Conservative victory occurred after the votes were counted. In the meantime, both the pro- and anti-free trade advertizing of business, labour and other organizations certainly contributed to raising the overall profile of the issue, ensuring that it remained securely at the centre of media coverage of the election's last weeks.

The *indirect* influence of advocacy advertising—its potential for shaping the public agenda through media reporting that picks up on the messages conveyed by the advertizer—is perhaps the most important political consequence of this activity. At the level of individual advertizing campaigns, the impression and the reality are of enormous diversity in the messages conveyed, the media strategy used and the publics at which they are targeted. But at the more general level of those interests that most businesses have in common (see Chapter One), corporate use of advocacy advertizing, along with corporate sponsorship of academic think tanks and their research, may well serve to reinforce popular consensus on the values that underpin the capitalist system. A member of the U.S.-based, ideologically conservative Heritage Foundation likens these vehicles for getting business's political message across to product advertizing for toothpaste: "They sell it and resell it every day by keeping the product fresh in the consumer's mind."[55] Advocacy advertizing and the dissemination of sympathetic "expert" opinion can play the same role, helping to keep public policy debate, as it affects business, "within its proper perspective."[56]

BUSINESS AND THE MEDIA: ANTAGONISTS OR ALLIES?

We started this discussion of business-media relations by showing the wide gulf that exists between the beliefs that journalists and business people hold about one another. At the level of attitudes, these groups resemble "two solitudes" in much the same way as business people and state officials appear to be separated by a wall of divergent beliefs (see Chapter One). Business spokespersons often complain that media coverage of corporate activities tends to be unfairly negative, based on journalists' weak grasp of economics, their anti-business political values and the media's penchant for the sensational. The growth of advocacy advertizing and other public relations techniques (see the discussion of lobbying in Chapter Seven) is largely a response to business's perception that it cannot count on the media for a fair, let alone a sympathetic, hearing. To add insult to injury, entertainment programming tends to portray business people as "crooks, con-artists or clowns,"[57] thus reinforcing the negative messages about business that are conveyed through news reporting.

But are business and media really antagonists? The privately-owned media is itself a business, for whom the "bottom line" is no less important than for other industries. Some structural characteristics of the mass media, notably concentrated ownership, dependence on advertizing income, sourcing of the news and advocacy advertizing, are often pointed to as factors that bias the media *in favour* of business. This argument is made most forcefully by the "propaganda model" of the media, "gatekeeper models" being less categorical about the direction of media bias. As one writer observes, the fact that business people often believe that they are mistreated by the media does not make it so:

> The considerable volume of corporate advocacy and promotional fluff that business manages to get into print and on the air tends to offset coverage that puts business in a negative light. Business's case against the media might be more convincing if it acknowledged this, as well as the general support for business positions that newspaper editorials provide.[58]

For us to conclude that business and the media are not irreconcilable adversaries, it is not necessary that we accept the extreme version of the propaganda model, in which the mass media are the ideological instruments of powerful corporate interests. These opposing images of the media-business relationship can be squared by disaggregating "business" into two levels: that of individual business people, corporations or industries; and that of capitalism or market economics. Media coverage of business people, corporations and industries undeniably contains negative messages. When television broadcasts images of protesters marching in front of Shell service stations to register their disapproval of that company's investments in South Africa, or when the logging industry operating on the British Columbia coast is portrayed as indifferent, even hostile, to the interests of native North Americans and environmentalists, there is no denying that the media are not sweeping controversy under the rug. Likewise, shady business dealings like the fraud perpetrated on investors during the 1980s by the Alberta-based Principal Group, or accusations of insider trading receive extensive media coverage; above-board practices have a far weaker chance of making the nightly news. Whether the balance between negative and positive messages is "fair" is a question that is not easily answered and probably depends, in part, upon one's own ideological point of view. How else can "fair" have any meaning in such an evaluation?

But even at this level of media coverage the claim that the media are antibusiness is surely exaggerated. It is unlikely that the media are any less critical of other major social institutions, like the state and labour unions. Moreover, we have seen that corporations, business associations and state agencies are important sources of the material that finds its way into media reporting on business.

When it comes to the second level of business interests, that of capitalism, there can be hardly any doubt that the media reinforce the values and institutions of the market economy. They do so by providing a reflection of the dominant culture; both in terms of the structural characteristics of the mass media—dominated by privately-owned, profit-oriented corporations—and in terms of the assumptions that influence how journalists, producers and others who have a hand in the final media product view the world and report on it. Even if one accepts the plausible claim that journalists are more likely to have leftist political leanings than are business people, their differences need to be understood in the context of what "left" and "right" mean in Canadian society. "Left" does not mean serious reservations about the basic institutions of the capitalist economy. To be on the left in the predominantly liberal societies of Canada and the United States has always meant to be ambivalent about business: to distrust excessive concentrations of economic power and to believe that business must be regulated, while accepting the superiority (in most circumstances) of private property and the market system of allocation. But this is the ambivalence of family members who do not see eye to eye on all matters at all times. It is not a perspective that is fundamentally hostile to business.

PUBLIC RELATIONS AND CORPORATE PHILANTHROPY

Dealings with the media have come to occupy an increasingly prominent place in corporate public relations. But at the same time, the more traditional ways in which businesses attempt to project a positive corporate image remain important. These include shareholder relations and philanthropic activities. Their importance varies between firms, depending on such factors as the corporation's size, what it produces, how it produces its products(s) and where its production/investment activities are located. An event like the Bhopal chemical disaster (Union Carbide, India), the nuclear meltdown at Three Mile Island (Pennsylvania), the Exxon tanker disaster off the Alaskan coast, or a more general development like increased public consciousness of apartheid in South Africa or environmental degradation, can result in a dramatic leap in the importance of a corporation's public relation activities. When the unplanned happens, advertizing and media relations will usually be the first line of a corporation's or industry's damage control efforts. But this should not obscure the importance of other public relations activities during both normal and unusual times.

Investor Relations

Corporation annual reports and prospectuses communicate information about the firm that is required by law. But they are intended to do more than this. They are also instruments for selling the corporation to the investing public and for promoting or reinforcing confidence in its prospects and profitability. In response to the growing importance of large institutional investors, most large North American corporations have established an investor relations bureau as part of their communications department.[59] One estimate suggests that the communications/public relations department of a "typical" large firm spends about 30 per cent of its time on investor relations, compared to 35 per cent on relations with employees, 25 per cent on government relations and 10 per cent on interactions with the media.[60]

Investor relations have increasingly become a field for political conflict. Probably the most prominent instance of this in recent years has involved the issue of corporate links with South Africa. Church groups and other organizations and individuals opposed to such links have become shareholders in corporations that have investment or other business ties to that country's economy. This enables them to express their opposition to the South African connection at the annual shareholders' meeting, an event normally devoid of media interest except when it is expected that political controversy will be raised.

When these shareholder protests occur against a larger backdrop of instability that threatens a corporation's public image or its profitability—for example, an organized boycott of its products—shareholder relations may become a tool for defusing political controversy. Some large businesses, Coca-Cola being one, have chosen to sell off their South African investments, an action that can be communicated to shareholders and the wider public as proof of the corporation's social conscience. As a general rule, the more exposed a firm's product(s) is to an organized consumer boycott the more responsive the firm is likely to be to shareholder protests.

Events like the chemical gas leak that killed and maimed thousands of people in Bhopal and nuclear energy disasters like Three Mile Island (U.S.A.) and Chernobyl (USSR) can result in falling share values as investors flee from a company or industry whose prospects are clouded by huge lawsuits or negative public opinion. In such circumstances shareholder relations become a necessary tool for restoring investor confidence. Their importance should not be underestimated. Immediately after an out of court settlement between Union Carbide and the government of India, the company's low share price left it the target of a takeover attempt. Union Carbide reacted by attempting to convince investors directly and through the media that the company was in sound condition. Its share price increased sharply, helping to prevent a hostile takeover.

Corporate Philanthropy

Business people may often lament the press they receive, the abuse they take from the uninformed and their caricatured portrayals in films and television programmes. But there is abundant evidence to suggest that they are among capitalist society's most esteemed citizens, if we may judge by their participation on the boards of symphonies and universities, in fund-raising drives like the United Way, and in a variety of cultural and charitable institutions. The fact that their participation is often solicited by these organizations is due to their usefulness in an organization's efforts to extract money from the business community. Charitable and cultural institutions are often dependent on corporate patronage for their survival. The fact that business people are willing to participate requires a more complex explanation. In most cases they probably believe in the value of the work done by a charitable organization like the United Way, or they may be an enthusiastic devotee of the performing arts, or they may simply like the social prestige of being a university chancellor or member of its board of governors. Individual motivations are doubtless complex. But it is also the case that corporate philanthropy serves a public relations function, a fact that has long been recognized by members of the corporate elite. Charity and patronage of the arts and higher learning are good business and are recognized as such.

By linking themselves to these community services, whether they be cultural diversions for the affluent or provision of life's necessities for the needy, corporations and capitalists may generate public goodwill. Visibility is crucial if corporate philanthropy is to have this effect. Examples include Toronto's O'Keefe Centre (built by O'Keefe Breweries); Calgary's Jack Singer Hall (Singer is the patriarch of one of Alberta's wealthiest families); corporate sponsorship of plays at the Stratford festival, opera productions, symphony orchestras, special exhibitions and permanent collections at museums and art galleries; and donations to universities in return for some public recognition (like the corporate donor plaques that are affixed to the back walls of business school classrooms at the University of Calgary). The public relations value of highly visible giving is not a discovery of modern corporate image-makers. Almost a century ago, the famous American industrialist Andrew Carnegie gave his name to hundreds of municipal libraries across North America, founded with money he provided.

In the language of corporate boosterism, these are "win-win" situations: business is associated with a "worthwhile" and perhaps even popular cultural activity, while for their part, arts and cultural organizations receive funding. But not everyone agrees that corporate sponsorship is without its costs for the organizations that depend on business largesse. As arts journalist Bronwyn Drainie observes, "Corporations almost always seek out safe, successful, uplifting and non-controversial events to sponsor, which automatically rules out vast areas of the arts."[61] "Blockbuster culture," the critics charge, is the inevitable product of dependence on corporate funding for the arts. On the face of it, this might appear to be no more than a dispute over whether the popularization—vulgarization, some would say—of culture is desirable. But there is an important political dimension to this longstanding arts-funding controversy. If corporate sponsorship of the arts and culture discourages the production and diffusion of works that criticize the capitalist system, it can on that account be argued to stifle controversy and the critical examination of capitalism's effects. In other words, corporate funding may operate as a form of indirect censorship on cultural expression, just as advertizing influences the behaviour of the mass media (see the discussion earlier in this chapter).

Charitable philanthropy also has a public relations dimension. In Judeo-Christian societies like ours, "doing good works" is considered to be virtuous and a mark of a developed social conscience. Corporations and individual business people who devote money, time and fundraising abilities to charitable causes are generally viewed as performing a public service. As is true of all corporate philanthropy, charitable work that is not visible has no public relations value. The Ronald Macdonald Houses that exist in most major cities for the families of children hospitalized for cancer are a classic example of corporate philanthropy harnessed to a corporate image. Who can complain if corporations get some goodwill mileage and publicity out of charitable activities?

Critics of private philanthropy claim that whatever social benefits are provided by private charities could be better delivered by the public sector. Not only would dependence on the generosity of corporate donors be eliminated, they argue, but also the responsibility of an economic system that generates huge inequalities in income would not be masked by the PR of corporate giving. Charitable philanthropy is, in the eyes of these critics, an investment in the legitimacy of the capitalist economy rather than being part of any real solution to the social problems it pretends to address. Indeed, there is evidence that the corporate elite has in the past viewed their support of private charity as a way of preventing the growth of a more interventionist welfare state.[62]

In all modern industrial societies the scope of the state's welfare activities has come to dwarf those of private charitable organizations. It is therefore unlikely that business's charitable philanthropy continues to be motivated by a desire to preclude the state from occupying a larger role in social affairs. Far more important today is the public relations role of private charity. In a society where giving carries a presumption of generosity, there is no doubt that charitable philanthropy generates goodwill toward the giver. The link between such activities and the benefits they carry appears clear and direct, whereas the critics of business philanthropy have the more difficult task of explaining how giving can have insidious consequences.

ENDNOTES

1. Louis Filler, *The Muckrakers* (University Park: Pennsylvania State University Press, 1976).
2. Walter Lippman, *Public Opinion* (London: Allen & Unwin, 1922), 345.
3. A study conducted for the 1981 Royal Commission on Newspapers found that the average Canadian claims to spend 40 per cent of his or her waking hours either watching television, listening to the radio or reading a newspaper. See Canada, Royal Commission on Newspapers, *Newspaper and their Readers* (Ottawa: Supply and Services, 1981), 13, 17.
4. *Ibid.*, Table 19.
5. Stanley Rothman and S. Robert Lichter, "Personality, Ideology and World View: A Comparison of Media and Business Elites," *British Journal of Political Science* 15:1 (1984), 29-49.

6. *Ibid.*, 42.

7. It should be added, however, that their liberalism was not hostile to capitalism, as shown by the fact that only 13 per cent agreed that "big corporations should be publicly owned" and 63 per cent agreed that "less regulation of business would be good for the USA." See *ibid.*, Table 2, 36.

8. *Ibid.*, 46.

9. Public choice theory explains behaviour in terms of individual self-interest.

10. See Michael J. Trebilcock, et al., *The Choice of Government Instrument* (Ottawa: Economic Council of Canada, 1982), 15-17.

11. John G. Udell, "Economics and Freedom of the Press," in Craig E. Aronoff, ed., *Business and the Media* (Santa Monica: Goodyear Publishing Company, 1979), 214.

12. Walter I. Romanow, et al., "Correlates of Newspaper Coverage of the 1979 Canadian Election: Chain-Ownership, Competitiveness of Market, and Circulation," study done for the Royal Commission on Newspapers (Ottawa: Supply and Services, 1981).

13. See Richard S. Stoddart, "A Look from the Corporate Side," in *Business and the Media*, 183-95.

14. On contemporary neo-conservatism, see Barry Cooper et al., eds., *The Resurgence of Conservatism in Anglo-American Democracies* (Durham, N.C.: Duke University Press, 1988).

15. This phrase appears in the *Constitution Act*, 1982, s.3.

16. Lippman, *Public Opinion,* 248.

17. *Ibid.*, 248.

18. Edward S. Herman and Noam Chomsky, *Manufacturing Consent: The Political Economy of the Mass Media* (New York: Pantheon Books, 1988).

19. *Ibid.*, 2.

20. Canada, Royal Commission on Newspapers, *Report* (Ottawa: Supply and Services, 1981), 92.

21. Canada, *Report of the Task Force on Broadcasting Policy* (Ottawa: Supply and Services, 1986), Table 27.4, 628.

22. *Ibid.*, Table 27.3, 626.

23. *Ibid.*, Table 27.5, 631.

24. *Ibid.*, Table 27.1, 620-21.

25. *Ibid.*, Table 27.2, 622-23.

26. Paul Audley, *Canada's Cultural Industries* (Toronto: Lorimer, 1983), 261.

27. *Ibid.*, 99.

28. *Report of the Task Force on Broadcasting*, 96, 99.

29. See T.L. McPhail and P. Mercer, *Deregulation Trends in International Broadcasting: A Canadian Perspective* (Ottawa: Department of Communications, 1988), 25.

30. Quoted in Diane Francis, *Controlling Interest* (Toronto: Collins, 1985), 17.

31. Southam Incorporated, *Annual Report*, 1987

32. The Royal Commission on Newspapers expressed this view, although only the Irving case was cited explicitly. See also comments of former premier of Saskatchewan, Allan Blakeney, in Francis, *Controlling Interest*, 316.

33. Herman and Chomsky, *Manufacturing Consent*, 8.

34. James Curran and Jean Seaton, *Power Without Responsibility: The Press and Broadcasting in Britain*, 2nd edition (London: Meuthen, 1985).

35. These were the *Chicago Day Book* with which poet Carl Sandberg was associated and a new York daily called *PM*.

36. See Morris Wolfe, *Jolts: The American Media Wasteland and the Canadian Oasis* (Toronto: Lorimer, 1985).

37. The analogy belongs to Curran and Seaton, *Power Without Responsibility*, 41.

38. Quoted in Herman and Chomsky, *Manufacturing Consent*, 16.

39. See the discussion of this influence in Curtis D. MacDougall, "Business's Friend, the Media," 45, and Mark Green, "How Business Sways the Media," 58-59, both in Aronoff, *Business and the Media*. See also *Manufacturing Consent*, ibid., 17.

40. Erik Barnouw, *The Sponsor* (New York: Oxford University Press, 1978).

41. See Stevie Cameron, "Satirists' barbs fly thick and fast as federal election campaign rolls on," *Globe and Mail* (3 November, 1988), A2.

42. Quoted in Dian Cohen and Kristin Shannon, *The Next Canadian Economy* (Montreal: Eden Press, 1984), 34.

43. A weekly column on small business that the Canadian Federation of Independent Business produces is carried by over 600 community newspapers in Canada.

44. Mark Fishman, *Manufacturing the News* (Austin: University of Texas Press, 1980), 153.

45. S. Prakash Sethi, *Handbook of Advocacy Advertising* (Cambridge, Mass.: Ballinger Publishing, 1987), 20.

46. A good discussion of PACs is provided in Larry Sabato, *The Rise of Political Consultants* (New York: Basic books, 1981), 268-84.

47. These observations on PACs are made by Sabato, *ibid.*, 268-83.

48. Quoted in Duncan McDowall, ed., *Advocacy Advertising: Propaganda or Democratic Right?* (Ottawa: Conference Board of Canada, 1982), v.

49. For example, a former federal minister of justice defended his government's advertising on proposed constitutional reforms by saying, "Government is too complex nowadays to rely on 'policy by press release.' Programmes must be explained—not by reporters but by people who created them." *Ibid.*, 7.

50. Seymour Martin Lipset and William Schneider, *The Confidence Gap*, revised edition (Baltimore: Johns Hopkins University Press, 1987), 366.

51. A 1978 American survey found that advocacy ads had the lowest credibility of all opinion sources, with 51.5 per cent of those surveyed saying that they never or seldom believed such ads. Cited in *ibid.*, 364.

52. Sethi, *Handbook of Advocacy Advertizing*, chapter one, and the references in footnote #38, 94.

53. They note, however, that business has benefited from the growth in anti-government sentiment, so that "improvement in public attitudes toward business are most visible in questions involving regulation, taxation, government control, blame for inflation and relative power—that is, in questions where business is judged vis-à-vis the state." *Ibid.*, 369.

54. See the case studies in Sethi, *Handbook of Advocacy Advertizing*, particularly "Aims of Industry, United Kingdom," "Canadian Petroleum Association, Canada," "W.R. Grace and company, New York," and "United Technologies Corporation, Hartford, Ct."

55. Quoted in Herman and Chomsky, *Manufacturing Consent*, 23-24.

56. *Ibid.*, 24.

57. This is based on a study by the corporate-sponsored Media Institute, which surveyed 200 American television programmes broadcast during the 1979-80 season. This study has often been cited by business spokespersons as evidence of media bias. See Sethi, *Handbook of Advocacy Advertizing*, Exhibit 9, 112.

58. A. Kent MacDougall, *Ninety Seconds to Tell It All: Big Business and the News Media* (Homewood, Illinois: Dow Jones-Irwin, 1981), 138.

59. *Economist*, "Corporate eyes, ears and mouths," (18 March, 1989), 67-68.

60. *Ibid.*, 68.

61. Bronwyn Drainie, "Everybody loves a winner," *Globe and Mail* (15 April, 1989).

62. John Porter, *The Vertical Mosaic* (Toronto: University of Toronto Press, 1965), 302-303.

Chapter 9

Business and Political Parties

When the Conservative Party came to power in the 1984 election, this was widely viewed as a victory for business. The previous Liberal government had alienated some segments of the business community with policies like the NEP, the ill-fated budget reforms proposed by Finance Minister Allan MacEachan in 1981, and a policy-making style—embodied in the person of Pierre Elliot Trudeau—that was perceived by many in the business community as being insensitive, if not downright hostile, to business interests.[1] John Turner's brief tenure as Liberal prime minister marked the beginning of a "thaw" in the climate of relations between Ottawa and the business community. But it was the election of the Conservatives under Brian Mulroney—formerly president of the American-owned Iron Ore Company of Canada—that appeared to herald a new dawn for business-government relations. In addition to the prime minister himself, several of his key cabinet ministers, including Michael Wilson, Sinclair Stevens, Robert de Cotret and Barbara McDougall, had close ties to the business community. The change in the party forming the government was expected to make a difference for policies affecting business.

How much difference does the party in power make for the way business interests are treated by government? The answer is, "It depends." Sometimes the difference can be quite large, as shown by the sweeping nationalizations in finance and industry when the socialist government came to power in France (1981), followed by extensive privatizations and economic deregulation under French Prime Minister Jacques Chirac and the conservative legislature elected in 1985. The 1979 election of Britain's Conservative Party under Margaret Thatcher and the 1980 victory of Ronald Reagan in the United States both are usually thought of as political turning-points towards more conservative, pro-business policies. In Canada, the Conservatives' 1984 victory was followed by government advertising informing potential foreign investors that Canada was "open for business." Some of the policies that had most irritated foreign capital were quickly dismantled, as was the NEP, or transformed, as was FIRA, which was rechristened Investment Canada, with a reduced screening role and a new investment promotion function. These were, however, changes that might well have transpired under a Liberal government led by John Turner.

The relationship of business to political parties may take several forms. Probably the most studied of these, in Canada at least, are business's contribution to *party finances* and the related issue of *patronage*. But other important dimensions of the relationship include the *ideological links* between parties and business, and the *personal connections* between state corporate elites. These dimensions overlap; for example, patterns of corporate donations to political parties are to some degree influenced by what donors and parties share ideologically. For our purposes, we will examine each dimension separately.

BUSINESS AND PARTY FINANCE

Combined spending by Canada's three main political parties during the 1988 national election came to $19.6 million.[2] Total spending by individual candidates came to $31.3 million. Election campaigns are, obviously, expensive affairs. In order to pay for them, and for party activities between elections, money must be raised from somewhere. Corporations have traditionally been one of the major sources of party revenue for the Liberal and Conservative Parties, though not for the NDP.[3] The idea that the votes may be on "Main Street," but the money to influence them is on Bay Street, captures the uneasiness that surrounds parties' financial dependence on special interests. Why do these interests contribute to political parties? What do they receive in return? When does a political contribution become a bribe or a kickback?

The history of party finance in Canada is punctuated by some spectacular cases of corporations "buying" influence through party contributions. The revelation that Prime Minister John A. Macdonald had promised the presidency of the new Pacific railway charter to Montreal businessman Hugh Allen, who gave $350,000 (several million in today's dollars) to the Conservative Party's 1872 election coffers, contributed to the Conservative government's defeat and to a temporary—though only temporary—blackening of Macdonald's political reputation. An equally notorious scandal erupted in the 1930s. The Beauharnois Power Corporation donated about $700,000 to the Liberal Party in 1930,[4] apparently expecting that this generosity would be repaid by a lucrative power contract. As Reg Whitaker observes, the Beauharnois scandal "created in the public mind [the impression] of a thoroughgoing interrelationship of the Liberal Party with a large corporation willing to dispense vast sums of money to corrupt the democratic process."[5] In Quebec, the Union Nationale Party under Maurice Duplessis maintained a close and mutually profitable relationship with business interests big and small, operating a network of patronage reminiscent of 19th century clientelist politics. Everyone knew that support for the governing UN was a condition for receiving government contracts, and the premier himself took no pains to disguise the fact.[6] These are simply a few of the more prominent cases where business's political contributions looked remarkably like bribes or kickbacks.

Scandals on the scale of Beauharnois no longer surface in Canadian politics. The public disclosure provisions in laws that regulate contributions to parties are by themselves sufficient to discourage donations on such a grand scale.[7] Nonetheless, concern over the role of money in politics continues to be expressed from time to time. These concerns follow two tracks. One of these involves *patronage*, the practice of rewarding donors with contracts, appointments and other material benefits that a party in power is able to distribute. The other involves *policy influence*, the possibility that money may purchase privileged levels of access and sympathy among elected decision-makers. Of the two, patronage is probably the easiest to spot and it has received the lion's share of attention, but it may well be the less important form of money's influence.

PATRONAGE: "LES ELECTIONS NE SE FONT PAS AVEC DES PRIERES" ("ELECTIONS ARE NOT FOUGHT WITH PRAYERS")[8]

Elections cost money. They cost more money now than they did when Liberal Cabinet minister Israel Tarte observed that they are not fought with prayers. But even from the first competitive elections, parties have needed to find sources of revenue to pay for their organizational and campaign activities. When in office, a party presides over a state that has material rewards to distribute. It is the nexus between parties' financial needs and the interests of businesses that stand to gain from the contracting, licensing and purchasing activities of government that explains business patronage. Even though reform of national and provincial election expenses laws has reduced the dependence of parties on corporate contributions, corporations and business people continue to be important sources of party funding.

When Canada's party system was taking shape in the decades after Confederation, patronage was very much about parties rewarding their financial supporters with contracts for buildings, roads, bridges and piers (and, as the size of the state bureaucracy grew, office supplies and services). Patronage also involved practices such as giving civil service positions and honorific titles to party faithful, attempting to buy votes with petty favours, and pork-barrelling—in other words, "the use of government discretion to influence whole communities."[9] But it is the patronage relationship between business and parties that concerns us here.

This business dimension of patronage still greases the wheels of party finance in the 20th century. Although patronage in its pork-barrelling and appointments forms tend to receive more attention from the media, if only because they are more openly practised, patronage relationships between business and parties continue to be important.

The practice of *tollgating*—payments to the governing party as a condition for receiving contracts or licences—was widely practised in Canada until well into this century (longer in certain provinces like Quebec). As Jeffrey Simpson observes, the tollgating of liquor companies by provincial governments that determined what products would be allowed on the shelves of provincially-owned retail monopolies was a common practice of both Liberals and Conservatives.[10] As recently as the late 1970s, an elaborate and very precise system of tollgating government contractors came to light in New Brunswick.[11]

A more subtle form of linking contracts to political contributions developed in the national Liberal Party during the 1930s, after the Beauharnois scandal. Under party president Norman Lambert, there developed a system of collecting donations from businesses that had *already* received government contracts. As Reg Whitaker explains, "When a contract had been let, Lambert would approach the successful bidder and suggest, in effect, that they might demonstrate a suitable degree of gratefulness to the government which had made possible their good fortune."[12] Suitable gratitude usually meant between 1.5 to 2.5 per cent of the value of the contract. This contract levy system that Lambert instituted in the mid-1930s, according to Whitaker, continued and widened during the following two decades of Liberal government. Increased defense spending during World War II and the Cold War that followed, and a generally expanding public sector, provided the opportunity for the growth of this patronage network. As Canadian politics began to make the transition to the electronic media age, the cost of political campaigning increased. Parties were caught between, on the one hand, their need for more and more funds and, on the other hand, decreasing public tolerance of traditional methods of raising these funds. This bind led to increasing pressure for electoral reform during the 1960s, finally culminating in the Election Expenses Act of 1974.

Although the contract levy system does not involve any illegal behaviour, it clearly offends contemporary political morals. As Jeffrey Simpson observes about the system under the Liberals, "The implicit assumption remained that if firms refused to contribute *post facto*, they could all but forget about another contract."[13] Such payments are perceived as "kickbacks" that subvert the process of competitive tendering and, potentially, impose costs on the taxpayers who ultimately pay for the goods and services government buys. Despite public censure, this form of patronage continues to surface from time to time. When it does, as happened in 1987 when the CBC reported on a party given for Roch

Lasalle while he was Minister of Public Works—a party attended by thirty business people who each paid a $5,000 entrance fee—the resignation of the offending government member is almost certain. This case actually came to light two years after it took place, and only because some of the business people who paid $5,000 to attend felt they had not received value for their money. They did not get any contracts!

Is there a relationship between the patterns of corporate political donations and the awarding of government contracts? Joseph Wearing has recently investigated this question from two angles. He first looked at corporations that gave significantly more to one of the two older parties than to the other, in order to see whether these contributors benefit more than other businesses when "their" party is in power. Wearing found only weak evidence of discrimination between "Conservative" and "Liberal" donors in the awarding of supply contracts between 1984 and 1986, with the predictable exception of government advertizing. Here, patronage shifted overwhelmingly to agencies with close ties to the Conservative Party.[14] Outside of advertizing, only a handful of "Conservative" donors experienced a sharp improvement in their government billings after the 1984 change in government. In the case of construction contracts, Wearing notes that most of the firms that won these contracts between 1984-86 were not big donors to either party.[15]

Wearing next approached the patronage question from the angle of the corporations that received big contracts. Here again, with the exception of advertizing, the evidence for linkage between government contracts and corporate giving was generally weak. Of the 25 law firms with the highest government billings in 1984-85, only 4 had party contributions that strongly favoured the Conservatives during this period. As the Conservatives' term in office went on, however, an increasing share of government legal work was shifted to firms and lawyers with Conservative connections.[16] Based on the assumption that the recipients of large grants from the Department of Regional Industrial Expansion might be inclined to show their gratitude to the party in power, Wearing then looked at the donations of the 20 textile and clothing firms that received DRIE grants of $400,000 in 1983-84. There was no tendency for these firms to favour the governing Liberal Party in their political contributions; about 40 per cent of them contributed to neither of the older parties over the 1983-85 period.[17]

Despite the adverse media coverage and public censure that inevitably follow disclosures of political patronage, and despite election financing reform that has made the Liberal and Progressive Conservative Parties less dependent on corporate donations, there is abundant evidence that old-style politics of patronage continue to link government to business in a complex web of patron-client relations. It is, and always has been, a web of reciprocal obligations in which each side—business and the party in power—has controlled something valued by the other. Two recent books on the subject by Canadian journalists, Jeffrey Simpson's *Spoils of Power*[18] and Claire Hoy's *Friends in High Places*, [19] paint a picture of rampant patronage in the relations between parties in power and business interests. Among the examples they cite are the following:

Contracts. The Montreal-based newspaper *Le Devoir* found that half of the contractors for the federally financed renovation of the old port at Quebec City, a project costing $115 million over five years, had contributed money to the Liberal Party. As Jeffrey Simpson observes, this probably only reflects a sort of pragmatic understanding among contractors that they should contribute to the governing party.[20] Nonetheless, the fact that they would consider this a prudent and perhaps even necessary "investment" in getting government contracts suggests that public contracting is influenced by patronage. The *Le Devoir* finding appears to contradict Wearing's conclusion, cited earlier, that there is not much evidence of linkage between political contributions and the awarding of construction contracts. Contracts under $30,000 can be distributed without competitive bidding. This alone is an important source of patronage for businesses selling office supplies, legal services, consulting work and other goods and services that governments purchase. But larger contracts may also be awarded without tender. Claire Hoy reports that of the approximately 2,200 federal contracts larger than $30,000 that were awarded between September 1984 and May 1985, about 1,000 were not tendered.[21]

Advertizing. The federal government is the single largest advertizer in Canada. When the Conservatives came to power in 1984, a $30 million tourism advertizing account was given, without competitive tendering, to Camp Associates Advertizing, headed by the co-chairman of the PC's 1984 election campaign. The links between advertizing companies and the two largest parties began in a major way in the 1950s and 1960s, when television and Madison Avenue advertizing techniques started to change the face of campaigning and governing. Patronage remains an important factor in the awarding of lucrative advertizing contracts for all political parties.[22] It is not, however, the only professional service where government contracting decisions are influenced by partisan connections. Decisions about polling services, legal and accounting work and consulting services are often taken outside the competitive tender process, and are widely recognized to be influenced by partisan considerations. Hoy provides numerous examples from the Mulroney government's first term in office.[23]

Business Patrons. Prime ministers, premiers and other elected officials who have the capacity to influence government contracts and policy affecting business have often had corporate benefactors. Mackenzie King's political career was launched with a trust fund established by several wealthy business-men.[24] Two former premiers from recent times, Gerald Regan in Nova Scotia and Richard Hatfield in New Brunswick, had their public incomes supplement-ed with money contributed by wealthy private benefactors.[25] The appropriate-ness of gifts and favours, like the swimming pool installed for former Prime Minister Trudeau at 24 Sussex or Prime Minister Mulroney's occasional use of a Palm Beach home owned by Power Corporation chief Paul Desmarais, has been questioned by those who believe that people in power should not appear beholden to private interests which might stand to benefit from government action (or inaction). But perhaps the most controversial form of corporate largesse involves the financing of party leadership campaigns. The issue first achieved national prominence during the 1977 PC national leadership cam-paign. Combined spending by the eight main contenders came to about two mil-lion dollars. Between 20-25 per cent of that was accounted for by Brian Mulroney's unsuccessful bid for the leadership, and indeed Mulroney's oppo-nents and the media portrayed him as the candidate of big corporate interests.

The "taint" of undisclosed corporate backing again became an issue leading up to the 1983 PC leadership convention. Stories about financial backing from financier Walter Wolf were widely circulated by journalists.[26] Each of the main contenders for the PC leadership (Mulroney, Clark, Crosbie and Pocklington) spent close to $1 million—spending levels that were surpassed by the two frontrunners in the 1984 Liberal leadership campaign (John Turner and Jean Chretien each spent close to the $1.6 million ceiling established by the party). The Liberals' idea of openness was to require disclosure of the names of donors who con-tributed more than $500 to a candidate, but not the amount they contributed. In the 1990 Liberal leadership campaign the candidate spending limit was raised to $1.7 million, and the threshold at which donors' names had to be disclosed was lowered to $100. But as in the past, the amount actually contributed remained secret.

In defense of leadership candidates, the money for their campaigns has to come from somewhere, and contributions are not tax deductible as is true of donations to political parties. But the support of wealthy backers is bound to create an impression—warranted or not—that the beneficiary "owes" something to the benefactor.

To be fair, the scale of these forms of political patronage is certainly smaller than that of the pork-barrelling variety directed at voters in constituencies and regions designated for some particular government expenditure. The decisions to build Mirabel Airport, to award a multi-million dollar patrol frigate contract to a New Brunswick shipbuilding firm, to give the CF-18 maintenance contract to Montreal-based Bombardier instead of Winnipeg-based Bristol Aerospace, and to build a new prison in the physically remote riding of Manicougan instead of in Drummondville are only a few of the very expensive choices federal governments have made in recent years on the basis of what appear to most observers (including the federal auditor general) to be political support criteria. It is arguable, however, that regional pork-barrel politics is at least consistent (some of the time) with the longstanding Canadian acceptance of regional redistribution. A similar defense cannot be made of patronage that involves an exchange of favours between particular businesses or individuals, on the one hand, and the party in power on the other. In this case, anything that interferes with open and competitive bidding for government business has the appearance of private gain at public expense.

What are we to make of this morally gray web of patronage relations between business and parties? Is the recent preoccupation with the patronage issue—a preoccupation that dates from Pierre Trudeau's farewell spate of appointments in 1984, and which gathered steam throughout the Conservatives' first term in office—just an aberration caused by the defeat of the Liberal Party after two decades of almost continuous rule and its replacement by a Conservative Party long deprived of the spoils of power? Is Reg Whitaker right when he says, "The age of patronage is gone. That of bureaucrats, lobbyists, and PR specialists has succeeded."[27] We would argue that, far from being dead, the patronage relations between business and parties have assumed new and more subtle forms. The old-style patronage still emerges from time to time, and when it does public censure and even criminal prosecution follow. Instead of looking for kickbacks and influence-peddling, we should think of modern patronage relations in terms of the privileged access that money may buy, and how this reinforces the other instruments of business influence that we discussed in Chapter Seven.

CANADIAN PARTY FINANCE TODAY

The situation before reform of Canada's election expenses legislation in 1974 can be described in a very few words. The two older parties were heavily dependent on corporate contributors to finance their activities. The NDP, by contrast, depended mainly on contributions from individuals and on the financial support of affiliated trade unions. Corporate donations to the national NDP were minuscule, and have remained so during most years since the 1974 reforms.

It is difficult to attach precise numbers to party finances before 1974, for the simple reason that parties were not legally required to disclose their sources of revenue. A study done for the federally-appointed Committee on Election Expenses (1966) estimated that in the 1953 election the Liberal Party received 50 per cent of its revenues from corporations, 40 per cent from business people associated with particular firms and 10 per cent from individuals.[28] More generally, Khayyam Paltiel estimates that before the 1974 reforms the older parties were dependent on business contributions for between 75 and 90 per cent of their incomes,[29] a figure that does not even include the value of services in kind that they received from businesses, particularly from advertizing and polling firms during election campaigns.[30] Not only were the Liberal and Conservative Parties dependent on business for all but a small share of their revenue, most of this corporate money was collected from big businesses in Toronto and Montreal.[31] Other students of party finances have confirmed this historical pattern of dependence on big financial and industrial capital.[32]

Passage of the Election Expenses Act, 1974 signalled a watershed in Canadian party finance. The Act included spending limits for individual candidates and political parties during election campaigns, changes to the Broadcasting Act requiring radio and television stations to make available to the parties represented in the House of Commons both paid and free broadcast time during election campaigns[33] and a system of reimbursement for candidates who receive at least 15 per cent of the popular vote for part of their expenses. This last reform has the effect of subsidizing the three main parties at taxpayer expense, a consequence that can only be defended on the grounds that this public subsidy helps to weaken their financial dependence on special interests.

But from the standpoint of the parties' sources of income, the most important reforms brought in by the Election Expenses Act involve tax credits for political contributions and public disclosure requirements for candidates and political parties. On the first count, changes to the Income Tax Act allow individuals or organizations to deduct, from their taxable income, a percentage of their donation to a registered political party or candidate, up to a maximum tax credit of $500. There is no limit on the size of political donations, but the maximum tax credit is reached with a donation of $1,150.[34] On the second count, parties and candidates are required to provide the chief electoral officer with a list of all donors who have contributed $100 or more in money or services in kind, as well as an itemized account of their expenditures. Openness has its limits, however. Parties are not required to disclose how much they spend on important activities such as fundraising and polling, although available evidence suggests that these are very expensive inter-election functions.[35]

Perhaps the most striking consequence of the 1974 reforms has been the dramatic increase in the importance of donations by individuals. These contributions were always the mainstay of NDP finances. Now, because of the tax credit for political donations and the older parties' adoption of sophisticated direct-mail techniques of fundraising, first developed in the United States,[36] contributions by individuals are a major source of income for all three main political parties. Contributions from individuals exceeded business contributions to the PC Party in 7 of the 14 years after the tax credit came into effect (1975-1988), and in 5 of those years for the Liberal Party. In view of their previous dependence on corporate money, this represents a remarkable change. Tables 9.1, 9.2 and 9.3 provide a breakdown of party finances for each of the three main parties between 1975 and 1988.

A broadly similar picture exists in the case of candidates' revenue. Over the four general election years since 1979, PC candidates have depended on contributions from individuals for an average of 42.1% of the total value of contributions, compared to 34.9% from business donations. In the case of Liberal candidates, the averages are 32.1% from individual contributions and 26.3% from business contributions. NDP candidates receive very little, if anything, from corporate donors. To some extent this lack of business support is made up by union contributions, which increase sharply during election years. Figure 9.1 shows the distribution of candidate contributions for the three main parties during each of the last four general election years.

Table 9.1

Sources of Contributions to the Progressive Conservative Party 1975-1988				
Year	Individuals	Corporations and Commercial Organizations	Other	Total ($'000)
1975	45.8%	**51.8%**	2.4%	$2,794
1976	48.9	**49.3**	1.8	3,907
1977	**49.2**	48.6	2.2	3,545
1978	**49.6**	49.0	1.4	5,363
1979(E)	38.0	**59.9**	2.1	8,376
1980(E)	40.2	**57.8**	2.0	7,564
1981	**62.2**	37.0	0.8	6,950
1982	**60.8**	27.5	11.7	8,521
1983	**64.5**	34.2	1.3	14,108
1984(E)	48.0	**52.0**	0.0	21,145
1985	**54.0**	46.0	0.0	14,565
1986	**50.4**	46.7	3.0	15,639
1987	47.5	**52.4**	0.1	12,761
1988(E)	41.5	**58.4**	0.1	24,542

NOTE: The single largest source of party funds for each year is indicated in bold type. (E) indicates election years.

Source: Canada, Report of the Chief Electoral Officer Respecting Election Expenses, various years; and annual returns filed by the parties with the Chief Electoral Officer of Canada, 1988.

Table 9.2

Sources of Contributions to the Liberal Party 1975-1988				
Year	Individuals	Corporations and Commercial Organizations	Other	Total ($'000)
1975	**51.4%**	46.2%	2.4%	$2,149
1976	**52.8**	46.0	1.2	5,599
1977	44.9	**51.8**	3.3	4,424
1978	44.0	**52.1**	3.9	4,780
1979(E)	22.7	**74.3**	3.0	5,221
1980(E)	36.7	**60.0**	3.3	6,218
1981	41.2	**53.1**	5.7	5,095
1982	**52.3**	41.3	6.4	6,104
1983	44.8	**48.6**	6.6	7,285
1984(E)	49.1	**52.6**	0.3	10,553
1985	**56.2**	43.7	0.2	5,571
1986	**54.2**	45.6	0.2	10,619
1987	39.3	**60.5**	0.2	8,832
1988(E)	35.9	**64.0**	0.1	13,211

NOTE: The single largest source of party funds for each year is indicated in bold
type. (E) indicates election years.

Source: Canada, *Report of the Chief Electoral Officer Respecting Election Expenses*, various years; and
annual returns filed by the parties with the Chief Electoral Officer of Canada, 1988.

The increased importance of individuals as a source of party revenue can
also be seen from the number of individual contributors. In 1974, the last year
before the tax credit came into effect, the NDP led the way with 27,910 individual contributors. The PC Party had 6,423 and the Liberal Party 9,882. In 1988,
the figures were as follows: NDP, 118,390; PC Party, 53,893; Liberal Party,
30,642. All three parties now have far more individual contributors than before
the 1974 reforms, but it has been the PC Party that has profited most from the
possibilities opened up by the political tax credit. As Khayyam Paltiel
observes, "The Tories have identified a new class of givers drawn from
upwardly mobile professionals and the managerial echelons of corporate enterprise."[37] The PC Party received more individual contributions than even the
NDP during 1983 and 1984. The average size of contributions by individuals to
the two older parties is considerably greater than to the NDP, confirming
Paltiel's observation about the comparatively affluent character of their new
financial support base. Figure 9.2 shows the growth in the number of individual
contributors to each party for selected years.

Table 9.3

Year	Individuals	Corporations and Commercial Organizations	Trade Unions	Provincial NDP Organizations*	Other	Total ($'000)
		Sources of Contributions to the New Democratic Party 1975-1988				
1975	**80.2%**	5.6%	14.2%		2.4%	$2,580
1976	**80.4**	4.2	15.3		0.1	2,206
1977	**77.3**	6.6	15.2		0.9	2,861
1978	**78.3**	6.4	15.0		0.3	3,259
1979(E)	**59.2**	3.7	37.0		0.1	4,597
1980(E)	**46.2**	1.6	27.9	19.3	0.1	6,101
1981	**47.0**	18.2	8.6	35.8	6.0	6,003
1982	**53.1**	2.0	6.7	32.9	5.3	7,108
1983	**57.7**	0.5	7.3	31.1	3.4	8,669
1984(E)	**39.5**	0.5	20.5	30.0	9.5	10,513
1985	45.4	0.6		**54.0**		10,152
1986	34.4	1.2		**64.4**		14,639
1987	**71.4**	0.7		27.9		6,679
1988(E)	**67.0**	2.2	23.2	N.A.	7.6	11,719

   *   This category includes contributions from individuals, trade unions and some businesses to provincial wings of the NDP.

NOTE: The single largest source of party funds for each year is indicated in bold type. (E) indicates election years.

Source: Canada, *Report of the Chief Electoral Officer Respecting Election Expenses*, various years; and annual returns filed by the parties with the Chief Electoral Officer of Canada, 1988.

On the face of it, then, the Liberal and Conservative Parties' traditional financial dependence on business appears to have been diluted. This should not not blind us, however, to the continuing importance of corporate donations for the older parties. They still account for close to half of total contributions during election years, and roughly 40-50 per cent between elections. Moreover, the average size of corporate contributions during most years is 3 to 6 times larger than the average contribution by individuals. Even more striking is the fact that the number of very large corporate contributions is far greater, and accounts for a much bigger share of total contributions, than is true of the largest donations from individuals.[38]

If we follow William Stanbury in defining a large corporate donation as one that is at least $10,000, we find that these contributions have accounted for about 15 to 30 per cent of total contributors for each of the Liberal and Conservative Parties over the last few years. This is a dramatic change from the

FIGURE 9.1

Sources of Candidate Contributions
for the 1979, 1980, 1984 and 1988 General Elections

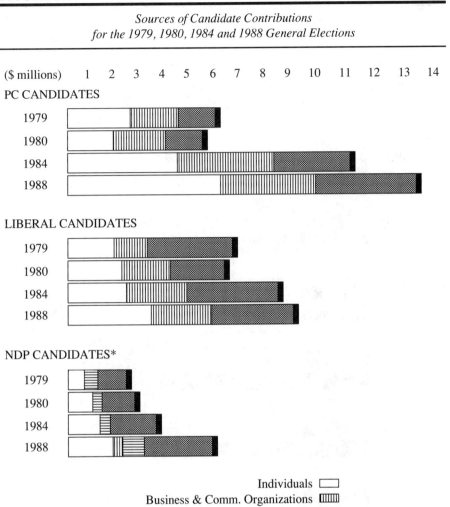

($ millions)   1   2   3   4   5   6   7   8   9   10   11   12   13   14

PC CANDIDATES

1979

1980

1984

1988

LIBERAL CANDIDATES

1979

1980

1984

1988

NDP CANDIDATES*

1979

1980

1984

1988

Individuals
Business & Comm. Organizations
Unions
Political Organizations & Registered Parties
Other

* Business contributions to NDP candidates are grouped together with "other" contributions

Source: Calculated from data in *Report of the Chief Electoral Office Respecting Election Expenses,* 1979, 1980, 1984, 1988.

FIGURE 9.2

*Number and Average Size of Contributions
by Individuals to the Three Major Parties,
1974-1988 (selected years)*

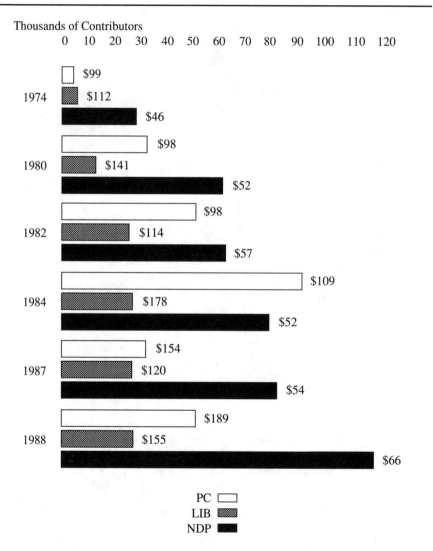

Thousands of Contributors

* The dollar figure beside each bar represents the average size of contributions by individuals.

Source: Based on data provided in *Report of the Chief Electoral Office Respecting Election Expenses,* various years.

days when all but a small fraction of party funds was collected by party "bag-men" from the Toronto and Montreal corporate elites. Figure 9.3 shows the share of Liberal and Conservative Party contributions accounted for by large ($10,000+) business donations for the last two election years. Table 9.4 identi-fies the largest business contributors to each of the two older parties for 1988.

A couple of final observations about the pattern of corporate contributions are in order. First, many large corporations donate nothing or very little to polit-ical parties (1988), 30 contributed to the Liberal Party during the 1988 election year and 32 to the governing PC Party. The amount of these donations ranged from the hefty $79,500 given by Canadian Pacific Ltd. (4th largest company in Canada) to the Liberal Party, to the puny $250 donated by Varity (39th) to the Conservatives. The five major banks are more uniformly generous, being perennially among the largest contributors to the two older parties. In 1988, their average donation to each of the two older parties was slightly more than $80,000. Other financial institutions are much less inclined to contribute money.[39]

A second observation concerns the differences in corporate giving to the Liberal and PC Parties. The conventional wisdom from the days before public disclosure was that big corporate contributors split their total donation 60/40 between the two older parties, with the party in power receiving the larger share. Whatever the historical accuracy of this claim might be, it does not char-acterize the contemporary pattern of corporate donations. There *is* a tendency for large corporate donors to give money to both of the older parties. The major banks, for example, generally give equal amounts to the Liberals and the Conservatives. If there is a "rule" of corporate giving, it appears to be that those large businesses that contribute to political parties split their donations between the Liberals and Conservatives. *How* they split their political donation is anoth-er matter. Looking at the 1984 election year, Stanbury found that "15 of the 52 firms [among Canada's top 100 firms] who made contributions to both parties gave the Tories 50 per cent more than they gave to the Liberals, who formed the government until June 1984, while for only four firms was the reverse the case."[40]

The 1988 election year was an unusual one, in that the two older parties were clearly distinguishable on the free trade issue. The FTA negotiated with the United States by the Conservative government was supported by most of Canada's corporate elite, with some important exceptions like the chartered banks. The Liberal Party opposed the FTA. In these circumstances, how did the big corporate contributors split their donation between the older parties? We have already seen that the major banks continued their tradition of even-handed generosity. Other corporations were much more likely to play favourites. Of the 25 firms that gave a donation of $50,000 or more to one of the parties, 12 gave at least twice as much to the PC Party as to the Liberals. Only 2 of these big corporate donors did the reverse (see Table 9.5).

FIGURE 9.3

*Liberal and Conservative Party Dependence
on Large ($10,000 +) Corporate Donations,
1984 and 1988*

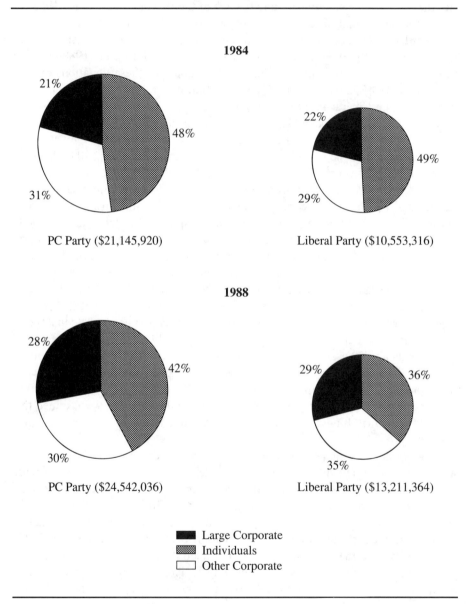

1984

21%
48%
31%

PC Party ($21,145,920)

22%
49%
29%

Liberal Party ($10,553,316)

1988

28%
42%
30%

PC Party ($24,542,036)

29%
36%
35%

Liberal Party ($13,211,364)

Large Corporate
Individuals
Other Corporate

Table 9.4

Largest Corporate and Contributions ($50,000+) and Contributions by the Major Banks, to the Liberal and PC Parties, 1988

Liberal Party		PC Party	
Canadian Pacific Ltd.	$79,500.00	Brascan Ltd.	$50,362.92
Clarkson, Gordon & Comp.	$69,750.41	Budget Rent-A-Car of Canada	$100,000.00
Coopers & Lybrand	$52,181.80	Burns Fry Ltd.	$5,456.94
John Labatt Ltd.	$52,553.00	Canadian Pacific Ltd.	$74,300.32
Lavalin Inc.	$72,135.50	Cast North American (1983) Inc.	$51,000.00
Le Groupe SNC Inc.	$62,782.65		
Peat Marwick Mitchell & Comp.	$55,719.28	Coopers & Lybrand	$57,983.40
		Eaton's of Canada Ltd.	$81,463.52
Power Corporation	$76,202.40	First City Financial Corp. Ltd	$51,480.60
RBC Dominion Securities Inc.	$51,888.68	J.D. Irving Ltd.	$60,000.00
Thorne, Ernst & Whinney	$69,969.21	John Labatt Ltd.	$51,812.62
		Merrill Lynch Canada Inc.	$105,469.11
Bank of Montreal	$80,510.60	Nabisco Brands Ltd.	$102,983.40
Canadian Imperial Bank of Commerce	$82,510.60	Northern Telecom Ltd.	$52,000.00
Bank of Nova Scotia	$80,000.00	Nova Corporation of Alberta	$50,000.00
Royal Bank of Canada	$80,000.00	Olympia & York Developments	$51,180.00
Toronto-Dominion Bank	$80,000.00	Peat Marwick	$54,000.00
		Power Corporation	$72,143.00
		Quebec North Shore & Labrador Railway	$100,000.00
		Royal Trust Corporation of Canada	$76,866.00
		RBC Dominion Securities Ltd.	$50,343.94
		Thorne, Ernst & Whinney	$52,000.00
		Wood Gundy Inc.	$66,394.82
		Bank of Nova Scotia	$80,000.00
		Bank of Montreal	$80,000.00
		Royal Bank of Canada	$80,000.00
		Canadian Imperial Bank of Commerce	$83,383.42
		Toronto-Dominion Bank	$86,067.38

Source: Elections Canada, *Registered Parties Fiscal Period Returns 1988*, Volume 1.

Table 9.5

Pattern of Corporate Giving to the Liberal and PC Parties, by the Largest Corporate Contributors [a], *in 1988*

Company	To the Liberal Party	To the PC Party
Brascan Ltd.	$24,319.90	**$50.362.92**
Budget Rent-A-Car of Canada	590.53	**100,000.00**
Burns Fry Ltd.	21,621.68	**56,456.94**
Canadian Pacific Ltd.	79,500.00	74,300.32
Cast North America (1983) Inc.	20,000.00	**51,000.00**
Clarkson, Gordon & Comp.	**69,750.41**	32,805.64
Coopers & Lybrand	52,181.80	57,983,40
Eaton's of Canada Ltd.		**81,463.52**
First City Financial Corp.	28,944.48	51,480.60
J.D. Irving Ltd.		**60,000.00**
John Labatt Ltd.	52,553.00	51,812.62
Lavalin Ltd.	**72,135.50**	24,972.55
Le Groupe SNC Inc.	62,782.65	32,375.74
Merrill Lynch Canada Inc.	43,781.80	**105,469.11**
Nabisco Brands Ltd.	25,000.00	**102,983.40**
Northern Telecom Ltd.	32,000.00	52,000.00
Nova Corporation of Alberta	25,000.00	**50,000.00**
Olympia & York Developments	41,281.59[b]	51,180.00
Peat Marwick	55,719.28	54,000.00
Power Corporation	76,202.40	72,143.40
Quebec North Shore & Labrador Railway	10,000.00	**100,000.00**
Royal Trust Corporation of Canada	26,000.00	**76,866.84**
RBC Dominion Securities Inc.	51,888.68	50,343.94
Thorne, Ernst & Whinney	69,969.21	52,000.00
Wood Gundy Inc.	25,534.84	**66,394.82**

a   These are defined here as corporations that gave at least $50,000.00 to one of the parties.

b   This donation represents $20,300 given by Olympia & York Developments Ltd., and $20,981.59 contributed by wholly-owned subsidiary Olympic & York Enterprises.

Note: The contributions in bold type are ones where the donor gave at least twice as much to one of the parties compared to the other.

Source: Elections Canada, *Registered Parties Fiscal Period Returns 1988*, Volume 1.

ACCESS AND INFLUENCE

Earlier in this chapter we suggested that the most important consequence of business contributions to parties and individual politicians may be the access it buys to political decision-makers. The shadow of Beauharnois is kept alive by periodic instances of influence-peddling in Canada and abroad.[41] But in most-cases it is a mistake to think of political contributions as a form of bribery, as payments offered in the expectation of receiving some particular favour in return. There are, no doubt, instances where firms that rely on government contracts for some part of their revenue, or hope to receive government business in the future, find it prudent to donate money to parties or candidates. But for most corporate contributors, and certainly for large donors like the banks and those leading industrial firms that are perennial contributors to the two older parties, there is no expectation of a specific *quid pro quo*.

So why do they bother? One explanation is that corporate political donations represent a sort of insurance premium. As Conservative strategist and political adviser Dalton Camp puts it:

> For the wise donor, the financing of the political system may very well be a duty and an obligation to the system, but it is, as well, insurance against the unlikely—such as the ascendancy of socialism—or against occasional political aberration, a Walter Gordon budget, say, or a Carter report on tax reform. When such contingencies arise, the price for *access* is modest indeed.[42]

Another way of expressing this is to say that big corporate donations represent an investment in two-party dominance. Business interests are often at loggerheads with both Liberal and Conservative governments over specific policies. But generally speaking, both of the two older parties are congenial towards corporate enterprise. Business can live with either a Liberal or Conservative government, and has a material interest in supporting the centrist politics that characterize the Canadian political system and in avoiding the polarization of party politics between the right and the left (as happened in the United Kingdom several decades ago). For what it is worth (and it probably is reliable), we have the testimony of party "bagmen" who claim that their pitch to prospective business donors stresses that party donations are akin to a form of civic obligation for leading corporate citizens. Requests for something specific in return are, they claim, extremely rare and are always rejected.[43]

In addition to helping finance a party system that is generally congenial to business interests, it has long been understood that donations buy access. On both sides of the transaction—party apparatchiks and corporate donors—this tacit understanding exists. In the words of Conservative political adviser Dalton Camp: "Toronto money merely [sic!] maintains access to the parties, keeping open essential lines of communication, corporate hotlines, so to speak, to the right ears at appropriate times."[44] This pragmatic view is echoed by an American party official: "Access. Access. That's the name of the game. [Big donors] meet with the leadership and the chairmen of the [congressional] committees. We don't sell legislation; we sell the opportunity to be heard."[45] In many cases the sheer size and importance of a corporation will be sufficient to ensure a hearing when the corporation feels its interests are at stake. And as we noted earlier, close to half of the largest 100 industrial firms in Canada do not even contribute to either of the two older parties. It would be ridiculous to conclude that their lack of generosity cuts them off from direct access to political decision-makers. But all things being equal, contributions probably open the door a bit wider.

Is the distinction between bribery—contributions given in the expectation of a specific favour—and paying for access really a piece of hairsplitting sophistry? After all, if we acknowledge that contributions confer on the donor an advantage that is not available to those who cannot afford to donate thousands of dollars to political parties, are we not thereby acknowledging that party donations reinforce inequalities based on money? It is widely accepted that access is an important component of influence on policy. The fact that corporate donations are neither given nor received in the expectation that a particular contract or a specific legislative or regulatory output will ensue does not mean that there is no exchange. Money helps buy access. Obviously it does not always ensure a sympathetic hearing. But in a political system in which groups are clamouring to be heard, so that they may make their case to those who will ultimately make policy decisions, access to political decision-makers is a valuable commodity. As Dalton Camp observes, party donations are a modest price to pay for this advantage.

The link between party contributions and access has become more controversial with the increasing prominence of "paid access opportunities." These are fundraising events like dinners and cocktail parties where, for an admission price that can range up to about $2,000, donors receive the opportunity to rub shoulders and exchange views with party leaders and other members of the government. Money obviously acts as a filter in determining who is likely to participate in such events, as does the party's invitation list. These fundraising events have been supplemented by an American invention, special clubs for large contributors. Both the Republican and Democratic Parties have operated such clubs for years, where for an individual contribution of thousands of dollars (higher for a corporate membership) the donor receives the chance to meet with important politicians like congressional committee chairpersons.[46] Canada's PC Party—the most adept of Canadian parties at learning from the marketing and finance innovations of American parties—was the first to establish such a club, the "500 Club." Membership requires an annual donation of $1,000, and included

2,511 contributors in 1988.[47] The national Liberal Party operates a similar paid-admission elite network, as do many provincial parties.

In the eyes of some, paid access opportunities such as these raise an ethical question: at what point does the ability to pay for special access to political decision-makers subvert the democratic process by favouring those with the money to make their views known directly? The dilemma is the familiar one captured in Israel Tarte's wry observation that elections are not fought with prayers. Parties need funds in order to carry out their activities. Even with a tax credit for political contributions, only a small portion of all Canadian taxpayers contribute money directly to parties or candidates. The money has to come from somewhere, and developments like paid access opportunities represent the parties' innovative search for stable sources of funds. One alternative would be to impose severe restrictions on how much money parties can spend, so that the relatively small contributions from individuals (publicly subsidized by the tax credit) and the public subsidy that candidates receive from the reimbursement provision of the Election Expenses Act would be sufficient to finance their activities. This would require that current levels of spending by the major parties be cut back. Of course the public subsidy to the parties could be increased. But this would serve to institutionalize the existing party system further, a criticism that has already been made of the public subsidies provided for in the 1974 reforms.[48]

After all is said and done, we should not exaggerate the importance of corporate political contributions as a lever of influence on the behaviour of parties when in power. As Jeffrey Simpson observes:

> Even large corporations, in the era after reforms to the Elections Act, often spent more money on trade associations, the Business Council on National Issues, or lobbying firms than they did contributing to the non-socialist political parties. For them political contributions are a kind of civic duty whereas the money spent on lobbyists and the like can directly reward self-interest.[49]

Political contributions are simply one lever—and usually not the most important one—that businesses may employ to influence government. Simpson mentions the lobbying and associational activities of corporations as more direct pathways of political influence, and as we saw in Chapter Seven, business is highly mobilized and continuously vigilant through these means. Party donations are not an important instrument in the repertoire of business associations. Stanbury found that, in the 1984 election year, some of the most important associations donated paltry sums—if they gave anything at all! In fact, business associations were open-handed in 1984 compared to the 1988 election year. In 1988, none of this country's major general business associations[50] gave anything to either the Liberals or the Conservatives. At the sectoral level, associations were hardly more inclined to give. The Pharmaceutical Manufacturers' Association was the chief exception, donating $4,231 to the Liberal Party and $7,000 to the governing Conservatives. Its rival association, the Canadian Drug Manufacturers' Association, gave $1,021 to the Liberals and nothing to the Conservatives. The few other cases of contributions from business associations included $1,215 from the Canadian Football League to the PC Party, $200 from the Canadian Recording Industry Association to the Conservatives and $181.11 to the PCs from the Canadian Wine Institute.

In the United States, that country's Federal Election Campaign Act has provided the basis for the proliferation of political action committees (PACs). As Khayyam Paltiel observes, "Designed to check the political effect of large contributions, [this legislation has], ironically, increased the impact of the corporate sector, trade associations, single issue groups, and [conservative] ideological groups."[51] The majority of these, and certainly the best endowed ones financially, are corporate PACs. Anticipating the growth of PACs and their political influence in Canada, legislation was passed in 1983 (by a unanimous vote in the House of Commons) that would have banned campaign advertizing by groups other than registered political parties and candidates. The law was challenged by Canada's most prominent PAC, the ideologically conservative National Citizens' Coalition (NCC), and was struck down by the Alberta Supreme Court as violating the constitutional guarantee of freedom of expression. In the court's judgment, the restriction could not be justified under the Charter of Rights and Freedoms' "reasonable limits" provision (Constitution Act 1982, s. 1).

Before and even during the NCC court challenge, some of Canada's leading experts on parties and elections warned that third-party spending by pressure groups would have two undesirable consequences. First, the campaign spending limitations imposed on candidates and parties since 1974 would be rendered pointless if pressure groups were permitted to spend without restriction. Second, groups are very unequal in terms of their financial resources. Without limits on third-party spending, a group's ability to get its policy and ideological messages across to voters would depend on the size of its war chest. Business groups would be at an obvious advantage.

Until the 1988 general election, the fears of those who defended restrictions on third-party spending seemed to be unfounded. PACs had not proliferated in Canada as they had in the United States, a difference that reflected the greater independence of individual legislators in the United States, who thus became crucial targets for both friendly and hostile PACs. But Canada's 1988 "free trade" election produced renewed calls for some form of restriction on third-party spending. The reason was simple enough. Combined spending on advertizing by groups opposed to and in favour of the FTA amounted to millions of dollars. Exactly how much was spent by these groups is not clear, but some estimates place the total above the combined spending of the political parties. Much of the third-party expenditure on advertizing was by coalitions that came together for the express purpose of influencing voters' choices in the election. Two of these *ad hoc* associations were the Pro-Canada Network ($750,000 against the FTA) and the Canadian Alliance for Trade and Job Opportunities ($1.5 million for the FTA).[52] Dozens of business associations entered the fray with their own advertizing campaigns (for example, the pro-FTA Tourism Industry Association of Canada spent $25,000 in the last week of the campaign). While the numbers may be in doubt, it is clear that the vast majority of this third-party spending was by business groups that supported the FTA. It appeared to many commentators, including Chief Electoral Officer Jean Hamel, that the most affluent interests—who happened to be corporate supporters of the FTA—were able to outspend their opponents by a large margin in the battle to influence voters' thinking on the free trade issue (which was, of course, tied to the question of who to vote for). Respect for freedom of expression, so the critics claim, needs to be set against the hard fact that groups are very uneven in their ability to pay for the advertizing that gets their messages across.

PERSONAL LINKS BETWEEN PARTIES AND BUSINESS

In the decades immediately following Confederation there was no sharp division between business and political elites. They were often the same people in an era when public office was not even remotely a full-time occupation for all but a few politicians, and salaries were not considered adequate to live on. In addition, the business of government was largely—even principally—about patronage.[53] Public works, such as railroads, ports, bridges, roads and buildings, as well as contracts for the supplies required by the bureaucracy and the military, were the vital stakes in an era before the state had assumed extensive responsibilities in social policy and economic regulation. The political morality of the time tolerated what we today would consider blatant conflicts of interest. No less a figure than Sir John A. Macdonald was president of Manufacturers' Life while serving as Conservative prime minister. In fact, it was not unusual for private companies to include cabinet ministers on their boards of directors, partly because of their potential value as personal contacts with the government, but in some cases because of the implied guarantee of stability conveyed by a company's formal association with prominent members of the government.[54]

Railroads explain part of the extensive overlap of business and political elites during this early period. Some of Canada's most prominent politicians, men like Allan McNab, Joseph Howe, Francis Hincks, Alexander Galt, Donald Smith and George-Etienne Cartier, had direct personal stakes in the railroad companies whose charters and public subsidies occupied such a central place in early Canadian politics. But more general factors were also at work, including the part-time nature of most public offices, the fact that politics was largely about patronage and the much lower level of what sociologists call "institutional specialization" (the differentiation and functional specialization of social institutions that is one of the hallmarks of modernization). As the scope of government expanded and the time requirements of public office increased, it became less and less feasible for business people to divide their time between politics and business. This was accompanied by growing public sensibility about individuals using public office for private gain. By the middle of the 20th century there was relatively little career overlap between members of Canada's corporate and political elites.[55]

Nonetheless, some notable personal links between these elites have persisted in modern times. If we look at the group of party politicians who have held the positions of prime minister, minister of finance, president of the treasury board and minister of industry, trade and commerce between 1945 and 1989, we find that 20 of the 41 individuals in this group had ties to the corporate elite before entering public life, or entered it after leaving politics. This group of key government members with links to the world of big business does not include Pierre Trudeau, Jean Chrétien and Marc Lalonde, all of whom joined elite law firms after their departure from the House of Commons, and who could therefore be argued to have moved into the network of the corporate elite.

A broadly similar picture of heavy business representation is found in many of the provincial legislatures. For example, the 1989 Liberal government in Quebec includes several members with close ties to that province's corporate elite. Among them are the premier, Robert Bourassa; the president of the treasury board, Paul Gobeil; the minister responsible for finances and privatization, Pierre Fortier; and the minister of industry and commerce, Daniel Johnson. The chief difference between the pattern of business representation in provincial governments compared to that in Ottawa is that provincial cabinet ministers with business backgrounds are far more likely to be connected to small business.[56]

Do these personal linkages between parties in power and the business community matter? Structural marxist theory takes the position that they do not (see Chapter Three). In fact, Nicos Poulantzas argues that the fewer personal ties existing between the dominant class and those who govern, the more effectively the state can serve the interests of capital. The reasoning behind this proposition is that the absence of personal links between capital and the state gives the democratic impression of a state that is not dependent on the capitalist class, but that is in fact constrained by ideological and structural forces.

Others maintain that personal linkages matter. For example, political scientist Stephen Clarkson has argued that Prime Minister Brian Mulroney's background as a multinational mining company executive, raised in a community whose economy was based on American capital, has formed his views on politics and public policy. We should not view social and professional experiences as completely deterministic of how individuals will behave in political life. Nonetheless, it seems reasonable to expect that those who have similar backgrounds will have an affinity of views. Moreover, the network of personal contacts that party politicians, drawn from the corporate elite, carry with them into government is a factor that reinforces the superior access that business has to political decision-makers.

Table 9.6

Professional Backgrounds of Key Federal Cabinet Ministers with Economic Responsibilities*, 1945-1989

		Number
A.	Big business (Corporation executive, corporate lawyer, corporate director)	20
B.	Small Business and Law	10
C.	Professors, Teachers and other Professionals	7
D.	Public Servants	2
E.	Farmers	2
	Total	41

* This group of 41 individuals includes prime ministers, ministers of finance, treasury board presidents and ministers of industry, trade and commerce. This last portfolio has undergone many organizational changes since 1945. We have included under this heading ministers of industry, ministers of trade and commerce, ministers of industry, trade and commerce, ministers of state for economic development, and ministers of regional industrial expansion.

Source: Various editions of *Canadian Parliamentary Guide* and *Canadian Who's Who.*

ENDNOTES

1. An interpretation of business perceptions of the Trudeau government is provided in James Gilles, "Where Business Fails Revisited," in V. Murray, ed., *Theories of Business-Government Relations* (Toronto: York University, 1985).
2. Unless otherwise indicated, all spending data are taken from Canada, Chief

Electoral Officer, *Registered Parties Fiscal Period Returns 1988* (Ottawa: Elections Canada, July 1989) or From CEO, *Report of the Chief Electoral Officer Respecting Election Expenses 1988* (Ottawa: Elections Canada, September 1989).

3. Trade unions are an important source of revenue for the New Democratic Party, especially during election years. They contribute a mere pittance ($7,053 in 1988) to the coffers of the two older parties.

4. As Reg Whitaker notes, this sum was more than twice what the Liberal Party was able to raise from all Bay Street sources during each of the 1935 and 1940 elections. Reg Whitaker *The Government Party: Organizing and Financing the Liberal Party of Canada, 1930-1958* (Toronto: University of Toronto Press, 1977), 12.

5. *Ibid.*,20

6. See Jeffrey Simpson, *Spoils of Power* (Toronto: Collins, 1988), chapter eleven.

7. Conflict-of-interest scandals, on the other hand, involving the unethical or even criminal misuse of the public trust for private gain, remain a feature of Canadian politics. The two most notable in recent years have been the Sinclair Stevens affair, which precipitated a judicial inquiry, and a real estate transaction that led to the firing of André Bissonnette from the Conservative Cabinet and subsequent criminal charges against him.

8. This phrase was coined by Israel Tarte, one-time Minister of Public Works in the Liberal government of Wilfred Laurier.

9. Jeffrey Simpson, "Political Patronage," in *Queen's Quarterly* 95:2, 392.

10. *Ibid.*, 388.

11. Simpson, *Spoils of Power*, 185-90.

12. Whitaker, *The Government Party*, 104.

13. Simpson, *Spoils of Power*, 140.

14. Joseph Wearing, "Political Bucks and Government Billings: A preliminary enquiry into the question of linkage between party donations by business and government contracts," in *Journal of Canadian Studies*, 22:2 (Summer 1987), 144-145.

15. *Ibid.*,145.

16. Fourteen of the top billing firms for 1984-85 were not on the list for 1985-86, and nine of these firms had clearly favoured the Liberals in their political donations, See *ibid.*, 147-48.

17. *Ibid.*, 148.

18. Simpson, *Spoils of Power*.

19. Claire Hoy, *Friends in High Places* (Toronto: Key Porter Books, 1987).

20. Simpson, *Spoils of Power*, 343.

21. Hoy, *Friends in High Places*.

22. As Khayyam Paltiel writes: "Although the New Democrats have not established an umbrella [media services buying] agency of their own, their relationship with their admen follows a pattern similar to that of the old parties, their publicists also benefiting from patronage contracts awarded by the provincial governments, under NDP

control." Khayyam Paltiel, "Political Marketing, Party Finance and the Decline of Canadian Parties," in Alain G. Gagnon and A. Brian Tanguay, eds., *Canadian Parties in Transition* (Toronto: Nelson, 1989), 340.

23. Hoy, *Friends in High Places*, 273, 275, 281-82, 283, 285, 286, 298, 302.

24. Whitaker, *The Government Party*, 18.

25. Simpson, *Spoils of Power*, 138.

26. See *ibid.*, 358 and Hoy, *Friends in High Places*, 341.

27. Whitaker, "Between Patronage and Bureaucracy: Democratic Politics in Transition," in *Journal of Canadian Studies*, 22:2 (Summer, 1987), 69.

28. Cited in Simpson, *Spoils of Power*, 140.

29. See Khayyam Paltiel, *Political Party Financing in Canada* (Toronto: McGraw-Hill Ryerson, 1970), 19-75.

30. These services are discussed by Whitaker, *The Government Party*, 204-206 and 216-63.

31. According to Paltiel, "For the 1972 [national] election half the funds raised in Ontario by the Liberal Party were collected personally by the chairman of the party's Treasury Committee from 90 large corporations." "Campaign Financing in Canada and its Reform," in Penniman, ed., *Canada at the Polls: The General Election of 1974* (Washington: American Enterprise Institute, 1975), 182.

32. See A.B. Stevenson, *Canadian Election Reform: Dialogue on Issues and Effects* (Toronto: Ontario Commission on Election Contributions and Expenses, 1982) and Whitaker, *The Governing Party*.

33. The number of hours per network, and the division of time between the parties is determined by the CRTC. In deciding how much time each party receives the CRTC is guided by a formula that is weighted according to each party's share of the seats and popular vote in the previous election.

34. The Income Tax Act includes a graduated schedule of tax credits: 75 per cent for donations up to $100; 50 per cent for contributions between $100 and $550; and 33.3 per cent for amounts over $550, to a maximum tax credit of $500.

35. Paltiel, "Political Marketing, Party Finance, and the Decline of Political Parties," 342.

36. See Sabato, *The Rise of Political Consultants*, especially chapter four.

37. Paltiel, "Political Marketing, Party Finance and the Decline of Political Parties," 344.

38. Stanbury calculates that contributions of $2,000 or more by individuals accounted for 1.5 per cent of all contributions by individuals to the PC Party in 1983, 10.7 per cent in 1984, 4.6 per cent in 1985 and 2.5 per cent in 1986. In the case of the Liberal Party, the percentages for these years were 4.4, 1.7, 1.7 and 5.8. See Stanbury, "Financing the Federal Political Parties in Canada, 1974-1986," in *Canadian Parties in Transition*, 365.

39. This pattern of corporate giving is consistent with Stanbury's findings for the 1983-86 period. See *ibid.*, 368-71.

40. *Ibid.*, 371.

41. Perhaps the most spectacular instance of influence-peddling in recent years was Japan's *Recruit* scandal, which played an important part in the fall of that country's Liberal government after over thirty years in power.

42. Dalton Camp, *Points of Departure* (Toronto: Deneau and Greenberg, 1979), 91.

43. In the words of former Liberal Senator John Godfrey: "When I was in charge of raising money in Ontario for the 1968 federal election all canvassers were instructed to approach prospective donors on the basis that giving a donation was merely being a good corporate citizen...and that they should give equally to the party in power and the official opposition...Since I became involved in 1968 I can recall four instances in which a prospective donor stated that what he might give would be influenced by some action, legislative or otherwise, which he wanted the government to take. I can recall how startled these gentlemen were when I told them forcefully and in no uncertain terms that the Liberal Party was not for sale, the government was not for sale, and that was not the basis upon which the Liberal Party raised or accepted money." Quoted in Ian Urquhart, "The Bucks Stop Here: Behind Every Great Leader is an Equally Great Bagman," *Maclean's*, (15 May, 1978), 45.

44. Camp, *Points of Departure*, 91.

45. Elizabeth Drew, *Politics and Money* (New York: Macmillan, 1983), #49.

46. Sabato, *The Rise of Political Consultants*, 279.

47. Calculated from Chief Electoral Officer of Canada, *Registered Parties Fiscal Period Returns* 1988, Vol. 1.

48. Paltiel, "Political Marketing, Party Finance and the Decline of Political Parties," 348.

49. Simpson, *Spoils of Power*, 372.

50. This list includes the Canadian Chamber of Commerce, the Canadian Manufacturers' Association, the Business Council on National Issues, the Canadian Federation of Independent Business, the Canada Organization of Business, the Business Council of British Columbia and the Conseil du Patronat du Québec.

51. Paltiel, "Political Marketing, Party Finance and the Decline of Political Parties," 337.

52. *Maclean's*, 101, No. 50 (5 December, 1988), 26.

53. See Simpson, *Spoils of Power* and Gordon Stewart, *The Origins of Canadian Politics* (Vancouver: University of British Columbia Press, 1986).

54. This was particularly true of the fledgling insurance industry. See Michael Bliss, *Northern Enterprise* (Toronto: McClelland and Stewart, 1988), 273.

55. Of the 611 Canadian-born members of the group John Porter identified as the economic elite (1955), 56 had been Liberal or Conservative Party politicians at some point in their working lives. *The Vertical Mosaic* (Toronto: University of Toronto Press, 1965), 298.

56. This observation is based on the author's own survey of the professional backgrounds of provincial cabinet ministers in 1988.

PART 5

PUBLIC POLICY

Chapter 10

Competition Policy

If we examine actual corporate behaviour it quickly becomes apparent that most businesses are not great lovers of competition, at least not for themselves. Despite the rhetoric about the alleged virtues of combative, rugged, individualist, risk-taking entrepreneurship, the reality of corporate activity is more prosaic and less favourably inclined towards competition. There is nothing particularly surprising about this because competition is a stressful and threatening process. For the mature corporation, competition threatens to steal customers, undermine profits, force price-cutting, reduce commissions, lower dividends, restrict cash-flow and eliminate people's jobs. If competition is too intense, then the corporation may even be threatened with bankruptcy. The tougher the competition, the harder executives and managers have to work, and the more they have to worry.

Where competition is inescapable, corporations spend large amounts of time and money trying to reduce it by eliminating their competitors, and naturally enough their competitors try to do the same. Whatever the social utility of such competition, a corporate war of all against all brings stress and insecurity for the participants, makes the business environment more unpredictable and makes corporate planning more difficult, though more necessary. Consequently, it becomes tempting to seek a truce in this warfare by trying to reach some sort of collective accommodation amongst formally competitive enterprises, or to reduce competition by some other means.

TYPES OF ANTI-COMPETITIVE BEHAVIOUR

One of the principal forms of anti-competitive behaviour is collusion between firms to restrain trade. This includes agreements to fix prices, to rig bids for contracts, to limit production, to divide up markets, either regionally or by agreeing to sell non-competing products, and to restrain trade in other ways.

In Adam Smith's often quoted words, written in the eighteenth century: "People of the same trade seldom meet together, even for merriment and diversion, but the conversation ends in a conspiracy against the public, or in some contrivance to raise prices."[1]

Today, conspiracies in restraint of trade are illegal, but there are still ways for companies to reduce competition while avoiding prosecution. One practice, which does not involve an explicit conspiracy, is known as *conscious parallelism*. This sometimes occurs in industries that are dominated by a small number of large producers (oligopolies). It takes place when corporations all set their prices at about the same level, and raise them at the same time, in parallel. One firm (normally the largest) is recognized as the price leader, and when that company raises its prices, all the others take the hint and follow suit. Conscious parallelism, itself, is not illegal, and firms cannot be charged with conspiracy because no actual collusion, or meeting, has taken place.

An alternative strategy for reducing competition, which also avoids the charge of conspiracy, is to take over or merge with a competing firm. Rivalry is eliminated, and the single enterprise that emerges can hardly be charged with conspiracy because conspiracy requires at least two participants. However, mergers that would substantially lessen competition can still be prohibited by government under certain circumstances.

If a company has a dominant position in a market, that is, if it has substantial monopoly control, then a variety of anti-competitive practices can be employed to maintain this position and undermine smaller competitors. For instance, the company might require its suppliers to shun these smaller competitors, by cutting them off or raising their costs. Alternatively, the dominant company may introduce "fighting brands" on a selective and temporary basis in order to push a smaller firm's products out of the market. These and other abuses of a dominant position are also forbidden by the Canadian government.

Finally, individual companies can engage in anti-competitive behaviour even if they do not have a monopolistic position. This includes such things as *"predatory pricing,"* where a company charges an unreasonably low price for a product in order to eliminate a competitor; *"resale price maintenance,"* where a supplier of a product requires retailers to keep their prices above a certain level; and *"exclusive dealing,"* where a supplier requires a customer to refrain from dealing with other suppliers as a condition of trade.

Most of the above practices are illegal in Canada (with a number of qualifications and exemptions), and currently the rules governing conspiracy, merger, abuse of dominant position, and miscellaneous restrictive practices constitute the essence of Canada's competition law enshrined in the Competition Act and the Competition Tribunal Act of 1986.[2] Before looking at the development of competition policy in Canada, it is first necessary to examine the basic goals that provide the rationale for this area of government intervention.

THE GOALS OF COMPETITION POLICY

Anti-competitive behaviour and high levels of corporate concentration create a number of different problems for capitalist democracies such as Canada. Not all of these problems have been given equal weight by government in the formation of competition policy, and the specific character of Canadian competition policy reflects the priority given to some concerns over others.

One objective that has *not* been given high priority by government in Canada is to ban the existence of monopolies, giant mergers and high concentrations of corporate power. We noted in Chapter Five that many areas of Canadian industry are dominated by a small number of large corporations, and that vast conglomerate enterprises spread their tentacles across much of the Canadian economic landscape. Part of the reason for this is that governments have taken a very permissive attitude towards corporate size and the overall concentration of economic power in Canadian society. Legislation in this araa has been weak. Government authority has not been used to restrict monopolies and concentrated economic power *per se*. Instead government has adopted a much more limited goal of trying to ensure that such concentrated power is not abused or exploited to restrain trade in certain ways.[3]

While such an approach does address the problem of specific anti-competitive abuses, it ignores the broader issues raised by the very existence of high concentrations of private economic power. In this regard, it is important to recognize that economic power is also intrinsically political. Control over production and distribution means that corporations continually make decisions that have a direct impact on people's livelihoods. These include decisions about who gets hired and who doesn't; whether production is expanded or workers are laid off; whether a plant will be closed down in this community or that one; whether a new factory will be located in one province or the next; and so on. These decisions are political ones because they directly affect "who gets what,"[4] and they are left largely to the discretion of private sector corporations. As Charles Lindblom points out, the use of such discretion creates problems for popular control:

> Corporate discretion poses an increasingly serious threat to popular control as the business enterprise grows in size. The discretionary decision of a single large corporation (to move in or out) can create or destroy a town, pollute the air for an entire city, upset the balance of payments between countries, and wipe out the livelihoods of thousands of employees.[5]

When this economic authority becomes concentrated in fewer and fewer hands we move closer towards a society in which the distribution of power is more centralized and less democratic.

Corporate concentration and the growth of giant conglomerates also increase the power of business over public policy. It is very hard for policy-makers to ignore the interests of corporations that control substantial segments of the economy, especially if these corporations are "rootless" multinationals that can move capital out of the country without too much difficulty. Governments must be more deferential to large employers, and corporate "giantism" weakens the hand of government in bargaining with business.

A further problem, illuminated by Milton Friedman, is that monopolies restrict liberty by reducing the alternatives available to individuals and inhibiting freedom of exchange.[6] However, Friedman is so hostile towards government that he rejects state intervention, even when it is designed to break up monopolies. He accuses government itself of being the most important source of monopoly power, and says that while private unregulated monopolies may be evil, government regulation is worse.[7] Friedman also contends that regulation is not required because the extent of monopoly, at least in the United States, has been overestimated.[8]

In Canada, the extent of corporate concentration has already been illustrated, but the broad political concerns about the power of monopolies and oligopolies have not figured prominently among government priorities. Instead, more narrowly defined economic goals have been emphasized. Paul Gorecki and W.T. Stanbury have analyzed the objectives of Canadian competition policy over a period of almost a century, and they conclude that three major goals stand out.[9] First, legislation has attempted to prevent abuses of economic power, such as predatory pricing, in order to protect the interests of consumers and competing business people. Second, the maintenance of free competition has been perceived, notably by the judiciary, as a virtue in itself which serves to protect the public interest. And third, a more recent goal of competition policy has been to promote economic efficiency, based on the belief that the efficient allocation of resources depends on the existence of competitive markets.[10] They also identify a number of lesser objectives that have arisen from time to time, such as fighting inflation, promoting small business and preserving the "free enterprise" system.

On a somewhat different plane, Joseph Schumpeter argues that giant industrial units are a threat to capitalism. Individual entrepreneurship will be destroyed and replaced by mechanistic bureaucracies and salaried administrators, and the entrepreneurial class will lose its crucial function of invention and innovation. In conjunction with other forces, capitalism will crumble, and socialism will be the likely outcome.[12]

> The perfectly bureaucratized giant industrial unit not only ousts the small and medium-sized firm and 'expropriates' its owners, but in the end it also

ousts the entrepreneur and expropriates the bourgeoisie as a class which in
the process stands to lose not only its income but also what is infinitely
more important, its function. The true pacemakers of socialism were not
the intellectuals or agitators who preached it but the Vanderbilts, Carnegies
and Rockefellers.[13]

However, it must be noted that Schumpeter is not defending "perfect" competition here, nor attacking monopolies for leading to economic stagnation. In
fact, Schumpeter sees monopolies as often being economically superior to competitive markets, and he staunchly defends some monopolistic practices. The
argument is not that capitalism will be destroyed by market failure and poor
economic performance, but ironically, that it will be destroyed by its own economic success.

None of this reasoning has troubled Canadian policy-makers unduly, and a
similar lack of concern has greeted marxist analysis about the growing centralization of capital. For Marx, the laws of capitalist production mean that larger
and stronger capitalists will continually "gobble up" and destroy their weaker
brethren—in Marx's words, "One capitalist always kills many."[14] As the number of capitalists who benefit from the system diminishes constantly and the
mass of proletarian misery grows, so the working-class becomes more politicized and revolutionary. The monopolization of capital and the growth of working class consciousness together provide the conditions that will eventually tear
the capitalist system asunder.[15] Needless to say this has not yet happened in
Canada, in part because "proletarian misery" has been attenuated both by the
economic successes of capitalism and by the intervention of the welfare state.
Class consciousness has generally been weak, and any destructive tendencies of
monopolization have not yet come to fruition. Consequently, there has been little
immediate incentive for the state to react to this "threat" with stringent anti-
monopoly policies.

THE HISTORY OF CANADIAN COMPETITION POLICY

The first attempts to legislate against uncompetitive business practices took
place at approximately the same time in both Canada and the United States. In
1889 Canada's first anti-combines law was passed, and in 1890 the United
States passed the Sherman Antitrust Act, outlawing conspiracies and combinations in restraint of trade, and banning monopolies or attempts to create monopolies. This proximity in timing, however, did not mean that the two laws were
similar. At the very outset U.S. competition law was stricter and more comprehensive than its Canadian counterpart, and this situation continued throughout
the subsequent history of competition policy. Although U.S. legislation has
been far from successful in preventing large concentrations of economic power,
it is generally recognized that Canadian law has been even weaker.

The Anti-Combinations Act of 1889

The Canadian legislation of 1889 was a response to public criticism of price-fixing by certain groups of merchants and producers, especially the Dominion Wholesale Grocers' Guild which controlled sugar, starch, baking soda, tobacco and other goods.[16] Domestic price-fixing had become easier since 1879, when the National Policy tariffs restricted imports, and pressure was mounting on the Conservative government to do something about it. In a calculated attempt to deflect this criticism, the government grudgingly passed the Act,[17] though not before it had been watered down following heavy business lobbying.[18]

The new law made it a criminal offence for businesses to conspire to restrain trade or lessen competition, but the actual wording of the law was so heavily qualified that it was unenforcable and useless. Business people and corporations could only be prosecuted if they conspired or combined *unlawfully* to lessen competition, production or distribution *unduly*, or to enhance prices *unreasonably*. The use of so many qualifiers provided corporations with a variety of legal loopholes, and over the next 14 years there was not a single successful prosecution. This was despite the fact that "the Dominion Wholesale Grocers' Guild was still recording its price-fixing arrangements in its minute books."[19] It was only after 1900, when the word "unlawfully" was dropped, that prosecutions became marginally easier, although there were still only four successful prosecutions between 1900 and 1910 when the Combines Investigation Act was passed.[20]

The Combines Investigation Act of 1910

Besides its overall weakness, the legislation of 1889 suffered from two other specific defects. Firstly, it failed to establish any institutional mechanisms for enforcing the law; responsibility for bringing cases to trial was simply passed off on to the provincial attorneys general.[21] Secondly, it had not dealt with the problem of monopolies and mergers.

The new Act, which was introduced by the Minister of Labour, Mackenzie King, tried to remedy both of these shortcomings. As an enforcement mechanism, any six people could now petition a judge to investigate an alleged business combination. After a hearing, the judge could then direct the Ministry of Labour to appoint a three-person commission, consisting of a representative of each party and a judge as chairperson. An inquiry would then be held to examine evidence, call witnesses, etc., and a report would eventually be given to the minister and published. If businesses were found to be acting criminally, then they could be fined.[22] As for the second defect, the definition of a combine was expanded to include trusts, monopolies and mergers.[23]

Mackenzie King was himself no great champion of business competition law, and he saw most mergers as conducive to economic efficiency.[24] Yet, the Liberal government was facing public pressure over a series of business combinations that were blamed for creating inflation.[25] Mergers abounded, including a major cotton merger to form Dominion Textiles in 1904; the consolidation of 24 Ontario factories to form Canadian Canneries Co. in 1905; and the merger of 23 cement producers by Max Aitken (later Lord Beaverbrook) to form Canada Cement in 1909.[26] The main merger wave, however, occurred in the period 1909-1912 when 58 industrial amalgamations took place.[27] The Combines Investigation Act had little impact on this movement, and in fact only one case was actually pursued between 1910 and 1919 when the Act was amended. On paper the scope of competition law had been extended, but in practice the impact had, if anything, been reduced.

The Amendments of 1919

The law of 1910 suffered from two main shortcomings which reduced its effectiveness. First, too many burdens had been placed on the complainants themselves in initiating and pursuing cases; and second, the enforcement procedures existed only on an *ad hoc* basis, with commissions of enquiry being set up, and then disbanded, for each particular case. In 1919 amendments were passed that established a permanent tribunal (the Board of Commerce) to examine suspected combines, with powers to initiate investigations of its own accord.[28] These improvements were short-lived. In 1921, some of the Board's activities were ruled *ultra vires*, i.e. outside the jurisdiction of the federal government, and the whole legislation was abandoned. A new act was drawn up in 1923.

The Combines Investigation Act of 1923

For over 30 years, competition policy in Canada had been almost completely ineffective, and passage of a new law in 1923 changed things only slightly. Essentially, the Act consolidated previous legislation, including a definition of combines that covered conspiracies, monopolies and mergers if they lessened competition unduly, and established a permanent registrar to investigate complaints. Combinations still fell under criminal law, where individuals could be fined up to $10,000 or imprisoned for up to two years. Corporations could be fined up to $25,000.

Typically, businesses reacted with hostility to the new law and lobbied against it,[29] though some may have been reassured by Prime Minister Mackenzie King's statement that:

The legislation does not seek in any way to restrict just combinations or agreements between business and industrial houses or firms, but it does seek to protect the public against the possible ill effects of these combinations.[30]

On average, between 1923 and 1942, less than one case per year was launched by the Crown.[31] For most of the 1930s, federal governments were more concerned with pushing prices up, as a stimulus to economic recovery, than with encouraging further price reductions. In the Great Depression, R.B. Bennett's government was generally unsympathetic to the Act, and it was not vigorously implemented. Reports of investigations were suppressed, and funding was cut.[32]

With some subsequent amendments the Combines Investigation Act provided the basis for Canadian competition law up until 1986. In 1935 the notion of detriment to the public interest was introduced, along with provisions on price discrimination; in 1952 resale price maintenance was banned; in 1960 restrictions were placed on misleading advertizing; and in 1976 the law was extended to cover service industries. However, up to 1986, the record is characterized more by the failure of reform than by its success. Most notably, a long saga of failed reform attempts followed the introduction of Bill C-256 in June 1971.

Attempts at Reform

The Initial Thrust: Bill C-256

Bill C-256 was a sweeping set of proposals to reform Canada's competition law, based on a 1969 report of the Economic Council of Canada.[33] In comparison with earlier reforms, it was far-reaching and radical, though this was not difficult given the limited nature of previous efforts. The essence of the proposals was threefold. Firstly, a range of business practices involving conspiracy would become criminal offences per se, without the Crown having to prove that they lessened competition unduly. Agreements between businesses to fix prices, allocate markets, limit production or engage in a variety of other anti-competitive practices would become criminal acts without qualification.[34] Convictions would now be much easier to obtain. Secondly, prohibitions against monopolization, resale price maintenance and misleading advertizing would be broadened in scope. These would also become indictable offences under criminal law.[35] Finally, provisions concerning mergers and certain restrictive practices would be transferred from criminal law to civil law, and cases would be adjudicated by a tribunal. As a result, the standard of proof would be reduced from "beyond reasonable doubt" under criminal law to "on the balance of probabilities" under civil law. Judgements against business would now be easier to achieve, though civil procedures also meant that the penalties would be less severe.

The potential impact of Bill C-256 on business was indicated by the ferocity with which the corporate world attacked it. Throughout the history of competition policy, big business had always opposed any strengthening of the law, but this time the reaction was particularly fierce. Individual corporations and business groups were immoderate in their criticisms, and targeted not just the bill itself but also its instigator, Minister of Consumer and Corporate Affairs, Ron Basford. By January 1972 that department had received 217 briefs or suggested amendments to the bill, most coming from producer groups, and virtually all being hostile.[36]

Faced with this business opposition, and with an election coming up in 1972, the Trudeau government started to get cold feet. It was reported that financial contributions from business were starting to swing in the Conservative's favour,[37] and this may have led Trudeau to replace Ron Basford early in 1972 and to back pedal on the legislation. The bill did not get as far as second reading in the House of Commons, and in the words of William Stanbury, "The intense narrowly focussed interest of business easily defeated the broader and diffuse interests of consumers."[38]

In 1973, in the wake of the failure of C-256, new reform proposals were put forward in two stages. Stage I revamped the least controversial sections of the Basford bill, including resale price maintenance, misleading advertizing and the conspiracy sections, although the word "unduly" was now retained. This stage was passed in 1975. Stage II, including revised sections on mergers and monopolies, was postponed until 1977 when it was introduced as Bill C-42.

Stage II: Bill C-42.

Bill C-42 included many of the same basic provisions concerning monopolies and mergers as C-256, including the use of both criminal and civil law and the creation of a tribunal. However, monopolistic firms would now be allowed an exemption if their actions resulted from superior economic efficiency. In another revision, some attempt was made to deal with the problem of "conscious parallelism" by removing the necessity for a formal agreement between firms.

Once again business went on the offensive and lobbied hard to water down or defeat the bill. Parliament provided a principal forum for this battle, and committees in the House and Senate turned into arenas for business opposition. In the Senate, the Committee on Banking, Trade and Commerce, after listening exclusively to business groups, concluded that almost every provision needed changing.[39] In the House, the Committee on Finance, Trade and Economic

Affairs made 94 recommendations, most of which would have reduced the effectiveness of the Act.[40]

Like C-256, the bill was so heavily criticized that it was withdrawn and in its place yet another set of proposals was drafted, namely Bill C-13.

Stage II Again: Bill C-13

Bill C-13 was introduced in November 1977 by Warren Allmand, who was the eighth Minister of Consumer and Corporate Affairs in ten years. The bill itself was a paler reflection of C-42 and incorporated some of the suggestions made by business at the earlier stages. One significant change was a provision that would allow businesses to appeal decisions of the competition tribunal to Cabinet. This meant that decisions about mergers that were formed by an impartial tribunal based on expert analysis could be overturned by ministers responding to "backstairs" political pressure from business interests.[41]

Even the new toned-down version of Stage II received the (by now) predictable hostility of corporate interests. Business groups not only engaged in lobbying themselves, but were able to mobilize both the provincial governments of Ontario and Quebec in opposition to the bill in order to delay it.[42] In the face of irate business interests, and with a federal election once again on the horizon, the bill was allowed to die.

Following the Liberal Party's defeat in March 1979, no attempt was made by the Conservative minority government to reform competition policy. The battle was only taken up again after the Liberals were returned to power in 1980.

Reform Proposals 1980-84.

In 1981 the Minister of Consumer and Corporate Affairs, André Ouellet, set out new proposals for revising Canada's competition policy.[43] These proposals would have used clear pre-established thresholds for determining whether mergers or monopolizations were illegal, and would also have removed the word "unduly" from consideration. In addition, the idea of a tribunal was to be scrapped, and instead matters would be transferred to the civil court system.

Two attempts were made to introduce a bill based on these proposals—one in 1982 and one in 1983. Each time Finance Minister Marc Lalonde intervened against the legislation in an attempt to soothe the relationship between business and the Liberal government which had suffered as a result of the conflict over the National Energy Program.[44] Finally, after consultation with the major business interest groups, yet another new Minister of Consumer and Corporate Affairs, Judy Erola, introduced Bill C-29 which was essentially a more qualified and insipid version of the Ouellet proposals. But when John Turner called the election in June 1984, the bill automatically died.

To this point, the reform of competition policy had been mostly a saga of frustration and false starts, and consequently any competition cases still had to be pursued under the old Combines Investigation Act, which made the Crown's task very difficult. Before looking at the changes that eventually did occur with the passage of the Competition Act of 1986, it is useful to look briefly at the case record, and at some examples that have come before the courts.

CASES IN COMPETITION POLICY

The slow and stumbling pace of reform has meant that, for most of this century, business has lived with a set of competition laws that is weak and difficult to enforce, and this has been reflected in the paucity of prosecutions and convictions. As can be seen from Table 10.1, the number of prosecutions and convictions under the Combines Investigation Act has been especially paltry in merger and monopoly cases. Some notable cases are outlined briefly below, as well as a more recent example of a merger case under the new Competition Act of 1986.

Table 10.1

Combines Prosecutions and Convictions* 1889-1986						
	Conspiracy		Merger/Monopoly		RPM/Refusal to sell	
	Prosecutions	Convictions	Prosecutions	Convictions	Prosecutions	Convictions
1889-1910	8	5	—	—	—	—
1911-1923	1	0	—	—	—	—
1924-1940	12	11	1	0	—	—
1941-1955	9	8	1	2	2	
1956-1960	13	13	2	0	1	1
1961-1965	7	7	0	0	10	9
1966-1970	16	15	1	1	7	7
1971-1975	18	11	4	3	15	13
1976-1980	18	10	2	0	47	36
1981-1983	11	4	0	0	26	15
1984-1986	16	9	1	1	45	32

*   Includes prohibition orders.

Sources: P.K. Gorecki and W.I. Stanbury, *The Objectives of Canadian Competition Policy 1888-1983* (Montreal: The Institute for Research on Public Policy, 1984), Appendix B; and Canada, Department of Consumer and Corporate Affairs, *Annual Reports: Director of Investigation and Research, Combines Investigation Act Competition Act* (1984-87).

K.C. Irving

K.C. Irving, one of the richest men in North America, owns a vast conglomerate empire based in New Brunswick. Because his companies are privately-owned, information about them is generally shrouded in secrecy, but it has been estimated that he controls around 400 companies with assets of up to $8 billion, representing approximately one-quarter of New Brunswick's gross provincial-product.[45] These companies are involved in a wide variety of industries, such as oil refining and distribution, mining, forestry, pulp and paper, shipping, and building, construction and—of direct interest here—the media.

Between 1944 and 1971, Irving had bought all five English-language daily newspapers in New Brunswick, and in 1972 the Crown charged Irving's companies with merger and monopoly offences. The case went to court, and in 1974 convictions were handed down. The trial judge found that free competition had been "absolutely stifled," and that such a complete monopoly was necessarily detrimental to the public under the law.[46] The companies were fined $150,000 and Irving was ordered to sell two of the newspapers. He appealed.

The appeal judge did not accept that public detriment could automatically be assumed from the formation or operation of a monopoly, and the original verdict was overturned. The judge argued that the public had not been harmed because the newspapers had kept their prices and advertizing rates down and had introduced a number of improvements. (However, it was clear that some of the main beneficiaries of low advertizing rates and wider circulation were Irving's other companies themselves.) Furthermore, there was no evidence of any direct interference by Mr. Irving with the independence of editors or publishers, and thus the judge found no detriment to the public from this monopoly. The Crown then took the case to the Supreme Court which upheld the Appeal Court's judgement unanimously.

As Reschenthaler and Stanbury point out, the Supreme Court took a very narrow view of public detriment, focussing on specific economic factors such as prices and advertizing rates. This was at the expense of broader political concerns about the freedom and independence of the press in New Brunswick, where Irving also owned a radio station and two television stations.[47] Reschenthaler and Stanbury argue that the Appeal and Supreme Courts were being naive in putting so much faith in the autonomy of editors and publishers in this situation. In their words:

> To believe, as the Appeal and Supreme Courts did, that the editors and publishers of five newspapers, owned by one of Canada's largest companies and the largest industrial firm complex in the province of New Brunswick, will operate in complete autonomy asks too much ... Will they need to be formally directed not to investigate assiduously the labour, environmental and other policies of the Irving companies?[48]

In this regard, Louis Robichaud, the former premier of New Brunswick, may have wondered about editorial independence when he crossed swords with K.C. Irving in the 1960s and found himself, and his policies, vehemently attacked by Irving's newspapers.[49]

Overall, the decision of the Supreme Court was significant because it meant that detriment to the public could not be presumed even where a complete monopoly existed. Instead, specific instances of public harm would have to be demonstrated, which would make the Crown's task even more difficult. This judgement further weakened a law that was never designed to do very much about concentrated corporate power in the first place.

Atlantic Sugar

The Atlantic Sugar case was one of the most renowned prosecutions ever initiated under the conspiracy provisions of the Combines Investigation Act. It involved three sugar refineries, namely Atlantic Sugar Refineries, Redpath Industries and St. Lawrence Sugar, who together controlled over 90 per cent of the sugar market in Central and Eastern Canada. In 1975, they were charged with eight separate competition related offences,[50] most notably with conspiracy to lessen competition unduly by agreeing to maintain market shares and fix prices throughout the 1960s and 1970s.

In 1958, the largest firm, Redpath, began a policy of price-cutting in an attempt to increase its market share, following the opening of its new refinery in Toronto. Temporarily, Redpath's market share did increase, but the other two firms soon responded to push it down again, and then Redpath's profits and share values started to decline. In 1959, it was taken over by the British multinational corporation, Tate and Lyle, who promptly ended the price war and introduced a new policy.[51] A not-too-secret formula was established for pricing refined sugar, based on the daily price of raw sugar set in London, England. These prices were then posted every day in the lobby of Redpath's offices where they could be discovered without too much difficulty.[52] The other two firms would then get hold of this information and set their own prices in parallel with Redpath's, thus coordinating the price without resorting to actual collusion.[53]

At the trial, the Crown accused the companies of price-fixing, agreeing to maintain their traditional market shares and refusing to compete. But the trial judge ruled that the pricing practices were no more than "conscious parallelism" that did not violate the law, and although there was a tacit agreement to maintain traditional market shares, it had "not been shown that this agreement was arrived at with the *intention* of unduly preventing or lessening competition."[54] Although the judgement went in favour of the companies, the Crown successfully appealed, only to have the original decision reinstated by the Supreme Court.

This case showed that it was not enough for the Crown to prove beyond reasonable doubt that companies agreed to maintain their traditional market shares, but it also had to prove that they *intended* to lessen competition unduly. In addition, it affirmed that companies are at liberty to set their prices in parallel.

Southam/Thomson

Thomson and Southam are two giants of the North American newspaper publishing industry. Thomson Newspapers Ltd. owns 160 newspapers across Canada and the United States, including *The Globe and Mail* and the *Winnipeg Free Press*, and is itself a part of an international conglomerate controlled by Toronto businessman Kenneth Thomson. The Southam Newspaper Group claims to be Canada's largest daily newspaper chain, measured by circulation, and it publishes 15 daily papers across the country, including *The Gazette* (Montreal), *The Ottawa Citizen*, the Vancouver *Sun* and the *Province* (Vancouver). Like Thomson Newspapers Ltd., it too is part of a large diversified corporation, namely Southam Inc., which is involved in communications and information services.

In June 1982 Thomson and Southam, along with some of their subsidiaries, were indicted by the federal government on eight counts of conspiracy, merger and monopoly under the Combines Investigation Act.

Prior to 1980 Southam and Thomson published competing English daily newspapers in Ottawa, Montreal, Winnipeg and Vancouver. But on August 27, 1980, Southam closed down the *Winnipeg Tribune* and sold the assets to Thomson's *Winnipeg Free Press* which was the only major English daily left. That same day Thomson closed the *Ottawa Journal*, leaving Southam's *Ottawa Citizen* on its own. In addition, Thomson sold its 50 per cent stake in Pacific Press, which published the *Sun* and the *Province* in Vancouver, to Southam, and Southam bought out Thomson's minority share in the Montreal *Gazette*. Earlier the *Montreal Star* had been closed by FP Publications (which was taken over by Thomson in 1980), and the *Star's* assets were acquired by *The Gazette*. As a result, Thomson now had the only English daily paper in Winnipeg, while Southam published the only English dailies in Vancouver, Ottawa and Montreal.

At the trial, the Crown charged that the decisions to close the newspapers were not made independently but were part of an unlawful agreement to lessen competition unduly. Combines investigators from the Department of Consumer and Corporate Affairs had raided Southam's offices and had found shredded documents in the wastepaper baskets.[55] They testified that one of the torn-up documents, which had been patched together by the investigators, was found in the office of Southam vice-president, George Meadows.[56] It was headed "Thomson" and said: (1) They get out of Ottawa; (2) They get out of Montreal; (3) They get out of Vancouver; (4) They get control of Winnipeg.[57]

The Crown said that other shredded documents had been found at Southam's headquarters, including one allegedly written by another Southam vice-president, William Carradine, which analyzed the potential profits from the "deal."[58] One of the combines investigators testified that he had found Carradine tearing up sheets of paper when he visited his office during the investigation.[59]

The Crown had hoped to prove that the two chains had conspired to divide up Canadian newspaper markets based on evidence from 230 documents seized from the offices of Thomson and Southam, but the judge acquitted the accused on all eight charges and rejected the inferences drawn by the prosecution.[60] He ruled that the companies' actions were arrived at independently and were a product of good business sense rather than conspiracy.[61] Regarding the merger charge, when Thomson bought the assets of the *Winnipeg Tribune*, the judge said that a conviction could only be obtained following the "acquisition of a business," but the *Tribune* had folded several hours prior to the sale of its assets, and thus was no longer "a going concern."[62].

The acquittals were initially appealed, but three months later, in February 1984, following a review of the decisions of the Supreme Court of Ontario, the Crown gave up and abandoned its legal actions.[63]

Southam's 1987 Annual Report proclaims: "Democracy must listen to many voices."[64] But for readers of English-language daily newspapers in Vancouver, Winnipeg, Ottawa and Montreal, the voices had been reduced.

Imperial Oil/Texaco Canada

In January 1989 Imperial Oil, the Canadian subsidiary of Exxon Corp. of New York, announced its five billion dollar takeover of Texaco Canada—a subsidiary of Texaco Inc., also of New York. Texaco was the fourth largest oil company in Canada, and Imperial was the largest. The merger would mean that competition amongst major gasoline refiners and retailers would be dominated by three giant companies.

However, before the deal could be finalized, Imperial needed to get approval from the Canadian Bureau of Competition Policy, which had to determine whether competition would be substantially lessened. This was one of the first multi-billion dollar mergers to come before the Bureau under the new Competition Act (see below). If the Bureau could not strike a satisfactory bargain with Imperial concerning the divestiture of some assets, then the matter would be referred to a separate Competition Tribunal for public hearing and adjudication. In practice, very few cases get that far: between June 1986 and October 1990 only seven merger cases were actually sent to the Tribunal, out of 711 that were examined in a significant fashion.[65]

The main issues in this case concerned the concentration of ownership of refineries and gas stations in Central and Eastern Canada. Imperial would dramatically increase its refining capacity with the acquisition of Texaco's billion-dollar refinery at Nanticoke, Ontario, while its power over the retail market would be greatly strengthened by the purchase of Texaco's 1800 gas stations. There were fears that this would undermine competition from independent dealers, and have a negative impact on consumers.

Negotiations took place throughout the first half of 1989, and at an early point the Bureau's director indicated that any divestiture deal would eventually be submitted to the Competition Tribunal for approval.[66] By June a deal had been struck with the Bureau in which Imperial would sell off 543 gas stations and a refinery in Dartmouth, Nova Scotia. This was then put before the Tribunal.

At the beginning of the hearings, Imperial announced that it would be selling another 68 Quebec gas stations, to bring the total divestiture up to 611 stations nation-wide. But despite this extra concession, the Tribunal made a provisional ruling criticizing both Imperial and the Bureau of Competition Policy, and preventing the merger unless further changes were made. In particular, the Tribunal was worried that independent gas stations would not have assured supply once Imperial had taken over Texaco's Nanticoke refinery. In addition, the Tribunal was also concerned that the assets divested in Atlantic Canada should go to a viable and strong competitor. Consequently, the Bureau was asked to work out a new deal with Imperial.

By December, Imperial had agreed to give guarantees to independent stations concerning supply from the Nanticoke refinery, as well as consenting to sell three more stations in Atlantic Canada. However, this new deal was still unsatisfactory to the Tribunal. In January 1990 the Tribunal again withheld its approval, and ruled that Imperial needed to divest itself of more gas stations in the Atlantic provinces, not just the low-volume, low-profit ones that it would have sold off in any case. In response, Imperial capitulated and agreed to sell another 24 Atlantic stations, bringing the total divestiture to 638 stations across the country. In February, this reconstructed merger was finally approved by the Competition Tribunal.

The whole process had taken over a year to resolve, and the decision was widely heralded as evidence that competition policy would be vigorously enforced. Certainly, this process of negotiation under civil law had more success than previous cases under criminal law (it could hardly have had less success!), and some positive changes were achieved. Yet, the final outcome still left Imperial with 4,400 gas stations in Canada, including most of the outlets formerly owned by Texaco. As a result, corporate concentration increased significantly.

THE COMPETITION ACT 1986

The Competition Act and the Competition Tribunal Act became law in June 1986, bringing with them several significant changes to Canadian competition policy. The Acts contain a mixture of provisions, some of which place greater restrictions on business activity by tightening up the law and making it easier to enforce, while others provide for more lenient treatment and offer businesses a number of loopholes.

Conspiracy

Under the new law, conspiracy in restraint of trade is still a criminal offence rather than a civil matter, which means that the prosecution must still prove its case "beyond reasonable doubt." The new Act also retains the word "unduly," and it is not enough for businesses to conspire to lessen competition, but such a lessening must also be judged by the courts as undue. This is a major difference from U.S. law where agreements to fix prices, keep out competitors, and divide up markets are illegal *per se*.

While these sections of Canadian law remain the same, others have changed:

Penalties   The maximum fine for conviction has been increased from $1 million to $10 million, and offenders can still be imprisoned for up to 5 years. In practice, the actual level of fines never come close to the $1 million ceiling, so extending the limit may have little real impact.

Circumstantial evidence   The courts can now infer that a conspiracy exists even if the evidence is only circumstantial. No direct evidence or "smoking gun" is necessary. However, in conspiracy cases direct evidence is normally hard to come by, and in the past the courts have sometimes had to rely on circumstantial evidence anyway. Consequently, this change may not mean very much, although past practice has now become explicitly permitted in law.

Intent   Previous judicial rulings had created uncertainty about the question of intent. The accused companies had to intend to enter an agreement, but did they also have to intend to lessen competition unduly? The new law makes it clear that the Crown does not have to prove the second intention. This addresses the problem that the Crown had faced in the *Atlantic Sugar* case.

Exports   The Competition Act gives companies increased protection from prosecution when they come together to form an export consortium.

Mergers

One of the major changes in the new legislation is that the provisions against mergers have been transferred from criminal law to civil law. Under the previous system, mergers that lessened competition to the detriment of the public had to be prosecuted through the criminal courts, and this had failed to produce even one contested conviction in 75 years. Now this system has been replaced by a Competition Tribunal which is a civil body with the power to review mergers that might lessen competition substantially.

A merger or proposed merger is first examined by the Director of Investigation and Research in the Bureau of Competition Policy at the Department of Consumer and Corporate Affairs, and if he or she finds that there are sufficient grounds, the case will then be referred to the Competition Tribunal. Alternatively, the director may close the case without proceeding, or may reach a negotiated settlement in which the companies are required to make some adjustments. If the director is satisfied, then an Advance Ruling Certificate can be issued, giving companies prior approval of the merger and preventing a subsequent challenge by the Competition Tribunal. If the director does decide to refer a case to the Tribunal, and the Tribunal finds a substantial lessening of competition, then it can break up a merger or prevent one from taking place. Although this sounds like a powerful mandate, the Tribunal's authority is subject to a number of restrictions concerning the merger provisions.

Restrictions on the Merger Provisions

Assessing Competition   The Tribunal cannot make decisions about a lessening of competition based solely on an analysis of corporate concentration or market share. In the United States, mergers are automatically reviewed if the new company's market share goes beyond certain pre-determined levels. In Canada, the Tribunal must also consider other factors, which can include the availability of substitute products, the level of imports, interprovincial trade barriers, government regulation, etc. Businesses will thus be given the opportunity to argue that a substantial lessening of competition has not taken place even in cases where the level of corporate concentration is extremely high.

Efficiency   A merger cannot be prevented or broken up by the Tribunal if it is likely to bring about gains in efficiency that will exceed and offset any lessening of competition. The Tribunal will thus be required to do a form of cost-benefit analysis, weighing increased efficiency against reduced competition in each case. This may be difficult because "efficiency" and "level of competition" are different concepts and cannot be measured in the same units on the same scale.[67] How much increased efficiency is equivalent to how much loss of competition? One does not simply "offset" the other, and answers to this question may well be decided arbitrarily. The aim of competition policy should not be solely to promote economic efficiency, but also to prevent excessive concentrations of corporate power. However, under this provision monopolies can be created with impunity, provided they are efficient. Furthermore, efficiency is measured in a strange fashion as "a significant increase in the real value of exports; or a significant substitution of domestic products for imported products."[68] The problem here is that levels of exports and imports are influenced by a multitude of factors, such as shifting exchange rates, alterations in foreign and domestic trade barriers, transfers of products between Canadian branch plants and their foreign parents and changing levels of production and capacity in other countries. These things do not reflect real changes in the productive efficiency of domestic firms, and there are just too many variables involved for the Tribunal to make an accurate calculation of future "efficiency" gains on this basis.

Joint Ventures   Joint ventures for specific projects or for research and development are exempt from the anti-merger provisions, and the Tribunal is not permitted to prevent or disallow these collective corporate activities.

Pre-notification

In some cases, companies involved in acquisitions or mergers must give advance warning of their intentions to the Bureau of Competition Policy. If the companies involved have combined Canadian assets or annual sales of more than $400 million, and if the target company has assets or sales of over $35 million ($70 million in the case of an amalgamation) then they must notify the Bureau. Pre-notification must take place at least seven days before the deal goes through, though in some cases 21 days notice is required.

The Bureau also offers a voluntary compliance program under which proposed mergers are discussed with corporations at an early stage, and advice is given to help the companies structure the merger in such a way that it complies with the law.[69] It is a practice that relies more on consultation than confrontation and, along with the use of civil review rather than criminal prosecution, constitutes a move away from judicial conflict between business and government. This cooperative emphasis is also reflected in the small number of cases that are actually sent to the Competition Tribunal by the Bureau. As mentioned previously, from June 1986 (when the Act was passed) to October 1990, 711 mergers were reviewed in a substantial fashion by the Bureau of Competition Policy, and only 7 were referred to the Tribunal.[70]

Monopolies

The word "monopoly" does not appear in the new legislation, and instead monopoly practices are dealt with under a section entitled "Abuse of Dominant Position."[71] This clearly recognizes that monopolies themselves are not illegal, and that the law is only trying to prohibit certain anti-competitive abuses that might stem from a dominant (monopoly) position in the market place.

As with mergers, the Competition Act transfers the monopoly provisions from criminal to civil law, and turns over the adjudication process to the

Competition Tribunal. Criminal penalties have thus been dropped, which is no great loss in practice because the previous criminal law was virtually unworkable. Under civil law the Tribunal can order monopolies to stop whatever anti-competitive acts in which they are engaged, and if this does not restore competition then the Tribunal can take sterner measures, such as ordering a divestiture of the corporation's assets. However, the use of this option would require a particularly courageous and crusading Tribunal and a particularly stubborn and self-destructive corporation. We do not anticipate that this option will be much used.

In general, remedies against abuse of dominant position may not be easy to achieve. In the first place, the Tribunal can only make rulings on cases referred to it by the Director of Investigation and Research in the Bureau of Competition Policy, who acts as a filter. If the record with mergers is any indication, then not many cases will get as far as the Tribunal.

Secondly, the Tribunal has to prove three separate things before it can issue a prohibition order: (1) A class of business must be completely or substantially controlled by one or more persons; (2) Anti-competitive acts must also be taking place; (3) These anti-competitive acts must prevent or lessen competition substantially, or be likely to do so. None of these things is particularly easy to determine in itself, and the Tribunal must find all three in conjunction.

Thirdly, it seems evident that the Tribunal must also prove intent on the part of the company or companies concerned. This is not explicitly stated in the legislation, but the new law gives a long list of examples of anti-competitive acts, virtually all of which imply some form of intention to lessen competition. For example:

- Pre-emption of scarce facilities or resources required by a competitor for the operation of a business, *with the object* of withholding the facilities or resources from a market.

- Adoption of product specifications that are incompatible with products produced by any other person and *are designed* to prevent his entry into, or to eliminate him from, a market.

- Requiring or inducing a supplier to sell only or primarily to certain customers, or to refrain from selling to a competitor, *with the object* of preventing a competitor's entry into, or expansion in, a market.

- Selling articles at a price lower than the acquisition cost *for the purpose* of disciplining or eliminating a competitor.[72] [Emphasis added]

Intent is a notoriously difficult thing to prove, which may hamper any efforts to remedy such monopolistic abuses.

Finally, in making rulings about lessening of competition the Tribunal is compelled to consider whether a reduction in competition was merely the result of "superior competitive performance." If this is the case, then the Tribunal is provided with an excuse for not prohibiting anti-competitive acts by monopolies. The cumulative effect of these provisions and limitations will probably make it difficult to control monopolistic abuses, and it may turn out that the new law is no better at eliminating these practices than the old one.

The Competition Tribunal

The Competition Tribunal is the federal agency responsible for reviewing cases under the civil law provisions of the Competition Act. It consists of up to 12 people appointed by Cabinet for seven-year terms, and attempts to combine judicial expertise with business experience by having a mixture of federal court judges and lay people serve as members. Individual cases are reviewed by panels of three to five people drawn from the full Tribunal, and each panel, like the Tribunal itself, must be chaired by a judicial member. Even though it appears that the lay members have a secondary role on the Tribunal, the inclusion of business people as members may help to colour the overall sympathies of the Tribunal. Business representatives have been co-opted on to a government agency with responsibility for policing business itself, which constitutes a partial delegation of public authority to the private sector.

The Tribunal is a quasi-judicial body and its decisions can be appealed through the Federal Court of Appeal when either matters of law or matters of fact are in dispute. This was one of the few areas where big business groups were unsuccessful in influencing the course of the legislation. Groups such as the Canadian Manufacturers' Association, the Canadian Chamber of Commerce and the Business Council on National Issues wanted to appeal Tribunal decisions to the Cabinet, which would have thrown every case into the political arena. Such a provision would have given businesses an opportunity to put pressure on cabinet ministers and pull some political strings to influence decisions in their favour. Big business lost this battle because it was felt that Cabinet appeals of judges' decisions would have undermined judicial independence.[73]

However, judicial challenges to Tribunal decisions can still provide business with a potentially fruitful means of obstructing these civil law rulings. In this regard there have recently been two significant challenges to the Competition Tribunal. The first case involved Alex Couture Inc., and the second involved Chrysler Canada Ltd.

Alex Couture Inc.

Alex Couture is a Quebec-based firm engaged in the rendering business, recycling animal waste. In 1986 it took over Lomex Inc., another rendering firm also based in Quebec, giving it control over roughly 85 per cent of the Quebec market. Early in 1987 the Bureau of Competition Policy began a lengthy investigation and concluded that this merger "would prevent or lessen competition substantially in the relevant market." [74] The case was referred to the Competition Tribunal for adjudication. However, Couture took the case to the Quebec Superior Court and challenged the jurisdiction of the federal government in this area of policy. The company also argued that the Canadian Charter of Rights and Freedoms had been infringed, and that the Competition Tribunal was not impartial due to the participation of non-judicial members. In April 1990 the Court brought down its judgement. Although the federal government's jurisdiction was upheld, the Court struck down three sections of the Competition Act, ruling that the Charter had been violated and that the Tribunal lacked impartiality.

Chrysler Canada Ltd.

Richard Brunet Co. is a small Montreal autoparts distributor which specializes in selling Chrysler parts in certain foreign markets. In 1988 Chrysler Canada, operating under instructions from the United States, cut off supplies to Brunet because it was competing with Chrysler's attempts to supply these foreign markets directly. The case was brought before the Competition Tribunal, which ruled in favour of Brunet and ordered Chrysler to resume supplies. Chrysler did not accept this ruling, and the Bureau of Competition Policy was forced to initiate contempt proceedings in an attempt to enforce the Tribunal's decision. However, in July 1990, the Federal Court of Appeal halted the contempt proceedings, ruling that the Tribunal had no power to enforce its own decisions.

These two cases have seriously undermined the authority of the Bureau of Competition Policy and the Competition Tribunal, and until these matters are finally resolved through the judicial appeal process, other cases will likely be called into question. One recent example is the NutraSweet case. NutraSweet Co. markets artificial sweetener and controls over 95 per cent of the market for Aspartame. But in October 1990, the Competition Tribunal rule that NutraSweet had abused its dominant position in the Canadian market, and had inserted clauses in its supply contracts that prevented customers from dealing with NutraSweet's competitors. This ruling was initially seen as an important victory for consumers, but in light of the Couture and Chrysler decisions, NutraSweet is in the process of appealing the decision on constitutional grounds. As a result, policy implementation has been delayed and the outcome of the whole process has become uncertain.

The weakening of the Competition Tribunal means that corporations have less to fear if they do not cooperate with the Bureau of Competition Policy. If the Tribunal has little effective power, then corporations will be less concerned when the Bureau threatens to refer cases to it. Consequently, the Bureau's bargaining position is weakened and negotiations are more likely to take place on terms dictated by business. Interaction between the Bureau and individual corporations may well fall into a pattern of cooperative "clientele" relations (as outlined in Chapter Three), where the corporations themselves have the strongest voice in determining competition policy decisions. This prospect is something that is encouraged by the whole thrust of the Competition Act which moves away from a system of criminal penalties and prosecution, towards a regime of negotiated settlements.

Overall, the Act represents a compromise between the need for reform and the political power of big business. Years of failure in achieving reform were made worse by judicial decisions that further hobbled an already weak law. In important areas, such as mergers and monopolies, the law was almost completely helpless and business concentration was unrestrained. Now we have a system that, at least in principle, seems more workable. Yet this has been achieved by decriminalizing major areas of the law and abandoning attempts to confront business head on. Instead, government has put its faith in a more conciliatory and consensual approach where business itself is invited to participate and cooperate. Whether this faith is misplaced remains to be seen.

COMPETITION AND GOVERNMENT INTERVENTION

Opposition to corporate concentration in Canada is by no means universal, and it is sometimes claimed that high levels of concentration are conducive to efficiency. The Macdonald Commission has been one of the most prominent advocates of this view, arguing that corporate concentration results in larger size and more efficient plants which are better able to exploit economies of scale. In order to take advantage of long production runs and other economies of scale, domestic firms must be large relative to the size of the Canadian market. For this reason the Commission welcomes even greater levels of concentration in some industries.[75]

According to the Commission, Government policies to enforce competition are rarely necessary and that the best way to promote competition is to rely on trade liberalization and deregulation. Unrestricted imports will increase the competition for domestic producers, and deregulation will make it easier for new competitors to enter the market.[76] In sectors where this takes place, "there is little need for public policy to restrict mergers of domestic companies, concentration within particular domestic industries, or co-operative arrangements among domestic suppliers."[77] Restrictions on mergers, monopolies and conspiracies would thus be superfluous.

These prescriptions on competition policy are rooted in the neo-conservative philosophy of writers such as Milton Friedman, particularly where blame for monopolies and corporate concentration is attributed largely to government regulation, with the accompanying conclusion that such problems can then be solved by deregulatlon.[78] However, high levels of corporate concentration are widespread in Canada and are not just restricted to industries where entry is regulated by government. They also characterize sectors where regulation is comparatively slight and where government is actively trying to encourage new participants.

Historically, Canada has seen waves of mergers and growth in concentrated ownership at times when the scope of government regulation was minimal by contemporary standards, such as the early part of this century prior to World War I. This was a period in which regulation was weak, while mergers and the formation of corporate monopolies really took off. Regulation is thus not a necessary condition for the growth of monopolies, and consequently the supposed linkage between corporate concentration and government regulation is suspect.

Even in more modern times and in sectors where concentration and regulation exist simultaneously, we cannot make general assumptions about which factor causes the other. Regulation may be a symptom of private monopolies rather than a cause, as with natural monopolies, where government resorts to regulation for the very reason that competitive pressures are weak.

Rather than pinning all the blame on government, it is necessary to recognize that the desire for power and market domination is an important motive behind takeovers and monopoly practices. Established firms desire to keep out new competitors and are sometimes prepared to use anti-competitive practices to do so. This motivation has little to do with the state of government regulation in an industry, and small businesses and the public have a right to be protected from these corporate abuses of power.

Arguments that rely on trade liberalization as a bulwark against corporate concentration also have their shortcomings. Firstly, these arguments focus exclusively on the structure of *sales* in a domestic market, rather than on the structure of *production*. Increased imports may mean that there is a greater variety of goods in the stores and that domestic firms are more constrained in their price increases, but imports have little direct impact on the concentrated ownership of productive resources, i.e. on the number of people who own and control major elements of the Canadian economy.

Control over the productive process in Canada is a crucial form of social power, one that has largely been delegated to the private sector with little direct accountability either to employees or to the public. Decisions about the production and distribution of goods and services have an enormous impact on people's lives particularly when corporations decide to lay off workers, close plants or move out altogether. When this sort of decision-making power becomes concentrated in the hands of fewer and fewer individuals or corporate enterprises, we end up with an economy that is increasingly dominated by a corporate elite.

This is not to say that factors such as choice, price and efficiency are unimportant, but there is another dimension to corporate concentration almost completely ignored by neo-conservative advocates like the Macdonald Commission, namely, concentration of production. It is this aspect of corporate concentration that is not remedied by trade liberalization.

Nor is efficiency necessarily enhanced by the centralization of ownership and the growth of corporate empires. Canadian business has become dominated by the growth of massive conglomerate enterprises spanning across many different industries, and there is no necessary connection between the scope of conglomerate power and the size of individual plants in any of the diverse industries that are controlled. It is quite possible for corporate empires to be created through the acquisition of different companies without increasing the scale of operations at the plant level, and without any expansion of production or improvements in efficiency. On the contrary, the amount of debt required to finance many of these corporate buyouts makes it more difficult to provide funds for expansion. Efficiency, like trade liberalization, cannot be relied upon to compensate for concentrated power over production.

Reliance on trade liberalization also has other problems. In the postwar period, Canada has experienced successive reductions in tariffs due to multilateral agreements under the General Agreement on Tariffs and Trade (GATT). Yet high levels of concentration still persist in the Canadian economy, even in sectors where trade barriers have been reduced. Secondly, in industries where Canadian producers have a strong comparative advantage over foreign rivals, the impact of reduced import barriers is likely to have only a small effect on domestic competition. Thirdly, we cannot always rely on importers themselves to be competitive, and perhaps the most notable example here is the manipulation of oil production and prices by the Organization of Petroleum Exporting Countries (OPEC) in the 1970s. A seven-year study by the Bureau of Competition Policy concluded, in 1981, that producers in Canada had charged Canadians an excess of over $12 billion during this period—a finding that was naturally contested by the oil companies.[79]

Finally, the use of trade liberalization and deregulation to achieve goals of competition policy makes unrealistic assumptions about the capacity for policy coordination in Canada. Policies concerning trade protection and government regulation are subject to their own separate determinants and political pressures that frequently take little account of the objectives of competition policy. Changes in these areas have their own impetus and cannot be relied upon to serve other goals, especially as jurisdiction for many regulatory policies and some forms of trade policy is divided amongst the provinces and the federal government. The federal government's objectives concerning competition policy may be thwarted by provincial regulations that have been established with other goals in mind.

The Macdonald Commission's recommendations thus suffer from a number of problems, and while a laissez-faire attitude to competition policy fits in well with other elements of a neo-conservative agenda that includes privatization, deregulation, free trade and unrestricted foreign investment, the prospects for achieving any significant reduction in corporate concentration by this strategy must be rated as slim.

CONCLUSION

Competition policy in Canada has been weak throughout its history and at no time has there been a vigorous and determined attempt to deal with the problem of concentrated corporate power. Even half-hearted attempts to bring about limited reforms met with the vehement opposition of big business, which was normally fatal for the proposed reform. In key areas the system had become virtually unworkable due to a series of judicial decisions that made it very difficult for the Crown to get convictions under criminal law. Rulings in cases like K.C. Irving, Atlantic Sugar, and Southam/Thomson revealed the problems of trying to confront business through the courts under the Combines Investigation Act.

The new Competition Act of 1986 adopts a very different approach to competition policy by decriminalizing major elements and transferring them to civil law to be adjudicated by the Competition Tribunal. Emphasis is now on finding remedies for abuses rather than punishing criminal activity. The new Act reflects a different philosophy towards the administration of competition policy—one that places greater stress on consultation and cooperation with business rather than on confrontation.

Although previous legislation was largely impotent in areas such as mergers and monopolies, it is doubtful whether the Competition Act will lead to much substantial improvement. The provisions in these areas are constrained and qualified by such things as the "efficiency defence" and the evident need to prove intent in cases involving abuse of dominant position. In addition, the consensual and consultative approach on behalf of the Bureau of Competition Policy may just turn out to be a consensus on business' terms.

Finally, competition policy has almost completely ignored political concerns raised by the concentration of corporate power in Canadian society, and the growth of private conglomerate empires has never been addressed by Canadian competition law. Instead the law has focussed on more narrowly defined economic factors, such as price, entry, efficiency and abuse of dominant position. Even here, government controls have historically been weak and difficult to administer, and it is unlikely that the 1986 reforms will improve matters greatly. While lip service has been paid to competition, the concentration of corporate power remains largely unchecked, and the most fitting epitaph for Canadian competition policy is still "Big Business as Usual."

ENDNOTES

1. Adam Smith, *The Wealth of Nations*, Book 1, Part 2 (first pub. 1776), chapter 10.
2. The Competition Act also includes measures against various illegal trade practices such as misleading advertizing and "pyramid" selling that do not directly relate to the state of competition between firms.
3. Paul K. Gorecki and W.T. Stanbury, *The Objectives of Canadian Competition Policy 1888-1983* (Montreal: The Institute for Research on Public Policy, 1984), xvii-xix.
4. Harold D. Lasswell, *Politics: Who Gets What, When, How* (Whittlesay House, McGraw-Hill, 1936).
5. Charles Lindblom, *Politics and Markets* (New York: Basic Books, 1977), 155.
6. Milton Friedman, *Capitalism and Freedom* (Chicago: University of Chicago Press, 1962), 28.
7. *Ibid.*, 128-29.
8. *Ibid.*, 122-23.
9. Gorecki and Stanbury, *The Objectives of Canadian Competition Policy 1883-1983*.
10. *Ibid.*, 164-68.
11. *Ibid.*, 169.
12. Joseph A. Schumpeter, *Capitalism, Socialism and Democracy* (New York: Harper Torchbooks, 1976. Original publication 1942.), 131-34.
13. *Ibid.*, 134.
14. Karl Marx, *Capital*, Vol. 1 (New York: International Publishers Co. Inc., 1967), 763.
15. *Ibid.*, 789.
16. Michael Bliss, *A Living Profit: Studies in the Social History of Canadian Business, 1883-1911* (Toronto: McClelland and Stewart, 1974), 33-34.
17. Michael Bliss, "Another Antitrust Tradition: Canadian Anti-Combines Policy 1889-1910," *Business History Review*, Vol. 47, No. 2 (Summer 1973), 182-83.
18. Lloyd G. Reynolds, *The Control of Competition in Canada* (Cambridge, Mass.: Harvard University Press, 1940), 134.
19. Bliss, "Another Antitrust Tradition," 185.
20. Report on the Committee to Study Combines Legislation (1952), "Historical Development of the Legislation," in L.A. Skeoch, ed., *Restrictive Trade Practices in Canada* (Toronto: McClelland and Stewart, 1966), 7.
21. Reynolds, *The Control of Competition in Canada*, 136.
22. Report, "Historical Development of the Legislation," 7-8.
23. *Ibid.*, 7.
24. Bliss, "Another Antitrust Tradition," 185.
25. *Ibid.*, 184.

26. Tom Naylor, *The History of Canadian Business 1867-1914*, Vol. 2 (Toronto: James Lorimer and Co., 1975), 170, 181, 189-90.

27. *Ibid.*, 189.

28. Reynolds, *The Control of Competition in Canada*, 141-42.

29. *Ibid.*, 145.

30. Canada, *Debates in the House of Commons*, Vol. 157, 2520-2667 in Skeoch, *Restrictive Trade Practices in Canada*, 30.

31. W.T. Stanbury, *Business Interests and the Reform of Canadian Competition Policy, 1971-1975* (Toronto: Carswell/Methuen, 1977), 51.

32. Reynolds, *The Control of Competition in Canada*, 147.

33. The Economic Council of Canada, *Interim Report on Competition Policy* (1969).

34. G.B. Reschenthaler, "The Proposed Competition Act of 1971: The Ascendency of the Consumer Interest," in chapter Seven of W.T. Stanbury, *Business Interests*, 76.

35. *Ibid.*, 79-80.

36. Stanbury, *Business Interests*, 113.

37. Stanbury, *Business Interests*, 112-13.

38. *Ibid.*, 133.

39. W. T. Stanbury, "Monopoly, Monopolization and Joint Monopolization: Policy Development and Bill C-13," in J.W. Rowley and W.T. Stanbury, eds., *Competition Policy in Canada: Stage II, Bill C-13* (Montreal: Institute for Research on Public Policy, 1978), 159.

40. *Ibid.*, 160.

41. M.T. MacCrimmon and W.T. Stanbury, "The Reform of Canada's Merger Law and the Provisions of Bill C-13," in Rowley and Stanbury, eds., *Competition Policy*, 102.

42. Stanbury, "The Background of Bill C-13."

43. Canada, Department of Consumer and Corporate Affairs, "Proposals for Amending the Combines Investigation Act," (April 1981).

44. W.T. Stanbury, "The New Competition Act and Competition Tribunal Act: Not With a Bang, but a Whimper," in *Canadian Business Law Review*, Vol. 12 (1986-87).

45. Diane Francis, *Controlling Interests: Who Owns Canada?* (Toronto: Macmillan of Canada, 1986), 14.

46. G.B. Reschenthaler and W.T. Stanbury, "Benign Monopoly: Canadian Merger Policy and K.C. Irving Case," in *Canadian Business Law Review* Vol. 2 (1977-78), 154.

47. *Ibid.*, 163.

48. *Ibid.*, 167.

49. Francis, *Controlling Interest*, 21.

50. Donald E. Armstrong, "The Sugar Case as a Reason for 'Strengthening' the Combines Act: An Economic Perspective," in Walter Block, ed., *Reaction: The*

New Combines Investigation Act (Vancouver: The Fraser Institute, 1986), 72.

51. Colin Irving, "The 'Errors' in Atlantic Sugar et al. v. R." in Block, ed., *Reaction*, 96.

52. *Ibid.*

53. W.T. Stanbury and G.B. Reschenthaler, "Oligopoly and Conscious Parallelism: Theory, Policy and the Canadian Cases," in *Osgoode Hall Law Journal*, Vol. 5, No. 3 (1977), 646-47.

54. Regina vs. Atlantic Sugar Refineries Co. Ltd. et al. (1975), 96.

55. *The Gazette* (28 September, 1983), B8.

56. *Ibid.*

57. *Ibid.*

58. *The Globe and Mail* (21 September, 1983), 4.

59. *The Gazette* (28 September, 1983), B8.

60. *The Globe and Mail* (10 December, 1983), 5.

61. *Macleans*, (19 December, 1983), 34-35.

62. *The Globe and Mail* (19 December, 1983), 5.

63. Canada, Department of Consumer and Corporate Affairs, *Annual Report: Director of Investigation and Research, Combines Investigation Act* (31 March, 1984), 60.

64. Southam Inc., *Annual Report 1987*, 2.

65. Data kindly provided to us by the Bureau of Competition Policy.

66. *The Globe and Mail*, (6 March, 1989), B2.

67. Stanbury, "The New Competition Act," 19.

68. The Competition Act, R.S.C., C-23 (1986), Sec. 68(2).

69. George N. Addy, "Competition Act: Effective Tool or Bureaucratic Nightmare?," in *Canadian Business Review* (Winter 1987), 36.

70. Data kindly provided to us by the Bureau of Competition Policy.

71. Competition Act, R.S.C., C-23 (1986), Sec. 50.

72. *Ibid.*

73. Lawson Hunter, *The New Competition Law* (Don Mills, Ontario: CCH Canadian Ltd., 1986), 13.

74. Consumer and Corporate Affairs Canada, Bureau of Competition Policy, *Annual Report* (1988), 11.

75. Canada, The Royal Commission on the Economic Union and Development Prospects for Canada, *Report*, Vol. 2, 218.

76. *Ibid.*, 220.

77. *Ibid.*

78. Friedman, *Capitalism and Freedom*, 125-28.

79. Canada, Department of Consumer and Corporate Affairs, Bureau of Competition Policy, *The State of Competition in the Canadian Petroleum Industry* (Bertrand Report), February 1981.

Chapter 11

Business Regulation

Regulation of social and economic activity is one of the principal functions performed by governments in all industrialized countries. Along with increased public expenditure, taxation and public ownership, regulation has been a central component of the state's expansion in the twentieth century. The scope of government regulation is part of the reality of modern capitalism, and it is a reality that differs markedly from theories of laissez-faire economics and free-market competition. In all industrialized countries, the state has become an integral part of the system of production, distribution and planning, and government's regulatory role is just one aspect of this.

In Canada, as in other industrial countries, the pervasiveness of regulation is readily apparent. A study by the Economic Council of Canada was hard pressed to find areas of activity that were not regulated by government in some way, and the Council depicted regulation as a dawn-to-dusk phenomenon:

> In the morning the clock radio awakens us with the sound of music subject to Canadian content regulations. The price, at the farm gate, of the eggs we eat for breakfast has been set by a government marketing board. We drive to work on tires that must meet federal minimum safety standards and in a car whose exhaust is subject to pollution emission regulations. At lunch, the restaurant in which we eat has been subject to the scrutiny of public health inspectors. The monthly rate for the telephone we use at the office is set by a federal or provincial regulatory agency. Shopping in the supermarket on the way home, we note the unpronounceable names of certain chemical preservatives that, by government regulation, are disclosed to us on a finely printed label. As we turn down the thermostat before retiring, we are confident that a government agency has protected our purse by setting the price we will be charged by the local monopoly supplier of natural gas.[1]

Businesses frequently complain about the burdens of this pervasive regulation, and, certainly, many regulations do impose costs on business. Yet we should also realize that some forms of regulation have the effect of promoting or "stabilizing" business interests. For instance, rules that restrict the entry of new competitors into an industry serve to protect those firms that are already established. Such government regulation of "entry" has characterized a variety of businesses, from the federal regulation of banking to the municipal licensing of street vendors. Despite the general business rhetoric against regulation, we must appreciate that different types of regulation have different objectives and effects, and that some are heartily welcomed by regulated firms. Later in this chapter we discuss the different types of regulation, and the various reasons why governments regulate business activity.

The fact that regulation can actually serve business interests also raises questions about the relationship between business and regulatory agencies. Are regulatory agencies really intent on "policing" industry on behalf of the public, or are they more concerned with promoting and defending the industries they regulate? Has the relationship between regulatory agencies and their business "clients" become too close and too cooperative? Have regulatory agencies, in effect, been "captured" by the corporate interests they are supposed to regulate? These issues are examined in another section of this chapter, along with questions about the political accountability of regulatory agencies.

In Canada, another important set of issues revolves around the division of regulatory authority between different levels of government. Regulation of business takes place at federal, provincial and municipal levels of government, and this can create problems for both the regulators and the regulated. Jurisdictional disputes can result in time-consuming battles between regulators at different levels, and the regulatory process can become deadlocked by intergovernmental conflict. In addition to jurisdictional disputes, the division of authority offers plenty of scope for contradiction, inconsistency and overlap in the network of regulations affecting business, and the whole system can become extremely confusing and frustrating for firms that are trying to comply with a multitude of different rules. The section, "Regulation and the Canadian Federal System," addresses some of these concerns.

The final section of the chapter deals with the contemporary backlash against regulation that has formed part of the overall neo-conservative attack on the state. Over the last decade there has been a movement, in a number of Western countries, to deregulate some areas of business activity, and this section looks at the recent Canadian experience and assesses the arguments for and against deregulation. However, before dealing with these several themes, it is important to examine the concept of regulation itself, in an attempt to define the principal characteristics that set it apart from other instruments of government policy.

THE CONCEPT OF REGULATION

The extent of regulation in Canada suggests that this category of government activity is a very broad one, and indeed, regulation is sometimes seen as encompassing virtually everything government does. Douglas Hartle, for example, sees regulation as "the essential function of government," and claims that "to examine government regulation is to examine the role and function of government itself."[2] While there is some merit in adopting a comprehensive definition for a multifaceted topic, one can take things a little too far. A definition that encompasses everything is really a lack of definition because it includes all government functions and activities in just one category.

Numerous other definitions have been put forward, and Schultz and Alexandroff provide a useful survey of some recent ones. [3] The authors note the confusing array of differing conceptions, and they offer their own understanding of regulation that includes two important themes. First, regulation involves some sort of government restriction or constraint on the behaviour of businesses and individuals. Second, regulation involves the use of state coercion rather than incentives, with the proviso that regulated firms do not necessarily object to such coercion. These characteristics are essential in distinguishing regulation from other forms of government intervention in the economy, such as public ownership or taxation.[4]

Regulation is just one of a number of possible instruments by which governments seek to achieve their ends, and several writers categorize government activities according to the choice of policy instrument, i.e. the means rather than end.[5] Generalizing from these perspectives, when government intervenes in business activity, five main instruments can be used:

(1) *Persuasion* — where government tries to convince business to do something voluntarily, with no rewards or penalties attached.

(2) *Expenditures* — where government tries to alter business behaviour through subsidies, loans, tax concessions or other financial incentives.

(3) *Taxation* — where government uses taxes, tariffs and other compulsory payments as a financial levy on business activity.

(4) *Regulation* — where government directs business behaviour through mandatory rules and sanctions, ultimately enforced through state coercion.

(5) *Public Ownership* — where government takes a business out of private hands and runs it as a state agency.

Governments use these instruments either individually or in conjunction with one another, yet each is conceptually distinct.

Regulation differs from persuasion or expenditures because of its coercive character. Businesses are under no obligation to be persuaded or to accept subsidies, but they must comply with legally enforceable regulations. Unlike taxation, regulation is not primarily a mechanism for raising government revenues, and most regulations do not involve financial payments from business to government—although regulations often do impose costs on business.

Finally, regulation differs from the most intrusive and coercive policy instrument, namely public ownership, because the state seeks only to constrain and direct business behaviour, while allowing ownership to remain in private hands. However, public enterprise, like private firms, can be subject to state regulation. In tying these various elements together, we arrive at the following definition of business regulation: A system of compulsory constraints, imposed by government on firms in either the private or public sector, backed by the coercive power and legal authority of the state, and relying primarily on directives rather than incentives, taxation or public ownership.

Within this overall definition, different types of regulation can be accommodated, and the next section investigates some of these distinctions.

TYPES OF REGULATION

Regulation is commonly divided into two broad types.[6] The first is *economic (or direct) regulation*, which is concerned primarily with regulating the conditions of business competition within particular "targeted" industries, such as railways or public utilities. If there is too little competition, then government regulation can keep prices down in order to protect consumers. If there is too much competition, then government regulation of entry or output can impose some stability on the industry. Where market competition does not exist, or where it fails to achieve the desired ends, government regulation may be the only viable substitute. This form of regulation, and the market failures that provoke it, are both extensive and longstanding.

The second type of regulation, namely *social regulation*, is generally of more recent origin, and is concerned primarily with achieving social goals such as environmental protection, product safety or fairness in employment practices. Many businesses, if left to their own devices, would ignore such goals (especially if they increased business costs), and consequently, government regulation is necessary to ensure that steps are taken to address these issues.

Economic Regulation

Economic regulation can be subdivided into a number of different categories according to the type of economic behaviour that is being regulated.

These are discussed below.

Prices and Rates of Return Here government regulates the rates or prices that certain businesses can charge their customers. Frequently this occurs when a company has a monopoly or a dominant position in a market, as for example with telephone rates, cable television rates or tolls charged by gas pipeline companies. However, prices can also be regulated where competition exists, as with rent controls or the regulation of taxi fares. In most cases, this type of regulation is designed to prevent consumers from being unduly exploited, but in some instances price regulation can have the opposite effect. For example, the regulation of domestic airline fares (prior to deregulation) served to protect and stabilize the airline industry by inhibiting price competition, at the expense of air travellers.

Entry In several industries, regulations exist that restrict new competitors from entering into business. In broadcasting, for instance, radio and TV stations cannot operate without a licence from the Canadian Radio-Television and Telecommunications Commission (CRTC), which must be periodically renewed. This prevents the airwaves from being swamped by too many signals, and allows the CRTC to enforce certain standards of performance. In banking and the domestic airline industry, regulations restrict the entry of foreign competitors, while many professional groups (such as lawyers and doctors) enjoy delegated authority to limit new entrants through a system of registration.

Exit Regulations can also prevent companies from getting out of a business, or some section of it. This is particularly applicable to the transport and telecommunications industries, where the freedom of regulated corporations to abandon unprofitable services (for instance, in remote communities) is subject to government controls. Another example is in the brewing industry, where beer companies must maintain a brewery within a province if they want to have access to that provincial market. In this way, regulation prevents beer companies from centralizing their production and "exiting" from some provinces.

Output Government limitations can also be placed on the quantity of production, through quota or licensing systems. In the fishing industry, the allocation of quotas, and the restrictions on the number and size of vessels and the sorts of fishing gear that can be used, aim to conserve stocks and protect incomes by limiting competition. A similar sort of regulation occurs with agricultural marketing boards that are responsible for managing supply, such as the Canadian Wheat Board.

Many of the above forms of economic regulation have come under attack in recent years, and steps towards deregulation have been taken in a number of industries, including airlines, trucking, telecommunications and the financial sector. However, this trend has been less evident in the area of social regulation.

Social Regulation

Although still applied to business, social regulation is not directly concerned with the conditions of competition within particular industries. Instead, it focusses on issues such as health, safety, quality of life and fairness and honesty in the way business deals with workers, consumers and the general public. In addition, it addresses issues of cultural protection, national autonomy and the wider impact of business on society. In one of the most useful analyses of regulation, the Economic Council of Canada divides social regulation into four basic groups:[7]

Health and Safety   This includes the safety of consumer goods, the handling and quality of edible products, the transportation of hazardous materials and safety in the workplace. For instance, toy manufacturers are regulated under the Hazardous Products Act to ensure that children's toys meet safety standards concerning flammability, toxicity and other risks. Food processing companies are regulated under the Canadian Agricultural Products Standards Act (amongst other statutes), and this covers numerous areas of their operations, including plant sanitary conditions, standards for fruit and vegetable products, packaging requirements and marketing rules. Regulations often involve very detailed standards, such as how many square inches of tomato skin are allowed in a 20 ounce can of tomatoes. Yet with this issue, and with many other regulations, the food processors support government imposed rules. In this case, the rules help to keep out lower-cost imports.[8]

Environmental Regulation   This covers pollution of the air and water, land-use regulation and environmental aspects of resource development, such as the destruction of forests or the protection of endangered species and habitats. Environmental issues have developed a high political profile in recent years, and the trend is towards stricter control over polluters by both federal and provincial levels of government. New Brunswick, for example, passed its Clean Water Act in 1989, which allows fines of up to one million dollars per day for polluters.

Fairness Regulation   This deals with such things as truth in advertizing, disclosure of information, accurate product labelling, minimum wage legislation and rules against discrimination in hiring. One recent example of "fairness" regulation is Ontario's 1988 pay equity law, which requires employers to provide equal pay for work of equal value.

Cultural Regulation   This is a rather nebulous category, incorporating things like Canadian content requirements for the broadcasting industry, restrictions on the foreign ownership of Canadian cultural industries and language laws such as Quebec's Bill 178 which bans bilingual signs on the outside of stores. Cultural regulation also encompasses rules about commercialism and the extent to which our society has become oriented towards a "culture of consumerism." Examples here include Quebec's regulation against advertizing that is aimed at young children, and the restriction in many Ontario municipalities against Sunday shopping.

Some types of social regulation have been in place for a considerable period of time, but many others have been introduced in recent decades, especially in the 1970s when there was an upsurge of concern about environmental issues, cultural protection, etc. It was in this period that Canadian businesses also became more politically mobilized, as they faced these new demands for increased regulation and felt themselves to be under attack. Even in the current atmosphere of deregulation, these social forms of regulation have shown considerable staying power, notably in the area of environmental protection, where the scope of regulation seems destined to increase as serious concern about environmental damage continues to grow.

REASONS FOR REGULATION

Listing the various types of economic and social regulations also provides us with a catalogue of rationales for regulating business—regulation is established to compensate for market failures, or to protect the environment, or to ensure product safety, etc. Yet this list really just describes what government does, rather than addressing the basic motivations for government action. In our view, the reasons for government regulation of business can be divided into three primary categories, based on different driving forces. These are (a) business needs, (b) public pressure, and (c) bureaucratic initiative.

Business Needs

One of the basic requirements of government in any modern capitalist society is to provide the conditions for the continued profitability of business. By regulating key elements of the national economic infrastructure, such as the transportation system, the banking system, the communications system and the energy production and transmission system, government can achieve two important goals. First, it can preserve the economic health and long-term viability of these crucial sectors by regulating the conditions of competition through controls over entry, prices and rates of return. Second, it can prevent firms in these key sectors from overcharging their customers (many of whom are other businesses), thus keeping costs down for the rest of Canadian industry.

However, these two goals can conflict, because increased profits for one industry often means increased costs for another. Government does not want to jeopardize fundamental industries, but neither does it want to penalize the rest of business. Thus, government regulation must try to reconcile these competing objectives, and balance the interests of different segments of the business community.

One alternative to the regulation of key economic sectors is to bring these industries (or parts of them) under direct state control by creating crown corporations. In this respect, regulation is a substitute for public ownership, and is a way of reconciling state economic management with an economic system based largely on private ownership. Another alternative is to rely more extensively on market competition as a "regulatory mechanism." But in some industries, such as the transmission of electricity, water supply and natural gas, it is more efficient to have just one operator for any geographic area. For instance, we would not want several competing companies digging up roads, laying cables or building duplicate networks of pipelines and electricity towers across the country. In these so-called "natural monopolies," regulation or public ownership are the only real alternatives.

Government can also serve the needs of producers through the regulation of output. By restricting collective output, as with agricultural marketing boards, producers enjoy higher prices and incomes. In addition, the longer-term prospect for the stability of some industries is enhanced by government licensing that is designed to prevent resource depletion. Examples of this occur in fishing and logging. In the case of marketing boards, it is individual consumers who ultimately pay the price for this form of regulation. The political power of farmers has taken precedence over consumers who are politically weaker, less geographically concentrated, and on the whole, less intensely and consistently interested in food prices.

Public Pressure

Pressure from the public, or from well-organized sections of it, provides a strong impetus for much government regulation. Where a regulatory issue, such as environmental protection, becomes politically popular, then parties compete with one another in regulating business in order to maximize voter appeal. Pressure from environmental groups, women's organizations, unions and other groups, over issues such as pollution, pay equity or occupational safety, provides a spur to government action. Frequently the issues are in the realm of social regulation, which can impose real costs on business in the form of capital expenditures, increased labour costs, changes in work practices or product standards, as well as the increased burden of paperwork that any new regulation entails.

The dilemma for government with this type of regulatory policy lies in trying to satisfy business demands for lower costs, and at the same time satisfy public demands for greater regulation. In this situation, it is tempting for government to take symbolic measures rather than substantive ones, in order to assuage public opinion without raising business costs. Naturally, where real and serious problems exist, as with environmental pollution, this recourse will have damaging consequences.

This dilemma is particularly difficult when companies are competing with industries in other countries, or other provinces, where the regulatory burden is lower. Here business opposition to social regulation can be intense, and government comes under pressure to create a "level playing field" by reducing the regulatory burden. In current circumstances, when capital is becoming more internationally mobile, governments must face the threat of businesses moving to other jurisdictions where policy environment is more favourable. Necessarily, this threat must be taken into account when regulatory policies are being considered.

Because of the competitive business environment, companies will sometimes welcome further regulation, even if it imposes greater costs. A company will gain an advantage if the regulatory costs are disproportionately high for competing firms. For example, when the federal government was considering legislation on hazardous products, one of the relevant trade associations, the Canadian Manufacturers of Chemical Specialties Association (CMCSA), lobbied for strict regulations on product labelling. The CMCSA already abided by a voluntary code of labelling ethics, and mandatory government regulations would place the greatest burden on those companies that were not CMCSA members.[9]

As far as government is concerned, one of the chief advantages of regulation over other governing instruments is that it can be a relatively cheap way of satisfying public demands and winning electoral support. In some cases, new regulations impose significant costs on government, for example, in hiring and training new inspectors and administrators, but in many instances, the bulk of the regulatory cost is shouldered by business. Government can be seen to take the initiative in promoting desirable social ends, without requiring major new spending programs or new taxation. Government can thus take the credit without directly paying the cost. This factor pushes government towards an expansion of regulation.

In capitalist societies, democratic governments have two principal considerations in formulating regulatory policy. One is to reconcile public demands for regulation with business needs to keep costs down. The other is to reconcile the regulatory needs of one segment of capital with those of other segments, or with the perceived needs of the economy as a whole. However, there is also another force at work.

Bureaucratic Initiative

The third explanation for government regulation focusses on the bureaucracy. Regulatory initiatives in this category do not stem from public pressure or necessarily from business needs. Instead, regulation is instigated from within the public bureaucracy by those who are most directly involved with administering and evaluating public programmes. Those who have the most specialized knowledge and expertise in any area of public policy are in the best position to identify problems in existing programmes and to recommend solutions. Some of these solutions involve increased regulation of business, and to a large extent, government regulations reflect the state of bureaucratic learning about various social and economic problems.

Bureaucratic initiative on specific issues occurs even where public pressure is largely absent, or where the general public is not even aware that a problem exists. At the same time, regulations that are proposed to deal with newly identified problems can increase the costs to business. However, bureaucratic proposals that place severe burdens on business, or that go against a main current of public opinion, face an uphill battle, and as a motive force for government regulation, bureaucratic initiative is generally weaker than the other two factors. Although such initiatives are quite common, they typically involve a large array of fairly minor and uncontroversial areas of activity. In these cases, the bureaucracy itself is the most credible factor in accounting for the development of regulatory programmes.

If one looks through the *Federal Regulatory Plan*, it is not difficult to find examples where the level of public awareness is low, and where costs are simultaneously imposed on business. A few examples, taken from just one page of this 442 page catalogue of federal regulatory proposals, serve to illustrate the point. For instance, the Department of Consumer and Corporate Affairs (CCA) determined that tent fires were responsible for approximately eight deaths or injuries each year, mostly involving children. In response, the Department proposed new regulations requiring warning labels and less flammable tent fabrics. In another example, the CCA received numerous complaints about exploding cigarette lighters and subsequently proposed regulations requiring "that lighters meet more stringent performance criteria." Finally, the Department also became concerned about injuries to young children from poorly designed baby walkers, and has been developing new safety standards to meet this danger.[10]

None of the above examples is an especially prominent issue, and public awareness is almost certainly very low. In addition, these regulations impose some additional costs on business (in the case of tents, costs could rise by as much as 20 per cent), and they can hardly be seen as a response to business needs. Instead, these cases provide examples of what might be termed "low-level regulation," where the bureaucracy plays a lead role in trying to correct particular small-scale problems that have been identified by the administrators themselves. This is an extremely common form of regulatory activity, although by the same token, the issues involved are not momentous. Whatever the broad pressures behind regulation, the form and effectiveness of regulatory activity is crucially affected by the relationship between business and the government regulators. This involves regulation that is carried out within the structure of government departments, and regulation that has been placed in the hands of separate government institutions known as regulatory agencies. These agencies, and their relations with regulated businesses, provide the focus of the next section.

REGULATORY AGENCIES

Regulatory agencies are commissions, boards or other government bodies set up to regulate business, with some degree of independence from departmental ministers or Cabinet as a whole. Regulatory agencies can be established at different levels of government, and in addition to their regulatory function, they often perform other roles, such as advising government or adjudicating between competing interests.[11]

The use of regulatory agencies has some advantages over regular departments. Regulatory decisions often involve a specialized evaluation of complex technical issues, and it is useful to have this process conducted by a body of experts who are somewhat removed from the political spotlight. If a cabinet minister has direct responsibility, then partisan political considerations could intrude on decisions that ought to be determined on their technical merits. The use of semi-autonomous agencies helps to prevent regulatory decisions from becoming "political footballs."

By the same token, the use of regulatory agencies also takes decision-making further away from parliamentary scrutiny. It is harder to hold ministers accountable for regulatory decisions if their departments are not directly involved in the decision-making process. As a result, ministerial responsibility is diminished, and decisions are removed a step further from democratic control.

Some examples of prominent regulatory agencies, at the federal level of government, are outlined below.

The Canadian Radio-Television and Telecommunications Commission (CRTC)

The CRTC is responsible for the regulation of all Canadian broadcasting, including television, AM and FM radio, as well as cable TV, Pay TV and specialty services. It also regulates the telecommunications companies that are under federal jurisdiction and that make up the bulk of the industry (Bell Canada, B.C. Tel, CNCP, Teleglobe Canada and Telesat Canada). Telephone companies in the Prairie and Atlantic provinces have been regulated by provincial governments, which has given rise to occasional jurisdictional disputes. However, a recent Supreme Court decision has given the CRTC jurisdiction over all domestic telephone companies.[12]

In broadcasting, the CRTC holds public hearings and issues licences, subject to specific conditions, and it can suspend or revoke the licence if the conditions are not fulfilled. In addition to rules against foreign ownership, the conditions cover a variety of topics, such as Canadian content requirements, closed caption services for the deaf and the elimination of sex-role stereotyping. Instead of removing a station's licence altogether, the CRTC can invoke less severe penalties. For example, in 1988 CKFM-FM Toronto was found to have breached the conditions of its licence by playing too much "hit music." By way of punishment, the CRTC suspended the station's right to broadcast commercials for three days.[13]

In telecommunications, regulated companies must get CRTC approval for any changes in rates, conditions of service, share issues and other aspects of their operations. For example, in 1988 the CRTC forced Bell Canada to reduce its long-distance charges, because it was making too much profit, and in 1989, the Commission forced another rate reduction because of Bell's lowered corporate tax rates. Also in 1989, the Supreme Court upheld an earlier CRTC ruling that Bell should give a $206 million rebate to its subscribers.[14]

The National Energy Board (NEB)

The NEB is a quasi-judicial tribunal with a variety of regulatory functions. It issues licences for the export of oil, natural gas and electricity; it issues certificates for the construction and operation of international and inter-provincial pipelines and powerlines; it regulates the tolls and tariffs that pipeline companies can charge; it oversees approved energy projects; and it administers occupational health and safety rules relating to the operation of pipelines. It also acts in an advisory capacity to the federal government on energy matters.[15]

The National Transportation Agency (NTA)

The NTA was set up by the National Transportation Act of 1987, and replaced the Canadian Transport Commission as the federal body concerned with transport regulation. It is responsible for resolving disputes over rates and services among transportation companies and their customers; it reviews large mergers or acquisitions in the transport industry to see if they are in the public interest; it issues transportation licences; and it deals with matters of railway safety. For instance, in December 1988, in response to a complaint by the bus companies, the NTA prevented Via Rail from offering discount fares on its routes between Toronto, Ottawa and Montreal.[16] In addition to these regulatory functions, the NTA also reviews legislation and pays out transport subsidies.[17]

The Life Cycle of Regulatory Agencies

Regulatory agencies in Canada and other countries are sometimes accused of being too closely associated with the industries they are supposed to be regulating. In this view, the regulatory bodies have lost sight of the public interest and have become "captured" by the regulated industries.[18] One of the most prominent advocates of this theory is Marver Bernstein, who suggests that regulatory agencies go through a "life cycle."[19]

Based on an analysis of American regulatory agencies, Bernstein argues that these bodies go through four phases in their life cycle. In the first phase (gestation), the agency is established following political agitation from reform-minded elements in society, who demand legislation to deal with "abusive business practices." Often this is a lengthy political struggle.[20]

In the second phase (youth), the agency has "an aggressive, crusading spirit," and takes a vigorous approach to regulating business. However, the agency's staff is inexperienced because it is involved in a new area of regulation, and some mistakes are inevitably made. The regulated industry tries to ingratiate itself with agency appointees, sometimes holding out the prospect of lucrative employment in the industry at some future date. It also tries to block appointment of anyone too unsympathetic to the industry. The agency faces the problem of legal challenges to its authority from the industry, and its energetic regulatory efforts can be tied up in the courts. As this happens, the initial thrust of public enthusiasm for the agency's regulatory activity starts to dissipate.

In phase three (maturity), the agency starts to lose much of its initial vitality, and becomes a more passive and accepted part of the status quo. The agency begins to develop a good working relationship with the regulated industry, and "its functions are less those of a policeman and more like that of a manager of an industry." Public concern for the agency's role has vanished; it becomes harder to get new funds or new staff; and the agency is too weighed down with a backlog of work to even think about new regulatory activities.[22]

In the final phase (old age), "passivity deepens into debility." The agency becomes lethargic and preoccupied with maintaining the status quo. The bureaucratic arteries have hardened, and any creative force has been drained. It is "recognized as the protector of the industry," and it increasingly relies on the industry to supply it with staff. Agencies, in this senescent stage, "become the servants rather than the governors of the industries which they regulate." In short, they have become "captured."[23]

Bernstein's theory pre-dates much of the new social regulation that was established around the 1970s, and the life-cycle theory was applied principally to agencies involved with "older-style" economic regulation. In this area of activity, where regulation of prices, entry, output, etc. can benefit the regulated firms, critics of Bernstein argue that regulation was actually initiated at the behest of industry. Gabriel Kolko, for example, claims that U.S. federal regulation, in the early part of this century, was not a response to "progressive" public reformism. Instead, government interventions "were usually motivated by the needs of interested businesses," and were "frequently merely a response to the demands of particular businessmen."[24] Businesses demanded regulation in an attempt to control the growing competition that was threatening to undermine profits.[25] The implication for Bernstein's theory is that regulatory agencies did not *become* captured by business—they served business interests from the start. This view has been challenged by writers such as Paul Quirk and James Q. Wilson, who argue that Kolko ignores regulations that impose costs on business, such as consumer protection and environmental regulation, and that he underestimates the extent of business opposition to regulation.[26]

In Canada, Tom Traves argues that business attitudes toward growing state regulation, in the interwar period, were ambivalent.[27] Manufacturers hesitantly sought government regulation to preserve their economic security, which was threatened by surplus capacity and growing competition. At the same time, increased regulation was also a source of frustration and unease for business, and different sections of business had conflicting needs with regard to regulation.[28] Where business was divided, politicians had greater autonomy to formulate policy in accordance with the "national interest," which was frequently defined in terms of their own personal political goals.[29] On issues that inspired public concern, "politicians had to tread carefully between powerful corporate interests and outraged public opinion," and in the whole area of state intervention, "there was never a simple translation of economic might into political power."[30]

Divisions within the business community also shape the character of regulatory agencies in a more contemporary period. Writing from a marxist perspective,

Rianne Mahon argues that these agencies have a dual, and sometimes contradictory, role.[31] On the one hand, they represent the interests of the regulated industry, but at the same time, these narrow industry concerns must be subordinated to the long-term interests of the dominant class.[32] Regulatory agencies, like other parts of the state bureaucracy, must arrange the compromises between the long-term needs of capital and the narrow interests of particular industries. Agencies "represent" industries, but they also "discipline" them on behalf of the "national interest."[33]

In addition, Mahon sees regulatory agencies as providing a way of accommodating political challenges to the rights of capital (eg. from subordinate classes in society). The right of capital to make decisions about production, exports, investment, etc., is infringed by regulation, and by creating a special structure (the regulatory agency) to perform this function, the infringement is "politically insulated" as an "exceptional" phenomenon or a special case.[34] Thus, from this neomarxist perspective, regulatory agencies are not simple "captives" of the industries they regulate. Instead, they fulfill a more complex function—constructing the particular compromises between regulated industries, dominant class interests and challenges from below.[35]

A complex characterization of business relations with regulatory agencies is also indicated by evidence of both conflict and cooperation in this relationship. The cooperative aspects suggest that regulatory agencies are attentive to at least some of the needs of regulated industries. The aspects of conflict suggest that agencies have not been totally captured, and that other considerations, besides the needs of the regulated, are also important.

Cooperation is based on a mutual dependency between regulated industries and government agencies, which tends to promote clientele relations (see Chapter Three). The agency needs specialized information from the industry, as well as cooperation in complying with regulations and political support in battles with other sections of government. The industry, in turn, needs good access to policy-makers, and favourable policy outputs. As indicated in Chapter Three, the prospects for the development of clientelism vary according to the specific circumstances of each case.

In Canada, one factor that works against "agency capture" or "clientelism," lies in the recruitment pattern of agency personnel. In the United States, there is a greater likelihood that regulators will be recruited from the industry itself, or will take up jobs in regulated firms after they leave the public service. This phenomenon, known as the "revolving door," is not totally absent from the Canadian political scene, but it is far less common than in the United States. It is much more likely that Canadian regulators will be recruited from within the public bureaucracy itself.[36]

Regulatory policy is also given a distinctively Canadian flavour by the division of authority between different levels of government. Jurisdiction over regulatory policy exists at federal, provincial and municipal levels of government. In many cases responsibility for particular areas of regulatory policy is shared, rather than clearly divided, which creates a number of problems in the regulatory process.

REGULATION AND THE CANADIAN FEDERAL SYSTEM

The division (and sharing) of regulatory authority among different levels of government creates problems both for business and for government. However, the jurisdictional patchwork can also work to business' advantage.

Where regulatory jurisdiction exists at the provincial or municipal levels, business can be faced with an array of different rules across the country. Businesses that operate nationwide must adapt to regulations that vary from one province or municipality to the next. Not only does this make life more complicated, it also makes it harder for business to influence regulatory policy. It requires more time and effort to lobby several different governments, than to focus attention on just one. For example, when Ontario transferred authority over Sunday shopping to the municipalities in February 1989, the major supermarkets had to take their lobbying campaign to each individual municipality in an attempt to get their stores open on Sunday.

Although this means greater costs, it also provides an advantage because individual municipalities can be played off against one another. If one municipality does not want to have Sunday shopping, then retailers can threaten to move to a neighbouring jurisdiction. If one municipality allows Sunday shopping, then retailers in nearby "closed" municipalities will lose business. Pressure can be brought to bear on politicians, and on a grander scale, with other regulatory issues, this sort of leverage can be used against individual provincial governments in an attempt to extract policy concessions. The same concern applies at the international level, where competition to attract and retain business investment limits the extent to which any individual country can place regulatory burdens on business. The key factor in all of this is the mobility of capital, and the vulnerability of the state to private business decisions about where to invest.

Within Canada, the overlapping regulatory authority between Ottawa and the provinces raises a number of problems for business. First, it leads to confusion about "who does what." It is not always clear which level of government has authority over various aspects of regulatory policy. In a political environment where new regulations are continually being formulated, and where existing regulatory regimes are subject to change, this problem can be especially acute. In the energy sector, for example, overlapping is particularly complicated because utility systems cut across provincial boundaries and fall under both federal and provincial regulatory authority.[37] Second, where overlap exists, business faces the problem of trying to conform to regulations that may contradict one another, or that do not mesh very well together. And finally, even where regulations are compatible, business must deal with the administrative costs of interacting with regulators at different levels of government. This includes such things as providing information, filling out forms, writing reports, attending hearings and dealing with government inspectors.

These problems of regulatory overlap can be very frustrating for business, especially if business plans are held up while approval is sought from more than one set of regulators. For example, in municipal development, companies must comply with provincial regulations as well as municipal bylaws. Every year, provinces create around one hundred new land-use regulations, and most provinces require zoning bylaws and development plans to be cleared with the provincial government.[38] In addition, building construction must comply with national and provincial regulations, and building contractors frequently complain about the lack of uniformity in these standards.[39]

Besides the difficulties associated with overlapping regulations, there is also the problem of jurisdictional disputes. Conflicts between Ottawa and the provinces over regulatory jurisdiction result in uncertainty for business about which sets of regulations to follow. As the Economic Council has put it, this "can lead to protracted negotiations between departments or governments, leaving firms caught in the middle to bear the brunt of the costly delays."[40]

Federal-provincial negotiation also requires an extensive network of intergovernmental committees aimed at resolving disputes, and where disputes cannot be resolved through negotiation, then federal and provincial regulators must fight it out in the courts. This not only means more delay and uncertainty for business, but it also weakens the effectiveness of regulation by creating a jurisdictional vacuum until the dispute is resolved.

One area that provides a good example of the complex pattern of federal-provincial regulation in Canada is in financial services. The federal government has exclusive jurisdiction over banks, while the provinces have exclusive jurisdiction over credit unions and the securities market. In the areas of insurance and trust companies, jurisdiction is shared between the federal and provincial governments.[41]

This picture is complicated enough in itself, but in recent years two developments have muddied the waters even further. First, there has been a trend towards integration of the four "pillars" of the financial system (banks, trust companies, insurance companies and investment dealers). Technological developments in computerization and telecommunications, along with corporate mergers, are leading to an integration of financial institutions throughout the world. In Canada, as in other countries, the barriers between different sorts of financial institutions are becoming less distinct.[42] Banks are already established in the mortgage business, which was formerly the prerogative of trust and insurance companies, and now they are moving into the securities business as well. Trust companies and investment dealers now provide cheque-writing facilities similar to banks; insurance and trust companies are trying to get into the commercial lending market; and "everyone seems to be vying for retail deposits and consumer credit."[43] In addition, the banks are pressuring government in an attempt to get into the insurance business.

The second factor is that Ottawa and various provinces are changing the rules in different ways, with no coordination between the different governments. In December 1986, the federal government's White Paper outlined a number of measures, including a proposal to permit financial institutions to engage in activities outside of their "core" areas.[44] However, the proposals were subsequently stalled. In 1989, British Columbia took a step away from such integration when it introduced a law banning financial "supermarkets," where trust companies, credit unions and insurance companies operate together. Quebec, on the other hand, is moving in the opposite direction, and in 1988, the province revealed a plan to allow different sorts of financial institutions to operate under the same roof. As Quebec was deregulating, Ontario was tightening the reins, and in the same year it placed new restrictions on trust companies, following a number of financial failures. Thus in Canada, the financial system, which is the backbone of any capitalist economy, is in a state of regulatory chaos. Jurisdictional divisions have produced conflict and inconsistency, and there is a clear need for greater regulatory harmonization in the face of growing international competition.[45]

Regulatory harmonization between Ottawa and the provinces is by no means impossible; for instance, an agreement was reached in 1985 which harmonized trucking regulations. However, agreement in this area was possible because there was little transfer of authority from one level of government to the other. Instead, both levels of government agreed to a more consistent and minimal regime through deregulation. Deregulation can thus provide the lowest common denominator for federal-provincial harmony in regulatory policy, and it is possible that "harmonization" could become a pseudonym for mutual deregulation. The movement towards deregulation, and the arguments surrounding this issue, are examined in the next section.

DEREGULATION

Over the last decade or so, several Western industrialized nations mounted an attack against some forms of state intervention. Under the neo-conservative governments of Margaret Thatcher and Ronald Reagan, Britain and the United States were in the vanguard of this movement, while Canada, under Brian

Mulroney, followed behind. The attack on the state has varied in its extent and emphasis among different countries, but in general it has involved cuts in social spending and some other domestic programs; lower corporate tax rates; the privatization of state-owned companies; the deregulation of certain areas of business activity; and an overall movement towards unrestrained market competition as opposed to state economic planning. Deregulation has thus been one element in a broader economic strategy.

In Canada, deregulation has become part of the contemporary political vocabulary, and has given rise to some debate. Yet in practice, the extent of deregulation has, so far, remained fairly limited. Its main thrust has been in the area of "economic" regulation, involving prices, output, entry, etc., rather than in "social" regulation, where issues such as health, safety, fairness and the environment are involved. Deregulation has been more concerned with exposing regulated industries to new competition, than with reducing the costs of social responsibility. But even in the realm of economic regulation, action has only been taken in a few industries, and not always in a comprehensive fashion. These industries include transportation, some aspects of financial services, and limited areas of in telecommunications and energy.

With regard to social regulation, the general trend, if any, has been towards increased state controls rather than deregulation. In this area most people accept that a lot of regulatory activity is necessary and appropriate. Few people would suggest that we take a more permissive attitude towards workplace injuries, unsafe consumer products, fraudulent advertizing, unsanitary food processing, aircraft safety, toxic waste disposal or racial discrimination in employment. In these cases, market competition cannot function as an effective regulator in protecting the public. It would be ludicrous to suggest that if consumers get food-poisoning from one company's products, they should simply try a different brand next time, or that victims of plane crashes should use an airline with a better maintenance record in future. The costs of getting advance information are too prohibitive for most consumers, and the consequences are too severe to permit the public to learn by its mistakes.

For an insight into the unsavoury side of unregulated production, we need go no further than Upton Sinclair's classic novel, *The Jungle*. This work describes conditions in the meat-packing houses of Chicago at the turn of the century, and was itself instrumental in provoking a federal investigation:

> There was never the least attention paid to what was cut up for sausage; there would come all the way back from Europe old sausage that had been rejected, and that was moldy and white—it would be dosed with borax and glycerine, and dumped into the hoppers, and made over again for home consumption. There would be meat that had tumbled out on the floor, in the dirt and sawdust, where the workers had tramped and spit uncounted

billions of consumption germs. There would be meat stored in great piles in rooms; and the water from leaky roofs would drip over it, and thousands of rats would race about on it. It was too dark in these storage places to see well, but a man could run his hand over these piles of meat and sweep off handfuls of dried dung of rats. These rats were nuisances, and the packers would put poisoned bread out for them, they would die, and then rats, bread, and meat would go into the hoppers together. This is no fairy story and no joke; the meat would be shoveled into carts, and the man who did the shoveling would not trouble to lift out a rat even when he saw one— there were things that went into the sausage in comparison with which a poisoned rat was a tidbit. There was no place for the men to wash their hands before they ate their dinner, and so they made a practice of washing them in the water that was to be ladled into the sausage. There were the butt-ends of smoked meat, and the scraps of corned beef, and all the odds and ends of the waste of the plants, that would be dumped into old barrels in the cellar and left there. Under the system of rigid economy which the packers enforced, there were some jobs that it only paid to do once in a long time, and among these was the cleaning out of the waste barrels. Every spring they did it; and in the barrels would be dirt and rust and old nails and stale water—and cart load after cart load of it would be taken up and dumped into the hoppers with fresh meat, and sent out to the public's breakfast.[46]

This is a pretty powerful argument in favour of strong social regulation (especially if you happen to be reading this over breakfast). But in other areas of regulatory policy, deregulation can have both advantages and disadvantages. These are illustrated with regard to one of the most prominent areas of Canadian deregulation, namely the transportation industry.

Deregulation and the Canadian Transportation Industry

In 1987 the federal government passed two new laws that deregulated key elements of Canada's transportation system. These were the National Transportation Act and the Motor Vehicle Transport Act. This new legislation was based on the belief that competition and market forces were the best mechanisms for achieving efficient, low-cost transportation. The federal government sought to promote competition by keeping regulation to a minimum.[47] In an attempt to achieve this objective, the Acts introduced a number of significant changes in regulatory policy.

For airlines, it is now much easier to get a licence for domestic service. Previously, airlines had to fulfill an array of conditions concerning such things as fares, schedules and routes, before a licence would be issued. They also had to demonstrate that the new service was needed according to a criterion of "public convenience and necessity."[48] These conditions had the effect of limiting competition by restricting entry and maintaining higher prices. Under the new rules, airlines only have to show that they are "fit, willing and able," to provide a service, which means that they must meet safety standards, be insured and in most cases be Canadian-owned.

It is also easier for airlines to "exit" through reducing services or abandoning unprofitable routes. Companies can now remove the service to a community simply by giving four months notice. For Northern and remote communities, some of the old regulations still remain, and if an air service is no longer profitable, the federal government can choose to provide subsidies to keep one going.[49]

For railways, shippers are now allowed to arrange confidential contracts with railway companies, which reduces the potential for collective rate-setting by the railways and encourages greater competition. New rules also make it easier for shippers to switch over to competitive lines, and it is now simpler for railways to abandon uneconomic routes.

In road transportation, the federal government has the power to regulate 'extra-provincial' trucking, but in the past this authority was delegated to the provinces. In accordance with a federal-provincial agreement, truckers no longer have to get government approval for their rates, and it is much easier to get a licence. As with airlines, new entrants now only have to show that they are "fit, willing and able," rather than passing the stricter test of "public convenience and necessity."[50]

According to the federal government, these regulatory changes will bring new competition, greater efficiency, lower rates, better service, increased income and more jobs.[51] However, this rosy assessment ignores a number of potential problems.

In the short-term, competition is likely to grow, as regulations against new entrants are loosened and the number of firms increases. This should also lead to price cutting. Unless firms quickly improve their efficiency, increased competition and lower prices will mean reduced profits and greater commercial instability. After deregulation in the United States, the trucking industry suffered a series of bankruptcies, and in Canada things may be going the same way, as trucking firms try to survive on wafer-thin profit margins.[51]

In the U.S. airline industry, deregulation initially resulted in more competition and cheaper fares as the number of airlines quickly jumped from 30 to 200. Then, as prices dropped and airlines started losing money, a wave of bankruptcies and mergers took place. By 1989, fares were rising and concentration in the industry had actually increased, with the five largest companies controlling over 70 per cent of the market—as opposed to 60 per cent before deregulation.[52]

In Canada, despite initial fare-cutting, industry concentration quickly increased as Wardair got into financial difficulties and was bought out by PWA. After the first year of deregulation, competition was reduced, fares had risen and the two top airlines, Air Canada and PWA (which owns Canadian Airlines International), controlled 98 per cent of the domestic market.[53] For passenger travel, this situation is now worse due to the extensive cuts in Via Rail, which further reduce the level of transport competition.

In freight shipping, deregulation has resulted in greater competition, as the railway companies try to fend off attacks by the trucking industry. Both CN and CP have been selling off non-rail assets in an attempt to cope with a deregulated system that neither of them wanted. In one case, CN sold its trucking division to the private sector, but the new trucking company was unable to deal with deregulation, and despite a $20 million modernization, it went bankrupt in 1988.[54]

The new competitive pressures for railways and truckers also come from the United States, because the Canadian market has now been opened up to U.S. competition. American transport companies can ship goods between cities within Canadian provinces, even though 43 U.S. states prevent Canadian truckers from doing the same thing south of the border.[55]

Deregulation is also likely to create problems in industrial relations, as competition forces companies to cut costs by keeping wages down, cutting staff and generally squeezing more out of their workforce. In the U.S., the experience of Eastern Airlines has not been a salutary example. The airline lost over one billion dollars since deregulation, and attempts to cut staff, salaries and routes met with massive labour unrest. Eventually, Eastern had to file for bankruptcy.[56]

Another problem with transport deregulation is "cream-skimming." Since government regulations have been relaxed, it is easier for airlines and railways to abandon less profitable routes in favour of more lucrative markets. Companies have the opportunity to "skim the cream" off the market by concentrating on heavy-traffic routes such as Toronto to Montreal, while more marginal routes are cut back or closed down.

This could have serious consequences for communities across Canada that depend on these transportation services. In a vast country with a small population, a comprehensive transportation network is a vital link in promoting national unity. Where this requirement clashes with profit-making, then national goals will not be well served by unregulated market competition.

Finally, deregulation generates pressures on transport companies to reduce costs by cutting corners on safety. Firms that are struggling to remain in business may be tempted to cut back on expensive repairs, or to reduce maintenance staff or to postpone equipment renewals. In the United States, truck safety has been deteriorating in the wake of deregulation, because maintenance standards have slipped, and drivers have pushed themselves beyond the limits of fatigue.[57] In Canada, a new highway safety code will attempt to address this problem, although the strain of competition will inevitably give rise to violations.

Pressure for deregulation of the transportation industry has stemmed from the fact that transport is a major element in the cost structure of Canadian business. By trying to inspire new competition, government has made life harder for existing transport companies, with the objective of benefiting other industries. However, we must also consider the longer-term effects of deregulation, and the risks of instability, bankruptcy and increased concentration, which ultimately may reduce competition and raise costs. Moreover, we face the prospect of reduced services in some areas, as well as increased labour unrest, and potential safety problems, as the deregulated competitive battle runs its course.

The whole issue of regulatory policy frequently pits the interests of one section of business against those of other sections, and government must try to balance and reconcile these conflicting needs. In addition, the requirements of business must be weighed against public demands for continued, or greater, regulation in certain areas of business activity. Government officials must continually manoeuvre between the twin imperatives of business profitability and democratic pressure, as well as trying to accommodate their own self-determined objectives.

ENDNOTES

1. Economic Council of Canada, *Responsible Regulation* (Ottawa: Minister of Supply and Services Canada, 1979), xi.
2. Douglas Hartle, *Public Policy, Decision Making and Regulation* (Montreal: The Institute for Research on Public Policy, 1979), 1.
3. Richard Schultz and Alan Alexandroff, *Economic Regulation and the Federal System* (Toronto: The Royal Commission on the Economic Union and Developmant Prospects for Canada, 1985), 2-5.
4. *Ibid.*, 4.
5. See G. Bruce Doern and V. Seymour Wilson, "Conclusions and Observations," in G. Bruce Doern and V. Seymour Wilson, eds., *Issues in Canadian Public Policy* (Toronto: Macmillan of Canada, 1974), 337-45; Margot Priest, W.T. Stanbury and Fred Thompson, "On the Definition of Economic Regulation," in W.T. Stanbury, ed., *Government Regulation: Scope, Growth, Process* (Montreal: The Institute for

Research on Public Policy, 1980), 1-16; Economic Council, *Responsible Regulation*; M.J. Trebilcock, et al., *The Choice of Governing Instrument*, A Study prepared for the Economic Council of Canada (Ottawa: Minister of Supply and Services Canada, 1982); G. Bruce Doern and Richard W. Phidd, *Canadian Public Policy: Ideas, Structure, Process* (Toronto: Methuen, 1983); and Nicolas Baxter-Moore, "Policy Implementation and the Role of the State: A Revised Approach to the Study of Policy Instruments," in Robert J. Jackson, Doreen Jackson, and Nicolas Baxter-Moore, eds., *Contemporary Canadian Politics: Readings and Notes* (Scarborough, Ont.: Prentice-Hall Canada, 1987), 336- 55.

6. See for example Economic Council, *Responsible Regulation*; Priest, Stanbury and Thompson, "On the Definition of Economic Regulation," 4; and Trebilcock et al., *The Choice of Governing Instruments*, 87.

7. Economic Council, *Responsible Regulation*, 45.

8. Canadian Food Processors Association, "Submission to Agriculture Canada on the Proposed Revision to the Processed Tomato Peel Standards" (August, 1987), 6.

9. David E. Osborn, "Hazardous Products Legislation in Canada (A)," in Mark C. Baetz and Donald H. Thain, eds., *Canadian Cases in Business-Government Relations* (Toronto: Methuen, 1985), 40.

10. Canada, Office of Privatization and Regulatory Affairs, *Federal Regulatory Plan, 1988* (Ottawa: Minister of Supply and Services, 1987), 63.

11. G. Bruce Doern, "Introduction: The Regulatory Process in Canada," in G. Bruce Doern, ed., *The Regulatory Process in Canada* (Toronto: MacMillan of Canada, 1978), 1-33.

12. *Globe and Mail* (15 August, 1989), B1.

13. CRTC, *Annual Report* (1988-89), 21.

14. *Ibid.*, 35 and 48.

15. NEB, *Annual Report*, 1987; NEB, *Regulatory Agenda* (June 1988); and *Federal Regulatory Plan*, 1988.

16. *Globe and Mail* (20 December, 1988), B1 and B4.

17. NTA, *The National Transportation Agency of Canada*, 1988; and Transport Canada, *Freedom to Move* (Ottawa: Minister of Supply and Services, 1988).

18. See, Marver H. Bernstein, *Regulating Business by Independent Commission* (Princeton, N.J.: Princeton University Press, 1955) and G.J. Stigler, "The Theory of Economic Regulation," in *Bell Journal of Economics and Management Science* (Spring 1971), 3-21.

19. Bernstein, *ibid.*

20. *Ibid.*, 74-77.

21. *Ibid.*, 79-84

22. *Ibid.*, 86-91.

23. *Ibid.*, 91-95.

24. Gabriel Kolko, *The Triumph of Conservatism: A Reinterpretation of American History, 1900-1916* (New York: The Free Press, 1963), 2.

25. *Ibid.*, 4.

26. P.J. Quirk, *Industry Influence in Federal Regulatory Agencies* (Princeton, N.J.: Princeton University Press, 1981) and James Q. Wilson, "The Politics of Regulation," in James W. McKie, ed., *Social Responsibility and the Business Predicament* (Washington, D.C.: The Brookings Institution, 1974), 135-68.

27. Tom Traves, *The State and Enterprise: Canadian Manufacturers and the Federal Government, 1917-1931* (Toronto: University of Toronto Press, 1979).

28. *Ibid.*, 7-11.

29. *Ibid.*, 9.

30. *Ibid.*

31. Rianne Mahon, "Regulatory Agencies: Captive Agents or Hegemonic Apparatuses," in *Studies in Political Economy*, 1 (1979), 162-200.

32. *Ibid.*, 174.

33. *Ibid.*, 171.

34. *Ibid.*, 175.

35. *Ibid.*, 175-76.

36. Doern, "Introduction: The Regulatory Process in Canada," 29; T.G. Kane, *Consumers and Regulators: Intervention in the Federal Regulatory Process* (Montreal: Institute for Research on Public Policy, 1980), 28; and Richard Schultz, "Regulatory Agencies," in Michael S. Whittington and Glen Williams, eds., *Canadian Politics in the 1980s*, 2nd edition (Toronto: Methuen, 1984), 437.

37. Richard Schultz, "The Regulatory Process and Federal-Provincial Relations," in Doern, ed., *The Regulatory Process*, 133.

38. The Economic Council of Canada, *Reforming Regulation* (Ottawa: Minister of Supply and Services Canada, 1981), 129.

39. *Ibid.*,

40. *Ibid.*, 128.

41. Stephen Handfield-Jones, *Harmonization of Financial Regulation in Canada*, Conference Board of Canada, Report No. 42-89 (June 1989), 1.

42. Handfield-Jones, *Harmonization*, v; The Economic Council of Canada *Competition and Solvency: A Framework for Financial Regulation* (Ottawa: Minister of Supply and Services Canada, 1986), 3 and B. Zafiriou, *The Regulation of Financial Institutions: Recent Proposals for Reform*, Library of Parliament, Current Issue Review, No. 86-24E (Ottawa: Minister of Supply and Services Canada, 1988), 1.

43. Zafiriou, *The Regulation of Financial Institutions*, 1.

44. *Ibid.*, 15.

45. Handfield-Jones, *Harmonization*, 8.
46. Upton Sinclair, *The Jungle* (New York: Airmont Publishing Company, Inc., 1965), 129. First published 1906.
47. Canada, Transport Canada, *Freedom to Move in Canada's New Transportation Environment* (Ottawa: Minister of Supply and Services Canada, 1988), 4.
48. *Ibid.*, 6.
49. *Ibid.*, 6 and 9.
50. *Ibid.*, 8.
51. *Globe and Mail* (13 September, 1988), B1.
52. *Financial Post* (18 January, 1989), 11.
53. *Globe and Mail* (8 June, 1989), B4.
54. *Globe and Mail* (13 September, 1988), B1.
55. *Globe and Mail* (4 January, 1988), B12.
56. *Globe and Mail* (23 July, 1988), B4 and (14 March, 1989), A7.
57. *Globe and Mail* (4 January, 1988), B12.

Chapter 12

International Trade Policy

International trade has been of vital significance to Canada throughout its history, and today the dependency on exports and imports is becoming even more pronounced. By 1989 Canada's merchandise exports accounted for 21.6 per cent of Gross Domestic Product, compared with 19.3 per cent in 1975 and 15.3 per cent in 1965.[1] As exports rose, so imports also increased. In 1965 imports were equivalent to 15.1 per cent of GDP, rising to 20.4 per cent in 1975, and 21.1 per cent in 1989.[2]

This growing dependency on international trade is not unique to Canada, but has been part of a global trend affecting most developed countries in the last half of the twentieth century. National economies have become increasingly integrated through trade and other linkages, such as foreign investment, satellite communications and global computer networks, and countries are increasingly affected by each other's trade and economic policies. For Canada and other countries, national autonomy and economic independence have been in retreat.

As can be seen from Table 12.1, exports have become substantially more important since 1965 for most of the major economies, although this trend has generally slowed since 1975. In 1989, Canada ranked second in terms of export dependency in comparison with the other major economies. In contrast, the United States has the lowest level of dependency, due to its large domestic market, and it can afford to be more aggressive than most of its trading partners when it comes to protectionism. This is necessarily worrying for a country such as Canada that is heavily reliant on access to the U.S. market.

Increasing international trade brings about a growth of export revenues, but on the other side of the coin, increased imports compete with domestic products and can have a severe impact on production, profits and jobs in some industries. When this occurs, policy-makers face demands for increased protection through tariffs or other trade barriers. These demands are frequently difficult for governments to ignore, especially if important industries are jeopardized, and lots of jobs (and votes) are threatened.

Table 12.1

		Merchandise Exports as a Percentage of GDP, Selected Countries, 1965, 1975 and 1989	
	1965	1975	1989
Canada	15.3	19.3	21.6
United States	3.9	6.7	7.1
Japan	9.3	11.2	9.7
France	10.1	15.1	18.9
West Germany	15.6	21.5	28.5
Italy	10.0	15.7	16.3
United Kingdom	13.2	18.8	18.5

Source: OECD, *Main Economic Indicators*; UN, *Monthly Bulletins of Statistics*.

Trade policy thus involves both export promotion and import protection, and these two things are closely related. It is difficult to persuade other countries to lower their trade barriers unless Canada is prepared to make reciprocal concessions, and thus there is tension and contradiction between the twin goals of promoting exports and protecting domestic industries against imports. The need to choose between these two goals, or to find some way of reconciling them, is a fundamental problem in international trade policy.

In Canada, trade policy has not always been consistent, and its emphasis has shifted between the two goals at different periods in Canadian history. The changes that have taken place will be examined in a later section of this chapter, including a brief history of Canadian trade policy, as well as an analysis of more recent developments. This will be followed by a chapter devoted specifically to the Canada-United States Free Trade Agreement.

But first it is useful to look both at the contemporary pattern of Canada's international trade, and at some of the different types of measures that fall under the heading of international trade policy.

CANADA'S TRADE PATTERN

Canada's trade pattern can be examined along four dimensions. First, we are concerned with the balance of international trade—do we export more than we import or vice versa? Second, we should look at the direction of trade—which countries are the major markets for our exports, and which are our principal suppliers of imports? Third, we need to be aware of the content of international trade—what products do we export most, and which do we import most? And finally, it is important to consider the regional significance of international trade in Canada—for instance, are some provinces much more dependent on foreign trade than others, and do different regions have conflicting interests over trade policy?

The Balance of International Trade

The balance of international trade is the difference between a country's exports and its imports. Naturally, all countries would like to have a surplus of exports over imports, but obviously it is not possible for every country to have a positive balance. Figure 12.1 shows that over the last two decades Canada has typically experienced a surplus in terms of merchandise trade, but has continually suffered a deficit in "invisible" trade, which includes services, investment income and transfer payments. For most years the invisible deficit has outweighed the surplus on visible merchandise, and the balance of payments on the current account (trade in goods and services plus investment income and transfer payments) has commonly been in the red. In 1989, the invisible deficit was so great that Canada's overall balance of trade was more than $19 billion in deficit.

In Chapter Four we saw that the structure of the Canadian economy, along with other developed countries, has shifted away from goods production towards services. This means that the world's major economies are moving away from an area of relative Canadian strength in international trade (i.e. goods

FIGURE 12.1

Canada's Balance of International Trade (Current Account) 1970-89

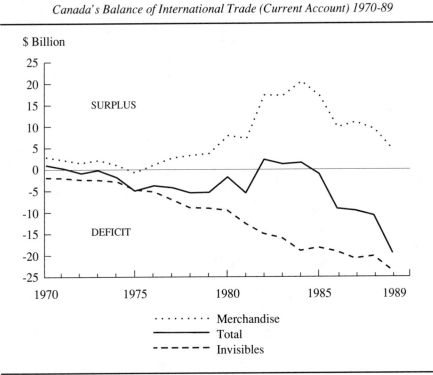

Source: Statistics Canada, 67-001.

production) to one of Canadian weakness (i.e. services). Unless there is some change in these trends, the long-term prospects for Canada's international trade balance are not encouraging.

The Direction of Canadian Trade

One of the most outstanding features of Canada's international trade is its overwhelming dependency on one other country, namely the United States. For both exports and imports, the U.S. is of far greater importance to Canada than the rest of the world combined. In 1989 Canada's merchandise exports to the United States amounted to $103.7 billion, which constituted 74.7 per cent of the total. In the same year imports stood at $93.3 billion, or 69.5 per cent of the total.[3]

This severe dependency on the United States has developed over the course of the twentieth century, as Britain's importance as a trading partner has waned. In 1901, 52.5 per cent of Canada's exports went to Britain, but by 1989 Britain accounted for only 2.5 per cent of the total.[4] Figure 12.2 illustrates the shift in focus that has taken place since the beginning of the century. Before the Second World War, Britain was still just ahead of the U.S. in importance, but as Britain's world economic power declined, so Canada turned increasingly to the United States as a trading partner. This shift became more pronounced in the postwar period as American capital expanded and the Canadian and U.S. economies became more integrated. At the same time, Britain was trading more with Europe, and this was reinforced in 1973 when it joined the European Economic Community (EEC). For Canada, the old colonial power of Britain has been superceded by the giant American economy which now sucks in nearly three-quarters of Canadian exports.

The inordinate dependency on the American market means that Canada is extremely vulnerable to policy developments in the United States. If access to the U.S. market were seriously restricted, then the economic consequences for Canada would be catastrophic. We have reached a situation where Canada's export eggs have been placed largely in one basket, and that basket is in the hands of U.S. policy-makers. As a result, Canadian government policies must necessarily be sensitive to adverse reactions in the United States, and this serves to limit the options that can realistically be pursued. Severe constraints exist on Canadian autonomy, and these extend to other areas of foreign and domestic policy besides trade.

In the future, this trade dependency on the United States will almost certainly continue to increase because the Free Trade Agreement will orient Canadian business even further toward the U.S. market. In addition, the 1992 removal of trade barriers within the EEC, and the competitive restructuring of European

FIGURE 12.2

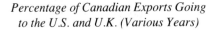

*Percentage of Canadian Exports Going
to the U.S. and U.K. (Various Years)*

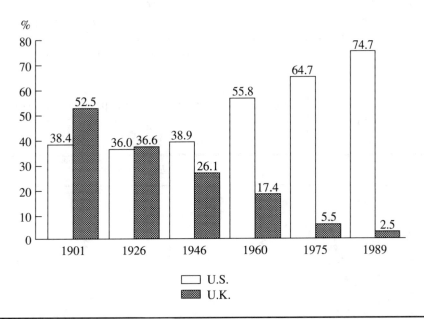

Sources: F.H. Leacy, *Historical Statistics of Canada, 2nd ed.* (Ottawa: Statistics Canada, 1983); and
Statistics Canada, 67-001.

industry that is likely to follow, will make it tougher for Canadian companies to
compete within that regional trading bloc.

The Content of Canada's Trade

Canada's international trade covers both physical merchandise and less tangible services, such as insurance, shipping and freight, travel and business services. While the overall structure of the economy has shifted toward services, the
proportion of Canadian exports taken up by services has actually declined. In
1960, services accounted for 22.8 per cent of Canadian exports, but this figure
dropped to 16.2 per cent in 1970, and by 1989 it was down to 12.8 per cent. [5]
Canada has regularly had a trade deficit in services (see Figure 12.1), and a large
proportion of this is accounted for by business services. Seventy per cent of
external payments for business services go to the United States, largely for royalties, patents, trademarks and management and administrative fees.[6]

For merchandise trade, Canada's exports are composed predominantly of end products and fabricated materials. These categories include such things as motor vehicles and parts, wood products and paper, metals and ores, oil and gas, chemicals and fertilizer, and industrial machinery. As shown in Chapter Four, end products and fabricated materials together account for over 75 per cent of Canadian exports, and the proportion of exports taken up by primary products has declined significantly over the last 30 years. However, this should not disguise the fact that Canada has a massive trade deficit in end products, amounting to $32.5 billion in 1989.[7]

Canada's leading merchandise exports are shown in Figure 12.3, and it is clear that Canada does not have a very diversified pattern of exports. Automotive products and wood products dominate the list, and these two cate-

FIGURE 12.3

Canada's Leading Merchandise Exports, 1989

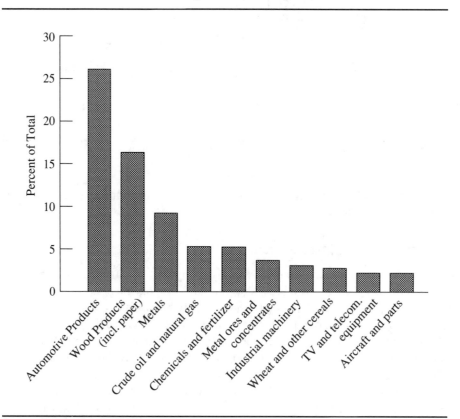

Source: Statistics Canada, 65-001.

gories account for over 42 per cent of Canadian exports. In all, the 10 sets of products shown on the bar chart comprise more than 76 per cent of Canadian exports. Thus Canada is not only highly dependent on a single foreign market, it is also highly dependent on a narrow range of products. If there is a drop in world demand for these products, due to technological change or changing tastes, then Canadian exports could be seriously hurt. Canada must also be concerned if there is growing international competition in these product areas, such as from Japanese and Korean automobiles, or in the form of international subsidy wars for wheat exports. Furthermore, in the areas of wood products, metal ores and oil and gas, there is the problem of resource depletion and the boom-bust cycle of commodity prices. Dependency on a small range of products may provide the benefits of specialization, but it also makes Canada more vulnerable to global economic change.

Regional Significance

International trade policy has been a longstanding source of conflict between different provinces in Canada. In particular, the "hinterland" provinces of Atlantic Canada and the West have argued continually that Canadian tariffs and other protectionist measures have been mechanisms for maintaining the economic dominance of the "heartland" provinces of Ontario and Quebec. Protectionism for manufactured goods has been viewed as a way of assisting industries in Central Canada, where most manufacturing takes place, while the hinterland provinces must pay higher prices both for imports and for goods manufactured behind tariff walls in Ontario and Quebec.[8]

It is also suggested that, in comparison with Central Canada, the hinterland provinces have tended to favour free trade because of their greater export orientation.[9] However, if we look at Figure 12.4, no clear regional division emerges. The most export-oriented provinces are Saskatchewan, New Brunswick, Ontario and British Columbia, in that order. The least export-oriented are Prince Edward Island, Manitoba, Nova Scotia and Quebec. Even within a particular province, generalization is not easy. Regional attitudes towards protectionism tend to vary depending on which products are being discussed and whether they are produced in a particular region. For instance, as Hamilton and Whalley point out, in the mid-1980s the West wanted better access to Japanese cars, and at the same time sought greater protection against meat imports from the United States.[10] Thus, provinces can be pulled in two directions at once.

When it comes to manufacturing, the regional conflicts over trade protection are a little clearer for the simple reason that most manufacturing is located in Ontario and Quebec. Yet, even here, some qualifications are necessary. First, the central provinces have a large number of consumers as well as producers,

FIGURE 12.4

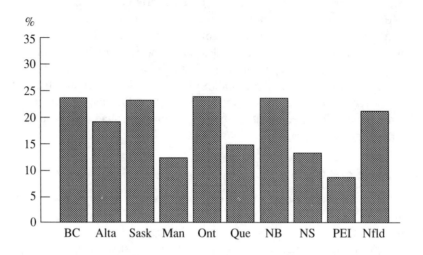

*Provincial Merchandise Exports as a
Percentage of Provincial GDP, 1989*

Source: Statistics Canada, 13-213P and 65-202.

and if prices were lowered due to a reduction in trade barriers, then consumers in Ontario and Quebec would also benefit.

Second, those manufacturing industries in Ontario and Quebec that use imported products in the production process would become more competitive as their costs were reduced. Protection for one industry often means higher costs for other industries. In a study for the Macdonald Commission, economist Ronald Shearer recognizes that "resource-based regions bear heavy costs as a result of Canada's restrictive international trade policies,"[11] but he concludes that with trade liberalization "there would probably be income gains in all regions."[12]

Finally, the attitudes of provincial governments toward trade liberalization are not simply determined by an analysis of economic costs and benefits. Ideological factors are also important, and provincial policy on free trade is influenced heavily by partisan predispositions. Provincial government attitudes can be radically altered by a change in the governing party, even if the economic considerations remain pretty much the same. And this applies just as much to the federal level of government as it does to the provinces.

One further noteworthy feature of Canada's trade pattern is that a high proportion of international trade takes place between companies that are related in some way. This frequently involves transactions between foreign multinationals and their Canadian subsidiaries, which is a function of the high level of foreign ownership in the Canadian economy. Unlike "arms-length" transactions between unrelated parties, these transfers are not always subject to normal commercial considerations or normal pricing practices. This injects an unknown element of distortion into Canada's trade figures.

TYPES OF TRADE POLICY

As suggested earlier, international trade policy can be divided into two broad types: those designed to promote exports, and those designed to impose barriers against imports. A substantial number of different measures come under each of these headings, and we will briefly mention some of the most significant ones, without claiming to draw up a comprehensive list.

Promotion

Governments in Canada play an active role in promoting exports in a variety of ways, and some of the chief methods are set out below.

Negotiating Access

One of the principal means by which Canadian policy-makers promote exports is by negotiating better access to foreign markets. This is done both on a multilateral basis, for instance at meetings of the General Agreement on Tariffs and Trade (GATT), and on a bilateral basis, where the most obvious recent example is the Free Trade Agreement with the United States. In either case, Canada has to reciprocate by providing freer access to its own market in return for concessions from other countries.

Subsidies

Both federal and provincial governments provide a wide range of export assistance programmes for private industry, including loans and grants. Some of these programmes are funded jointly by different levels of government, such as British Columbia's Cooperative Overseas Market Development Program which promotes exports of B.C.'s wood products, and which spends over $23 million a year. Others are funded by the federal government alone, or by individual provinces. Most provinces provide assistance to businesses for participation in trade fairs and missions, and British Columbia even provides free airline tickets for business people to go looking for export markets.

By subsidizing the costs of market development, government gives industry the opportunity to charge lower prices for its products, and thus be more competitive against foreign rivals. The danger here is that foreign governments will see such subsidies as a form of unfair trade and will impose countervailing duties against any exports that are judged to be subsidized. For instance, in the late 1960s and early 1970s, Michelin Tire received extensive public assistance from all levels of government to set up and expand production in Nova Scotia. The bulk of this production was scheduled to be exported, but the U.S. government subsequently ruled that these exports were unfairly subsidized and placed a countervailing duty on them. In another example, the U.S. Department of Commerce ruled in 1986 that the Canadian softwood lumber industry was being subsidized by government because it was not being charged enough for the privilege of chopping down trees. Before a countervailing duty could be levied, the Canadian federal government imposed a 15 per cent export tax on softwood lumber to appease the U.S. officials.

The Export Development Corporation

The Export Development Corporation is a federal crown corporation that assists Canadian companies in making export sales. It provides insurance for Canadian exporters against various risks entailed in making sales abroad—for instance, the failure of a purchaser to pay up, or the halting of payment for political reasons. Because the Canadian government absorbs these risks, export costs are reduced for Canadian business. In addition, the EDC also extends lines of credit to foreign purchasers to make it easier for them to buy Canadian goods. The EDC is a truly massive undertaking, and in 1989 it was one of the largest financial institutions in Canada, with assets of $6.6 billion.[13]

The Canadian Commercial Corporation

The Canadian Commercial Corporation was set up by an Act of Parliament in 1946 to "assist in the development of trade between Canada and other nations."[14] The CCC helps Canadian companies win export contracts from foreign governments and international agencies such as the United Nations. It acts as a go-between in cases where these institutional purchasers would prefer the security of dealing with another government, rather than dealing directly with private contractors. It is especially concerned with winning U.S. defense contracts under the Canada/U.S. Defence Production Sharing Arrangements. The CCC is funded out of general tax revenues, and in 1989-90 it helped 300 exporters and generated $739 million in export business for Canadian industry.[15]

The Programme for Export Market Development

This is a substantial export assistance programme administered by the Department of External Affairs. Under the PEMD, money is given to Canadian companies for various activities designed to increase their exports. The PEMD shares the costs of bidding for foreign contracts; it provides money for business people to travel abroad looking for new markets; it sponsors participation by Canadian companies in foreign trade fairs and exhibitions; it pays for potential foreign buyers to come to Canada; it helps companies establish marketing facilities abroad; it encourages the formation of export consortia; and it generally helps to develop export markets. In 1988-89, sales from PEMD-assisted marketing activities were over one billion dollars.[16] The effect of the PEMD is to reduce the risk for Canadian firms wanting to sell their products abroad. If a company is successful, then its profits will cover the costs of market development; if it is unsuccessful, then the federal government will help pay the bill. This programme is just one of many instances where risk-taking by the private sector has been attenuated by a system of government sponsorship and socialization of business costs.

Information and Advice

Government provides an array of information and advice to business about exporting. The Department of External Affairs, for example, has a planning and tracking system that provides information on market opportunities abroad, and it runs a programme called "WIN Exports," which is a computerized data base of Canadian exporters used by government officials in helping to win export contracts. The Department also organizes numerous seminars for businesses across the country; it puts on an annual exposition called Canada Export Trade Month, involving information sessions, exhibits, workshops, presentations, etc.; it helps businesses handle the necessary documentation and procedures for exporting; it provides export awards; it sponsors university programmes aimed at turning out students familiar with international business; it publishes a free bi-monthly newsletter called CanadExport to tell companies about foreign business opportunities and trade fairs; etc … , etc … On top of this, External Affairs also maintains trade commissioners in posts throughout the world who act as troubleshooters and advisers for Canadian businesses.

Overall, it is clear that a large chunk of the External Affairs bureaucracy is primarily concerned with promoting exports on behalf of the Canadian private sector. This effort by the federal government is, in many instances, duplicated by provincial governments, each of which is concerned with promoting exports from its own provincially-based firms.

Trade and Aid

Official development assistance to Third World countries is not just a humanitarian gesture by Canada; it has significant trade implications as well. As the Department of External Affairs has admitted, "An important direct and indirect benefit of Canadian official development assistance is to support

Canadian export interests in food, manufactured goods and services."[17] Official aid is channelled through the Canadian International Development Agency (CIDA), which cooperates closely with the Canadian business community. Like the Export Development Corporation, CIDA also provides cheap export financing for Canadian companies.

Canadian aid often comes with conditions attached, and a substantial amount is "tied" to the purchase of Canadian products by the recipients. The Department of Finance has estimated that 66.6 per cent of Canadian bilateral aid to developing countries is tied to purchases of Canadian products.[18] In the words of the Department of External Affairs, "One of the criteria for receipt of Canadian official development assistance is the commercial significance of the country for Canada."[19]

The whole gamut of these export promotion activities, orchestrated and funded by Canadian governments, constitutes a substantial area of state intervention on behalf of business. This is by no means unique to Canada, and all other developed countries have comparable, or even more extensive, export sponsorship programmes. The international battle for exports is far removed from any classical notions of laissez faire or free enterprise, in which government is supposed to play little or no role. In all countries, and on a massive scale, the state is involved extensively in helping private business compete in international markets.

Import Barriers

Trade barriers erected against imports are a common feature of government industrial policy throughout the world, and Canada is no exception in this regard. Trade barriers are normally divided into two categories, namely tariffs and non-tariff barriers (NTBs).

Tariffs

A tariff is a tax placed on some foreign goods when they enter the country. Each category of products imported into Canada will have its own specific tariff rate (sometimes zero), and this rate can also vary depending on the country of origin. Canada has several different tariff rates for products from different countries:

General   This is the highest tariff rate and is applied only to a few countries that are not participants in the General Agreement on Tariffs and Trade (GATT).

Most Favoured Nation   This rate applies to GATT members, and covers most imports into Canada, with the recent exception of the United States. These rates have been declining successively throughout the postwar period as a result of multilateral negotiations under the GATT.

British Preferential Tariff   Originally designed as a preferential tariff rate for Britain and the Commonwealth, it now only applies to goods from Australia and New Zealand.

General Preferential Tariff   This is a special low tariff rate for Third World countries, aimed at helping their economic development. Unfortunately, many Third World products are excluded from this category because they compete vigorously with Canadian goods, e.g. textiles, clothing, footwear and electronics. Only a very small proportion of all imports into Canada are granted this concession tariff rate.

United States Tariff   This is a special series of rates for U.S. goods as a result of the Free Trade Agreement. The remaining duties are temporary ones and will be reduced in stages up to 1999.

Today the tariff is normally seen as a device for protecting industries from foreign competition, but in the days before income tax, one of the primary functions of the tariff was to raise revenue for government. This function has now dwindled in significance as other sources of government revenue have expanded. In recent decades Canadian tariff rates have been substantially reduced as a result of multilateral and bilateral negotiations with other countries, and even prior to the FTA, 80 per cent of trade with Canada's largest partner was duty free.

In general, tariffs are no longer such a formidable barrier in international trade, and protectionism in the modern world has increasingly come to rely on non-tariff barriers. The use of these has gone up as tariff rates have come down.

Non-Tariff Barriers

NTBs come in many forms, and some of the more prominent ones are discussed below:

Quotas   Quotas are restrictions on the quantity of a product that can be imported. They have the effect of restricting supply in the domestic market, thus keeping prices higher than they otherwise would be. Compulsory quotas against foreign goods are commonly considered to be one of the most restrictive forms of trade barrier, and except for special circumstances, quotas violate international agreements under the GATT. For these reasons quotas tend to be used only rarely, such as when Canada placed a quota on fabric and clothing from South Africa in 1988, or when the federal government initiated a programme of global quotas for footwear in 1977.

One major set of special circumstances is the Multi-Fibre Arrangement (MFA). This is a special provision of the GATT that allows countries to put quotas on textile and clothing imports. Canada maintains such restrictions against 22 countries, mostly in the Third World, because cheap imports from these sources would pose a serious threat to Canadian production.

Antidumping Duties   Dumping is a practice where producers sell their goods in foreign markets at less than their fair value. This does not necessarily mean selling below the cost of production—exporters are also guilty of dumping merely if they sell a product abroad at a price lower than in the home market. It is a reasonably common occurence in world trade, and most countries (including Canada) maintain the ability to impose extra duties on dumped goods from abroad, in order to bring their price up to a fair level.

Before antidumping duties (ADs) can be applied, an investigation must be conducted, usually in response to a complaint from a domestic industry. In Canada (and in the U.S.) this involves a two-part procedure where the complainant must prove (a) that goods have been dumped, and (b) that this dumping has caused, or is likely to cause, injury to a domestic industry. Some recent examples of Canadian ADs against foreign products include steel reinforcing bars and structural steel from the United States and Mexico in 1987; dry wall screws from France in 1988; and photo albums from several countries in 1988.

Countervailing Duties   These are a similar sort of measure to ADs—only this time the target is unfair foreign subsidies rather than dumping. The procedures for applying CVDs are comparable to those for ADs, but there is a lot of disagreement about what exactly constitutes an unfair export subsidy. One recent example of a Canadian CVD was against corn imports from the United States in 1987, when the U.S. government was judged to be giving its exporters unfair assistance.

Emergency Safeguards   If a Canadian industry is suffering from serious injury as a result of increased imports, then protectionist measures, such as extra tariffs or quotas, can be applied on a temporary basis. This can happen even if imports are perfectly fair. In accordance with GATT agreements, emergency safeguards can only be imposed after a thorough investigation has taken place, and protectionist measures cannot discriminate against individual countries, but must be applied on a global basis. For instance, Canada, along with other countries, has been subject to emergency safeguards imposed by the U.S. on specialty steel and cedar shakes and shingles.

Voluntary Restraint Agreements   VRAs are bilateral agreements in which one country "voluntarily" agrees to limit its exports to the other. Why would a country agree to such a self-imposed quota? The reason is that harsher and less voluntary barriers might be erected if the voluntary restraints were not accepted. VRAs are usually applied in response to some immediate problem, such as a surge in imports of a certain product. In the past Canada has negotiated VRAs over imports of leather footwear and Japanese automobiles. Voluntary restraints have become fairly common instruments of contemporary trade policy throughout the world, and they allow some flexibility of administration, and they can be removed quickly if circumstances change.

Government Procurement Government purchasing at the federal and provincial levels constitutes a multi-billion dollar market for business. However, this market is not equally open to all suppliers. At the federal level, although there is no explicit "Buy Canadian Act," the two biggest civilian purchasing agencies, the Department of Supply and Services and the Department of Public Works, both have a system of preferences designed to discriminate in favour of Canadian companies.[20] At the provincial level, preferences exist favouring provincial or Canadian suppliers, which can penalize goods from other provinces as well as those from outside the country.[21]

Other Non-Tariff Measures Anything that makes life harder for importers can be seen as a non-tariff barrier, and quite a variety of things can be involved here. The list includes administrative delays at the border; lengthy inspection procedures for imported goods; complex paperwork and documentation requirements; customs "user" fees; and many other measures. For example, in 1984 a U.S. regulation was established that required imported steel pipes to have the country of origin actually stamped into the metal, instead of just painted on. But stamping damaged the pipes and made them weaker, as well as more expensive. Consequently, they were not as competitive with U.S. products. Subsequently, this regulation was revised in the face of widespread international protest.

Trade barriers constitute a major form of government involvement in economic activity, and they have been used repeatedly as a leading component of industrial policy in Canada and other countries. Naturally, businesses that benefit from protectionism do not normally complain about this form of state intervention, but import barriers can mean higher prices for consumers and higher costs for industries that use imported products. This leads to conflicts between industries over import policy, such as the conflict between the Canadian textile industry which wants extensive protection, and the clothing industry which uses imported cloth. Government must then choose between these competing business interests, or find some way of reconciling them.

CANADIAN TRADE POLICY IN HISTORICAL PERSPECTIVE

From the time of the earliest staple industries, Canada's economic development has relied heavily on trade. Early immigrants depended on imports from Europe for many basic manufactured goods, and in order to pay for these items it was necessary to sell something in return. The abundant natural resources of the new country provided the needed commodities for export, and the colony became a supplier, first of fish and fur and then of timber and wheat, for the old world (see Chapter Two).

The 18th century fur trade and the later expansion of the timber trade required the development of a commercial and transportation infrastructure, so that staple products could be exported and manufactured goods imported. Along with this trade grew a class of mercantile capitalists who made their money from buying, selling, shipping and financing, rather than from building factories or developing manufacturing industry. It was this class, associated with transport, finance and trade, that dominated Canadian business for most of the 19th century.

In the first half of the century, the timber trade provided a focus for most of the commercial activity in Canada, and British tariff policy was instrumental in encouraging this development. Prior to the 1800s Canada did not supply Britain with much timber because it was too expensive to ship it across the Atlantic. Britain also had a cheaper and competing source of supply in the Baltic countries. The situation changed in the first decade of the century during the Napoleonic wars with France. By 1808 Napoleon's trade embargo, known as the "Continental System," had succeeded in blocking Britain off from much European trade—including trade with the Baltic. In response, Britain turned to its remaining North American colonies. The development of the timber trade in New Brunswick and Quebec was a product of this demand, and the patterns of trade established during this period were maintained even after the Continental System was disbanded. Britain wanted to encourage the development of these Canadian supplies, and one crucial factor that made this possible was a massive British tariff on timber from which Canada was exempt. The result was a commercial boom for the timber-producing provinces.

Up until 1846 Canada enjoyed preferential British tariffs on both timber and wheat, but as Britain moved to a regime of free trade these preferences ended. The result was a severe setback for Canadian commerce. The Montreal-based commercial elite now started looking to the United States as a possible alternative, and in an attempt to get better access to the U.S. market, hundreds of Montreal merchants signed a manifesto in 1849 proposing that Canada be annexed to the United States. This idea did not appeal much to the Americans or the British at the time, and Canadian dissatisfaction was subsequently rechannelled into official efforts to negotiate a free trade treaty. By 1854 the Reciprocity Treaty had been signed, granting Canada free trade in natural resources, and giving the United States access to Nova Scotia's fishing waters.

The Treaty resulted in a big expansion of Canadian exports, but in 1866 the United States unilaterally terminated the agreement following the end of the American Civil War. Part of the reason was that the growing industrial interests of the American North were becoming more protectionist, but there was also resentment against Britain's pro-Southern sympathies during the war. In addition, Canada had already raised its own tariffs against manufactured goods in the late 1850s and this further alienated American manufacturers.[22] The Canadian tariff increases of 1858 and 1859, which were imposed by Finance Minister Alexander Galt, were essentially a revenue-raising mechanism to help pay the mounting public debt. Much of this debt had been incurred bankrolling the Grand Trunk Railway, with which Galt himself was associated.[23] In this period, and in subsequent decades, railway magnates and Canadian politicians enjoyed more than just cozy relations—they were often the same people.[24]

The American decision of 1866 was one of the influences that helped push the Canadian provinces into Confederation in 1867. As access to the American market became more restricted, so the prospect of an enlarged domestic market, united behind protective tariffs, became more attractive. Yet both before and after Confederation, the American market was a considerable lure, and repeated efforts were made by Canadian governments to renegotiate reciprocity with the United States. Throughout the remainder of the century these attempts were repeatedly rebuffed.

The continual failure to alleviate U.S. protectionism provoked growing demands for higher tariffs in Canada, particularly from the emerging manufacturing sector which lobbied intensely for greater protection. By the election of 1878, John A. Macdonald had become convinced that reciprocity was impossible unless Americans saw that they had something to gain from it.[25] To this end he campaigned on a platform of substantial Canadian tariff increases. With the support of most manufacturing interests, Macdonald and the Conservatives were elected, and one year later the National Policy Tariffs were enacted.

The National Policy Tariffs 1879

The National Policy Tariffs placed duties of up to 35 per cent on a wide range of manufactured and primary products entering Canada. The tariffs were an integral part of a wider strategy for national economic development that also included a commitment to complete a Canadian Pacific railway and a vigorous attempt to maintain a high level of permanent immigrants.

The new protectionist measures were designed to achieve a number of goals. First, they would protect infant industries against strenuous American competition, and thus nurture the development of Canadian business. Second, the resulting growth of Canadian manufacturing would provide more jobs and higher wages, which in turn would attract more immigrants. Third, tariffs would increase government revenues and provide at least some of the money necessary for projects such as the transcontinental railway. Fourth, East-West trade within Canada would be encouraged as North-South trade became more expensive. The tariff would thus promote national integration. Fifth, the higher tariffs would provide a greater incentive for the United States to consider a reciprocity treaty with Canada because the U.S. would now have something substantial to gain. And sixth, higher prices and increased profits for Canadian manufacturers would reward those interests that had generously supported Macdonald's election campaign in 1878. In addition to these motivations, a crucial long-term effect of the National Policy was that U.S. companies were encouraged to set up branch plants in Canada in order to jump the tariff walls. This became increasingly apparent over the next few decades, and the impact on foreign ownership and the structure of the Canadian economy was considerable.

Attempts at Free Trade

Despite the overall protectionist thrust of the National Policy, periodic attempts were still made to negotiate free trade with the United States, and these efforts continued, off and on, well into the 20th century.

By the first decade of the new century, the growth of the Prairie population and the boom in wheat production had put new demands on the federal government over trade policy. Because of protectionism, the new farming population had to pay artificially high prices for most things (including agricultural implements), and for the first time there was some serious political opposition to the high tariff policies that had favoured Central Canada. The Liberal government of Wilfrid Laurier was pressured to negotiate for free trade, and in 1911 the government announced that an agreement for a wide-ranging reciprocity treaty had been achieved with the United States.

Although supported by Western farmers, it soon became apparent that many other sections of the country opposed reciprocity. The Conservative opposition in Parliament blocked the legislation necessary to pass the treaty, and Laurier was forced to call an election on the issue. In contrast with the situation in 1988, both the Conservatives and the bulk of the business community were opposed to free trade, and in the campaign of 1911 most of the newspapers took a stand against reciprocity as well. In Central Canada, the National Policy had been associated for a long time with prosperity and industrial development, and the reciprocity agreement was portrayed as both a threat to the economy and to Canada's traditional links with Britain. Amidst the clamour of anti-American flag-waving, Laurier and free trade went down to defeat, largely at the hands of voters in Ontario.

Protectionism and the Great Depression

The affirmation of ties with Britain, and the rejection of free trade with the United States, came at a time when Britain was already in decline as an economic power. Countries that industrialized later, especially the United States, were in a process of leaving Britain behind in terms of technology and manufacturing prowess. By the end of World War I, the United States was emerging as the world's dominant economy, and a growing level of investment in Canada now came from the U.S. rather than Britain.

Contrary to laissez faire ideology, American industrialization had not occurred under conditions that in any way resembled liberal international trade. U.S. industrial development in the last quarter of the 19th century had taken place behind the skirts of the state's highly protective tariffs. Apart from a brief respite prior to World War I, this high tariff policy was maintained or increased through to the mid-1930s, as U.S. manufacturers continued to exert influence over Congress.

Canadian trade policy was largely a reaction to developments in other countries—a position that has characterized much of Canada's international economic relations before and since. In the 1920s, Canada reacted to rising U.S. protectionism by raising its own tariffs against U.S. goods, and at the same time looking towards Britain in the hope of establishing special concessionary tariffs.

By the end of the decade, the stock market crash of 1929 and the onset of the Great Depression coincided with one of the most wide-ranging and restrictive tariff laws in U.S. history, namely the Smoot-Hawley Tariff of 1930. This tariff revision increased rates of duty on approximately 20,000 items, resulting in an average tariff rate of over 50 per cent on dutiable items.[26] Other countries retaliated, including Canada, and world trade nosedived. Britain moved away from earlier free trade policies to a system of Commonwealth tariff preferences in 1932, and this further entrenched the global trade crisis.

It soon became evident that "beggar-thy-neighbour" policies of severe protectionism were only making the Depression worse, and the new Roosevelt Administration in the U.S. began making efforts to reverse this trend. In 1934 the Reciprocal Trade Agreements Act was passed, authorizing the President to negotiate bilateral reductions in trade barriers, and in 1935 a limited agreement was worked out with Canada. The agreement was opposed by the Canadian Manufacturers' Association, and the federal government's attempts to reinvigorate Canadian capitalism were thus resisted in a short-sighted fashion by a major section of organized capital. In effect, the state had to ignore short-term business demands in order to serve long-term business needs.

Subsequent trade negotiations took place in 1937-38, and the scope was widened to include a number of countries at once. Progress was slow, but eventually an agreement was reached to reduce tariffs further. This collection of bilateral agreements was a harbinger of the more developed system of international negotiations, known as the General Agreement on Tariffs and Trade (GATT), which came to dominate the global trading environment following World War II.

The GATT and the Early Postwar Period

After the end of World War II there was a fear that the world would once again slump into an economic depression. A recession had occurred soon after World War I, and memories of the Great Depression of the 1930s were still fresh in people's minds. Protectionist policies at that time had helped to prolong and deepen the economic catastrophe, and in the early postwar period the goal of more harmonious trade relations seemed very attractive.

The postwar world was, however, a very different sort of environment. European and Japanese industry had been devastated by bombing, and it would be a long time before their shaky economies could be reconstructed. Any claim that Britain had to world economic leadership had long since vanished, and the United States was by far the most dominant, or hegemonic, capitalist power. With the Soviet Army occupying half of Europe, and strong communist parties in some other European countries, the economic and political future of Europe was unclear. In this environment the United States became the prime mover in re-establishing an international economic order favourable to the maintenance of capitalism in general and U.S. interests in particular. Under U.S. guidance, international economic institutions were established after the war to encourage the growth of a liberal, market-oriented, capitalist system of production and trade. These institutions included the International Monetary Fund and the World Bank, as well as the GATT.

The GATT was signed in 1947 between 23 founding nations, including Canada. It established a set of common rules governing international trade among its members, and it provided a means for reducing tariffs and controlling non-tariff barriers on a multilateral basis. It operated (with some imperfections) according to two basic principles, namely *national treatment* and *non-discrimination*. *National treatment* meant that once a foreign country's goods had crossed the border into another country (and had paid the appropriate duty), they should be treated just the same as domestic products. *Non-discrimination* meant that any trade concessions made available to one country had to be made available to all countries equally. Among other things this would make it difficult for Britain to discriminate against the U.S. by establishing new trade preferences based on the Commonwealth.

In the first round of GATT negotiations held in 1948, trade concessions covered 45,000 tariff items and constituted a major step towards trade liberalization. Such a reduction in trade barriers started to open up domestic markets to the freer play of international competition at a period when the United States was by far the most competitive country around. Thus, the U.S. had a vested interest in the GATT.

In successive rounds of GATT negotiations (and there have been eight including the most recent Uruguay round), tariffs have been reduced further and more countries have been included in the arrangement. The later rounds have also tried to deal more specifically with non-tariff barriers, and have set up rules governing the operation of such things as antidumping and countervailing duties. In the climate of greater protectionist pressures in the 1980s and 1990s, the GATT has become increasingly concerned with managing trade barriers and dealing with disputes, rather than with just trying to reduce tariffs. Its trade liberalizing function has come under some pressure, especially as many U.S. policymakers have become concerned with protecting their own declining industries.

Despite the recent pressures on the GATT, Canada has consistently maintained its support for this international institution for three main reasons. First, as a medium-sized economic power, Canada has greater clout in trade negotiations if it teams up with other countries that have similar interests. Second, the non-discrimination principle of the GATT prevents Canada from getting picked on by the economic superpowers. And third, the GATT provides a set of rules that brings some degree of order and stability to international trade relations, which is of course important for a country that depends heavily on trade.

Under the regime of trade liberalization engineered in the first decades of the GATT's history, Canada's international trade grew significantly. Exports increased by about four per cent per year in the 1950s, and by nine per cent per year in the 1960s.[27] However, in addition to multilateral trade negotiations, Canada has also had to deal bilaterally with its main trading partner, the United States. Here, one policy measure has had a major impact on Canadian trade, and this was the Auto Pact of 1965.

The Auto Pact

The Canada-U.S. Automotive Products Trade Agreement, better known as the Auto Pact, was signed in 1965, and has had a profound influence on Canada's trade patterns. The Auto Pact is simultaneously two things. First, it is a sectoral free trade agreement, in which cross-border tariffs on new vehicles and original equipment parts are waived for qualified producers. Second, it is an interventionist industrial policy designed to influence the level of auto production in Canada through government regulation and incentives.

In order to get tariff-free access, auto assemblers that are included under the Pact (dominated by GM, Ford and Chrysler) had to manufacture one car in Canada for every one they imported. They also had to ensure that the Canadian value-added in their car production was equivalent to at least 60 per cent of their sales in Canada. If they failed to comply with these safeguards then the tariff could be reimposed. Rules also applied for duty-free access to the United States. Vehicles and parts from Canada could only cross the border duty-free if they had at least 50 per cent North American content, which was an attempt to close the door against non-North American manufacturers.

The Auto Pact resulted in a massive restructuring of the North American auto industry. Previously, the U.S. and Canadian industries had each operated more or less separately, despite the fact that they were both dominated by the same giant corporations.[28] High tariffs had resulted in a typical branch plant structure, with the Canadian subsidiaries of U.S. automakers each producing a large range of models just for the Canadian market. The small size of this Canadian market meant that production runs were short, and Canadian automaking was expensive and inefficient. As John Holmes points out, by the early 1960s the Canadian auto industry was facing a crisis of "declining competitiveness and profitability, falling output and employment, increased import penetration from the US, and a growing trade deficit."[29]

After the Auto Pact, the Canadian industry was transformed. Canadian assembly plants now turned out a much smaller range of models, but these were sold throughout the entire continent. This meant longer production runs, greater efficiency, a rise in productivity and increased exports. At the same time, many of the models that had formerly been made in Canada were now imported from the U.S. In the parts section of the industry, over $500 million in new investment took place in Canada from 1964 to 1969, with more than 230 new plants being set up. Employment in this segment of the industry jumped from 29,000 to 42,000, and productivity increased by more than 50 per cent.[30] For the industry as a whole, the impact on international trade was substantial. From 1966 to 1970, exports of vehicles and parts to the United States grew from $872 million to $3.1 billion, and total auto trade with the U.S. increased by over 21 per cent.[31]

However, the safeguards that have existed for Canadian production levels and value-added have not affected the industry uniformly. They have had a greater impact on vehicle assembly than on parts production. While the Big Three automakers have been required to assemble a fixed proportion of their vehicles in Canada, they have had more flexibility with regard to parts. The trend in corporate policy has been to use more parts from non-unionized cheap-labour plants located in the southern United States, in preference to higher cost Canadian sources. As a result, while Canada has a trade surplus in assembled autos, it has a trade deficit in parts.

For the automakers, the Auto Pact has been enormously beneficial in allowing them to achieve greater efficiencies by rationalizing production on a continental basis. Although the Canadian safeguards have limited their freedom somewhat, this has been an acceptable price to pay for the tariff waivers. For the Canadian government and Canadian autoworkers, the Auto Pact provided the benefits of continental rationalization but with important restrictions that deter the auto companies from moving production out of Canada. While these safeguards still exist on paper, the deterrent effect has been substantially reduced as a result of the Free Trade Agreement (see Chapter 13). This has worrisome implications in an age of rapid economic restructuring, where capital has become increasingly mobile, and where the auto companies have shown no reluctance to move their operations to new locations, if it were more profitable to do so.

Changes in the structure of the world economy have had a wider impact on Canadian trade policy throughout the 1970s and 1980s, especially as these conditions have affected the position and policies of the United States.

CANADIAN TRADE POLICY AND GLOBAL ECONOMIC CHANGE

For roughly a quarter of a century after the Second World War, the United States enjoyed a position of economic supremacy. But by the 1970s this hegemony was in decline, and U.S. industry was starting to experience serious competitive problems. Japan and newly industrializing countries were fighting vigorously for a larger share of the U.S. market, and were undermining U.S. dominance at home and abroad. In many industries these new actors had considerable advantages in technology, labour costs, productivity, and in the way the production process was organized. Traditionally strong industries in the United States, such as steel, autos, and appliances, began to feel the pinch of international competition. Along with new sources of supply and new competition, U.S. industries also had to face general conditions of weakening demand and slower growth, which threatened to undermine both profits and employment.

In response to these changing terms of competition, industries in the United States and other Western countries put pressure on their governments for increased trade protection. As U.S. hegemony continued to decline and trade deficits rose, this threat became stronger, and countries like Canada that rely on access to the U.S. market became increasingly concerned. The multilateral system of GATT negotiations no longer seemed so capable of maintaining and extending trade liberalization, and world economic relations seemed well on the road to a new protectionism.

This developing trend had some early ramifications for Canada. In 1971, when the United States faced a severe balance of payments crisis, President Nixon unilaterally imposed a temporary 10 per cent surcharge on all dutiable imports across the board. Previously, Canada had had some success in gaining exemptions from such general U.S. measures, but this time the supposed "special relationship" between Canada and the United States did not seem much in evidence. Given the volume of exports from Canada, this extra tariff would be very costly for the Canadian economy, and in the wake of the American decision, the Canadian federal government decided to conduct a hasty reassessment of its trade policy options.

In a paper drawn up by the Department of External Affairs in 1972, three options were outlined for Canada in its relations with the United States:[32]

(1) Try to maintain the status quo and deal with individual problems on an ad hoc basis.

(2) Seek closer economic integration with the United States.

(3) Promote greater geographic diversity of Canadian trade, and develop a comprehensive long-range plan to reduce Canada's dependency on the U.S.

The paper argued strongly for the third option, and this option eventually became the basis for much of the federal government's trade and industrial policy in the 1970s and early 1980s.

However, as a trade strategy the third option had a number of problems. If Canada was to diversify its international trade, which other markets should be targeted? Europe was one possibility; but the European Community was becoming increasingly preoccupied with its own internal trade, and there were plenty of protectionist forces within the EC that made it difficult for external competitors. Japan was another possibility; but Japanese manufacturers were very competitive in foreign markets, and even more so at home. In areas other than natural resource products, many of which are not found in Japan, Canada has had great difficulty breaking into the Japanese market. Finally, there was the Third World; but here two things impeded export expansion. First, most developing countries are not rich enough to buy Canada's exports in great quantities, and second, Canada maintains protectionist barriers of its own against many imports from the Third World, which tends to provoke reciprocal protectionism. The third option's emphasis on diversifying trade away from the United States thus became difficult to put into practice due to the lack of realistic alternatives.

Another problem was that trade patterns do not simply change in accordance with the government's wishes. Decisions about imports and exports are made every day by a multitude of different private actors who take many different considerations into account. These actors are influenced by government incentives, regulations, tax breaks, tariffs, etc., but they are unlikely to restructure established trade patterns just because government wants them to. Without a massive program of incentives, government could not easily get private capital to move in a new direction. This reluctance was further entrenched by patterns of intra-corporate trade within multinational corporations. Cross-border transfers between American parent corporations and their Canadian branch plants would not change much unless there was some significant change in the structure of foreign ownership in the Canadian economy. In the Trudeau era, efforts were made to address the problem of foreign ownership through policies such as the Foreign Investment Review Agency and the National Energy Program.

Although some limited changes in ownership were achieved, Canada's trade dependency on the United States continued to increase.

By the end of the 1970s, it had already become apparent that Canada's trade options had effectively been reduced to two. Moreover, the structural changes that had been occurring in the world economy, coupled with growing protectionism in the United States, meant that the "status quo" was being redefined in an uncertain fashion. Today, global economic change has presented Canada with a number of problems in the area of international trade policy. The problems of declining U.S. economic hegemony and the threat of non-tariff barriers have already been mentioned. Canada is especially vulnerable to these U.S. developments due to its enormous trade dependency on the American market. However, many of the same forces that shape conditions in the United States also have a direct impact on Canada itself.

One such problem is the growth of competition from newly industrializing countries. Countries with low wages, low corporate taxes, few regulations and few social programmes are able to produce things cheaply in competition with domestic Canadian industries. As these countries move production from less sophisticated products to more sophisticated, higher-value ones, important sections of Canadian industry will have to restructure if they are to survive. Selective trade protection for threatened industries may work as a temporary stop-gap measure, but eventually it will push foreign competitors into other areas of production that will threaten other domestic industries.

Like other Western countries, Canada's vulnerability to shifts in the global pattern of production has been heightened by the growing interdependence of the world economy. Not only has the volume of world trade increased, but securities and financial markets have become more integrated, and there has been a growing interpenetration of investment flows between countries. These developments have been encouraged by several factors in the postwar period, including multilateral tariff reductions; export-oriented production from newly industrializing countries; the growth of giant multinational enterprises; improvements in transportation and communications; and the problems of surplus capacity in some industries.

The changing conditions of global competition have provoked a response from business in two important areas (in addition to protectionist demands from some firms). One area is automation, where companies seek to replace high cost labour by machines. The other is the growing mobility of capital, as companies seek to relocate production to lower-cost areas of the world. Neither of these responses offers much consolation to workers whose jobs may be threatened.

As capital becomes more "footloose," governments are also put under pressure, and they are faced with the central problem of how to attract and retain capital within their national or provincial boundaries. One possible government response is suggested by Jeanne Laux and Maureen Molot. They argue that "in a world economy characterized by the internationalization of production, policy-makers in Canada as elsewhere sought to counteract their vulnerability to external change and assert greater control over domestic resources by extending the direct role of the state as investor and producer."[33] The problem with this interventionist option (if adopted on any significant scale) is that it is liable to provoke a hostile reaction from business. In addition to simple ideological opposition, elaborate state intervention also carries the prospect of higher taxation and competition with established private enterprise. The use of more "coercive" instruments of government policy is likely to make a country less attractive for business, and where capital is highly mobile, this can have adverse economic consequences. This option thus has costs that reduce its attractiveness to government.

An alternative government reaction to "globalization" is to move public policy in the opposite direction, selectively reducing the scope of state intervention where business demands it, and competing with other countries to provide the most alluring policies for business. One area where this is reflected is in corporate taxation. The proportion of Canadian revenues from corporate income tax dropped from 20 per cent to 11 per cent in the period 1961-1986, while at the same time, the proportion from personal income tax rose from 39 per cent to 54 per cent.[34] As Laurent Desbois notes, "60 percent of corporations and 46 percent of profitable firms do not pay corporate income tax. This is because of the variety of deductions and credits introduced to provide incentives to invest and thus create economic activity."[35] However, the reaction to capital mobility has also become manifest in other policy areas, such as deregulation, privatization, reductions in social programmes and free trade—all of which have come to the forefront of the Canadian political agenda. It was concern about Canada's trading position in the face of global economic change that inspired moves toward the Canada-United States Free Trade Agreement, which is the subject of the next chapter.

ENDNOTES

1. OECD, *National Accounts: Main Aggregates*; OECD, *Main Economic Indicators*; UN, *Monthly Bulletins of Statistics*.
2. *Ibid.*
3. Statistics Canada, 67-001.
4. F.H. Leacy, *Historical Statistics of Canada*, 2nd edition (Ottawa: Statistics Canada, 1983) and Statistics Canada, 67-001.

5. Statistics Canada, 67-001.

6. Philip Cross, "The Growth of Services in the Canadian Economy," in *Canadian Economic Observer* (Ottawa: Supply and Services Canada, January 1988), 35.

7. Statistics Canada, 65-001.

8. Colleen Hamilton and John Whalley, "Regional Considerations and Canadian Trade Policy," in John Whalley, ed., *Canada-United States Free Trade* (Toronto: The Royal Commission on the Economic Union and Development Prospects for Canada, 1985), 295.

9. F.J. Chambers, "The Emerging Cost Structure of Canadian Firms: Some Implications for International Economic Policy," in Denis Stairs and Gilbert R. Winham, eds., *Selected Problems in Formulating Foreign Economic Policy* (Toronto: The Royal Commission on the Economic Union and Development Prospects for Canada, 1985), 125.

10. Hamilton and Whalley, "Regional Considerations and Trade Policy," 300.

11. Ronald A. Shearer, "Regionalism and International Trade Policy," in John Whalley, ed., *Canada-United States Free Trade*, 343.

12. *Ibid.*

13. *Financial Post 500*, 1990.

14. Canadian Commercial Corporation, *Annual Report* (1989-90), 3.

15. *Ibid.,* 4

16. Department of External Affairs, *Annual Report*, (1988-89), 23.

17. The Department of External Affairs, *A Review of Canadian Trade Policy* (Ottawa: Supply and Services Canada, 1983), 162-63.

18. Canada, Department of Finance, *1989-90 Estimates: Canadian International Development Agency*, Part 3 (Ottawa: Department of Finance, 1988), 31.

19. External Affairs, A *Review of Canadian Trade Policy*, 163.

20. Andrew R. Moroz, "Some Observations on Non-Tariff Barriers and their Use in Canada," in John Whalley, ed., *Canada-United States Free Trade*, 252.

21. *Ibid.*, 253.

22. R.T. Naylor, *Canada in the European Age 1435-1919* (Vancouver: New Star Books, 1987), 262.

23. *Ibid.*, 274-75.

24. For more detailed accounts of these linkages see R.T. Naylor, *Canada in the European Age* and Michael Bliss, *Northern Enterprise: Five Centuries of Canadian Business* (Toronto: McClelland and Stewart, 1987).

25. J.L. Granatstein, "Free Trade between Canada and the United States: The Issue That Will not Go Away," in Denis Stairs and Gilbert R. Winham, eds., *The Politics of Canada's Economic Relationship with the United States* (Toronto: The Royal Commission on the Economic Union and Development Prospects for Canada, 1985), 17.

26. Robert A. Pastor, *Congress and the Politics of U.S. Foreign Economic Policy* (Berkeley, Calif.: University of California Press, 1980), 77-78.

27. Canada, Department of External Affairs, *A Review of Canadian Trade Policy* (Ottawa: Supply and Services Canada, 1983), 21.

28. John Holmes, "Contemporary Restructuring of Canadian Industry," paper presented to the Workshop on Development in the 1980s: Canada in the Western Hemisphere, sponsored by the Programme of Studies in National and International Development (Queen's University, Kingston, May 10-13, 1984), 43.

29. *Ibid.*, 44.

30. *Ibid.*, 46.

31. Ross Perry, *The Future of Canada's Auto Industry* (Ottawa: Canadian Institute for Economic Policy, 1982), 118-19.

32. Mitchell Sharp, Secretary of State for External Affairs, "Canada-U.S. Relations: Options for the Future," *International Perspectives*, Special Issue (October 1972), 13.

33. Jeanne Kirk Laux and Maureen Appel Molot, *State Capitalism: Public Enterprise in Canada* (Ithaca and London: Cornell University Press, 1988), 4.

34. Laurent Desbois, *Reform of the Corporate Income Tax System* (Ottawa: Minister of Supply and Services Canada, 1987), 3

35. *Ibid.*

Chapter 13

Canada-United States Free Trade Agreement

In the 1970s and 1980s, the economic problems of stagflation, new international competition, energy crises, U.S. trade deficits and the threat of rising U.S. protectionism provoked a reassessment of Canada's trade relations with the United States. The failure of the Third Option (see Chapter Twelve) had left Canadian trade policy with little central direction other than trying to prop up the GATT. Yet, as a system of international agreements, the GATT was increasingly beleaguered by protectionist pressures. Rapid, and frequently unwelcome, changes in the international political economy had made it more and more difficult to maintain status quo trade policies, and Canada's attempts to manage particular trade problems with the United States on an ad hoc basis were starting to falter.

Against this background, calls for a formal free trade agreement became stronger. In particular, both the Economic Council of Canada and the Senate Committee on Foreign Affairs issued reports recommending bilateral free trade, in addition to the GATT, as a way of preserving access to the U.S. market and ensuring Canadian competitiveness.[1] Some efforts were made in 1983 to negotiate with the United States for free trade in a limited number of sectors, including steel, urban transit equipment, agricultural machinery and informatics, but these negotiations ran into problems, largely because it was difficult to find "matching" sectors where both sides could agree that mutual gains would occur.[2]

The movement towards a more comprehensive agreement was given a large boost in 1985 when a Royal Commission, chaired by former Liberal Cabinet minister Donald Macdonald, issued its report advocating bilateral free trade as one of its chief recommendations.[3] This recommendation was well received by the new Conservative government which was already committed to improving Canada-U.S. relations, and which was leaning towards a more market-oriented view of industrial policy, incorporating deregulation, privatization and free trade. By September 1985, the Canadian federal government formally committed itself to seeking a comprehensive bilateral free trade agreement with the United States.

For the Reagan administration, a free trade deal with Canada would provide an opportunity to get rid of some barriers to the free flow of American trade and investment, and it would also hamper any future resurgence of Canadian economic nationalism, which (inevitably) would be directed against the United States. It would thus make Trudeau-style "socialistic" government intervention more difficult, and would fit in nicely with the Reagan administration's overall free-market ideology. Bilateral negotiations could also be used as a testing ground for the U.S. agenda at the next round of the GATT.[4] In addition, the Canadian deal could put pressure on America's other trading partners to be more accommodating at the multilateral negotiations. If the U.S. was frustrated at the GATT, then it could conceivably move towards a series of one-to-one deals with separate countries, with a better chance of dominating each relationship.[5]

Formal discussions began in May 1986 following the U.S. Senate's decision to put negotiations on a "fast-track" for U.S. legislative approval, and the two negotiating teams were given a deadline of October 3, 1987 to complete the deal. Canada's team was led by Simon Reisman, a former senior bureaucrat with a long experience of trade negotiations, while the American team was led by Peter Murphy, a relatively junior official who was a virtual rookie in comparison with Reisman. These choices reflected different levels of importance that each country attached to the negotiations: for Canada, the FTA was a central chapter in trade history, while for the United States it was a footnote.

The deal was barely completed before the deadline, and it took another two months before the final legal text was ready for inspection. Three weeks later, on January 2, 1988, it was signed by President Reagan and Prime Minister Mulroney.

The implementing legislation passed relatively quickly and quietly in the U.S., but in Canada, amidst intense national controversy, the Senate refused to pass the legislation. The Senate clearly has the constitutional authority to do this, although the power is rarely used in practice. But if the Senate means anything as a body of "sober second thought," then an issue of this magnitude was probably a good one on which to exercise its formal powers. As a result of this action, a general election was called for November 21.

The Free Trade Agreement provoked more labour militancy than had been seen in Canada since the 1976 "Day of Protest" against the anti-inflation controls (estimated to have involved close to a million workers). The FTA was opposed by all major labour organizations on the grounds that it would lead to a loss of jobs in Canada, to a downward pressure on Canadian wages and to an erosion of social benefits that Canadian workers currently enjoy.[6] Resolutions rejecting the FTA passed at the annual convention of the Canadian Labour Congress and by nine of the ten provincial federations of labour (P.E.I. was the exception) in the year leading up to the 1988 "free trade election."[7] Labour organizations spent an unprecedented amount of money on advocacy advertizing that year (see Chapter Eight), in an attempt to mobilize Canadians against the FTA.

While free trade was rejected outright by the Canadian labour movement, business was, on the whole, supportive of the deal.[8] And major business associations, representing the heavy hitters of the Canadian corporate world, were solidly behind free trade. Thus, the FTA opened a deep rift between labour and capital on the trade issue where, historically, they had found common cause. The National Policy tariffs, for example, had been supported by both the manufacturers, who stood to gain from a protected domestic market, and their workers. This alliance of interests stood up through most of the 20th century. But it fell apart when the increasingly continental character of Canadian business and the fear of being excluded from the American market by protectionist trade laws combined to increase business support for free trade.

The policy of free trade polarized business and labour at two related levels. At the *macro level*, labour portrayed the FTA as part of a neo-conservative political agenda being advocated by business associations like the Business Council on National Issues.[9] Other parts of this agenda, according to labour leaders, included privatization and downsizing of the public sector, rolling back social benefits as a means of deficit reduction and reducing labour costs for Canadian employers to enable them to better compete with foreign businesses. At the *micro level*, they argued that the FTA would contribute to this larger political agenda by shifting the balance of industrial relations in favour of employers. The "level playing field" of free trade would increase the pressures on Canadian employers, and ultimately on Canadian governments, to reduce the standard of income benefits received by Canadian workers to the level of their American counterparts. In addition to wage levels, benefits like health insurance and Unemployment Insurance, to which employers contribute, would ultimately be forced down. The opponents of the FTA, and particularly NDP leader Ed Broadbent, during the election campaign quoted extensively from Canadian business leaders to demonstrate that this downward harmonization of wages and benefits was exactly what Canadian business expected. For example, the Grocery Products Manufacturers said this about free trade:

> Some product sectors in Canada are at a disadvantage because the comparative U.S. industries are not as unionized. Therefore, some fundamental realignment in legislated benefits programs and labour union organizations will be required. As well, Canadian workers' income expectations will have to be substantially lowered.[10]

The president of the Canadian Manufacturers' Association expressed similar expectations:

> It's simply a fact that, as we ask our industries to compete toe to toe with American industries... we in Canada are obviously forced to create the same conditions in Canada that exist in the U.S., whether it is the Unemployment Insurance scheme, Workmen's Compensation, the cost of government, the level of taxation, or whatever.[11]

The results of the election were somewhat ironic. The NDP and the Liberals both opposed the Agreement, and the Conservatives received only a minority of the popular vote. However, because of the nature of the Canadian electoral system, this translated into a majority of seats in the House of Commons. The Conservatives and the pro-free-trade forces had won: the Senate dropped its obstruction; the implementing legislation was rapidly passed; and the FTA came into force on January 2, 1989.

OVERVIEW OF THE AGREEMENT

The FTA is indeed a comprehensive agreement. It covers virtually all areas of trade, as well as other aspects of bilateral economic relations, such as investment, the movement of personnel and the management of energy policy. For Canada, the Agreement also has broad implications for the future development of industrial, social and cultural policies, and the FTA is rightly seen, by proponents and opponents alike, as a momentous step in Canadian history.

In its broad outline the FTA encompasses a wide range of provisions, including tariffs, non-tariff barriers (NTBs) and other measures, not all of which can be examined in detail here. The main elements of the Agreement cover the following:

Tariffs   All tariffs between the two countries will be eliminated. Some are eliminated immediately; some will be eliminated gradually over a five-year period; and the remainder will be phased out over a 10-year period. The pace of this tariff elimination can subsequently be stepped up if both sides agree.

Antidumping and Countervailing Duties   Both countries retain the right to penalize the other's exports if they are unfairly dumped or subsidized, and are causing injury to a domestic industry. What has changed is the appeal process. Previously, these decisions could be appealed through each nation's domestic court system, but now appeals will be heard by a bi-national panel. Agreement was also reached to draw up more effective rules against government subsidies over a period of five to seven years.

Emergency Safeguards   Each country retains the right to impose emergency protection for a domestic industry in serious trouble from increased imports. Such protection is imposed on a global basis (i.e. against all countries at once), including the other FTA partner. The main change is that the other FTA partner will be exempted from the emergency protection if imports from that country are not substantial. This is defined as being up to five to ten per cent of total imports for the industry in question.

Government Procurement   Federal government purchasing in both countries discriminates against foreign suppliers. In accordance with GATT agreements, only government contracts above US$171,000 were open to competitive and equitable bidding, and individual governments place exclusions on various areas of purchasing. Under the FTA this threshold is reduced to US$25,000, and there will be a review body to handle bidding disputes.

Other NTBs   With some exceptions, the FTA prohibits export taxes, customs-user fees, tariff drawbacks and waivers for exporters, and quantitative restrictions and embargoes. Canada and the U.S. have also agreed to try to harmonize their technical standards, concerning such things as inspection, labelling and packaging, to prevent these regulations from being used as trade barriers.

Investment   The FTA liberalizes investment flows between the two countries and generally provides "national treatment" for foreign investors. In both countries, some areas of investment are still excluded to foreigners. As far as Investment Canada is concerned, U.S. companies can now take over Canadian companies with assets of up to $150 million without having to undergo a review. Previously the ceiling was $5 million.

Sectors   Various specific measures pertain to individual sectors of the economy, including energy, autos, services, agriculture, wine and spirits and cultural industries. A number of these sectors are analyzed in greater detail later in this chapter.

Consultation and Dispute Settlement   Each country agrees to give the other advance notice of any measures that may affect the operation of the FTA, and mechanisms will be set up for arbitration of disputes. Chief amongst these is the Canada-U.S. Trade Commission, which is a bi-national body charged with interpreting the Agreement and trying to resolve disputes.

Termination   The FTA can be terminated by either party on six months notice.

The following sections examine aspects of the FTA in greater detail in an attempt to evaluate the strengths and weaknesses of the Agreement, and discuss some of the possible implications for Canada.

TARIFFS, NON-TARIFF BARRIERS AND MARKET ACCESS

One of the principal reasons for entering into a bilateral free trade agreement with the United States was to get guaranteed access to the U.S. market and to circumvent the growing mood of protectionism in American trade policy. As the Department of External Affairs proclaimed, under the heading "WHAT IT'S ALL ABOUT," the negotiations were concerned with "market access for our exports; security and predictability of access; better and broader access to bigger markets for Canadian goods and services."[12] So, to what extent did Canada get better and more secure access to the U.S. market as a result of the FTA? This question is best answered by looking at the principal areas of trade protection covered by the Agreement.

Tariffs

The elimination of U.S. tariffs over a maximum 10-year period will certainly provide Canadian companies with easier access to the U.S. market for some products. In areas such as railway freight cars, petrochemicals, metal alloys and clothing, U.S. tariffs were at levels over 15 per cent. The reduction of these tariffs to zero thus constitutes a significant improvement in access for these industries. Not only does it make Canadian exports more competitive vis-à-vis American products, it also gives them an extra edge against firms in other countries which still have to pay the tariff when they compete in the U.S. market.

However, we must also recognize that the bulk of Canadian exports to the United States was already duty-free before the FTA came into force. As economist Milton Moore points out, 80 per cent of Canada's exports enter the U.S. with a zero tariff rate, while another 15 per cent enter at a rate lower than 5 per cent.[13] In contrast, only about two-thirds of American imports enter Canada duty-free.

Tariff rates in both countries have come down throughout the postwar period as a result of the GATT agreements, and it is quite possible that further reductions will occur in subsequent rounds of multilateral negotiations. Thus, despite the significance for a limited number of industries, the U.S. tariff reductions in the FTA cover only about one-fifth of Canadian exports, and for most of these the reductions are small.

Naturally, Canada had to eliminate its own tariffs on U.S. imports in order to get the reciprocal concession, and the Canadian reductions were much larger than those of the United States because, on average, Canada's tariffs were a lot higher to start with. In 1988, Canada's average tariff rate on dutiable imports was 11.2 per cent, while the U.S. average was 6.5 per cent.[14] The Canadian concession was thus nearly twice as great. In some sectors, such as textiles and clothing, furniture, footwear and tobacco, the Canadian tariffs were quite high, and U.S. competition will have a serious impact.

Antidumping and Countervailing Duties

One of Canada's goals in the trade negotiating process was to put limits on the U.S. recourse to contingency protection measures, namely antidumping duties (AD), countervailing duties (CVD) and emergency safeguards.[15] However, in regard to AD and CVD, it is hard to be very enthusiastic about the outcome of the negotiations. Article 1902 of the FTA states that each party retains the full right to apply its AD/CVD laws against the other country's goods, and each country also has the right to pass further laws in the area of trade protection. Canadian exporters (all of whom are saint-like fair traders) still have to face the "judicial harassment" of having to fight AD/CVD cases, and they still have to pay the duties if they are caught injuriously dumping or being subsidized.

However, despite this generally disappointing picture, some positive (albeit limited) changes were achieved. First, Canada obtained the right to be notified and consulted if the U.S. decides to change its AD/CVD laws, although this does not necessarily affect the substance of any changes. Nor does it affect the way the U.S. laws operate at present. Second, changes in the law can be reviewed by a bi-national panel, and this body has the power to recommend modifications to U.S. legislation (Article 1903). If the panel's recommendations are ignored, then Canada is allowed either to pass equivalent measures or to terminate the whole FTA. Unfortunately, the first option is not much of a sanction, and the second is too severe to be used as a credible threat. Third, although no agreement was reached concerning detailed codes for defining unfair subsidies, discussions will continue for five to seven years after the introduction of the FTA. Even strong advocates of the FTA admit that this was a bit of a disappointment,[16] but the door is nevertheless open to further negotiations in this area.

Finally, there is the much heralded, binding review mechanism for AD and CVD cases (Article 1904). Under the pre-existing procedures, AD and CVD cases (in both countries) were subject to judicial review by the domestic courts. Under the new system, this judicial review process has been placed in the hands of a bi-national panel of five individuals (normally lawyers), with two from each country and one chosen by consensus or by lot. According to Simon Reisman, Canada's chief negotiator, "We have established a watchdog to ensure that the laws are interpreted fairly and applied properly and that there is no arbitrariness in the application of those laws."[17]

The problem here is that the watchdog has a rather short leash. It cannot turn back an AD/CVD decision just because it thinks the decision is wrong; the panel can only remand a U.S. decision if it has been made illegally, according to U.S. law. This restriction places the focus on the process rather than the substance of the decision, and is no real improvement on the pre-existing judicial review procedure, which was undertaken by the U.S. Court of International

Trade. There is little basis for the assumption that the former review process was biased or arbitrary, and it is unlikely that the new watchdog will have any better eyesight in discovering impropriety by trade officials. The main advantage of the new system is that it may offer a speedier review process than was previously the case.

Emergency Safeguards

Both countries retain the right to take emergency action to protect industries that are seriously injured as a result of increased imports (Article 1102). These measures can include global tariffs and quotas, and Canadian negotiators were anxious to get an exemption from this aspect of U.S. trade law. In this area some success was achieved—Canada does get an exemption from U.S. emergency safeguards. However, the exemption only applies if imports from Canada are less than five to ten per cent of the total. Thus Canada would not have gotten an exemption for woodshakes and shingles in 1986, because Canada was the major importer, but it would have prevented Canada from being "sideswiped" when the U.S. placed emergency tariffs and quotas on specialty steel in 1983. Therefore Canada gets an exemption, but only if U.S. imports from Canada do not amount to very much.

In general, a lot of fuss has been made over U.S. contingency protection measures, but as Robert Young points out, the real impact of these measures on Canada has been small.[18] He estimates that between 1980 and 1987, the direct cost of CVD and emergency safeguard actions has been $1 billion per year at most. With exports to the U.S. of $93.18 billion in 1986, this has been equivalent to a tariff of only 1.07 percent.[19] Even the Department of Finance's own figures show that, from 1980 to 1987, most U.S. contingency protection cases against Canada failed. In cases where protection was imposed, the total value of Canadian exports affected has been $6.2 billion—or less than $1 billion per year.[20] This contrasts with more than $2 billion per year in lost revenues that will result from the elimination of Canadian tariffs.

Government Procurement

In the free trade negotiations, Canada sought a big procurement deal covering all government purchases for both civil and military equipment at federal and state/provincial levels.[21] Nothing this sweeping was actually achieved, although some smaller changes have been negotiated. Basically, there has been a reaffirmation of rights already established under the GATT, plus a lowering of the thresholds for bidding on government contracts. The decision-making process for government contracting has also been made a little more transparent.

Firms on both sides of the border can now bid on an equal basis for federal government contracts as small as US$25,000. Previously, the threshold was US$171,000. The result is that the Canadian government is opening up roughly $650 million in new contracts to American bids, while the American government is opening up nearly $4 billion to Canadian companies.[22]

Although this is potentially a large market, the actual gains for Canada are not likely to be substantial. At the federal level, U.S. defense contracting is largely unchanged, and important areas of transport and telecommunications are closed off. Procurement at the state/provincial and municipal levels is not directly included under the FTA, largely because the federal governments of both countries have difficulty in ensuring compliance from these subnational jurisdictions. According to the Economic Council of Canada, Canadian exports will probably increase by about $141 million, while imports will rise by about $128 million.[23] These figures are far from monumental, and even the ECC (which was staunchly pro-free-trade) admitted that the trade effects of the FTA's procurement provisions "are likely to be small."[24]

Other Barriers

Under this heading, limitations are placed on the ability of either government to engage in certain types of industrial policies. Governments cannot put a tax on exports unless the same tax also applies to sales in the home market (Article 408); with some exceptions, duty waivers and drawbacks are eliminated (Articles 404 and 405); and U.S. Customs user fees are removed (Article 403). User fees were only 17 cents for every $100, and could be challenged under the GATT in any case.

Conclusion

Better access to the U.S. market has certainly been secured for roughly 20 per cent of Canadian exports as a result of tariff eliminations, but in most cases the gain is not huge and GATT negotiations may well have reduced some of these rates on a multilateral basis. Antidumping and countervailing duties still exist as before, and unless enormous weight is attached to the new bi-national review mechanism, the benefit in this area is slight. Unfortunately, the review panel has very narrow terms of reference, and its judicial character may yield results that are not much different from the existing judicial review mechanism. With regard to emergency safeguards, Canada only gets an exemption if its products constitute less than five to ten per cent of U.S. imports, and even defenders of the FTA admit that the procurement provisions are disappointing. Thus, although access has improved, the progress in important non-tariff barriers has not been dramatic.

THE ECONOMIC IMPACT

Nobody knows with any semblance of precision what the overall economic impact of the FTA will be—there are just too many intangibles to be taken into account. Exchange rates, for example, have an enormous impact on the balance of imports and exports. These are affected by a wide variety of external and internal factors, and are extremely difficult to predict over any length of time. Such changes could easily offset the effects of trade liberalization. In fact, some economists argue that we need not worry about adverse economic consequences from the FTA for this very reason. If the Canadian economy started to falter due to the FTA, then a weakening Canadian dollar would "limit the damage" by making our exports more competitive, and by making investment in Canada more attractive.[25] However, the double-edged nature of this argument is not always noted: if the Canadian economy performs well due to the FTA, then a strengthening Canadian dollar would serve to limit the gain.

Other factors are also uncertain. No one can be really sure about the extent to which investment will increase or decrease, or about the extent to which Canadian businesses will "gear up" their production for the continental market. Predictions of productivity growth rest on the assumption that a significant restructuring of Canadian production will take place, involving greater specialization, larger plants and greater economies of scale. It is by no means certain that Canadian businesses will be willing and able to do this, especially if they are small businesses. Business confidence is a factor here, and given that several NTBs still remain, and that the FTA can be revoked on 6 months notice, Canadian firms may still have some reluctance about making continental commitments. Furthermore, the scope, form and sectoral targets of future U.S. trade measures are hard to calculate (with or without the FTA) due to the uncertainty and complexity of the U.S. political process. If companies are going to take the risk and "gear up" production, they may figure that it is safer to do this in the larger market south of the border, and supply the entire continent from there.

It is uncertain how all these variables will turn out, and the picture of the post-FTA economy is still unclear. Weather forecasting is probably more of an exact science than economic forecasting, and the FTA has required a substantial leap of faith. Needless to say, the problems of prediction have not prevented some considerable speculation, from different quarters, about the possible consequences for economic growth, national income and employment.

One of the most frequently cited economic forecasts was made by David Cox and Richard Harris before the FTA was signed or even negotiated. Based on the assumption that all tariffs and export subsidies would be eliminated, they estimated that trade with the United States would increase by more than 98 per cent, and that there would be a 9 per cent growth in real income.[26]

Other estimates have subsequently been less optimistic. For instance, the Economic Council of Canada ran four different simulations based on the assumption that bilateral free trade would be implemented, and concluded that by 1998 exports would be 0.9 - 2.2 per cent higher than without the FTA, and that real income would be 0.7 - 2.8 per cent higher.[27] These figures were themselves notably different from ECC estimates conducted six months earlier.[28]

The Council also produced two detailed forecasts of employment based, in the first case, on the assumption that trade barriers would be removed, and in the second, on the assumption that productivity would also increase. In the first simulation, 76,000 new jobs would be created over 10 years (including a net loss of 26,000 jobs in manufacturing), and in the second simulation 251,300 new jobs would be created over the same period.[29] These estimates seem to have been incorporated into official forecasts that long-term real income will increase by 2.5 percent and that 120,000 new jobs will be created over 5 years.[30]

Even the Council's own forecasts were not unanimous, but were challenged in a dissenting minority report. The dissenting report questioned the assumption that tariff reductions would be fully passed on to consumers, rather than being kept by manufacturers, importers or retailers as an extra margin of profit. Evidence for productivity gains was also questioned, and the minority report charged that "the Council simply assumes, without a shred of evidence, that manufacturing productivity will increase by 0.6 per cent annually under the FTA."[31] Despite substantial trade liberalization that has already taken place under the GATT, "the Canada-U.S. manufacturing productivity gap is about the same level as it was 25 years ago."[32] Consequently, we have little historical evidence that a further trade liberalization would improve the position.[33] Even if one accepts the Council's more optimistic projection, an annual increase of 25,000 new jobs is not much in the context of a total labour force of over 13 million.

Predictions by critics of the FTA that hundreds of thousands of jobs will be lost are also unreliable. As Cameron and Mackenzie point out, it is relatively easy to identify Canadian manufacturing industries where jobs will be threatened when protection is removed—these include "food processing, furniture, textiles, clothing, leather goods, footwear, plastics, paper products and household appliances"—but it is more difficult to say how many firms will emerge or expand to take advantage of new market opportunities.[34]

INVESTMENT

The FTA's chapter on investment (Chapter 16) establishes a principle that foreign investment from the other country must be given "national treatment" without discrimination. However, in both countries, some sectors are still subject to restrictions, such as transport and communications.

In Canada, the high level of foreign ownership of the economy has been a major source of concern, and in 1973 the Foreign Investment Review Agency was set up (see Chapter Four). Foreign takeovers of Canadian companies with assets over $250,000 were reviewed, and this threshold was raised to $5 million when FIRA became Investment Canada in 1985. Under the FTA, this threshold has now been raised to $150 million, and thus only U.S acquisitions of very large Canadian companies will be subject to review. However, it is important to note that the pre-existing review thresholds for oil and gas and uranium industries have been retained. In addition, U.S. investment in Canadian cultural industries is still subject to special review. It has been estimated that roughly 80 per cent of acquisitions previously subject to review will now fall below the threshold, which has led some analysts to suggest that Investment Canada is unlikely to continue in its current form.[35]

As a result of the higher thresholds, U.S. ownership of the Canadian economy is likely to increase. American corporate raiders and leveraged buy-out specialists have been eyeing Canadian companies for some time because Canadian stocks have generally been undervalued compared with prices in the United States.[36] By reducing the barriers to U.S. takeovers, the FTA makes Canadian companies a little more vulnerable to U.S. corporate "bargain-hunters."

Overall, the investment provisions are likely to promote a greater mobility of capital across the border in both directions, which is something predicted by critics and supporters alike.[37] Business now has greater freedom to move capital around with fewer restrictions, and as Mel Watkins notes, this strengthens the hand of business in bargaining with labour and the state. The threat of pulling up stakes and moving away is a lever that can be used both in wage negotiations and in lobbying for favourable government policies.[38]

ENERGY

The energy provisions of the FTA are concerned with liberalizing bilateral trade, but in a way that is different from most of the rest of the Agreement. For most products, the FTA is aimed at reducing government restrictions on *imports*; but for energy products, the FTA is largely concerned with reducing government restrictions on *exports*. This affects Canada disproportionately because, in bilateral trade, Canada is overwhelmingly the bigger exporter of energy.

International trade in energy is already subject to some regulations under the GATT, but the FTA goes beyond these rules in two important respects. First, under Article 903, Canada is forbidden from putting export taxes on energy products unless the same charges are also applied to domestic consumption. Second, under Article 904, Canada guarantees to keep providing the United States with the same proportion of crude oil, gas, electricity, etc. relative to domestic supply, even if there is a domestic shortage. The same conditions apply (with less relevance) to the United States.

What are the implications of these measures? Principally, the effect of these provisions is to make government intervention in energy more difficult, especially the sort of nationalistic interventions of the Trudeau era. In the past, when world prices soared, the federal government stepped in to regulate domestic prices and give Canadian consumers a break. Now the government can only do this if it is prepared to offer the United States the same cheap rates. This means that the Canadian government would be subsidizing American consumers, which would be particularly galling for Canadian firms that compete against American energy-consuming industries. Alternatively, the government could maintain a laissez faire position and let Canadian energy prices rise to world levels. While this would undoubtedly benefit the large oil companies in Canada (most of which are foreign-owned), it could impose severe costs on Canadian consumers. For instance, Thomas Gunton calculates that "the inability to regulate energy prices during the last decade...would have cost Canadian consumers approximately $93 billion more in payments for natural gas and oil." [39] If Canadian consumers were faced with this bill, then they might well decide to impose severe electoral costs on the incumbent politicians. Neither of these two alternatives is particularly attractive, and when energy prices soar again, then the Canadian government will be caught in a dilemma of its own creation.

Another problem concerns the depletion of Canadian energy resources and the possibility of future shortages. If Canada wanted to restrict production for conservation purposes, it could not do this just by restricting exports to the United States. Exports to the United States can only be reduced to the extent that supply to Canadians is reduced by the same proportion. This principle of proportionality means that American consumers will be better insulated against any future energy shortages but, by the same token, fewer energy supplies will be available to insulate Canadian consumers. If oil supplies were to get seriously depleted, Canada would be unable to restrict its exports to the U.S. in order to maintain the same level of domestic supply.

One grey area in the whole energy question is the position of crown corporations such as the provincial hydro utilities. The FTA's energy provisions put restrictions on government policy, but if these state-owned corporations choose (of their own volition) to charge higher prices to U.S. customers or to restrict exports in favour of domestic users, then there may be little that the U.S. government can do under the FTA. It is not yet clear if the U.S. government will see things this way.

Another provision of the energy section provides a specific benefit for the uranium industry (located largely in Saskatchewan) by exempting Canada from U.S. restrictions on foreign uranium enrichment. In return, Canada removes a requirement that uranium be upgraded in Canada prior to shipping to the United States.

Finally, Canada gets an exemption from a U.S. embargo on crude oil from Alaska's North Slope, and Canadian refineries are now allowed to import up to 50,000 barrels per day. This may have been a bit of a hollow concession because it appeared that no Canadian refineries wanted Alaskan oil in any case.[40]

AUTOS

One of the fears expressed during the trade negotiations was that the Auto Pact would be adversely affected. In particular there was a concern that the safeguards for Canadian production would be weakened. Under the terms of the Auto Pact, Canadian automakers must produce one car in Canada for every one they import, and there must be at least 60 per cent Canadian content. If manufacturers fail to meet these safeguards then a tariff of 9.2 per cent is applied to their imports. Under the FTA, the production safeguards still exist on paper, but the penalty tariff is eliminated. Thus U.S. automakers have less real incentive to comply with the safeguards and maintain production levels in Canada. Although nominally still in force, the production safeguards have actually been seriously weakened, and consequently the Auto Pact itself has been compromised.

In practice, Canada has dispensed with an instrument of industrial policy and has put its faith in free-market economics, with fewer real conditions imposed on American automakers. This may not mean very much immediately, but if Canadian labour and production costs rise, for instance, as a result of a strengthening Canadian dollar, then the Big Three automakers may conclude that greater advantages can be realized by producing in another location, such as the southern United States. If this happens then production in Canada could be scaled back. Before the FTA, this threat was less credible because the tariffs would have been reapplied and the companies would have been heavily penalized, but now the prospect has become more realistic. Naturally, the threat of moving away can be used by the corporations in the bargaining process with Canadian autoworkers and Canadian politicians. The one remaining deterrent is that the Big Three automakers bring products into Canada from countries other than the United States. Under the Auto Pact these imports are also duty-free, but if the companies violate the safeguards, then these duties will be applied.

Also contained in the FTA is a new rule concerning North American content. Fifty per cent of direct manufacturing costs for vehicles and new parts must now be incurred in North America, otherwise they cannot be shipped across the border duty-free. This penalizes Japanese auto firms that assemble vehicles in Canada, but which do not use a high proportion of domestic parts. Free trade is denied to them unless they improve their domestic sourcing. This could mean that more Canadian parts will be used, but alternatively it may just make it less attractive for offshore automakers to set up assembly plants in Canada.[41]

One further result of the FTA is that Canada gives up the right to offer import duty waivers to non-North American automakers as an incentive to produce cars in Canada or export cars from Canada. This is another curtailment of industrial incentives for foreign car makers to establish production in Canada.

In total, the automotive provisions of the FTA are very favourable to the Big Three automakers. Industrial policies that restrict their freedom (ie. the safeguards) have been weakened in practice, and the vulnerability of labour has been increased. At the same time, regulations imposed on non-North American producers have been increased, and some incentives for foreign car makers have been eliminated. It is a restructuring of industrial policy that enhances the power and freedom of the Big Three auto companies over foreign competitors, labour and the state.

CULTURAL INDUSTRIES

One of the perennial fears of many anglophone Canadians is that Canada's cultural distinctiveness will be homogenized by the giant cultural blender to the South. The fear surfaced once again during the free trade debate and, despite repeated assurances to the contrary, there was a continual concern that cultural industries would be "on the table."

In many respects Canada lives in the cultural shadow of the United States, but, in our view, the FTA itself has little specific impact on this pattern of dominance. Article 2005 of the FTA states that "cultural industries are exempt from the provisions of this Agreement," and this includes publishing, music, film, video, broadcasting and cable. There are nevertheless a few exceptions to this rule. First, tariffs will be eliminated on printed material, tapes, records and films. Second, if a U.S company indirectly acquires a Canadian subsidiary in a cultural industry when it buys another U.S. company, then Canada can still demand that the subsidiary be sold off to Canadians. If this happens, the FTA says that the U.S. company should be paid a fair market value. Third, if a Canadian cable TV station retransmits a copyrighted U.S. programme, then it should pay for it. Finally, Canadian firms can now get a tax break for advertizing in Canadian editions of U.S. periodicals, even if the periodicals are printed in the United States.

On the whole, it is difficult to see these exceptions as a tremendous threat to Canadian culture. The tariff eliminations have a limited impact because there were not many tariffs in cultural industries even before the FTA, and it seems reasonable that a fair price be paid for indirect acquisitions. The retransmission clause may even offer some further protection for Canadian culture by making it less attractive for Canadian cable TV companies to show U.S. programmes. The advertizing tax break will hurt some Canadian magazines, but it is important to note that advertizing on U.S. border TV and radio stations has not been included here.

One last concern with the FTA's culture provisions is that the U.S. has the right to "take measures of equivalent commercial effect" if Canada does anything to protect its cultural industries that is inconsistent with the FTA. This does not really weaken the Canadian position because there was little to stop the U.S. retaliating against Canadian cultural protectionism in the first place. At least now U.S. retaliation may be restricted to "equivalent" measures, rather than excessive ones.

INSTITUTIONAL PROVISIONS

In addition to the bi-national dispute mechanism for antidumping and countervailing duty cases, the FTA establishes other institutional mechanisms for dealing with problems that may arise from the operation of the Agreement.

First, each country is required to notify the other about any proposed measures that affect the FTA, and information must be provided about such measures. Second, either country can request consultation about anything that may affect the Agreement. Third, if problems are not solved by consultation, they can be referred to a new Canada-U.S. Trade Commission, which is a bi-national body responsible for the binding arbitration of disputes. If the Commission's findings are not implemented by one party, then the other country can retaliate by suspending equivalent benefits.

Although the Commission will try to arrive at mutually satisfactory solutions, there will inevitably be times when the different national representatives on the Commission are in conflict. As Stephen Clarkson suggests, the Commission's decision-making functions are likely to be highly politicized, possibly to the extent of paralysis.[42] In addition, the vast scope of the FTA means that an enormous bureaucratic effort will be necessary to deal with all the notification, consultation, arbitration and information collation that is likely to take place. Far from "downsizing" government, the bureaucracy is liable to increase.[43]

WIDER IMPLICATIONS: SOCIAL PROGRAMMES, POLICY HARMONIZATION AND SOVEREIGNTY

During the debate on the FTA, some of the fiercest criticisms were directed, not so much at specific measures, but at the implications of the Agreement as a whole. In particular, critics argued that the FTA would generate inexorable pressures for the "harmonization" of Canadian social and industrial policies with those existing in the United States. It was argued that Canada's sovereignty over its own public policy would be restricted, and that we would be forced to sacrifice our more generous social programmes and more interventionist industrial policies, in order to bring them into line with U.S. practice.

The logic behind this argument is twofold. First, there would be external pressures from the United States to limit a wide variety of industrial support programmes on the grounds that they were unfair subsidies. These might include loans, loan guarantees, grants, tax rebates, research incentives, export assistance programmes, regional development measures and even some forms of social programmes such as unemployment insurance for fishermen. Some critics of the FTA go even further, claiming that virtually all Canada's social programmes, including medicare, pensions, workers' compensation and unemployment insurance, could be defined by the U.S. as unfair subsidies, and thus be subject to countervailing duties.[44]

The second argument is that there would be internal pressure from Canadian business to cut back social programmes or any other programmes that impose greater costs on corporations in Canada than in the United States. This could involve environmental regulations, minimum wage laws, corporate taxation levels, occupational health and safety laws, unemployment insurance, etc. With free trade, Canadian businesses could now argue that they need a "level playing field" in the realm of public policy, so that they can compete on equal terms with companies in the United States. If this policy harmonization did not take place then Canadian businesses would have a strong incentive for moving south of the border.

Looking initially at the external pressures, a couple of points are worth noting. First, as Thomas Courchene suggests, little has really changed with regard to subsidies and countervailing duties. Any Canadian programmes that are countervailable now, were already countervailable prior to the FTA.[45] American industries could already launch CVD cases against Canada, and this right has not been expanded under the Agreement. However, the agreement to negotiate a subsidies code over the next 5-7 years will put many Canadian industrial programmes under the U.S. microscope. Little is now likely to be overlooked, and American CVD cases against Canada may actually increase as a result of the FTA, which would be an ironic twist.

Second, most of Canada's social policies are general programmes that are not targeted towards specific industries or firms. Under international law, the national availability of social policy benefits means that they do not count as unfair subsidies.[46] Thus the arguments about increased external pressures are unconvincing.

In contrast, the fears about increased internal pressure for policy harmonization are a little more troubling. Greater exposure to American competition will make Canadian businesses highly sensitive to any advantages enjoyed by U.S.

companies, and the relative costs and benefits of government policies will inevitably be part of this calculation. With U.S. companies generally enjoying lower taxes, weaker environmental regulations, low or non-existent minimum wage laws, stronger anti-union legislation and lower costs for unemployment insurance and workers' compensation, Canadian companies will undoubtedly feel that the playing field is sharply tilted. If Canada does not "harmonize" its policies, then Canadian businesses may find competition more difficult, especially against companies located in the U.S. "Sunbelt" where labour costs are already lower.

Worse still, Canadian companies may decide that the simplest solution is to shift production to a cheaper location in the U.S., and supply the entire North American market from there. Once Canadian profits, jobs, growth and tax revenues start to disappear, then government would not wait to be pressured by business; it would make the necessary policy adjustments without prompting.

The effect of the FTA may be to push Canada (willingly or unwillingly) towards the sort of 'neo-conservative' policies more characteristic of the United States, and away from policies of industrial planning and business regulation. If competitive forces mean that there is little option but to follow the American lead in important areas of industrial and social policy, then Canadian sovereignty has effectively been diminished.

This does not mean that all policy areas are equally threatened, and economist Thomas Courchene points out that the financing of some Canadian social policies, such as health care and old age pensions, "bestows a very substantial advantage on Canadian industries." Consequently, business will not want to alter these programmes.[47] However, this implies that social programmes may be in trouble if they do not confer benefits on business, and this forces us to distort our priorities in designing or modifying social policies. Policy becomes more concerned with fulfilling the needs of business, rather than the needs of recipients such as the sick and the elderly.

In conclusion, it is not surprising that most businesses are enthusiastic about the FTA. The Agreement enhances business mobility and freedom, and places labour in a more vulnerable position. It also puts further pressure on future governments to shape public policy in accordance with business interests. It is now harder for government to choose some policy options in regard to industrial planning, foreign ownership, business regulation, social programmes, etc., and the power of business has been increased relative to both labour and the state. Canadian public policy has taken a significant step to the political right, and has moved more in line with a market vision of how an economy should operate. Despite the six months termination clause, once the FTA has become entrenched, continental integration will become even more highly structured, and it will be increasingly difficult for any future government to reverse the process. The Free Trade Agreement is a turning point in Canadian history; and Canada has turned towards the United States.

ENDNOTES

1. Economic Council of Canada, *Looking Outward: A New Trade Strategy for Canada* (Ottawa: Information Canada, 1975) and Canada, Senate Committee on Foreign Affairs, *Canada-United States Relations*, Vol. II, "Canada's Trade Relations with the United States" (Ottawa: Queen's Printer, 1978).
2. Earl H. Fry, "Trends in Canada-U.S. Free-Trade Discussions 1911-1986," in A.R. Riggs and Tom Velk, eds., *Canadian-American Free Trade: Historical, Political and Economic Dimensions* (Halifax: Institute for Research on Public Policy, 1987), 38.
3. Canada, The Royal Commission on the Economic Union and Development Prospects for Canada, *Report*, Vol. I (Ottawa: Minister of Supply and Services, 1985), 382-84.
4. Giles Gherson, "Washington's Agenda," in Duncan Cameron, ed., *The Free Trade Deal* (Toronto: James Lorimer and Co., 1988), 3.
5. Albert Breton, "The Political Economy of Free Trade," paper presented to the Atlantic Canada Economics Association, Sackville, New Brunswick (October 24, 1986), cited in R.A. Young, " Canada-United States Free Trade: Economic Realities and Political Choices," in Riggs and Velk, eds., *Canadian-American Free Trade*, 118.
6. Pradeep Kumar et al., *The Current Industrial Relations Scene in Canada, 1988* (Kingston, Industrial Relations Centre, Queen's University, 1988), 50-57.
7. *Ibid.*, 52-60.
8. The FTA was opposed by firms in industries expected to lose from continental restructuring of production. Many of these firms organized under the umbrella of the Business Council for Fair Trade to oppose the FTA.
9. This argument is put forward in John W. Warnock, *Free Trade and the New Right Agenda* (Vancouver: New Star Books, 1988).
10. Quoted in Michael Lynk, "Labour Law Erosion," in Ed Finn, ed., *The Fact of Free Trade* (Toronto: James Lorimer and Co., 1988), 72-77.
11. *Ibid.*, 75.
12. Canada, Department of External Affairs, *Trade Negotiations: Securing Canada's Future* (Ottawa: Department of External Affairs, 1987), 4.
13. A. Milton Moore, "The Case for Tariffs," *Policy Options* (July/August, 1988), 40.
14. Economic Council of Canada, *Venturing Forth: An Assessment of the Canada-U.S. Trade Agreement* (Ottawa: Minister of Supply and Services Canada, 1988), 8.
15. External Affairs, *Trade Negotiations*, 4.
16. Richard C. Lipsey and Robert C. York, "Tariffs and Other Border Measures", in John Crispo, ed., *Free Trade: The Real Story* (Toronto: Gage, 1988), 28 and Debra P. Steger, "Dispute Settlement," in *Ibid.*, 88.

17. Simon Reisman, "The Nature of the Canada-U.S. Trade Agreement," in Murray G. Smith and Frank Stone, eds., *Assessing the Canada-U.S. Free Trade Agreement* (Halifax: Institute for Research on Public Policy, 1987), 44.

18. Robert A. Young, "Breaking the Free Trade Coils," *Policy Options* (March, 1988), 10.

19. *Ibid.*

20. Canada, Department of Finance, *The Canada-U.S. Free Trade Agreement: An Economic Assessment* (Ottawa, Department of Finance, 1988), 22.

21. Reisman, "The Nature of the Canada-U.S. Trade Agreement," 43.

22. *Ibid.*, 44.

23. Economic Council of Canada, *Venturing Forth*, 14.

24. *Ibid.*

25. See for example, A.E. Safarian, "Foreign Direct Investment," in Crispo, ed., *Free Trade* and Richard Lipsey, "Sovereignty and the Canadian American Free Trade Agreement," in *Assessing the Canada-U.S. Free Trade Agreement*, 255.

26. David Cox and Richard G. Harris, "A Quantitative Assessment of the Economic Impact on Canada of Sectoral Free Trade with the United States," paper presented to the Royal Commission on the Economic Union and Development Prospects For Canada, and summarized in John Whalley, ed., *Canada-United States Free Trade* (Toronto: Royal Commission on the Economic Union and Development Prospects for Canada, 1985), 172-73.

27. Economic Council of Canada, *Venturing Forth*, 18.

28. S. Magun, S. Rao and B. Lodh, "The Impact of Canada-U.S. Free Trade on the Canadian Economy," Economic Council of Canada, *Discussion Paper* 331 (Ottawa: August 1987).

29. Economic Council , *Venturing Forth*, 22.

30. Department of Finance, *The Canada-U.S. Free Trade Agreement: An Economic Assessment*, 30 and Department of Finance, "Information," 88-03 (Ottawa: January 14, 1988), 1.

31. Raymond Koskie, "Dissent," in Economic Council of Canada, *Venturing Forth*, 34.

32. *Ibid.*

33. *Ibid.*

34. Duncan Cameron and Hugh Mackenzie, "Manufacturing," in Cameron, ed., *The Free Trade Deal*, 118-19.

35. George N. Addy, "Investment," in John D. Richard and Richard G. Deardon, eds., *The Canada-U.S. Free Trade Agreement: Final Text and Analysis* (Don Mills, Ont.: CCH Canadian Ltd., 1988), 53.

36. *Globe and Mail*, (3 August, 1989), B1.

37. Safarian, "Foreign Direct Investment," 77, and Mel Watkins, "Investment," in Cameron, ed., *The Free Trade Deal*, 90.

38. Watkins, *ibid.*

39. Thomas Gunton, "A Cautionary Note on Resources," in *Policy Options*, Vol. 9, No. 9 (November 1988), 26.

40. John Dillon, "Continental Energy Policy," in Cameron, ed., *The Free Trade Deal*, 113.

41. David Petras and Scott Fairley, "Automotive Trade," in Richard and Dearden, eds., *The Canada-U.S. Free Trade Agreement*, 38.

42. Stephen Clarkson, "The Canada-United States Trade Commission," in Cameron, ed., *The Free Trade Deal*, 38 and 40.

43. *Ibid.*, 31.

44. See for example, United Auto Workers-Canada, *Free Trade Could Cost Us Canada* (Willowdale, Ont.: UAW-Canada, 1986) and Marjorie Bowker, *What Will the Free Trade Agreement Mean to You and to Canada?* (Edmonton, July 1988), 36-37.

45. Thomas Courchene, "Social Policy and Regional Development," in Crispo, ed., *Free Trade*, 144.

46. *Ibid.*, 136.

47. *Ibid.*

Chapter 14

Industrial Relations

In the relations between capital and labour, between employers and employees, we find the elements of a major political drama. Those who buy the labour of others, in order to produce a good or provide a service, are not indifferent about the terms under which this labour is employed. Wages, working conditions (including hours of work), vacations, severance pay and employee benefits are all matters that affect an employer's costs, and therefore an employer's ability to compete with other businesses selling similar goods or services. Those who sell their labour to an employer, as their only or principal means of earning a living, likewise have a clear interest in their terms of employment. The interests of employees and their employers often conflict, and because vital matters such as jobs and incomes and profits are at stake, these conflicts can be passionate—and on occasion violent. Governments are not mere spectators, looking on as labour and capital slog it out. Indeed, they are intimately involved in setting and enforcing the ground rules under which these relations unfold. Governments are, in addition, major employers, and their employment policies often have repercussions beyond the public sector.

Industrial relations is the term generally used to designate the broad set of relationships between employers and employees. These relationships have three main dimensions: economic, legal-political and social. On the economic front, it is immediately obvious that the hard core of the employer-employee relationship is the willingness of one party to sell his or her time and skills to another in return for money. This transaction—what Marx called the "cold, cash nexus" between labour and capital—is hedged in by laws that establish the rights of the respective parties, and by state structures that mediate and enforce these laws. Finally, the employer-employee relationship unfolds against a backdrop of social forces that affect the capacity of each party to successfully pursue its material interests. These social forces include broad developments in the organization and technologies of production, in the structure of society and in the cultural-ideological setting. The legal-political dimension of industrial relations, and the economic muscle of labour and capital, are determined by these broader social forces. The interrelated character of these dimensions will become clearer as we examine the historical development and current state of industrial relations in Canada.

INDUSTRIAL CHANGE, THE WORKPLACE AND THE STATE

Industrial relations, in the broad sense of the term, predated industrial society. Even before smokestacks, factories and railroads became the characteristic landscape of the industrial age, the relations between employers and employees were matters of public policy. The rules of employment set by medieval guilds were enforced by the state against those who violated them. Slavery was an important pillar of the plantation economy in many parts of the world, and it enjoyed the protection of the law. The feudal obligations that existed between landowners and their farming tenants were enforced by agents of the crown. In each of these examples, the state's intervention in the relations between workers and employers was based on its defense of the particular economic institutions that existed at the time. Maintenance of the existing social order—or protection of the "public interest," as it is more likely to be called—has long provided a basis for this intervention.

Industrialization was accompanied by increasing disharmony between labour and capital. The emergence of factory production spawned the growth of the industrial city in which the urban labour force congregated. In combination with the development of labour-saving agricultural machines, the rise of factory production changed the face of industrializing societies. The balance of population shifted from the countryside to the cities, and class structures were altered dramatically by industrial capitalism's need for a large pool of unskilled workers based in the cities. The new production technologies also required skilled workers, and the divisions between skilled and unskilled, and between different types of skilled workers, influenced the course of labour union development and the political organization of workers.

The impact of industrialization on the relations between labour and capital was enormous. Those relations were placed under increasing strain as employees and their employers attempted to come to grips with change. Inside the workplace, the safety of workers, their hours of employment, the substitution of machines for people and the rates of pay were issues around which the pressures for workers to act collectively coalesced. Outside the factory gates, industrialization gave rise to new social tensions. These centred around the living conditions of the industrial working class, the new phenomenon of urban unemployment and the exclusion of the propertyless workers from full democratic rights. At the extreme, these tensions exploded into riots and violent repression, such as occurred in the Homestead steel strike in the United States. Immigration to the United States, Canada and other new world societies relieved some of these social tensions, particularly in the case of Great Britain. The western frontier performed a similar "safety valve" function in North America during the 19th century. But immigration and western expansionism provided inadequate and only temporary relief from the class tensions developing between labour and capital in the industrial cities.

State response to the challenges that industrialization posed to social order varied between countries. Generally speaking, social reforms like public pensions, industrial accident insurance, unemployment insurance and public health insurance were implemented earlier in societies in which labour was most organized for industrial and political action. This begs the question, of course, as to what explains these national differences in labour's organization and political activity. An intriguing, though only partial, answer was given by German sociologist Werner Sombart and by Frederick Engels at the turn of the last century. They both concluded that the more quiescent industrial relations scene in North America, as compared to Western Europe, was due to a combination of lower barriers to class mobility in North America society, greater affluence of workers there than in Europe and a dominant culture that loudly proclaimed the classlessness of society.[1] These factors, they argued, contributed to the "embourgeoisement" of the working class, and to the development of comparatively tame labour unions that eschewed direct political action.

Whatever the explanation might be, governments in both Europe and North America were confronted with a growing challenge to social order, posed by the changing relations between labour and capital that industrialization spawned. In order to preserve "industrial peace" these governments became more heavily involved in the regulation of the workplace and, more generally, in attempting to reconcile the capitalist economy—which itself was undergoing enormous changes in production technology and management practices—with the popular demands of workers. In the jargon of marxian political economy (see Chapter Three), the state resorted to legitimation policies in order to contain class conflict that threatened to spill over from the workplace to undermine the market economy and the stability of a social order founded on capitalist relations of production. But the motives of governments were seldom Machiavellian. Instead, they usually were responding to democratic pressures for reforms like minimum wage laws, regulations governing the hours of work, industrial accident insurance and collective bargaining rights. Their response was limited, however, by the power of business and by a dominant ideology that did not question the fundamental goodness of the capitalist economy. Industrial relations policy was also influenced by the political strength of organized labour, as well as some more idiosyncratic factors like the ideas of those state officials who had a hand in making labour policy. We turn now to an analysis of the formative period of

Canadian industrial relations, and the factors that shaped government policies in this area.

ESTABLISHING THE NEW GROUNDRULES, 1872-1948

Trade unions were legalized with the passage of the Trade Unions Act, 1872. Before then, unions were illegal in the eyes of the law, on the grounds that they were combinations in restraint of trade. This they were, and still are. But the attitude of society and government toward them has changed in recognition of the gross imbalance that exists between the power of an employer and that of any single employee. The legalization of trade unions in 1872 did not, however, signal this change. Unions were no longer illegal, but employers were under absolutely no obligation to recognize them or bargain with employees through them. Moreover, employers were free to dismiss workers who went on strike. As business historian Michael Bliss puts it:

> The much trumpeted business "recognition" of trade unionism before World War I reduced itself to this: workingmen had a right to try to bargain with employers, to try to shut down a firm by going on strike ... Employers had equal rights to refuse any concessions, to fire workers who went out on strike, and to smash unions by bringing in strikebreakers.[2]

With rare exceptions, the businessmen of this epoch were opposed to dealing with their employees through unions. To bargain with a union, they believed, interfered with a man's right to determine how his business should be run. Few principles were insisted on more strenuously than the sanctity of businessmen's property rights. If employees wanted to join a union and to strike that was their own affair. But for his part, the typical businessman of the era was adamant that who he hired and fired, rates of pay and conditions of employment—within the very loose constraints imposed by the law—were up to him, and no one else, to decide.

The relations between labour and capital in Canada were undergoing the strains produced by the transformation of a predominantly rural economy, in which manufacturing was typically carried out on a small scale, into an increasingly industrial economy characterized by larger enterprises. The average size of business establishments was increasing, as was the importance of these larger corporations to the overall economy (see Chapter Two). As a result, the relations between employers and employees were becoming increasingly impersonal. The implications of this trend were apparent to many in the business community. An 1896 editorial in the *Monetary Times* lamented that:

> The decay of domestic industry has well-nigh severed the bonds of sympathy that had from time immemorial united master and man ... Under the fac-

tory system, many employers fail to recognize an essential difference between machines and the human labor by which they are operated; kindly interest and consistent devotion have been replaced by indifference and distrust. The outcome has been strikes, lockouts and riots.[3]

But while businessmen recognized that the world had changed (rhapsodies about the traditional harmony between "master and man" were certainly exaggerated), they reacted to the new tensions that existed between labour and capital with the same strategies and approaches that businessmen had traditionally used in dealing with workers. These ranged from paternalistic employment practices to authoritarian discipline, both of these extremes coming to light during hearings of the 1886 Royal Commission on the Relations of Labour and Capital.[4] Collective bargaining between employers and unions was not viewed by businessmen as a reasonable response to the changed industrial environment.

Despite the generally unreceptive attitude of employers toward labour unions, modest inroads were made in organizing Canadian workers. By 1911 about eight per cent of the non-agricultural labour force, or 133,000 workers, belonged to unions.[5] American-based labour organizations like the Knights of Labour, the American Federation of Labour and the United Mine Workers of America were active in Canada, and the Canadian labour movement was in fact dominated by American-based international unions during this early period. American labour organizers were particularly despised by Canadian businessmen, on the grounds that the interests they looked after were those of the American competitors of Canadian industry.[6] The influence of international unions has also been a source of conflict within the Canadian labour movement, as we will see later in this chapter. The extent of unionization in Canada, and the proportion of union members belonging to national and international unions are shown in Figures 14.1 and 14.2.

The systematic collection of data on the Canadian labour force and industrial relations only began after the creation of the Department of Labour in 1900. It was established in response to the demands of unions, particularly the Trades and Labour Congress, and it appears that the Liberal government's expectations for the new department were not very ambitious. As it happened, however, the Labour Department's first director, Mackenzie King, saw the department as "a great agency of industrial peace."[7] Under King's active direction, and guided by his personal philosophy of industrial relations, the Department went well beyond the collection of statistics and the publication of the monthly *Labour Gazette* to become involved in the conciliation of labour disputes. And there appears to be strong qualitative evidence (hard data are missing for the years before 1901) that the period around the turn of the century was marked by an increasing number of strikes and lockouts in Canada, as in other industrial economies at the time. Between 1901 and 1911, the Department of Labour recorded 1,303 strikes and lockouts involving 7,096 employers. Most of the dis-

FIGURE 14.1

Union Membership in Canada and the United States,
as Percentage of Non-Agricultural Labour Force,
1911 to 1987 (selected years)

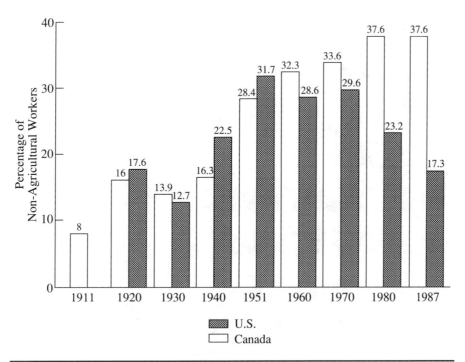

Source: Adapted from data in Pradeep Kumar et al., *The Current Industrial Relations Scene in Canada,*
1988 (Kingston: Industrial Relations Centre, Queen's University, 1988), 447.

putes were of little or no consequence for the overall state of the economy. But
some, such as those in the transportation sector, had the potential of paralyzing
or at least seriously disrupting the activities of other businesses. These disputes
were the focus of Canada's early industrial relations policy, a policy whose central principle was the prevention of strikes that threatened the social order. The
Industrial Disputes Investigation Act (IDIA) of 1907 was the concrete embodiment of this principle.

The IDIA created a legal mechanism for compulsory investigation of labour
disputes involving public utilities. By "public utilities" the government had in
mind "those industries and classes of industries upon the continuous and unin-
terrupted operation of which the welfare of the general public and other industries are dependent."[8] This very general conception of public utilities—one

FIGURE 14.2

Union Membership in Canada,
Including Share in Unions with International Affiliation,
1911 to 1987 (selected years)

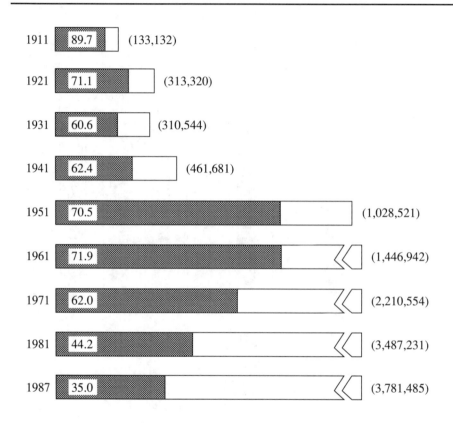

NOTE: The shaded area of each column represents the share of union members belonging to internationally affiliated unions, with the percentage indicated. The number in parentheses after each row represents the total union membership in Canada for that year.

Source: Adapted from data in Pradeep Kumar et al., *The Current Industrial Relations Scene in Canada, 1988* (Kingston: Industrial Relations Centre, Queen's University, 1988),448.

broad enough to encompass such businesses as coal mines and textile firms, in addition to those sectors like electricity, gas, water and transportation that are more commonly thought of as utilities—reflected the industrial relations philosophy of the Act's chief architect, Mackenzie King. No strike or lockout could take place at a firm determined by the government as falling under the Act, before a report on the dispute had been handed down by a tripartite council. This council would consist of a member nominated by the employer, another nominated by the union and a chairperson agreed to jointly or selected by the government. While the board's report was not binding on the parties, it was intended to bring the weight of public opinion to bear on recalcitrant workers or employers by exposing the "facts" of a dispute. It turned out that publicity was seldom used as a means for settling disputes. In fact it was usually avoided when the IDIA was invoked in a dispute.[9]

As the centrepiece of Canadian industrial relations policy throughout the first half of this century, the IDIA was important in three ways. First, it embodied the state's preoccupation with social-industrial peace, being designed to prevent or at least shorten disruptive labour-management disputes. Second, it expanded the role of government in the field of employee-employer relations. Although the Act fell far short of compulsory binding arbitration of disputes (neither employers nor unions would have accepted this), and its reach was limited to "public utilities," it marked a new level of state intervention in the affairs of individual firms and their workers. Third, the fundamental principles and mechanisms contained in the Act (with variations and more recent additions) continue to be expressed in the industrial relations laws of federal and provincial governments in Canada. Compulsory dispute conciliation before a strike, tripartite boards and special groundrules for disputes involving the "public interest" are all standard features of Canada's current industrial relations scene.

The IDIA and the principles it embodies represent a liberal solution to the "problem" of industrial peace. It is worth quoting from Mackenzie King, main author of the Act, to give a sense of the broader philosophy that underlay the development of industrial relations policy. In his book *Industry and Humanity*, King observes that "all industrial strife is a form of anarchy."[10] The remedy, according to him, was the full public exposure of the facts of a dispute, thereby bringing "Reason" to bear on the behaviour of parties whose self-interest might blind them to the interests of the larger community. In King's words, "There is no right superior to that of the community as a whole."[11] The community's interest, he believed, lay in industrial peace, and anything that threatened to disrupt the social order was necessarily bad. To ensure that the public interest would triumph over the narrower interests of the immediate parties to an industrial dispute, government would have to step in. In the liberal spirit, King assumed that there was no necessary antipathy of interests between labour and capital, but that in fact they had a common interest in the well-functioning economy. At one point King writes: "However opposed the interests of the parties may seem to be as respects the distribution of income derivable from total production, as respects production itself they are concurrent, since it is to the advantage of each that the total available for distribution should be as large as possible."[12] But it needs to be emphasized that the harmony of interests that

King had in mind was one based on the capitalist economy, the individual's right to private property and the businessman's freedom to manage his affairs as he saw fit. All of these are, of course, components of liberal ideology (see Chapter One). Concepts like "labour solidarity" or "capitalist class" had no meaning for King, and they run against the concept of "public interest" that continues to occupy a central place in industrial relations policy.

Ottawa's jurisdiction over industrial relations was dealt a serious blow by the 1925 court decision, *Toronto Electrical Commissioners v. Snider*.[13] This ruling of Britain's Judicial Committee of the Privy Council (see Chapter Six) held that the relations between employers and employees were matters of property and civil rights, therefore falling under the authority of the provinces. As a result, the federal government has been left with responsibility for industrial relations in industries that fall under its constitutional authority (including banks, railways, airlines and some telephone systems) and in the federal public service and crown corporations. This leaves approximately 90 per cent of Canadian workers under the regulatory jurisdiction of provincial labour law.

The immediate aftermath of *Snider* for industrial relations policy was fairly limited. Some provincial governments simply went ahead and passed provincial versions of the IDIA. Later on, however, as provincial public sectors expanded and as the scope of their economic activities increased, the provinces' authority over most industrial relations would provide the basis for a variety of legal and administrative responses. An up-to-date inventory of policies in different jurisdictions is provided in the annual edition of *The Current Industrial Relations Scene in Canada*, produced by the Industrial Relations Centre at Queen's University.

Not all of the state's interventions in industrial disputes were as gentle as conciliation under the IDIA. The use of the military and civilian militia to enforce court injunctions against picketing of an enterprise, and to enable strikebreakers to enter an employer's premises, was quite common. Historian Desmond Morton has recorded 33 such interventions between 1867 and 1914.[14] Some of these interventions were accompanied by violent confrontation between the strikers and the military, as happened in the 1903 dispute between the Western Federation of Miners and Dominion Coal Mines at Ladysmith, B.C.; in the 1909-10 dispute, at Springhill, N.S. when the Dominion Coal Company resisted the entry of the United Mine Workers of America into that province's coalfields; and in the Winnipeg General Strike of 1919. The Winnipeg Strike, in particular, has been portrayed by labour historians as a pivotal confrontation between workers and employers (abetted by the state), in which the stakes were nothing less than union recognition and the right to collective bargaining.[15] The strike was put down and several of its leaders jailed.

Neither business nor labour stood idly by as the terrain of industrial relations changed under their feet. Labour leaders responded by attempting to organize workers into unions, and by pressing demands on governments for legislation on such matters as hours of work, minimum wages, public pensions and disability compensation. Their organizing successes were limited, however, as unionization made slow progress in Canada before World War II (see Figure 14.1). Politically, labour had little direct representation in either Ottawa or the provincial legislatures. There were several reasons for this, the most important of which were, first, the labour movement's general rejection of direct participation in electoral politics and, second, the fact that the Canadian electoral system discriminates against minor political parties whose support base is spread across the country (as unionists were).[16] To this we need to add the comparatively low level of working-class consciousness in Canada—with some regional exceptions, notably in the "company-town" province of British Columbia and in the heavily working-class north of Winnipeg—and the fact that the Liberal and Conservative Parties proved flexible enough to adopt some of the reforms advocated by the labour movement into their own policy platforms.

On the legislative front, labour did win some concessions. These included minimum wage laws, first passed in the 1920s; workers' compensation, first implemented by the Ontario government in 1914 and followed by most other provinces by the end of World War I;[17] public old-age pensions in 1927, extended to all provinces by 1937; and statutory regulations of hours of work, starting in 1893. But the crucial breakthrough for labour, the right to collective bargaining with employers, had not been achieved. Without this right the bargaining leverage of workers was undermined by the fact that employers could simply refuse to negotiate with a union, and replace striking workers with new permanent employees.

For their part, employers reacted to the changing workplace environment—the increasing size of the firm and the new technologies of production—with new approaches to dealing with workers. The end of the 19th century had already witnessed a proliferation of "welfare work" innovations. These included company pension plans, improved safety and ventilation in the workplace, recreational facilities for employees and, in some cases, low-cost housing for workers. These were frankly defended by business spokespersons on the grounds of enlightened self-interest, "as the surest safeguard against the more aggressive and most objectionable demands of socialists and labor agitators."[18] Welfare work measures represented, however, simply an extension of the paternalistic style of employer-employee relations, designed to encourage workers' loyalty to the firm. More sophisticated techniques of worker control emerged in the industrial relations scene in the early 20th century.

Before examining these techniques we need to understand the political importance of the internal practices of the firm. Except in rare instances, work is seldom organized democratically. This is true of capitalist and non-capitalist economies, of modern and pre-modern societies. The division of work into separate tasks and the need to coordinate the activities of those who are performing these tasks provides the basis for unequal relationships between members of an organization. Some will have more say about what gets done, and how, than others. The politically important questions then become, "Who has the authority to direct the actions of others?" and "How do those with authority compel the obedience of their subordinates?"

The traditional answers to these questions were: 1) the owner of the enterprise has unlimited authority to make all decisions concerning the activities of those in his employ; and 2) the methods for ensuring the cooperation of workers may range from authoritarian discipline (the stick, or at least the threat of it) to paternalistic generosity to promote subordinates' loyalty (the carrot). But when workplace relationships became more complicated because of the increasing size of enterprises and the introduction of new production technologies, the old answers were not always adequate. One of the characteristic features of the modern industrial economy taking shape at the turn of the century was the growth of management functions within the firm—the emergence of a white collar salariat of engineers, accountants and efficiency experts (and somewhat later, human resources staff, marketing specialists, public relations personnel and computer experts). The direction of an enterprise became less a one-person affair and more the responsibility of an hierarchically-arranged management team.

Thus, the rise of management tended to dilute the authority of the owner, not in any formal or legal sense, but simply because owners were increasingly dependent on administrative and technical experts to run their businesses. Politically, this development had the effect of complicating class relations by interposing between labour and capital a new and increasingly large management layer which was not made up of capitalists or workers in the usual sense of these terms. The influence that these managers had on the behaviour of the firm was based on their professional skills and their positions within the hierarchy of the firm. Authority based on these attributes, and not on ownership of the enterprise, formed the basis of the *scientific management movement* that began in the United States and spread to Canada and elsewhere.

Scientific management—or "Taylorism" as it is often called, after its founder the American engineer Frederick Winslow Taylor—claimed that the proper management of an enterprise was a matter that could, and should, be determined by technical experts. Taylor argued that "both sides [employers and employees] must recognize as essential the substitution of exact scientific investigation and knowledge for the old individual judgment or opinion, either of the workman or the boss."[19] According to scientific management, there could be no conflict of interest between employer and employee once management had determined the technically best way of performing the enterprise's tasks. The workplace would be governed by "natural laws," discovered by the time-and-motion study experts, engineers and other administrative personnel who comprised the brain of the enterprise. The ideological content of scientific management came down to this: the interests of labour and capital were in essential harmony, and should be orchestrated by management. In terms of what this meant for industrial relations, labour unions and anything that restricted management's freedom to determine how a business should be run were viewed negatively.

The critics of scientific management have always insisted that it simply papered over the conflicting interests of employers and employees *on the employer's terms*, behind a façade of "scientific" neutrality. In any event, scientific management was not the only employer response to the changing industrial relations scene. A vast outpouring of work on human relations in organizations began in roughly the 1920s, and has continued unabated to the present day. Between Elton Mayo's *The Human Problems of an Industrial Civilization* (1933)[20] and Thomas Peter and Robert Waterman's *In Search of Excellence: Lessons from America's Best-Run Companies* (1982),[21] there stretches a concern with the social and psychological dimensions of the work milieu, and how these can best be shaped so as to maximize the productivity of employees and the competitiveness of an enterprise. Where scientific management emphasized the physical and technological conditions under which work takes place, the human relations tradition has seen in emotional contentment and psychological fulfillment the best guarantees that employees' behaviour will coincide with the employer's interests. But both scientific management and human relations approaches have this in common: they are techniques that aim to influence the behaviour of workers in ways that are expected to help the firm achieve its goals. Even the most "progressive" contemporary solutions for antagonistic industrial relations—profit-sharing, worker participation on the board of directors (co-determination as it is called in West Germany, where the practice is popular), Japanese-style labour practices—do not alter the fundamental inequality between labour and capital in the economic marketplace (see Chapter One).

We may summarize developments during this formative period in Canadian industrial relations under the following headings.

Employees An increasingly large share of the Canadian labour force belonged to unions, although the vast majority of workers remained unorganized. While employees had the right to belong to a union and to go on strike, they could not compel their employer to bargain with them through their union. Most employers would not. Moreover, a striking worker took the chance that he or she would be permanently replaced, there being no law guaranteeing a worker's right to return to the job he or she held before going on strike. Collective bargaining between employers and employees had not yet arrived.

The labour movement's demands for legislation regulating the conditions of employment and for social reforms like public pensions and workers' compensation were met to some degree by Ottawa and the provinces. These reforms were limited, however, and were implemented unevenly across Canada because of provincial jurisdiction over most areas of industrial relations and social policy.

Employers   Business people reacted to the changing industrial scene in various ways. Scientific management techniques, and eventually human relations approaches, were adopted by some firms. Others responded with welfare work schemes, which represented an updating of the traditional paternalism that had long characterized employee-employer relations. All of these were attempts at promoting peace in the workplace, and were often deliberately aimed at undermining the attractiveness of unions.

When it came to dealing with unions, the general attitude of employers was hostility. They saw no reason to negotiate on matters that they felt were theirs, and theirs alone, to determine. The Canadian Manufacturers' Association even launched a legal campaign to have unions made legally responsible for strikers' actions, by requiring that they be incorporated (this had happened in Great Britain as a result of the 1901 *Taff Vale* court decision). This effort was unsuccessful. Anti-union activity appears to have been common at the level of municipal trade associations,[22] and the use of detective agencies, spies, blacklists and strikebreaking agencies were not uncommon, although probably less widespread than in the United States.

Government   Canadian governments reacted in a couple of ways to the strife that industrialization generated. One was by adopting the role of "umpire" in industrial relations, a role that assumed concrete form with the 1907 passage of the Industrial Disputes Investigation Act. Whether the state was really an "impartial umpire," as Mackenzie King believed, was another matter. The emphasis of early industrial relations policy was on minimizing the economic disruption caused by strikes and lockouts, so that one could argue that state intervention was in defense of the existing capitalist social order, and therefore served the interests of owners more than those of workers. This was more starkly apparent in those numerous instances when the militia was called upon to defend the property interests of employers against their striking employees.

To be fair, we need to acknowledge that governments did respond positively to a number of labour's demands. Unions had been legalized in 1872, and were exempted from prosecution under the Combines Investigation Act. Their effectiveness was limited, however, by the frequent use of court injunctions to ban or limit picketing by strikers, and by the refusal of either governments or the courts to guarantee the right of collective bargaining. On the other hand, both Ottawa and the provinces had begun to legislate on such matters as hours of work, minimum wages, workers' compensation and public pensions, all of which were reforms advocated by the labour movement. Governments' responsiveness to these pressures took forms that did not fundamentally challenge the prerogatives of employers. Workers' compensation, for example, was made palatable to business because it required that workers forfeit the right to sue their employers for personal injury. (This is the case in all provinces and is unlike the "two-tiered" system in the United States where workers' compensation schemes do not deprive an injured worker of the right to sue in the courts.)

THE MODERN ERA IN CANADIAN INDUSTRIAL RELATIONS: 1946 TO THE PRESENT

The Winnipeg General Strike had dealt a major setback to the Canadian labour movement. It provided a convincing demonstration of the ability of employers, backed up by the military power of the state, to resist demands that they recognize and negotiate with unions. The aftermath saw an actual decline in union membership during the 1920s, and an even sharper drop in the share of Canadian workers belonging to unions.[23] The massive unemployment of the Great Depression undermined even further the limited power of organized labour. The bargaining position of workers has always been strongest when the demand for labour has been high relative to supply. The 1930s was, on the contrary, a buyer's market for labour, and real wages fell as a result.[24] The labour movement's fortunes, and its power vis-à-vis capital, were at low ebb.

The turnaround for labour came toward the end of World War II. The demand for labour was pushed up by the wartime economy and by the mobilization of thousands of men for military service. This increased the bargaining leverage of Canadian workers. The number of strikes and lockouts more than doubled in 1942-43 from their pre-war levels, reaching 352 in 1942 and 402 in 1943, compared to an annual average of 148 between 1931-1940.[25] The duration of these work stoppages tended, however, to be short, reflecting the increased bargaining power of labour. Union membership increased from 18 per cent of the non-agricultural workforce in 1941 to 24.2 per cent in 1945.[26] The demobilization that followed the war was not accompanied by the high unemployment that most people expected. Consequently, the gains made by unions during the war were not undermined by market forces.

But favourable market conditions were only part of the story. The social climate had also changed by mid-century, providing more receptive ground for labour's demands. One indication of this change was increased popular support for the politically left-wing Cooperative Commonwealth Federation (CCF), the predecessor to the New Democratic Party (NDP). A 1943 Gallup poll placed the CCF ahead of the Liberal and Conservative Parties in popular support. The Ontario CCF finished second in that province's 1943 election, and in Saskatchewan the party was elected to office in 1944. National support for the CCF dissipated somewhat by war's end, but the party still captured an unprecedented 28 seats and 15.6 per cent of the popular vote in the 1945 general election. While it would be going too far to claim that the Canadian population was turning "pink," there was widespread support for the welfare state policies advocated by the CCF and the labour movement. Unshackled by rigid ideological principles, the governing Liberal Party and its leader Mackenzie King were able to integrate many of these reforms into their own policies, thereby undermining popular support for the CCF.[27] But the important point is simply this: labour's political agenda was increasingly in tune with the mainstream of Canadian attitudes.

It was in these circumstances that collective bargaining finally arrived on the Canadian industrial relations scene. *Collective bargaining* is a method for establishing the terms of employment, arrived at through negotiations between organized employees on one side and their employer (or an organization of employers) on the other. Out of this bargaining emerges a contract of a set duration which, in addition to such matters as rates of pay and employee benefits, typically includes provisions regarding union recognition and procedures for resolving grievances. In terms of the balance of power between employers and employees, the crucial change that collective bargaining introduced was employers' recognition of the union as the sole legitimate representative of employees for purposes of determining working conditions. This status had always been resisted by employers on the grounds that it interfered with an owner's right to decide who they employed and how their business was run.

Collective bargaining—the labour movement's longstanding demand for it, and business's equally persistent opposition to it—was about power. When it arrived at the end of World War II, it was the direct result of Privy Council Order 1003, a 1944 wartime measure passed by Ottawa. This order set down the groundrules for union certification and recognition, bargaining procedures and third-party dispute settlement. This wartime measure was replaced by the legal protections for collective bargaining contained in the Industrial Relations and Dispute Investigation Act, 1948 and the Canada Labour Code. It also provided the basis for subsequent provincial laws regulating industrial relations.

But giving legal sanction to collective bargaining was not by itself sufficient to provide unions with real clout in bargaining with employers. Whatever leverage unions have in collective bargaining ultimately rests on the right to strike and on employee solidarity to back up union demands. A union's legal right to bargain collectively with an employer is hollow without the *necessary means* to persuade workers to support the union and to compel the employer to take the union's demands seriously.

This question of means was dealt with in a 1946 arbitration decision by Justice Ivan Rand. After a long and bitter dispute between the Ford Motor Company and the UAW at Windsor, Ontario—during which the efforts of the provincial police to break the union's picket lines were resisted by massive civil disobedience (striking workers blocked the streets of downtown Windsor and those leading to the Ford plant with their locked and abandoned cars)—the union and the company agreed to submit the dispute to binding arbitration. Justice Rand's ruling denied the union's demand for a closed shop (i.e., where the employer would be forced to hire from the union's membership). But it provided the labour movement with a major victory by requiring that all members of a bargaining unit pay union dues regardless of whether or not they choose to belong to the union. In exchange, unions would be legally prevented from striking during the term of a collective agreement. This has come to be known as the *Rand Formula*. The compulsory check-off of union dues was critical in providing unions with the financial resources needed to pay for strikes (striking workers with no income are unlikely to maintain their resolve for long) and to finance the union's negotiating and other functions. These "other" functions have become controversial in recent years, as we explain later in this chapter.

The 1946 Rand decision embodied the changed social climate of industrial relations. Noting that Ottawa and most of the provinces had legislated the machinery of collective bargaining, Justice Rand argued that "the corollary from it is that the labour unions should become strong in order to carry on the functions for which they are intended."[28] "Social justice," according to Rand, required that labour's power vis-à-vis capital be increased. This idea that the union is fundamentally important to all workers, and should therefore be provided with the necessary means to bargain with employers on their behalf, was no longer revolutionary. It was in tune with the greater willingness to interfere with market forces that was characteristic of postwar capitalist societies the world over. The Keynesian welfare state that emerged after World War II embodied a new "deal" between labour and capital, and legal protections for unions' right to bargain with employers was part of this deal.

It needs to be emphasized that this new deal did not threaten the interests of employers. On the contrary, governments expected that the extension of collective bargaining would actually stabilize industrial activity (by reducing work stoppages) and promote economic growth (through higher wages and consumer purchasing power). These expectations were clearly expressed when the United States Congress passed the National Labor Relations Act, 1935 (the Wagner Act), which made collective bargaining official government policy in that country. The preamble to the Wagner Act explains why collective bargaining is desirable:

> The inequality of bargaining power between employees who do not possess full freedom of association or actual liberty of contract, and employers who are organized in the corporate or other forms of ownership association substantially burdens and affects the flow of commerce, and *tends to aggrevate recurrent business depressions*, by depressing wage rates and the purchasing power of wage earners in industry and by preventing the stabilization of

competitive wage rates and working conditions within and between industries.

Experience has proved that protection by law of the right of employees to organize and bargain collectively *safeguards commerce from injury, impairment, or interruption, and promotes the flow of commerce* by removing certain recognized sources of industrial strife and unrest, by encouraging practices fundamental to the friendly adjustment of industrial disputes...[29]

We have quoted this justification at length for two reasons. First, the Wagner Act and the philosophy of industrial peace behind it influenced the legislative framework for collective bargaining that was implemented in Canada by P.C. 1003 (1944) and the Industrial Relations and Dispute Investigation Act, 1948. As Joseph Weiler observes, it is not clear that Canadian policy-makers were persuaded by the economic growth arguments that inspired the American Wagner Act.[30] But there is hardly any doubt that they, like their American counterparts, saw in collective bargaining the promise of fewer and less disruptive work stoppages. This had been the main goal of Canadian industrial relations policy from the IDIA, 1907. And in any case, increased labour militancy during the war and growing public support for the CCF made it politically expedient to legislate such reforms. Second, the reasoning that was used in passing the Wagner Act has been reputiated by business interest groups, most economists and many governments in more recent years. As we will see later in this chapter, some observers of the North American industrial relations scene claim that collective bargaining rights have been eroded by governments that have come to view them as obstacles to competitive economic performance.

The legal protections and encouragement that federal and provincial laws provided for collective bargaining after World War II had the predictable result of making labour unions more popular among Canadian workers. Between 1946 and 1956, the percentage of non-agricultural workers belonging to unions increased from 27.9 to 33.3 per cent. This level of unionization began to flag in the 1960s, because of the declining share of total employment in the industrial sectors of the economy. It received a major boost again during the 1970s with the extension of collective bargaining rights to most federal and provincial public servants.

Putting state employees on a similar industrial relations footing as their private sector counterparts may have had important consequences for the broader employer-employee relations scene in Canada and for the Canadian economy. We stress the "may" because the alleged effects of extending collective bargaining to the public sector are open to dispute. With this warning in mind, here are some of the claims that have been made:

(1) *Wage and benefit settlements in the public and private sectors are often related.* The extension of collective bargaining to state employees, and the correlative right to strike, has increased the bargaining leverage of these workers. Their compensation gains have to some degree spilled over into the private sector, at times fuelling inflationary pressures in the economy. This was widely felt to be the case in the early 1970s, when public sector wage settlements were outstripping those in the private sector, leading Ottawa to react with temporary legislative controls on wage settlements between 1975 and 1978.[31]

Ottawa again imposed wage controls in 1982, this time on federal public sector employees only. This policy of public sector wage restraint was emulated by several provincial governments. As in the case of the 1975-78 controls, the official justification was the need to dampen inflationary pressures. Even though the 1982-84 controls did not extend to the private sector, they were widely perceived by business as a signal for wage restraint. Whether these controls actually had a "demonstration effect" on private sector settlements is another question. High unemployment was certainly a more important factor limiting the bargaining leverage and therefore wage gains of private sector workers. More generally, the empirical evidence for the argued "spill-over" effect is weak.[32]

(2) *Public sector unionization and collective bargaining have increased the rigidity of the Canadian labour market, and have therefore burdened the economy with additional costs.* This argument is based on a couple of related claims. One is that public sector unionization has been accompanied by significant wage gains for public sector workers. The evidence for this appears irrefutable, although the public sector's wage advantage over the private sector has declined since the late 1970s, probably due to increased government restraint.[33] The second claim—and this is the one that provides the basis for most attacks on public sector collective bargaining—is that public sector wages are less responsive to changes in the health of the economy than are wages in the private sector. If this is true, it represents an important source of

cost rigidity in the Canadian economy because one of every four members of the Canadian labour force is employed in the public sector. [34] The empirical record, however, does not support this claim. Especially since the end of the anti-inflation controls (1978) the average level of wage settlements in the public and private sectors has been quite similar on a year-to-year basis.[35]

(3) *Extending the right to strike to public sector workers has increased the economic disruption that results when essential services are suspended.* This claim is a difficult one to assess. The level of successful negotiation (i.e., settlement without a strike) is in fact much higher in the public than in the private sector.[36] The propensity to strike is highest in the mining, construction and manufacturing industries, all of which are predominantly in the private sector. Nonetheless, there is the possibility that the character of some public sector services is such that their interruption carries greater costs for other sectors of the economy than would most strikes in the private sector. Postal strikes, for example, invariably bring forth business complaints about the costs they suffer from the interruption of this service. In fact, many of the public sector strikes that occasion public demands for back-to-work legislation and for the protection of essential services are ones with social, rather than mainly economic, consequences. Nurses' strikes, such as occurred in British Columbia and Quebec in 1989, and teachers' strikes are prominent examples. Some public sector disputes, like those involving air traffic controllers and public transit, straddle the line between economic and social consequences.

But many of the most economically disruptive work stoppages involve disputes between employers and unions in the private sector. At the federal level, all but a few of the twenty back-to-work laws passed between 1950 and 1987 involved railways and shipping, where disputes were usually between private sector parties.

Provincial back-to-work legislation has much more often been used against public sector unions, but this largely reflects provincial jurisdiction over health care institutions and schools, which together accounted for 23 of the 62 provincial back-to-work laws passed between 1959 and 1987.37 We should not, therefore, jump to the conclusion that public sector work stoppages are more likely to be disruptive for the overall economy than those in the private sector.

"Back-to-work" laws, "essential services," and "wage controls" all involve limitations on the bargaining rights of affected employees. These limitations have been imposed with increasing frequency by Ottawa and the provinces over the last couple of decades (see Figure 14.3). Likewise in the case of "essential services," some provincial governments have reduced the range of public sector collective bargaining by expanding the number of positions designated as essential to the public interest, whose occupants cannot strike in support of their demands. Legislated wage controls represent another obvious limitation on collective bargaining, a limitation that before the 1975-78 anti-inflation controls had only been applied during wartime. What is the explanation for this trend toward restricting collective bargaining rights?

According to some, the explanation lies in the changing world economy. As economist W. Craig Riddell says, "The increasingly competitive external environment for tradeable goods has increased employee concerns about job security and employer concerns about product market competitiveness."38 More concretely, many private sector employers have sought workers' concessions on wages and benefits, hours of work, scheduling, job classifications; all of which affect a business's costs. The terms "rollback" and "concession bargaining" entered the lexicon of industrial relations during the late 1970s. Before then, it was generally assumed that negotiations between unions and employers accepted previous employee gains as the baseline for talks about future contracts. When Chrysler negotiated wage concessions with its UAW workers at the end of the 1970s, when the automaker was recording huge losses and its market share was declining, it became clear that the postwar belief in upward-ratcheting worker gains was not a reliable guide to the future of industrial relations.

Public sector employers have likewise been increasingly keen on controlling their wage bill. This has been done through formal controls like those instituted by Ottawa and most provinces in the early 1980s, pay restraint, and reduction in the size of state bureaucracies through eliminating positions, contracting out services to the private sector, and privatizing crown corporations. Whereas private sector employers have been able to use the pressures of competition and rapidly changing technology as levers in bargaining with their workers, public sector employers have relied on legislative restrictions on collective bargaining

FIGURE 14.3

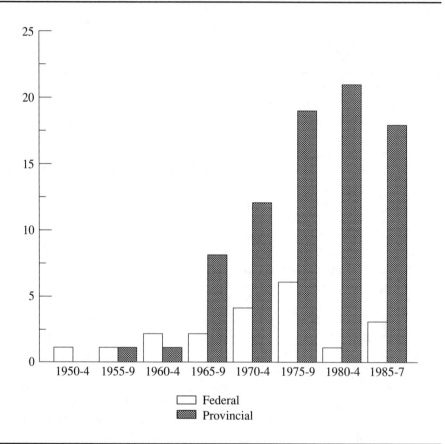

Back-to-Work Legislation in Canada
by Jurisdiction,
1950-87

Source: Labour Canada, Federal-Provincial Relations Division, "Emergency Legislation and Orders
Suspending the Right to Strike or to Lock Out", 1987

and employees' right to strike, and on public opinion that is unsympathetic to
public sector workers. The 1988 edition of *The Current Industrial Relations
Scene in Canada* describes governments' recent approach this way:

> In contrast to the growing management desire in the private sector for
> working together with labour, the public sector management approach is

hard-line bargaining and confrontation using government's legislative and executive fiat powers to enforce their bargaining agenda. This neo-conservative attitude appears particularly prevalent at the federal level and in the provinces of Saskatchewan, Alberta and British Columbia.[39]

How have employees and their unions reacted to employers' demands for concessions and pay restraint? The answer is mixed. Concessions have been accepted by unions. In 1986, 22 per cent of private sector settlements involved wage freezes or cutbacks, a figure that declined to 4 per cent in 1987. In the public sector, the comparable figures were 6 and 2 per cent.[40] But in return, unions have increasingly demanded job and income guarantees like no-layoff provisions, longer advance notice of lay-offs and plant closures, better income security programmes for laid-off workers (like supplemental unemployment benefits and severance pay), limitations on the use of part-time workers and, in the special case of public sector workers, restrictions on privatization and contracting out services to private sector businesses. Unions have for the most part rejected management offers of profit-sharing and employee stock ownership plans, favoured by some employers as an alternative to conventional pay increases.

More aggressive demands by employers for pay rollbacks and freezes aggravated the long-simmering tensions between the Canadian sections of U.S.-based unions and their American parents. American labour leaders and their union memberships have been more willing than their Canadian counterparts to accept pay concessions. This difference in bargaining orientations exploded during the 1985 negotiations between the UAW and the Big Three auto companies. The result was the 1986 decision of the Canadian section to split away from the American-based UAW to form the Canadian Auto Workers under the leadership of Bob White. Another major split followed in 1987 when the Canadian arm of International Woodworkers of America broke away to form the IWA-Canada. The Canadian section of the United Food and Commercial Workers Union (which, along with the United Steel Workers of America, is the largest international union in Canada) has also moved towards greater autonomy from its U.S. parent.[41]

The changing environment of industrial relations has crystallized around several important policy issues in Canada. We have already mentioned the formal wage controls implemented by Ottawa in 1975-78 and again, in the case of public sector employees, in 1982-84 (followed by most of the provinces). Other policy issues have included corporatism (see Chapter Three), free trade, the right to strike, unions' political activities and equity in the workplace. We look at each of these in turn.

Corporatism

Beginning in the 1960s, the federal government made some limited efforts to institutionalize joint labour and business participation in economic decision-making. This was to take place through bodies like the Economic Council of Canada (ECC) and the Canada Labour Relations Board (CLRB), and through attempts to achieve business and labour cooperation on prices and incomes policy between 1969, when the Canadian Prices and Incomes Commission was created, and the 1975-78 mandatory controls period. By the mid-1970s the words *tripartism* and *co-determination* were being used by the Trudeau government, and it was apparent that Ottawa then viewed the mandatory controls programme as a step towards a new and less confrontational system of industrial relations in Canada. The government's official policy statement on the anti-inflation controls, *Attack on Inflation* (October 14, 1975), singled out fragmented collective bargaining as a factor contributing to upward ratcheting of wages and disruptive industrial relations. The government stopped short of explicitly advocating measures like industry-wide bargaining, but it did refer to the tripartite CLRB as a step toward solving the "problem" of fragmented bargaining in Canadian industry.

Ad hoc measures aimed at bringing together representatives of business and labour with government have also been used by Ottawa and some of the provinces. Labour and business representation on task forces and royal commissions provide opportunities for this sort of collaboration. Conferences on economic problems provide another forum for limited forays into corporatist decision-making. In 1985, the federal Conservative government held a summit on the economy, in which dozens of business and labour organizations, along with other groups, were invited to participate. But perhaps the most ambitious attempt at state-sponsored business-labour collaboration was the series of 18 conferences on the Quebec economy organized by the Parti Québécois government during its first term in power (1976-80). Like Ottawa's 1985 summit on the economy, the PQ's policy of *concertation* extended beyond business and labour to include women's groups, consumer associations and other interests. There is not much evidence to suggest, however, that these exercises in collaboration have delivered the goods in terms of more harmonious industrial relations.[42] Nevertheless, they may perform a public relations function for governments that are keen to advertize their openness.

The Right to Strike

The right to strike was dealt with head on by the Supreme Court of Canada in a set of related cases decided on April 9, 1987.[43] The majority decision of the court was that "the constitutional guarantee of freedom of association ... does not include, in the case of a trade union, a guarantee of the right to bargain collectively and the right to strike."[44] The right to bargain collectively and to strike are not, the court rules, fundamental rights or freedoms that deserve the constitutional protection of section 2(d) of the Charter. "They are," the court said, "the creation of legislation, involving a balance of competing interests,"[45] and their scope and limitations are appropriately determined by legislatures. To put it very simply, economic rights were viewed as subordinate to political ones. The Court said as much: "[T]he overwhelming preoccupation of the Charter is with individual, political, and democratic rights with conspicuous inattention to economic and property rights."[46]

In arriving at this decision, the majority on the court was sensitive, as Rand had been, to the socio-economic context of their ruling. It is worth quoting from the majority decision written by Justice McIntyre in order to convey the broader considerations that influenced the court:

> Great changes—economic, social, and industrial—are afoot, not only in Canada and North America, but as well in other parts of the world. Changes in the Canadian national economy...have resulted in great pressures to reassess the traditional approaches to economic and industrial questions, including questions of labour law and policy... To intervene in that dynamic at this early stage by implying constitutional protection for the right to strike, would, in my view, give to one of the contending forces an economic weapon removed from and made immune, subject to s.1, to legislative control which could go far toward freezing the development of labour relations and curtailing that process of evolution necessary to meet the changing circumstances of a modern society in the modern world.[47]

The dissenting opinions of Chief Justice Dickson and Justice Wilson in the *Alberta Reference* case were very much in the spirit of the Rand decision. Chief Justice Dickson observed that "throughout history, workers have associated to overcome their vulnerability as individuals to the strength of their employers. The capacity to bargain collectively has long been recognized as one of the integral and primary functions of associations of working people."[48] Collective bargaining, according to Dickson, requires that workers have the right to strike. His argument was simple: "If freedom of association only protects the joining together of persons for common purposes, but not the pursuit of the very activities for which the association was formed, then the freedom is indeed legalistic, ungenerous, indeed vapid."[49]

What are we to conclude, then, about the current status of the right to strike in Canada? The answer appears to be that it is not viewed by the courts as a necessary corollary to the freedom of association that is guaranteed in the Charter. Some commentators view this as a regrettable step backwards by a Supreme Court more concerned with individual rights and freedoms than with the economic relationships between labour and capital.[50] But as the Court's reasoning makes clear, its current interpretation of the right to strike is influenced by broad socio-economic considerations just as Justice Rand's was four decades ago. One might argue that the Supreme Court's 1987 decision on the right to strike is broadly in tune with the attitudes of a majority of Canadians, who have long been ambivalent about unions and opposed to the right to strike for public sector employees and workers in "essential industries." While a clear majority of Canadians agree that workers should have the right to strike, they are equally emphatic that this right should not extend to workers in essential industries.[51] When asked whether public servants should have the right to strike, a majority of respondents say "no," a turnaround from the 1960s when a majority of Canadians favoured the right to strike for state employees.[52] A study on public attitudes carried out for the Macdonald Commission arrived at this conclusion: "[U]nions as an institution are not popular by any standard, but we cannot say unequivocally that unions have become less popular than they were before."[53]

Unions' Political Activities

Freedom of association was also the issue in a 1986 Ontario Supreme Court decision on unions and their activities. In the *Lavigne* case, a community college teacher, financed by the ideologically conservative National Citizens' Coalition,[54] challenged the Rand formula requirement that he pay dues to the union that represented him, even though he had chosen not to belong to the union. Lavigne argued that this violated his freedom of association under the Charter, because some of his union dues went towards political party contributions and other political purposes that had nothing to do with the union's bargaining function. The Court agreed.

The *Lavigne* decision left untouched, however, the compulsory dues requirement that is at the heart of the Rand Formula and which provides the financial basis for unions' collective bargaining efforts. Only political activities were affected, and here the Court proved much more sympathetic to unions than the NCC had hoped.[55] Justice White ruled that union members have the right to "opt out" of that portion of their union dues that goes towards non-collective bargaining purposes with which they disagree. Otherwise there exists a presumption of consent. The 1987 decision establishing this rule gave a fairly broad interpretation to "collective bargaining purposes," so that it included activities intended to promote union solidarity (for example, Justice White determined that union payments to striking UK miners was a proper use of union dues). So the loss of union dues as a result of the *Lavigne* decision will almost certainly be small. (As this is written, the *Lavigne* case is still before the courts, currently in the Ontario Court of Appeals.)

The larger significance of the *Lavigne* decision for business-government relations in Canada lies in the fact that it places limits on the political activities of labour organizations that do not exist in the case of associations representing business interests. We saw in Chapter Nine that the NCC successfully challenged the third-party election spending rules contained in the Canada Elections Act. Business's right to spend money promoting causes it believes in is protected by the freedom of expression guarantee in the Charter. The right of labour unions to spend money on political activities is, on the other hand, limited by their members' willingness to pay for these activities. In practice, this may amount to no more than a technical difference (Will a significant number of unionists actually exercise their "opt-out" right, thereby crippling the political activities of unions?).

Equity in the Workplace

It is well known that female workers earn less than males. The major factor accounting for this difference is the segregation of work into jobs that are predominantly held by women and those that are dominated by men. Female-dominated occupations—"pink-collar ghettoes" as they have been called—tend to pay substantially less, a fact that has given rise to demands that governments step in to legislate pay equity for jobs of comparable value. Human rights tribunals and courts have also been called on to determine whether men and women have been treated equally by employers. The issue of employment equity, including equal pay for work of equal value, has introduced an important new twist to the relationship between employers and employees.

Ottawa and several of the provinces have passed pay equity laws. The most far-reaching of these laws is Ontario's Pay Equity Act, 1987. Unlike the pay equity systems established by other governments, Ontario's includes both public sector employees and private sector businesses with 10 or more employees. It establishes the Pay Equity Commission of Ontario which is empowered to investigate claims of gender-based pay differences, and to establish and monitor pay equity plans for employers. In determining what constitutes work of equal value, the Commission considers the skill, effort and responsibility associated with the work, as well as the conditions under which it is performed. Pay differences owing to such factors as performance merit, seniority and skills shortages that inflate compensation in an occupation are considered "reasonable" by the Commission. Moreover, there are ceilings on the pay increases that an employer would be required to implement under a Commission decision, and the allowable period for instituting a pay equity plan ranges from three years for very large firms (500 or more employees) to six years for the smallest businesses covered by the Act (10-49 employees). Employers and employees cannot negotiate a contract that contravenes the terms of a pay equity plan.

Pay equity schemes like that being implemented in Ontario represent an obvious interference with the market mechanism. The detractors of pay equity argue that it flouts the laws of supply and demand, and therefore introduces costly distortions into the economy. On the other hand, it has to be admitted that legal guarantees for collective bargaining, employee reinstatement after a strike and state conciliation of industrial relations disputes also interfere with the market mechanism. The precise point we have been making in this chapter is that the state has become progressively more involved in regulating the employee-employer relationship. Thus, the real issue at stake in the case of pay equity is whether this particular interference in the labour market is worth whatever costs it might carry. The proponents of pay equity claim that the market mechanism can produce injustices, because of social attitudes that have undervalued "women's work." Like collective bargaining, the pay equity issue involves a balance of economic and social considerations. There is, consequently, no "correct" answer to whether pay equity is a good thing; just accommodations between different interests.

Regardless of our personal views on pay equity, we should keep in mind that no equal pay/value law in Canada compels employers to increase their total wage bills or reduce profits in order to implement a pay equity plan. Michael Mandel, a firm supporter of pay equity, explains the economics of this reform:

> That money [to bring the pay of women up to that of men performing jobs of equal value] has to come from somewhere. Employers are not going to be more easygoing at the bargaining table because of pay equity. Nor is business competition going to ease because of it ... [B]arring a fundamental realignment in the structure of social power—increases for working women will be entirely at the expense of working men.[56]

Gender-based differences in hiring have also come under close scrutiny in recent years. In a 1987 ruling, the Supreme Court of Canada upheld a human rights tribunal decision that Canadian National Railways was guilty of *systemic discrimination* because of its failure to hire women for blue-collar positions. The Court required CNR to implement the tribunal's requirement that one of every four new hirings in "non-traditional" job categories be filled by a woman until 13 per cent of its blue-collar workers are female. Similar rulings by human rights tribunals have been issued since then, including Canadian Human Rights Commission rulings in 1989 against Bell Canada and the Canadian Broadcasting Corporation.

INDUSTRIAL RELATIONS TODAY

The present state of industrial relations in this country contains elements of continuity and change. The major institutions of Canadian industrial relations have been in place for decades—third-party conciliation before a strike, collective bargaining, the Rand Formula, limitations on the right to strike in the case of "essential services"—but recent years have seen some important modifications and some additions under the pressure of economic, social and political changes. Foremost among these changes has been the increasingly competitive world economy. The spate of plant closures at the end of the 1970s and the deep economic recession in the early 1980s marked a turning point in employer-employee relations. Businesses generally became more aggressive in negotiating with their employees, and the bargaining power of unions was seriously weakened. The number of settlements involving wage rollbacks or freezes has declined as the economy has recovered. But the attitude forged in the crucible of the recession continues to prevail. It is an attitude that sees wage demands as a problem from the standpoint of Canada's ability to compete in the global economy.

Economic change is the most important part of the background to recent developments in industrial relations, but it is not the whole story. Social and political changes have also affected these relations. The demands of the women's movement influenced both the equality section (s.15) of the Charter and provincial charters of human rights. These equality guarantees have, in turn, been used by the courts and by human rights tribunals to require some employers to implement affirmative action policies in hiring. Pay equity laws represent another interference in the labour market to promote gender equality.

More generally, the political discourse of post-Charter Canada is increasingly a discourse inspired by the rights and freedoms set out in the Charter. Both the right to strike and the political activities of unions have been challenged in recent years, using the s.2 guarantees of the Charter. And in both cases the court's ruling has generally been viewed as a setback for organized labour. This is not surprising. The Charter makes explicit reference to *individual* rights and freedoms. The *collective* rights it recognizes are associated with gender, age, race, language, ethnicity and aboriginal status, not with class. As the Supreme Court said in the 1987 right to strike decision, the Charter is characterized by a "conspicuous inattention to economic and property rights."[57]

Against this background of economic, social and political developments, the hard core of industrial relations in Canada remains largely unchanged. It continues to involve an adversarial relationship between those who sell their labour and those who buy it, presided over by the state. Collective bargaining institutionalizes the adversarial relationship between labour and capital, bringing their conflicts out in the open. There are, however, other methods of managing industrial relations. The supposedly less confrontational approaches found in economies like those of Japan, Sweden and West Germany are often pointed to as holding lessons for Canada. The following comments are fairly typical:

> We in Canada need to recognize that our essentially adversarial industrial
> relations system is increasingly anachronistic in the new environment in

which we find ourselves. We have failed to appreciate the nature and extent of the challenge—especially from those countries where a genuine labor/management/government co-partnership prevails. Both unions and employers need to recognize that the real adversaries are the enterprises of Tokyo, Osaka, Seoul and Taipei.[58]

The reality is, however, that neither business nor labour has shown much enthusiasm for the importation of these techniques into Canada.

ENDNOTES

1. Werner Sombart, *Why There Is No Socialism in the United States* (1905). Frederick Engels' arguments are presented in Seymour Martin Lipset, "Radicalism in North America: A Comparative View of the Party Systems in Canada and the United States," in *Transactions of the Royal Society of Canada*, Series IV, Vol. XIV, 1976.

2. Michael Bliss, *A Living Profit* (Toronto: McClelland and Stewart, 1974), 87.

3. Quoted in *ibid.*, 75.

4. The Commission's findings are discussed in *ibid.*, chapter three.

5. Calculated from the data in F.H. Leacy, ed., *Historical Statistics of Canada*, Dl-7 and E175-177.

6. For a discussion of American labour expansionism, see R.H. Babcock, *Gompers in Canada* (Toronto: University of Toronto Press, 1974).

7. Paul Craven, *'An Impartial Umpire': Industrial Relations and the Canadian State 1900-1911* (Toronto: University of Toronto Press, 1980), 209.

8. Quoted from Labour Minister R. Lemieux in *Ibid.*, 288.

9. *Ibid.*, 299-301.

10. W.L. Mackenzie King, *Industry and Humanity: A Study in the Principles Underlying Industrial Reconstruction* (Toronto: University of Toronto Press, 1973), 313.

11. *Ibid.*, 329.

12. *Ibid.*, 98.

13. Discussed in Peter Russell, *Leading Constitutional Decisions*, 4th edition (Ottawa: Carleton University Press, 1988), No. 9.

14. Cited in Bryan D. Palmer, *Working-Class Experience* (Toronto: Butterworths, 1983), 143.

15. See the interpretation in Kenneth McNaught and David J. Bercuson, *The Winnipeg General Strike: 1919* (Don Mills: Longman, 1974).

16. The classic exposition of the effects that Canada's electoral system has had on the representation of different interests is Allan Cairns, "The Electoral System and the Party System in Canada, 1921-1965," in Cairns, *Constitution, Government, and Society in Canada* (Toronto: McClelland and Stewart, 1988), 111- 138.

17. Nova Scotia, 1915; British Columbia, 1916; Alberta, 1918; New Brunswick, 1918.

18. Quoted from the business magazine *Industrial Canada* in Bliss, *A Living Profit*, 90.

19. Quoted in Reg Whitaker, "Scientific Management Theory as Political Ideology," in *Studies in Political Economy*, 86.

20. Elton Mayo, *The Human Problems of an Industrial Civilization* (New York: Viking Press, 1960).

21. Thomas J. Peters and Robert H. Waterman, Jr., *In Search of Excellence* (New York: Warner Books, 1982).

22. This is Michael Bliss's view, based on his review of the minutes of several trade associations. *A Living Profit*, 94.

23. Total union membership went from 313,000 in 1921 to 275,000 in 1926, or from 18.4 to 13.6 percent of the non-agricultural workforce. Industrial Relations Centre, Queen's University, *The Current Industrial Relations Scene in Canada, 1988*, 446.

24. Total labour income fell from $2.94 billion in 1929 to $1.79 billion in 1933, and only attained its pre-Depression level in 1940. Leacy, ed., *Historical Statistics of Canada*, E14-29.

25. *Ibid.*, E190-197.

26. *Ibid.*, E175-177.

27. The CCF had other problems as well, including its association in the minds of many with communism. This was a serious liability in the Cold War era that followed World War II, and "red scare" tactics were commonly used by other parties where the CCF-NDP posed a credible threat.

28. Quoted in Leo Panitch and Donald Swartz, *The Assault on Trade Union Freedoms* (Toronto: Garamond Press, 1988), 19.

29. Quoted in Joseph Weiler, "The Role of the Law in Labour Relations," in Ivan Bernier and Andrée Lajoie, research coordinators, *Labour Law and Urban Law in Canada* (Toronto: University of Toronto Press, 1986), 7.

30. *Ibid.*, 15.

31. Prices were also controlled under the Anti-Inflation Act, but virtually all serious commentaries on the AIB controls agree that the government's real intention was to control wages, and that price controls had at best a marginal impact on inflation.

32. A summary of studies on this issue is provided in W. Craig Riddell, "Canadian Labour Relations: An Overview," in Riddell, research coordinator, *Canadian Labour Relations* (Toronto: Unversity of Toronto Press, 1986), 23-27.

33. *Ibid.*, 22-23.

34. This is using a broad definition of the public sector that includes schools, hospitals

and other organizations that are financed mainly or exclusively by the state.

35. Riddell, *Canadian labour Relations*, 24-26.

36. R. Lacroix, "Strike Activity in Canada," in Riddell, *Canadian Labour Relations*, 176-177, Tables 3-3, 3-4.

37. Calculated from Panitch and Swartz, *The Assault on Trade Union Freedoms*, 127-29.

38. Riddell, *Canadian Labour Relations*, 4.

39. Queen's University, *The Current Industrial Relations Scene in Canada, 1988*, 2.

40. *Ibid.*, 60.

41. On the Canadian autonomy movement, see *ibid.*, 43-44.

42. See for example, A. Brian Tanguay, "Concerted Action in Quebec, 1976-83: a dialogue of the deaf," in Alain G. Gagnon, ed., *Quebec: State and Society* (Toronto: Methuen, 1985), 365-385.

43. *Reference re Public Service Employment Relations Act* (Alta.) (1987), 38 D.L.R. (4th) 161; *Public Service Alliance of Canada v. Canada* (1987), 38 D.L.R. (4th) 249; and *Government of Saskatchewan et al. v. Retail, Wholesale & Department Store Union, Locals 544, 635 & 955 et al.* (1987) 38 D.L.R. (4th) 277; all in the Supreme Court of Canada.

44. Quoted in Panitch and Swartz, *The Assault on Trade Union Freedoms*.

45. *Ibid,* 58.

46. Quoted in Michael Mandel, *The Charter of Rights and the Legalization of Politics in Canada* (Toronto: Wall & Thompson, 1989), 191. The Court had an additional, very practical, consideration in mind. Giving constitutional status to the right to strike would, the Court feared, effectively transfer to judges the responsibility for determining the "reasonability," under s.1 of the Charter, of legislative restrictions on the right to strike. This would, the Court believed, involve judges in complex political, economic and social matters that are better decided by specialized labour tribunals and legislatures. See *Re Public Service Employees Relations Act* (Alberta), 1987: 232-235.

47. Quoted in Panitch and Swartz, *The Assault on Trade Union Freedoms*, 60.

48. Quoted in Mandel, *The Charter of Rights and the Legalization of Policies in Canada*, 194.

49. Quoted in Panitch and Swartz, *The Assault on Trade Union Freedoms*, 61.

50. This is clearly the critical position taken by Panitch and Swartz, and by Mandel.

51. Queen's University, *The Current Industrial Relations Scene in Canada*, 555.

52. See Pradeep Kumar, "Union Growth in Canada: Retrospect and Prospect," in Riddell, *Canadian Labour Relations*, 105.

53. Richard Johnston, *Public Opinion and Public Policy in Canada* (Toronto: University of Toronto Press, 1986), 166.

54. It is estimated that the NCC spent $400,000 on the case. *Globe and Mail*, 8 July 1986, A3.

55. In its submission after the 1986 decision, the NCC advocated that union members should be required to agree beforehand to any political uses of dues proposed by their union.

56. Mandel, *The Charter of Rights and the Legalization of Politics*, 267-68.

57. *Re Public Service Employees Relations Act [Alberta]* [1987], 1 SCR, 232.

58. Jim Armstrong, "Labor/management battles an exercise in cutting our own throats," *Globe and Mail*, 24 June 1989, B2.

PART 6

CONCLUSION

Chapter 15

Business and Government in the 1990s

As this century draws to a close, the business of forecasting the future has already reached a feverish pitch. Pick up any business magazine and chances are good that it will include at least one article on coming to grips with change, prognosticating the future or profiting from uncertainty. "Corporate restructuring," "globalization" and "internationalization of capital" are some of the buzzwords used to capture this consensus that the future will not be like the past, and that change is the only certainty. Anticipating, managing and profiting from change are the topics of virtually all bestselling business books of the last decade.[1] Auguries of change and sharp breaks with the past and visions for the future have always been more glamorous than those which predict more of the same. Even so, the recent explosion in the market for explanations of what is happening, predictions of where we are heading, and advice on how to cope with it all, reflects something more than the age-old fear of the future. It is solidly rooted in the accelerated pace of economic and technological change that is the hallmark of the late twentieth century.

These changes have been unfolding at both the micro and the macro levels. At the micro level, technological innovation has been transforming the workplace and traditional industrial/commercial practices. The new conventional wisdom on business management values adaptability, responsiveness and decentralized authority structures, while tending to vilify "bigness" as the outdated characteristic of industrial dinosaurs. Today's workers are told that they can expect to change careers four to five times over their working life. Consumers, as a group, are becoming more affluent and more sophisticated in their tastes, resulting in the splintering of product and service markets into smaller, more specialized parts. The sectoral balance of advanced capitalist economies continues to shift away from blue-collar manufacturing industries to white-collar service ones. And while big business takeovers, mergers and leveraged buyouts capture most of the headlines, small businesses have accounted for most of the recent growth in jobs and GNP.

At the macro level, the 1970s preoccupation with the "crisis" of industrial capitalism and "deindustrialization" has lost some of its pessimistic stridency, as the internationalization of production and capital have become recognized as facts of economic life. This is a world in which, as business historian Michael Bliss puts it, "there [is] less place to hide."[2] This is undoubtedly true, but business and governments have not stopped trying. Tariff barriers to trade have fallen dramatically since World War II, but their decline has been offset by a proliferating jungle of non-tariff barriers to trade (NTBs) that protect domestic producers from foreign competition (see Chapter Twelve). The political temptation to protect industries and workers who obviously are threatened by imports (with the cost passed on less obviously to consumers) is hard to resist, and the greater subtlety of NTBs than tariffs makes them attractive to governments. "Fair trade" and "managed trade" are some of the current euphemisms for protectionism that the Japanese challenge and the economic muscle of the NICs have spawned in Western economies. There are, nonetheless, some countertrends. The Free Trade Agreement between Canada and the United States, and the European Common Market scheduled for 1992 represent the two most ambitious developments in the direction of freer trade.

The economic changes that business and government must grapple with are both profound and global in their scope. They are, however, only part—albeit the most important part—of the shifting constellation of forces that are shaping the future trajectory of business-government relations. Social and political circumstances in their own backyards also influence how governments respond to the changing economic scene. Indeed, it is popular to blame existing political institutions and entrenched social practices and attitudes for the alleged failure of governments to come to grips with the new multipolar economic order. As Robert B. Reich observes in *The Next American Frontier*:

> Every group is reluctant to risk change in its economic status for fear that the burden of change in the economy as a whole will fall disproportionately upon it. But the collective unwillingness of all participants to risk economic change is dooming everyone. America's impasse is rooted in the incapacity of its political institutions to ensure that the burdens and benefits of adjustment will be allocated fairly.[3]

Reich is speaking of the United States, but his argument could equally be applied to Canada, Britain, France or any other capitalist democracy. Sudden policy swings are rare, because of the vested economic, political and bureaucratic interests that stand to lose from withdrawal of the supports on which they depend.

How have the relations between business and government in Canada been affected by the economic, social and political changes unfolding in our own backyard? We argued in Chapter One that business enjoys a "privileged position" in the politics of capitalist societies, Canadian politics included. A combination of structural and cultural factors, along with the sheer political muscle that superior financial resources can buy, ensure that business is perched atop the pecking order of social interests. Has the privileged position of business been changed by the transformations taking place on the economic, social and political fronts? As Canada approaches the 21st century, can we divine the future of business-government relations from the entrails of the present?

Prediction is a perilous enterprise. Just how perilous it can be is brought home by the long list of very wrong guesses about the future by people who might have been expected to know better. In the mid-1970s the president of Digital Equipment Corporation (one of the largest makers of computers) proclaimed that "there is no reason for any individual to have a computer [at] home."[4] A little more than a decade ago, some seers were predicting that Brazil would be an economic giant by the end of this century (instead of what it is now—a hobbling economy burdened with foreign indebtedness and racked with political and social instability). Before peering into the future one would do well to reflect on a humbling adage from the volatile feature film industry: "No one knows anything."

Our aim in the remainder of this chapter is less ambitious than prediction. It is, instead, to highlight a couple key developments—public opinion and structural economic change—affecting business power in Canada. This should at least provide some idea of the tendencies and forces that are shaping the business-government relationship as we move toward this century's end.

PUBLIC OPINION AND BUSINESS

Public attitudes toward business have been plumbed less deeply in Canada than in the United States. Lacking the attitudinal surveys that abound south of the border, we have been left to rely upon the inferences that can be drawn from historical and impressionistic accounts of business in society and on some scattered surveys of public opinion. There is no reason to believe that the results of a poll will necessarily reveal more about community attitudes than would a thoughtful assessment of non-numeric evidence. Nonetheless, survey results at least have the virtue of enabling us to spot trends in public attitudes with a minimum of guesswork. Fortunately, there are a couple of Canadian organizations that have collected trend data on public attitudes toward business. The most important of these is Decima Research, which generously provided access to data from the *Decima Quarterly Report*.

Using these data we can get an idea of changing public attitudes towards business in comparison with other institutions. In general, attitudes towards both business and unions have improved, in relative terms, as public sympathy towards government plummeted. Table 15.1 shows that between 1984 and 1988, the percentage of people who saw "big government" as the greatest threat rose from 33 per cent to 47 per cent. Fear of "big labour" declined relatively, while perceptions of "big business" stayed the same. Table 15.2 also shows a dramatic deterioration in attitudes toward government. In 1984, 49 per cent of the population thought that government best looked after their economic interests. By 1989 this figure had fallen to only 25 per cent. In comparison with government, the figures for business improved dramatically in this period. Overall, Tables 15.1 and 15.2 show that in 1988/89 attitudes towards business were substantially more favourable than those towards government or unions.

It is noteworthy that this comparatively low level of public concern with "big business" has persisted during a decade in which the pace of corporate mergers and the decline of domestic competition in several major sectors of the economy have been rapid, and media coverage of the trend toward greater corporate concentration has generally been unfavourable.

Table 15.1

	Biggest Threat: Business, Labour, Government?		
Year	Biggest Threat		"Don't Know"
	"Big Business" "Big Labour" "Big Government"		
1978	21%	38%	35%	12%
1984	17	34	33	16
1988	17	24	47	11

Source: Canadian Institute of Public Opinion (CIPO)
Items: Speaking of the future, which do you think will be the biggest threat to Canada in years to come
— big business, big labour or big government?

Table 15.2

	Government, Business and Unions: Which of These Sectors Best Looks After Your Economic Interests?				
Year	Government	Business	Unions	Don't Know, No Opinion	(N)
1984	49%	32%	10%	9%	1500
1986	42	31	13	14	1500
1989	25	50	15	10	1500

(N) Number of respondents in the survey.

Source: The Maclean's/Decima Poll, in Maclean's (1 January, 1990), 26

As we observed in Chapter Fourteen, labour unions have never been popular among Canadians. Unions receive the lowest public confidence rating of all the institutions listed in the *Decima Quarterly Report* (see Table 15.3). Some business sectors do not fare much better, but the point is this: Canadian public opinion is not solidly behind organizations whose *raison d'être* is to wrest a better deal from employers for workers. There is even a fair-sized slice of the population, ranging from about a quarter to a third, which would take away the right to strike.[5] This is a rather back-door way of measuring attitudes toward business. But we are probably on safe ground in thinking that those who feel negatively toward unions, and even more emphatically those who would ban the right to strike for workers, believe that unions are often disruptive and make irresponsible demands on the economy.

Although business as a whole comes off rather well (at least compared to other major institutions), some sectors of the business community have a definite image problem. Oil, tobacco and insurance companies, as well as multinationals, all rank toward the bottom of the public confidence ladder along with labour unions and the federal government (see Table 15.3). Other sectors, including banking, forestry and mining, receive positive ratings. Whether public opinion is an asset or a liability for business associations and individual corporations in their dealings with governments that are sensitive to the popular mood, depends on the industry in question. Negative public opinion may indeed render an industry more vulnerable to antagonistic public policies. The ability and willingness of the federal Liberal government to impose the National Energy Program (1980) in the face of outraged howls from the multinational oil companies, the Alberta government and American politicians, was surely made easier by the petroleum industry's bad image (prompting the Canadian Petroleum Association to spend millions of dollars on a media compaign to improve that image). The more recent travails of the tobacco industry, under attack by a wide and vocal anti-smoking coalition, provides a classic illustration of a business group fighting a vigorous rear-guard action against rampant public opinion.

Perhaps the most striking feature of the public confidence ratings in Table 15.3 is that most of them are negative. Government, labour, several industries and some other social institutions all receive negative confidence ratings. This is also true in the United States, where the trends and correlates of public attitudes toward social institutions have been studied far more thoroughly. These American studies have found that there has been a *general* decline in public confidence in institutions since the mid-1960s.[6] Richard Johnston suggests that a similar phenomenon exists in Canada, with public confidence ratings of different institutions tending to move in the same direction.[7] But the evidence is much less strong than in the well-documented American case.

Table 15.3

Average Confidence Ratings of Institutions, 1980-88			
Institution	Hardly Any	Some	Great Deal	No Opinion
Forest industry	13%	53%	30%	4%
Airlines	14	54	30	2
Schools	17	54	28	1
Banks	19	53	28	1
Courts	21	51	27	2
Railways	19	54	24	3
Beer companies	25	48	22	4
Organized religion	27	47	23	3
Mining industry	15	59	22	4
Newspapers	20	60	19	1
Chemical industry	32	49	15	4
Insurance companies	32	50	17	1
Television	25	57	17	1
Provincial government	23	59	17	1
Civil service	27	56	15	2
Multinational corporations	31	52	13	4
Tobacco industry	41	43	12	4
Oil companies	35	50	14	2
Federal government	31	56	12	1
Labour unions	46	43	10	1

Source: *Decima Quarterly Report*
Item: *Now I'm going to name some institutions in this country and I'd like you to consider the people who run these institutions. How about the people who run...(ROTATE ITEMS).* Would you say you have a great deal of confidence in them, only some confidence in them, or hardly any confidence in them?

If the limited Canadian data available to us will bear any conclusion, it is that the climate of public opinion within which business operates is not menacing. Canadians are much less disposed to fret about the danger posed by "big business" than they are about "big labour" and especially "big government." A solid majority place greater confidence in private industry than in government as most likely to promote the country's economic well-being. The unpopularity of labour unions suggests that there is no groundswell of class sentiment that might challenge the rights of capital. Some industries are viewed negatively by the Canadian public, and many reasons for more regulation of business are supported by it. But overall, there appear to be no grounds for believing that Canadians question either the legitimacy or the effectiveness of their capitalist economic system. The cultural/ideological dominance of business thus appears to be well entrenched.

THE STRUCTURAL POWER OF CAPITAL

Did the political victory of free trade in Canada represent a symbolic watershed in the balance of social forces in this country? Leaving aside the economists and the governments that supported it, free trade's most ardent advocates were representatives of big business. As we observed in Chapter Thirteen, this was a dramatic turnaround from the traditional opposition of organizations like the Canadian Manufacturers' Association to the dismantling of protectionist walls. It is hardly conceivable that the free trade initiative would have gotten off the ground, let alone succeeded politically, without the backing of the business community. Public opinion far from endorsed free trade in 1985, when Ottawa first launched the idea. Three years later, the Conservative Party's re-election in the "free trade election" and opinion surveys showed that Canadian society remained divided on the issue. Does the victory of free trade in Canada tell us anything about the power of business, and about the forces that determine business's ability to influence government actions?

We would answer "yes." The FTA was one of those symbolic moments in Canadian history, like the National Policy of 1879, the "reciprocity election" of 1911 and the 1945 White Paper on Reconstruction that committed Ottawa to the adoption of Keynesianism and the liberal welfare state.[8] The greater formal integration of the Canadian and American economies that the FTA represents, and which the most powerful elements of this country's business community support, is in a sense the political culmination of economic changes that have been underway for years now. We have discussed these changes and some of their social and political consequences at various points in this book. In particular, we have argued that the growing internationalization of capital has tended to strengthen the political hand of business interests, while at the same time weakening the political strength of organized labour and those interests most committed to the Keynesian welfare state. It has done so by leaving governments more exposed to international economic forces that they cannot control, but which affect their ability to regulate the domestic economy and to finance existing state programmes.

As international competitive pressures intensify, corporations will be forced into a process of substantial restructuring. In this process, relocation to areas of lower production costs will be an increasingly attractive option. This process has already been underway for some time, and many large firms have shifted their production to cheap wage areas, such as to the *maquiladoras* in Mexico where labour can be bought for as little as one dollar per hour. In addition, the movement of capital has also been taking place within the United States, with companies relocating from the northern "rust belt" to the lower wage, less unionized "sun belt" of the south and the west. The overall effect is to increase the vulnerability and dependency of governments and workers. While capital moves around the world fairly freely, labour faces many more obstacles, and the state cannot move at all. This permits business to use the threat of relocation to extract concessions from both labour and government in countries such as Canada.

Governments are not the only ones affected by international economic restructuring. Businesses also find that their ability to compete for markets and investment capital is influenced by economic developments beyond their national borders. Some of these businesses lose, unable to compete with their foreign rivals without hefty state subsidies. Their demands for protection often receive a sympathetic hearing from governments who are keen to preserve jobs, and who see no politically acceptable way of avoiding the subsidies bidding game that internationally mobile business investors are able to work to their advantage. Organized labour usually supports these subsidies, valuing the jobs associated with any new investment, no matter how it is attracted, more than the costs that paying for it may impose on taxpayers, consumers, and the overall economy.

There are, however, some limits to business mobility. Some sectors of the economy, like insurance, banking, and communications, typically are hedged in with all sorts of restrictions that limit foreign entry into the domestic market. Moreover, the world economy continues to bristle with a staggering array of protectionist measures that have thus far eluded to GATT's efforts to lower barriers to international trade. Nevertheless, by any measure, the world economy has become a more interdependent place (see Chapter Twelve), and the icon of the current economic age is the transnational corporation.

For those businesses whose markets are international and which are able to shift production between countries with relative ease in response to economic incentives (cheaper wages, weaker unions, government subsidies), the new economic order presents enormous opportunities. Other businesses require greater and greater protection just to hold on to their existing domestic market in the face of tough foreign competition. The internationalization of capital produces winners and losers in the business community. But its impact on governments is more uniform. Broadly speaking, governments in advanced capitalist societies have two options. They can respond to intense foreign competition and mobile business investment by offering various forms of protection to domestic producers. The more dependent an economy is on international trade, the less viable this option will be. Alternatively, they can choose to provide a business environment that attracts capital investment because of its competitive advantages. Deregulation of industry, lower corporate taxation and downward pressure on wages are ways in which this may be done.

Both of these options strengthen the political hand of business. The increased protectionism route benefits the vested corporate interests that see in state protection their best hope (sometimes their only hope) for survival. The

competitive advantage route benefits business by reducing the costs of producing in a particular country. Governments do not consciously choose between
these options: the policy-making process is far messier than that. And there is
nothing to prevent governments from moving simultaneously in both of these
directions: protecting domestic producers from foreign competition and at the
same time bringing the costs of doing business more into line with what they
are in countries jostling for the same investment capital. Most commentators
argue that this is precisely what has happened in the United States over the last
decade. Whether a government leans more towards the increased protectionism
or the lower business costs option depends on the particular mix of domestic
politics and ideologies, as well as on the calculation of costs and benefits to the
economy as a whole.

The FTA between Canada and the United States is a response to the restructuring going on in the world economy. Corporate supporters of free trade see in
it the promise of improved access to the huge American market (which is a
springboard to other international markets), as well as a possible lever for bringing production costs in Canada more into line with the level of our major trading partner. On the political side, both the business advocates of free trade and
the governments which support it have argued that there is no alternative; that
Canada's trade dependence on the United States and our vulnerability to protectionist American laws, combined with the intensity of global competition, mean
that there is literally "no place to hide."

Despite the conflicting arguments over the FTA, one point seems relatively
uncontroversial, namely that free trade shifts the balance of social forces
towards those whose interests lie primarily with the market and not with the
state. When we think about who opposed and who supported the FTA it is clear
that most of free trade's opponents were groups who counted on government
interference with the market (most of Canada's cultural community; farmers in
marketing board sectors of agriculture; environmentalists; heavily regulated/pro-
tected industries like food processing or furniture; supporters of Canadian social
programmes) or in the case of labour, those who feared the effects that unleash-
ing market forces might have on jobs and wages in Canada. For these groups,
the FTA appeared to be more a menace than a blessing. Pro-free trade groups
have not always dismissed these concerns, but as the C.D. Howe Institute puts
it:

> Debates about the potential impact of a Canadian-U.S. free trade area on
> jobs, on Canadian cultural industries, and on Canadian sovereignty are
> important; but there is a risk that this will turn out to have been like debat-
> ing the deck chair arrangement on the Titanic as it approached the fateful
> iceberg.[9]

On the other hand, the support of all the major business associations in this country was based on their expectation that a freer North American market would be to their advantage. The division between the defenders and the detractors of the FTA, therefore, came down to a fundamental difference of attitude toward the market.

In general, business sympathies lie with a political system that imposes the fewest limitations on its ability to expand and adapt to changing profit opportunities. But at the same time, business also benefits from forms of state intervention that subsidize costs of production, provide insurance against business failure and restrict challenges from other sections of society. Business support for free markets and free trade thus only goes so far. It does not extend to the elimination of key areas of state intervention such as the establishment of a transportation infrastructure; the provision of state-subsidized education; government restrictions on the right to strike; the protection of private property; the maintenance of social stability; or interventions in a variety of other areas such as trade promotion and government procurement. The movement towards free markets, of which the FTA is a part, is thus a selective one. Core areas of state support for business are excluded from the forces of liberalization, while the scope for public control of business activity is simultaneously reduced.

In response to the growing international mobility of capital, the orientation of public policy is being pushed in a direction more attractive to business. The globalization of business activity has increased the vulnerability of the Canadian state, and the policy agenda has been reshaped in accordance with the competitive battle to attract "footloose" capital. In the 1990s we can thus expect a continued growth in the structural power of business as governments battle to attract corporate investment in an increasingly mobile and competitive international environment.

ENDNOTES

1. Included in this list would be Thomas J. Peters and Robert H. Waterman, Jr., *In Search of Excellence* (New York: Harper & Row, 1982); William G. Ouchi, *Theory Z: How American Business Can Meet the Japanese Challenge* (New York: Avon Books, 1981); Ouchi, *The M-Form Society: How American Teamwork Can Recapture the Competitive Edge* (Reading, Mass.: Addison-Wesley, 1984); Peter Drucker, *The New Realities* (New York: Heinemann, 1989); and Robert B. Reich, *The Next American Frontier* (New York: Times Books, 1983).

2. Michael Bliss, *Northern Enterprise* (Toronto: McClelland and Stewart, 1987). This

is the title of Chapter 19, and is taken from a remark made in the 1985 Report of the Macdonald Commission.

3. Robert B. Reich, "The Next American Frontier," in *The Atlantic Monthly* (April 1983), 107.

4. Quoted in Marie José Drouin, "The outlook is rosy ... maybe," in *The Financial Post Report on the Nation* (Winter 1988-89), 68.

5. Richard Johnston, *Public Opinion* and *Public Policy in Canada* (Toronto: University of Toronto Press, 1986), Table 5-24, 166.

6. Seymour Martin Lipset and William Schneider, *The Confidence Gap: Business, Labor, and Government in the Public Mind*, revised edition (Baltimore: John Hopkins University Press, 1987), chapter one.

7. Johnston, *Public Opinion and Public Policy in Canada*, 55-59.

8. Some would add to this list the 1963 defeat of the Diefenbaker Conservatives, and the return to power of the Liberal Party. In his *Lament for a Nation*, nationalist guru George Grant argues that the defeat of Diefenbaker sounded the death knell for the possibility of an independent Canada. The election of the Liberal Party, in his view, represented the victory of American continentalism, cultural and economic, and the final absorption of Canada into the American liberal empire.

9. Edward A. Carmichael, *Confronting Global Challenges* (Toronto: C.D. Howe Institute, 1986), 73.

APPENDIX

THE MACHINERY OF CANADIAN GOVERNMENT

In writing this book we have assumed that most readers have probably taken an introductory level course in Canadian politics and government. They are already familiar with terms like "parliament," "cabinet," and "bureaucracy," which are scattered throughout the text without an explanation of their meaning. But for others, particularly those students in commerce or business administration programmes, this may be their first formal exposure to the study of Canadian politics. It is mainly for these students that the following pages are written, although others may also wish to refresh their knowledge of how the machinery of government operates in Canada.

Just as a crash-course in French will not enable a non-francophone to leaf through Balzac with easy confidence, this brief survey will not produce "fluency" in the language of Canadian government. Some conversational skills are all that can be expected. For those who want or require the immersion approach, there are many useful books dealing with Canadian politics, government institutions or public administration. The following ones are widely used:

> Robert J. Jackson and Doreen Jackson, *Politics in Canada: Culture, Institutions, Behaviour and Public Policy, second edition* (Scarborough, Ont.: Prentice-Hall Canada, Inc., 1990).

> J.R. Mallory, *The Structure of Canadian Government*, revised edition (Toronto: Gage, 1984).

> Norman Ward, *Dawson's Government of Canada*, sixth edition (Toronto: University of Toronto Press, 1987).

> Robert F. Adie and Paul G. Thomas, *Canadian Public Administration: Problematical Perspectives* (Scarborough, Ont.: Prentice-Hall Canada, Inc., 1987).

> Kenneth Kernaghan and David Siegel, *Public Administration in Canada: A Text* (Toronto: Methuen, 1987).

A short and very readable introduction to Canadian government is provided in Eugene A. Forsey, *How Canadians Govern Themselves* (Ottawa: Minister of Supply and Services Canada, 1982), and an excellent account of how institutions interact with the informal political process is provided by Robert M. Campbell and Leslie A. Pal, *The Real Worlds of Canadian Politics* (Peterborough: Broadview Press, 1989). Campbell and Pal examine six recent cases in Canadian policy-making, enabling them to explore how institutions and processes affect policy outcomes in different issue areas.

THE CONSTITUTION

Canada's constitution consists of the various Constitution Acts passed since 1867, and the unwritten rules—or *conventions*—associated with British-style parliamentary democracy and with federalism. We may divide these constitutional rules into three categories: 1) those that relate to the machinery of government; 2) those that define the legislative division of powers between Ottawa and the provinces; and 3) those that establish the rights and freedoms of the citizen, and groups of citizens, vis-à-vis the state. The first category will be discussed later in the section on "The Formal Structure of Canadian Government." We turn our attention now to the categories of federalism and citizens' rights and freedoms.

Federalism

A federal political system is one in which the authority to pass laws is divided in some measure between the national and regional governments, where neither level of government is able, unilaterally, to alter or eliminate the powers of the other. Besides Canada, examples of federal systems include Australia, the United States and the Federal Republic of Germany. Federal systems can be contrasted with unitary systems, such as Britain, France or Sweden, where authority is centralized in the hands of a national government, and where any regional or local governments clearly have a subordinate status. The British North America Act 1867—renamed Constitution Act 1867 in 1982—created Canada as a federal system. The heart of the division of powers between Ottawa and the provinces is laid out in sections 91 and 92 of the *Act*. Other sections of the original *Act*, and some of its subsequent amendments, also bear upon federal-provincial relations (see Chapter Six).

Initially, the Canadian federal system was highly centralized. Most of the important mechanisms for raising revenue were controlled by the federal government, and with the exception of agriculture and immigration, where jurisdiction was shared, the most important areas of public policy were allocated to the federal government. The provinces had control over "matters of a merely local or private nature" (s. 92), and over things such as education, health care, local works, municipal institutions, natural resources, property and civil rights. In an era before Keynesian economics, or the emergence of the welfare state, or Albertan oil, many of these areas were of limited significance by modern standards.

In addition to the biases in revenue-raising and policy jurisdiction, the federal government was also granted residual powers. The federal government could pass laws for the "peace, order and good government of Canada" on any matters not specifically allocated to the provinces (s.91). This remains the case today. Furthermore, the federal government could disallow any provincial legislation, and in the late nineteenth century (unlike today) this power was actually used.

This early version of centralized federalism has been transformed over the course of the twentieth century, and today Canada is generally recognized as one of the world's most *decentralized* federal systems. However, this change has not been a smooth or constant one. By the early decades of the twentieth century, the British Judicial Committee of the Privy Council had made a number of legal interpretations of the Constitution which shifted power a bit more towards the provinces. Moreover, by the 1920s, areas of social and economic policy under provincial jurisdiction were starting to become more significant. Provincial responsibilities were becoming more onerous, and with the onset of the Great Depression, the provinces had extreme difficulty in coping financially with the problems of mass unemployment and economic collapse. Some were even on the verge of bankruptcy. As a result of the Depression, the provinces became more dependent on Ottawa for financial support. There was also a greater tension in federal-provincial relations, with a competitive scrambling for revenues amongst different governments. The tension was resolved temporarily by the Second World War, and as with the First World War, hostilities brought an emergency centralization of power in the hands of the federal government.

Following the war, fear of another Depression, and belief in Keynesian economics, provoked an upsurge of federal spending in areas of provincial jurisdiction. This was achieved through the extensive use of shared-cost programmes and conditional grants to the provinces. The relative prosperity of the postwar years coincided with a period of paternalistic federalism, which was characterized by reasonably harmonious intergovernmental relations dominated by Ottawa. But by the mid-1960s this situation was changing. The provinces were becoming more powerful, and intergovernmental relations were becoming more conflictual. Several factors contributed to this trend: the growth of Quebec nationalism; the development of bigger and more competent provincial bureaucracies; the assumption of greater taxing authority by the provinces; the right of provinces to "opt out" of federal shared-cost programmes (with compensation); and some degree of federal disillusion with conditional grants and shared-cost programmes which were increasingly expensive for the federal government, but which did not give Ottawa much credit or control. The partial retreat from shared-cost programmes continued into the 1970s, and by the end of the decade some of the major programmes had been replaced by unconditional block grants. These allowed greater restraint on Ottawa's spending, but also passed more responsibility onto the provinces. This decentralizing tendency was exacerbated by demands for separatism in Quebec, by the growth of resource revenues in some provinces, by provincial attempts to stimulate regional growth, and by Western alienation from a federal government that was seen as dominated by central Canada. Today, pressure on Ottawa to reduce the budget deficit has put additional strain on the role of the national government, and has produced further incentives to reduce transfer payments to the provinces. In addition, the failure of the Meech Lake accord has now made it difficult for Quebec to accept Canadian federalism without a further substantial devolution of authority. And perhaps even this will not be enough.

The evolution of Canadian federalism has thus witnessed a transformation from an early system of federal domination and relatively distinct areas of jurisdiction, to a much more decentralized system in which jurisdiction is now effectively shared with the provinces in most areas of policy. Today, both levels of government are active in the fields of economic, social and cultural policy. Jurisdiction is thoroughly mixed. In some cases the Constitution clearly provides a basis for joint occupancy of a policy area, as is true of taxation, regulation of business, agriculture, immigration, public pensions, and administration of justice. In other cases the constitutional authority to legislate rests more or less squarely with provincial governments, but Ottawa is able to influence policy because it provides much—often half—of the funding for these provincial programmes. This is true of major health care and social assistance programmes, post-secondary education and economic development in less affluent regions. Finally, jurisdiction is sometimes effectively divided because of political compromises and/or the need for administrative cooperation between the levels of government. Trucking, cable television and control over offshore resources are matters that the courts have ruled fall under Ottawa's authority, but the federal government has chosen to either give the responsibility to the provinces (trucking) or divide it with them (cable, offshore resources). Shared-cost programmes, and the ongoing tax collection and financial transfer agreements that are renegotiated on a periodic basis, necessitate administrative cooperation across a broad range of policy fields.

The reality of overlapping jurisdictions and the interdependence of federal and provincial governments have given rise to an elaborate institutional machinery for managing intergovernmental relations. At the bureaucratic level, there is a network of intergovernmental committees as well as a coterie of officials in individual government departments who are concerned with intergovernmental liaison. Most provinces have a ministry of intergovernmental affairs (or equivalent), and in Ottawa, the Federal-Provincial Relations Office is a key agency in managing relations with the provinces. At the political level, there are regular formal meetings between federal ministers and their provincial counterparts, in addition to more informal contacts. At the highest level, the most open and visible mechanism for intergovernmental relations is the First Minister's Conference. These televised conferences are both forums for national debate and confrontation, as well as mechanisms for (occasionally) achieving agreement and compromise on important national issues. This whole system of intergovernmental relations, involving bureaucrats and politicians from the federal government and all the provinces, has come to be known as "executive federalism".

It is a form of federalism that reflects the growing need for intergovernmental cooperation, and a blurring of the jurisdictional lines between Ottawa and the provinces on many issues.

Citizens' Rights and Freedoms

Citizens' rights and freedoms are also an integral part of Canada's constitution. Before passage of the Constitution Act 1982, they were guaranteed mainly by the constitutional conventions that developed over the centuries in Anglo-American liberal democracies. Freedom of religion, association and expression, freedom from discrimination, and fundamental democratic rights (e.g., the right to vote) and legal rights (e.g., habeas corpus; right to a trial; presumption of innocence) were important components of this political tradition, whose meanings were amplified through actual judicial decisions (i.e., the common law). The Canadian Bill of Rights (1960) and various provincial analogues gave statutory recognition to these rights and freedoms, but courts were reluctant to use these laws to strike down other laws. Generally speaking, so long as a government was not impinging upon the jurisdiction of the other level of government, the courts rarely challenged the supremacy of parliament to do as it chose. This has changed dramatically. The Charter of Rights and Freedoms that comprises sections 1 to 35 of the Constitution Act 1982 entrenches in Canada's written constitution the rights and freedoms that had previously been protected by political tradition and statute law. The Charter adds some new categories of individual rights, like mobility rights and equality based on gender. But most of the rights and freedoms it guarantees are codifications of ones that existed, albeit more tenuously, before 1982. Entrenchment in the Charter, however, has made an important difference. Individuals and organizations are now much more likely to use the courts in fighting laws to which they object. The courts, for their part, have assumed a more active role in the political process. Their traditional deference to the will of elected legislatures has receded, and they have shown themselves quite prepared to use the Charter to strike down impugned laws.

The Constitution also includes guarantees for group rights. These guarantees date from pre-Confederation, as in the 1774 Quebec Act recognition of the status of the Catholic church and the French-language *code civil* in Quebec. Recognition of language rights and the educational rights of religious denominations were contained in the British North America Act passed in 1867 (sections 93 and 133). Section 93 of that Act has been used by the courts to uphold the constitutionality of public funding for denominational schools. The official equality of the French and English languages that s.133 of the BNA Act guarantees is extended by the Charter to include federal public services (where the demand or nature of the service warrants bilingualism) and the right to primary and secondary school instruction in the language of the English or French linguistic minority of a province (again, where numbers warrant). The rights of the aboriginal peoples of Canada, including their treaty rights and those rights established under land claims agreements, are also recognized by the Charter.

Constitutional Amendment

As a general rule, written constitutions usually are not easy to change. The process of constitutional amendment is deliberately more difficult, and requires a higher level of agreement than is the case in passing a simple law. Before 1982 the heart of the Canadian constitution was a series of laws passed by the British parliament in Westminster. This was the British North America Act, 1867 and its subsequent amendments. In order to change the BNA Act the Canadian government had to approach the British parliament which then amended this British statute. Although it was quite clear that the Westminister parliament would not change the BNA Act except at the request of the Canadian government, the process on this side of the ocean was far from settled. Did all provinces have to agree to a change that affected their powers? Did Quebec, Ontario or any other province have a veto over constitutional change? While there was agreement among Canadian constitutional experts that provincial consent was required for amendments affecting the division of powers, the extent and nature of that consent was not agreed upon.

One of the things that the 1982 Constitution Act accomplished was the patriation of Canada's constitution; transforming the BNA Act and its amendments into Canadian constitutional laws, and thus eliminating Britain's custodial relationship to the Canadian constitution. Amending the Constitution now takes place (or doesn't take place) entirely in Canada, according to one of the four formulas laid down in Part V of the Constitution Act 1982. Different categories of constitutional change are subject to different amendment procedures. There is also a provision (s.40), perhaps uniquely Canadian, that would enable a provincial government to opt out of an amendment passed under the general procedure for changing the Constitution (s.38[1]). These changes have not made constitutional amendment easier than it was before 1982. The failure of the Meech Lake Accord—the first attempt to change the Constitution using the new rules—was testimony to the enormous difficulties involved in making any significant amendment to the Canadian Constitution.

THE FORMAL STRUCTURE OF CANADIAN GOVERNMENT

The Government of Canada publishes an organization chart that lays out the formal relationships between the various institutions that comprise Canada's system of government. A simplified version of this chart is provided in Figure A.1.

The three branches of Canadian government are the *executive*, the *legislature* and the *judiciary*. The executive includes the monarch (currently Elizabeth II), whose powers are exercised by the governor general; the prime minister and cabinet, commonly referred to as the government; and the bureaucratic departments and agencies that fall under the control of cabinet. Canada's legislative branch of government includes the elected House of Commons and the appointed Senate. The judiciary encompasses the Supreme Court of Canada, the Federal Court of Canada and the various provincial courts, all of which are federally-appointed.

The Monarch and Governor General

Her Majesty Queen Elizabeth II is Canada's head of state. Although this position is principally a ceremonial one, some of the monarch's formal duties are nevertheless significant. All legislation in Canada must receive Royal Assent before it can become law, and the Queen is also responsible for dissolving Parliament, and for appointing the prime minister. When one party has a majority of seats in the House of Commons, the choice of prime minister is obvious and automatic. And when no party has a majority, then the leader of the largest party is the normal choice. However, circumstances can arise when a minority government is forced to resign, and instead of agreeing to call a general election, the monarch can conceivably call on the leader of the opposition to try to form a government. This remains a possibility, although it almost never happens.

The Queen herself does not normally perform her duties in Canada, but delegates these responsibilities to surrogates. At the federal level this is the governor general who is appointed by the Queen on the recommendation of the Canadian prime minister. At the provincial level, the lieutenant-governors are the Queen's representatives. Currently, the Governor General is former Conservative cabinet minister, Ray Hnatyshyn.

The Prime Minister and the Cabinet

In Canada, as in Britain, the prime minister is the chief executive of government. In contrast with the United States, where the chief executive (President) is elected separately by the people every four years, the Canadian prime minister is simply the leader of the dominant political party in the House of Commons at any particular time. Normally, this is the party that has won a majority of seats in a general election (held at least once every five years, with no fixed date), but occasionally the biggest party still only has a minority of seats. Joe Clark's government (1979-80) and Pierre Trudeau's government (1972-74) were both minority governments.

The prime minister chooses the people who will be cabinet ministers, and who will be responsible for the various departments of government. Ministers can be hired, fired or given different jobs, as and when the P.M. sees fit. This places a lot of power and patronage in the hands of the P.M., and is one of the mechanisms by which prime ministers exert discipline over the party's MPs (known collectively as the "caucus"). Most MPs want jobs in government and are unlikely to antagonize the prime minister by voting against the government's programme in the House of Commons. The result is a *fusion of powers* between the executive and the legislature in Canada. In times of majority government, the House of Commons generally conforms to the will of the P.M. and the Cabinet due to the constraint of *party discipline.*

The government is, however, collectively responsible to Parliament, and must maintain the support of the majority of the House of Commons. If a government loses a "no-confidence" motion put forward by one of the opposition parties, or if it is defeated in the Commons on a supply motion (proposing the spending of money) or on an important piece of legislation, the prime minister

FIGURE A.1

The Formal Organization of Canadian Government

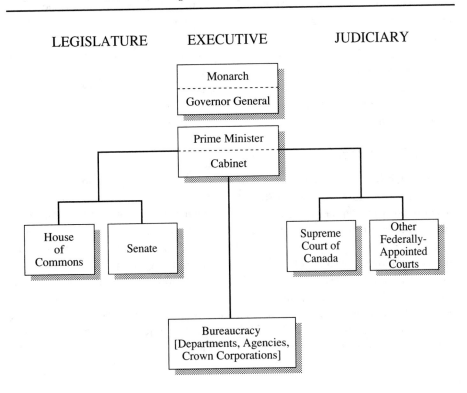

LEGISLATURE   EXECUTIVE   JUDICIARY

and cabinet must resign. The governor-general could then call upon one of the opposition parties to try to form a government that can command majority support in the Commons or, far more likely, dissolve parliament and call for a fresh election. Responsible government means, then, that a government does not hold office for a fixed term of years, but only as long as it has majority support in the Commons.

Cabinet ministers are also individually accountable to Parliament. They must take responsibility for the actions of their Department and answer questions in the House of Commons. If serious mistakes are made by the Department's officials, or if illegal acts have occurred, then by convention the minister should take the blame and resign. In practice, this rarely happens unless the minister was directly and personally involved.

In modern times, Cabinets have 30-40 ministers, and it is very difficult for the whole Cabinet to meet regularly to discuss issues and make decisions. As a result, the work of Cabinet is divided up into committees. There are currently 15 Cabinet committees, and each deals either with a broad area of public policy (e.g. Economic Policy, Foreign and Defence Policy, or the Environment), or with some important aspect of government activity (e.g. Legislation and House Planning, or Government Operations). Of all the committees, the most important is the Committee on Priorities and Planning, which is chaired by the P.M., and which sets the long-term agenda of government and coordinates the work of other committees.

Even when the work is divided up into committees, ministers still do not have very much time to consider policy options in detail. Furthermore, ministers generally have little specialized knowledge or expertise in the area of policy for which they are responsible. Consequently, all ministers rely heavily on advice from the bureaucracy.

The Bureaucracy

The public bureaucracy consists of appointed officials who are responsible for formulating policy proposals, advising elected policy-makers, implementing government programmes, and running the machinery of state. In Canada, most bureaucrats are professional career civil servants who remain in their jobs even when the party in power changes. In the course of their duties, civil servants have the opportunity to develop a considerable amount of experience and expertise in a particular area of policy and administration. Commonly, they interact on a regular basis with the principal interest groups and private sector organizations in their policy field, as well as with their political "masters", the public and other bureaucrats. This level of knowledge and proficiency gives the bureaucracy a key role in the process of policy-making, even if it is the politicians who are formally responsible. Business organizations and other interest groups recognize this fact, and the bureaucracy is an important target for lobbying (see Chapter Seven).

At both the federal and provincial levels, the public bureaucracy is organized into a variety of different structures. The principal ones will be mentioned briefly here, with a focus on the federal level of government.

Departments

The bulk of government functions are organized into separate *departments*, for instance, the Department of Consumer and Corporate Affairs, the Department of Industry, Science and Technology or the Department of Communications. While the minister is the political head of a department, a *deputy minister* is the administrative head. Deputy ministers (DMs) are normally long-serving, non-partisan, career officials who have worked their way up through the bureaucratic ranks. They are crucial links between ministers and their departments, and they have a considerable impact on policy development. Below the DM is a broadly hierarchical arrangement of ranks and bureaus, each with a particular competency in some specialized area or policy. Just as ministers rely on advice from deputy ministers, so DMs rely on policy advice and research from lower levels of the department. Middle-level bureaucrats can thus be an important source of policy recommendations.

In addition to regular departments, there are also ministries of state. These are smaller than most other departments, although they are still under the direct responsibility of a minister. They are generally set up either as an adjunct to a larger department (in order to relieve some of the workload), or else to fulfill some specific and relatively narrow function. Current examples include the Ministry of State for Small Businesses and Tourism, and the Ministry of State for Science and Technology.

Agencies, Commissions and Tribunals

Some functions of government are organized into non-departmental structures, such as regulatory agencies, commissions, and tribunals. These bodies are normally concerned with one limited area of administration, and they have a greater degree of independence from direct ministerial control than a department does. Frequently, they have quasi-judicial functions, requiring them to make adjudicatory decisions, such as setting telephone rates or giving approval for pipeline construction. These two things are part of the responsibilities of the Canadian Radio-television and Telecommunications Commission (CRTC) and the National Energy Board (NEB) respectively. Issues concerning regulatory agencies are discussed more fully in Chapter Eleven.

Crown Corporations

Crown corporations are bodies owned by the federal or provincial government, but which have a separate legal status of their own, and which operate with a substantial amount of independence from ministerial direction. Some, such as Canadian National Railways and Sydney Steel, are designed to operate largely as commercial enterprises in competition with the private sector. Others, such as the Atomic Energy Control Board and the Canada Mortgage and Housing Corporation, act more like regulatory agencies or mini-departments, with less of a commercial mandate. Over recent years there has been a movement towards privatizing a number of crown corporations including Canadair, Teleglobe Canada, Air Canada, Petro Canada and Saskatchewan Potash, as governments have sought to scale down the size of the state sector. Crown corporations and privatization are discussed further in Chapter Four.

Central Agencies

One of the problems of any complex organization like government is in coordinating the work of different divisions and departments. At the centre of Canadian federal government there are a number of relatively small agencies whose jurisdiction cuts across the whole range of government activity, and whose work is concerned with this coordination function. These include the Prime Minister's Office, the Privy Council Office, The Federal-Provincial Relations Office, and the Treasury Board Secretariat. The Department of Finance, although very extensive, is sometimes included as a central agency due to its centrally important financial and fiscal role.

The Prime Minister's Office   The PMO is a publicly-funded agency consisting of partisan political appointees loyal to the prime minister. It is the P.M.'s personal bureaucracy, and one of its main responsibilities is to ensure that policy direction is sensitive to the party's political considerations. It also has other duties such as managing the P.M.'s schedule, dealing with the press, and making recommendations for government appointments.

The Privy Council Office   The PCO is an agency, staffed by non-partisan career bureaucrats, that provides policy advice to the prime minister, the Cabinet and the Cabinet committees. It is responsible for trying to coordinate the policies and programmes of all government departments and agencies. Needless to say, this is no easy task. The PCO is one of the most important bureaucratic agencies in government, and the Clerk of the Privy Council is generally recognized as the head of the federal civil service.

The Federal-Provincial Relations Office   The FPRO's main responsibilities are to coordinate the federal government's relations with the provinces, to organize federal-provincial negotiations and to advise Cabinet on the implications of federal policy for relations with provincial governments.

The Treasury Board Secretariat   The TBS is the body of civil servants that advises the Treasury Board (which is an important Cabinet committee). The Treasury Board is responsible for granting or withholding approval for departmental spending programmes, and for financial and personnel management in the civil service. In times of budgetary restraint, it frequently denies or restricts departmental spending proposals, and consequently, it is not always very popular. It is a powerful institution, headed by a senior cabinet minister, with a mandate ranging across the whole federal government machine. Because of its extensive duties, the Treasury Board's ministers are highly dependent on the Secretariat for research and advice.

In general, the modern role of these central agencies is a response to the growing complexity of government, and an attempt to achieve a greater degree of coherence in federal government policy. Because of their limited resources and broad mandates, these agencies are normally too busy to be very accessible for frequent consultations with private sector groups.

The Supreme Court

Canada's founding constitutional document, the Constitution Act 1867, gave the federal government the authority to establish a "General Court of Appeal for Canada" (s.101). This was done in 1875 with the passage of the Supreme Court Act. The Supreme Court of Canada did not become the highest court of appeal for this country until 1949. Until then, the Judicial Committee of the Privy Council (a committee of the British House of Lords) was the supreme arbiter of Canadian constitutional law.

Judges of the Supreme Court—for that matter all judges in Canada—are appointed by the government when a vacancy occurs. Their salaries are determined by Parliament, and the structure of the court system, including the Supreme Court of Canada, can be changed simply by the passage of a law. These limitations on the judiciary's independence are more apparent than real. Superior court judges at both the federal and provincial levels have permanent tenure until the age of seventy-five. Although they can be removed before then, if majorities in both the Senate and the House of Commons decide to do so, this has never happened. The bulwark of judicial independence in Canada are the traditions of parliamentary government and Anglo-American jurisprudence, which prohibit political interference with judicial decision-making.

The Supreme Court of Canada is the final arbiter of Canada's constitution. It has historically played an important role in determining the division of legislative powers between Ottawa and the provinces (see Chapter Six). Since the passage of the Constitution Act 1982, which entrenched the Charter of Rights and Freedoms in the Constitution, the Court has also played an increasingly prominent role in defining the relationships between citizens and the state.

Parliament

The Canadian Parliament is bicameral, consisting of the elected House of Commons and the appointed Senate. Since the 1988 election, the House of Commons has 295 members, each of whom represents a single constituency (riding) of roughly equal size (by population). The distribution of MPs as of January 1990 is shown in Table A.1.

Between them, Ontario and Quebec have the majority of the seats in the House, and federal elections are typically won or lost in central Canada. The Senate has 104 seats, with a fixed number from each province (Ontario and Quebec have 24 each, Nova Scotia and New Brunswick have 10 each, the Western provinces and Newfoundland have 6 each, P.E.I. has 4, and the Northwest Territories and the Yukon have one each). The prime minister has the constitutional power to appoint an additional eight senators, and this has recently been exercised, bringing the total to 112. The Conservatives now have a slim majority in the Senate.

On paper, the legislative powers of each chamber are very similar, and both bodies must give approval to a bill before it can become law. However, all statutes

Table A.1

	P.C.	Lib	N.D.P.	Other/Vacant	Total
	The Regional and Party Balance in the House of Commons, after the 1988 Election.				
Newfoundland	2	5	—	—	7
Prince Edward Island	—	4	—	—	4
Nova Scotia	5	6	—	—	11
New Brunswick	5	5	—	—	10
Quebec	63	12	—	—	75
Ontario	46	43	10	—	99
Manitoba	7	5	2	—	14
Saskatchewan	4	—	10	—	14
Alberta	24	—	1	1*	26
British Columbia	12	1	19	—	32
Yukon	—	—	1	—	1
Northwest Territories	—	2	—	—	2
Total	168	83	43	1	295

*   One P.C. Member died before being sworn in.

Source: InfoGlobe, *Canadian Parliamentary Guide.*

proposing the raising or spending of public revenue must be introduced in the House of Commons. When it comes to amending the Constitution, the majority approval of the Commons is required, but Senate rejection can only delay passage of an amendment resolution for 100 days. After that, the House of Commons can repass the resolution without the need for Senate approval.

In practice, the rough equality of the two chambers does not exist. The Commons is by far the more important body, and the Senate rarely obstructs legislation that has been passed by the House. However, between 1984 and 1990 the Liberal-dominated Senate was less compliant in dealing with bills from the Conservative-dominated House of Commons. This culminated in the battle to stop the Goods and Services Tax in the fall of 1990, when Liberal Senators (now in a minority) tried to block the GST by a variety of procedural and disruptive measures, including blowing kazoos.

Besides its legislative function, the House of Commons also provides a forum for (i) debating national issues, (ii) publicizing differences between the parties, (iii) scrutinizing public expenditures, (iv) conducting special investigations, (v) holding ministers and their departments accountable at Question Period, (vi) legitimizing the government's actions, and (vii) providing responsible government.

The House is divided up into committees, and this is where most of the real work takes place. There are several different types of committees, and since the system was reformed in 1985, two of the more important types are (a) *standing committees* and (b) *legislative committees*. Standing committees conduct investigations, examine evidence, call witnesses, and make recommendations on particular areas of public policy. There are at present 19 of these committees, each with a specific policy jurisdiction. Legislative committees are set up on an ad hoc basis to consider the details of individual bills and to propose amendments. Parties are represented on committees in rough proportion to the partisan balance in the House as a whole. This allows a majority government to dominate the work of each committee by imposing party discipline - just as it dominates the whole House.

HOW A LAW IS PASSED

The law takes various forms. A statute passed by the House of Commons and the Senate, and given royal assent by the governor general, is clearly a law. But decisions taken by Cabinet, that have not been approved in the legislature, also have the force of law. These are called "orders-in-council." Thousands of them are issued each year, and they are published in the *Canada Gazette*. The decisions of agencies, boards and commissions that receive their regulatory powers from a statute also have the force of law. Finally, there are the regulations and guidelines issued and enforced by the departmental bureaucracy in accordance with the discretionary powers delegated to them under a statute. These also have the force of law.

In a strictly numerical sense the statutes passed annually by Parliament represent only the tip of the iceberg of laws promulgated each year. Nevertheless, virtually all major policy decisions—including budget measures, and the laws that assign discretionary power to the bureaucracy—come before the legislature. The only exception is when the normal process of government is suspended by passage of the War Measures Act, which requires parliamentary approval in order to be invoked. This happened during World War I, again during World War II, and briefly in 1970 when Ottawa proclaimed the Act after two political kidnappings in Quebec by the *Front de libération du Québec*.

During normal times the law-making process involves several stages and opportunities for debate and amendment. The steps from the introduction of a bill in Parliament to the final proclamation of a *statute* are set out in Figure A.2.

There are two types of bills, namely *private members' bills* and *government bills*. Private member' bills originate from any individual MP, and unless they get the backing of government, they have little chance of passing. Government bills dominate parliament's legislative agenda, and when major legislation is being proposed, such a bill is sometimes preceded by a *white paper*. This is a report for discussion, based on research by the bureaucracy (and sometimes the legislature as well), and is a statement of the government's legislative intentions.

Once a bill has been drafted by government, it is introduced into the Senate, or more usually, into the House of Commons. Here it is given *first reading*, which is just a formality and involves no debate. Then the bill goes to *second reading*, where the main principles of the bill are debated, and a vote is taken. If the bill passes second reading, it then moves to the *committee stage*, where the details of the bill are considered clause by clause. Occasionally, the whole House sits as a committee to consider this stage, but more often a bill is sent to a smaller legislative committee. At this stage, amendments can be made, but the principle of the bill cannot be altered. The bill is then reported back to the House, where all aspects are debated, including any amendments. At this *report stage* new amendments can also be introduced. If a bill passes this hurdle it then goes to *third reading* where a final vote is taken, sometimes after further debate. Once a bill has been passed in the House, it is then sent to the Senate where a virtually identical process takes place. If a bill was first introduced in the Senate, then it would now be sent to the House. Finally, a bill that has been passed in both the House and the Senate can be given royal assent and become law.

FIGURE A.2

From Bill to Statute

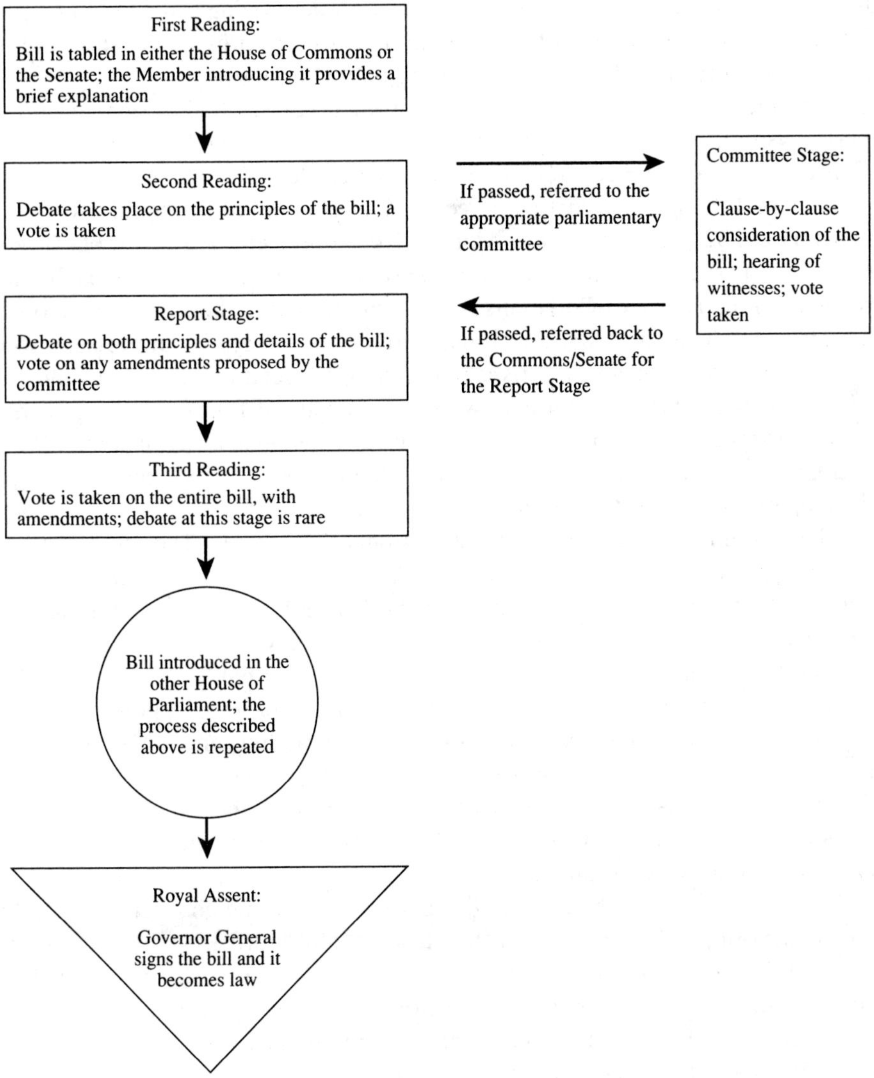

First Reading: Bill is tabled in either the House of Commons or the Senate; the Member introducing it provides a brief explanation

↓

Second Reading: Debate takes place on the principles of the bill; a vote is taken

If passed, referred to the appropriate parliamentary committee →

Committee Stage: Clause-by-clause consideration of the bill; hearing of witnesses; vote taken

Report Stage: Debate on both principles and details of the bill; vote on any amendments proposed by the committee

← If passed, referred back to the Commons/Senate for the Report Stage

↓

Third Reading: Vote is taken on the entire bill, with amendments; debate at this stage is rare

↓

Bill introduced in the other House of Parliament; the process described above is repeated

↓

Royal Assent:

Governor General signs the bill and it becomes law

POLITICAL PARTIES

Disciplined political parties are an important ingredient in the Canadian parliamentary system, and are a central plank in the organization of democratic politics in Canada. They fulfill an important function in collectivizing and representing the interests of broad sections of the population, as well as providing a structure for recruiting political leaders and formulating policy proposals.

The federal party system in Canada is sometimes labelled a "two-and-a-half party system," consisting of the two major parties, namely the Progressive Conservatives and the Liberals, plus the smaller New Democratic Party. In the election of 1988 the Conservatives received 43 per cent of the popular vote; the Liberals got 32 per cent and the NDP polled 20 per cent. However, because of Canada's "first-past-the-post" electoral system, the number of seats each party receives in the House of Commons is not proportional to their percentage of the popular vote. Thus in 1988, the Conservatives got a majority of the seats with only a minority of the votes. This is not an unusual occurrence in Canadian politics. Today, the party system may well be in a state of flux with the growth of support for the Western-based Reform Party, and the breakaway of some Liberal and Conservative MPs to form the Bloc Quebecois. The full impact of these developments remains to be seen.

The national figures also disguise regional differences. The NDP virtually are unrepresented in Quebec or Eastern Canada; the Liberals continue to have very few MPs from the West; and until the leadership of Brian Mulroney, the Conservatives typically had great difficulty winning seats in Quebec. This pattern both reflects and reinforces the underlying regionalism of the Canadian political system. In addition, it is not uncommon for provincial political parties to disagree with their federal counterparts, thus adding another string to the regional discord. Perhaps the most discordant string amongst Canada's parties is the Parti Quebecois, which was elected to office in Quebec in 1976 and 1981. Although now in Opposition, the PQ still remains the strong voice of Francophone Quebec nationalism and separatism.

At the federal level, both the major parties have strong connections with the business world, and although the Liberals are slightly further to the left, the ideological distance between the Liberals and the Conservatives is not great. Both compete in a reasonably pragmatic fashion for the electoral middle ground. In this regard, the Liberals have generally had more success, and have been the governing party for most of the twentieth century.

The NDP started life as the Co-operative Commonwealth Federation (CCF), founded in 1933. From its radical agrarian roots in the West, it has subsequently moved towards the political centre and has been successful in gaining support in Central Canada. It has developed links with Canada's fairly conservative trade union movement, and it has repeatedly backed away from earlier socialist rhetoric in an attempt to broaden its appeal. The NDP has become a social democratic party rather than a socialist party in that it seeks to enact some moderate reforms while accepting the existence of a capitalist economy. At the federal level, the NDP customarily pools around 20 per cent of the national vote, and it has never risen beyond third party status. However, it has formed governments at the provincial level in Saskatchewan, Manitoba, British Columbia and recently in Ontario.

PROVINCIAL AND MUNICIPAL GOVERNMENTS

Combined revenues and spending of provincial and municipal governments in Canada surpass those of the federal government. Many of the public services that Canadians receive, and most of those with which they have daily contact (roads and sidewalks, schools, water and electricity, garbage removal, sewers, police and fire protection, to name a few) are provided at the provincial or municipal level. Municipalities and other local authorities (townships, counties, regions) have no independent status under the Constitution. They are created by provincial governments and receive their powers from provincial laws.

The formal structure of provincial government very closely resembles that of the national government. Laws are introduced and passed in the same manner, and party discipline determines legislative behaviour. There is, however, no provincial equivalent of the Senate. All provincial legislatures are comprised of a single, elected house in which constituencies (the districts in which an election for a particular seat in the legislature takes place) are determined on the basis of population. Although the Constitution Act 1867 gives Ottawa the formal power to withhold assent from a provincially-passed law, this should not be interpreted as meaning that the provincial level of government is subordinate or in any way inferior to the federal level. This federal power was last used in 1943, and it is generally considered a dead letter of the Constitution.

The structure of local government looks quite different from the parliamentary system that operates in Ottawa and in the provincial capitals. Mayors, municipal councils, school boards and public utilities commissions (and sometimes other bodies) are all elected separately, and clear party lines are still relatively rare in local politics. More common are "pro-" and "anti-development" factions, or other divisions based on local controversies.

INDEX